THE
CONTEMPORARY
CONCORDANCE
OF
BIBLE TOPICS

THE Contemporary

CONCORDANCE
OF BIBLE TOPICS

The entire Bible indexed by subject matter.
Edited and compiled by

KEN ANDERSON

VICTOR BOOKS.®

A DIVISION OF SCRIPTURE PRESS PUBLICATIONS INC.
USA CANADA ENGLAND

Second printing, 1988

The primary source for this book was the *Holy Bible, New International Version,* © 1973, 1978, 1984, International Bible Society. Used by permission of Zondervan Bible Publishers. The *King James Version* was also used.

Recommended Dewey Decimal Classification: 220.2
Suggested Subject Headings: BIBLE, CONCORDANCE, INDEX

Library of Congress Catalog Card Number: 87-62609
ISBN: 0-89693-438-1

The Why of This Book

The Contemporary Concordance of Bible Topics began as a private indices, a compilation of Scripture portions which illustrate or relate to subjects not readily found by using a word content concordance. For example, "ecology" does not appear in any Bible text. Yet references listed in this book relate to that topic.

The book is in no way exhaustive. Others, reading their Bibles, would likely discover illustrative material unlisted here. This is, then, one Christian layman's store of topics and subjects which he found illustrated or emphasized in the Word of God.

Rather than to provide in-depth coverage of a given topic, the objective was to list a variety of representative texts. Thus, in preparing an oral presentation, written study, or lesson, the user has a variety of options for use in illustration and reinforcement.

In essence, then, this book supplements, rather than supplants, existing reference sources.

Hopefully, *The Contemporary Concordance of Bible Topics* will provide pastors, Bible teachers, lay students, and others a source of illustrations and quotations relevant to contemporary vocabulary and interests. Thus this volume will best be used as a supplement, an extension to sources and methods previously used.

The friends, clergymen, and Bible teachers who scanned the manuscript in its developing stages gave me much encouragement and incentive. Several of them suggested entries, even topics. Ginger Caswell typed and assembled the initial draft, checking each reference. My daughter Margaret tirelessly entered subsequent drafts on the word processor. Barbara Williams edited the final copy, offering timely suggestions as she prepared the material for typesetting. Her competence, rapport, and repartee enhanced the many hours of final proofreading and revision.

If the enrichment I received from the many readings of the Bible and the consequent development of this material can enrich the lives and ministry of those who use *The Contemporary Concordance,* I shall be grateful.

Ken Anderson
Winona Lake, Indiana, 1988

To
Dr. John Haggai and the multitude
of world leaders
he has permitted me to meet
through the ministry of
Haggai Institute.

A

ABANDONED
Mankind abandoned, Genesis 6:11-13.
Joseph's temporary abandonment,
    Genesis 37:23-28.
Abandoned city, 1 Samuel 30:1-6;
    Lamentations 1:1.
Shunned by friends, Psalm 38:11.
Abandoned Son of God, Matthew 27:46;
    John 16:32. (See Ps. 22:1.)
Abandoning ship, Acts 27:41-44.
Deserted apostle, 2 Timothy 4:16.
See *Desolate, Forsaken, Loneliness.*

ABHOR
Abhoring laws, Leviticus 26:15.
Rejecting idols, Deuteronomy 7:25-26.
Attitude toward aliens, Deuteronomy 23:7.
Self-hatred, Job 42:6.
Learn to hate evil, Romans 12:9.
See *Hatred.*

ABILITY
Lost skill of farming, Genesis 4:9-12.
Building Tower of Babel, Genesis 11:1-6.
Talent and ability come from God, Exodus
    4:10-12. (See 6:30.)
Sanballat's ridicule of Jewish capability,
    Nehemiah 4:1-10.
Faith greater than physical strength, Psalm
    147:10-11.
Race not to swift or strong, Ecclesiastes
    9:11.
What God requires, God provides, Isaiah
    2:3.
Capable of evil, Micah 2:1.
Relationship between ability and call to
    service, Romans 11:29.
Competence comes from God,
    2 Corinthians 3:4-5.
Do not neglect your gift, 1 Timothy 4:14.
Prepared by God to succeed, Hebrews

13:20-21.
See *Agility, Artist, Athletics, Capability,
    Skill, Talent.*

ABNORMAL
Multiple fingers and toes, 2 Samuel 21:20.
Illicit relationship of two sisters, Ezekiel
    23:1-49.
See *Disfigure, Handicap.*

ABOLISH
Idolatry, Isaiah 2:18.
Conclusion to politics and government,
    1 Corinthians 15:24.
Death destroyed, 1 Corinthians 15:26.
Old Covenant, 2 Corinthians 3:13-15.

ABOMINATION
Pagan sacrifices, Exodus 8:26.
Heathen lifestyle, Deuteronomy 18:9-12.
A people defiled, Jeremiah 3:1-3.
For continued sinning, certain judgment,
    Amos 1:3, 6, 9, 11, 13; 2:1, 4, 6. (Note
    the nature of sin in each of these
    judgments.)
See *Degradation, Depravity, Dissipation.*

ABORTION
Accidental abortion, Exodus 21:22-25.
Onan's procedure toward command of
    Judah, Genesis 38:8-10.
Desired by Job, Job 3:16.
Message for the unborn, Psalm 102:18.
Blessing of producing children, Psalm
    127:5.
Destiny of unborn, Psalm 139:15-16;
    Jeremiah 1:5.
End of infant mortality in future, Isaiah
    65:20.
Son in the body of his ancestor, Hebrews
    7:9-10.

See *Children, Infanticide, Infertility, Pregnancy.*

ABRASION
How to deal with divisive person, Titus 3:10.
Methods of disruptive hypocrite in church, 3 John 9-10.
See *Discontent, Friction, Hurt, Irritation, Malcontent.*

ABSENCE
The joy of purposeful separation from loved ones, John 14:28.
Paul was fearful of reunion with the Corinthians, 2 Corinthians 12:20-21.
Separated believers, Philippians 1:25-26.
Remembering those who are absent, 1 Thessalonians 2:17.
See *Attendance.*

ABSOLUTE
The Lord reigns forever, Psalm 9:7-8.
Absolute trust in divine deliverance, Daniel 3:16-18.
The God who does not change, Malachi 3:6. (See Rom. 11:29.)
Believe the Good News, Mark 1:14-15.
One gate to sheep pen, John 10:1-21.
Only one way, John 14:6.
Divine decisions irrevocable, Romans 11:29.
Undying love, Ephesians 6:24.
Meaning of "today" in God's reckoning, Hebrews 4:7.
Kingdom that cannot be shaken, Hebrews 12:28-29.
Changeless Christ, Hebrews 13:8.
Past, present, and future of Jesus, Revelation 1:4.

ABSOLUTION
See *Forgiveness.*

ABSTINENCE
Marital continence, Exodus 19:15; 1 Corinthians 7:1-5.
Requirement for priests, Leviticus 10:9.
Clean and unclean animals for food, Leviticus 11:1-47.
Abstaining from both wine and all fruit of the grape, Numbers 6:2-4.
Covenant to avoid lust, Job 31:1.
Refusal to drink wine, Jeremiah 35:1-14.

Daniel's resolve, Daniel 1:8.
Example of John the Baptist, Luke 1:15.
Abstinence for witness, Romans 14:21.
Abstaining from meat, Romans 14:23; 1 Corinthians 8:1-13; 1 Timothy 4:3.
Drinking of wine, 1 Timothy 5:23.
See *Alcohol, Beer, Drunkenness, Intemperance, Wine.*

ABUNDANCE
River with four sources, Genesis 2:10-14.
Abundance of grain in Egypt, Genesis 41:49.
Giving to the Lord in overabundance, Exodus 36:2-7.
Year-around harvest, Leviticus 26:5; Amos 9:13; Revelation 22:2.
Responsibility in good times, Deuteronomy 28:47-48.
God-given prosperity, Deuteronomy 30:9; Isaiah 30:23.
Abundant blessing of nature, Deuteronomy 33:13-16.
Making much of little, 2 Kings 4:1-7.
Abundant riches, Psalm 52:7.
After willingness and obedience, Isaiah 1:19.
Abundance of silver and chariots, Isaiah 2:7.
God's righteousness lasts forever, Isaiah 51:8.
Plenty to eat, Joel 2:26.
Here today, gone tomorrow, Luke 12:13-21.
Streams of living water from within, John 7:38-39.
The full life Christ gives, John 10:10.
Overflowing with hope through the Holy Spirit, Romans 15:13.
Lavished with blessing, Ephesians1:7-8.
Abundant powers, Ephesians 3:20.
Good land and unproductive land, Hebrews 6:7-8.
All we need to live life of godliness, 2 Peter 1:3.
See *Affluence, Contentment, Greed, Harvest, Plenty, Wealth.*

ABUSE
Moral perversion, Genesis 19:5-9, 31-38.
Abused authority, Numbers 20:10-13.
Corrupted ordinances, 1 Samuel 2:12-17; 1 Corinthians 11:17-22.
Perverting truth, 2 Peter 2:10-22.

See *Torture.*

ACADEMIC
Regret of poor student, Proverbs 5:12-13.
Seeing and hearing but not understanding, Mark 4:11-12.
Folly of intellectual pride, 1 Corinthians 3:18-20.
Passing exam, 2 Corinthians 13:5-6.
See *College, Education, Students, Teacher, Teaching.*

ACCEPTANCE
Of necessity, King Saul accepted David, 1 Samuel 18:5. (Note chap. 17 and 18:6-9.)
Sowing seed on various kinds of soil, Mark 4:3-20.
Mary doubted, then believed angelic announcement, Luke 1:28-38.
Accepting and rejecting the Messiah, John 7:25-31.
Disciples slow to accept converted Saul, Acts 9:26.
Only a few converts at Athens, Acts 17:34.
Accepting one another, Romans 15:7. (See 2 Cor. 7:2.)
Accepting either married or unmarried state, 1 Corinthians 7:32-35.
Paul and Barnabas given right hand of fellowship, Galatians 2:9-10.
See *Camaraderie, Rapport, Receptive, Self-acceptance.*

ACCESS
Importance of gates, Nehemiah 3:1-32.
Those who may ascend, Psalm 24:3-4.
Divinely opened gates, Isaiah 26:2.
Jesus, the gate, John 10:9.
Access to God, Romans 5:2; Ephesians 2:18; 3:12.
Mediator between God and men, 1 Timothy 2:5.
See *Authorization.*

ACCIDENT
Cause of accidental death, Numbers 35:22-25.
Death caused by accident, Deuteronomy 19:4-7.
Baby crippled by nurse's fall, 2 Samuel 4:4.
Injured by freak accident, 2 Kings 1:2.
Perilous activities, Ecclesiastes 10:9.
See *Fortuity, Injury, Misfortune.*

ACCLAIM
No prophet like Moses, Deuteronomy 34:10-12.
God's commendation of Job, Job 1:8.
Nature and people praise the Lord, Psalm 148:1-14.
Honor of strong people, Isaiah 25:3.
See *Accolade, Applause, Citation, Honor, Praise.*

ACCLAMATION
Choice of Jesus or Barabbas, Matthew 27:15-26.
See *Plebiscite, Unanimity, Vote.*

ACCOLADE
Honor not fitting for a fool, Proverbs 26:1.
Whatever measure of success, glory belongs to God alone, 1 Corinthians 3:7.
Boasting about perseverance and faith of others, 2 Thessalonians 1:4.
See *Applause, Citation, Honor, Praise.*

ACCOMMODATIONS
Prophet's chamber, 2 Kings 4:8-10.
Small beds for tall people, Isaiah 28:20.
Accommodations for priests, Ezekiel 41:9-10.
See *Guests, Hospitality, House.*

ACCOMPANIMENT
Prophecy to sound of music, 2 Kings 3:15-16.
Reciting proverbs to musical accompaniment, Psalm 49:4.
See *Music, Singing, Solo.*

ACCOMPLICE
Jason accused of being an accomplice to Paul and Silas, Acts 17:5-9.

ACCOMPLISHMENT
God saw that His work was good, Genesis 1:10, 12, 18, 21, 25, 31.
Performing wonders by power of God, Exodus 34:10.
Those who want to share honors in military victory, Judges 12:1-3.
Giving God glory for success, Psalm 118:23.
End better than beginning, Ecclesiastes 7:8.
God, who sees all, rewards the good,

Jeremiah 32:19.
Something beyond belief, Habakkuk 1:5.
Vine and fruit, John 15:1-8.
Speaking only of what Christ has done in us, Romans 15:18-19.
Whatever the measure of success, glory belongs to God alone, 1 Corinthians 3:7.
The runner and the prize, 1 Corinthians 9:24-27.
Let the Lord commend, 2 Corinthians 10:17-18.
See *Achievement, Performance, Success.*

ACCORD
See *Rapport, Unity.*

ACCOUNTABILITY
Family accountability, Joshua 7:1-26.
Children and age of accountability, 1 Samuel 3:7.
Personally accountable, 2 Samuel 12:1-15.
Those able to understand, Nehemiah 8:2-3.
Responsibility for conversation, Matthew 12:36.
All responsible before God, Romans 14:12.
Human responsibility for evil, James 1:13-15.
Responsibility in judgment, 1 Peter 4:4-5.
Those who take Scriptures to heart, Revelation 1:3.
See *Obligation, Responsibility.*

ACCREDITATION
Wisdom of Solomon, 1 Kings 4:29-34.
Provision for safe conduct, Nehemiah 2:7.
Prophet's certainty of voice of the Lord, Jeremiah 32:1-12.
Status of John the Baptist and Christ, Luke 3:15-17.
Prophet not accepted in home community, Luke 4:23-24.
Jesus had no need for human credentials, John 5:31-40.
Genuineness of faith made known, 1 Thessalonians 1:1-10.
Approved by God rather than men, 1 Thessalonians 2:4-6.
New identity for slave, Philemon 17.
See *Approval.*

ACCURACY
Splitting a hair, Judges 20:16.
Faulty bow, Hosea 7:16.

Loss of right eye, Zechariah 11:17.

ACCUSATION
King Saul's accusation and Ahimelech's innocence, 1 Samuel 22:11-15.
Satanic tirade, Job 1:6-12.
Forced to restore what one did not steal, Psalm 69:4.
False charges, Daniel 6:5-24.
Satan's role as accuser, Zechariah 3:1-2.
Silence of Jesus before accusers, Matthew 26:57-67; 27:12-14.
Members of Jesus' own family thought Him out of His mind, Mark 3:20-21. (Note v. 31.)
Given words to respond to accusers, Luke 12:11-12.
Woman caught in adultery, John 8:3-11.
Death of Stephen, Acts 6:8–7:60.
Jealous backlash, Acts 16:16-24.
Accusations which could not be proved, Acts 25:7.
Accusing others of sins we ourselves commit, Romans 2:1.
Accusations must have two or three witnesses, 1 Timothy 5:19.
See *Criticism, Demean, Gossip, Guilt.*

ACHIEVEMENT
No success outside God's will, Numbers 14:41-45.
The Lord's demands are within reach, Deuteronomy 30:11.
No prophet like Moses, Deuteronomy 34:10-12.
Taking credit for God's blessing, Judges 7:2-3.
Report to a mother-in-law, Ruth 3:16-17.
A son seeks to impress his father, 1 Samuel 14:1-14.
Lavish display of wealth, Esther 1:4-8.
Display of good talent, Psalm 45:1.
Skilled in one's work, Proverbs 22:29.
The emptiness of success and affluence, Ecclesiastes 2:4-11.
Assurance of achievement, Isaiah 54:2-3.
Skilled at art of seduction, Jeremiah 2:33.
Something to boast about, Jeremiah 9:23-24.
God the Creator and gods who perish, Jeremiah 10:11-12.
Ashamed of the idols he had made, Jeremiah 10:14-15.
Riches gained unjustly, Jeremiah 17:11.

The skill of Daniel and his young friends, Daniel 1:20.
Giving God glory for personal achievement, Romans 15:17-19.
Let the Lord commend, 2 Corinthians 10:17-18.
Forgetting the past, pressing forward to the goal, Philippians 3:12-16.
Good purpose fulfilled, 2 Thessalonians 1:11.
See *Accomplishment, Performance, Success, Victory.*

ACKNOWLEDGMENT
Nebuchadnezzar acknowledged the wisdom God had given Daniel, Daniel 2:46-47.
Nebuchadnezzar's recognition of a sovereign God, Daniel 4:34-37.
Paul's wise use of names of followers, Colossians 4:7-17.
See *Admit, Awareness, Recognition.*

ACOUSTICS
Teaching from a boat, Luke 5:1-3.

ACQUITTAL
Longing for pardon, Job 7:21.
Fear after being found guilty, Job 9:28-31.
Guilt must be punished, Nahum 1:3.
See *Pardon.*

ACROPHOBIA
Fear of height, Ecclesiastes 12:5.

ACROSTIC
Hebrew language example, Psalm 119:1-176.

ACTIONS
Defiled by one's actions, Psalm 106:39.
Path of righteous and way of wicked, Proverbs 4:18-19.
Evil deeds and motives likened to eggs, Isaiah 59:4-5.
Tree known by fruit, Matthew 12:33-35.
Actions validate inner change, Luke 19:8-9.
Reap what you sow, Galatians 6:7-10.
Whatever you say or do, Colossians 3:17.
Put scriptural teaching into action, James 1:22-25.
See *Conduct, Deeds, Performance.*

ADDICTION
Man a slave to whatever masters him, 2 Peter 2:19.
See *Drunkenness, Habits.*

ADEQUATE
Labor and good food, Ecclesiastes 5:18-20.
What God requires, He provides, Isaiah 2:3.
All-sufficiency of our Lord, Isaiah 44:24-28.
God's righteousness lasts forever, Isaiah 51:8.
Nothing too hard for God, Jeremiah 32:27.
See *Plenty, Sufficient, Supply.*

ADHESIVE
Tar instead of mortar, Genesis 11:3.

ADMINISTRATION
Advice of father-in-law, Exodus 18:15-27.
Unhappy with present leadership, Numbers 16:1-4.
No prophet like Moses, Deuteronomy 34:10-12.
Commander of the Lord's army, Joshua 5:13-15.
Well-organized Israelites, Joshua 7:14.
Leader among trees, Judges 9:7-15.
Leadership under divine guidance, 2 Chronicles 31:20-21.
Once-faithful city, Isaiah 1:21-23.
More than wealth makes a king, Jeremiah 22:14-15.
Family of David to be always on throne, Jeremiah 33:17.
Daniel distinguished himself as administrator, Daniel 6:1-4.
See *Bureaucracy, Government, Leadership, Politics.*

ADMIRATION
See *Appreciation, Love, Respect.*

ADMIT
King Saul's admission of David's righteousness, 1 Samuel 24:16-17.
Nebuchadnezzar admitted superior power of Hebrew God, Daniel 3:28-30.
See *Confession.*

ADMONITION
Wounds of a friend, Proverbs 27:6.
Worth of honest rebuke, Proverbs 28:23.
Jesus scolding an evil spirit, Mark 1:23-26.

Paul admonished those he would never see again, Acts 20:25-38.
Admonishing fellow laborers, Romans 15:14-16.
Penetrating correspondence, 1 Corinthians 4:14.
Word to parents, Ephesians 6:4.
Paul's admonition to followers, Colossians 3:16; 4:17.
Encourage weak and timid, 1 Thessalonians 5:14.
Divisive person warned, Titus 3:10.
See *Prophecy, Sermon, Warning.*

ADOLESCENCE
Generation in spiritual ignorance, Judges 2:10.
Sacrifice of daughter, Judges 11:30-40.
Boy ministering in temple, 1 Samuel 2:18.
Twelve-year-old king, 2 Kings 21:1. (See 22:1.)
Covenant to avoid lust, Job 31:1.
Service of a child, Jeremiah 1:4-7.
Hard labor for young boys, Lamentations 5:13.
Ezekiel's description of puberty, Ezekiel 16:5-9.
Communicating God's message to children, Joel 1:1-3.
Holy Spirit and youth, Joel 2:28.
Boy with an evil spirit, Mark 9:14-29.
See *Children, Juvenile delinquent, Puberty.*

ADOPTION
Adopted children, Genesis 15:3; 48:5; Exodus 2:10; Esther 2:7.
Selected as a nation, Deuteronomy 14:1-2.
Becoming children of God, John 1:12; Romans 8:15; 2 Corinthians 6:18; Galatians 4:3-7.

ADORATION
See *Worship.*

ADULATION
Avoiding partiality and flattery, Job 31:21-22.
Flattering lips speak deception, Psalm 12:2.
Nature and people praise the Lord, Psalm 148:1-14.
The God who is pure ego, Isaiah 42:8.
Herod called a god, not a man, Acts 12:22.
See *Accolade, Infatuation, Worship.*

ADULTERY
Adulteress foiled, Genesis 39:7-20.
Seventh commandment, Exodus 20:14.
Neighborhood relationship, Leviticus 20:10.
Cover of darkness, Job 24:15.
Folly of simpleton, Proverbs 7:6-23.
Adultery committed in profusion, Jeremiah 3:6.
Adultery and lust in heart and mind, Ezekiel 6:9; Matthew 5:27-28.
Wife who preferred strangers to her husband, Ezekiel 16:32.
Hosea's instructions to marry an adulterous wife, Hosea 1:2-3.
Divine forgiveness, John 8:1-11.
See *Immorality, Lust, Passion.*

ADVERSARY
Enemies of Israel, Joshua 5:13.
Counselors hired to frustrate plans for building temple, Ezra 4:5.
At peace with one's enemies, Proverbs 16:7.
Mob of bad characters incited against Paul and Silas, Acts 17:5-7.
Enemies of the Gospel, 1 Corinthians 16:9.
See *Antagonism, Demons, Enemy, Opponent, Satan, Soldier.*

ADVERSITY
Penalty for wickedness, Leviticus 26:14-16; Deuteronomy 28:45-48; 32:24.
Judgment brings righteousness, Isaiah 26:9.
Frying pan to fire, Amos 5:19.
Persecution implements spread of Gospel, Acts 8:3-4.
Always a silver lining, Romans 8:28.
Chastening and correction, Hebrews 12:5-11.
Vitalizing faith, 1 Peter 1:5-8.
See *Misfortune, Testing, Trauma, Trouble.*

ADVICE
Well-meaning advice leads to tragedy, Genesis 37:14-20.
Moses took advice of father-in-law, Exodus 18:13-26.
Rehoboam rejected advice of elders, 1 Kings 12:1-11.
Good advice, 2 Kings 5:13-14.
National guidance, Proverbs 11:14.
Fools spurn counsel, Proverbs 12:15.

Plans fail for lack of counsel, Proverbs 15:22.
Value of good advice, Proverbs 24:5-6.
Paul's counsel and sad parting with friends at Ephesus, Acts 20:25-28.
See *Counsel, Counseling.*

ADVOCATE

Looking out for welfare of people, Esther 10:3.
Speak up for those who cannot help themselves, Proverbs 31:8-9.
Paul's plea for Onesimus, Philemon 8-21.
Our High Priest in heaven, Hebrews 8:1-2.
Present place of Jesus in heaven, 1 Peter 3:22.
Our advocate with Heavenly Father, 1 John 2:1-2.
See *Mediator.*

AESTHETICS

Temple fragrance not for personal enjoyment, Exodus 30:34-38.
Aroma from altar, Leviticus 2:9.
Pleasing aroma, Numbers 15:7.
Food with pleasant aroma, Numbers 28:2.
Prophecy to sound of music, 2 Kings 3:15-16.
Matching colors on garment, Luke 5:36.
Residence by the sea, Acts 10:6.
See *Ambrosia, Beauty, Emotion, Music, Sensitivity.*

AFFECTATION

Egotist's parade, Esther 6:6-9.
Hypocrisy on display, Matthew 6:1-2, 16.
Empty sincerity of the Pharisees, Mark 12:15-17.
Ego displayed by teachers of Law, Mark 12:38-40.
Phoniness exposed, 1 Corinthians 4:6-8.
False humility, Colossians 2:18.
Mark of false teachers, 2 Peter 2:18-19.
Making false claim of holy life, 1 John 1:8-10.
See *Hypocrisy, Pretense, Sham.*

AFFECTION

Frustrated grandfather, Genesis 31:28.
Turning to rejected brother in time of need, Judges 11:1-10.
Love of David and Jonathan, 2 Samuel 1:26.
Kiss of death, 2 Samuel 20:9-10.

Our Lord's enduring love, Psalm 136:1-26.
Loved with everlasting love, Jeremiah 31:3.
False affection of Judas, Matthew 26:47-48.
Love expressed through anguish, 2 Corinthians 2:4.
Paul's deep love for Onesimus, Philemon 12.
Love each other deeply, 1 Peter 4:8.
Kiss of love, 1 Peter 5:14.
Love in the truth, 3 John 1.
See *Camaraderie, Emotion, Love, Rapport.*

AFFINITY

Rapport between believers, Psalm 119:63.
Two in agreement, Amos 3:3.
Commanded to love one another, John 13:34; 15:12.
Serving in unity, Acts 1:4; 2:44-47.
Perfect affinity, 1 Corinthians 1:10.
Sharing of both suffering and comfort, 2 Corinthians 1:7.
Bearing each other's burdens, Galatians 6:2.
Paul's concern for spiritual development of followers, Colossians 2:1-5.
Daily exhortation, Hebrews 3:13.
All of one mind, 1 Peter 3:8.
Love for each other,1 John 3:14; 4:7-13.
See *Camaraderie, Companionship, Compatibility, Unity.*

AFFLICTION

Divine concern for those suffering, Exodus 3:7.
Receiving both good and evil, Job 2:10; 5:17; Lamentations 3:22-39.
Longing for oblivion, Job 10:18-19.
A kind of birthright, Job 14:1.
Role of testing, Job 23:10; Psalm 66:10; Isaiah 48:10; 2 Corinthians 4:17; 1 Peter 1:7.
Scripture and suffering, Psalm 119:50, 67, 143.
Desperate times, Psalm 60:3.
Afflicted for a purpose, Psalm 119:75.
Furnace of affliction, Isaiah 48:10.
A place of disease and death, Jeremiah 16:1-13.
Glory in tribulation, Romans 5:3; 12:12.
Acceptance of affliction, 2 Corinthians 6:4-10; 7:4.
Sufficient grace, 2 Corinthians 12:9.
See *Calamity, Disease, Distress, Illness, Persecution, Sickness.*

AFFLUENCE

Wealthy Abram, Genesis 13:2.

Envy caused by wealth, Genesis 26:12-14.

God-given ability to produce wealth, Deuteronomy 8:18.

Wealth a test of spirituality, Deuteronomy 28:47-48.

Solomon's prayer for wisdom rather than material gain, 1 Kings 3:1-15.

Palace and temple, 1 Kings 7:1-51.

Wealth of King Solomon, 1 Kings 10:23.

Danger of riches and bribes, Job 36:18-19.

Wealth can numb thoughts of God, Psalm 10:3-6.

Lending money without interest, Psalm 15:5.

Discovery of eternal wealth, Psalm 19:8-11.

Trusting solely in the Lord, Psalm 20:7.

All earth belongs to the Lord, Psalm 24:1-2.

Better little with righteousness than wealth with wickedness, Psalm 37:16-17.

Prosperity of wicked short-lived, Psalm 37:35-36.

Danger of coveting good fortune of wicked, Psalm 73:2-5.

Greatest of all wealth, Psalm 119:14.

Wealth worthless in day of wrath, Proverbs 11:4.

Riches not to be trusted, Proverbs 11:28.

Pretending to be wealthy, Proverbs 13:7.

Value of little with faith over much with turmoil, Proverbs 15:16.

Better simple food with peace and quiet, Proverbs 17:1.

Those who lack character to go with wealth, Proverbs 19:10.

Rich and poor have common origin, Proverbs 22:2.

Emptiness of success and affluence, Ecclesiastes 2:4-11.

Dangers of national wealth, Isaiah 2:7-8.

Ruin of rich, Isaiah 5:17.

No desire for silver and gold, Isaiah 13:17.

Rejecting one's own idols of silver and gold, Isaiah 31:7.

That which money cannot buy, Isaiah 55:1-2.

Potential harm of great wealth and power, Jeremiah 5:27-28.

Wealth given away in judgment, Jeremiah 17:3.

Great wealth does not insure greatness, Jeremiah 22:14-15.

Poor people of Judah discovered true wealth, Jeremiah 39:10; 40:11-12.

Boasting and trusting in wealth, Jeremiah 48:7; 49:4.

Wealth into hands of enemy, Lamentations 1:10.

Gold loses luster, Lamentations 4:1.

Silver, gold, jewelry lose value, Ezekiel 7:19-20.

Good life swept away in judgment, Ezekiel 26:12-13.

Wealth numbs conscience, Hosea 12:8.

Loss of summer house because of disobedience, Amos 3:15.

Disobedient not allowed to enjoy materialistic possessions, Amos 6:11.

Silver and gold of no value when judgment falls, Zephaniah 1:18.

Silver and gold like dust and dirt, Zechariah 9:3.

Gain the world, forfeit the soul, Matthew 16:25-26.

Wealth a hindrance to salvation, Matthew 19:16-26.

Jesus accused of luxury, Matthew 26:6-13.

Deceitfulness of wealth, Mark 4:19.

Rich young man who kept the Law, Mark 10:17-27.

Widow's two small coins, Mark 12:41-44.

Rich receive less blessing than poor, Luke 6:20, 24-25.

Greed over one's possessions, Luke 12:13-15.

Wealthy hospitable to wealthy, Luke 14:12-14.

Rich man and Lazarus, Luke 16:19-31.

Spiritual perils of rich man, Luke 18:24.

He who was rich became poor, 2 Corinthians 8:9.

We bring nothing into the world, take nothing out, 1 Timothy 6:6-8.

Monetary wealth and the wealth of good deeds, 1 Timothy 6:11-19.

Love of money, Hebrews 13:5.

What seems a high position is instead low, James 1:10.

Clothes do not necessarily make the man, James 2:1-5.

Corrosion of gold and silver, James 5:1-3.

Our eternal inheritance, 1 Peter 1:3-4.

Sharing material possessions with others, 1 John 3:17.

True wealth, Revelation 2:9.

Difference between temporal wealth and spiritual wealth, Revelation 3:15-18.

See *Possessions, Property, Wealth.*

AFFRONT
Satanic defiance of Creator, Genesis 3:1-5;
Job 1:6-12; 2:1-7.
Speaking out against the Lord, Exodus
17:7; Numbers 21:5.
Pseudo-sympathizers, Job 2:11-13.
Challenging the Lord, Isaiah 5:18-25; 45:9-
10.
Affronting the prophets, Isaiah 30:10;
Amos 2:12.
Opposition to rebuilding temple, Ezra 4:4-
5.
Plot against a city, Nehemiah 4:7-9.
Affronting the one who affronts, Zechariah
3:1-2.
Affronting an enemy of truth, Acts 13:4-12.
Decisive resistance to opposition, Acts
18:6.
Reluctance of archangel to affront Satan,
Jude 9.
See *Defiance, Opposition.*

AFRAID
See *Apprehension, Fear.*

AGE
Age of Old Testament father, Genesis
11:10-26.
Assured longevity, Genesis 15:15.
Life as a pilgrimage, Genesis 47:9.
Value established by person's age,
Leviticus 27:1-8.
Vigor in old age, Deuteronomy 34:7;
Joshua 14:11; Job 5:26; 11:17; Psalm
92:14; Luke 2:36-37.
Marriage between young and old, Ruth
3:10.
Conclusion of a full life, 1 Chronicles
29:28.
Fear of old age, Psalm 71:9.
Assigned number of years, Psalm 90:10.
Prestige of gray hair, Proverbs 16:31.
Gamut of age, Isaiah 46:4.
Darius became king at age 62, Daniel 5:30-
31.
Old and young received angelic
announcements concerning births of
John the Baptist and Jesus, Luke 1:5-38.
Discipline for the aged, Titus 2:2-3.
Respect for those who are older, 1 Peter
5:5.
See *Birth, Birth certificate, Birthday,*

Geriatrics, Old age, Time.

AGGRESSIVE
Demanding a blessing, Genesis 32:26.
Eager for salvation, Mark 10:17.
Making most of every opportunity,
Ephesians 5:15-16; Colossians 4:5.
See *Ambition, Energy, Initiative,
Leadership.*

AGILITY
Soldiers agile with either hand,
1 Chronicles 12:1-2.
Feet of a deer, 2 Samuel 22:34; Song of
Songs 2:17.
See *Athletics, Skill.*

AGITATE
Counselors hired to frustrate plans for
building temple, Ezra 4:5.
Marks of an evil character, Proverbs 6:16-
19.
Jealous Jewish leaders, Acts 13:45-51.
See *Abrasion, Irritation, Meddle.*

AGNOSTIC
Claiming wisdom superior to God's, Psalm
73:6-11.
God makes Himself known through
judgment, Ezekiel 11:7-12.
Seeing and hearing but not understanding,
Mark 4:11-12.
Validity of Jesus questioned, John 8:12-30.
Doubt augmented by hearing the truth,
John 8:45-47.
See *Apostasy, Atheism, Cynical, Irreligious,
Skepticism, Unbelief.*

AGONY
Rich man in hades, Luke 16:23.
Spiritual misery, 2 Corinthians 1:8-9.
Agonizing prayer, Colossians 4:12.
Those who wish to die but cannot,
Revelation 9:4-6.
Torment forever, Revelation 14:11; 20:10.
Suffering increases rejection, Revelation
16:10-11.
See *Pain, Suffering, Torment, Torture.*

AGREEMENT
Treaty between Abraham and Abimelech,
Genesis 21:22-34.
Rebekah's consent to go to Isaac, Genesis
24:57-58.

Wrong kind of unanimity, Exodus 16:2.
Agreement voiced by congregation as the
Law declared, Deuteronomy 27:14-26.
Those who broke faith with God,
Deuteronomy 32:51.
Removal of sandal to finalize transaction,
Ruth 4:7.
Importance of treaty, 1 Kings 20:34.
Penalty for disobeying covenant, Jeremiah
11:1-5.
"Amen" of agreement to God's message,
Jeremiah 28:5-6.
Legal conflicts resulting from false oaths,
Hosea 10:4.
Judas under contract to betray Jesus,
Matthew 26:14-16.
Agreeing in united mind and thought,
1 Corinthians 1:10.
See *Approval, Concur, Rapport, Unanimity.*

AGRICULTURE

Let the land produce, Genesis 1:11-12.
Mankind's first vocation, Genesis 2:15;
3:23.
Laborious task of producing food, Genesis
3:17-19.
Ancient farmers, Genesis 4:2; 9:20; 1 Kings
19:19; 1 Chronicles 27:26; 2 Chronicles
26:10.
Lost skill for farming, Genesis 4:9-12.
Livestock farmer, Genesis 4:20.
Seedtime and harvest, Genesis 8:22.
Man of soil, Genesis 9:20.
Earning a fortune from farming, Genesis
13:2.
Limited fertility in Negev, Genesis 13:5-9.
Desire for best farmland, Genesis 13:10-11.
Isaac's abundant harvest, Genesis 26:12.
Identification of farm animals, Genesis
30:37-43.
Discerning sheaves, Genesis 37:7.
Abundance of grain in Egypt, Genesis
41:49.
Seventh-year rest for fields, Exodus 23:10-
11.
Rainless sky and parched earth, Leviticus
26:19-20.
Stolen crops, Deuteronomy 28:33.
David's kindness to son of Jonathan,
2 Samuel 9:10.
Solomon's knowledge of plant life, 1 Kings
4:33.
Farmer unable to manage wild ox, Job
39:9-13.

God provides rain for crops and pastures,
Psalm 65:9-13.
God's blessing on those who praise Him,
Psalm 67:5-6.
Finest of wheat, Psalm 81:16.
Promise of harvest, Psalm 85:12.
God's blessing on fields and herds, Psalm
107:37-38.
Creator entrusted earth to man, Psalm
115:16.
Grass on the housetops, Psalm 129:6-7.
Barns filled and flocks abundant, Psalm
144:13.
How to farm successfully, Proverbs 3:9-10.
He who hoards grain, Proverbs 11:26.
Abundance for good farmer, Proverbs
12:11.
Need of good animals to produce harvest,
Proverbs 14:4.
Importance of first things first, Proverbs
24:27.
Taking good care of farm animals,
Proverbs 27:23-27.
Driving rain of little value, Proverbs 28:3.
Tilling land or chasing fantasies, Proverbs
28:19.
Woman purchases field, Proverbs 31:16.
Crops not planted and harvested by
looking at sky, Ecclesiastes 11:4.
Fields robbed by foreigners, Isaiah 1:7.
Bad harvest, Isaiah 5:10.
Weeds take place of vines, Isaiah 7:23.
Grain of Nile brought to Tyre, Isaiah 23:3.
Making fertilizer, Isaiah 25:10.
The Lord watches over fruitful vineyard,
Isaiah 27:2-3.
God guides farmer, Isaiah 28:24-26.
Promise of rain, Isaiah 30:23.
Grain-growing volunteer, Isaiah 37:30.
Barren land made fertile, Isaiah 41:18-20.
Meadow grass and thriving trees, Isaiah
44:4.
Deserts become gardens, Isaiah 51:3.
Flesh of pigs equated with rats, Isaiah
66:17.
Israel likened to a harvest, Jeremiah 2:1-3.
Defilement of fertile land, Jeremiah 2:7.
Choice vine becomes corrupt, Jeremiah
2:21.
Break up unplowed ground, Jeremiah 4:3.
Vineyards ravaged because of
disobedience, Jeremiah 5:10.
Refusing to glorify God for harvest,
Jeremiah 5:24.

Harvest taken from disobedient, Jeremiah 8:13.

Promise of land "flowing with milk and honey," Jeremiah 11:5; 32:22.

Sow wheat but reap thorns, Jeremiah 12:13.

Extreme drought makes land barren, Jeremiah 14:4-6.

Joy of restoration in Israel, Jeremiah 31:5-6.

Well-watered garden, Jeremiah 31:12.

Beautiful heifer and gadfly, Jeremiah 46:20.

Scatter salt on condemned land, Jeremiah 48:9.

Land made desolate, Ezekiel 6:14.

God promises good crops to His people, Ezekiel 36:29-30.

Farmers weeping for lost harvest, Joel 1:11.

Seeds that will not sprout, Joel 1:17.

Land like Garden of Eden becomes desert waste, Joel 2:3.

Abundant rain brings abundant harvest, Joel 2:23-24.

Scant rainfall during growing season, Amos 4:7.

Sad time for farmers, Amos 5:16.

Confusion of seasons in the field, Amos 9:13.

Swords beaten into plowshares, Micah 4:3.

Planting but not harvesting, Micah 6:15.

Though crops fail, trust the Lord, Habakkuk 3:17-18.

Place of salt pits, Zephaniah 2:9.

Good crops withheld, Haggai 1:10-11.

Promise of blessing on harvest, Haggai 2:19.

Good seed and crops, Zechariah 8:12.

Praying for rain in springtime, Zechariah 10:1.

Prophets turned farmers, Zechariah 13:1-5.

Parable of Sower, Matthew 13:1-23; Luke 8:4-15.

Weeds and wheat, Matthew 13:24-30, 37-43.

Seedtime to harvest, miracle of growth, Mark 4:26-29.

Proper procedure for fertilizing tree, Luke 13:8.

Vine and fruit, John 15:1-8.

Blessing of rain and good crops, Acts 14:17.

Fruit of labor, 1 Corinthians 9:7.

God's blessing on seed and harvest, 2 Corinthians 9:10.

Reap what you sow, Galatians 6:7-10.

Farmer receives first share of crop, 2 Timothy 2:6.

Blessing of God on farming, Hebrews 6:7-8.

Farmer's patience as he waits for crop, James 5:7.

Grain for a day's wages, Revelation 6:6.

Locusts who do not harm grass, plant, or tree, Revelation 9:3-4.

Great harvest of earth in final days, Revelation 14:14-20.

Crop to harvest every month of year, Revelation 22:2.

See *Animals, Cattle, Farmer, Gleaners, Harvest, Nature, Seed, Soil, Weather.*

AIRCRAFT
Possible prophecy of airplanes, Isaiah 60:8. (See also 31:5; Ezek. 1:19.)

ALARM
Sudden attack, Judges 7:20-23.

ALCHEMY
Turned into gold, Job 23:10.

ALCOHOL
Noah's drunkenness and nudity, Genesis 9:18-27.

Lot and his two daughters, Genesis 19:30-38.

Sobriety in worship, Leviticus 10:8-10.

Wine offered as sacrifice, Numbers 15:5-7.

Alcoholic beverage other than wine, Judges 13:7.

Drink put Boaz in good spirits, Ruth 3:7.

Joy beyond levity of wine, Psalm 4:7.

Alcohol can lead astray, Proverbs 20:1.

Too much wine and food brings laziness, Proverbs 23:20-21.

Lingering over wine, Proverbs 23:30-33.

Sobriety and good government, Proverbs 31:4-7.

Champion bartenders, Isaiah 5:22.

Crying out for wine, Isaiah 24:7-13.

Festive use of wine, Isaiah 25:6.

Those laid low by wine, Isaiah 28:1, 7.

Drunkenness makes good decisions difficult, Isaiah 28:7.

Drunk but not with wine, Isaiah 51:21.

False sense of values, Isaiah 56:10-12.

Wine and divine judgment, Jeremiah

13:12-14.
Forefather's example of sobriety, Jeremiah 35:1-16.
False joy of drunkenness, Jeremiah 51:39.
Wine forbidden in temple, Ezekiel 44:21.
Weeping drunkard, Joel 1:5.
Forcing Nazarites to break vow, Amos 2:12.
Women who drink, Amos 4:1.
Abundance of wine and beer, Micah 2:11.
Drunk from too much wine, Nahum 1:10.
Betrayed by wine, Habakkuk 2:5.
Causing neighbor to become drunk, Habakkuk 2:15.
Correct method for storing wine, Matthew 9:17; Mark 2:22.
Wine at the Crucifixion, Mark 15:23.
Changing water into wine, John 2:1-11.
Causing another to stumble, Romans 14:20-23.
Drunk on wine or filled with the Spirit, Ephesians 5:18.
Drinking of wine, 1 Timothy 5:23.
An elder must not be given too much wine, Titus 1:7.
Women who drink wine, Titus 2:3.
Man a slave to whatever masters him, 2 Peter 2:19.
Babylon, drunk with blood of saints, Revelation 17:6.
See *Abstinence, Beer, Drunkenness, Intemperance, Liquor, Wine.*

ALERT
Not found sleeping when the Lord returns, Mark 13:35-37.
Making the most of every opportunity, Ephesians 5:15-16.
Ready to serve and witness, Ephesians 6:15.
Awake in time of judgment, Revelation 16:15.
See *Awareness, Perception.*

ALIEN
See *Foreigner, Intruder, Race, Racism, Stranger, Xenophobia.*

ALLEGORY
Understandable communication, Numbers 12:8.
Short story with moral for disobedient man, 2 Samuel 12:1-4.
From ignominious birth to royal beauty,

Ezekiel 16:4-29.
Two eagles and the vine, Ezekiel 17:1-24.
See *Literature, Parable.*

ALMS
See *Philanthropy, Welfare.*

ALTERNATIVE
Wavering between two opinions, 1 Kings 18:21.
A better option, Isaiah 1:18.
Choice of Jesus or Barabbas, Matthew 27:15-26.
Gain world or lose soul, Mark 8:36.
No alternative to Jesus, John 6:66-69.
See *Choice, Escape, Freewill, Option, Rescue.*

ALTRUISTIC
One brother's unselfish attitude toward another, Genesis 33:1-11.
Brother returns good for evil, Genesis 50:15-21.
Providing for strangers and poor, Leviticus 23:22.
Providing for need of another, Ruth 2:15-16.
Men of bad circumstances share good fortune with others, 2 Kings 7:3-9.
Unselfish prayer of wise king, 2 Chronicles 1:7-12.
Joseph's altruistic concern for Mary, Matthew 1:19.
Greatest in the kingdom, Luke 9:46-48.
Woman who helped the poor, Acts 9:36-42.
Basic premise is love, 1 Corinthians 13:1-13.
See *Unselfishness.*

AMATEUR
Father assisting inexperienced son, 1 Chronicles 22:5; 29:1.
See *Athletics, Novice.*

AMAZEMENT
Vindication by earthquake, Numbers 16:28-34.
Ezekiel overwhelmed, Ezekiel 3:15.
Awesome acts of God, Joel 1:13-20.
See *Awe, Emotion, Serendipity.*

AMBASSADOR
Moses made like God to Pharaoh, Exodus

7:1-2.
Messengers and envoys dispatched,
Numbers 20:14; 21:21; 2 Samuel 5:11;
1 Kings 5:1; 20:2-3; 2 Kings 14:8; 16:7;
Ezekiel 17:13-15.
Highest of all appointments, 2 Corinthians
5:20.
See *Missionary.*

AMBIDEXTROUS
Soldiers agile with either hand,
1 Chronicles 12:1-2.

AMBIENT
See *Aura.*

AMBIGUOUS
Confusion of languages, Genesis 11:1-8.
Avoiding ambiguity, Habakkuk 2:2.
Followers of Jesus unable to understand
the coming Crucifixion, Luke 9:44-45.
Paul accused of babbling, Acts 17:18.
Trumpet's uncertain sound, 1 Corinthians
14:8.
Ambiguous gospel, Galatians 1:6-7.
See *Vague.*

AMBITION
Ambition of a secular society, Genesis
11:1-4.
Campaigning for office, 2 Samuel 15:1-4.
Desire for full obedience, Psalm 119:1-5.
David's determination to fulfill his destiny,
Psalm 132:1-5.
Man's plans and God's purposes, Proverbs
16:1; 19:21.
Desire to keep ahead of one's neighbor,
Ecclesiastes 4:4.
Seeking great things in rebellion against
God, Jeremiah 45:4-5.
Indulgent mother, Matthew 20:21.
Desire for religious prominence, Luke
22:24.
Continual lust for more, Ephesians 4:19.
Making most of every opportunity,
Ephesians 5:15-16.
Ready to serve and witness, Ephesians
6:15.
Paul's supreme desire, Philippians 3:7-11.
Make the most of every opportunity,
Colossians 4:5.
Motivated to a truly Christian lifestyle,
1 Thessalonians 4:11-12.
Desire to be an overseer, 1 Timothy 3:1.

Danger of motivation toward wealth,
1 Timothy 6:9-10.
Uncertainty of tomorrow, James 4:13-16.
See *Initiative, Motivation.*

AMBIVALENCE
Amnon's hatred for Tamar, whom he had
loved, 2 Samuel 13:12-19.
Accusation against King David, 2 Samuel
19:6.
Renegade pleads for his life from the one
he would harm, Esther 7:7.
Complaint and praise, Psalm 22:1-11, 22-
31.
Beloved and yet seen as wicked, Jeremiah
11:15.
Accusing the Lord, then praising Him,
Jeremiah 20:7, 11-13.
Negative attitude toward God's blessing on
His message, Jonah 4:1-11.
Divine love and hatred, Malachi 1:2-3.
Pharisees alleged concern for safety of
Jesus, Luke 13:31.
See *Affection, Hatred, Hypocrisy, Love.*

AMBROSIA
Food in presence of enemies, Psalm 23:5.
Satisfying fare of good things, Psalm 103:5.
Deceptive delicacies, Proverbs 23:3.
See *Aesthetics, Delicacy.*

AMBUSH
Joshua's tactic, Joshua 8:12.
Citizen's ambush, Judges 9:25.
Murder by deceit, 2 Samuel 3:27.
Attacking enemy from rear, 2 Samuel
5:22-25.
Setting traps for men, Jeremiah 5:26.
Fear of walking in public places, Jeremiah
6:25.
Led into false security, Jeremiah 41:4-7.

AMENITIES
Amenities to visitors, Genesis 18:3-5.
Abundant blessings of nature,
Deuteronomy 33:13-16.
See *Courtesy, Hospitality.*

AMNESTY
No qualification for amnesty, Genesis
18:16-33.
No death penalty for one day, 1 Samuel
11:13.
Leave revenge to God's timing, 1 Samuel

26:1-11.
Death penalty waived, 2 Samuel 19:16-23.
Amnesty by public choice, Matthew 27:16-26; Mark 15:7-15; Luke 23:18; John 18:40.
Divine amnesty, Romans 6:23; Ephesians 2:1-9.
See *Pardon, Parole.*

AMUSEMENT
When laughter is out of place, Genesis 18:10-15.
Wicked games, Exodus 32:6.
Samson's performance, Judges 16:25.
Boxing and wrestling matches, 2 Samuel 2:14.
Dancing children, Job 21:11-12.
Entertainment with no thought of spiritual need, Isaiah 5:12.
Strumming on harps, Amos 6:5.
Worship of fishing, Habakkuk 1:16.
Children playing, Zechariah 8:5.
See *Hedonism, Laughter, Playboy, Pleasure, Relaxation.*

ANALOGY
Likeness of a fool, Proverbs 26:1-11.
Heavens illustrate divine thought and purpose, Isaiah 55:9.
Two baskets of figs, Jeremiah 24:1-10.
Jesus used figures of speech, Mark 8:14-21.
Human body likened to temple, John 2:18-22.

ANARCHY
Contempt for church and state, Deuteronomy 17:12; Ezra 7:26.
Positive anarchy of the ant, Proverbs 6:6-8.
Many rulers during rebellion, Proverbs 28:2.
People turning against each other, Isaiah 3:5-7.
Overabundance of shepherds, Jeremiah 12:10.
Fish have no ruler, Habakkuk 1:14.
Slaves turn against masters, Zechariah 2:9.
Neighbor against neighbor, Zechariah 8:10.
Men attacking each other, Zechariah 14:13.

ANCESTORS
Suffering penalty of ancestor's sin, Exodus 20:5-7.

Confessing sins of ancestors, Nehemiah 9:2.
Genealogy of Jesus, Matthew 1:1-17; Luke 3:23-38.
Hypocrisy toward ancestors, Matthew 23:29-32.
See *Forefathers, Heritage, History, Influence.*

ANESTHETIC
First use of anesthetic, Genesis 2:21.
Satanic anesthesia, Ephesians 5:14.

ANGELS
Abraham's heavenly visitors, Genesis 18:1-10.
Offering mortal amenities to angels, Genesis 19:1-4.
Angels spoken of as men, Genesis 19:1-13.
Guidance by personal angel, Genesis 24:40.
Donkey who saw an angel, Numbers 22:23-28.
Commander of army of the Lord, Joshua 5:13-15.
Angel unrecognized, Judges 13:16-18.
Mistaking an angel for God Himself, Judges 13:21-23.
Deliverance to those in need, Psalm 34:7.
Bread of angels, Psalm 78:25.
Role of guardian angels, Psalm 91:9-12. (See Ex. 23:20.)
Angels obedient to the Lord, Psalm 103:20.
Angel of the Lord destroyed enemy soldiers, Isaiah 37:36.
Appearance of Gabriel to Daniel, Daniel 9:20-21.
Strength from an angel, Daniel 10:15-19.
Angels, dreams, and visions, Zechariah 1:7-17.
Ministry of angel to prophet, Zechariah 1:8-21. (Note also continuing chapters.)
Angel described as "a young man," Mark 16:5.
Miraculous births of Jesus and John the Baptist foretold by angel, Luke 1:5-38.
Frightened at sight of angel, Luke 1:11-12.
Gabriel on two assignments, Luke 1:11-38.
Angel named newborn son, Luke 1:13.
Philip guided by angel, Acts 8:26.
Seen in a vision and recognized as representative of the Lord, Acts 10:3-4.
Ministry of angels in time of need, Acts 12:8-10; 27:21-25.

Peter's personal angel, Acts 12:15. (See v. 11.)

Demons masquerade as angels of light, 2 Corinthians 11:14-15.

Christ superior to angels, Hebrews 1:4-8.

Ministering spirits, Hebrews 1:14.

Entertaining angels without knowing it, Hebrews 13:2.

Curiosity of angels, 1 Peter 1:12.

Book of Revelation given by an angel, Revelation 1:1.

Great choir of angels, Revelation 5:11-12.

Illumination of an angel's presence, Revelation 18:1.

One angel capable of overpowering Satan, Revelation 20:1-3.

Fellow servants not to be worshiped, Revelation 22:8-9.

See *Demons, Guardian.*

ANGER

Anger that led to murder, Genesis 4:3-8.

Angry at a song, Genesis 18:6-15.

Things done in rage, Deuteronomy 19:4-7.

Danger of hot temper, Judges 18:25. (See also Prov. 22:24-25.)

Anger at divine remedy, 2 Kings 5:1-12.

Anger without sin, Psalm 4:4.

Anger turned away by gentle words, Proverbs 15:1.

Using words with restraint, Proverbs 17:27.

Lacking self-control, Proverbs 25:28.

A fool and a wise man, Proverbs 29:11.

Angry man stirs up dissension, Proverbs 29:22.

Stirring up anger, Proverbs 30:33.

Cup of God's wrath, Jeremiah 25:15-29.

Continual anger, Amos 1:11.

Anger a form of murder, Matthew 5:21-22.

Resentment to spiritual truth, Acts 5:30-33.

Anger at sunset, Ephesians 4:26.

See *Disgust, Hatred, Reaction, Temper.*

ANGUISH

No song for heavy heart, Proverbs 25:20.

Joy turns to sorrow, Lamentations 5:15.

Prayer in Gethsemane, Mark 14:35-36. (Note: Some believe Jesus was praying His body would be able to bear humanity's guilt until He could get to the cross!)

Gnashing teeth, Acts 7:54.

Those who wish to die but cannot, Revelation 9:4-6.

Agony of those who refuse to repent, Revelation 16:10-11.

See *Anxiety, Pain, Persecution, Stress, Suffering, Torment, Torture.*

ANIMALS

God created both domestic and wild animals, Genesis 1:24-25.

Man and animals vegetarian, Genesis 1:29-30.

Intelligence of the serpent, Genesis 3:1.

Experiment in animal breeding, Genesis 30:37-39.

Liability for treacherous animal, Exodus 21:28-32.

Distinction between animal life and human life, Leviticus 24:21.

Cruelty to horses, 2 Samuel 8:4.

Mountains rich with game, Psalm 76:4.

More responsive to obedience than humans, Isaiah 1:3.

One day all nature will again be in harmony, Isaiah 11:6-9; 65:25.

Courage of a lion, Isaiah 31:4.

Lions, wolves, and leopards, Jeremiah 5:6.

Anger of bear robbed of cubs, Hosea 13:8.

Relationship of wild animals to God, Joel 2:22.

Security in lion's habitat, Nahum 2:11.

Four beautiful horses, Zechariah 6:2-3.

Donkey chosen to serve Jesus, Matthew 21:1-7; Mark 11:1-7.

Concern for one lost sheep, Luke 15:1-7.

Men and animals of different flesh, 1 Corinthians 15:39.

Trained animals, James 3:7.

See *Carnivorous, Donkey, Dragon, Horse.*

ANIMISM

Worship of nature forbidden, Deuteronomy 4:15-20; 17:2-7.

Nature as teacher, Job 12:7-16.

Homage to sun and moon, Job 31:26-28.

Worshiping wood and stone, Jeremiah 2:27.

Worship of the sun, Ezekiel 8:16.

Worshiping the stars, Zephaniah 1:5.

ANIMOSITY

Unanimous complaint, Exodus 16:2.

Jealous wife, 1 Samuel 1:3-7.

Wealth and prestige could not numb Haman's resentment, Esther 5:10-14.

At odds with one's Maker, Isaiah 45:9.

See *Covet, Hatred, Jealousy.*

ANNIVERSARY
Looking back over many years of blessing,
Deuteronomy 2:7.
Recording date of completion of Jerusalem
wall, Nehemiah 6:15.
Date to remember, Haggai 2:18.
See *Birthday, Celebration, Commemorate.*

ANNOUNCEMENT
Letters of invitation, 2 Chronicles 30:1-5.
Royal announcement, Ezra 1:2-4.
Advance notice, Isaiah 40:3.
Proclaiming year of the Lord, Isaiah 61:1-3.
Royal decree to disobey God, Daniel 3:4-7.
Preaching of John the Baptist, Matthew
3:1-3.
Angelic announcement of births of Jesus
and John the Baptist, Luke 1:5-38.

ANNOY
Disturbing privacy of others, Proverbs
25:17.

ANOINTING
David's respect for King Saul's position
and anointing, 1 Samuel 24:1-7. (See
26:7-11.)
Hand of the Lord on Ezekiel, Ezekiel 1:3.
Anointed to serve the Lord worldwide,
Zechariah 4:14.
Sending out the Twelve to minister, Luke
9:1-6.
Sanctifying truth, John 17:17.
See *Commitment, Consecration, Holy Spirit,
Ordination.*

ANONYMITY
Grave of Moses, Deuteronomy 34:6.
Peter's act of violence almost an act of
anonymity, Matthew 26:51-52; Mark
14:47; Luke 22:49-51; John 18:10-11.
Jesus could not keep His presence secret,
Mark 7:24.
Jesus disappeared through the crowd,
Luke 4:30.
Anonymous heroes of faith, Hebrews
11:35-39.
Unknown name, Revelation 19:12.
See *Secrecy, Stranger, Unknown.*

ANSWER
Nonverbal response, Judges 6:36-40;

1 Kings 18:37-38.
Answer delayed 10 days, Jeremiah 42:7.
Daniel looked to God for knowledge,
Daniel 2:14-28.
Abraham waited patiently for God's
promise, Hebrews 6:13-14.
See *Response.*

ANTAGONISM
Wealth and prestige could not numb
Haman's resentment, Esther 5:10-
14.
Multitude of demons, Luke 8:26-31.
Bad characters incited against Paul and
Silas, Acts 17:5-7.
See *Adversary, Demons, Enemy,
Opposition, Satan.*

ANTICHRIST
Many will come claiming to be Christ,
Matthew 24:4-5.
Description of man of sin, 2 Thessalonians
2:1-11.
Deceivers in the world, 2 John 7-11.
See *Millennium, Second Coming,
Tribulation.*

ANTICIPATION
Spiritual preparation for future victory,
Joshua 3:5.
Preparing to receive promised water,
2 Kings 3:15-17.
Longing fulfilled, Proverbs 13:12, 19.
Watchmen on walls, Isaiah 62:6.
Behind devastation, ahead anticipation,
Joel 2:3.
Aged Simeon saw promised Saviour, Luke
2:25-32.
That which God has prepared for those
who love Him, 1 Corinthians 2:9-10.
Abraham anticipated salvation of Jew and
Gentile by faith, Galatians 3:6-9.
Asking God for wisdom and believing it
will be granted, James 1:5-7.
Eternal inheritance, 1 Peter 1:3-4.
See *Aspiration, Expectation,
Hope, Horizons.*

ANTI-SEMITISM
Punishment decreed on enemies of Israel,
Jeremiah 30:16-17.
Mixing human blood with sacrifices, Luke
13:1.
See *Islam, Israel, Prejudice, Racism.*

ANXIETY

Trusting God in face of insurmountable opposition, Exodus 14:5-14.

Description of anxiety, Deuteronomy 28:66-67.

Sure rest in the Lord's protection, Deuteronomy 33:12.

Courage is God's command, Joshua 1:9.

David as counselor of distressed and discontented, 1 Samuel 22:2.

Lifted out of deep waters, 2 Samuel 22:17.

Lamp of the Lord, 2 Samuel 22:29.

Desire for peace and security, 2 Kings 20:19.

Curdled like cheese, Job 10:10.

Endless internal tension, Job 30:27.

Totally trusting the Lord whatever the circumstances, Psalm 3:1-8.

Wrestling one's thoughts, Psalm 13:2, 5.

God is ever present, Psalm 14:4-5.

God's light overcomes darkness, Psalm 18:28.

Relaxation in the Lord, Psalm 37:7.

Songs in the night, Psalm 42:8.

Be still and know, Psalm 46:10.

Fear of the future, Psalm 55:4-5.

Casting all care on the Lord, Psalm 55:22.

Finding rest in God alone, Psalm 62:5-8.

God bears daily burdens, Psalm 68:19.

Consolation brings joy to the soul, Psalm 94:19.

God delivers from distress, Psalm 107:6.

Calling out to God in time of deep depression, Psalms 116:1-4; 120:1.

Release from anguish, Psalm 118:5.

Secret to true relaxation, Proverbs 19:23.

Learn to banish anxiety, Ecclesiastes 11:10.

Fearing wrong things, Isaiah 8:12-14.

Kept in perfect peace, Isaiah 26:3.

Strength and repose from the Lord, Isaiah 35:3-4.

Purpose of tension for God's glory, Isaiah 38:15-16.

Mount up on wings like eagles, Isaiah 40:29-31.

Gladness and joy overtake sorrow, Isaiah 51:11.

Anguish of guilt, Jeremiah 4:18-19.

Blessed are those who trust in the Lord, Jeremiah 17:7-8.

Safest place in times of trouble, Jeremiah 42:1-22.

Inner torment, Lamentations 1:20.

Anxiety caused by circumstances, Ezekiel 4:16-17.

Plight of those who rebel against the Lord, Ezekiel 12:19.

Quiet rejoicing in the Lord, Zephaniah 3:17.

Nonproductive worry, Matthew 6:27.

Rest for the weary and burdened, Matthew 11:28-30.

Permitting worry to blind one's eyes to truth of Scripture, Matthew 13:22.

Needless fear in time of storm, Mark 4:35-41.

Power of faith over fear, Mark 5:36.

Circumstances should not hinder confidence of faith, Luke 8:22-25.

At peace before authorities, Luke 12:11-12.

Antidote for troubled hearts, John 14:1.

Surest therapy for anxious hearts, John 16:33.

The Lord who is always at hand, Acts 2:25-28.

Evil spirits cause torment, Acts 5:16.

Going without food in times of duress, Acts 27:33-34.

Exercising hope when no basis for hope, Romans 4:18-22.

Nothing can separate us from love of God, Romans 8:37-39.

Christ, who is faithful, will keep you strong, 1 Corinthians 1:8-9.

Turning to the God of all comfort, 2 Corinthians 1:3-4.

Love expressed through anguish, 2 Corinthians 2:4.

Secret of deliverance, 2 Corinthians 4:7-18.

Paul experienced anxiety, Philippians 2:28.

Prayer that brings peace, Philippians 4:6-7.

Motivated by joy given by Holy Spirit, 1 Thessalonians 1:6.

Jesus knows our weaknesses, promises help in time of trouble, Hebrews 4:14-16.

Grace and peace in abundance, 1 Peter 1:2.

Be self-controlled, 1 Peter 1:13.

Cast all cares on the Lord, 1 Peter 5:7.

Abundant grace and peace, 2 Peter 1:2.

God's best in abundance, Jude 2.

Tears forever wiped away, Revelation 7:17; 21:4.

See *Apprehension, Danger, Despondency, Distress, Stress, Tension, Worry.*

APATHY
Complacent women, Isaiah 32:9.
Those who pass by, Lamentations 1:12.
Heart of flesh or heart of stone, Ezekiel 11:19.
Refusing to see and hear, Ezekiel 12:1-2.
Relegating prophetic judgment to distant future, Ezekiel 12:26-28.
Complacency in Zion, Amos 6:1.
Those who neither seek the Lord nor ask about Him, Zephaniah 1:6.
Fate of carefree people, Zephaniah 2:15.
Hearts hard as flint, Zechariah 7:11-12.
Rejecting wedding invitation, Matthew 22:1-14.
Spiritual love grown cold, Matthew 24:10-13.
Caring neither for God nor man, Luke 18:1-5.
See *Backsliding, Carnality, Unconcerned, Worldliness.*

APHORISM
Origin of a saying, 1 Samuel 10:11-12.
Deeds reveal person, 1 Samuel 24:13.
"Freedom," a play on words, Jeremiah 34:17.
See *Figure of speech.*

APOLOGETICS
Jesus challenged to prove His divinity, John 10:22-39.
Challenge to prove all things, 1 Thessalonians 5:21.

APOSTASY
No God, no priest, no Law in Israel, 2 Chronicles 15:3.
Nations resisting Law of God, Psalm 2:3.
Truth that perished, Jeremiah 7:28.
Ministration of evil prophets, Jeremiah 23:10-14.
Tree known by fruit, Matthew 12:33-35.
Weeds among wheat, Matthew 13:24-30.
Turning away from faith, Matthew 24:10.
Peter and John persecuted for proclaiming resurrection, Acts 4:1-4.
Stephen resorted to history for his defense, Acts 7:1-60.
Holding onto faith, 1 Timothy 1:18; 4:1; Hebrews 3:12; 2 Peter 3:17.
Those who deserted Paul, 2 Timothy 1:15.
Turning away from the living God, Hebrews 3:12.

Those who fall away from truth, Hebrews 6:4-6.
Those who go out from the body, 1 John 2:18-19.
Those who experienced deliverance but did not believe, Jude 5.
Feigning life when spiritually dead, Revelation 3:1.
See *Liberalism, Modernism, Syncretism, Unbelief.*

APPEARANCE
Physique and appearance of Joseph, Genesis 39:6-7.
Samson's mother described angel who came to her, Judges 13:6.
Outward appearance, 1 Samuel 16:7; 2 Corinthians 5:12.
Appearance of the boy David, 1 Samuel 16:12.
Neglecting one's personal appearance, 2 Samuel 19:24.
Happy heart makes cheerful face, Proverbs 15:13.
Prophecy concerning Jesus, Isaiah 53:2.
Variation of facial appearance, Ezekiel 1:10.
Whitewashed tombs, Matthew 23:27; John 7:24.
See *Countenance.*

APPEASE
Provision for grumbling people, Exodus 16:2-18.
A sacrifice for sin, Micah 6:7.
Refusing to appease those who dilute Gospel message, Galatians 1:9-10.

APPETITE
Man and animals originally vegetarian, Genesis 1:29-30. (See also 2:16.)
Angels presumed to have appetites, Genesis 19:1-3.
Taste for game influenced Isaac's feelings toward Esau, Genesis 25:27-28.
Loss of appetite, 1 Samuel 1:7; 20:34; Psalms 102:4; 107:18.
Too much food and drink, Proverbs 23:20.
Too lazy to eat, Proverbs 26:15.
Bitterness tastes sweet when hungry, Proverbs 27:7.
Dogs with big appetites, Isaiah 56:11.
The king who lost his appetite, Daniel 6:18.
Hunger and thirst for righteousness,

Matthew 5:6.

Four thousand who had not eaten for three days, Mark 8:1-9.

Too much concern for food and drink, Luke 12:29.

Peter, while hungry, fell into trance, Acts 10:10.

Continual lust for more, Ephesians 4:19.

Appetite for spiritual food, 1 Peter 2:2-3.

Sweet in the mouth, sour to the stomach, Revelation 10:9-10.

See *Cooking, Famine, Food, Gourmet, Hunger.*

APPLAUSE

Coronation applause, 2 Kings 11:12.

Applause of scorn, Job 34:37; Lamentations 2:15.

Nature applauds, Psalm 98:8; Isaiah 55:12.

Rejoicing in malice, Ezekiel 25:6-7.

Clapping hands at fate of Nineveh, Nahum 3:19.

See *Accolade, Praise.*

APPOINTMENT

Commission with encouragement, Deuteronomy 3:28.

Moses told where to go for his death, Deuteronomy 32:48-50.

Daniel's request for appointment with the king, Daniel 2:16.

Joshua chosen to build the temple, Zechariah 6:9-15.

APPRAISAL

Counting the cost, Luke 14:28-30.

Honest appraisal of oneself, James 1:22-24.

APPRECIATION

Vicarious appreciation, 2 Samuel 9:1; 10:2.

Gratitude for great forgiveness, Luke 7:39-50.

Appreciation not shown to servant, Luke 17:7-10.

The 10 healed of leprosy, Luke 17:12-18.

See *Gratitude, Thanksgiving.*

APPREHENSION

Adonijah's unnecessary fear, 1 Kings 1:50-53.

David's fear of God in a given circumstance, 1 Chronicles 13:12.

No fear of bad news, Psalm 112:7.

Danger of fearing wrong things, Isaiah 8:12-14.

Needlessness of worry, Matthew 6:25-27.

Role of holy fear as motivating factor, Hebrews 11:7.

Reverent fear, 1 Peter 1:17.

See *Fear, Indecision, Uncertainty.*

APPRENTICE

Prior to his time of leadership, Joshua obeyed commands of Moses, Exodus 17:10.

Moses given formula for perfume, Exodus 30:22-25.

Divinely acquired skills, Exodus 31:1-5.

Training Joshua for future leadership, Numbers 27:18-23.

Father assists inexperienced son, 1 Chronicles 22:5; 29:1.

Paul and Timothy, 2 Timothy 2:1-2.

See *Novice, Skill, Teaching.*

APPROPRIATE

Appropriate role in kingdom, Esther 4:14.

Proper time and procedure, Ecclesiastes 8:5-6.

Doing what she could, Mark 14:8.

See *Tact, Timing.*

APPROVAL

People respond with one voice, Exodus 24:3.

Removal of sandal to finalize transaction, Ruth 4:7.

Nehemiah's authorization from king for travel to Jerusalem, Nehemiah 2:1-8.

Honor of strong people, Isaiah 25:3.

God's total approval of His Son, Matthew 3:17.

Empty sincerity of Pharisees, Mark 12:15-17.

Receive praise from God, 1 Corinthians 4:5.

Paul's recognition of followers, Colossians 4:7-17.

APTITUDE

What God requires, He provides, Isaiah 2:3.

Victory involves more than ability, Isaiah 25:11.

Choice of candidates for service in Babylonian government, Daniel 1:3-5.

See *Ability, Intelligence, Skill, Talent.*

ARAB
See *Islam.*

ARBITRATION
Divine provision in property dispute,
Genesis 26:19-22.
Divine surveillance, Genesis 31:48-50.
Mediation of a king between two mothers,
1 Kings 3:16-28.
Deliverance from conflict beyond mortal
strength, Romans 7:15-25.

ARBOR
Abraham's tree planting, Genesis 21:33.
Choosing king from among trees, Judges
9:7-20.
See *Trees.*

ARCHEOLOGY
Ruins rebuilt, Isaiah 58:12; 61:4.

ARCHITECTURE
Building Tower of Babel, Genesis 11:1-6.
Threshing floor site for altar, 2 Samuel
24:18-25.
Solomon's organization for building
temple, 1 Kings 5:12-18.
Nehemiah's skill in rebuilding wall,
Nehemiah 6:1.
Measuring new temple area, Ezekiel 40:5-
49.
Lack of permanence in temple, Mark 13:1-
2.
Builder has greater honor than building,
Hebrews 3:3.
See *Building, Carpenter, Construction,
Design, Plan.*

AREA
Measuring width and length of Jerusalem,
Zechariah 2:1-2.
See *Property.*

ARGUMENT
Futility of strife among brothers, 2 Samuel
2:27-28.
Let the Lord make your cause valid, Psalm
37:6.
Anger turned away by gentle words,
Proverbs 15:1.
Good counsel when tempted to quarrel,
Proverbs 17:14.
Sin of loving a quarrel, Proverbs 17:19.
Wisdom of silence elevates fool, Proverbs

17:28.
An honor to avoid strife, Proverbs 20:3.
Evidence turns against accuser, Proverbs
25:8.
Speaking with gentle tongue, Proverbs
25:15.
Meddling in a quarrel, Proverbs 26:17.
Disputing mercy and justice of God's ways,
Ezekiel 33:10-20.
How to handle dispute, Romans 14:1.
Avoid foolish arguments, 2 Timothy 2:23.
Basic rules for teacher in handling dispute,
2 Timothy 2:23-26.
Keep one's head in all situations,
2 Timothy 4:5.
Avoid foolish arguments about the Law,
Titus 3:9.
See *Debate, Quarrel.*

ARID
No water to nurture crops, Leviticus 26:18-
20.
Land that produces sparingly, Isaiah 5:10.
Drought during growing season, Amos 4:7-
8.
Dry top soil, Mark 4:5-6.
See *Desert, Weather.*

ARMAGEDDON
Inevitable fate of world governments,
Psalm 2:7-9.
Description of great battle to come, Daniel
11:36-45.
See *Antichrist, Rapture, Second Coming.*

ARMAMENT
Threat of iron chariots, Judges 1:19.
Futility of war, 2 Samuel 1:27.
See *Army, Military, Pacifism, Soldier, War,
Weapons.*

ARMY
David's army of chosen men, 2 Samuel
6:1.
See *Armament.*

ARREST
Apprehended by manner of speech,
Judges 12:5-6.
Held in custody for Sabbath-breaking,
Numbers 15:34.
City of refuge, Numbers 35:6-15.
Imprisoned for tax evasion, 2 Kings 17:4.
Posting bond following arrest, Acts 17:9.

Paul under house arrest, Acts 28:16.
Angel to arrest and chain Satan, Revelation 20:1-3.
See *Indictment, Jail, Prison.*

ARROGANCE
Arrogant before the Lord, 1 Samuel 2:3.
Thinking it easy to face an enemy, Deuteronomy 1:41-45.
Flattering lips and boastful tongue, Psalm 12:4.
Haughty and ruthless, Isaiah 13:11.
Those who do not know how to blush, Jeremiah 6:15.
Boast only about the Lord, Jeremiah 9:23-24.
Pride and arrogance of Moab, Jeremiah 48:29.
Pride of conqueror brought down, Jeremiah 50:11-12.
Paul's ironical evaluation of weak Christians, 1 Corinthians 4:8-18.
Evil queen refuses to admit sin, Revelation 18:7-8.
See *Pride, Rebellion, Self-image, Vanity.*

ARSON
Samson's method for burning fields of Philistines, Judges 15:4-5.
See *Fire.*

ART
Divine portrayal, Psalm 19:1.
Wall murals, Ezekiel 8:7-12; 23:14.

ARTESIAN
Water pouring from well, Jeremiah 6:7.

ARTHRITIS
Filled with searing pain, Psalm 38:7.

ARTIFACTS
Articles from sanctuary taken into battle, Numbers 31:6.
David kept weapons of Goliath, 1 Samuel 17:54.

ARTIFICIAL
Ego displayed by teachers of the Law, Mark 12:38-40.
False humility, Colossians 2:18.
See *Insincerity, Sham.*

ARTIST
Separating light from darkness, Genesis 1:4, 17-18.
Talents provided by Holy Spirit, Exodus 31:1-5.
Chisel at work, Deuteronomy 10:1.
Skilled at his work, Proverbs 22:29.
Idol-maker burns wood from carving, Isaiah 44:15-17.
Decor of temple, Ezekiel 41:17-20.
See *Skill, Talent.*

ASCENSION
Elijah to heaven in whirlwind, 2 Kings 2:11.
Ascension foretold, Psalm 68:18.
Ascension event, Mark 16:19; Acts 1:9.
Ascension impact, Hebrews 4:14; 9:24; 1 Peter 3:22.

ASHAMED
Ashamed to mention name of the Lord, Amos 6:10.
Hiding the light, Matthew 5:15.
Guilt of Judas, Matthew 27:3.
See *Humiliation, Repentance.*

ASPIRATION
Desire for full obedience, Psalm 119:1-5.
Greatest in kingdom, Luke 9:46-48.
See *Ambition, Determination, Vision.*

ASSASSINATION
Death of a king, Judges 3:21.
Death of King Saul, 2 Samuel 1:1-16.
A brother avenged, 2 Samuel 3:27.
Recruited to turn against their own king, 2 Kings 9:14-24.
King destroyed by associates, 2 Kings 12:19-20.
Slain at temple worship, 2 Kings 19:37.
See *Murder.*

ASSERTIVE
Insisting on God's blessing, Genesis 32:26.
Suggesting conditions for answered prayer, Exodus 32:31-32.
Admission of weakness as a demand for blessing, 1 Kings 3:7-9.
Approach to God on the basis of His character, Psalm 51:1-7.
Repetitious prayer, Luke 11:5-13.

ASSESSMENT

Thinking it easy to face an enemy, Deuteronomy 1:41-42.

Sanballat's ridicule of Jewish capability, Nehemiah 4:1-10.

Realizing what believers have in Christ, Ephesians 1:18-23.

Good land and unproductive land, Hebrews 6:7-8.

See *Evaluation, Inventory.*

ASSIGNMENT

Trustworthy messenger, Proverbs 25:13.

One threshes grain, one grinds flour, Isaiah 28:28.

Joshua chosen to build temple, Zechariah 6:9-15.

Paul's extended ministry, Acts 18:11.

ASSISTANCE

God's presence in time of trouble, Psalm 14:4-5.

The Saviour left with no one to help Him, Psalm 22:1.

Man who assisted Paul in his ministry, 2 Timothy 1:16-18.

ASSOCIATION

Satan's association with angels in heaven, Job 1:6; 2:1.

Separated from evil by choice, Psalm 1:2.

Two in agreement, Amos 3:3.

Jesus called those He wanted, Mark 3:13.

United to follow Jesus, Luke 8:1-3.

Bad company and good character, 1 Corinthians 15:33.

Do not share sins of other, 1 Timothy 5:22.

See *Camaraderie, Cooperation, Fellowship, Teamwork.*

ASSURANCE

God's promise to Abram, Genesis 12:2-3; 15:1; 17:1.

Jacob reassured by God to enter Egypt, Genesis 46:1-4.

David's assurance of divine guidance, 2 Samuel 5:12.

Our refuge and strength, Psalm 46:1-3.

Confidence in the Lord rather than men, Isaiah 36:4-10.

Those called by His name need fear no danger, Isaiah 43:1-2.

God makes a new thing, Isaiah 43:19.

God knows end from beginning, Isaiah 46:10-11.

The God who knows what is best, Isaiah 48:17-18.

Walking with confidence in the dark, Isaiah 50:10.

Material universe vanishes but salvation endures, Isaiah 51:6.

God fulfills His promises, Jeremiah 29:10-11.

Nothing too hard for God, Jeremiah 32:27.

Love and faithfulness day by day, Lamentations 3:22-24.

Confidence of Daniel's friends in deliverance from fiery furnace, Daniel 3:16-17.

Believe the Good News, Mark 1:14-15.

Assurance to those who come to the Lord for help, John 6:37.

The Lord who is always at hand, Acts 2:25-28.

Paul assured of divine protection, Acts 18:9-11.

Pagans certain of erroneous belief, Acts 19:35-36.

Standing at end of struggle, Ephesians 6:13.

Good work begun will be completed, Philippians 1:6.

Standing firm whatever circumstances, Philippians 1:27-30.

Spiritual need totally fulfilled in Christ, Colossians 1:15-23.

Full comprehension, Colossians 2:2.

Deep conviction, 1 Thessalonians 1:5.

Assurance of eternal encouragement, 2 Thessalonians 2:16-17.

Absolute confidence in the One whom we believe, 2 Timothy 1:12.

Our Lord remains faithful, 2 Timothy 2:13.

Coming to our High Priest with confidence, Hebrews 4:14-16.

God, who cannot lie, provides an anchor for the soul, Hebrews 6:18-20.

Jesus our guarantee, Hebrews 7:22.

Coming to God in full assurance, Hebrews 10:9-23.

Perfect Saviour offers perfect salvation, Hebrews 10:11-14.

Certainty of faith, Hebrews 11:1.

Going in obedience toward unknown objective, Hebrews 11:8.

Confident now of God's fulfillment of His promises in the future, Hebrews 11:13.

Confidence in our salvation, 1 John 3:24.

Shielded from evil, 1 John 5:18.
The God who keeps and provides, Jude 24-25.
See *Confidence.*

ASTOUNDED
See *Awe, Serendipity.*

ASTROLOGY
Astronomy versus astrology, Deuteronomy 4:19.
Worship of stars, 2 Kings 21:3, 5; Zephaniah 1:5.
Bones of star-worshipers exhumed, Jeremiah 8:1-2.
Signs in the sky, Jeremiah 10:2.
So-called men of wisdom in Nebuchadnezzar's court, Daniel 2:1-4.
See *Zodiac.*

ASTRONAUT
Elijah to heaven in whirlwind, 2 Kings 2:11.
Nest among the stars, Obadiah 4.

ASTRONOMY
Creation of sky, Genesis 1:8, 14-17.
Vastness of creation, Genesis 2:1.
Star of Bethlehem, Numbers 24:17; Matthew 2:1-8.
Sun, moon, and stars not to be worshiped, Deuteronomy 4:19.
Strength of rising sun, Judges 5:31.
Homage to sun and moon, Job 31:26-28.
Unable to look at the sun, Job 37:21.
God speaks to Job of His creation, Job 38:4-13, 31-33.
Greatness of heavens attest to smallness of man, Psalm 8:3-4.
Sky proclaims glory of God, Psalm 19:1-6 (Note how role of sky has similarity in function of Scripture, vv. 7-11.)
Rising and setting of sun, Psalm 50:1.
Ancient skies, Psalm 68:32-33.
Moon designates seasons, Psalm 104:19.
All of space cannot contain God's love, Psalm 108:4-5.
Stars numbered and named, Psalm 147:4.
Earth and sky show wisdom of God, Proverbs 3:19-20.
Wisdom came before all Creation, Proverbs 8:24-31.
Sun, moon, and stars darkened, Isaiah 13:10.

Reversing shadow of the sun, Isaiah 38:7-8.
Heavens and the hand of God, Isaiah 40:12.
Each star named, Isaiah 40:26.
Creator cares for creation, Isaiah 42:5-7.
When sun and moon no longer needed, Isaiah 60:19.
God of all nature, Jeremiah 31:35.
Christ the Creator, Colossians 1:15-17.
Given the morning star, Revelation 2:28.
Stars falling to earth, Revelation 6:13.
Falling star of judgment, Revelation 9:1.
Hailstones from sky, Revelation 16:21.
Earth and sky flee from the eternal, Revelation 20:11.
No sun or moon over the New Jerusalem, Revelation 21:23-24.
Bright Morning Star, Revelation 22:16.
See *Morning star, Sky, Space, Space/time.*

ASTUTE
Proper time and procedure, Ecclesiastes 8:5-6.
Wisdom of Gamaliel, Acts 5:30-40.
Eyes of the heart, Ephesians 1:18-19.
Guidance in discerning good from evil, Hebrews 5:11-14.
See *Tact, Wisdom.*

ASYLUM
No place to hide, Leviticus 26:25.
Cities of refuge, Numbers 35:6; Deuteronomy 4:41-43; 19:1-14; Joshua 20:1-9; 1 Chronicles 6:67.
Conditions for protecting Rahab and family, Joshua 2:17-21.
David's retreat from Saul, 1 Samuel 27:1-12.
See *Hiding place, Protection.*

ATHEISM
No God in Israel, 2 Kings 1:3.
No God, no priest, no Law, 2 Chronicles 15:3.
No room for God, Psalm 10:4.
Voice of the fool, Psalms 14:1; 53:1.
Those who live under non-Christian government, Isaiah 26:13.
God makes Himself known through judgment, Ezekiel 11:7-12.
Doubt augmented by hearing truth, John 8:45-47.
See *Agnostic, Irreligious, Skepticism, Unbelief.*

ATHLETICS
Ishmael, the archer, Genesis 21:20.
Wrestling with God, Genesis 32:22-30.
(Note injury, vv. 25, 31-32.)
Physique and appearance of Joseph,
Genesis 39:6-7.
Strong and tall, Deuteronomy 9:2.
Strong man's need for liquid, Judges
15:17-19.
Splitting a hair, Judges 20:16.
Stature of King Saul, 1 Samuel 10:23-24.
David realized strength and agility came
from God, 2 Samuel 22:33-37.
Feet of deer, 2 Samuel 22:34.
Soldiers agile with either hand,
1 Chronicles 12:1-2.
God as pugilist, Psalm 3:7.
Spreading hands to swim, Isaiah 25:11.
Men on foot cannot compete with horses,
Jeremiah 12:5.
Disciple who outran Peter, John 20:4.
Runner and prize, 1 Corinthians 9:24-27.
In the arena, 1 Corinthians 9:26.
Hindered from running good race,
Galatians 5:7.
Physical training and godliness, 1 Timothy
4:7-8.
Playing according to rules, 2 Timothy 2:5.
Finishing the race, 2 Timothy 4:7.
Faithfully running race, Hebrews 12:1-
2.
See *Competition, Physical, Running,
Sportsman.*

ATONEMENT
He who bore our sins, Isaiah 53:4-12.
Cleansing fountain, Zechariah 13:1.
Blood shed for us, Matthew 26:28.
Disciples could not understand, Mark 9:30-
32.
Mixing blood of man with sacrificial blood,
Luke 13:1.
The Lamb of God, John 1:29.
Death and resurrection of Redeemer, Acts
17:2-3; 1 Corinthians 15:3-5.
Divine propitiation, Romans 3:24-26.
Justifying redemption, Romans 5:1-21.
Redeeming work of Christ, Ephesians 2:1-
18.
Power and meaning of blood of Christ,
Hebrews 7:23-28.
Our advocate with the Heavenly Father,
1 John 2:1-2.
See *Cross, Redeemer.*

ATTACK
Go to neighbor for help, Proverbs 27:10.
Fear of walking in public places, Jeremiah
6:25.
See *Adversary, Enemy, Opposition.*

ATTAINMENT
No success outside God's will, Numbers
14:41-45.
Future accomplishment assured, Numbers
21:34.
Son seeks to impress father, 1 Samuel
14:1-14.
Ambition of humble man, Proverbs 30:7-8.
Riches gained unjustly, Jeremiah 17:11.
Authority over demons, Luke 10:17-20.
More than conquerors, Romans 8:28-39.
Good purpose fulfilled, 2 Thessalonians
1:11.
See *Ambition, Goal.*

ATTENDANCE
Guilty people frightened of place of
worship, Numbers 17:12-13.
Vast assembly, 1 Kings 8:65.
Constant attendance, Luke 2:36-37; 24:53.
Customary Sabbath attendance, Luke 4:16.
Unable to get through the crowd, Luke
8:19-21.

ATTENTION
Call for attention to those who need to
hear, Isaiah 28:14.
Paying close attention to important
information, Ezekiel 40:4.
Careful listening, Luke 8:18.
How the Lord got Saul's attention, Acts
9:1-5.
See *Heed, Response, Students, Teaching.*

ATTESTATION
Paul's wise use of names of followers,
Colossians 4:7-17.
Work of God reported widely,
1 Thessalonians 1:8-10.
Trustworthy saying, 1 Timothy 4:9-10.
Signs, wonders, and miracles verified
message, Hebrews 2:4.

ATTITUDE
Negative attitude of Cain, Genesis 4:3-7.
Abram's attitude toward Lot, Genesis 13:8-
9.
Servant's attitude toward unfair employer,

Genesis 16:1-10.
Positive attitude in worship, Leviticus 22:29.
David's willingness to accept rebuke, 2 Samuel 16:5-12.
Boastful attitude of King Rehoboam, 1 Kings 12:13-14.
Pagan king persuaded to permit rebuilding of temple, Ezra 1:1-4, 7-8; 5:8–6:12; 7:13-26.
Nehemiah's prayer, Nehemiah 1:4-11.
Experiencing suffering and reversal without blaming God, Job 1:22.
Willingness to accept truth of wrongdoing, Job 6:24.
Serve the Lord with gladness, Psalm 100:1-2.
Rejoicing in the day the Lord has made, Psalm 118:24.
Positive attitude toward problems, Psalm 119:71. (See Prov. 24:10.)
God's attitude to the proud and humble, Psalm 138:6.
Happy heart makes cheerful face, Proverbs 15:13, 30; 17:22.
Pride brings destruction, Proverbs 16:18.
Do not rejoice in failure of enemy, Proverbs 24:17-18.
Value of sorrow over laughter, Ecclesiastes 7:3-4.
Value of positive lifestyle, Ecclesiastes 8:15.
Thanking God in midst of adverse circumstances, Jeremiah 33:10-11.
Pride and arrogance of Moab, Jeremiah 48:29.
Ezekiel's bitterness and anger, Ezekiel 3:14.
Jonah's sour grapes, Jonah 4:1-11.
Effect of attitudes on understanding, Matthew 13:14-15.
Nature of kingdom of heaven, Matthew 19:14.
"Salt" of a truly spiritual personality, Mark 9:50.
True humility, Luke 7:6-7.
Willing to accept rebuke, Acts 7:51-58.
Paul evaluates weak and strong, Romans 14:1-8.
Wrong attitudes in worship do more harm than good, 1 Corinthians 11:17-32.
Refreshing spirit of others, 1 Corinthians 16:18.
Facial radiance, 2 Corinthians 3:18.
Making room in the heart for acceptance of others, 2 Corinthians 7:2.
New awareness in the hearts of Corinthians, 2 Corinthians 7:10-13.
Do not grieve the Holy Spirit, Ephesians 4:30.
Paul's attitude toward those who opposed him, Philippians 1:15-18.
Gentleness always, Philippians 4:5.
Mental attitude dictates lifestyle, Philippians 4:8-9.
Enmity in the mind against God, Colossians 1:21.
Keys to a positive attitude, 1 Thessalonians 5:16-18.
Paul's attitude toward those who deserted him, 2 Timothy 4:16.
Christian attitude toward persecution and suffering, James 1:2-6.
Clear the mind of negative thoughts, 1 Peter 2:1.
See *Disposition, Frame of reference.*

ATTRIBUTES
Heart realities, Proverbs 27:19.
Attributes of mature Christian life, 2 Peter 1:5-9.

AUDACITY
Misunderstanding gesture of goodwill, 2 Samuel 10:1-4.
Defiance of the fool, Psalm 14:1.
Deliberate falsehoods concerning law of the Lord, Jeremiah 8:8.
See *Discourtesy, Impertinence, Rudeness.*

AUDIENCE
Let the earth hear, Isaiah 34:1.
Some listen, some refuse, Ezekiel 3:27.
Large crowd forced Jesus into boat, Matthew 13:1-2.
Jesus told parable as crowd gathered to hear Him preach, Luke 8:4-15.
Jesus' own mother and brothers unable to get through crowd, Luke 8:19-21.
Crowd of thousands, Luke 12:1.
People curious to see miracles performed, John 6:1-2.
Relatives and friends of Cornelius, Acts 10:24-27.
Bereans listened with eagerness to Paul's message, Acts 17:11-12.
Paul changed audience from Jews to Gentiles, Acts 18:4-6.
Jews wanted miracles; Greeks, wisdom,

1 Corinthians 1:22-24.
Importance of welcoming the message,
1 Thessalonians 1:6.
See *Congregation, Mob psychology, Students.*

AUDIOVISUAL
Moses and the burning bush, Exodus 3:1-6.

AURA
Radiating the presence of the Lord, Exodus 34:29.
Glory filling the tabernacle, Exodus 40:34.
Glory over all the earth, Numbers 14:21; Habakkuk 3:3.
Radiant faces, Psalm 34:5; Ecclesiastes 8:1; Acts 6:15.
Path of the righteous, Proverbs 4:18.
Reflected glory, Daniel 12:3; 2 Corinthians 3:18.
Ambient glow of Christmas, Luke 2:9.
Flashing light from heaven, Acts 22:6.
No need for sunlight, Revelation 22:5.

AUTHENTICITY
Failure of Nebuchadnezzar's wise men, Daniel 2:1-11.
John the Baptist looked for authentic Messiah, Matthew 11:1-5.
Pharisees wanted sign from heaven, Mark 8:11-12.
Living by truth, John 3:21.
Validity of Jesus questioned, John 8:12-30.
Those who could not accept identity of Jesus, John 10:24-30.
Pilate and the King of the Jews, John 19:19-22.
Paul's recognition of his writings as authentic Scripture, 1 Corinthians 14:37-38.
See *Genuine, Honesty, Truth.*

AUTHOR
Words given by Holy Spirit, 2 Samuel 23:2.
Solomon's many proverbs and songs, 1 Kings 4:32.
Pen of skillful writer, Psalm 44:1.
Finding the right word, Ecclesiastes 12:10.
Diamond-pointed pen, Jeremiah 17:1 (KJV).
Instructions to write a book, Jeremiah 30:2.
Danger of writing the truth, Jeremiah 36:4-32.
Writing kit, Ezekiel 9:2, 11.

Many writers attempted to record New Testament events, Luke 1:1-4.
Luke speaks of his writings, Acts 1:1-2.
The author of Scripture, 2 Peter 1:20-21.
One author commends another, 2 Peter 3:15-16.
Reluctance to write, 2 John 12.
Message conveyed by an angel, Revelation 1:1-3.
Command given to John, Revelation 1:10-11.
See *Communication, Fiction, Literature, Writing.*

AUTHORITY
Authority of the Creator's command, Genesis 1:3, 6, 9, 14-15, 20, 24, 26.
Man given authority over Creation, Genesis 1:26-29.
The Lord made Moses like God to Pharaoh, Exodus 7:1-2.
Speaking by divine authority, Leviticus 23:1-2, 9-10, 23-24.
King Saul's long reign over Israel, 1 Samuel 13:1.
David's power over subjects and foreigners, 2 Samuel 22:44-46.
Boastful attitude of King Rehoboam, 1 Kings 12:10-11, 14.
Hesitant to exert authority, 1 Kings 21:1-16.
Power of God's name, Psalm 54:1.
Wealth as authority symbol, Proverbs 22:7.
God speaks and acts, Isaiah 44:24-28.
Jeremiah's fear and reluctance of proclaiming God's message, Jeremiah 1:1-10, 17-18.
Recognize authority of teachers and masters, Matthew 10:24.
Authority of Jesus and authority of Beelzebub, Matthew 12:22-32.
Finger of God, Luke 11:20.
Jesus obeyed what His Father told Him to do, John 12:50.
Jesus accused of disrespect, John 18:19-24.
God's authority greater than man's, John 19:8-11.
Authority of Christians to heal sick, Acts 3:11-16.
Scriptures as authority concerning Jesus, Acts 18:28.
Demons unmoved by those whose message lacked authority, Acts 19:13-16.

Insulting someone of high rank, Acts 23:4-5.

Truth declared with power, Romans 1:4.

Relationship of men and women, 1 Corinthians 11:2-16.

Witnessing effective only through the Holy Spirit, 1 Corinthians 12:3.

Ministry with spiritual weapons, 2 Corinthians 10:1-5.

Wives and husbands relating to each other, Ephesians 5:22-23.

Qualifications of Christ as Saviour and King, Colossians 1:15-20.

Christ, the Head over all, Colossians 2:9-10.

Means by which the Lord Jesus will overthrow man of sin, 2 Thessalonians 2:8.

Desire to be an overseer, 1 Timothy 3:1.

God does not lie, Titus 1:2.

Leadership with authority, Titus 2:15.

God's Son superior to angels, Hebrews 1:3-4.

Ministering in name of the Lord, 3 John 7.

Wrong kind of authority in congregation, 3 John 9-10.

Only authority over evil, Jude 9.

Sovereignty of Jesus over all the earth, Revelation 1:5.

Delegation of satanic authority, Revelation 13:2.

Temporary authority of the beast, Revelation 13:5.

One-hour reign of 10 kings, Revelation 17:12.

See *Dictator, Leadership, Politics, Royalty, Scripture.*

AUTHORIZATION
Nehemiah's authorization from king for travel to Jerusalem, Nehemiah 2:1-8.

AUTOGRAPH
Paul's signature, Colossians 4:18; 2 Thessalonians 3:17.
See *Graphology.*

AUTOMOBILE
Verse some believe to be prophetic of modern automobiles, Nahum 2:4.

AUTUMN
Seasons designated, Genesis 1:14; Psalm 104:19.

Harvesttime, Genesis 8:22; Deuteronomy 24:19; Ruth 1:22; 2 Samuel 21:9.

Temple completion, 1 Kings 6:37-38. (Note: Ziv is May, Bul is November.)

Temple foundation completed in October, 1 Kings 8:2. (Note: Ethanim is October.)

September completion of project, Nehemiah 6:15. (Note: Elul is the month of September.)

Harvest diligence a picture of evangelism, Proverbs 10:5.

Birds know when to migrate, Jeremiah 8:7.
See *Seasons.*

AVANT-GARDE
See *Original, Unprecedented.*

AVENGE
When not to do as others have done, Proverbs 24:29.

Showing love to those who cause grief, 2 Corinthians 2:5-11.

Leave revenge in God's hands, 2 Thessalonians 1:6-7.
See *Retribution, Revenge.*

AWAKENING
See *Evangelism, Revival.*

AWARENESS
Adam's discovery of nakedness, Genesis 3:8-11.

Joseph recognized his brothers, Genesis 42:7.

Aware of future potential, Genesis 48:17-20.

Guilt by daylight, Exodus 22:2-3.

Responsibility of being aware, Leviticus 5:1.

Donkey saw what man did not, Numbers 22:25.

Boy recognized the word of the Lord, 1 Samuel 3:3-18.

Aware of another's loyalty, 1 Samuel 24:1-22.

Something to boast about, Jeremiah 9:23-24.

Knowing who is the Lord, Ezekiel 6:10, 14; 7:4, 9, 27; 12:16, 20; 13:9, 23.

Recognizing Jesus as Son of God, Mark 15:39.

Seeing and understanding what others never knew, Luke 10:23-24.

Those who do not understand, Luke 18:31-

34.
John immediately recognized identity of Jesus, John 1:29-31.
New awareness in hearts of Corinthians, 2 Corinthians 7:10-13.
Comprehending dimensions of faith, Ephesians 3:14-19.
Aware of false prophets, 1 John 4:1-6.
See *Discovery, Frame-of- reference, Intellectual, Sensitivity.*

AWE
Standing on holy ground, Exodus 3:1-6.
Astounding fall, Lamentations 1:9.
Ezekiel overwhelmed, Ezekiel 3:15.

Daniel awed by his vision, Daniel 10:7-8.
Talking to God, Daniel 10:15-21.
Silent earth, Habakkuk 2:20.
Be still before the Lord, Zechariah 2:13.
Contemplating resurrection and exaltation of Christ, Ephesians 1:18-23.
See *Amazement, Emotion, Reverence, Worship.*

AWKWARD
See *Inexperience, Novice.*

AXIOM
Origin of a saying, 1 Samuel 10:11-12.

B

BACHELOR
Joshua's family name recorded but no
record of a family of his own, Joshua
1:1.
Promise to eunuchs, Isaiah 56:3-5.
Marriage renounced, Matthew 19:12.
Marriage counsel from a bachelor,
1 Corinthians 7:27-28.
The 144,000, Revelation 14:1-5.
See *Eunuch, Marriage, Single.*

BACKBITING
See *Slander.*

BACKGROUND
Sons of a sorceress, Isaiah 57:3.
Prophet from Galilee, John 7:41-52.
Military background of Cornelius caused
him to express respect for Peter, Acts
10:25-26.
Paul's resumé of Old Testament events,
Acts 13:16-41.
See *Ancestors, Family, Heritage.*

BACKSLAPPING
Flattery to a king, 2 Samuel 14:5-17.
Partiality to none, Job 32:21.
Flattering lips speak deception, Psalm 12:2.
Rebuke better than flattery, Proverbs
28:23; 29:5.
Tongues of hypocrisy, Luke 20:20-26; Acts
12:19-23.
See *Applause, Approval, Commendation,
Exaggeration, Insincerity.*

BACKSLIDING
Causes of backsliding, Exodus 17:7;
Deuteronomy 8:11-14; Psalm 106:14;
Proverbs 16:18; Mark 4:18-19;
1 Timothy 6:10; 2 Peter 1:9.
Decline caused by absence of good leader,
Exodus 32:1-6.
Wayward community, Deuteronomy
13:12-18.
Journey one should never make again,
Deuteronomy 28:68.
Sobering question to wayward Israel,
Joshua 22:18.
People quick to backslide, Judges 2:18-19.
Backslider returning to the Lord, 1 Samuel
15:24-25.
Turning spiritual failure into success,
1 Kings 8:33-34.
Old age and spiritual decline, 1 Kings 11:4.
Turning away, 1 Kings 11:9.
Secretly disobeying the Lord, 2 Kings 17:9.
So quickly God's blessings forgotten,
Psalm 106:13.
Once astray, now obedient, Psalm 119:67.
Choosing evil, Psalm 125:5.
Equity of rewards for conduct, Proverbs
14:14.
Massive backsliding of Israel, Isaiah 1:1-4.
Grieving the Holy Spirit, Isaiah 63:10.
Divinely hardened hearts, Isaiah 63:17.
Israel turned to idols, ignoring the God
who led them through the wilderness,
Jeremiah 2:5-8.
Turning their backs to God, Jeremiah 2:27.
Spiritual vagabonds, Jeremiah 2:31.
Cure for waywardness, Jeremiah 3:22.
Leaders and people alike turn against the
Lord, Jeremiah 5:3-5.
Conspiracy against the Lord, Jeremiah
17:13.
Desire to return to Egypt, Jeremiah 42:1-
22. (Note 43:1-7.)
Inevitable judgment to those who disobey
God, Jeremiah 44:15-28.
Righteous man turns from righteousness,
Ezekiel 3:20-21.
Contrast between backsliding and

repentance, Ezekiel 18:24-28.

Way of backslider and way of convert, Ezekiel 33:17-20.

Reasoning of people who turned away from God, Ezeki 1 33:21-33.

Israel forgot God, Hosea 8:14.

Certain judgment for those who turn from faithfulness, Hosea 9:7.

Potential of blessing lost to idols, Hosea 9:10.

Israel's bent toward backsliding, Hosea 11:7.

Abundant blessing can turn to backsliding, Hosea 13:6.

Sin and boasting, Amos 4:4-5.

Hearts hard as flint, Zechariah 7:11-12.

Salt that loses its flavor and lights that are hidden, Matthew 5:13-16.

No one can serve two masters, Matthew 6:24.

Witnessing miracles with hard hearts, Matthew 11:20.

Love grown cold, Matthew 24:12.

Peter's pledge not to betray Christ, Mark 14:27-31, 66-72.

Those who look back, Luke 9:62; Galatians 4:9.

Backsliding disciples, John 6:66-69.

Seeking pleasure from those things which cause spiritual death, Romans 6:21.

Paul's description of those who thought they had attained spiritual success, 1 Corinthians 4:1-21.

Waywardness among believers, 1 Corinthians 5:9-12.

Paul astonished at Galatians, Galatians 1:6-9.

Returning to the weak and miserable, Galatians 4:9.

Helping someone who has sinned, Galatians 6:1.

Those who could not hold true to faith, 1 Timothy 1:18-20.

Those who deserted Paul, 2 Timothy 1:15; 4:10.

Those who wander from truth, 2 Timothy 2:17-18.

Love for world greater than love of ministry, 2 Timothy 4:9.

Hearts always going astray, Hebrews 3:10.

Sinful and unbelieving hearts, Hebrews 3:12.

Those who fall away from truth, Hebrews 6:4-6.

Danger of continuing in sin, Hebrews 10:26-27.

Restoring backslider to fellowship, James 5:19-20.

Warning not to return to evil desires, 1 Peter 1:14.

Those who turn their backs, 2 Peter 2:20-22.

Those who go out from the body, 1 John 2:18-19.

Danger of losing full reward, 2 John 8.

Plight of Ephesus, Revelation 2:4-5.

Those in danger of being erased from the Book of Life, Revelation 3:2-5.

Neither cold nor hot, Revelation 3:15-16.

See *Carnality*.

BAD NEWS

Penalty for giving bad report, Numbers 14:36-37.

Learning truth from God's prophet, 1 Kings 14:1-18.

Good news or bad news, the Lord is obeyed, Jeremiah 42:6.

One message after another of bad news, Jeremiah 51:31-32.

BAIL

Posting bond for release from custody, Acts 17:9.

BAKING

Fast food, Genesis 18:6.

Bible bakers, Genesis 40:1; Jeremiah 37:21; Hosea 7:4.

Ten bakers, one oven, Leviticus 26:26.

Vitality of loaf of bread, Judges 7:13-15.

Food defiled because of unclean fuel, Ezekiel 4:12-15.

Yeast as spiritual example, Matthew 13:33.

BALANCE

Constructing idol that will not fall, Isaiah 40:20.

Those who easily stumble, Jeremiah 12:5.

Balanced life of Jesus, Luke 2:52.

Sense of balance toward gifts of the Spirit, 1 Corinthians 12:27-30.

Be self-controlled, 1 Peter 1:13.

BALM

Balm in Gilead, Genesis 37:25; Jeremiah 8:22; 46:11.

Therapy for pain, Jeremiah 51:8.

BANKER
Generous loan policy, Deuteronomy 15:7-8.
Mortgaging land, Nehemiah 5:3.
Rich versus poor, Proverbs 22:7.
Commercial centers in Ezekiel's time, Ezekiel 27:12-23.
Value and designation of currency, Ezekiel 45:12.
Storing treasures, Matthew 6:19-20.
Money changers in temple, Matthew 21:12; Mark 11:15; John 2:15.
See *Currency, Money, Mortgage, Treasure, Wages.*

BANKRUPTCY
Lacking power to help one's self, Job 6:13.
Prosperity forgotten, Lamentations 3:17.
Fortunes restored, Zephaniah 2:7.
Unable to pay debt, Matthew 18:21-35.
See *Failure.*

BANNER
See *Flag.*

BANQUET
Egyptian birthday, Genesis 40:20.
Eating with rejoicing, Deuteronomy 27:7.
Pagan temple feast, Judges 9:27.
Banquet for enemies, 2 Kings 6:18-23.
Job's concern over family festivity, Job 1:4-5.
Blessing better than richest of food, Psalm 63:5.
Banner of love at banquet hall, Song of Songs 2:4.
Five thousand guests at Belshazzar's banquet, Daniel 5:1.
Eating to complete satisfaction, Joel 2:26.
Feeding the 5,000, Matthew 14:13-21; Mark 6:30-44; Luke 9:10-17; John 6:1-13.
Birthday banquet, Mark 6:21.
Banquet for Jesus, Luke 5:27-35.
Desiring place of honor at table, Luke 14:7-11.
Miracle at Cana, John 2:1-11.
Eating a time to express love, John 13:1-2.
Wedding supper in heaven, Revelation 19:9.
See *Feast, Festivity, Food, Gourmet.*

BAPTISM
Believer's baptism, Matthew 28:19; Mark 16:16; Acts 2:38; 10:48; Galatians 3:27; Colossians 2:12.
Belief prior to baptism, Acts 2:41.
Eagerness of Ethiopian eunuch to be baptized, Acts 8:36-37.

BARBER
Strange rite at time of death, Deuteronomy 14:1-2.
Samson's uncut hair, Judges 13:4-5.
Wait until your beards grow long, 1 Chronicles 19:5.
Divine barbering, Isaiah 7:20.
Cutting off hair to show remorse, Jeremiah 7:29.
Heads shaved and beards cut off, Jeremiah 48:37.
Sharp sword used for shaving, Ezekiel 5:1.
Barber in the temple, Ezekiel 44:20.
Shaving the head in mourning, Micah 1:16.
Hairs of the head numbered, Luke 12:7.
Paul's haircut in response to a vow, Acts 18:18.
See *Coiffure, Hair.*

BARGAINING
Abraham's bargaining with God on behalf of Lot, Genesis 18:20-33.
Esau's birthright offered at a bargain, Genesis 25:27-34.
Life for a life, Joshua 2:14.
Getting best price, Proverbs 20:14.
God's great bargain, Isaiah 55:1-2.
Losing in bad exchange, Jeremiah 2:11.
Sadistic bargaining, Matthew 14:7-10.
Infamy of Judas, Matthew 26:14-16.

BARREN
Reproach of childlessness, Genesis 16:1-4; 29:31-34; 30:1-24; 1 Samuel 1:1-20; Isaiah 4:1; Luke 1:5-25.
Infertility in the household of Abimelech, Genesis 20:17-18.
Motherhood for barren woman, Psalm 113:9.
Wombs that miscarry, Hosea 9:14.
See *Childless, Infertility.*

BARTER
Animals, land, and people used in place of money, Genesis 47:16-21.
Trading lumber for food, 1 Kings 5:10-11.
Losing in bad exchange, Jeremiah 2:11.
Commercial centers in Ezekiel's time,

Ezekiel 27:12-23.
Barley for a wife, Hosea 3:2.

BASHFUL
Tongues stick to roof of mouth, Job 29:10.
Paul could be timid and bold,
2 Corinthians 10:1.
Do not be ashamed to testify, 2 Timothy
1:8-9.
See *Reticent, Shy, Timidity.*

BASICS
Need for food and water, Job 22:7-8.
Day of small things, Zechariah 4:10.

BATH
Washing feet common for those who
traveled on foot, Genesis 18:4; 19:2.
Pharaoh's daughter, Exodus 2:5.
Ceremonial cleansing, Leviticus 14:8;
2 Kings 5:10-14.
Place for washing prostitutes and chariots,
1 Kings 22:38.
Soda and soap, Jeremiah 2:22.
See *Cleanliness, Cleansing, Soap, Washing.*

BEACH
Waterside audience, Matthew 13:2.
Fisherman's catch, Matthew 13:48.
Broiling fish, John 21:9.
Kneeling in the sand, Acts 21:5.
Miracle by seaside, Acts 28:1-6.

BEARD
See *Whiskers.*

BEASTS
See *Animals.*

BEAUTY
Means to personal safety, Deuteronomy
21:10-14.
Beauty only skin deep, Proverbs 11:22;
31:30.
Naughty women of Zion become bald,
Isaiah 3:16-17.
Allegory of Jerusalem from ignominious
birth to royal beauty, Ezekiel 16:4-14.
Beauty in nature, Hosea 14:5-6; Matthew
6:28-29.
Beautiful young women, Zechariah 9:17.
Mountain of Transfiguration, Matthew
17:1-8.
Physical appearance comes from God,

1 Corinthians 4:7.
Radiant face of Moses, 2 Corinthians 3:7-8.
Flowers that wither, 1 Peter 1:24-25.
Inner beauty, 1 Peter 3:3-4.

BED
Earth and stone, Genesis 28:11.
King-sized, Deuteronomy 3:11.
Gold and silver, Esther 1:6.
Ivory, Amos 6:4.
All the family, Luke 11:7.

BEER
Alcoholic beverage other than wine,
Judges 13:7.
See *Alcohol.*

BEGGING
Children as beggars, Psalms 37:25; 109:10.
Made necessary by handicap, Mark 10:46-
52; John 9:1-12.
Rich man and beggar, Luke 16:19-31.
Surprised beggar, Acts 3:1-8.

BEGINNER
See *Inexperience, Novice.*

BEHAVIOR
Path of righteous and way of wicked,
Proverbs 4:18-19.
Exemplary behavior, 1 Corinthians 13:1-
13; Philippians 1:9-10; 2 Thessalonians
3:7-10; 1 Timothy 3:2; Titus 2.
Judged by observance of legalism,
Colossians 2:16.
Lifestyle of those risen with Christ,
Colossians 3:1-17.
Tactful in conversation with others,
Colossians 4:6.
Attributes of mature Christian, 2 Peter 1:5-
9.
See *Character, Conduct, Frame of
reference.*

BELIEVER
Idols in the heart, Ezekiel 14:1-11.
The believer's body is the Holy Spirit's
temple, 1 Corinthians 3:16-17.
Only faith pleases God, Hebrews 11:6.
Those clean in a society of deceit,
Revelation 3:4. (See also v. 10.)
Those gathered from all tribes and nations,
Revelation 7:9-10.
See *Congregation, Convert, Followers.*

BELOVED
Sacrifice of a daughter, Judges 11:30-40.
Dawn of love, Ruth 3:1-18.
Beloved, but barren, 1 Samuel 1:2-11.
Mutual love between friends, 1 Samuel 20:17.
Esteemed of the Lord, Isaiah 66:2.
Becoming like the Lord's signet ring, Haggai 2:23.
Marriage on earth compared to relationship in heaven, Mark 12:18-27.
Communicating with gentle spirit of mother, 1 Thessalonians 2:7-8.

BENEDICTION
First divine blessings, Genesis 1:22, 28.
Melchizedek's blessing of Abram, Genesis 14:18-20.
Blessing given Rebekah, Genesis 24:60.
Blessing the people, Leviticus 9:22; Joshua 22:6; 2 Samuel 6:18.
Priestly blessing, Numbers 6:24-26.
Assigned to pronounce blessings, Deuteronomy 10:8.
Joshua's blessing and warning as his death approached, Joshua 23:14-16.
Mother-in-law's benediction, Ruth 1:8-9.
Blessing populace, 2 Samuel 6:18.
Prayer of Jesus, John 17:1-5.
Paul's parting with the elders of the church at Ephesus, Acts 20:17-38.
Brief benedictions, Romans 15:33; Galatians 6:18; 2 Thessalonians 3:18.
Call to world evangelism, Romans 16:25-27.
Grace, love, and fellowship of the Trinity, 2 Corinthians 13:14.
To the King eternal, 1 Timothy 1:17.
Grace, mercy, and peace, 2 John 3.
God keeps and provides, Jude 24-25.
Prelude to prophecy, Revelation 1:4-6.
Outcry of praise to God, Revelation 7:11-12.
Concluding proclamation of faith in God, Revelation 15:3-4.
Great rejoicing in heaven over destruction in Babylon, Revelation 19:6-8.
Conclusion of the Bible, Revelation 22:20-21.

BENEFACTOR
Divine benefactor, Deuteronomy 7:6-26; Acts 14:15-18; Philippians 4:19.

BENEFICIARY
Beneficiaries by command, Joshua 17:4.
Beneficiaries of divine goodness, Isaiah 57:13; Romans 4:13; Colossians 1:12.
Conditions for exercising a will, Hebrews 9:16-17.
See *Heir, Inheritance, Legacy.*

BENEFITS
Enjoying benefits developed by others, Joshua 24:13.

BENEVOLENCE
Job's concern for those in need, Job 29:16.
Do good to those who deserve it, Proverbs 3:27.
Reward to generosity, Proverbs 11:25; 22:9.
Opportune giving, Proverbs 18:16.
Giving to the poor is lending to the Lord, Proverbs 19:17.
Sensitivity to needs of others, Proverbs 21:13.
Concern for an enemy, Proverbs 25:21.
Benevolence and personal needs, Proverbs 28:27.
Care of others, Isaiah 58:10.
Giving in privacy, Matthew 6:2-4.
Benevolence of Heavenly Father, Matthew 7:1-11.
Reward for looking after needs of others, Matthew 25:34-40.
Sharing with others, Luke 3:11.
Principle of stewardship, Luke 6:38.
Good Samaritan, Luke 10:30-37.
Putting first things first, Luke 10:38-42.
Hospitality to those who cannot reciprocate, Luke 14:12-14.
Woman who helped the poor, Acts 9:36-42.
Kindness to poor recognized by the Lord, Acts 10:4.
Reaching out to help others in need, Acts 11:27-30.
More blessed to give than receive, Acts 20:35.
Caring for the poor, Romans 12:13; Galatians 2:10; Ephesians 4:28.
Sharing spiritual blessings and material blessings, Romans 15:26-27.
Generosity of Macedonian churches, 2 Corinthians 8:1-5.
Sharing with those in need, 1 John 3:17.
See *Charity, Philanthropy, Transmutation, Welfare.*

BEREAVEMENT

Grief for wife, Genesis 23:1-4.
Jacob's sorrow, Genesis 37:32-35; 42:38.
Overt mourning, Exodus 12:29-30;
   2 Samuel 18:33.
Shaving head of mourner, Deuteronomy
   14:1-2.
United in sorrow, Ruth 1:1-9.
Employed to mourn, Amos 5:16-17.
Mourning to music, Matthew 9:23.
Sorrowing mother, Luke 7:12.
Sorrow of Jesus, John 11:35.
Loving sorrow, Acts 9:39.
Comforted by truth, 1 Corinthians 15:12-
   20.
Hope beyond death, 1 Thessalonians 4:13-
   18.
Tears wiped away, Revelation 21:3-4.
See *Death, Grief, Sorrow.*

BETRAYAL

Captive gives information about enemy,
   Judges 8:13-14.
Delilah's deceit, Judges 16:15-19.
Man who turns against his friends, Job
   17:5.
Close friend deceived, Psalms 41:9; 55:12-
   14.
Betrayed by one's friends, Lamentations
   1:19.
Family dishonor, Micah 7:6; Matthew
   10:21.
Prophecy of the cross, Zechariah 12:10-11.
Jesus betrayed for 30 silver coins, Matthew
   26:14-16, 47-50; Mark 14:43-46; Luke
   22:3-6. (See Zech. 11:12-13.)
Peter's denial of his Lord, Matthew 26:31-
   35, 69-75.
Jesus used morsel of bread to implicate
   Judas, John 13:21-27.

BEWILDERED

Walking about in darkness, Psalm 82:5.
A spirit of dizziness, Isaiah 19:14.

BIAS

Negative and positive viewpoints,
   Numbers 13:17-33.
Favoring one man against another,
   1 Corinthians 4:6.
See *Fanaticism, Opinion.*

BIBLE

Sweeter than honey, Psalms 19:10;
   119:103.
Lamp and light, Psalm 119:105.
Rain and snow, Isaiah 55:10-11.
Fire and hammer, Jeremiah 23:29.
Cleansing water, Ephesians 5:26.
Spirit's sword, Ephesians 6:17.
Milk and solid food, Hebrews 5:12; 1 Peter
   2:2.
Divine mirror, James 1:23-25.
See *Scripture.*

BIGOTRY

Nationalism, Esther 3:8-9.
Attitude of Pharisees, John 8:33-38.
Name-calling, John 8:48-49.
Spiritual blindness, John 9:39-41.
Justification for bigotry, Philippians 3:4-6.
Caused by ignorance, 1 Timothy 1:13.
See *Prejudice, Racism, Xenophobia.*

BIOGRAPHY

Thumbnail biography of Ishmael, Genesis
   25:12-18.
Example of limited biography, 2 Kings
   15:13-15.
Biography from beginning to end,
   1 Chronicles 29:29-30.

BIRDS

Types of birds, Genesis 8:8; Leviticus
   11:13-19; Numbers 11:31-32;
   Deuteronomy 14:12-18; Job 28:7;
   30:29; 38:41; 39:13, 27; Psalms 84:3;
   102:6; Song of Songs 2:12; Isaiah 14:23;
   34:15; Jeremiah 8:7; Matthew 10:29-31;
   23:37; 26:34.
Subservient to man, Genesis 9:2.
Carried on eagle's wings, Exodus 19:4;
   2 Samuel 1:23; Proverbs 23:5; Isaiah
   40:30-31.
Inedible birds, Leviticus 11:13-19;
   Deuteronomy 14:12-18.
Birds of prey, Leviticus 11:14;
   Deuteronomy 14:13; Job 28:7; Isaiah
   34:15.
Avoid endangering species, Deuteronomy
   22:6-7.
Hawk flies south, Job 39:26.
Nesting sites, Psalms 84:3; 104:16-17;
   Isaiah 34:13-15; Matthew 8:20.
Way of an eagle, Proverbs 30:18-19.
No protest when judgment comes, Isaiah
   10:14.
Birds know when to migrate, Jeremiah 8:7.

Surrogate mother among birds, Jeremiah
17:11.
Value of a sparrow and value of a soul,
Matthew 10:29-31.
Peter and crowing rooster, Mark 14:29-31,
66-72.

BIRTH
Births known in advance, Genesis 16:11;
18:10; Judges 13:3; 1 Kings 13:2;
2 Kings 4:16; Isaiah 9:6.
Death of Rachel in childbirth, Genesis
35:16-20.
Animals of nature born in secret, Job 39:1.
Regretted birth, Ecclesiastes 7:1.
Time of birth, Isaiah 26:17.
Improper care of newborn, Ezekiel 16:4-5.
Dramatic events at time of birth, Luke
1:57-66.
See *Abortion, Childbirth, Pregnancy.*

BIRTH CERTIFICATE
Problem of pregnancy with two prostitutes,
1 Kings 3:16-28.
Loss of family records, Nehemiah 7:64.
God's command to increase population,
Jeremiah 29:4-6.

BIRTHDAY
Age of Old Testament fathers, Genesis
11:10-26.
Birthday parties, Genesis 40:20; Matthew
14:6-11.
Remembering family birthdays, Genesis
43:33.
Lamenting one's birth, Job 3:1-26;
Jeremiah 15:10; 20:14-18.
Length of life determined, Job 14:5.
Years pass quickly, Job 16:22.
Carefully counting one's days, Psalm
90:12.

BIRTHRIGHT
Esau sold his birthright, Genesis 25:29-34;
Hebrews 12:16-17.
Ranked by time of birth, Genesis 43:33.
Right of firstborn, Deuteronomy 21:15-16;
2 Chronicles 21:3.
See *Citizenship.*

BITTERNESS
Bitterness of soul, Job 3:20; Proverbs
14:10.
Bitterness of forsaking the Lord, Jeremiah

2:19.
Punishment of conscience, Jeremiah 4:18.
Gall of bitterness, Lamentations 3:15.
Bitterness overcome, Ephesians 4:31.
Bitter roots, Hebrews 12:15.
Harbored in heart, James 3:14.

BLACK
Skin and hair, Song of Songs 1:5; 5:11.
Black man helped Jesus carry the cross,
Mark 15:21. (Note: Cyrene is a city in
North Africa.)

BLACKMAIL
Joseph's initial attitude to brothers,
Genesis 42:1-34.
Delilah's exploitation of Samson's love,
Judges 16:4-21.
Conniving against Daniel, Daniel 6:3-24.
Judas' misuse of relationship with Jesus,
Matthew 26:47-50; Mark 14:43-46;
Luke 22:47-48; John 18:1-4.

BLACKOUT
Egyptian darkness, Exodus 10:21-23.
Majestic Sinai, Deuteronomy 4:11.
Time of Crucifixion, Matthew 27:45.
Eternal blackout, Jude 6.

BLAME
Passing blame to others, Genesis 3:8-13.
Pardon for bloodguilt of a nation, Joel 3:21.
Guilt of Judas, Matthew 27:3.
Those who look for something to criticize,
Mark 3:2.
Danger of seeing light but walking in
darkness, 2 Peter 2:21.
See *Conscience, Guilt, Responsibility.*

BLASPHEMY
Pharaoh dared to defy God, Exodus 5:2.
God's name not to be misused, Exodus
20:7; Leviticus 19:12; Matthew 5:34-36;
James 5:12.
Examples of blasphemy, Leviticus 24:11;
2 Chronicles 32:16; Isaiah 65:6-7;
Daniel 7:25; Acts 13:45; 18:6.
Putting blame on God, 2 Kings 6:33.
Insulting the Lord, 2 Chronicles 32:17.
Blasphemous vanity, Psalm 73:9-11.
Sin of challenging God, Isaiah 5:18-19.
True God spoken of as if He were one of
many gods, Isaiah 37:10. (See vv. 6, 23.)
Ultimate defamation, Isaiah 44:7.

God does not yield His glory to another, Isaiah 48:11.
Accusing the Lord of deception, Jeremiah 4:10.
Conspiracy against the Lord, Jeremiah 11:9-10.
Boasting against the Lord, Ezekiel 35:13.
Self-declared diety, Daniel 11:36-37; 2 Thessalonians 2:4.
Speaking against the God of gods, Daniel 11:36.
Laughing at truth spoken by Jesus, Matthew 9:23-24.
Jesus accused of satanic power, Matthew 9:32-34.
Unpardonable sin, Matthew 12:20-32; Mark 3:28-30.
Mockery against Jesus, Mark 15:16-20, 29-32. (Note v. 19.)
Accusing Jesus of demon-possession and madness, John 10:19-21.
Accepting praise belonging only to God, Acts 12:22-23.
Antichrist exalting himself above God, 2 Thessalonians 2:4.
Endeavoring to make God a liar, 1 John 1:8-10.
Pride and blasphemy, Revelation 13:5.
Agony of those who refuse to repent, Revelation 16:10-11.
See *Curse.*

BLEMISH
Young lady's life blemished by stranger, Genesis 34:1-24.
Avoid blemished meat, Exodus 22:31.
Skin infection, Leviticus 13:1-3.
Priests to be without blemish, Leviticus 21:17-24.
Gouging out an eye, 1 Samuel 11:1-2.
Unblemished restoration, Nehemiah 6:1.
Silver to dross, wine to water, Isaiah 1:22.
Mutilated lamb, Amos 3:12.
Loss of arm and eye, Zechariah 11:17.
See *Disfigure, Handicap, Injury.*

BLESSING
God's blessing and protection for Ishmael, Genesis 21:9-21.
Performing wonder by divine power, Exodus 34:10.
Requirements for God's blessing, 1 Kings 8:56-61.
Promise of blessing, warning against disobedience, 1 Kings 9:1-9.
Abundance of God's goodness, Nehemiah 9:25.
Personal righteousness a means to God's blessing, Psalm 18:20-21.
Experiencing divine wonders before death, Psalm 88:10-12.
God's blessing dependent on obedience to covenant, Jeremiah 11:1-5.
Greater blessing causes lesser blessing to be forgotten, Jeremiah 16:14-15.
Abundant blessing can turn to backsliding, Hosea 13:6.
Reward of good stewardship, Malachi 3:8-10.
Woman who touched Jesus, Mark 5:24-30.
Prophet and widow, Luke 4:23-26.
Good things God gives for daily life, Acts 14:17.
Those who refresh the spirit, 1 Corinthians 16:18.
Paul a channel of much blessing to Philippians, Philippians 1:25-26.
Every good gift is from above, James 1:16-17.
Grace and peace in abundance, 1 Peter 1:2.
God's best in abundance, Jude 2.
Final statement of Scripture, Revelation 22:21.
See *Abundance, Affluence, Anointing, Goodness, Provision.*

BLINDNESS
Kindness to blind people, Leviticus 19:14; Deuteronomy 27:18.
No blind clergy, Leviticus 21:16-23.
Eli likely suffered from cataracts, 1 Samuel 4:14-15.
Partial blindness inflicted as disgrace, 1 Samuel 11:2-11.
Healing blind, deaf, and dumb, Isaiah 35:5-6.
Spiritual blindness, Isaiah 59:10; Matthew 6:23; 15:14; Ephesians 4:18; 1 John 2:11.
Last healing of Jesus prior to Crucifixion, Matthew 20:29-34.
Active faith of blind Bartimaeus, Mark 10:46-52.
Seeing and hearing but not understanding, Luke 10:24.
Blindness of Jews to Messiah, John 7:25-36.

Validity of Jesus questioned, John 8:12-30.
Blindness and a sorcerer, Acts 13:6-12.
Pagans certain of erroneous belief, Acts 19:35-36.
Witnessing to those blinded by Satan, 2 Corinthians 4:1-6.
See *Eyes, Sight.*

BLISS
Ignorance is bliss, Ecclesiastes 1:18.

BLOOD
Eating food containing blood, 1 Samuel 14:31-33.
Mixing human blood with sacrifices, Luke 13:1.
Beverage of judgment, Revelation 16:5-6.

BLOODSHED
Brutal human sacrifice, Deuteronomy 18:9-12.
Guilt of innocent blood, 1 Kings 2:31; Isaiah 59:7.
Saturated city, 2 Kings 21:16.
Foot wash in enemy blood, Psalm 58:10.
Righteous victims, Lamentations 4:13; Joel 3:19.
Sacrificial bloodshed, Hebrews 9:22.
See *Carnage.*

BLOSSOM
Aaron's rod, Numbers 17:5, 8.
Fruitful nation, Isaiah 27:6.
Living desert, Isaiah 35:1-2.
Fig tree, Habakkuk 3:17.

BLUEPRINT
The Lord plans far in advance, Isaiah 25:1.
God's prenatal plan for Jeremiah, Jeremiah 1:4-5.
Drawing plan for battle, Ezekiel 4:1-3.

BLUSH
Embarrassed Ezra, Ezra 9:6.
Those who do not know how to blush, Jeremiah 6:15; 8:12.
See *Embarrassment, Shame.*

BOASTING
Goliath's macho, 1 Samuel 17:44.
Hedonistic boasting, Psalm 10:3.
Giving praise to God's Word, Psalm 56:10.
Clouds without rain, Proverbs 25:14.
Future plans, Proverbs 27:1.

Satan's taunts, Isaiah 14:12-15; Ezekiel 28:12-19.
Boasting only in the Lord, Jeremiah 9:23-24.
Peter could not live up to claims of loyalty, Matthew 26:31-35, 69-75; Mark 14:27-31, 66-72; John 13:37-38; 18:15-18, 25-27.
Proud sorcerer, Acts 8:9-10.
Self-praise and commendation from the Lord, 2 Corinthians 10:13-18.
See *Bragging, Vanity.*

BOAT
Apparent use of ferry, 2 Samuel 19:18.
Conveyance for audience, John 6:22-23.
Use of lifeboat, Acts 27:30.

BODY
Demons' need for physical bodies, Matthew 8:31.
The believer's body is the Holy Spirit's temple, 1 Corinthians 3:16-17.
See *Athletics, Physique.*

BODYGUARD
Trained men in Abram's household, Genesis 14:14.
Shielded by God's power, 1 Peter 1:5.
See *Protection.*

BODY OF CHRIST
Many invited to wedding banquet, few chosen, Matthew 22:1-14.
Context of one's spiritual family, Luke 8:19-21.
New relationships in Christ, John 19:26-27.
Jews and a centurion, Acts 10:22, 28, 34-35.
Peter and Gentiles, Acts 11:1-3.
Message to Gentiles, Acts 15:13-21.
Growing New Testament church, Acts 16:5.
Gospel message to Gentiles, Acts 18:6.
Paul's consistent prayer for other Christians, Romans 1:8-10; 1 Corinthians 1:4-9; Ephesians 1:11-23; Philippians 1:3-6; Colossians 1:3-14.
Function of various body members, Romans 12:4-8.
Honor others above yourself, Romans 12:10.
Result of a promise, Galatians 4:21-31.
Mystery which is the church, Ephesians

1:9-10; 3:2-3.
Members of God's family, Ephesians 2:19-22.
Paul considered himself a servant to the church, Colossians 1:24-26.
Christian community like a family, 1 Timothy 5:1-2.
Coming of the church as promised from beginning of time, Titus 1:1-3.
Slave who became a brother, Philemon 8-21.
Relationship in Christ, Hebrews 2:11-13.
Participants in divine nature, 2 Peter 1:4.
Becoming children of God, 1 John 3:1-3.
Love one another, 1 John 4:7-11.
The seven churches, Revelation 1:20.
See *Church, Congregation.*

BOLDNESS
Boldness of fearless preacher, 1 Kings 18:16-18.
Danger of fearing wrong things, Isaiah 8:12-14.
Jeremiah preached truth at threat of death, Jeremiah 26:12-16.
Ezekiel proclaimed God's message with boldness, Ezekiel 33:21-33.
Daring Daniel, Daniel 6:10.
Courage of ordinary men, Acts 4:13.
Approaching God in confidence, Ephesians 3:12; Hebrews 4:16; 10:19.
Standing firm whatever circumstances, Philippians 1:27-30.
Those not embarrassed because of Paul's chains, 2 Timothy 1:16-18.
Leadership with authority, Titus 2:15.
See *Bravery, Courage.*

BONDAGE
Israelites' right to be set free, Leviticus 25:47-55.
Jeremiah prophesied restoration of Israel, Jeremiah 30:8-17.
Conditional freedom, Jeremiah 34:8-11.
Free men ruled by slaves, Lamentations 5:8.
Those enslaved who foolishly think they are free, John 8:31-36.
Paul's chains increased his ministry, Philippians 1:12-14.
Binding of Satan, Revelation 20:1-3.
See *Slavery.*

BONES
Human bones desecrated, 2 Kings 23:13-14; Psalm 53:5; Jeremiah 8:1; Ezekiel 6:5.
Arms broken in judgment, Ezekiel 30:20-26.
Valley of dry bones, Ezekiel 37:1-14.

BOOK OF LIFE
Divine registry, Psalm 87:6.
Name in, Revelation 3:5; 20:15; 21:27.
Book opened, Revelation 20:12.

BOOKS
Dialogue immortalized, Job 19:23.
Endless supply of books, Ecclesiastes 12:12.
Scroll of remembrance, Malachi 3:16-18.
Source of joy, Luke 10:20.
Sorcery literature destroyed, Acts 19:19.
Believer's identity, Philippians 4:3.
Volumes of judgment, Revelation 20:12.
See *Author, Literature, Writing.*

BOREDOM
Meaningless activity, Ecclesiastes 2:1-11.

BORROWING
Injury or loss involving borrowed and rented property, Exodus 22:14; 2 Kings 6:5.
Lend to those in need, Deuteronomy 15:8; Psalms 37:26; 112:5; Matthew 5:42; Luke 6:35.
Borrowing but not repaying, Psalm 37:21.
Power of loaned money, Proverbs 22:7.

BOTHER
See *Disruption, Dissension, Meddle.*

BOTTOM LINE
Paul's "punch line" conclusion to appeal for stewardship, 2 Corinthians 9:15.

BOUNTIFUL
Abundant blessings of nature, Deuteronomy 33:13-16.
That which gives true contentment, Proverbs 30:7-9.
God's righteousness lasts forever, Isaiah 51:8.
No longer will the enemy plunder, Isaiah 62:8-9.
Eating to complete satisfaction, Joel 2:26.

God's grace lavished on us, Ephesians 1:7-8.

Good land and unproductive land, Hebrews 6:7-8.

See *Abundance, Affluence, Plenty, Wealth.*

BOXING
Hand-to-hand fighting, 2 Samuel 2:14.
Divine pugilism, Psalm 3:7.

BRACELET
Betrothal gift, Genesis 24:22.
Object of worldliness, Isaiah 3:19.
Worn by men, Ezekiel 16:11.

BRAGGING
Big mouths, Judges 9:38.
Proper time for boasting, 1 Samuel 2:1-3.
Affront to the Lord, Psalm 10:3.
Nothing to brag about, Psalm 49:6-9; 1 Corinthians 1:29; 2 Corinthians 4:6-7; Ephesians 2:8-10.
Dishonest stewardship, Proverbs 25:14.
Boast only about the Lord, Jeremiah 9:23-24.
Pharaoh only a loud noise, Jeremiah 46:17.
Peter could not live up to his claims of loyalty, Matthew 26:31-35, 69-75.
Evil boasting, James 4:16.

BRAVERY
Joshua's bravery, Numbers 14:6-9.
Bold Gideon, Judges 7:7-23.
David versus Goliath, 1 Samuel 17:1-51.
Nehemiah's boldness, Nehemiah 6:10-13.
Brave woman, Esther 4:13-16.
Imputed bravery, Proverbs 28:1; Ephesians 3:12; Hebrews 4:16.
Unwavering courage, Daniel 3:16-18.
Daniel's courage, Daniel 6:10.
Facing adversaries, Philippians 1:27-28.
See *Boldness, Courage.*

BRAWN
Mighty Samson, Judges 14:6; 16:3-30.
Bear and lion slain by hand, 1 Samuel 17:32-37.
Glory of youth, Proverbs 20:29.
Race not to swift or strong, Ecclesiastes 9:11.
See *Athletics, Physical, Physique, Strength.*

BREATH
Divine life, Genesis 2:7.

Blast of divine breath, 2 Samuel 22:16; Job 4:9; Psalm 18:15; Isaiah 30:33.
Job's bad breath, Job 19:17.
Creative breath, Psalm 33:6.
Valley of dry bones, Ezekiel 37:5.
See *Life, Mortality.*

BREVITY
Six-word obituary, Numbers 20:1.
Shortest short story, Ecclesiastes 9:13-15.
Short chapter with message of judgment and mercy, Jeremiah 45:1-5.
One-chapter books, Obadiah 1-21; Philemon 1-25; 2 John 1-13; 3 John 1-14; Jude 1-25.
Two-word command, Mark 2:14.
Blind man's simple request, Mark 10:46-52.
Verse with only two words, John 11:35.
Paul's brief sermon at Athens, Acts 17:22-31.
Profound truth briefly presented, Ephesians 3:1-3.
One-hour reign of 10 kings, Revelation 17:12.

BRIBERY
Taking bribes forbidden, Exodus 23:8.
Asking special favor, Judges 1:13-15.
Delilah bribed to deceive Samson, Judges 16:5.
Sons of Samuel, 1 Samuel 8:1-5.
International bribery, 1 Kings 15:19.
Anti-Semitic persuasion, Esther 3:8-9.
Danger of riches and bribes, Job 36:18-19.
Thwarting justice, Proverbs 17:23; Amos 5:12.
God accepts no price or reward, Isaiah 45:13.
Daniel's refusal of bribes or rewards, Daniel 5:17.
Hands skilled in doing evil, Micah 7:3.
Jesus betrayed for 30 silver coins, Matthew 26:14-16, 47-50; Mark 14:10-11; Luke 22:3-6. (See Zech. 11:12-13.)
Perjuring Resurrection, Matthew 28:11-15.
Desire for healing gift, Acts 8:9-24.
Felix wanted bribe from Paul, Acts 24:26.
Avoid any kind of partiality, 1 Timothy 5:21.
See *Cheating, Politics.*

BRIDE
Search for bride, Genesis 24:1-66; Esther

2:17.
Engagement to marriage, Deuteronomy
20:7.
Blessing of a good wife, Proverbs 18:22.
Remarriage, Romans 7:2-3; 1 Timothy
5:14.
See *Marriage, Wedding.*

BRIDEGROOM
Extended honeymoon, Deuteronomy 24:5.
Bridegroom's festivity, Judges 14:10.
Colorful appearance of bridegroom, Psalm
19:4-5.
See *Husband, Marriage, Wedding.*

BRIDGE
Bridge to cross Jordan, 2 Kings 2:13-14.

BRIERS
See *Thorns.*

BROTHER
Abraham's relationship to stepsister,
Genesis 20:12, 16.
Jacob and Esau, Genesis 25:21-26; 27:1-46.
Reunion between Jacob and Esau, Genesis
33:1-20.
Jealousy of younger brother, Genesis 37:1-
36.
Joseph and brothers in Egypt, Genesis
42–45.
Rejecting brother born of evil woman,
Judges 11:1-10.
Israel and Judah, Jeremiah 3:11.
Strife before birth, Hosea 12:3.
Jealousy within family, Luke 15:11-32.
One brother tells another, John 1:41.
See *Family.*

BROTHERHOOD
Becoming brother of Jesus, Matthew 12:50.
Love as the supreme identity of relation-
ship, John 13:34.
Brotherhood of believers, Acts 9:17; 21:20;
Romans 16:23-24.
Accepting one another, Romans 15:7.
Servant becomes brother, Philemon 16.
The darkness of hatred, 1 John 2:9-11.
See *Body of Christ, Church, Congregation.*

BRUTALITY
Mistreatment to slaves, Exodus 21:20-21.
People who become like animals in times
of distress, Deuteronomy 28:53-57.

Cutting off thumbs and big toes, Judges
1:7.
See *Cruelty, Sadistic, Torture.*

BUDGET
Estimating cost before starting to build,
Luke 14:28-30.

BUILDING
Threshing floor became site for altar,
2 Samuel 24:18-25.
Need for larger building, 2 Kings 6:1-2.
Tears of joy as foundation laid for temple,
Ezra 3:10-13.
Even the temple was temporary, Matthew
24:1-2.
By faith Noah built ark, Hebrews 11:7.
See *Architecture, Construction, Design,
Plan.*

BULLHEADED
Defiant sin, Numbers 15:30-31.
King who desecrated temple, 2 Chronicles
26:16-21.
Fool airs his own opinion, Proverbs 18:2.
See *Stubborn.*

BURDEN
Burdens lifted daily, Psalm 68:19.
Jeremiah's anguish, Jeremiah 4:19.
Heart of flesh or heart of stone, Ezekiel
11:19.
Mourning over a message, Daniel 10:1-3.
Burden made light, Matthew 11:28-30.
Paul's concern for Athens and its idolatry,
Acts 17:16.
Paul would himself be lost if it could mean
salvation of Israel, Romans 9:1-4. (See
10:1.)
Paul's relentless effort on behalf of
followers, Colossians 1:28-29.
Paul's concern for spiritual development
of followers, Colossians 2:1-5.
Paul eager for proper counsel with
Thessalonians, 1 Thessalonians 3:1-5.
See *Concern, Empathy.*

BUREAUCRACY
Politicians keep eyes on each other,
Ecclesiastes 5:8-9.
See *Administration, Government, Politics.*

BURIAL
Choice place for burial, Genesis 23:6.

Untouched graves, Numbers 19:16.
Disgrace of no burial, Deuteronomy 28:26; Psalm 79:2; Ecclesiastes 6:3; Jeremiah 7:33.
Burial sites, Judges 16:31; 1 Samuel 25:1; 31:13; 2 Kings 21:18; 1 Chronicles 10:11-12; 2 Chronicles 33:20; Jeremiah 26:23; Matthew 27:7, 57-59; Luke 23:50-53.
Old Testament significance of burial, 2 Samuel 2:4-6.
In a garden, 2 Kings 21:26.
Enemy buried alive, Psalm 55:15.
Disinterred body, Isaiah 14:19.
Graves hewn out of rock, Isaiah 22:16.
Burial in ignominy, Jeremiah 41:9.
Satanic opposition to body of Moses, Jude 9.
See *Cremation, Death, Exhume, Funeral, Grave, Tomb, Tombstone.*

BUSINESS
Do not take advantage of another, Leviticus 25:17.
Taking care of unfinished business, Deuteronomy 20:5-9.
Import and export in King Solomon's time, 1 Kings 10:28-29.
Merchandising on Sabbath, Nehemiah 10:31; 13:15-18.
When business is bad, Psalm 37:7, 16, 35-40.
Meaningless effort, Psalm 39:6.
Dishonest weights and measures, Proverbs 11:1; 20:10, 23. (See also Ezek. 45:9-10; Hosea 12:7.)
Woman skilled in business, Proverbs 31:16.
Industrial insomnia, Ecclesiastes 5:12.
Businessmen of Tyre, Isaiah 23:7-8.
Man who refuses bribes and related evil, Isaiah 33:15-16.
Purchasing field with silver, Jeremiah 32:25.
Judgment on buyer and seller, Ezekiel 7:12.

Prosperity of ancient Tyre taken away in judgment, Ezekiel 27:1-36.
Skill in business brings vanity of heart, Ezekiel 28:4-5.
Cheating in business, Amos 8:5-6.
Merchant's desecrated land, Nahum 3:17.
Time of economic collapse, Zephaniah 1:11.
No wages, no business opportunities, Zechariah 8:10.
Correct procedure in paying taxes, Mark 12:17.
Determining cost before expenditure, Luke 14:28-30.
Parable of shrewd management, Luke 16:1-8.
Lydia, businesswoman at Thyatira, Acts 16:13-15.
Business profit limited by integrity of converts, Acts 19:23-41.
Work more diligently for Christian employer, 1 Timothy 6:2.
Business of church, Titus 1:5.
Success in business succumbs to certainty of death, James 1:10-11.
Merchants of earth lament destruction of Babylon, Revelation 18:11-19.
See *Bargaining, Barter, Commerce, Merchandise.*

BUSYBODY
Strategy of Jesus in facing accusers, Matthew 21:25-27.
Pharisees looked for point against Jesus, Mark 3:1-6.
Jesus and Pharisees, Luke 14:1-6.
Debate between Jesus and teachers of darkness, John 8:13-59.
Pharisees and man born blind, John 9:13-34.
Arguing over point of doctrine, Acts 15:1-3.
Those teachings which cause controversy, 1 Timothy 1:3-4.
Pointless quarreling over words, 2 Timothy 2:14.

C

CALAMITY
Judgment brings righteousness, Isaiah 26:9.
One message after another of bad news, Jeremiah 51:31-32.
Young and old in dust of streets, Lamentations 2:21.
From frying pan into fire, Amos 5:19.
Persecution implements spread of Gospel, Acts 8:3-4.
Fear causes people to give glory to God, Revelation 11:13.
Greatest earthquake of all time, Revelation 16:18.
See *Disaster, Trauma.*

CALENDAR
Creation of days, Genesis 1:5.
Twelve months, 1 Chronicles 27:1-15.
Lunar designations, Psalm 104:19.
Time for everything, Ecclesiastes 3:1-8.
Dates measured by reign of kings, Jeremiah 1:2-3; Daniel 1:1; Haggai 1:1; Zechariah 1:1. (Note dates more generalized, Isa. 1:1; Micah 1:1; Zeph. 1:1.)
Recognizing specific date, Ezekiel 1:1.
Date related to earthquake, Amos 1:1.
Unknown date, Matthew 24:36; Mark 13:32.
See *Date.*

CALL
Call to ministry, Genesis 12:1; Exodus 3:2-10; Numbers 27:18-23; Deuteronomy 31:23; Joshua 1:1-9; 4:1-16; Judges 6:11-14; 1 Kings 19:19; Isaiah 6:8-10; Acts 26:16.
Calling of Samuel, 1 Samuel 3:4-10.
Rejecting God's call, Psalm 81:11; Isaiah 65:12; Jeremiah 7:13; Hosea 9:17;

Jonah 1:1-3.
Selection of priests and Levites, Isaiah 66:21.
Those whom the Lord did not call, Jeremiah 23:21.
Donkey chosen to serve Jesus, Matthew 21:1-7.
Calling of disciples, Mark 1:16-20; 2:13-17.
Paul's vision of Macedonian, Acts 16:9-10.
Relationship between ability and God's call to service, Romans 11:29.
Paul's credentials as apostle, Galatians 1:1, 15-17.
Christ Himself ordained by His Father, Hebrews 5:4-6.

CALLOUSED
Stubborn Pharaoh, Exodus 5:1-9.
Stiff neck and hard heart, 2 Chronicles 36:11-13; Nehemiah 9:17.
Hardness of heart, Psalms 78:32; 95:8; Proverbs 28:14; 29:1; Jeremiah 5:3; Zechariah 7:12.
Those who should have been weeping, Isaiah 22:12-13.
Calloused women, Isaiah 32:9.
Those who pass by, Lamentations 1:12.
Witnessing miracles with hard hearts, Matthew 11:20.
Cares of this world, Matthew 22:1-6.
Caring neither for God or man, Luke 18:1-5.
No concern for mistreatment of another, Acts 18:17.
See *Hardness, Indifference.*

CAMARADERIE
Wrong kind of camaraderie, Exodus 23:2.
Wrong kind of unanimity, Numbers 11:4-10.
Sharing same spirit, Numbers 11:16-17.

48

People united behind new leader, Joshua 1:16-18.

Mother-in-law and daughter-in-law, Ruth 1:16-19.

In unity, heart and soul, 1 Samuel 14:7.

Working diligently together, Nehemiah 4:6.

Abandoned by friends in time of trouble, Job 6:14-17.

Sharing with those who deserve, Proverbs 3:27-28.

Two better than one, Ecclesiastes 4:8-12.

Lover and beloved, Song of Songs 2:3-6.

Weeping and rejoicing with Jerusalem, Isaiah 66:10.

Two walking in agreement, Amos 3:3.

Return to the Lord and He will return to you, Zechariah 1:3.

Justice, mercy, and compassion for one another, Zechariah 7:8-10.

Mother, brothers, and sisters, Mark 3:32-35.

People at peace with each other, Mark 9:50.

Guest who remained three months, Luke 1:56.

Like teacher, like student, Luke 6:40.

United to follow Jesus, Luke 8:1-3.

United behind common goal, Luke 10:1-2.

Measure of friendship, Luke 11:5-8.

Communicating with gentle spirit of a mother, 1 Thessalonians 2:7-8.

No place for arguments and quarrels, 2 Timothy 2:24-26.

See *Brotherhood, Fellowship, Rapport, Unanimity.*

CAMOUFLAGE

Isaac deceived by Jacob in search of Esau's birthright, Genesis 27:1-46.

Judah deceived by daughter-in-law, Genesis 38:13-19.

Disguising true identity, Joshua 9:3-6.

David feigns madness, 1 Samuel 21:12-14.

King Herod and the magi, Matthew 2:7-8, 12.

CAMPAIGNING

Winning favor of people, 2 Samuel 15:1-6.

See *Politics.*

CAMPFIRE

Twigs set ablaze, Isaiah 64:1-2.

CANDIDATES

Candidates to replace Queen Vashti, Esther 2:1-4.

Two men proposed to replace Judas, Acts 1:21-26.

See *Politics.*

CANDOR

Worth of honest rebuke, Proverbs 28:23.

Wisdom of Gamaliel, Acts 5:34-40.

Paul willing to be accepted as a fool, 2 Corinthians 11:16-19.

CANNIBALISM

Eating sons and daughters, Deuteronomy 28:53; 2 Kings 6:28; Jeremiah 19:9; Lamentations 2:20; 4:10.

Eating one's own flesh, Isaiah 49:26.

Fathers and children eating each other, Ezekiel 5:10.

Nation butchered, Micah 3:1-3.

Eating flesh of kings, Revelation 19:18.

CAPABILITY

Special gifts from God through Holy Spirit, Exodus 31:1-5.

Sanballat's ridicule of Jewish capability, Nehemiah 4:1-3.

What God requires, He provides, Isaiah 2:3.

Victory requires more than ability, Isaiah 25:11.

Choice of candidates for service in Babylonian government, Daniel 1:3-5.

Capable of evil, Micah 2:1.

Qualifications of Christ as Saviour and King, Colossians 1:15-20.

Prepared by God to succeed as believer, Hebrews 13:20-21.

See *Ability, Talent.*

CAPITAL PUNISHMENT

Divine institution of capital punishment, Genesis 9:6.

Premeditated murder, Exodus 21:14.

Death to kidnappers, Exodus 21:16.

Death to idolater, Exodus 22:20; Deuteronomy 13:6-10.

Sabbath-breaker, Exodus 35:2.

Deterrent to crime, Ecclesiastes 8:11.

See *Stoning.*

CAPTIVE
Lot taken captive, Genesis 14:11-12.
Death to captives, Numbers 31:15-18;
Deuteronomy 20:16-20.
Enemy subjects and leaders put to death,
Joshua 10:16-27.
Samson's captivity, Judges 16:5-30.
Captives unharmed, 1 Samuel 30:1-2.
Captives put to work, 2 Samuel 12:29-31;
1 Chronicles 20:1-3.
King released and honored, 2 Kings 25:27-
30.
Brutality and indecency, Lamentations
5:11-13.
See *Prison.*

CAREER
Woodcutters and water carriers, Joshua
9:26-27.
Long reign of King David, 2 Samuel 5:4.
God's blessing on work of hands, Psalm
90:17.
Paul's advice to unmarried women,
1 Corinthians 7:25-26.
Ultimate career, a life of love, Ephesians
5:1-2.

CARELESS
Carelessness in duty, 1 Samuel 26:7-16;
2 Chronicles 24:5.
Lazy man's house, Ecclesiastes 10:18.
Lax in the Lord's work, Jeremiah 48:10.
Careless construction, Matthew 7:26.
Careless investment, Matthew 25:14-25.
See *Neglect.*

CARING
Providing for strangers and poor, Leviticus
23:22.
Preventive care for children, Job 1:4-5.
Sharing with those who deserve, Proverbs
3:27-28.
Looking after one's house, Ecclesiastes
10:18.
Jeremiah's broken heart, Jeremiah
23:9.
Heart of flesh or heart of stone, Ezekiel
11:19.
Faith of friends resulted in man's healing,
Mark 2:1-5; Luke 5:17-20.
Sincerely caring for poor, Luke 11:37-41.
Sharing with others, Luke 12:48.
Attitude of Pharisees toward helping
others on the Sabbath, Luke 13:10-17.

Pharisees false concern for safety of Jesus,
Luke 13:31.
Reaching out for those in need, Luke
14:12-14.
Hospitality toward unbeliever, Luke 15:1-2.
Father's loving heart, Luke 15:20.
Paul's reluctance in expressing deep
spiritual concern, Romans 9:1-2.
Not embarrassed by the misfortune of
friend, 2 Timothy 1:16-17.
See *Compassion, Empathy, Involvement.*

CARNAGE
Massive victory in battle, 2 Samuel 10:18.
Shields and uniforms red with blood,
Naham 2:3.
Third of mankind destroyed, Revelation
9:18.
See *Bloodshed, Destruction, War.*

CARNALITY
Reluctance of Lot to leave Sodom, Genesis
19:15-16.
Motherhood by incest, Genesis 19:30-38.
God's Spirit and one who practiced
sorcery, Numbers 24:1-2.
People quick to disobey God, Judges 2:10-
13; 3:7, 12; 4:1.
Wanton woman becomes unfaithful to
husband, Judges 19:1-3.
Unable to be near the ark of God, 1 Samuel
5:10-11.
Sin considered trivial, 1 Kings 16:31.
Doing right, but not wholeheartedly,
2 Chronicles 25:2.
Isaiah realized his own sinfulness, Isaiah
6:1-5.
Trying patience of God, Isaiah 7:13.
Those who should be weeping engage in
merriment, Isaiah 22:12-13.
Listeners who hear nothing, Isaiah 42:20.
Reasoning of people who had turned from
God, Ezekiel 33:21-33.
Hostility in house of God, Hosea 9:8.
Those who feed on the wind, Hosea 12:1.
Abundant blessing can turn to backsliding,
Hosea 13:6.
For continued sinning, certain judgment,
Amos 1:3, 6, 9, 11, 13; 2:1, 4, 6. (Note
the nature of sin in each of these
judgments.)
Those who neither seek the Lord nor ask
about Him, Zephaniah 1:6.
Defiled offerings from defiled people,

Haggai 2:13-14.
Preferring demons to deliverance,
Matthew 8:28-34. (Note especially v.
34.)
Witnessing miracles with hard hearts,
Matthew 11:20.
Cause for divorce, Matthew 19:8.
Marriage on earth compared to
relationship in heaven, Mark 12:18-27.
Those afraid to profess their faith, John
12:42-43.
Pleasures which cause spiritual death,
Romans 6:21.
Sinful passions aroused by the Law,
Romans 7:5.
Struggle between flesh and Spirit, Romans
7:15-18.
Outreaching grace to those who reject,
Romans 10:21.
Paul's description of those who thought
they had attained spiritual success,
1 Corinthians 4:1-21.
Pride over immorality, 1 Corinthians
5:1-2.
Danger of testing God, 1 Corinthians
10:14-22.
Those who live by standards of world,
2 Corinthians 10:2.
Reaping what is sown, Galatians 6:7-10.
Anger and the devil, Ephesians 4:26-27.
Enmity in mind against God, Colossians
1:21.
Unintentional sin, Hebrews 9:7.
Role of evil desire in causing one to sin,
James 1:13-15.
Bitter envy and selfish ambition, James
3:13-16.
Submit to God; resist the devil, James 4:7.
Suffering removes evil human desires,
1 Peter 4:1-2.
Evil desires, 2 Peter 1:4.
Danger of corrupt desire, 2 Peter 2:4-10.
Those who carouse, 2 Peter 2:13-16.
That which keeps us from will of God,
1 John 2:15-17.
Danger of losing one's full reward, 2 John
8.
Physical pollution, Jude 8.
Losing first love, Revelation 2:4.
Those with little strength, Revelation 3:8.
Neither cold nor hot, Revelation 3:15.
Refusing to repent, Revelation 9:20-21.
See *Backsliding, Flesh, Hedonism,*
Immorality, Lust, Materialism, Orgy.

CARNIVOROUS
Man and animals originally vegetarian,
Genesis 1:29-30. (See also 2:9.)
Lions, wolves, and leopards, Jeremiah 5:6.
Feast for animals following great battle in
Israel, Ezekiel 39:14-20.
Locusts who attack only people, Revelation
9:3-6.
Women's hair and lions' teeth, Revelation
9:8.

CAROUSING
Waiting for Moses, Exodus 32:1-6.
Torture for entertainment, Judges 16:23-
25.
From one sin to another, Jeremiah 9:3.
An end to noisy songs, Ezekiel 26:13.
Doing what pagans do, 1 Peter 4:3.

CARPENTER
Carpenters build palace, 2 Samuel 5:11.
Building temple, 2 Kings 12:11.
Carpentry of a lazy man, Ecclesiastes 10:18.
Selecting good wood to make idol, Isaiah
40:20.
Only a carpenter's Son, Matthew 13:55;
Mark 6:1-3.
Builder has greater honor than the
building, Hebrews 3:3.

CASH
Services paid for in cash, Deuteronomy
2:6.

CASTRATION
See *Eunuch.*

CATACLYSM
See *Catastrophe, Disaster.*

CATARACTS
Eli likely suffered from cataracts, 1 Samuel
4:14-15.

CATASTROPHE
God's promise to Noah, Genesis 9:8-16.
Gentle flowing waters or mighty flood
waters, Isaiah 8:6-7.
Judgment brings righteousness, Isaiah
26:9.
Persecution implements spread of Gospel,
Acts 8:3-4.
Destruction on earth and in sky, Revelation
6:12-14.

Fallen Babylon, Revelation 14:8.
Greatest earthquake of all time, Revelation 16:18-20.

CATERING
Food and drink provided in desert, 2 Samuel 16:1-4.

CATTLE
Creation of livestock, Genesis 1:25.
First record of veal for food, Genesis 18:7.
Cows and bulls as gifts, Genesis 32:13-15.
Israel's livestock preserved, Exodus 9:1-7.
Idolatrous golden calf, Exodus 32:1-4; Deuteronomy 9:15-16; Psalm 106:19.
Blessing for calves, Deuteronomy 7:13.
Cows as draft animals, 1 Samuel 6:7.
Jeroboam's golden calves, 1 Kings 12:28; 2 Kings 10:28-29; 17:16; 2 Chronicles 11:13-16.
Calf-idol of Beth Aven, Hosea 10:5.

CAUSE
God as first cause in Creation, Genesis 1:1.
Pure from impure, Job 14:4.
Righteousness caused by Scripture memorization, Psalm 119:11.
Out of heart, Matthew 15:10-20; Mark 7:20-23.
Good things stored in heart, Luke 6:45.
See *Frame of reference, Motivation.*

CELEBRATION
Feast on day of Isaac's weaning, Genesis 21:8.
Three festivals honoring God, Exodus 23:14-17.
Looking back over many years of blessing, Deuteronomy 2:7.
Dedication of temple, 1 Kings 8:62-66.
Time to rejoice and not weep, Nehemiah 8:9-10.
Town and country praising the Lord, Isaiah 42:11.
Banquet for Jesus, Luke 5:27-35.
Rejoicing in heaven when sinner repents, Luke 15:3-10.
Return of prodigal, Luke 15:22-24.
Dinner given in Jesus' honor, John 12:2.
Celebrating death of two witnesses, Revelation 11:7-11.
See *Commemorate, Festivity.*

CELEBRITY
No prophet in Israel like Moses, Deuteronomy 34:10-12.
Famous Joshua, Joshua 6:27.
Solomon's fame, 1 Kings 4:29-34; 10:1.
Local fame, 1 Chronicles 12:50.
David's fame, 1 Chronicles 14:17.
Seeking audience with ruler, Proverbs 29:26.
The Lord should be the celebrity, Isaiah 26:8.
Role of humility in greatness, Matthew 23:12.
Respect of Cornelius for Peter, Acts 10:25-26.
See *Fame.*

CELIBACY
Relationship of Joseph to Mary, Matthew 1:25.
Remarriage after divorce, Matthew 19:8-12.
Those who renounce marriage for spiritual service, Matthew 19:11-12.
Unmarried widows, 1 Corinthians 7:8.
Pauline advice, 1 Corinthians 7:27.
Observing strict celibacy, Revelation 14:4.
See *Eunuch.*

CENSURE
King's command to stop rebuilding temple, Ezra 4:18-22.
Refusal to obey king's edict, Esther 1:10-20.
He who helped others himself becomes discouraged, Job 4:3-5.
Wounds of a friend, Proverbs 27:6.
Futile effort to suppress truth, Jeremiah 38:1-6.
Those who look for something to criticize, Mark 3:2.
Christian method of rebuke, 2 Thessalonians 3:14-15.

CENSUS
Census in Israel, Numbers 1:2; 26:2.
Men of military age, 2 Samuel 24:2.
Census by satanic impetus, 1 Chronicles 21:1.
Enumeration of exiles returning from Babylon, Ezra 2:3-64.
God's command to increase population, Jeremiah 29:4-6.

Taking of census at time of the birth of Jesus, Luke 2:1-5.

CEREMONY
Circumcision at advanced age, Genesis 17:10-27.
Liturgy of a woman's purification, Numbers 5:11-31.
Improvised ceremony for new king, 2 Kings 9:11-13.
Illustration of religious works involved in idolatry, Isaiah 46:1.
Washing hands before eating, Matthew 15:1-9.
Great pomp of King Agrippa, Acts 25:23.
See *Protocol.*

CERTAINTY
Time for everything, Ecclesiastes 3:1-8.
Certainty of God's plans and purposes, Isaiah 14:24.
Promise of judgment fulfilled, Lamentations 2:17.
The Lord's love and faithfulness day-by-day, Lamentations 3:22-24.
Believe the Good News, Mark 1:14-15.
Divine decisions irrevocable, Romans 11:29.
The meaning of "today" in God's reckoning, Hebrews 4:7.
Jesus, our Guarantee, Hebrews 7:22.
Confident now of God's fulfillment of promises in future, Hebrews 11:13.
No lie comes from truth, 1 John 2:20-21.
See *Assurance.*

CERTIFICATION
See *Credentials, Documentation, Validity.*

CHAINS
See *Fetters.*

CHALLENGE
March on with strong soul, Judges 5:21.
Smallest and weakest, Judges 6:14-16.
Overcoming obstacles with God's help, 2 Samuel 22:30.
Confidence to face challenge, Psalm 18:29.
Sin of challenging God, Isaiah 5:18-19.
Challenge to work for divine cause, Haggai 2:4.
Becoming fishers of men, Matthew 4:19.
Jesus saw abundant fishing where there had been none, Luke 5:1-11.

CHAMPAGNE
Foaming wine with dregs, Psalm 75:8.

CHANCE
Death by measurement, 2 Samuel 8:2.
Death of a king by random arrow, 2 Chronicles 18:33-34.
Casting lots to determine guilt, Jonah 1:7.
Casting lots to determine God's will, Acts 1:23-26.
See *Fortuity, Happenstance.*

CHANGE
God's command to Abraham, Genesis 12:1-9.
Comparing old and new, Luke 5:36-39.
Paul fearful of reunion with Corinthians, 2 Corinthians 12:20-21.

CHAOS
Warriors stumbling over each other, Jeremiah 46:12.
Time of community despair, Ezekiel 7:27.
See *Destruction, Peril, War.*

CHARACTER
Righteous man without blame, Genesis 6:9.
Angel's tragic description of unborn Ishmael, Genesis 16:11-12.
Prenatal description, Genesis 25:21-34.
Father's predictions, Genesis 49:1-28.
Deeds reveal person, 1 Samuel 24:13.
David showed kindness to enemy, 2 Samuel 9:1-8.
David refused to drink water which had endangered lives of his men, 2 Samuel 23:15-17.
God's commendation of Job, Job 1:8.
Pure cannot come from impure, Job 14:4.
The Lord judges integrity, Psalm 7:8.
Characteristics of a holy life, Psalm 15:1-5.
Description of in-depth character, Psalm 51:6.
Marks of an evil character, Proverbs 6:16-19.
Those who lack character to go with wealth, Proverbs 19:10.
Childhood evidence, Proverbs 20:11.
The Lord knows the inmost being, Proverbs 20:27.
Disguising true self by false speech, Proverbs 26:24-26.
Sometimes better poor than rich, Proverbs

28:6.
Youth in building of character, Ecclesiastes 11:9.
Eloquent description of noble person, Isaiah 32:8.
Mark of righteous man, Isaiah 32:15-16.
Man who refused bribes and related evil, Isaiah 33:15-16.
Evil deeds and motives likened to eggs, Isaiah 59:4-5.
Some juice left in grapes, Isaiah 65:8.
Act of shame, Jeremiah 13:26.
Description of righteous man, Ezekiel 18:5-9.
Easily deceived, Hosea 7:11.
Mark of man who pleases the Lord, Micah 6:8.
Fasting in secret, Matthew 6:16-18.
Revealing thoughts of heart, Luke 2:34-35.
Balanced life of Jesus, Luke 2:52.
Good fruit and bad fruit, Luke 6:43-45.
Those of good character welcome truth, Luke 8:15.
Clean on outside, dirty on inside, Luke 11:37-41.
Jesus knew what was in men, John 2:24-25.
Good motivation of David, Acts 13:22.
Noble character of Bereans, Acts 17:11.
Character within a person, Romans 2:28-29.
Dual nature of man, Romans 7:21-25.
Always doing what is right, Romans 12:17.
Overcome evil with good, Romans 12:21.
Bad company and good character, 1 Corinthians 15:33.
Standing firm in the faith, 1 Corinthians 16:13-14.
Fruit of the Spirit, Galatians 5:22-23.
Ultimate career, a life of love, Ephesians 5:1-2.
Faithful service without pastoral supervision, Philippians 2:12-13.
Lifestyle of those risen with Christ, Colossians 3:1-17.
Providing for one's own needs, Titus 3:14.
Moses' choice to refuse pleasures of Egypt and identify with God's people, Hebrews 11:24-25.
Additions to faith, 2 Peter 1:5-9.
Continuity of evil and good in character, Revelation 22:11.
See *Conduct, Lifestyle.*

CHARACTER ASSASSINATION
Stripped of one's honor, Job 19:9.
See *Demean, Gossip, Slander.*

CHARIOT
Vehicle of distinction, Genesis 41:42-43.
Three thousand strong, 1 Samuel 13:5.
Community of chariots, 1 Kings 9:19.
Replacement order, 1 Kings 20:25.
Death vehicle, 1 Kings 22:35.
Chariot of fire, 2 Kings 2:11.

CHARISMATIC
Dreams and visions and Word of God, Jeremiah 23:25-32.
Speaking in new tongues, Mark 16:17.
Paul and the laying on of hands, Acts 19:1-7.
Paul's omission of healing and tongues in challenging Roman Christians, Romans 12:4-8. (See 15:17-19.)
Role of tongues in body of Christ, 1 Corinthians 12:27-31; 14:1-5.

CHARITY
Giving to poor is lending to the Lord, Proverbs 19:17.
Concern for poor, Proverbs 28:27.
Speak up for those who cannot help themselves, Proverbs 31:8-9.
Open arms to poor, Proverbs 31:20.
Real meaning of fasting, Isaiah 58:3-7.
Early Christians took care of those in need, Acts 4:32-35.
Woman who helped poor, Acts 9:36-42.
Devout centurion, Acts 10:2.
Kindness to poor recognized by the Lord, Acts 10:4.
Reaching out to help others in need, Acts 11:27-30.
The church looking after the needs of poor, Romans 15:26-27.
See *Benevolence, Welfare.*

CHASTITY
Proof of chastity, Deuteronomy 22:13-21.
Geriatric chastity, 1 Kings 1:1-4.
Those who looked after the king's harem, Esther 2:14.
Covenant of personal purity, Job 31:1.
Purity by determination, Proverbs 2:10-22; Colossians 3:5.
Lust in the heart, Proverbs 6:24-25; Matthew 5:28.

Ezekiel's description of puberty, Ezekiel 16:5-9.
Avoid evil associates, 1 Corinthians 5:11.
Temple of Holy Spirit, 1 Corinthians 6:13-19.
Not even a hint, Ephesians 5:3-4.
Challenge to purity, 1 Timothy 5:22.
See *Morality, Purity.*

CHAUVINISM
See *Husband, Women's rights.*

CHEATING
Dishonest scales, Deuteronomy 25:13; Proverbs 11:1; Hosea 12:7; Micah 6:11.
Deceptive purchasing, Proverbs 20:14.
Cheating in business, Amos 8:5-6.
Can dishonesty be acquitted? Micah 6:11.
Cheating the Lord, Malachi 3:8-9.
Expensive gain, Matthew 16:26.
Failing to pay workman his wages, James 5:4.
See *Dishonesty.*

CHEEK
Taking a slap, 1 Kings 22:24; Job 16:10.
Enduring patiently, Matthew 5:39.

CHEER
A cheer so loud it shook the ground, 1 Samuel 4:5.
Singing songs to a heavy heart, Proverbs 25:20.

CHEESE
Bread and cheese, 1 Samuel 17:17-18.
Cheese made from cow's milk, 2 Samuel 17:27-29.
Picture of anxiety, Job 10:10.

CHEMICALS
Chemicals cause land to become unproductive, Deuteronomy 29:23.

CHERISH
See *Affection, Love.*

CHILD ABUSE
Greed of Joseph's brothers, Genesis 37:12-36.
Threat of torture, 1 Kings 3:16-27.
Wartime slaughter, Isaiah 13:16.
Slaughter of children, Ezekiel 9:6; Matthew 2:13-18.

Boys traded for prostitutes, Joel 3:3.

CHILDBIRTH
Husband's death brings death to wife, 1 Samuel 4:19-20.
Bearing firstborn, Jeremiah 4:31.
Men suffering pains of childbirth, Jeremiah 30:6.
Woman in heaven who gave birth, Revelation 12:1-6.

CHILDISH
As senseless children, Jeremiah 4:22.
Spiritual infants, 1 Corinthians 3:1-2.
Marks of immaturity, 1 Corinthians 13:11.
Limited rights of immature, Galatians 4:1-3.
Acting like infants, Ephesians 4:14; Hebrews 5:12.
See *Immaturity.*

CHILDLESS
Barrenness of Abram and Sarai, Genesis 11:30; 15:2; 16:1-5; 21:1-7.
Infertility in the household of Abimelech, Genesis 20:17-18.
Lifetime infertility, 2 Samuel 6:23.
No son to carry Absalom's name, 2 Samuel 18:18.
Eunuch's name preserved more than with sons and daughters, Isaiah 56:3-5.
Elizabeth and Zechariah given son in declining years, Luke 1:5-25.
See *Barren, Impotence.*

CHILDREN
Adoptions, Genesis 15:3; 48:5; Exodus 2:10; Esther 2:7.
Births predicted in advance, Genesis 16:11; 18:10; Judges 13:3; 1 Kings 13:2; 2 Kings 4:16; Isaiah 9:6; Matthew 1:21; Luke 1:13.
Abraham's relationship to stepsister Sarah, Genesis 20:12, 16.
Children born in old age, Genesis 21:1-7.
Weaning of Isaac, Genesis 21:8.
Children learn by asking questions, Exodus 12:26-27.
Sin of father charged to children, Exodus 20:5-6; 34:6-7; Numbers 14:18.
Death to both women and children of the enemy, Numbers 31:7-18.
Divine promises to children, Deuteronomy 5:16; Psalm 27:10; Proverbs 8:32; Mark

10:14; Acts 2:39.

Threat to children if God's commands disobeyed, Joshua 6:26.

Good works performed by children, 1 Samuel 2:18; 2 Kings 5:2-3; 2 Chronicles 24:1-2; John 6:9.

Children who need conversion experience, 1 Samuel 3:7.

Son's influence over father, 1 Samuel 19:1-6.

David's many children, 2 Samuel 5:13-15.

God's promise to David, 2 Samuel 7:12.

Children offered in pagan sacrifices, 2 Kings 3:26-27; 16:1-3; 2 Chronicles 28:3; Isaiah 57:5; Jeremiah 19:5; Ezekiel 16:20.

Good children of evil fathers, 2 Kings 12:2; 18:3; 22:2; 2 Chronicles 34:3.

Josiah, child king, 2 Chronicles 34:1.

Those able to understand, Nehemiah 8:2-3.

Fate of father becomes the fate of his sons, Esther 9:12-14.

Children give praise to God, Psalm 8:2.

God looks after fatherless, Psalm 10:14.

Child given confidence in the Lord, Psalm 71:5-6, 17-18.

Relating God's greatness from generation to generation, Psalm 78:1-7.

Father's compassion for children, Psalm 103:13-14.

Barren woman becomes happy mother, Psalm 113:9.

Way of purity for young man, Psalm 119:9.

Children a special blessing from the Lord, Psalm 127:3-5.

Sadistic killing of children, Psalm 137:9.

Children should be proud of parents, Proverbs 17:6; Zechariah 10:7.

Discipline with words instead of whipping, Proverbs 17:10.

Hurt of foolish son, Proverbs 17:25.

Children who rob parents, Proverbs 19:26; 28:24.

Character begins with childhood, Proverbs 20:11.

Properly training child, Proverbs 22:6.

Folly in heart of child yields to discipline, Proverbs 22:15; 23:13-14.

Good children bring joy to father and mother, Proverbs 23:22-25.

Children can damage reputation of parents, Proverbs 27:11.

Those who dishonor parents, Proverbs 30:11.

Having 100 children, Ecclesiastes 6:3.

Government in hands of children, Isaiah 3:4.

Eunuch has name preserved more than with sons and daughters, Isaiah 56:3-5.

Those yet unborn, Jeremiah 1:4-5; Hebrews 7:1, 10.

Like father, like children, Jeremiah 16:10-13.

When it is better not to have had children, Jeremiah 22:30.

Obedience to father's command regarding drinking of wine, Jeremiah 35:1-14.

Protecting orphans and widows, Jeremiah 49:11.

Children dying in mothers' arms, Lamentations 2:12.

Children without food or drink, Lamentations 4:4.

Children eaten by mother, Lamentations 4:10.

Sons and daughters sacrificed to idols, Ezekiel 16:20; 23:37.

Unable to have children, Hosea 9:11.

Nineveh to have no descendants, Nahum 1:14.

Children playing in streets, Zechariah 8:5.

Gospel can turn children against parents, Matthew 10:32-36.

Jesus recognized wisdom of children, Matthew 11:25.

Jesus saw greatness in children, Matthew 18:1-6; Mark 9:42.

Those who fail to see importance of children, Matthew 19:13-15; Mark 10:13-16; Luke 18:15-17.

Children give praise to the Lord, Matthew 21:16.

Compassion of Jesus for daughter of Jairus, Mark 5:21-42.

Value and example of a child, Mark 9:36-37.

Joy and delight to parents, Luke 1:14-15.

Obedience of Child Jesus to His parents, Luke 2:41-52.

Balanced life of Jesus, Luke 2:52.

Concern for an only child, Luke 9:38.

Proper discipline of children, Ephesians 6:4.

Proper encouragement and instruction for children, Colossians 3:20-21.

Grandmother's faith passed on to daughter, Eunice, and grandson, Timothy, 2 Timothy 1:5.

Disobedience to parents, 2 Timothy 3:2.
Influence of Scriptures since childhood,
2 Timothy 3:14-15.
When the Lord takes His children by the
hand, Hebrews 8:9.
Importance of discipline, Hebrews 12:5-11.
Children of good parents, 2 John 4.
Children who are Christians, 3 John 4.
See *Daughter, Family, Names, Offspring,
Progeny, Son.*

CHIPS
When the chips are down, Isaiah 28:6.

CHIROPODIST
Foot problems, 2 Chronicles 16:12.

CHOICE
Choice of place to live, Genesis 13:10-13.
Some may think it undesirable to serve the
Lord, Joshua 24:15.
Loving choice, Ruth 1:16.
Given a choice, 1 Kings 3:5.
Choosing to follow way of truth, Psalm
119:30.
Better option than sins as scarlet, Isaiah
1:18.
Gentle flowing waters or mighty flood
waters, Isaiah 8:6-7.
Choice contrary to God's will, Isaiah 66:3.
Way of life and way of death, Jeremiah
21:8.
Valley of decision, Joel 3:14.
Barabbas or Christ, Matthew 27:15-26;
Mark 15:6-15; Luke 23:18-19, 25; John
18:38-40. (See Acts 3:14.)
Those who will receive and believe, John
1:12.
Jesus willingly lay down His life, John
10:17-18.
Man's choice and God's sovereignty,
Romans 9:14-21.
Moses' choice, Hebrews 11:24-25.
See *Decision, Predestination, Volition.*

CHOIR
Those in charge of temple music,
1 Chronicles 6:31-46.
Choir and orchestra, 1 Chronicles 15:16;
25:6-7.
Military music, 2 Chronicles 20:21.
Payment to choir members, Nehemiah
12:47.
Trees of forest singing, Psalm 96:12.

Great choir of angels, Revelation 5:11-12.

CHRIST
Type of sin-bearing, Numbers 21:6-9.
Names of Christ, Numbers 24:17; Joshua
5:15; Psalm 2:2; Song of Songs 2:1; 5:10;
Isaiah 9:6; 11:1; 53:3; 55:4; 63:9; Haggai
2:7; Zechariah 3:8; Matthew 11:19; John
1:1; 6:48; 10:7; Acts 10:36; Romans
10:12; Colossians 1:13; Hebrews 13:20;
Revelation 5:5-6, 8; 19:13.
Ezekiel's vision of the Lord, Ezekiel 1:26-
28.
Called "the Name," 3 John 7.
Beginning and End, Revelation 22:13.

CHRISTIAN
Biblical names for Christians, Matthew
5:13; John 10:27; 15:14-15;
1 Corinthians 12:18, 25; Ephesians 5:1;
2 Timothy 2:4; 1 Peter 2:11, 16; 3:7;
1 John 2:1.
First designation of Christians, Acts 11:26.
See *Believer, Body of Christ, Discipleship.*

CHRISTMAS
Initial forecast of Christ's birth, Genesis
3:15.
Star of Bethlehem, Numbers 24:17.
The One who came and was forgotten,
Ecclesiastes 9.14-15.
Prophecy of Virgin Birth, Isaiah 7:14.
Birth and coming of Messiah, Isaiah 9:1-7.
Similarity to Christmas tree, Jeremiah
10:3-5.
Prophecy of birth in Bethlehem, Micah 5:2.
See *Nativity.*

CHURCH
Generation away from potential extinction,
Judges 2:10.
Many invited to wedding banquet, few
chosen, Matthew 22:1-14.
Prayer of Jesus for His own, John 17:20-23.
Kingdom not of this world, John 18:36.
New relationships in Christ, John 19:26-27.
Message to Gentiles, Acts 15:13-21; 18:6.
Special greeting to house church, Romans
16:5.
The "mystery" which is the church,
Ephesians 1:9-10; 3:2-3.
Coming of church as promised from
beginning of time, Titus 1:1-3.
No churches in heaven, Revelation 21:22.

See *Congregation, Sanctuary*

CHURCH AND STATE
Jeremiah 37 and 38 illustrate Old
Testament role of religion in politics.
See *Citizenship, Government.*

CIRCUMCISION
All males included, Genesis 17:10, 14.
Requirement for Old Testament marriage,
Genesis 34:1-24.
Punishment for neglect, Exodus 4:24.
Circumcision knives, Joshua 5:3.
Wilderness delay, Joshua 5:7.
King Saul's vulgar request for dowry,
1 Samuel 18:25.
Performed on eighth day, Luke 1:59.
Subject of legalism, Acts 15:1; Galatians
5:2.
All things to all men, Acts 16:3; Galatians
5:12.

CIRCUMSTANCES
Childless Abram's promise of offspring,
Genesis 15:1-6.
God tested Abraham concerning covenant
of promise, Genesis 22:1-18. (See
13:16; 15:5.)
Circumstances caused Moses to doubt
God's guidance, Exodus 5:22-23.
Doubting goodness of God in times of
confusion and disappointment, Judges
6:11-13.
Circumstances are from the Lord, Psalm
16:5.
Those who change their way and direction
only under pressure of circumstances,
Psalm 32:9.
Waters up to neck, Psalm 69:1.
Recognizing that God has made each day
for His purpose, Psalm 118:24.
The Lord does as He pleases, Psalm 135:6.
Prosperity and disaster both in God's
control, Isaiah 45:7.
Do not question the Potter, Isaiah 45:9.
Success whatever circumstances,
Jeremiah 17:7-8.
Obey the Lord, whether circumstances
favorable or unfavorable, Jeremiah
32:6-7.
Thanking God in midst of adverse
circumstances, Jeremiah 33:10-11.
Though crops fail, trust in the Lord,
Habakkuk 3:17-18.

Circumstances should not hinder
confidence of faith, Luke 8:22-25.
Unpleasant circumstances turned to glory
of God, Acts 16:16-40.
Imprisonment made possible Paul's visit to
Rome, Romans 1:13.
All things work for good, Romans 8:28.
Nothing can separate us from God's love,
Romans 8:37-39.
Illness caused Paul to preach Gospel in
Galatia, Galatians 4:13-14.
Adverse circumstances can be special
blessing, Philippians 1:12-14.
Reason for circumstances, Philemon 15-
16.
Circumstances do not necessarily indicate
reality, Hebrews 11:11-12.
See *Fortuity, Happenstance.*

CIRCUS
Tamed animals as in circus, James 3:7.

CITATION
Honor not fitting for a fool, Proverbs 26:1.
Reward for good mother, Proverbs 31:31.
Jesus' evaluation of John the Baptist,
Matthew 11:11-14.
Let the Lord commend, 2 Corinthians
10:17-18.
See *Commendation, Honor.*

CITIZENSHIP
Duty of citizens to change in leadership,
Joshua 1:16-17.
Obedience to civil law, Ezra 7:26;
Ecclesiastes 8:2.
Rights of citizen, Nehemiah 5:4-13.
Search for one honest person in entire city,
Jeremiah 5:1.
Israel became as travelers in their own
country, Jeremiah 14:8.
Exiles in Babylon subjected themselves to
government of Babylon, Jeremiah 29:4-
7.
Daniel's prayer of repentance for himself
and his nation, Daniel 9:1-19.
Paying taxes, Matthew 17:27; 22:21; Luke
20:21-25.
Good words for the centurion, Luke 7:4-5.
Protection for Roman citizen, Acts 22:25-
29.
Respect for citizen of one's own country,
Acts 22:25-29.
Government authority divinely ordained,

Romans 13:1.
Praying for those in authority, 1 Timothy 2:1-4.
Christian citizenship, Titus 3:1; 1 Peter 2:13-14.
Citizens of New Jerusalem, Revelation 21:27.
See *Alien, Church and state, Xenophobia.*

CITY

Cities of refuge, Exodus 21:13; Numbers 35:6; Deuteronomy 4:42; 19:1-7; Joshua 20:2, 9; 1 Chronicles 6:67.
Babylon, as prophesied, now lies deserted, Isaiah 13:19-22.
Description of destroyed Jerusalem, Lamentations 1:1.
Nineveh considered large city, Jonah 3:3.
New Jerusalem, Revelation 21:2, 15-27.
See *Community, Neighborhood, Urban.*

CIVILITY

Example of Joseph, Genesis 47:1-10.
Christ's teaching, Luke 14:8-10.
Timothy's use of, Philippians 2:19-23.
Practiced by Gaius, 3 John 1-6.

CLARITY

Understandable communication, Numbers 12:8.
Inscribing Law of God clearly on stones, Deuteronomy 27:8.
Written with iron tool, Jeremiah 17:1-2.
Trampled grass and muddied water, Ezekiel 34:18-19.
Message written with clarity, Habakkuk 2:2.
Speaking without figures of speech, John 16:29-30.
Speaking effectively, Acts 14:1.
Spiritual truth communicated in human terms, Romans 6:19.
Clear call to action, 1 Corinthians 14:8.
Importance of being understood, 1 Corinthians 14:13-19.
Presenting message which can be understood, 2 Corinthians 1:13-14.
Clarity of Gospel message, Galatians 1:8.
Some things better spoken than written, 2 John 12; 3 John 13-14.
See *Communication, Eloquence, Speech.*

CLASS

Many simple people brought to Christ,

1 Corinthians 1:26-31.
No class distinction in Christ, Ephesians 6:9.
Paul could have boasted of former status, Philippians 3:2-11.
The wrong of discrimination, James 2:1-4.
See *Prejudice, Racism.*

CLAY

Brick-making, 2 Samuel 12:31.
Earth like clay seal, Job 38:14.
Used for pottery, Isaiah 41:25.
Miracle implement, John 9:6, 15.

CLEANLINESS

Washing feet common for those who traveled, Genesis 18:4; 19:2.
Clean clothes, Genesis 35:2.
Cleanliness next to godliness, Exodus 40:32.
Shower and shave, Numbers 8:7.
Feminine daintiness, Ruth 3:3.
Place for washing prostitutes and chariots, 1 Kings 22:38.
Priestly requirement, Isaiah 52:11.
Soda and soap, Jeremiah 2:22.
Laundry soap, Malachi 3:2.
Outward purity, Matthew 23:26.
Washing hands and utensils a necessary ceremony, Mark 7:1-4.
Washed with pure water, Hebrews 10:22.

CLEANSING

Whiter than snow, Psalm 51:7.
Prayer for inner peace and righteousness, Psalm 139:23-24.
Come let us reason, Isaiah 1:18.
Clean hearts and changed lives, Ezekiel 36:25-27.
Refined gold and silver, Malachi 3:2-4.
Need for discipline within congregation, 1 Corinthians 5:1-13.
Sanctifying work of the Spirit, 1 Peter 1:1-2.
Benefit of bodily suffering, 1 Peter 4:1-2.
See *Holiness, Purity.*

CLERGY

Holiness by virtue of occupation, Leviticus 21:8.
High quality lives for clergymen, Leviticus 21:17-23.
Speaking by divine authority, Leviticus 23:1-2, 9-10, 23-24.

Contesting clergy, Numbers 16:3-7.

Priests were to eat from that which was offered, Numbers 18:11-13.

Priests owned no property, Numbers 18:20.

Speaking what the Lord commands, Numbers 23:11-12.

Do not neglect Levites, Deuteronomy 12:19.

New clergy comes in earnestness, Deuteronomy 18:6-7.

Detecting words of false prophet, Deuteronomy 18:21-22.

Weakness of people left without spiritual guidance, Judges 2:18-19.

Priests who engaged in idol-worship, Judges 18:30-31.

Evil sons of a priest, 1 Samuel 2:12.

Eli's grief for ark of God greater than for death of sons, 1 Samuel 4:16-18.

Priest who served also as judge, 1 Samuel 7:15-16.

Looking back across exemplary life, 1 Samuel 12:3.

Refusal to turn against clergy, 1 Samuel 22:16-17.

Those unqualified for priesthood, 1 Kings 12:31.

Boldness of fearless preacher, 1 Kings 18:16-18.

Priest and king, 2 Kings 11:15-18.

Priest who consulted prophetess, 2 Kings 22:14.

No God, no priest, no Law in Israel, 2 Chronicles 15:3.

Book of the Law lost in temple, 2 Chronicles 34:14-15.

Mocking the preacher, 2 Chronicles 36:16.

Priests tax-free, Ezra 7:24.

Clergy wives, Ezra 9:1-2.

Ezra standing above people, Nehemiah 8:5.

Priests required to work to support themselves, Nehemiah 13:10-11.

Great company of those who proclaim God's Word, Psalm 68:11.

Do not touch God's anointed ones, Psalm 105:15.

Jesus a Priest forever, Psalm 110:4.

People and priests clothed with righteousness, Psalm 132:9, 16.

Ministry by night in house of the Lord, Psalm 134:1.

Ministry accompanied by praise, Psalm 135:1-2.

Isaiah answered call of God, Isaiah 6:8.

Blinded prophets and seers, Isaiah 29:10.

People ask for pleasant sermons, Isaiah 30:10.

Listeners who hear nothing, Isaiah 42:20.

Instructed tongue, Isaiah 50:4.

The Lord puts words in your mouth, Isaiah 51:16.

Touch no unclean thing, Isaiah 52:11.

The Lord selects priests and Levites, Isaiah 66:21.

Jeremiah's fear and reluctance of proclaiming God's message, Jeremiah 1:6-10.

Shepherds after God's own heart, Jeremiah 3:15.

Priests who rule by their own authority to delight of congregation, Jeremiah 5:31.

Total depravity of men and clergy, Jeremiah 8:10.

Shepherds who do not seek the Lord, Jeremiah 10:21.

Jeremiah attacked with words, Jeremiah 18:18.

Wicked priests who persecuted Jeremiah, Jeremiah 20:1-2.

Ministration of evil prophets, Jeremiah 23:10-14.

Jeremiah persecuted for prophesying truth, Jeremiah 37-38.

Shepherds who lead sheep astray, Jeremiah 50:6. (See also Micah 3:5-7.)

Perishing in search for food, Lamentations 1:19.

King and priest forsaken, Lamentations 2:6.

Jeremiah's burden for his people, Lamentations 3:40-51.

Priests and elders without honor, Lamentations 4:16.

Courage to minister under any circumstances, Ezekiel 2:6-7.

Responsibility of watchman, Ezekiel 33:1-9.

Shepherds who care more for themselves than for their flocks, Ezekiel 34:2. (Note content of chapter.)

Two functions of a priest, Ezekiel 40:44-46.

Accommodations for priests, Ezekiel 41:9-10; 42:13.

Garments worn by priests in temple, Ezekiel 42:14; 44:19.

Priests instructed to keep hair neatly trimmed, Ezekiel 44:20.

Paul's great compassion for Galatians, Galatians 4:19-20.
Penalty for misleading others, Galatians 5:10.
Less than the least, Ephesians 3:8-9.
Worthy of calling, Ephesians 4:1.
Speaking truth in love, Ephesians 4:15.
Praying for those who preach and teach, Ephesians 6:19-20; Colossians 4:3-4.
Paul's great love for his followers, Philippians 1:3-11; Colossians 1:28-29; 2:1-5.
Envy among those who preach Christ, Philippians 1:15.
Paul considered himself a servant to the church, Colossians 1:24-29.
Prayer for those who minister, Colossians 4:3.
Paul's clear motivation in preaching and teaching, 1 Thessalonians 2:1-6.
Ministering with gentleness, 1 Thessalonians 2:7.
Paul's spirit of love and fellowship in ministry, 1 Thessalonians 2:7-9.
Followers are joy and crown of those who present message, 1 Thessalonians 2:17-20.
Abundant praise to God for success in ministry, 1 Thessalonians 3:8-10.
Purpose and means of spiritual success, 2 Thessalonians 1:11-12.
Employment to support one's ministry, 2 Thessalonians 3:6-10.
Paul thanked his Lord for privilege of ministry, 1 Timothy 1:12-14.
Message Paul was called to proclaim, 1 Timothy 2:5-7.
Devoting yourself to preaching and teaching, 1 Timothy 4:13-14.
Payment for those in Christian work, 1 Timothy 5:17-18.
Description of those who take pride in false doctrine, 1 Timothy 6:3-5.
Called to be herald, apostle, and teacher, 2 Timothy 1:11.
God's plan for perpetuation of Gospel, 2 Timothy 2:1-4.
Paul's ministry mandate to Timothy, 2 Timothy 4:1-5.
Credentials for ministry, Titus 1:1-3.
Example of truly Christian leader, Titus 3:1-2.
High priest selected from among people shared in their weaknesses, Hebrews 5:1-3.
Jesus, the ultimate clergyman, Hebrews 7:23-28.
Service in sanctuary of ultimate High Priest, Hebrews 8:1-6.
Pastor as leader and example, Hebrews 13:7.
Searching prophets, 1 Peter 1:10-12.
Called to ministry of holiness, 1 Peter 1:15-16.
Speaking and serving to glory of God, 1 Peter 4:11.
Shepherds of God's flock, 1 Peter 5:1-4.
Continuing zeal of aging worker, 2 Peter 1:13-14.
Proclaiming angel, Revelation 14:6-7.

CLIMATE
Seasons after the Flood, Genesis 8:22.
Lord of time and seasons, Psalm 74:16-17.
One who governs wind and wave, Proverbs 30:4.
See *Meteorologist, Weather.*

CLOSENESS
Kept at a distance, Numbers 24:17.
Nearness of the Lord when we pray, Deuteronomy 4:7.
Nearness of God's Word, Deuteronomy 30:14.
Two inseparable women, Ruth 1:14-18.
Ever-present Good Shepherd, Psalm 23:1-4.
Nearness of the Lord according to Scripture, Psalm 119:151.
Coming close to God, James 4:8.
See *Affinity, Camaraderie, Fellowship, Intimacy.*

CLOTHING
Garments of skin, Genesis 3:21.
Deceitful apparel, Genesis 27:2-29.
Women not to wear men's clothing, Deuteronomy 22:5.
Mixed materials, Deuteronomy 22:11.
Costly clothing, 2 Samuel 1:24; 1 Peter 3:3-4.
Clothed with righteousness and faithfulness, Isaiah 11:5.
Clothes make the man, Daniel 5:29.
Proper repair of garment, Matthew 9:16.
Fine clothing belongs in kings' palaces, not on prophet in desert, Matthew 11:7-9.
Rich man, poor man, Luke 16:19-31.

Teachers of Law in flowing robes, Luke 20:46-47. (See also 21:1-4.)
Those wearing clean robes, Revelation 22:14.
See *Wardrobe.*

CLOUDS
Guiding cloud, Exodus 13:21.
Time of murmuring, Exodus 16:10.
Storage for rain, Ecclesiastes 1:7.

COGITATION
Bible-centered mentality, Psalm 1:2.
The glory of kings, Proverbs 25:2.
See *Concentration, Meditation, Thought.*

COIFFURE
Paul's haircut in response to vow, Acts 18:18.
Instruction relative to cutting hair, 1 Corinthians 11:14-15.
Hairstyles and jewelry, 1 Timothy 2:9-10.
See *Barber, Hair.*

COLD
Persistent coming of winter, Genesis 8:22.
David could not keep warm in old age, 1 Kings 1:1-4.
Driving winds, Job 37:9.
Icy blast, Psalm 147:17.
Use of warm fire, John 18:18.
Rain and cold, Acts 28:2.

COLLABORATION
Wrong kind of unanimity, Numbers 11:4-10.
Collaboration between mother-in-law and daughter-in-law, Ruth 3:1-18.
People working diligently together, Nehemiah 4:6.
As iron sharpens iron, Proverbs 27:17.
Two in agreement, Amos 3:3.
United behind common goal, Luke 10:1-2.
See *Cooperation.*

COLLATERAL
Reuben's guarantee to his father, Genesis 42:37.

COLLEGE
Three-year training program in Babylon, Daniel 1:3-5.

COLOR
Spectrum in the sky, Genesis 9:13-16.
Sky blue, Exodus 24:10.
Blue, purple, and scarlet, Exodus 25:3-5; 26:1, 31, 36; 38:18.
Blue cord, Exodus 28:28.
Reminder of divine commandments, Numbers 15:38-40.
Absence of color, Job 10:20-22.
Whiter than snow, Psalm 51:7.
Darkened skies, Joel 3:14-15.
Darkness of perdition, Matthew 8:12; 22:13; 25:30; 2 Peter 2:4.

COMBINATION
Avoid wrong combinations, Deuteronomy 22:10-11.

COMFORT
Springs and palm trees, Exodus 15:27.
In times of trouble, God ever-present, Psalm 14:4-5.
Importance of first things first, Proverbs 24:27.
Gladness and joy overcome sorrow and sighing, Isaiah 35:10.
Lambs and shepherd, Isaiah 40:11.
Mourning forbidden in time of judgment, Jeremiah 16:5-7.
Padding for Jeremiah's comfort in deliverance, Jeremiah 38:11-13.
No one to comfort, Lamentations 1:2.
Faithfulness and compassion of the Lord new every morning, Lamentations 3:22-23.
Shade provided for Jonah, Jonah 4:6.
Christ has overcome the world, John 16:33.
Sharing comfort through experience, 2 Corinthians 1:3-5.
Secret of deliverance, 2 Corinthians 4:7-18.
Assurance of eternal encouragement, 2 Thessalonians 2:16-17.
Christ suffered temptation so that He might help those who were tempted, Hebrews 2:18.
Eternal comfort in presence of God, Revelation 7:16.
Tears forever wiped away, Revelation 7:17.

COMMEMORATE
Three festivals honoring God, Exodus 23:14-17.
Purpose of Sabbath, Exodus 31:16.

Captured city named after its captor, Numbers 32:42.

COMMENDATION
High compliments for David, 1 Samuel 29:6-9.
Some good in Judah, 2 Chronicles 12:12.
God's commendation of Job, Job 1:8.
Job commended for speaking truth, Job 42:8.
Honor of strong people, Isaiah 25:3.
Evaluation of John the Baptist, Matthew 11:11-14.
God's commendation of His Son, Mark 1:10-11.
Let the Lord commend, 2 Corinthians 10:17-18.
Paul's commendation of Timothy, Philippians 2:19-23.
Paul's wise use of names of followers, Colossians 4:7-17.
See *Compliment, Honor.*

COMMERCE
Import and export in King Solomon's time, 1 Kings 10:28-29.
Local, national, and international, 2 Chronicles 9:21; Proverbs 31:14-18; Revelation 18:10-24.
Grain of Nile brought to Tyre, Isaiah 23:3.
Wealth to those who lived by many waters, Jeremiah 51:13.
Prosperity of ancient Tyre taken away, Ezekiel 27:1-36.
Using temple for business purposes, Mark 11:15-17; Luke 19:45-46; John 2:16.
Business profit limited by transformation of converts, Acts 19:23-28.
Luxury no longer for sale, Revelation 18:11-13.
See *Bargaining, Barter, Business, Trade.*

COMMISSION
Moses laid hands on Joshua, Deuteronomy 34:9.
Great Commission, Matthew 28:16-20.
Commission to preach and teach, Luke 4:14-21.
Paul commissioned to minister, Acts 23:11.
Entrusted with secret things of God, 1 Corinthians 4:1-2.
See *Dedication.*

COMMITMENT
Aroma of good sacrifice, Genesis 8:20-21. (See Lev. 23:18; 2 Cor. 2:15; Eph. 5:1-2.)
Test of father's love to God and his son, Genesis 22:1-14.
Servant for life, Exodus 21:2-6.
Anointing of objects, Exodus 40:9-10.
Dedicating one's house to the Lord, Leviticus 27:14.
Those who do not follow wholeheartedly, Numbers 32:11.
Preparation for future blessing, Joshua 3:5.
Joshua's call for total faithfulness, Joshua 24:14.
Mother's reward for giving son to the Lord, 1 Samuel 2:18-21.
Partial commitment of King Solomon, 1 Kings 3:3.
Incomplete faithfulness to God, 1 Kings 22:43.
Personal treasures to temple, 1 Chronicles 29:3-4.
Working from morning to night, Nehemiah 4:21.
Nehemiah's total commitment to rebuilding wall, Nehemiah 5:14-16.
Righteous in one's own eyes, Job 32:1.
Keeping one's vow to God, Psalm 65:1.
Prayer for an undivided heart, Psalm 86:11.
Fulfill a vow to God, Ecclesiastes 5:4-5.
Commitment of two loves, Song of Songs 6:3; 8:7.
Answering call of God, Isaiah 6:8.
Stand firm or not at all, Isaiah 7:9.
Meaningless oaths, Isaiah 48:1-2.
Coming to the Lord with clean vessel, Isaiah 66:20.
Vow to Babylonian Queen of Heaven, Jeremiah 44:24-30.
Someone to stand in gap, Ezekiel 22:30.
Disciples left occupation to follow Jesus, Matthew 4:20-22.
Counting the cost, Matthew 8:19-20.
Losing your life to find it again, Matthew 10:39.
Calling of Simon, Andrew, James, and John, Mark 1:16-20.
No looking back, Luke 9:62.
Paul's willingness to face persecution, Acts 21:10-14.
Once slaves to sin, now slaves to righteousness, Romans 6:18.
Living sacrifice, Romans 12:1-2.

In a race, only one wins. In serving God, all may win, 1 Corinthians 9:24-27.
Daily death of true commitment to Christ, 1 Corinthians 15:30-31.
Presence of Holy Spirit in life of commitment, 2 Corinthians 3:7-8.
Marks of disciple in service, 2 Corinthians 6:3-13.
Crucified with Christ, Galatians 2:20.
Loving Christ with undying love, Ephesians 6:24.
Poured out like drink offering, Philippians 2:17; 2 Timothy 4:6.
Filled with knowledge of God's will, Colossians 1:9-12.
Paul's description of true disciple, 2 Timothy 2:1-4.
Paul endured everything to help others, 2 Timothy 2:10.
Supreme commitment of Christ as Redeemer, Hebrews 10:5-7.
Enoch pleased God, Hebrews 11:5.
Willing to lay down one's life for others, 1 John 3:16.
See *Dedication, Discipleship.*

COMMITTEE
Value of many advisers, Proverbs 11:14; 12:15; 15:22; 24:5-6.

COMMONPLACE
Writing with ordinary pen, Isaiah 8:1.
Ordinary people, Jeremiah 26:23.
See *Ordinary, Value.*

COMMUNICATION
Example of nonverbal communication, Genesis 8:10-11; Ruth 4:8.
God's rainbow, Genesis 9:12-17.
Those who spoke one common language, Genesis 11:1, 5-9.
God spoke to Abram in deep sleep, Genesis 15:12-15.
Divine use of visions and dreams, Numbers 12:4-6.
Understandable communication, Numbers 12:8.
Place for words, Deuteronomy 27:2-3.
Inscribing Law of God clearly on stones, Deuteronomy 27:8.
Putting instructions in writing, Deuteronomy 31:9.
Putting foot to neck, Joshua 10:24.
Identification by manner of speech, Judges 12:5-6.
Communication with the dead, 1 Samuel 28:8-20.
Making sure someone is listening, 2 Samuel 20:17.
Speaking to inanimate object, 1 Kings 13:2.
Message from thistle to cedar tree, 2 Kings 14:9.
Methods of communication, 2 Chronicles 30:1-10; Esther 1:22.
Petition of protest to king and his response, Ezra 4:12-22.
Language confused by intermarriage, Nehemiah 13:23-37.
Seven-day silence, Job 2:13.
Testing of words, Job 12:11.
Tip of tongue, Job 33:2.
Communication with God, Psalm 18:25.
God speaks through nature and through His Word, Psalm 19:1-14.
Twisting of words, Psalm 56:5.
Iron sharpens iron, Proverbs 27:17.
Secret thoughts conveyed to others, Ecclesiastes 10:20.
Finding right words, Ecclesiastes 12:10.
Call for decision, Isaiah 16:3.
Trying to communicate to those too young to understand, Isaiah 28:9.
Farmer does not plow continuously, Isaiah 28:24.
Speaking in language understood, Isaiah 36:11.
God of Israel spoken of as "god" by pagan king, Isaiah 37:10.
Mouth like sharpened sword, Isaiah 49:2.
Instructed tongue, Isaiah 50:4.
Boldness of speech given by God, Jeremiah 1:6-10.
Those of strange language, Jeremiah 5:15.
Text of letter from Jeremiah to exiles in Babylon, Jeremiah 29:4-23.
Danger of writing the truth, Jeremiah 36:4-32.
Communicating to those who ought to be eager to listen, Ezekiel 3:4-9.
Young Hebrews taught culture, language, and literature of Babylon, Daniel 1:3-5.
Writing on wall, Daniel 5:5.
Message written with clarity, Habakkuk 2:2.
Gigantic scroll, Zechariah 5:1-2.
Lips that preserve knowledge, Malachi 2:7.

Effect of attitudes on understanding, Matthew 13:14-15.

Spectacular communication from heaven, Luke 2:8-14.

Jesus knew when He had been touched, Luke 8:43-48.

Followers of Jesus unable to understand coming Crucifixion, Luke 9:44-45.

When great truth sounds like nonsense, Luke 24:9-11.

No one spoke as Jesus spoke, John 7:45-46.

Some thought they heard thunder; others the voice of an angel, John 12:29.

Speaking without figures of speech, John 16:25-30.

Multilingual information, John 19:20.

Sufficient communication to convey message, John 20:30-31.

Day of Pentecost, Acts 2:1-12.

Lack of understanding what one reads, Acts 8:27-35.

Speaking effectively, Acts 14:1.

Gathering together for report of God's work among Gentiles, Acts 14:27.

Use of reasoning in teaching, Acts 17:1-3.

Resurrection message in opposition to idolatry, Acts 17:16-18.

Paul quoted poets of Athens, Acts 17:28.

Falling asleep during long sermon, Acts 20:7-12.

Effect of speaking in people's language, Acts 22:2.

Seeing light but not understanding voice, Acts 22:9.

Message communicated in nature, Romans 1:18-20.

Spiritual truth communicated in human terms, Romans 6:19.

Words beyond normal vocabulary, Romans 8:16, 26-27.

Paul asked for prayer that his service would be acceptable, Romans 15:31-32.

Conversation enriched in Christ, 1 Corinthians 1:5-6.

Clear call to action, 1 Corinthians 14:8.

Importance of being understood, 1 Corinthians 14:13-19; 2 Corinthians 1:13-14.

Tact in relating to unbelievers, 2 Corinthians 2:15-16.

Earning right to be heard, 2 Corinthians 4:1-2.

Lifestyle Paul communicated by example, 2 Corinthians 6:4-10.

Hearts opening to each other, 2 Corinthians 6:11-13.

Writing more effectively than speaking, 2 Corinthians 10:10.

Information without eloquence, 2 Corinthians 11:6.

Profound truth presented briefly, Ephesians 3:1-3.

Paul's insistence to his followers, Ephesians 4:17.

Fathers should not exasperate children, Ephesians 6:4.

Keeping in touch concerning each other's activity and welfare, Ephesians 6:21-22.

Good news between believers, Philippians 2:19.

Invisible made visible in Christ, Colossians 1:15.

Fullness of Deity in Christ, Colossians 2:9.

Successful communication of message requires prayer support, Colossians 4:3-4.

Paul's wise use of names of followers, Colossians 4:7-17.

Communication with followers, Colossians 4:8.

Paul's wise introduction of Onesimus to Colossians, Colossians 4:9. (See Phile. 10-11.)

Gospel communicated with words and power, 1 Thessalonians 1:4-5.

Importance of welcoming message, 1 Thessalonians 1:6.

Rising above opposition in proclaiming the Gospel, 1 Thessalonians 2:1-2.

Communicating with gentle spirit, 1 Thessalonians 2:7.

Responsibility of those who hear message, 1 Thessalonians 2:13.

Teaching by means of speech and writing, 2 Thessalonians 2:15; 1 Timothy 3:14-15.

Identified by handwriting, 2 Thessalonians 3:17.

Quarreling over words, 2 Timothy 2:14.

Responsibility to proclaim message God has given, Titus 1:1-3.

Make teaching attractive, Titus 2:10.

Ways of communicating God's message, Hebrews 1:1-2.

Faith is credibility to what is heard, Hebrews 4:2.

Penetrating impact of Scripture, Hebrews

4:12.

Short letter, Hebrews 13:22.

Solemn responsibility of proclaiming God's message, 1 Peter 4:11.

Divine purpose in giving Scriptures, 2 Peter 1:20-21.

Purpose of Peter's letters to friends, 2 Peter 3:1.

Writing difficult to understand, 2 Peter 3:15-16.

The world listens to those who have its viewpoint, 1 John 4:5.

In person rather than by correspondence, 2 John 12. (See also 3 John 13-14.)

Those who take the Scriptures to heart, Revelation 1:3.

Questions and answers between teacher and student, Revelation 7:13-17.

Sounding forth cry of doom, Revelation 8:13.

God in direct fellowship with men, Revelation 21:3-5.

Conclusion of Scripture record, Revelation 22:1-21.

See *Conversation, Message, Preaching, Teaching, Witness.*

COMMUNION

Aliens barred from Passover, Exodus 12:43-45.

Highest motive life can know, Psalm 27:4

Thirst for the living God, Psalm 42:1-2.

The Lord listens to those who listen, Zechariah 7:13.

Taking of the Lord's table, Matthew 26:17-30; Mark 14:12-26; Luke 22:7-38; 1 Corinthians 11:17-30.

Come near to God and He will come near to you, James 4:8.

Believing without seeing, 1 Peter 1:8-9.

See *Prayer, Worship.*

COMMUNISM

Godless king and nation, Daniel 11:36-39.

Christian kind of sharing, Acts 2:44.

See *Socialism.*

COMMUNITY

Building first city, Genesis 4:17.

Small town spared disaster of large city, Genesis 19:15-22.

Preventing infection from spreading, Leviticus 13:45-46.

Holy community, Numbers 16:3.

Well-situated city with poor water, 2 Kings 2:19-22.

Priest and king, 2 Kings 11:15-18.

Community in turmoil, Isaiah 22:2.

Town and country praising the Lord, Isaiah 42:11.

Depravity of one entire city, Jeremiah 5:1.

When God establishes a good community, Jeremiah 30:20.

Least and greatest, Jeremiah 42:1-3.

Total destruction of a community, Jeremiah 51:20-23.

Time of despair for entire community, Ezekiel 7:27.

Judgment on evil community, Zephaniah 3:1.

Salt and light in the world, Matthew 5:13-16.

Nazareth of low reputation, John 1:46.

Early Christian and his community, Acts 2:46-47.

Christians keeping in touch concerning each other's activities and welfare, Ephesians 6:21-22.

Coming community where all know the Lord, Hebrews 8:11.

Being example to unbelievers, 1 Peter 2:12.

Place of residence for demons and evil spirits, Revelation 18:2.

City of total integrity, Revelation 21:27.

See *City, Neighborhood, Urban.*

COMPANIONSHIP

Companions in danger, 1 Samuel 22:23.

Walking in good company, Proverbs 2:20; 13:20.

Two better than one, Ecclesiastes 4:9.

Disciples two-by-two, Luke 10:1; Acts 13:2.

Wife traveling with husband, 1 Corinthians 9:5.

Paul's desire for fellowship of Timothy, 2 Timothy 4:9-10.

See *Camaraderie, Fellowship.*

COMPARISON

Comparing sun and moon with the stars, Genesis 1:16.

Saul's thousands and David's tens of thousands, 1 Samuel 18:7. (See 21:11; 29:5.)

Beyond comparison, Psalm 89:6; Isaiah 46:5.

Comparison between two unfaithful

nations, Jeremiah 3:11.
Sufferings and glory, Romans 8:18.

COMPASSION

Concern of Pharaoh's daughter for baby Moses, Exodus 2:5-6.
David sought member of Saul's family to whom he could show love, 2 Samuel 9:1-13.
Caring for those who are weak, Psalm 41:1.
God's love never lessens, Isaiah 54:10.
Compassion of Jeremiah, Jeremiah 9:1.
The Lord's mercy follows the Lord's judgment, Jeremiah 12:14-17.
Crying out to those who reject God's Word, Jeremiah 22:29.
Loved with everlasting love, Jeremiah 31:3.
The Lord shows no pity in judgment, Lamentations 2:2.
Faithfulness and compassion new every morning, Lamentations 3:22-26.
Jeremiah's burden for his people, Lamentations 3:40-51.
Ezekiel feared all Israel would be destroyed, Ezekiel 11:13.
Heart of flesh or heart of stone, Ezekiel 11:19.
New heart and new spirit, Ezekiel 36:26.
Daniel's compassion for condemned wise men, Daniel 2:10-13, 24.
Joseph did not want to make Mary subject of public disgrace, Matthew 1:19.
Compassion of Jesus for people without a shepherd, Matthew 9:36.
Prayer of Jesus over rebellious Jerusalem, Matthew 23:37.
Good Samaritan, Luke 10:30-37.
Grief of Jesus over need of Jerusalem, Luke 13:34; 19:41-44.
Reaching out to help others in need, Acts 11:27-30.
Compassion of Paul's preaching, Acts 20:31.
Consideration shown to Paul, the prisoner, Acts 27:3.
Kind islanders, Acts 28:2.
Willing to pay the supreme price for salvation of others, Romans 9:1-4. (See 10:1.)
Divine compassion to disobedient, Romans 10:21.
Strong looking after weak, Romans 15:1.
Love expressed through anguish, 2 Corinthians 2:4.
Paul's great compassion for Galatians, Galatians 4:19-20.
Carrying each other's burdens, Galatians 6:2.
Concern for those who are ill, Philippians 2:26-27.
Paul struggled over his converts, Colossians 2:1.
Paul eager for proper counsel with Thessalonians, 1 Thessalonians 3:1-5.
Compassion of Paul for a slave, Philemon 8-21.
See *Concern, Empathy, Mercy, Sympathy.*

COMPATIBILITY

Agreement necessary for two to walk together, Amos 3:3.
Sharing of both suffering and comfort, 2 Corinthians 1:7.
See *Camaraderie, Rapport.*

COMPENSATION

Compensation for someone intentionally injured, Exodus 21:18-19.
God accepts no price or reward, Isaiah 45:13.
Stone rejected by builders, Matthew 21:42.
See *Honorarium, Salary, Stipend.*

COMPETENCE

Sanballat's ridicule of Jewish capability, Nehemiah 4:1-3.
Race not to swift or strong, Ecclesiastes 9:11.
When God sends, He guides, Isaiah 2:3.
Victory requires more than ability, Isaiah 25:11.
Least and greatest, Jeremiah 42:1-3.
Qualifications for following Jesus, Luke 9:23-26.
Competence comes from God, 2 Corinthians 3:4-5.
Qualifications of Christ as Saviour and King, Colossians 1:15-20.
Prepared by God to succeed as believer, Hebrews 13:20-21.
See *Ability, Skill, Talent.*

COMPETITION

Competing for father's love, Genesis 37:1-4; Luke 15:25-31.
David and Saul, 1 Samuel 18:8-16.
At peace with one's enemies, Proverbs

16:7.
Gloating over enemy's failure, Proverbs 24:17-18.
Jesus evaded accusation of competition with John, John 4:1-3.
Competition between Christians, Romans 13:13; Galatians 5:26.
Running a race, 1 Corinthians 9:24-27.
Ministry to Jews and ministry to Gentiles, Galatians 2:8.
See *Athletics, Covet, Jealousy.*

COMPLACENCY
Thinking it easy to face enemy, Deuteronomy 1:41-45.
Complacency and prosperity of wicked, Job 21:7-18.
A nation at ease, Jeremiah 49:31.
Those who pass by, Lamentations 1:12.
Relegating prophetic judgment to distant future, Ezekiel 12:26-28.
Abundant blessing can turn to backsliding, Hosea 13:6.
Jonah asleep during storm, Jonah 1:5-6.
God's displeasure with the complacent, Zechariah 1:14-15.
Sin of complacency, James 4:17.
See *Attitude, Careless, Carnality, Powerless, Undependable.*

COMPLAIN
Remembering Egypt instead of trusting God, Exodus 16:2-3.
Rehoboam rejected the advice of his elders, 1 Kings 12:1-11.
Bitterness against God, Job 23:2.
Complaining to the Lord, Psalm 142:1-2.
Howl like jackal, moan like owl, Micah 1:8.
Martha's discontent with Mary, Luke 10:38-42.
Do everything without complaint or argument, Philippians 2:14-15.
See *Friction.*

COMPLETION
Creation, a task well done, Genesis 1:31.
Frustrated project, Genesis 11:1-9.
Rebuilt temple, 2 Chronicles 6:10-11; Zechariah 4:9.
Dedication of Jerusalem wall, Nehemiah 12:27-43.
Termination of testing, Job 23:10.
Finished work of Jesus, John 19:30.

Good work begun and completed, Philippians 1:3-6.
Life's work completed, 2 Timothy 4:6-8.
Culmination of the Bible's message, Revelation 22:20-21.
See *Accomplishment, Ending, Finale.*

COMPLICITY
Aiding a thief, Psalm 50:18.
National guilt, Matthew 27:25.
Adam's sin, Romans 5:12.

COMPLIMENT
High compliments for David, 1 Samuel 29:6-9.
Public relations approach, 1 Kings 1:42.
Some good in Judah, 2 Chronicles 12:12.
Avoiding partiality and flattery, Job 32:21-22.
Flattering lips speak deception, Psalm 12:2.
Praise and glory belong only to God, Psalm 115:1.
A timely word, Proverbs 15:23.
Honor not fitting for a fool, Proverbs 26:1.
Folly of flattery, Proverbs 28:23.
Eloquent description of noble person, Isaiah 32:8.
Talented people encouraging each other, Isaiah 41:7.
Jesus' evaluation of John the Baptist, Matthew 11:11-14
Duty of true servant, Luke 17:7-10.
Paul complimented and encouraged followers, Acts 20:1-2; Romans 1:8; 2 Corinthians 1:13-14; Philippians 1:3-6; Colossians 2:5; 1 Thessalonians 1:3; 2 Thessalonians 1:3-4; 2 Timothy 1:3-5.
Giving compliments to friends, Romans 16:3-16.
Whatever measure of success, glory belongs to God alone, 1 Corinthians 3:7.
Paul's compliment to those who faithfully followed his teachings, 1 Corinthians 11:2.
Paul commended Corinthians, 2 Corinthians 7:4-7. (See also vv. 14-16.)
Paul's commendation of Timothy, Philippians 2:19-23.
Paul's wise use of names of his followers, Colossians 4:7-17.
Boasting about perseverance and faith of others, 2 Thessalonians 1:4.

One author commended another, 2 Peter
3:15-16.
Strength and weakness of church at
Ephesus, Revelation 2:1-6.
Commendation before reproof, Revelation
2:2-6, 13-16, 19-20.
One worthy of praise from all creation,
Revelation 5:13-14.
See *Commendation, Encouragement,
Praise.*

COMPOSURE
Facing the enemy, Nehemiah 4:1-23.
Lack of composure, Daniel 6:18-20.
Facing violent death, Acts 7:59-60.
Keeping courage, Acts 27:21-26.

COMPREHENSION
Eyes that see and ears that hear,
Deuteronomy 29:2-4.
Those able to understand, Nehemiah 8:2-3.
Full of words about a subject, Job 32:17-22.
Learning what cannot be seen, Job 34:32.
God-given ability to understand Scripture,
Psalm 119:125.
Those too young to understand, Isaiah
28:9.
Understanding brings terror, Isaiah 28:19.
Refusal and inability to read, Isaiah 29:11-
12.
Effect of attitudes on understanding,
Matthew 13:14-15.
Hearing but not understanding, Mark 4:11-
12.
Thoroughness of Jesus with disciples,
Mark 4:34.
Women too frightened to comprehend
Resurrection, Mark 16:1-8.
Simeon understood dual mission of
Saviour, Luke 2:28-32.
Joseph and Mary did not understand their
Son's conduct, Luke 2:41-50.
Use of parables to illustrate truth, Luke 8:9.
Followers of Jesus unable to understand
coming Crucifixion, Luke 9:44-45.
Seeing and hearing but not understanding,
Luke 10:24.
Those who could not accept identity of
Jesus, John 10:24-30.
Lack of understanding what one reads,
Acts 8:27-35.
Seeing light but not understanding voice,
Acts 22:9. (See 9:1-7.)
Spiritual truth communicated in human

terms, Romans 6:19.
That which God has prepared exceeds
human perception and experience,
1 Corinthians 2:9-10.
Folly of intellectual pride, 1 Corinthians
3:18-20.
Eyes of the heart, Ephesians 1:18-19.
That which is not understood, Jude 10.
See *Clarity, Communication, Frame of
reference, Hearing, Simplicity,
Understanding.*

COMPROMISE
After much pestilence, Pharaoh
compromised, Exodus 8:28.
Desire to be like unbelievers, 1 Samuel
8:1-22.
Abner's compromise with David,
2 Samuel 3:6-21.
Partial commitment of King Solomon,
1 Kings 3:3.
Heathen worship for Solomon's wives,
1 Kings 11:8.
Incomplete faithfulness to God, 1 Kings
22:43.
Failing to be completely obedient, 2 Kings
14:1-4. (See 15:1-4, 34-35.)
Secretly disobeying the Lord, 2 Kings 17:9.
Worshiping the Lord and other gods,
2 Kings 17:33.
Doing right but not wholeheartedly,
2 Chronicles 25:2.
Calling evil good and good evil, Isaiah 5:20.
Those who do not want to hear truth, Isaiah
30:10-11.
Hezekiah intimidated, Isaiah 36:4-10.
Desire to be like others, Ezekiel 20:32-38.
No one can serve two masters, Matthew
6:24.
Marriage between unbelievers and
believers, 1 Corinthians 7:16.
Do not take into your home those of false
teaching, 2 John 10-11.
Influence of Jezebel in church at Thyatira,
Revelation 2:20.
See *Cult, Syncretism, Worldliness.*

CONCEIT
Goliath's macho, 1 Samuel 17:42-44.
Haughtiness despised, 2 Samuel 22:28.
Taunts of Sanballat, Nehemiah 4:1-3.
Enemy's loss of self-confidence,
Nehemiah 6:16.
Conceited affluence, Psalm 49:5-6;

Proverbs 25:14.
Wise in one's own eyes, Proverbs 3:7; 26:5-16.
Conceited women, Isaiah 3:16.
Empty boasting, Isaiah 16:6.
Boast only about the Lord, Jeremiah 9:23-24.
Christian to avoid conceit, Romans 12:16.
Role of conceit in false doctrine, 1 Timothy 6:3-5.
Evil queen refused to admit sin, Revelation 18:7-8.
See *Pride, Vanity.*

CONCENTRATION
Listening carefully, Job 13:17.
Bible-centered mentality, Psalm 1:2.
Keeping eyes on the Lord, Psalm 25:15.
Glory of kings, Proverbs 25:2.
God gives motivation to His children, Jeremiah 32:39.
Paying attention to Scripture, Hebrews 2:1-3.
Fix thoughts on Jesus, Hebrews 3:1.
See *Cogitation, Thought.*

CONCERN
Taking care to check on family welfare, Exodus 4:18.
Neglecting one's personal appearance until sure of king's safety, 2 Samuel 19:24.
Heart of flesh or heart of stone, Ezekiel 11:19.
Love expressed through anguish, 2 Corinthians 2:4.
Christians keeping in touch concerning each other's activities and welfare, Ephesians 6:21-22.
Concern for the spiritual needs of others, Colossians 1:9.
See *Burden, Empathy, Rapport, Sympathy.*

CONCILIATORY
Abram's attitude toward Lot, Genesis 13:8-9.
Offering to make peace before battle, Deuteronomy 20:10.
See *Tact.*

CONCISE
Obituary of six words, Numbers 20:1.
Shortest short story, Ecclesiastes 9:13-15.
Two-word command, Mark 2:14.

Paul's concise resumé of God's plan through the ages, Romans 1:1-6.
See *Brevity.*

CONCLUSION
Last words of David, 2 Samuel 23:1-7.
Solomon's summation of his testimony, Ecclesiastes 12:13-14.
Ezekiel's prophecy of "the end," Ezekiel 7:2.
Last statement of great prophet, Ezekiel 48:35.
Prayer of Jesus, John 17:1-5.
Paul's "punch line" conclusion to appeal for stewardship, 2 Corinthians 9:15.
Conclusion of Bible, Revelation 22:20-21.
See *Ending, Finale.*

CONCUR
Agreement voiced by congregation as Law declared, Deuteronomy 27:14-26.
King Saul's admission of David's righteousness, 1 Samuel 24:16-17.
Two in agreement, Amos 3:3.
See *Agreement, Unanimity.*

CONDEMNATION
Self-condemnation, 2 Samuel 24:10; Job 9:20; 42:6.
Wounds of a friend, Proverbs 27:6.
No condemnation, Isaiah 50:9; Romans 8:1.
Second judgment on evil King Jehoiakim, Jeremiah 36:27-32.
For continued sinning, certain judgment, Amos 1:3, 6, 9, 11, 13; 2:1, 4, 6. (Note the nature of sin in each of these judgments.)
Those who look for something to criticize, Mark 3:2.
Redeemer also the Judge, John 5:22-24.
Falling into hands of a living God, Hebrews 10:31.
See *Gossip, Judgment.*

CONDITION
Divine ultimatum, Exodus 15:26.
Spiritual preparation for future victory, Joshua 3:5.
Conditions for God's blessing or judgment, 2 Chronicles 7:11-22.
God's blessing dependent on obedience to covenant, Jeremiah 11:1-5.
God's great invitation to call on Him,

Jeremiah 33:3.
For God to return to us, we must return to
Him, Zechariah 1:3.
Conditions of relationship with the Lord,
2 Timothy 2:11-13.
See *Blessing.*

CONDOLENCE
David's sympathy, 2 Samuel 10:2.
Job's friends, Job 2:11.
Mary and Jesus, John 11:23-35.

CONDUCT
Promise of answered prayer to those who
please the Lord, Exodus 33:17.
Lifestyle and example, Deuteronomy 4:9.
Defiled by one's actions, Psalm 106:39.
Path of righteous and way of wicked,
Proverbs 4:18-19.
The Lord hates pride, evil behavior, and
perverse speech, Proverbs 8:13.
Conduct and conversation linked together,
Proverbs 22:11.
Evil deeds and motives likened to eggs,
Isaiah 59:4-5.
Reward for good and evil conduct,
Jeremiah 22:3-5.
Practice what you preach, Ezekiel 33:31;
Luke 3:7-8.
Exploiting poor for personal gain, Amos
5:11.
False prophets recognized by their fruit,
Matthew 7:15-20.
Actions speak louder than words, Matthew
11:18-19.
Tree known by its fruit, Matthew 12:33-35;
Luke 6:43-45.
Jesus chose apostles and then gave them
specific guidelines for holy and
purposeful ministries, Luke 6:12-49.
Those who would teach others but need to
be taught themselves, Romans 1:17-23.
Reward for good works, Romans 2:5-11.
Seeking pleasure from those things which
cause spiritual death, Romans 6:21.
True measure of spirituality, Romans
14:17-18.
Doing all for glory of God, 1 Corinthians
10:31.
Wrong attitudes in worship do more harm
than good, 1 Corinthians 11:17-32.
Importance of conduct, 2 Corinthians 5:10.
You reap what you sow, Galatians 6:7-10.
Worthy of calling, Ephesians 4:1.

New lifestyle in Christ, Ephesians 4:22-24.
Right and wrong kind of attitude and
disposition, Ephesians 4:31-32.
Slaves and masters, Ephesians 6:5-9.
Judged by observance of legalism,
Colossians 2:16.
Lifestyle of those risen with Christ,
Colossians 3:1-17.
Captive to will of Satan, 2 Timothy 2:25-26.
Proper teaching for all ages, Titus 2:1-10.
Self-condemnation of those who cause
difficulty among believers, Titus 3:10-
11.
Instruction for living Christian life,
Hebrews 13:1-9.
Faith without works, James 2:14-18.
True faith demonstrated, James 3:13.
Those who sow in peace, James 3:18.
Attributes of mature Christian life, 2 Peter
1:5-9.
Doing what is right, 1 John 2:29.
Need to warn against false teaching and
wrong conduct, Jude 3-4.
See *Lifestyle, Performance, Walk.*

CONFERENCE
Dates for assembly, Exodus 12:16;
Numbers 28:18, 26; 29:7.
Israelite community assembled for
information, Exodus 35:1.
Vast assembly, 1 Kings 8:65.
Seeking consensus of leadership and then
the entire body, 1 Chronicles 13:1-4.
Day after day devoted to reading
Scriptures, Nehemiah 8:17-18.
Futile attempt to hold retreat, Luke 9:10-
11.
Gathering church members for ministry
report, Acts 14:27-28.
Paul's summary of ministry, Acts 21:19.
Good organization in church,
1 Corinthians 14:33-40.

CONFESSION
Nehemiah's prayer, Nehemiah 1:4-7.
Folly of concealing sin, Proverbs 28:13.
Ridden with remorse for betraying Jesus,
Judas hanged himself, Matthew 27:3-5.
Role of witness in salvation, Romans 10:9-
10.
Confess to each other, James 5:16.
Our Advocate with the Heavenly Father,
1 John 2:1-2.
See *Conscience, Guilt, Remorse.*

CONFIDENCE

God's word of assurance to Abram, Genesis 15:1.

Trusting God against insurmountable opposition, Exodus 14:5-14.

Confident in face of danger, Numbers 14:8-9.

March on with strong soul, Judges 5:21.

David's lack of confidence in face of danger, 1 Samuel 27:1.

David's fear of God in a given circumstance, 1 Chronicles 13:12.

David's sin in depending on number of fighting men, 1 Chronicles 21:17.

Sure of God's plan and purpose, Job 42:2.

Facing opposition with confidence, Psalm 3:6.

The Lord a sure refuge to all who come to Him, Psalm 9:9-10.

God's love unfailing, Psalm 13:5-6.

Confidence to face challenge, Psalm 18:29.

Sure faith, Psalm 27:1.

Certainty of deliverance in midst of trouble, Psalm 34:19.

Be still and wait, Psalm 37:7.

Confidence wrongly placed, Psalms 44:6; 49:6-7; 146:3; Jeremiah 17:5; 48:7; Ezekiel 33:13.

Steadfast heart, Psalm 57:7.

God's love and God's strength, Psalm 62:11-12.

No fear day or night, Psalm 91:4-6.

Sure that the Lord is God, Psalm 100:3.

Fear of man, Psalm 118:6-9.

Trusting God like a small child, Psalm 131:2.

The God who answers prayer, Psalm 138:1-3.

Prayer for instruction and confidence, Psalm 143:10.

Certainty of God's promises, Psalm 145:13.

Gossip betrays confidence, Proverbs 20:19.

Trustworthy messenger, Proverbs 25:13.

Fear of man a snare, Proverbs 29:25.

Danger of fearing wrong things, Isaiah 8:12-14.

Kept in perfect peace, Isaiah 26:3.

Tested stone in Zion, Isaiah 28:16.

Confidence in the Lord rather than men, Isaiah 36:4-10.

Dramatic use of silence, Isaiah 36:13-21.

Do not question the Potter, Isaiah 45:9.

Confident in one's own wickedness, Isaiah 47:10.

All in God's hands, Isaiah 49:4.

Certainty of answered prayer, Isaiah 49:8.

Walking with confidence in the dark, Isaiah 50:10.

Jeremiah's fear and reluctance of proclaiming God's message, Jeremiah 1:6-10.

Confidence in difficult times, Jeremiah 1:17.

Those who trust the Lord, Jeremiah 17:7-8.

The Lord like a mighty warrior, Jeremiah 20:11.

Nothing too hard for the Lord, Jeremiah 32:17.

Thanking God in midst of adverse circumstances, Jeremiah 33:10-11.

Safest place to be in times of trouble and persecution, Jeremiah 42:1-22; Ezekiel 34:25.

The Lord's mercies new each morning, Lamentations 3:22-26; Zephaniah 3:5.

Confidence of Daniel's friends facing fiery furnace, Daniel 3:16-18.

Mountains crumble but God's ways are eternal, Habakkuk 3:6.

Believe in the Good News, Mark 1:14-15.

In the presence of the One who bestows faith, disciples lacked faith, Mark 4:36-41.

No need to fear in the presence of Jesus, John 6:20.

Antidote for troubled hearts, John 14:1.

Pagans certain of erroneous belief, Acts 19:35-36.

Paul went with confidence into difficult places, Acts 20:22-24.

A man sure of his destiny, Acts 27:23-24.

Hope when no basis for hope, Romans 4:18-22.

Nothing can separate us from the love of God, Romans 8:37-39.

Confident of the Lord's full blessing, Romans 15:29.

Our competence comes from God, 2 Corinthians 3:4-5.

Confidence in unseen, 2 Corinthians 4:18.

Living by faith, not by sight, 2 Corinthians 5:1-7.

Paul admitted his lack of confidence, 2 Corinthians 10:1-2.

God can do more than we ask or imagine, Ephesians 3:20-21.

Still standing at end of struggle, Ephesians 6:13.

Standing firm whatever circumstances, Philippians 1:27-30.
Prayer that brings peace, Philippians 4:6-7.
Absolute confidence in the One whom we believe, 2 Timothy 1:12.
We come to our High Priest, the Lord Jesus, with confidence, Hebrews 4:14-16.
Going in obedience toward unknown objective, Hebrews 11:8.
Faith to believe what has not been received, Hebrews 11:13.
Kingdom that cannot be shaken, Hebrews 12:28-29.
Asking God for wisdom and believing it will be granted, James 1:5-7.
Grace and peace in abundance, 1 Peter 1:2.
God of all grace, 1 Peter 5:10.
No fear in love, 1 John 4:18.
Absolute confidence in one's salvation, 1 John 5:13.
See *Assurance, Certainty, Faith, Guidance, Promise, Trust.*

CONFIDENTIAL
Careful with words, Ecclesiastes 12:10.
Whispers to be proclaimed, Matthew 10:27.
Evil cannot be kept confidential, Luke 12:2-3.
See *Secrecy, Secret.*

CONFLICT
David fought the Lord's battles, 1 Samuel 25:28.
Futility of strife among brothers, 2 Samuel 2:27-28.
Struggle between strong and weak, 2 Samuel 3:1.
At peace with one's enemies, Proverbs 16:7.
Noise of battle and destruction, Jeremiah 50:22.
Love your enemy, Matthew 5:43-48.
Satan divided against himself, Matthew 12:22-32.
No peace on earth, Mark 13:6-8.
Clash of personalities between Paul and Barnabas, Acts 15:36-41.
Stress between evil and good in human nature, Romans 7:14-20.
Those who purposely cause trouble, Romans 16:17.

Lawsuits among believers, 1 Corinthians 6:1-8.
Purpose of trouble, 2 Corinthians 4:17-18.
Peter and Paul face-to-face, Galatians 2:11-21.
Handling conflict in church with firmness and love, 1 Timothy 1:3-7.
See *Argument, Discord, Dispute, Jealousy, Strife.*

CONFORMITY
Following wrong of others, Exodus 23:2; Deuteronomy 12:29-30.
Desiring same political structure as pagans, 1 Samuel 8:1-22.
Conforming to pagan ways, 2 Kings 17:13-15.
Conformity to Christ, Romans 8:29.
Conformed or transformed, Romans 12:1-2.
See *Influence, Syncretism.*

CONFUSION
Wandering Israelites, Exodus 14:1-4.
Lamp of the Lord, 2 Samuel 22:29.
Walking about in darkness, Psalm 82:5.
A fool does not know way to town, Ecclesiastes 10:15.
Spirit of dizziness, Isaiah 19:14.
Sick drunk, Isaiah 28:7.
Blind without guidance, Isaiah 59:10.
Warriors stumbling over each other, Jeremiah 46:12.
Nebuchadnezzar confused between admission of one true God and belief in many gods, Daniel 3:28-30; 4:18.
From one peril to another, Amos 5:19.
Herod's lack of perception, Luke 9:7-9.
Avoiding confusion in worship, 1 Corinthians 14:29-33, 40.

CONGENIAL
In-depth congeniality, Nehemiah 8:10-12.
Brief congeniality, Job 20:5.
Laughter and joy in abundance, Psalm 126:2; Philippians 1:26.
Medicinal attitude, Proverbs 17:22.
Time to laugh, Ecclesiastes 3:4.
Laughter of fools, Ecclesiastes 7:6.
Wells of salvation, Isaiah 12:3.
Gladness and joy, Isaiah 35:10.
Christian lifestyle, 1 Peter 1:8-9.
See *Attitude, Lifestyle, Optimism.*

CONGRATULATE

Whatever measure of success, glory belongs to God alone, 1 Corinthians 3:7.

Complimenting those who had been previously rebuked, 2 Corinthians 7:14.

See *Acclaim, Commendation, Praise.*

CONGREGATION

Passover forbidden to aliens, Exodus 12:43-45.

Wrong kind of unanimity, Exodus 16:2.

People responded with one voice, Exodus 24:1-7.

Gathering together, Leviticus 8:1-4; Numbers 1:17-18; 8:9; Joshua 18:1; Judges 20:1.

Leading disgruntled congregation, Numbers 11:4-15.

Every member a prophet, Numbers 11:26-30.

Holy community, Numbers 16:3.

One man brings guilt on entire assembly, Numbers 16:22.

Agreement voiced by congregation as Law is declared, Deuteronomy 27:14-26.

Uniting behind new leader, Joshua 1:16-18.

Weakness of people left without spiritual guidance, Judges 2:18-19.

David's army of chosen men, 2 Samuel 6:1.

Owning a share of the king, 2 Samuel 19:43.

David's mighty men, 2 Samuel 23:8-39.

Those who will not listen, 2 Kings 17:14.

Least and greatest in society, 2 Kings 23:2.

Multitude as one, Nehemiah 8:1.

In-depth obedience within congregation, Psalm 103:17-21.

All the people join in praise, Psalm 106:48.

Fulfilling one's vows to the Lord, Psalm 116:14, 18-19.

People and priests clothed with righteousness, Psalm 132:9, 16.

Glory of large population, Proverbs 14:28.

Those who do not want to hear truth, Isaiah 30:10-11.

Satisfied with deceitful priests, Jeremiah 5:31.

The "amen" of agreement to God's message, Jeremiah 28:5-6.

Those who disbelieved message Ezekiel proclaimed, Ezekiel 20:49.

Calling congregation together to pray, Joel 1:14; 2:16.

Those who dislike strong preaching, Amos 7:16.

Sheep without a shepherd, Mark 6:34.

People at peace with each other, Mark 9:50.

Jesus proclaimed depths of spiritual truth, John 6:60-69.

Prayer of Jesus for His own, John 17:20-23.

Dissension and jealousy in church, Acts 6:1.

Winning large number of people, Acts 14:21.

Gathering church members for report on ministry, Acts 14:27-28.

Growing New Testament church, Acts 16:5.

Paul's consistent prayer for other Christians, Romans 1:8-10; 1 Corinthians 1:4-9; Ephesians 1:11-23; Philippians 1:3-6; Colossians 1:3-14.

Function of various body members, Romans 12:4-8.

Honor others above yourself, Romans 12:10.

Live in harmony with others, Romans 12:16, 18.

Serving the Lord in unity, Romans 15:5-6.

Special greeting to house church, Romans 16:5.

Need for unity among believers, 1 Corinthians 1:10-17.

Serving together in effective cooperation, 1 Corinthians 3:1-16.

Discipline within congregation, 1 Corinthians 5:1-13.

Wrong attitudes in worship, 1 Corinthians 11:17-32.

Different kinds of gifts and service in the Lord's work, 1 Corinthians 12:4-11.

One body, many parts, 1 Corinthians 12:12-30.

Paul could boast about his converts, 2 Corinthians 10:8.

Need for stability in congregation, Galatians 1:6-9.

Carrying each other's burdens, Galatians 6:2. (See also v. 5.)

Relationships within fold, Galatians 6:10.

Members of God's family, Ephesians 2:19-22.

Serving God in unity, Ephesians 4:3.

Varied talents in body of Christ, Ephesians

4:11-13.

Imitators of God expressing love to others, Ephesians 5:1-2.

Conduct and activity in worship, Ephesians 5:19-21.

Praying for those who minister, Ephesians 6:19-20.

Like-minded people serving God in love, Philippians 2:1-2.

Faithful service without pastoral supervision, Philippians 2:12-13.

Paul's instruction on unity in Philippian church, Philippians 4:1-9.

Concern for pastor, Philippians 4:10-19; Colossians 4:3-4.

Paul's relentless effort on behalf of followers, Colossians 1:28-29.

Life centered in Christ, Colossians 3:1-17.

Care in one's conduct toward unbelievers, Colossians 4:5.

Importance of welcoming message, 1 Thessalonians 1:6.

Properly receiving the Word of God as it is, 1 Thessalonians 2:13.

Followers are joy and crown of those who present message, 1 Thessalonians 2:17-19.

Overflowing love among believers, 1 Thessalonians 3:12.

Thanking God for others, 2 Thessalonians 1:3.

Growing, persevering Christians, 2 Thessalonians 1:4.

Avoid making enemies of those who do wrong, 2 Thessalonians 3:14-15.

Praying together without dispute, 1 Timothy 2:8.

Christian community like a family, 1 Timothy 5:1-2.

Looking after needs of new congregation, Titus 1:5-9.

Proper teaching for all ages, Titus 2:1-10.

Singing God's praises in congregation, Hebrews 2:12.

Encouraging one another, Hebrews 3:13.

Confident of growth in followers, Hebrews 6:9.

Being an example to each other, Hebrews 10:24-25.

Brotherly love, Hebrews 13:1.

Showing hospitality to all who come to worship, James 2:1-4.

Cause of discord, James 4:1-2.

Do not grumble against each other, James 5:9.

Love one another deeply, 1 Peter 1:22; 1 John 4:7-11.

Living stones built of the Living Stone, 1 Peter 2:4-8.

Judgment begins with family of God, 1 Peter 4:17.

Message for all ages, 1 John 2:12-14.

Disruption in congregation, 3 John 9-10.

Disruptive people who slip in among believers, Jude 3-4.

Listening to Holy Spirit speak to churches, Revelation 2:29.

Measure temple, count worshipers, Revelation 11:1.

Song for exclusive congregation, Revelation 14:1-3.

No churches in heaven, Revelation 21:22.

Ministry of Holy Spirit and church in evangelism, Revelation 22:17.

See *Body of Christ, Church, Clergy, Discipline, Fellowship, Missionary, Preaching, Sanctuary, Soul-winning, Unity, Witness.*

CONNIVANCE

Premeditated murder, Exodus 21:14.

Compromising leadership, Exodus 32:1-2.

Augmenting evil, Psalm 50:18; Proverbs 24:24; 28:4; Romans 1:32.

Prophets who see nothing, Ezekiel 13:1-3.

Spineless Pilate, Matthew 27:17-26.

Pharisees suspected a deceitful Resurrection claim, Matthew 27:62-66. (See 28:11-15.)

Death of Stephen, Acts 8:1.

Paul's shadowed past, Acts 22:19-20.

See *Deceit, Deception.*

CONQUEST

Overcoming obstacles with God's help, 2 Samuel 22:30.

Laying land completely waste, 2 Kings 3:19.

Stark, bloody vengeance, Psalms 58:10; 68:23.

Lands of other nations, Psalm 111:6.

Victory requires more than ability, Isaiah 25:11.

Plundering with glee, Ezekiel 36:5.

Means by which the Lord Jesus will overthrow man of sin, 2 Thessalonians 2:8.

See *Victory.*

CONSCIENCE
Birth of conscience, Genesis 3:6-11.
Guilty conscience, Genesis 42:1-23; Ezra 9:6.
Much searching of heart, Judges 5:16.
David's clear conscience concerning King Saul, 1 Samuel 20:1; 24:1-7.
David the subject of convicting parable, 2 Samuel 12:1-10.
David's concern about his army rather than promises of God, 2 Samuel 24:10.
Things known in heart, 1 Kings 2:44.
Sin considered trivial, 1 Kings 16:31.
Tears of contrition and confession, Ezra 10:1.
A clear conscience, Job 27:6; 1 Corinthians 4:4; 1 John 3:19-20.
Role of Scripture, Psalm 19:7-11.
Agony of guilt, Psalm 38:4.
Indelible awareness of sin and guilt, Psalm 51:3.
Not always dependable, Proverbs 16:25.
Countenance betrays conscience, Isaiah 3:9.
Reaching to heart, Jeremiah 4:18.
Those who do not know how to blush, Jeremiah 6:15.
God tests heart and mind, Jeremiah 11:20.
Wealth numbs conscience, Hosea 12:8.
Those who hoard plunder become insensitive to right, Amos 3:10.
Remorse of Judas, Matthew 27:3-5.
Realization of sin in presence of Jesus, Luke 5:8.
Responsive conscience, Acts 2:37.
Hues of conscience, Acts 23:1;
1 Corinthians 8:7; 1 Timothy 3:9; 4:2; Hebrews 10:22.
Conscience toward God and men, Acts 24:16.
Those who do not have scriptural guidance, Romans 2:14-15.
Conscience in conflict, Romans 7:15-25.
Variety in conscience, Romans 14:1-23;
1 Corinthians 8:7-13; Titus 1:15.
Role of grief in repentance, 1 Corinthians 5:1-2.
New awareness in heart, 2 Corinthians 7:10-13.
Do not grieve the Holy Spirit, Ephesians 4:30.
Value of a good conscience, Hebrews 9:14.
Danger of seeing light but walking in darkness, 2 Peter 2:21.
Those who refuse to repent, Revelation 16:10-11.
See *Conviction, Guilt, Repentance, Wrong.*

CONSCIENTIOUS
Abraham's attitude toward Lot, Genesis 13:5-9.
Conscientious pagan maiden, Exodus 2:5-10.
Boaz and Ruth, Ruth 2:5-10; 3:7-18.
David's exemplary example, 2 Samuel 9:1-13.
Sympathy toward a father's loneliness, 2 Samuel 14:1-24.
Conscientious king, 1 Kings 20:32-34.
Right conscience of leadership, Nehemiah 5:8-19.
Mordecai and Esther, Esther 2:7.
Nebuchadnezzar's conduct in conquest, Jeremiah 39:1-14.
Joseph's initial attitude toward Mary, Matthew 1:18-19.
Good Samaritan, Luke 10:30-36.
See *Compassion, Kindness.*

CONSCRIPTION
Taking care of business, Deuteronomy 20:5-9.
Solomon's use of forced labor, 1 Kings 9:15.
United enemy, 2 Kings 3:21.
Chosen for temple service, Luke 1:8-9.

CONSECRATION
Threshing floor becomes site for altar, 2 Samuel 24:18-25.
National commitment, 2 Kings 23:3;
2 Chronicles 15:15.
With all the heart, Nehemiah 4:6.
Give heart to God, Psalm 40:7-8.
Coming to the Lord with clean vessel, Isaiah 66:20.
Dual responsibility, Acts 6:1-4.
Dying daily, 1 Corinthians 15:31.
To God and each other, 2 Corinthians 8:5.
See *Commitment, Dedication, Responsibility, Volition.*

CONSENSUS
Unanimous complaint, Exodus 16:2;
Numbers 11:4-6.
Seeking consensus of leadership and then of entire body, 1 Chronicles 13:1-4.

Wise put to shame, Jeremiah 8:9.
See *Unanimity.*

CONSENT
See *Agreement, Approval, Decision.*

CONSEQUENCES
Warning against disobedience, Genesis
2:17; Proverbs 13:15; Ezekiel 18:13;
Romans 2:9.
Consequences of righteousness, Genesis
7:1; Psalm 18:24.
Spoils of war, Joshua 7:11-12.
Humility delays disaster, 1 Kings 21:29.
Aftermath to spiritism, 1 Chronicles 10:13.
Unanswered prayer, Psalm 66:18; Isaiah
59:2.
Plight of fools, Psalm 107:17.
Guidance results from commitment,
Proverbs 3:5-6.
Pursuit of evil, Proverbs 11:19.
Certain judgment, Proverbs 11:21.
Misfortune and prosperity, Proverbs 13:21.
Delay of justice, Ecclesiastes 8:11.
Reward for tithing, Malachi 3:10. (See Luke
6:38.)
Beatitudes, Matthew 5:3-12.
Result of believing, Acts 16:31.
Consequence of Adam's sin, Romans 5:12;
6:23.
Diversified labor, 1 Corinthians 3:8.
No escape for ignoring salvation, Hebrews
2:3.
Faith rewarded, Hebrews 11:6.
See *Doubt, Judgment, Obedient, Results.*

CONSERVATION
Saving trees in conquered city,
Deuteronomy 20:19.
Jesus wanted nothing wasted, John 6:12.
See *Ecology.*

CONSERVATIVE
The wise incline to the right, Ecclesiastes
10:2.

CONSIDERATION
Returning neighbor's lost property,
Deuteronomy 22:1-3.
Padding for Jeremiah's comfort in
deliverance, Jeremiah 38:11-13.
Joseph did not want to make Mary subject
of public disgrace, Matthew 1:19.
Putting first things first, Luke 10:38-42.

Consideration shown to Paul, the prisoner,
Acts 27:3.
Being tactful in conversation with others,
Colossians 4:6.
Exercise tact in times of duress, James
1:19-20.

CONSISTENT
Abstaining from both wine and grapes,
Numbers 6:2-4.
Follow all of God's commands,
Deuteronomy 8:1.
When Israelites consistently did that which
was evil, Judges 13:1.
An undivided heart, Psalm 86:11.
Our Lord's enduring love, Psalm 136:1-26.
Jeremiah proclaimed message "again and
again," Jeremiah 25:3-4.
Loved with everlasting love, Jeremiah 31:3.
The Lord's love and faithfulness day by
day, Lamentations 3:22-24.
Undivided heart, Ezekiel 11:19.
Present or absent, Philippians 1:27-28.
Testimony of consistent life,
1 Thessalonians 4:11-12; James 3:13.
Persevere in life and doctrine, 1 Timothy
4:16.
See *Balance.*

CONSOLATION
Our rock and our song, Psalm 40:1-3.
Refuge and strength in trouble, Psalm
46:1-3.
Provision for thirst, help through the night,
Psalm 63:1-8.
Sheep of His pasture, Psalm 100:1-5.
Steadfast heart, Psalm 108:1-5.
Help in time of sorrow, Psalm 116:1-6,
15.
No song for heavy heart, Proverbs 25:20.
See *Comfort, Empathy.*

CONSPIRACY
Conspiracy of Joseph's brothers, Genesis
37:12-18.
Guards unwilling to follow king's
command to do evil, 1 Samuel 22:16-
17.
Conspiracy of Absalom, 2 Samuel 15:1-
12.
Murderous officials, 2 Kings 12:19-21;
14:19; Daniel 6:1-5.
Plot to kill Paul, Acts 23:12-22.
See *Deceit, Treachery.*

CONSTANT
Pledge of lifelong loyalty, Ruth 1:15-17;
1 Samuel 20:42.
Mercies new each morning, Lamentations
3:22-26.
One who never changes, Hebrews 1:10-12;
13:8.
See *Absolute, Consistent, Dependability.*

CONSTRUCTION
Man who built a city, Genesis 10:11-12.
Use of specific materials for building,
Genesis 11:3.
Solomon's organization for building
temple, 1 Kings 5:12-18.
Nehemiah's skill in rebuilding wall,
Nehemiah 6:1.
Grass on housetops, Psalm 129:6-7.
Carpentry of lazy man, Ecclesiastes 10:18.
No building programs, Jeremiah 51:26.
New temple in Jerusalem, Ezekiel 40–43.
Mortar and brickwork, Nahum 3:14.
Chosen to build temple, Zechariah 6:9-15.
Determining cost before expenditure,
Luke 14:28-30.
See *Architecture, Carpenter, Design.*

CONTEMPT
Burning with anger, 1 Samuel 17:28.
Opposition to rebuilding walls, Nehemiah
2:19; 4:3.
World against God, Psalm 2:1-3.
Defiance of a fool, Psalm 14:1; 53:1.
Scorn for acts of humility, Psalm 69:10-12.
Prayer for good attitude, Psalm 119:22.
False witness against Jesus, Mark 14:53-59.
Contempt for miracle, John 9:13-34.
See *Hatred.*

CONTENTMENT
Happiness during reign of King Solomon,
1 Kings 4:20.
Contented with little, Psalm 37:16-17.
Contentment of believer, Psalm 84:10-12.
Desires satisfied and strength renewed,
Psalm 103:5. (See 37:4.)
Satisfaction comes only from the Lord,
Psalm 107:8-9.
Rejoicing in day the Lord has made, Psalm
118:24.
Little with contentment, Proverbs 15:16.
Do not envy sinners, Proverbs 23:17.
Not envious of the wicked, Proverbs 24:19-
20.

Happiness from honesty and God's
provision, Proverbs 30:7-9.
Special gift of God, Ecclesiastes 3:12-13.
Labor and good food, Ecclesiastes 5:18-20.
Enjoyment of life, Ecclesiastes 8:15.
Live within income, Luke 3:14.
Secret of contentment, Philippians 4:11-
13.
Godliness with contentment, 1 Timothy
6:6-8; Hebrews 13:5.
Do not grumble against each other, James
5:9.
See *Peace, Rest, Satisfaction, Tranquility.*

CONTEXTUALIZATION
Message adaption to Greek mentality, John
1:1-14. (*Word* translated from Greek
logos, basic concept in Greek teaching
and philosophy.)
Divine witness in natural revelation, Acts
14:8-19.
Relating Gospel message through Old
Testament Scriptures, Acts 17:1-3;
Philippians 3:3-11.
Witnessing to intellectual, pagan
Athenians, Acts 17:16-34.
Paul's contextual approach to those of
other cultures and circumstances,
1 Corinthians 9:19-22.
See *Tact.*

CONTINENCE
David and women of palace, 2 Samuel
20:3.
Relationship of husband and wife,
1 Corinthians 7:1-7.
See *Abstinence, Eunuch, Morality,
Restraint.*

CONTINUITY
Joyful transfer of leadership on the throne
of Israel, 1 Kings 1:47-48.
One generation tells the next, Psalm 145:4.
God's message conveyed from generation
to generation, Isaiah 59:21.
God's plan for perpetuation of the Gospel,
2 Timothy 2:1-4.
The One who never changes, Hebrews
1:10-12.
See *Absolute, Dependability.*

CONTRACEPTION
Onan's procedure toward command of
Judah, Genesis 38:8-10.

CONTRACT
Treaty between Abraham and Abimelech, Genesis 21:22-34.
Gravesite covered by deed, Genesis 23:20.
Nonverbal contract, Genesis 24:2-4.
Daughter's contract altered by father's intervention, Numbers 30:3-5. (See also vv. 10-15.)
God's covenant through many generations, Deuteronomy 5:2-3.
Those who broke faith with God, Deuteronomy 32:51.
Fate of favorite daughter, an only child, Judges 11:29-39.
Symbol of transaction, Ruth 4:7.
Purchase order, 1 Kings 5:8-11.
Importance of treaty, 1 Kings 20:34.
Servants bound by contract, Isaiah 21:16.
Penalty for disobeying covenant, Jeremiah 11:1-5.
Documents of ownership, Jeremiah 32:14. (See vv. 6-15.)
Legal conflicts resulting from false oaths, Hosea 10:4.
Judas under contract to betray Jesus, Matthew 26:14-16.
See *Agreement, Guarantee, Mortgage.*

CONTRADICTION
Saying one thing, meaning another, Exodus 14:5-8; Psalms 55:12-23; 78:34-37; Proverbs 26:18-26; Isaiah 29:13-16.
Worship without true reverence, Amos 5:21-24.
Display of piety without sincerity of heart, Matthew 23:1-39; Mark 12:38-40; Luke 6:46; 11:39-52.
Practice what you preach, Romans 2:21-25.
See *Hypocrisy, Sham.*

CONTRAST
Light separated from darkness, Genesis 1:4-5.
Path of righteous and way of wicked, Proverbs 4:18-19.
Positives and negatives, Ecclesiastes 3:1-8.
Gentle flowing waters or mighty flood waters, Isaiah 8:6-7.
Wide contrast between temporal and spiritual, Isaiah 40:7-8.
Light shining in darkness, Isaiah 60:1-2.
Fate of good and evil, Isaiah 65:13-14.
Faithless Israel and unfaithful Judah, Jeremiah 3:11.
In midst of his lament, Jeremiah gave contrast of God's mercy and blessing, Lamentations 3:22-26.
Prophet an exception to those he warned, Micah 3:8.
Pagan nations and those who follow the Lord, Micah 4:5.
Reaction of Mary compared to that of shepherds, Luke 2:19-20.
Contrast between brother's and father's love, Luke 15:11-32.
Law of Moses and message of Christ, John 1:17.
Man's evil and God's righteousness, Romans 3:5-8.
That which is truly high and that which is truly low, James 1:9-10.
Women's hair and lions' teeth, Revelation 9:8.
See *Variety.*

CONTRIBUTION
Asking for much, 2 Kings 4:3.
Giving from continuity of desire to do so, 2 Corinthians 9:10-11.
No help from pagans, 3 John 7.
See *Participation, Philanthropy, Stewardship.*

CONTRITE
Man who felt unworthy of being in presence of king, 2 Samuel 19:24-28.
Broken hearts, crushed spirit, Psalms 34:18; 51:17.
Reverence before the Lord, Psalm 51:17; Isaiah 66:2.
Role of grief in repentance, Joel 2:13; 1 Corinthians 5:1-2; 2 Corinthians 7:10.
Guilt of Judas, Matthew 27:3.
See *Repentance.*

CONTROL
Desire to be overseer, 1 Timothy 3:1.
Man is a slave to whatever masters him, 2 Peter 2:19.

CONTROVERSY
Discontent with leadership, Numbers 14:1-4.
Divided into two factions, 1 Kings 16:21-22.
Strife caused by pride and hatred, Proverbs 10:12; 13:10.

Evidence turns against accuser, Proverbs
25:8.
Settle misunderstandings quickly, Matthew
5:25.
Foolish questions, 1 Timothy 6:4; Titus 3:9.
See *Abrasion, Argument, Dispute, Mob
psychology.*

CONVALESCENCE
Sustained on sick bed, Psalm 41:3.
Restored to health, Isaiah 38:16.
Illness and near death of Epaphroditus,
Philippians 2:25-30.
See *Health, Medicine, Physician, Therapy.*

CONVERSATION
Sometimes it is wisdom to speak neither
good nor evil, Genesis 31:24.
Spiritual matters, Deuteronomy 6:4-7.
Samson and Philistine woman, Judges
14:7.
Left with nothing to say, Nehemiah 5:8.
Job accused of not speaking sensibly, Job
18:2.
Resolving not to sin with one's mouth,
Psalm 17:3.
Keeping tongue from speaking wrong,
Psalm 39:1.
Words known before spoken, Psalm 139:4.
Tongues of serpents, Psalm 140:3.
How to avoid participation in gossip, Psalm
141:3.
Speech of righteous and wicked, Proverbs
10:11.
Good and evil tongue, Proverbs 10:31-32.
Fruit of one's lips, Proverbs 12:14.
Wisdom of silence elevates a fool, Proverbs
17:28.
Opinions of a fool, Proverbs 18:2.
Gossip by one who talks too much,
Proverbs 20:19.
Guarding tongue, Proverbs 21:23.
Conduct and conversation linked together,
Proverbs 22:11.
Words aptly spoken, Proverbs 25:11;
Ecclesiastes 5:2.
Disguising true self by false speech,
Proverbs 26:24-26.
Saying yes or no, Matthew 5:37.
Words condemn or acquit, Matthew 12:37.
Not what goes into the mouth but what
comes out, Matthew 15:10-20.
Use of gracious words, Luke 4:22.
Talking about latest ideas, Acts 17:21.

Conversation enriched in Christ,
1 Corinthians 1:5-6.
Foolish talk and coarse joking, Ephesians
5:4.
Words seasoned with salt, Colossians 4:6.
Avoid godless chatter, 2 Timothy 2:16.
Seriousness and soundness of speech,
Titus 2:7-8.
Deceit of unruly tongue, James 1:26.
Guard tongue well, James 3:3-6.
Speaking and serving to glory of God,
1 Peter 4:11.
Empty, boastful words, 2 Peter 2:18.
Some things better spoken than written,
2 John 12; 3 John 13-14.
Pride and blasphemy, Revelation 13:5.
See *Communication, Gossip, Silence,
Speech, Tact.*

CONVERSATIONAL CONTROL
Strategic control of speech, James 3:2-4.

CONVERSION
Wood used in pagan worship becomes fuel
for fire of altar to God, Judges 6:25-26.
Children who need conversion experience,
1 Samuel 3:7.
Saul changed into different person by
power of Holy Spirit, 1 Samuel 10:6-10.
Picture of conversion experience, Psalm
18:16-19.
David could see himself blameless before
the Lord, Psalm 26:1, 11.
David's song of transformation, Psalm
40:1-4.
Depth of mercy and forgiveness, Psalm
51:1-2.
Walking in the Way, Isaiah 35:8.
Light has come, Isaiah 60:1.
True repentance from disgrace of youth,
Jeremiah 31:19.
Repentance in tears, Jeremiah 50:4-5.
From heart of stone to heart of flesh,
Ezekiel 11:19.
Turning from wicked past, Ezekiel 16:59-
63.
New heart and spirit, Ezekiel 36:26.
Purified and made spotless, Daniel 12:10.
All who call will be saved, Joel 2:32.
Remembering date of decision, Haggai
2:18.
New garments for Joshua, Zechariah 3:1-7.
Levi celebrated calling to follow Jesus,
Luke 5:27-32.

Faith in Christ can bring family division,
Luke 12:49-53.
Need for repentance, Luke 13:3-5.
Being born again, John 3:1-8.
Man healed of blindness, John 9:1-7.
Turning to light before darkness comes,
John 12:35-36.
Salvation in no other name but Christ, Acts
4:12.
Simon, the sorcerer, Acts 8:9-13.
Conversion of Saul, Acts 9:1-19. (See 7:58;
8:1-3; 9:20-21.)
Conversion of Roman leader influenced by
sorcerer, Acts 13:6-12.
Conversion of jailer, Acts 16:25-34.
Conversion of ruler of synagogue, Acts
18:8.
Scrolls of value destroyed by converted
sorcerers, Acts 19:19.
King Agrippa would not be persuaded,
Acts 26:28.
Spiritual life follows natural life,
1 Corinthians 15:45-49.
New creation in Christ, 2 Corinthians 5:17.
Self-examination, 2 Corinthians 13:5.
Paul set apart from birth, Galatians 1:15-
17.
From darkness to light, Ephesians 5:8-10.
Those who have died with Christ,
Colossians 2:20-23.
Those risen with Christ, Colossians 3:1-17.
Paul the blasphemer becomes minister of
Gospel, 1 Timothy 1:12-14.
Example of God's grace to worst of
sinners, 1 Timothy 1:15-16.
Faith is credibility to what is heard,
Hebrews 4:2.
Birth through Word of truth, James 1:18.
Birth into living hope, 1 Peter 1:3-5.
Becoming chosen people, 1 Peter 2:9.
Walking in light, 1 John 1:5-7.
Doing what is right, 1 John 2:29.
Purifying privilege, 1 John 3:1-3.
Confidence in conversion, 1 John 3:24.
Wearing clean robes, Revelation 22:14.
See *Decision, Repentance, Salvation.*

CONVERT
Solomon's attitude toward foreigners who
came to temple, 1 Kings 8:41-43.
Lambs and shepherd, Isaiah 40:11.
Way of backslider and way of convert,
Ezekiel 33:17-20.
Burning stick snatched from fire,

Zechariah 3:2.
Worth of one lost sheep, Matthew 18:12-
14.
No evidence that Barabbas trusted Christ,
Mark 15:6-15.
Those who believed, John 10:42.
Secret believers, John 12:42-43.
Immaturity of new convert, Acts 8:13-24.
Centurion named Cornelius, Acts 10:1-33.
Do not make it difficult for new converts,
Acts 15:19.
Visiting places of ministry, Acts 15:36.
Prominent women choose to follow Christ,
Acts 17:4.
Only few converts at Athens, Acts 17:34.
Testimony of Christ confirmed in convert,
1 Corinthians 1:4-6.
Many simple people brought to Christ,
1 Corinthians 1:26-31.
One plants, one waters, God gives growth,
1 Corinthians 3:6-9.
Seal of apostleship, 1 Corinthians 9:1-2.
Convert was Paul's recommendation,
2 Corinthians 3:1-3.
Paul could boast about converts,
2 Corinthians 10:8.
Encouraged by news of new convert,
Galatians 1:23-24.
Recorded in Book of Life, Philippians 4:3.
Paul struggled over converts, Colossians
2:1.
Paul's glory and joy, 1 Thessalonians 2:19-
20.
Follow-up of converts, 1 Thessalonians
3:1-5.
True son in faith, 1 Timothy 1:2.
Persecution of new converts, Hebrews
10:32-33.
Redeemed from all nations, Revelation 7:9-
17.
See *Believer.*

CONVICTION
Much searching of heart, Judges 5:16.
Isaiah's conviction of sin, Isaiah 6:5.
Understanding brings terror, Isaiah 28:19.
Knowing what is right, Isaiah 51:7.
Power of holy words, Jeremiah 23:9.
Reaction to prophet's message, Ezekiel
21:7.
Wealth numbs conscience, Hosea 12:8.
Multitudes in valley of decision, Joel 3:14.
Pharisees knew Jesus was talking about
them, Matthew 21:33-46.

Ridden with remorse, Matthew 27:3-5.
Impact of spiritual power, Mark 5:17.
Revealing thoughts of heart, Luke 2:34-35.
Realization of sin in presence of Jesus,
Luke 5:8.
Drawn to Christ by Heavenly Father, John
6:44.
Day of Pentecost, Acts 2:37-38.
Awareness in hearts of Corinthians,
2 Corinthians 7:10-13.
Do not harden heart, Hebrews 3:7-8, 15.
God searches mind and heart, Revelation
2:23.
See *Conscience, Duress, Guilt.*

CONVINCING
Vindication by earthquake, Numbers
16:28-34.
Mouth like sharpened sword, Isaiah 49:2.
Preaching with authority, Luke 4:32.
Difficulty in convincing others, Romans
9:1-2.
See *Persuasion.*

COOKING
Implements for making food, Exodus 8:3;
Leviticus 2:5, 7; 1 Samuel 2:13-14;
1 Kings 17:12; Isaiah 47:2; Ezekiel 4:3;
Amos 6:6.
Broiled meat, Exodus 12:8.
Food with pleasant aroma, Numbers 28:2.
Ancient dishwashing, 2 Kings 21:13.
Cooking pots in the Lord's house,
Zechariah 14:20-21.
See *Food, Gourmet, Meals, Menu.*

COOPERATION
Ox and donkey cannot plow together,
Deuteronomy 22:10.
Nation united, Joshua 10:29-42.
People working with all their heart,
Nehemiah 4:6.
Living together in unity, Psalm 133:1-3.
As iron sharpens iron, Proverbs 27:17.
Saviour left with no one to help Him, Isaiah
63:5.
Two in agreement, Amos 3:3.
Mutual faith required for healing, Mark
6:4-6.
Those for and those against, Luke 11:23.
Barnabas and Saul set apart by laying on of
hands, Acts 13:1-3.
Agreeing with each other in united mind
and thought, 1 Corinthians 1:10.

Total function of body of Christ,
1 Corinthians 12:14-20.
Ministry to Jews and ministry to Gentiles in
harmony, Galatians 2:8.
Carrying one's own load, Galatians 6:5.
Philippians shared in ministry expense,
Philippians 4:15-19.
See *Camaraderie, Rapport, Unanimity.*

CORDIALITY
Warm salutation, 1 Samuel 25:6.
Mary questioned cordial greeting of angel
announcing miraculous pregnancy,
Luke 1:28-31.
Paul's many greetings to friends, Romans
16:3-16.

CORNERSTONE
Prophecy of Christ's rejection, Psalm
118:22.
Cornerstone in Zion, Isaiah 28:16.
Christ, the Cornerstone, 1 Peter 2:6-8.

CORPSE
Choice place for burial, Genesis 23:6.
Covering corpse, 2 Samuel 20:12.
See *Burial, Death, Funeral.*

CORRECTION
Rebuke of righteous man, Psalm 141:5.
Willingness to be disciplined and
corrected, Proverbs 10:17; 25:12.
Value of open rebuke, Proverbs 27:5.
Counsel of friend, Proverbs 27:9.
Those who refuse counsel, Proverbs 29:1.
Sins paid back, Isaiah 65:6.
The Lord guides and corrects those who
seek Him, Jeremiah 10:23-24.
Problem of legalism at Jerusalem, Acts
15:1-11.
Instruction in effective witness, Acts 18:24-
26.
Painfulness of good correction,
2 Corinthians 7:8-9.
Helping someone who has sinned,
Galatians 6:1.

CORRESPONDENCE
Seeking divine guidance concerning
correspondence, 2 Kings 19:14-19.
Letters to and from kings, Ezra 4:7-22; 5:8-
17; 7:11-26.
Good news from distant land, Proverbs
25:25.

Letter from Jeremiah to exiles in Babylon, Jeremiah 29:1-23.

Paul wrote convincing letters but lacked ability in public speaking, 2 Corinthians 10:10.

Sharing Paul's letters between churches, Colossians 4:16.

Identified by handwriting, 2 Thessalonians 3:17.

Paul's letter on behalf of slave, Philemon 1-25.

Short letter, Hebrews 13:22.

Purpose of Peter's letters to friends, 2 Peter 3:1.

Better spoken than written, 2 John 12; 3 John 13-14.

CORROSION
Oil as protection against rust, Isaiah 21:5.

Deteriorating material investment, Matthew 6:19-20.

CORRUPTION
Vanishing faithful, Psalm 12:1-2.

Corrupt from birth, Psalm 58:3.

Silver to dross, wine to water, Isaiah 1:22.

Ravages of wickedness, Isaiah 9:18.

Defiled with blood, Lamentations 4:14.

Anger beyond measure, Lamentations 5:21-22.

Despising those who tell truth, Amos 5:10.

Felix wanted bribe from Paul, Acts 24:26.

Gaining benefit by taking advantage of others, James 5:4-5.

Surviving in evil surroundings, 2 Peter 2:4-9.

Evil men who commit sin in broad daylight, 2 Peter 2:13-23.

Suggestion of social disease, Jude 7-8.

See *Bribery, Deceit, Dishonesty.*

COSMETICS
Aroma of romance, Ruth 3:3.

David's use of lotion, 2 Samuel 12:20.

Eye makeup, 2 Kings 9:30; Ezekiel 23:40.

Making clothing fragrant, Psalm 45:8.

Jewelry and cosmetics to be snatched away, Isaiah 3:18-24.

Eyeshade and makeup, Jeremiah 4:30.

The anointing of Jesus, Matthew 26:6-13; Mark 14:3-9.

Expensive perfume used on the feet of Jesus, John 12:1-8.

See *Fragrance, Myrrh, Perfume.*

COST
Cheap stewardship refused, 2 Samuel 24:21-24.

Food of stingy man, Proverbs 23:6-8.

Rejection of family a high cost of discipleship, Luke 14:26-27.

Need for counting cost, Luke 14:28-30.

See *Sacrifice, Stewardship.*

COSTUME
Clothed with righteousness and faithfulness, Isaiah 11:5.

Cloud for robe, rainbow for hat, Revelation 10:1.

Beautiful jewels adorning evil woman, Revelation 17:4.

See *Clothing, Wardrobe.*

COUNSEL
Aged father's counsel to son, 1 Kings 2:1-9.

Men from nations seek counsel, 1 Kings 4:34.

He who helped others himself becomes discouraged, Job 4:3-5.

Undergirding of God's Word gives credence to speech of righteous, Psalm 37:30-31.

Rebuke of righteous man, Psalm 141:5.

Wise listen to good counsel, Proverbs 9:9; 20:18.

Good and bad sources for advice, Proverbs 12:5.

Multitude of counselors, Proverbs 15:22.

Advice from friend, Proverbs 27:9.

Those who refuse counsel, Proverbs 29:1.

Paul's counsel and sad parting with friends at Ephesus, Acts 20:25-38.

Paul eager for proper counsel with Thessalonians, 1 Thessalonians 3:1-5.

Gently instruct backslider, 2 Timothy 2:23-26.

See *Advice.*

COUNSELING
Moses seated as judge, Exodus 18:13-24.

Priest who served also as judge, 1 Samuel 7:15-17.

David as counselor of distressed and discontented, 1 Samuel 22:2.

Advice as from God, 2 Samuel 16:23.

Guidance in king's court, 1 Chronicles 27:32-33.

Supreme choice of Counselor, Isaiah 9:6.

Instructed tongue, Isaiah 50:4.
Helping wayward believer, Ezekiel 3:20-21.
No message from counselor, Ezekiel 7:26.
Joseph of Arimathea, Mark 15:43; Luke 23:50-51.
Promised Counselor, John 14:16-17.
Counselor shares what has been experienced, 2 Corinthians 1:3-4.
Gentle like a mother, 1 Thessalonians 2:7.
Dealing gently with those who need guidance, Hebrews 5:2.
Restoring backslider to fellowship, James 5:19-20.
See *Guidance.*

COUNTENANCE

Variety of facial expressions, Genesis 4:5; 31:2 (KJV); Deuteronomy 28:50; Judges 13:6; 1 Samuel 16:12; Nehemiah 2:2-3; Proverbs 15:13; 25:23; Matthew 17:2; 2 Corinthians 3:7, 18.
Encouraging facial expression, Job 29:24.
Divine countenance, Psalms 4:6; 44:3.
Heart reflects in face, Proverbs 27:19.
Sad face, Ecclesiastes 7:3; Ezekiel 27:35.
Countenance betrays conscience, Isaiah 3:9.
Face set like flint, Isaiah 50:7.
Brazen look of prostitute, Jeremiah 3:3.
Variation of facial appearance, Ezekiel 1:10.
Master of intrigue, Daniel 8:23.
Face of an angel, Acts 6:15.
See *Attitude.*

COUNTERFEIT

Friends and brothers not to be trusted, Jeremiah 9:4-8.
False christs in later days, Matthew 24:4-5, 24.
Ego displayed by teachers of Law, Mark 12:38-40.
Ultimate identification of hypocrite, Luke 13:23-27.
Disciples could not believe Saul's conversion, Acts 9:26-27.
Counterfeit Christian leaders, 2 Corinthians 11:13-15.
False humility, Colossians 2:18.
Counterfeit intellectualism, 1 Timothy 6:20.
Deceitful claim of holy life, 1 John 1:8-10.
Feigning life when spiritually dead, Revelation 3:1.

COUP DE GRACE

Saul's suicide, 1 Samuel 31:4-6. (See 2 Sam. 1:1-16.)
Strange death of Absalom, 2 Samuel 18:9-15.

COURAGE

Courage at God's command, Joshua 1:9.
Courageous in old age, Joshua 14:10-12.
People who risked their lives, Judges 5:18.
March on with strong soul, Judges 5:21.
Facing big opposition, Judges 7:7-23; 1 Samuel 17:32, 50.
Courageous youth, 1 Samuel 14:6-45.
Strength from God, 2 Samuel 22:23.
Fearless horse in battle, Job 39:19, 25.
Moving ahead in spite of circumstances, Psalm 44:18.
Witness to those in authority, Psalm 119:46.
Bold and stouthearted, Psalm 138:3.
Courage in times of trouble, Proverbs 24:10.
Mighty lion, Proverbs 30:30.
Danger of fearing wrong things, Isaiah 8:12-14.
Sufficiency of our God, Isaiah 41:10.
Face set like flint, Isaiah 50:7.
Courage to face adverse circumstances, Ezekiel 2:6-7.
Witness in king's court, Daniel 3:8-18.
Courage of Daniel to point out sin of king, Daniel 5:18-28.
Faith ahead of loyalty to king, Daniel 6:5-11.
Peter's attempt to walk on water, Matthew 14:22-31.
Reward of standing firm, Luke 21:19.
Fear of authority, John 19:38.
Courageously preaching Christ, Acts 3:12-26.
Endeavoring to silence Peter and John, Acts 4:16-20.
Ministry under persecution, Acts 5:37-42; 8:1. (Note v. 4 as to activity of those who fled from Jerusalem.)
Going with confidence into difficult places, Acts 20:22-24.
Paul, arrested by soldiers, asked for opportunity to witness, Acts 21:37–22:21.
Admitting lack of courage, 2 Corinthians 10:1-2.
Paul prayed not to be ashamed, Philippians

1:20.
Standing firm whatever circumstances,
Philippians 1:27-30.
Facing opposition with boldness,
1 Thessalonians 2:1-2.
Not spirit of timidity but power and love,
2 Timothy 1:7.
Those not embarrassed because of Paul's
chains, 2 Timothy 1:16-18.
Faithful to point of death, Revelation 2:13.
Holding on to faith, Revelation 2:25.
See *Boldness, Hero, Martyr.*

COURT
Moses seated as judge, Exodus 18:13-
24.
Fairness in trials, Deuteronomy 1:15-17.
Securing verdict, Deuteronomy 17:9.
Venue, Deuteronomy 21:19; 25:7; Judges
4:5.
Circuit court, 1 Samuel 7:15-16.
Bringing theological dispute into secular
courtroom, Acts 18:12-17.
See *Justice, Lawyer, Verdict.*

COURTESY
A man's sister in strange country, Genesis
12:10-13.
Returning neighbor's lost property,
Deuteronomy 22:1-3.
Special courtesy to a stranger, Ruth 2:14-
18.
Gentleness of Boaz to Ruth, Ruth 3:7-15.
Wasted compliments, Proverbs 23:8.
Only 1 of 10 returned to thank Jesus, Luke
17:11-19.
Being tactful in conversation with others,
Colossians 4:6.
Show respect to everyone, 1 Peter 2:17.
See *Human relations.*

COURTSHIP
Arranged marriages, Genesis 21:21; 24:1-
67.
Seven-year wait, Genesis 29:18-20.
Samson and Philistine woman, Judges
14:1-7.
Kidnapped brides, Judges 21:23.
Women's initiative, Ruth 3:1-18.
Bargaining hearts, 1 Samuel 18:17.
Stealing heart, Song of Songs 4:9.
Males easily find wild donkey, Jeremiah
2:24.
See *Marriage, Romance.*

COVENANT
Everlasting covenant, Genesis 8:20-22.
God's promise to Abram, Genesis 13:14-
17; 15:1-25. (Note: Some see "dust of
the earth" as Jewish or earthly family
and "the stars" as future church or
heavenly family.)
Keeping covenant between people, Joshua
9:16-21.
Divine covenant with believers, Psalm
145:13, 18.
Freedom for slaves, Jeremiah 34:8-21.
Neither good nor evil transmitted from
father to son, Ezekiel 18:3-20.

COVET
Tenth commandment, Exodus 20:17.
Servant's greed, 2 Kings 5:20-27.
Evil heart's desire, Psalm 10:3; Proverbs
1:19.
Personal relationship with believers, Psalm
25:14.
Coveting good fortune of wicked, Psalm
73:2-5.
Longings of wicked, Psalm 112:10.
Antidote for covetousness, Psalm 119:36.
Covetousness compared to stewardship,
Proverbs 21:25-26.
Envying sinners, Proverbs 23:17; 24:19-20.
Never satisfied, Ecclesiastes 5:10-11.
Greedy dogs, Isaiah 56:11.
All greedy for gain, Jeremiah 6:13.
See *Greed, Self-interest, Selfishness.*

COWARD
Joseph's cowardly brothers, Genesis
42:21-28.
Frightened by falling leaf, Leviticus 26:36.
Feeling small like grasshoppers, Numbers
13:33.
Infectious cowardice, Deuteronomy 20:8.
Melting because of fear, Joshua 2:24.
Thousand flee from one enemy, Joshua
23:10; Isaiah 30:17.
Dubious loyalty, 1 Chronicles 12:19.
Turning away from battle, Psalm 78:9.
Fleeing from nothing, Proverbs 28:1.
Fear of man, Proverbs 29:25; Galatians
2:12.
Leaders captured without fight, Isaiah 22:3.
Plight of Egypt, Jeremiah 46:17-24.
Brave warriors flee naked, Amos 2:16.
Pharisees feared crowd, Matthew 21:45-46.
Peter's denial of his Lord, and frightened

disciples, Matthew 26:31-35, 69-75.
Coming to Jesus at night, John 3:2.
Those who dare not witness, John 7:12-13;
12:42-43.
Pharisees unable to face rebuke, John 8:1-
11.
Cowardly Christians, 2 Timothy 4:16.
See *Fear.*

CRAFTSMAN
God saw that His work was good, Genesis
1:10, 12, 18, 25.
Display of good talent, Psalm 45:1.
Skilled at his work, Proverbs 22:29.
Skillful detail and technique, Isaiah 44:12-
13.
Men have talent but God is sovereign,
Jeremiah 10:8-10.
Ashamed of idols he made, Jeremiah
10:14-15.
Potter and wheel, Jeremiah 18:1-12.
See *Ability, Skill, Talent.*

CRAFTY
Satan as cunning serpent, Genesis 3:1.
Mother's camouflage, Genesis 27:11-16.
Deception at Gilgal, Joshua 9:3-6.
Crafty tongue, Job 15:5.
King Herod and the magi, Matthew 2:7-8,
13.
Plot against Jesus, Matthew 26:4; Mark
14:1.
Jesus equal to the crafty Pharisees, Luke
20:41-47.
Deception in theology, Ephesians 4:14.
See *Deceit, Deception.*

CRAVING
Continual lust for more, Ephesians 4:19.

CREATION
Job's concept of space/time, Job 26:7-14.
Greatness of heavens attest to smallness of
man, Psalm 8:3-4.
Sky proclaims glory of God, Psalm 19:1-6
(Note how role of the sky has similarity
in function of Scripture, vv. 7-11.)
By the word of the Lord, Psalm 33:6.
Creation illustrates love of God, Psalm
36:5-6.
Ancient skies, Psalm 68:32-33.
Fearfully and wonderfully made, Psalm
139:14.
The Lord calls each star by name, Psalm

147:4.
Nature and people praise the Lord, Psalm
148:1-14.
Earth and sky show wisdom of God,
Proverbs 3:19-20; 8:24-31; Jeremiah
10:12.
Heavens and the hand of God, Isaiah 40:12.
God's purpose in creating earth, Isaiah
45:18.
New heaven and new earth, Isaiah 65:17.
God who made and sustains universe,
Jeremiah 51:15-16.
Christ as Creator, John 1:1-4, 10;
Colossians 1:15-17.
Creator continuing at work, John 5:17.
Ultimate purpose of Creation and human
life, Romans 8:18-23.
Men and animals of different flesh,
1 Corinthians 15:39.
Creator and Sustainer of all things,
Hebrews 1:3, 10-12.
Universe formed at God's command,
Hebrews 11:3.

CREATIVITY
Working with all the heart, Nehemiah 4:6.
Display of good talent, Psalm 45:1.
Producing and enjoying, Psalm 49:3-4.
Skilled in one's work, Proverbs 22:29.
Artist is mortal, Isaiah 44:11.
Ashamed of idols he had made, Jeremiah
10:14-15.
See *Ability, Skill.*

CREATOR
Power and authority of Creator, Job 9:1-10.
Creation proclaims God's righteousness,
Psalm 50:6.
Ruler over all nature, Psalm 89:8-13.
Eternal God predates His Creation, Psalm
90:1-2.
Difference between Creator and idols,
Psalm 96:5.
All nature praises Creator, Psalm 96:11-12.
Eternal God and temporal creation, Psalm
102:25-27.
Poem to God of nature, Psalm 104:1-26.
Each star known by name, Psalm 147:4.
Wisdom and greatness of Creator, Isaiah
40:12-28.
God who created and cares for His
creation, Isaiah 42:5-7.
God's purpose in creating earth, Isaiah
45:18.

Earth and sky reflect wisdom of God, Jeremiah 10:12.
God who is everywhere, Jeremiah 23:23-24.
Christ as Creator, John 1:1-4, 10; Colossians 1:15-17; Hebrews 1:3, 10-12.
Author of life itself, Acts 3:15.
One who fills universe, Ephesians 4:10.
Jesus Christ Himself, the Word of life, 1 John 1:1-4. (See John 1:1-3.)
Unique name for Jesus, Revelation 3:14.

CREDENTIALS
Jesus had no need for human credentials, John 5:31-40.
Credentials to visiting instructors, Acts 15:22-31.
Qualifications of Christ as Saviour and King, Colossians 1:15-20.
Paul's credentials in ministry, Titus 1:1-3.
Credentials of an elder, Titus 1:5-9.
See *Documentation.*

CREDIBILITY
Moses afraid he would not be believed, Exodus 4:1.
Seeing is believing, 1 Kings 10:6-9.
Some good in Judah, 2 Chronicles 12:12.
Certainty of God's plans and purposes, Isaiah 14:24.
The Lord's message revealed, Isaiah 53:1.
Despising those who tell truth, Amos 5:10.
Believe the Good News, Mark 1:14-15.
Preaching with authority, Luke 4:32.
Initial mistrust of Paul by other disciples, Acts 9:26.
Faith gives credibility to what is heard, Hebrews 4:2.
No lie comes from truth, 1 John 2:20-21.
Testimony of man and testimony of God, 1 John 5:9.
See *Dependability, Honesty, Integrity, Reputation.*

CREDIT
Loans to poor, Exodus 22:25-27.
Credit encouraged, Deuteronomy 15:8; Matthew 5:42.
No interest charge to countryman, Deuteronomy 23:19-20.
Security for loan or debt, Deuteronomy 24:6; Job 24:3.
Demands of cruel creditor, 2 Kings 4:1.
Lender rules over borrower, Proverbs 22:7.

Charging high interest, Proverbs 28:8.
Shrewd settlement, Luke 16:1-8.
Obligation to pay debts, Romans 13:8.
See *Borrowing, Finances, Foreclosure, Mortgage.*

CREED
Pagans certain of erroneous belief, Acts 19:35-36.
Futility of no resurrection message, 1 Corinthians 15:13-19.
Paul's concise thesis concerning Gospel, 1 Timothy 4:9-10.
See *Doctrine.*

CREMATION
Drama of Abraham and Isaac, Genesis 22:2.
Form of judgment, Leviticus 20:14; 21:9.
Sudden and massive cremation, Numbers 16:35.
Penalty for sacrilege, Joshua 7:15.
Stoned to death, then burned, Joshua 7:25.
Fiery death of daughter, Judges 11:30-40.
Saul and his sons, 1 Samuel 31:11-13.
Burning of human skeletons, 1 Kings 13:1-2.
Bones exhumed and burned, 2 Kings 23:16; 2 Chronicles 34:5.
Burned bones of a king, Amos 2:1.
Duty of relative, Amos 6:9-10.
Surrendered to flames, 1 Corinthians 13:3.

CRIMINAL
Habitual criminal, Ecclesiastes 8:12.
Pardon for bloodguilt of nation, Joel 3:21.
Cheating and polluting, Amos 8:5-6.

CRISIS
Bad advice, Job 2:9-10.
Sure refuge, Psalm 46:1-11.
Go to neighbor for help, Proverbs 27:10.
Silver and gold of no value when judgment falls, Zephaniah 1:18.
See *Calamity, Trauma.*

CRITICISM
Criticizing those whom the Lord has not denounced, Numbers 23:8.
Willingness to accept truth of wrongdoing, Job 6:24.
Job accused of not speaking sensibly, Job 18:2.
Zophar upset by criticism, Job 20:2-3.

Job's thick skin, Job 34:7.
Only God knows, Psalm 3:1-2.
Criticizing family members, Psalm 50:20.
Touching God's anointed ones, Psalm 105:15.
Accepting criticism peacefully, Psalm 119:165 (KJV).
Tongues of serpents, Psalm 140:3.
Rebuke of righteous man, Psalm 141:5.
Willingness to be disciplined and corrected, Proverbs 10:17.
Learning to keep silent when others err, Proverbs 11:12.
Healing tongue and deceitful tongue, Proverbs 15:4.
Faithful wounds of friend, Proverbs 27:6.
Valued counsel of friend, Proverbs 27:9.
Rebuke better than flattery, Proverbs 28:23.
Secret words of disdain, Ecclesiastes 7:21-22.
Waiting for friend to fail, Jeremiah 20:10.
Those who dislike strong preaching, Amos 7:16.
Satan's role as accuser, Zechariah 3:1-2.
Judging and criticizing others, Matthew 7:1-5.
Jesus criticized for fellowship with sinners, Matthew 9:10-12; Luke 5:27-31.
Slander spoken against Jesus, Matthew 11:18-19.
Jesus criticized for picking grain on Sabbath, Matthew 12:1-8.
Jesus criticized for casting out demons, Matthew 12:22-32.
Response of Jesus to critics, Matthew 21:23-27; Mark 14:53-62.
Jesus criticized on the cross, Matthew 27:39-44.
Jesus criticized for healing paralytic man, Mark 2:6-12.
Looking for something to criticize, Mark 3:1-6.
Members of Jesus' own family thought Him out of His mind, Mark 3:20-21. (Note v. 31.)
Ability of Jesus to confound critics, Mark 11:29-33.
Trying to catch Jesus in His own words, Mark 12:13-17.
Rejoice when criticized for faith, Luke 6:22-23.
Wrong of criticizing others, Luke 6:37; Romans 2:1.

Speck in brother's eye, plank in your own, Luke 6:41-42.
Folly of unfounded criticism, Luke 8:49-56.
Jesus carefully watched by Pharisees, Luke 14:1.
Judging mere appearances, John 7:24.
Dissension and jealousy in the church, Acts 6:1.
God the only Judge, Romans 8:33.
Proper attitude to those who are weak, Romans 14:1.
Judging others, Romans 14:13.
Help weak rather than criticize, Romans 15:1.
Unimportance of being judged by people, 1 Corinthians 4:3-4.
Criticizing conduct of another Christian, 1 Corinthians 10:27-33.
Judging one's self, 1 Corinthians 11:28-32.
Positive and productive criticism, 2 Corinthians 7:8-13.
Trying to please others, Galatians 1:10.
Fathers should not exasperate children, Ephesians 6:4.
Paul's attitude toward those who opposed him, Philippians 1:15-18.
Judged by food and drink, Colossians 2:16.
Conversation full of grace, Colossians 4:6.
Accusations must have two or three witnesses, 1 Timothy 5:19.
Living above criticism, Titus 2:8.
Remember one's own past before criticizing others, Titus 3:1-3.
Slander no one, James 4:11-12.
Do not grumble against each other, James 5:9.
Judgment begins with family of God, 1 Peter 4:17.
Commendation before reproof, Revelation 2:2-6, 13-16, 19-20.
See *Slander.*

CROCODILE
"Leviathan" believed by some to be the crocodile, Job 41:1-16.

CROSS
Redeemer and King, Isaiah 63:1.
Prophecy of Judas and 30 pieces of silver, Zechariah 11:12-13.
Disciples could not understand, Mark 9:30-32; Luke 9:44-45.
Jesus foretold death and Resurrection, Mark 10:32-34.

Parable of Vineyard, Mark 12:1-12.
Weight of sin, not pain of the cross, took life of Jesus, Mark 15:33-37, 44.
Jesus could not die before His time had come, Luke 4:28-30.
Jesus willingly lay down His life, John 10:17-18.
Prior to His own death, Jesus visited the one whom He had raised from the dead, John 12:1-10. (See 11:1-44.)
Jews had no right to crucify, John 18:28-32.
God's perfect timing in Christ, Romans 5:6.
Setting free from power of sin, Romans 8:1-4.
Jesus took penalty for all, Hebrews 2:9.
First covenant put into effect with blood, Hebrews 9:18-22.
Willingness to suffer with Christ, Hebrews 13:11-14.
John's vision of resurrected Christ, Revelation 1:17-18.
See *Atonement, Crucifixion, Redemption.*

CROSS-CULTURAL
Earth divided, people scattered, Genesis 10:5; 11:1-9.
Abraham, Lot, Sodom and Gomorrah, Genesis 18:20-33; 19:1-29.
Clash of moral viewpoints, Genesis 39:1-23.
Joseph's relevance to Pharaoh, Genesis 41:1-40.
Solomon and Queen of Sheba, 1 Kings 10:1-13.
Appeal of divine truth to all cultures, Isaiah 55:5; Micah 4:3-4; Romans 10:12-13.
Value of heathen culture, Jeremiah 10:1-5.
Supreme example of cross-cultural communication, John 4:4-26.
Philip and the Ethiopian eunuch, Acts 8:26-40.
Peter's lesson in cultural prejudice, Acts 10:9-23; 11:1-14.
Paul and the Athenians, Acts 17:16-27.
Cultural dissipation of revealed truth, Romans 1:21-32.
See *Alien, Contextualization, Prejudice, Racism, Xenophobia.*

CROWD
No place to hide, Leviticus 26:25.
God can single out individual, Deuteronomy 29:21.
A vast assembly, 1 Kings 8:65.

Jesus forced into boat, Matthew 13:1-2; Mark 4:1.
Triumphal Entry of Jesus into Jerusalem, Mark 11:1-10.
Potential mob violence during Passover, Mark 14:1-2.
Crowd stirred up against Jesus, Mark 15:11-15. (See 11:8-10.)
Crucifixion of Jesus, Mark 15:21-32.
Entry through roof, Luke 5:17-26.
Thronging thousands, Luke 12:1.
Enemies of Jesus wanted to avoid public opinion, Luke 22:3-6.
Curious to see miracles performed, John 6:1-2, 26-27.
Entire city in uproar, Acts 19:23-41.
City aroused by troublemakers, Acts 21:30.
See *Audience, Mob psychology.*

CROWNS
Priestly headpiece, Leviticus 8:9.
Crowns of vanquished kings, 2 Samuel 1:5-10; 12:29-31.
Crown and covenant, 2 Kings 11:12.
Crowned with glory and honor, Psalm 8:5.
Crowned with love and compassion, Psalm 103:3-4.
Crown of thorns, Matthew 27:29; Mark 15:17; John 19:5.
Believer's crown, 1 Corinthians 9:25; 2 Timothy 4:8; Revelation 3:11.
Crown of life, James 1:12; Revelation 2:10.
Crown of glory, 1 Peter 5:4.
Crowns laid before the Lord, Revelation 4:10.
See *Reward.*

CRUCIFIXION
Prophecy of cross, Psalm 22:1-8, 18.
Dying Saviour, Isaiah 53:1-12.
Seven sayings on the cross, Matthew 27:46; Luke 23:34, 43, 46; John 19:26-28, 30.
Jesus could not die before His time had come, Luke 4:28-30.
Prior to His own death, Jesus visited the one whom He had raised from the dead, John 12:1-10. (See 11:1-44.)
Jews had no right to crucify, John 18:28-32.
John's vision of resurrected Christ, Revelation 1:17-18.
See *Atonement, Cross, Redemption.*

CRUELTY
Brotherly brutality, Genesis 37:19-24.

Destruction of male infants, Exodus 1:22.
Mistreatment of animals, Numbers 22:27-28; 2 Samuel 8:4; 1 Chronicles 18:4; Proverbs 12:10.
Body mutilation, Judges 1:6; 1 Samuel 11:2; 2 Kings 25:7.
People burned to death, Judges 9:49.
Ignominy to a prophet, Jeremiah 38:6.
Into fiery furnace, Daniel 3:12-27.
Mental cruelty, Matthew 5:11; Acts 9:16.
Killing prisoners to prevent escape, Acts 27:42-43.
Bodily harm, Romans 8:17; 2 Corinthians 4:11; 1 Peter 2:20.
See *Brutality, Persecution, Sadistic.*

CULT
Wayward community, Deuteronomy 13:12-18.
Detecting words of false prophet, Deuteronomy 18:21-22.
Wrong interpretation of Scripture, Jeremiah 8:8.
Proclaiming dreams instead of word of God, Jeremiah 23:25-32.
Prophecy of imagination, Ezekiel 13:1-23.
Hindering others from entering kingdom of heaven, Matthew 23:13-15.
Many will come claiming to be Christ, Matthew 24:4-5, 11, 24; Mark 13:22-23.
Those who fast while others do not, Mark 2:18-20.
Only one gate to sheep pen, John 10:1-21.
Pagans certain of erroneous belief, Acts 19:35-36.
Futility of no resurrection message, 1 Corinthians 15:13-19.
Paul astonished at Galatians, Galatians 1:6-9.
False disciples dilute Gospel, Galatians 2:4-5.
Bewitched Galatians, Galatians 3:1.
Those who would alienate from truth, Galatians 4:17.
Danger of deceptive philosophy, Colossians 2:8.
Teachings which cause controversy, 1 Timothy 1:3-4.
Theology of demons, 1 Timothy 4:1-4.
Those who take pride in false doctrine, 1 Timothy 6:3-5.
Godless chatter and opposing ideas falsely called knowledge, 1 Timothy 6:20-21.
Wandering from truth, 2 Timothy 2:17-18.

Those who deceive others are themselves deceived, 2 Timothy 3:13.
Those who do not want sound doctrine, 2 Timothy 4:3-4.
Ministering for dishonest gain, Titus 1:10-16.
Careful of strange teachings, Hebrews 13:9.
Cleverly invented stories, 2 Peter 1:16.
False teachers and destructive heresies, 2 Peter 2:1-3.
Falling away from truth, 2 Peter 3:17.
Walking in darkness, 1 John 1:5-7.
Leading believers astray, 1 John 2:26.
Counterfeit anointing, 1 John 2:27.
Test of spirits of false prophets, 1 John 4:1.
Deceivers in the world, 2 John 7-11.
Do not welcome those of another teaching into house, 2 John 10-11.
Need to warn against false teaching and wrong conduct, Jude 3-4.
Discerning those who are false, Revelation 2:2.
Finality of Scripture record, Revelation 22:18-19.
See *Error, Heresy, Syncretism.*

CULTURE
Influence of nation on nation, Jeremiah 10:2.
Language and literature of Babylon, Daniel 1:3-4.
Noble character of Bereans, Acts 17:11.
Paul's sense of responsibility for ministry to all cultures, Romans 1:14-17.
Wisdom and foolishness, 1 Corinthians 1:18-21.
Adapting to culture, 1 Corinthians 9:19-23.
See *Cross-cultural.*

CURIOSITY
Plight of Lot's wife, Genesis 19:17, 26.
Massive death for looking into ark, 1 Samuel 6:19.
Eye and ear never satisfied, Ecclesiastes 1:8.
Curiosity by roadside, Jeremiah 48:19.
Those who pass by, Lamentations 1:12.
Waiting to see spectacle of judgment, Jonah 4:5.
Large crowds followed Jesus to witness miracles, Matthew 4:23-25; 8:1, 18; 19:2; Luke 14:25; John 6:1-2, 26-27.
Things people go to see, Luke 7:24-26.

Curiosity that led to blessing, Luke 18:35-43.

People who must see signs and wonders to believe, John 4:48.

Those wanting to see Lazarus and Jesus, John 12:9-11, 18.

Mind your own business, John 21:21-22.

Staring at those God uses, Acts 3:12.

Listening to latest ideas, Acts 17:21.

Following crowd in confusion, Acts 19:32.

Curiosity of angels, 1 Peter 1:12.

Suffering as meddler, 1 Peter 4:15.

CURRENCY

Gold as legal tender, Genesis 13:2; 1 Chronicles 21:25.

First use of money, Genesis 17:12-13, 23, 27.

Silver as legal tender, Genesis 20:16.

Services to be paid for in cash, Deuteronomy 2:6.

Silver not precious metal, 1 Kings 10:21, 27.

Purchasing field with silver, Jeremiah 32:25.

Value and designation of currency, Ezekiel 45:12.

Time of economic collapse, Zephaniah 1:11.

Small coin, Matthew 12:41-43; Luke 21:1-2.

Coin from fish's mouth, Matthew 17:27.

Legal currency, Mark 12:16; Luke 20:24.

See *Finances, Money.*

CURSE

Penalty for disobedience, Deuteronomy 28:15-68.

God instructed exiles in Babylon to use curse, Jeremiah 29:21-23.

See *Imprecation, Judgment.*

CUSTOM

See *Culture, Tradition.*

CYNICAL

Calamity hungered for Job, Job 18:12.

Youth chides wisdom of age, Job 32:6-9.

Likenesses of a fool, Proverbs 26:1-11.

Common destiny, Ecclesiastes 9:1-2.

Cynical tongues made silent, Luke 20:20-26.

See *Sarcasm.*

D

DAIRY
Curds and milk, Genesis 18:8; Deuteronomy 32:14.
Herd of cows, Genesis 32:15.
Animal plague, Exodus 9:2-3.
Large herds, Numbers 32:1.
Plentiful pasture needed, Joshua 14:3-4.
Milk as beverage, Judges 4:19.
Inexperienced cows, 1 Samuel 6:7.
Dairy product in desert, 2 Samuel 17:29.
Milk to butter, Proverbs 30:33.
Cow and goats, Isaiah 7:21-22.
Beautiful heifer and gadfly, Jeremiah 46:20.
See *Cheese, Milk.*

DAM
Miraculous stopping of river's flow, Joshua 3:15-16.

DANCING
Marching with lilting steps, Exodus 15:19-21.
Forbidden and permitted, Exodus 32:19; Psalm 30:11. (See 1 Sam. 18:6-7 and Matt. 14:6-12.)
Dancing as a dirge of death, Judges 11:30-39.
Leaping and dancing despised, 2 Samuel 6:14-16.
Dance of praise, Psalms 149:3; 150:4.
Appropriate dancing, Ecclesiastes 3:4.
Music but no dancing, Matthew 11:17.

DANGER
Holding hands in time of danger, Genesis 19:16.
Jacob reassured by God to enter Egypt, Genesis 46:1-4.
People who risked their lives, Judges 5:18.
Companions in danger, 1 Samuel 22:23.
Seemingly careless ways of ostrich, Job 39:13-17.
Wicked bend their bows, Psalm 11:2.
Danger of fearing wrong things, Isaiah 8:12-14.
Thousand flee from one enemy, Isaiah 30:17.
Fear of walking in public places, Jeremiah 6:25.
Snorting of enemy horses, Jeremiah 8:16.
Good news and bad news, Jeremiah 34:1-7.
Only loud noise, Jeremiah 46:17.
Responsibility of watchman, Ezekiel 33:1-9.
Safety in midst of peril, Ezekiel 34:25.
Neighbor turned against neighbor, Zechariah 8:10.
Jesus could not be harmed until His time had come, John 7:30.
Avoiding unnecessary danger, John 11:53-54.
Ministry of angel in time of danger, Acts 27:21-25.
Seeing light but walking in darkness, 2 Peter 2:21.
See *Peril, Persecution.*

DAREDEVIL
Careless about danger, Proverbs 22:3.

DARING
Daring Daniel, Daniel 6:10.

DARKNESS
Total darkness, Genesis 1:2-4.
Not traveling after sunset, Genesis 28:11.
The Lord our lamp, 2 Samuel 22:29.
No God, no priest, no Law in Israel, 2 Chronicles 15:3.
Time of day for evil, Job 24:14-17.

One who lights deepest darkness, Isaiah
9:2.
Darkness as light, Isaiah 42:16.
Light in darkness, Isaiah 50:10.
Evil under cover of darkness, Ezekiel 8:12.
Eternal darkness, Matthew 8:12.
Fear in the night, Luke 2:8-14.
Light and darkness in conflict, John 1:5;
Romans 13:12-13.
Nicodemus came to Jesus at night, John
3:2; 19:39.
Judas went out into night, John 13:27-30.
Spiritual darkness, Acts 13:8-11.
Safety of darkness, Acts 17:10.
From darkness to light, Acts 26:18.
Navigation at sea, Acts 27:27-29.
No hiding place, 1 Corinthians 4:5.
See *Night.*

DATA
See *Statistics.*

DATE
Recognizing specific date, Ezekiel 1:1.
Date to remember, Haggai 2:18.
Unknown date in future, Matthew 24:36;
25:13; Mark 13:32.
See *Calendar.*

DAUGHTER
Daughter's rights protected, Exodus 21:7-
10.
Daughter and mother involved in
marriage, Leviticus 20:14.
Father's authority over daughter, Numbers
30:3-5.
Given in marriage, Judges 1:12-13;
1 Samuel 17:25; 18:20-21.
Father's attitude toward affections of
daughters, Judges 15:1-2.

DAUGHTER-IN-LAW
Parents unhappy with daughters-in-law,
Genesis 26:34-35.
Ruth's love for mother-in-law, Ruth 1:8-
18.
Daughter-in-law worth seven sons, Ruth
4:13-15.

DAY
Working from morning to night, Nehemiah
4:21.
Dark days, Ecclesiastes 11:8.
Recognizing specific date, Ezekiel 1:1.

DAYDREAMING
Hard work and fantasy, Proverbs 28:19.

DEAFNESS
Consideration toward deaf people,
Leviticus 19:14.
Hearing impaired by age, 2 Samuel 19:35;
Ecclesiastes 12:4.
Dull ears, Isaiah 6:10.
Healing the blind, deaf, and dumb, Isaiah
35:5-6.
Those who refuse to hear the Word of the
Lord, Jeremiah 6:10.
Ears that refuse to hear, Ezekiel 12:2;
Zechariah 7:11; 2 Timothy 4:4.
Speaking with signing, Luke 1:62.
Seeing and hearing but not understanding,
Luke 10:24.
See *Hearing, Perception.*

DEATH
Place of burial for Abraham's wife, Genesis
23:1-20. (See 25:8-10.)
Desire for death, Exodus 16:2-3.
Joshua's blessing and warning as death
approached, Joshua 23:14-16.
Facing death, Judges 16:28.
Father and son together in death,
2 Samuel 1:23.
Dead cannot return, 2 Samuel 12:22-23.
Respect for dead bodies, 2 Samuel 21:13-
14.
Last words of David, 2 Samuel 23:1-7.
David's charge to Solomon, 1 Kings 2:1-
12.
Job's view of life after death, Job 14:7-14.
Finality of life's pursuits, Psalm 6:5.
End of life comes quickly, Psalm 39:4-6.
All wealth left behind at death, Psalm
49:16-20.
God becomes Father to fatherless, Psalm
68:5.
Strength broken and days shortened,
Psalm 102:23.
Righteous man remembered, Psalm 112:6.
Beauty and meaning of believer's death,
Psalm 116:15.
Death ends influence of secular leadership,
Psalm 146:3-4.
End of all for wicked man, Proverbs 11:7.
Born naked and leave naked, Ecclesiastes
5:15.
Death better than birth, Ecclesiastes, 7:1-2.
No power over day of death, Ecclesiastes

8:8.
Grave cannot praise God, Isaiah 38:18.
Ignominy to dead, Jeremiah 8:1-2.
Numerous widows, Jeremiah 15:8.
Mourning forbidden in time of judgment, Jeremiah 16:5-7.
Burial in ignominy, Jeremiah 22:19.
Promise of peaceful and honorable death, Jeremiah 34:4-5.
Inequity in life and death, Ezekiel 13:19.
Death never satisfied, Habakkuk 2:5.
Physical and spiritual death, Matthew 8:21-22.
Earthly relationships not same in heaven, Matthew 22:23-30.
Power of Creator over death, Mark 5:38-42.
Sin, not cross, took the life of Jesus, Mark 15:37, 44; John 19:28-30, 33.
Jesus could not die before His time had come, Luke 4:28-30; John 19:11.
True immortality, John 8:51.
Like beautiful sleep, John 11:11-15.
Prior to His own death, Jesus visited one He had raised from the dead, John 12:1-10. (See 11:1-44.)
Death of David, death of Christ, and messianic implications, Acts 2:29-35.
Beauty of martyr's death, Acts 7:54-56.
Enemy to be destroyed, 1 Corinthians 15:26.
That which is earthly and that which is eternal, 2 Corinthians 5:1.
Death is gain to those who live for Christ, Philippians 1:21.
Paul looked forward to finishing race victoriously, 2 Timothy 4:6-8.
Probate of a will, Hebrews 9:16-17.
Rich man passes away like wildflower, James 1:10-11.
Flowers and grass wither, 1 Peter 1:24-25.
Human body but a tent, 2 Peter 1:13.
Those who wish to die but cannot, Revelation 9:4-6.
Death in the Lord, Revelation 14:13.
Blood of a dead man, Revelation 16:3.
See *Mortality*.

DEBASE
World against God, Psalm 2:1-3.
Silver to dross, wine to water, Isaiah 1:22.
Defiled with blood, Lamentations 4:14.
See *Corruption, Defile, Demean*.

DEBATE
Wise put to shame, Jeremiah 8:9.
Debate concerning rank in kingdom, Luke 9:46-48.
Concise, brief debate, Luke 20:1-8.
Debate between Jesus and teachers of darkness, John 8:13-59.
Paul debated Jewish leaders, Acts 18:27-28.
See *Argument, Disagreement, Dispute*.

DEBAUCHERY
Cities given to debauchery, Genesis 18:16-33.
World against God, Psalm 2:1-3.
Corrupt from birth, Psalm 58:3.
Silver to dross, wine to water, Isaiah 1:22.
Ravages of wickedness, Isaiah 9:18.
Sick drunk, Isaiah 28:7.
Choice vine becomes corrupt, Jeremiah 2:21.
Running after foreign gods, Jeremiah 2:25.
From one sin to another, Jeremiah 9:3.
Utter depravity of two adulterous sisters, Ezekiel 23:1-49.
Sow the wind, Hosea 8:7.
Conditions prior to return of Christ, Matthew 24:37-38.
Continual lust for more, Ephesians 4:19.
Sin in broad daylight, 2 Peter 2:13-22.
See *Carnality, Immorality, Lust, Promiscuity*.

DEBILITY
Fear and discouragement debilitate good leadership, Joshua 1:9.
Melting because of fear, Joshua 2:24.
See *Fear, Weakness*.

DEBT
Abram refused to be obligated to the king of Sodom, Genesis 14:22-24.
Creditors seize all, Psalm 109:11.
Pay what you owe, Romans 13:7-8.
Debt owed by slave, Philemon 18-19.
See *Credit, Finances, Mortgage*.

DECADENT
Prone to idolatry, Exodus 32:19-26.
Destiny set for rebellious people, Numbers 14:35.
Defiant sin, Numbers 15:30-31.
Blatant display of immorality, Numbers 25:6-9.

Lack of discernment, Deuteronomy 32:28.
Homosexual activity, Judges 19:22.
Immoral use of place of worship, 1 Samuel
2:22-25.
Work of the Lord in decline, 1 Samuel 3:1.
Resorting to cannibalism, 2 Kings 6:24-29.
King who desecrated temple of the Lord,
2 Chronicles 26:16-21.
Renegade pleads for his own life, Esther
7:7.
Lamp of the wicked, Job 18:5-6.
Boasting of evil, Psalm 52:1-4.
All have turned away, Psalm 53:3.
Corrupt from birth, Psalm 58:3.
Like idol, like follower, Psalm 135:15-18.
Way of deep darkness, Proverbs 4:19.
Playing with fire, Proverbs 6:27-28.
Drunken folly, Proverbs 23:35.
Once-faithful city, Isaiah 1:21-23.
Haughty women, Isaiah 3:16.
Vileness from every mouth, Isaiah 9:17.
Powerless, cumbersome idols, Isaiah 46:1-
2.
Sin separates man from God, Isaiah 59:1-2.
End result of evil, Isaiah 59:7-8.
Skilled in art of seduction, Jeremiah 2:33.
Utterly defiled, Jeremiah 3:1-3.
Deliberately writing falsehoods concerning
Law of the Lord, Jeremiah 8:8.
Forgetting how to blush, Jeremiah 8:12.
Deceitful heart, Jeremiah 17:9.
Lifetime of evil, Jeremiah 32:30.
Pagan beyond redemption, Jeremiah 51:9.
Prophets who see nothing, Ezekiel 13:1-3.
Hindered from worship by evil heart,
Hosea 5:4.
Those who plan iniquity, Micah 2:1.
Drunk with blood of saints, Revelation
17:6.
See *Carnality, Hedonism.*

DECAY
Foul odor of disobedience, Exodus 16:19-
20. (See also vv. 22-24.)
Worms in dead bodies, Isaiah 66:24.
Old Testament object lesson, Jeremiah
13:1-11.

DECEIT
Abraham's deceitfulness concerning
Sarah, Genesis 20:1-18.
Isaac misled by Jacob in search of Esau's
birthright, Genesis 27:1-46.
Jacob deceived concerning Rachel,
Genesis 29:14-30.
Jealousy of younger brother, Genesis 37:1-
36.
Wayward community, Deuteronomy
13:12-18.
Rahab lied to protect two spies, Joshua 2:1-
6.
Wiles of Samson's wife in solving riddle,
Judges 14:11-19.
David's plot against Uriah, 2 Samuel
11:14-17.
Amnon and Tamar, 2 Samuel 13:1-14.
Kiss of death, 2 Samuel 20:9-10.
Adonijah's ill-fated request for a wife,
1 Kings 2:13-25.
Motives different from speech, Psalm
55:21; Proverbs 26:24-26.
No place for deceit in God's house, Psalm
101:7.
Sweetness of stolen things, Proverbs 9:17.
Pretending to be what one is not, Proverbs
12:9.
Hurt of being deceitful, Proverbs 26:28.
Truth nowhere to be found, Isaiah 59:15.
Those who cling to deceit, Jeremiah 8:5.
Speaking cordially with deceitful heart,
Jeremiah 9:8.
Those who speak well of you but betray
you, Jeremiah 12:6.
Slaves set free, then enslaved again,
Jeremiah 34:8-22.
Two kings lie to each other, Daniel 11:27.
Despising those who tell truth, Amos 5:10.
Dishonest scales and false weights, Micah
6:11.
Herod and the magi, Matthew 2:7-8, 13.
False affection of Judas, Matthew 26:47-48;
Mark 14:10-11, 43-46.
Pharisees suspected deceitful Resurrection
claim, Matthew 27:62-66. (See 28:11-
15.)
Pretending to be honest, Luke 20:20.
Ananias and Sapphira, Acts 5:1-11.
Deceitful plan to destroy Paul, Acts 23:12-
22.
Those who deceive others are themselves
deceived, 2 Timothy 3:13.
Preaching and teaching for dishonest gain,
Titus 1:10-16.
Gaining benefit by taking advantage of
others, James 5:4-5.
Cleverly invented stories, 2 Peter 1:16.
False teachers and destructive heresies,
2 Peter 2:1-3.

Those who follow their own desires, Jude
17-18.
Feigning life when spiritually dead,
Revelation 3:1.
See *Devious, Folly, Lie.*

DECEPTION
Listening to Satan's reasoning, Genesis
3:1-5.
Introducing wife as sister, Genesis 12:10-
20; 20:2; 26:7.
Brother impersonating brother, Genesis
27:6-23.
Rachel's hiding of father's gods, Genesis
31:31-35.
Circumcision for Shechem, Genesis 34:13-
31.
Joseph's deception of brothers, Genesis
42–44.
Murderous deceit, Judges 3:12-21.
Delilah and Samson, Judges 16:4-20.
David's pretense of madness, 1 Samuel
21:10-15.
Incest by deception, 2 Samuel 13:1-14.
Sanballat's effort to deceive Nehemiah,
Nehemiah 6:1-14.
Hurt of being deceptive, Proverbs 26:28.
Friends and brothers not to be trusted,
Jeremiah 9:4-8.
Believing a lie, Jeremiah 43:1-7.
Despising those who tell truth, Amos 5:10.
Herod's unsuccessful ploy, Matthew 2:7-
12.
Awkward effort of Pharisees, Matthew
22:15-22.
Contemplated deception, Mark 14:1.
Ananias and Sapphira, Acts 5:1-9.
See *Deceit, Lie.*

DECISION
Choice of place to live, Genesis 13:10-13.
Mistreating others because of one's own
decision, Genesis 16:1-6.
Rebekah permitted to make her own
decision, Genesis 24:54-58.
Making your own decision or asking God
for guidance, 1 Samuel 14:36-41.
Two options, 1 Kings 18:19-21.
Choosing to follow way of truth, Psalm
119:30.
An oath to follow Scripture, Psalm 119:106.
Thinking things through, Proverbs 4:25-
27.
Remembering specific date of decision,

Haggai 2:18.
Disciples immediately left occupations to
follow Jesus, Matthew 4:20-22.
Choice of Jesus or Barabbas, Matthew
27:15-26.
Night of prayer before important decision,
Luke 6:12-16.
Prepared in advance for persecution, Luke
21:12-15.
Deciding to turn back from following
Jesus, John 6:66-71.
Reaching out to God, Acts 17:27.
King Agrippa would not be persuaded,
Acts 26:28.
Challenge to hear and act, Hebrews 3:7-
14.
Resist Satan, 1 Peter 5:8-9.
See *Choice, Determination.*

DECODE
Let the earth hear, Isaiah 34:1.
Some thought they heard thunder, others
the voice of an angel, John 12:29.
See *Communication.*

DECREE
Stop work order on temple construction,
Ezra 4:17-23. (See counter decree of
King Darius, 6:1-5. Also the decree
issued by King Artaxerxes, 7:12-26.)
Sanballat's opposition to rebuilding wall,
Nehemiah 6:5-6.
Queen Vashti versus King Xerxes, Esther
1:10-22.
Political pressure against Daniel, Daniel
6:1-28.
Caesar Augustus' call for census-taking,
Luke 2:1-7.
Ecclesiastical decisions, Acts 16:1-5.
See *Announcement.*

DEDICATION
Anointing of objects, Exodus 40:9-10.
Committing all elements of sanctuary to
the Lord, Numbers 7:1.
King Solomon dedicated temple, 1 Kings
8:22-53, 62-66.
Dying daily, 1 Corinthians 15:31.
Filled with knowledge of God's will,
Colossians 1:9-12.
See *Commitment, Consecration.*

DEEDS
Documents of ownership, Jeremiah 32:14.

DEEPER LIFE

In constant communion, Psalm 1:1-3.
The life of full commitment, Psalm 37:4-7.
Undivided heart, Psalm 86:11.
Foundation in depth, Luke 6:46-49.
In-depth comprehension and
    commitment, Ephesians 3:14-21.
Filled with knowledge of God's will,
    Colossians 1:9-12.
See *Commitment, Discipleship.*

DEFAMATION

Stripped of one's honor, Job 19:9.
Misuse of goblets from temple, Daniel 5:1-4.
See *Desecration.*

DEFAULT

Loss of Edenic bliss, Genesis 3:22-24.
Forbidden entry to Promised Land
    because of disobedience, Numbers
    14:21-45; 20:9-12; Deuteronomy 32:48-52.
Rich young man missed eternal wealth,
    Matthew 19:16-22.
Denied rest because of disobedience,
    Hebrews 4:6.

DEFEAT

Journey one should never make again,
    Deuteronomy 28:68.
Death of King Saul on battlefield, 1 Samuel
    31:1-6. (See also 2 Sam. 1:1-12.)
Turning spiritual failure into success,
    1 Kings 8:33-34.
Description of utter defeat, 2 Kings 13:7.
Job looked to future and saw no hope, Job
    17:11.
Those with broken hearts and spirits,
    Psalm 34:18.
Scattered bones of enemy, Psalm 53:5.
Food for jackals, Psalm 63:10.
Leaders captured without fight, Isaiah 22:3.
Fortified city made desolate, Isaiah 27:10.
Certainty of defeat by Babylon, Jeremiah
    37:1-10; 38:14-28.
Cruel results of defeat, Jeremiah 39:1-7.
Warriors stumbling over one another,
    Jeremiah 46:12.
Defeat augmented by the Lord, Jeremiah
    46:15.
Hiss of fleeing serpent, Jeremiah 46:22.
One message after another of bad news,
    Jeremiah 51:31-32.

Giving up to enemy, Lamentations 1:5.
Nine out of 10 lost in battle, Amos 5:3.
Ruined beyond remedy, Micah 2:10.
Clapping hands at fate of Nineveh, Nahum
    3:19.

DEFECTIVE

Animals without defect, Exodus 12:5.
Unqualified for priesthood, Leviticus
    21:17-23.
Partial blindness inflicted as disgrace,
    1 Samuel 11:2-11.
Multiple fingers and toes, 2 Samuel 21:20.
A perfect church, Ephesians 5:25-27.
The perfect Lamb of God, 1 Peter 1:19.
See *Handicap, Maim.*

DEFENSE

Elimination of blacksmiths, 1 Samuel
    13:19.
Killing man in self-defense, 2 Samuel 2:22-23.
Half stood guard while other half worked,
    Nehemiah 4:21.
Israel today consists of unwalled villages,
    Ezekiel 38:10-12.
Gates wide open to enemy, Nahum 3:13.
Jerusalem a city without walls, Zechariah
    2:3-5.
Jesus avoided those who would take His
    life, John 7:1.
No one could harm Jesus until His time
    had come, John 7:30.
Young man who defended Paul, Acts
    23:16-22.
Paul's plea before Felix, Acts 24:1-21.
Shield of faith, Ephesians 6:16.

DEFENSIVE

Zophar upset by criticism, Job 20:2-3.

DEFIANCE

Pharaoh dared to defy God, Exodus 5:2.
Defiance of fool, Psalm 14:1.
Inevitable judgment to those who disobey
    God, Jeremiah 44:15-28.
See *Affront, Anarchy, Opposition.*

DEFILE

Guilty fingers, lying lips, Isaiah 59:3.
Broken jar no one wants, Jeremiah 48:38.
Pagans enter sanctuary, Lamentations
    1:10.
Evil comes from inside, Mark 7:23.

Corrupting influence of evil tongue, James 3:6.
Antidote to uncleanness, 1 John 3:1-3.
Temple court defiled, Revelation 11:1-2.

DEGENERATE
Corrupt from birth, Psalm 58:3.
Silver to dross, wine to water, Isaiah 1:22.
Defiled with blood, Lamentations 4:14.
Agony of those who refuse to repent, Revelation 16:10-11.
See *Debauchery.*

DEGRADATION
Desecration of the ark of God, 1 Samuel 5:1-2.
Blaming God, 2 Kings 6:33.
Infamy to daughter of king, 2 Kings 9:30-37.
Skilled at art of seduction, Jeremiah 2:33.
Place of disease and death, Jeremiah 16:1-13.
Drunkenness and vomit, Jeremiah 25:27.
Defiled with blood, Lamentations 4:14.
Women of Sodom, Ezekiel 16:49.
Promiscuity of two sisters, Ezekiel 23:1-49.
Treasures of the Lord in pagan temple, Daniel 1:2.
Alcohol and nudity, Habakkuk 2:15.
See *Carnality, Debauchery, Defile.*

DELAY
Dangerous procrastination, Genesis 19:12-16.
Enemy progress delayed, Exodus 14:24-25.
Waiting patiently for the Lord, Psalm 130:5-6.
When time will no longer be prolonged, Isaiah 13:22.
Noon schedule delayed until night, Jeremiah 6:4-5.
Those who said it was not time to rebuild temple, Haggai 1:3-4.
Jesus' delay in attending to Lazarus, John 11:6-44.
Time of death in the Lord's hands, John 21:20-23.
Delayed response to Gospel, Acts 24:25.
Paul endeavored to keep on schedule, 1 Timothy 3:14-15.
Abraham waited patiently for God's promise, Hebrews 6:13-15.
Return of Christ as scheduled, Hebrews 10:37.

See *Hindrance, Procrastination.*

DELEGATE
Delegating work to others, Exodus 18:17-27.
The Lord delegates responsibility, Deuteronomy 1:9-18.
Trustworthy messenger, Proverbs 25:13.
Organizing distribution of welfare to widows, Acts 6:1-4.
See *Organization, Responsibility.*

DELIBERATION
Keeping your eyes on the Lord, Psalm 25:15.
Eyes fixed directly ahead, Proverbs 4:25.
Glory of kings, Proverbs 25:2.
Fear and obey God, Ecclesiastes 12:13-14.
Those who plan iniquity, Micah 2:1.
See *Concentration.*

DELICACY
Sugar cane, Exodus 30:23.
Manna called bread of angels, Psalm 78:25.
Choice fruits and flavors, Song of Songs 4:13-14.
Imported sweets, Jeremiah 6:20.
Items of barter, Ezekiel 27:19.
Fruit from tree of life, Revelation 2:7.
Hidden manna, Revelation 2:17.
See *Ambrosia, Gourmet.*

DELINQUENCY
Sons of sorceress, Isaiah 57:3.
Sons unfaithful to father, Jeremiah 3:19.
Evil influence of fathers on children, Jeremiah 16:10-12.
Children who bring sorrow, Hosea 9:12.
God's love for errant child, Hosea 11:1-4.
Prodigal Son, Luke 15:11-32.

DELIVERANCE
Kidnapping and rescue of Lot, Genesis 14:12-16.
Joseph's prediction of deliverance from Egypt, Genesis 50:24-25.
Israelites escape from Egypt, Exodus 14:29. (See Ps. 105:38.)
Lamp of the Lord, 2 Samuel 22:29.
God, not man, can help in time of trouble, Psalm 60:11-12.
Power of God's name in time of trouble, Psalm 118:8-12.
God's promise to Hezekiah, Isaiah 37:33-

34.
Gladness and joy overtake sorrow, Isaiah 51:11.
Assurance to Israel in Egypt, Jeremiah 46:27.
Too little and too late, Amos 3:12.
Certainty that God's revelation will come to pass, Habakkuk 2:3.
Demons preferred to deliverance, Matthew 8:28-34. (Note especially v. 34.)
Delivered of many demons, Mark 5:15.
Murder thwarted by Jesus, Luke 4:28-30.
Jesus rebuked demon, Luke 4:33-36.
Angelic intervention, Acts 5:17-20; 12:4-11.
Paul bitten by snake, Acts 28:1-6.
Deliverance from sin through Christ alone, Romans 7:24-25; Hebrews 7:23-28.
Prostitute delivered by faith and obedience, Hebrews 11:31.
Set free from continual sin, 1 John 3:4-6.
Celebrating death of those who oppressed, Revelation 11:7-11.

DEMEAN
Humiliation of strong man, Judges 16:23-30.
Low estimation of a servant, 2 Kings 8:13.
Stripped of one's honor, Job 19:9.
Wounds of a friend, Proverbs 27:6.
See *Defamation, Insult.*

DEMOGRAPHICS
See *Population, Statistics.*

DEMONS
Guidance by divination, Genesis 30:27.
Demons counterfeit works of God, Exodus 7:6-12.
No curse on those who have been blessed, Numbers 22:12.
Origin of demons, 1 Samuel 16:15.
Evil spirits and poor health, 1 Samuel 16:16.
Demons driven out, Matthew 8:16.
Demons need bodies in which to reside, Matthew 8:28-33; Mark 5:1-15.
Jesus accused of satanic power, Matthew 9:32-34; John 8:48-52.
Power and authority over evil spirits and illness, Matthew 10:1-8.
Jesus criticized for casting out demons, Matthew 12:22-32.
Satan cannot drive out Satan, Mark 3:20-26.
Demons have names, Mark 5:8-9.
Demon recognized identity of Jesus, Luke 4:33-36, 41. (See vv. 22-24.)
Many demons in one man, Luke 8:30.
Evil spirit confronted Jesus, Luke 9:37-43.
Mute demon, Luke 11:14.
Illness caused by spirit, Luke 13:10-16.
Satan himself controlled Judas in betrayal of Jesus, Luke 22:3; John 13:27.
Evil spirits cause torment, Acts 5:16.
Deliverance from evil spirits, Acts 8:7.
Opposition of sorcerer, Acts 13:6-8.
Miracles in the ministry of Paul, Acts 19:11-12.
Physical harm caused by demons, Acts 19:13-16.
Nothing can separate us from love of God, Romans 8:37-39.
Pagan idols are actually demons, 1 Corinthians 10:20.
Demons masquerade as angels of light, 2 Corinthians 11:14-15.
Anger and the devil, Ephesians 4:26-27.
Armor of God, Ephesians 6:10-18.
Rescued from dominion of darkness, Colossians 1:13-14.
Cross triumphs over evil authority, Colossians 2:15.
Hindered by Satan, 1 Thessalonians 2:18.
Those handed over to Satan, 1 Timothy 1:18-20.
Theology of demons, 1 Timothy 4:1-4.
Widows turn away to follow Satan, 1 Timothy 5:15.
Satan's trap, 2 Timothy 2:25-26.
Submit to God, resist devil, James 4:7; 1 Peter 5:8-9.
Testing spirits for those that are false, 1 John 4:1-6.
Whole world controlled by evil one, 1 John 5:19.
Only authority over evil, Jude 9.
Demons unable to withstand Michael and his angels, Revelation 12:7-9.
Influence of demons over world leaders, Revelation 16:13-14.
Place of residence for demons and evil spirits, Revelation 18:2.
See *Exorcism.*

DENIAL
Those who deny Christ are disowned, Matthew 10:33; Mark 8:38; 2 Timothy

2:12.
Peter's denial, Matthew 26:34, 69-70, 73-74.
See *Ashamed, Rejection, Self-denial.*

DENOMINATION
Rules taught by men, Isaiah 29:13.
Disagreement as to ministry of Jesus, John 7:42-43.
Insisting on one interpretation of doctrine, Acts 15:1.
Need for proper credentials, Acts 15:22-31.
Theological dispute in secular courtroom, Acts 18:12-17.
Those of different views, Romans 14:1-3.
Disagreements among early believers, 1 Corinthians 1:10-17.
Following teachings of good men, 1 Corinthians 3:4.
Ministry to Jews and ministry to Gentiles in harmony, Galatians 2:8.
Envy among those who preach Christ, Philippians 1:15-19.
Preventing teaching of false doctrine, 1 Timothy 1:3-5.
Faith held in common, Titus 1:4.
See *Doctrine, Syncretism, Theology.*

DENTISTRY
Loss of tooth to be compensated, Exodus 21:27.
Teeth as fangs, Job 29:17.
Teeth of wicked broken, Psalm 3:7.
Bad tooth, Proverbs 25:19.
Becoming toothless, Ecclesiastes 12:3.
    (Note: Some believe "grinders" refer to teeth.)
Children's teeth set on edge, Jeremiah 31:29; Ezekiel 18:2.
Broken teeth, Lamentations 3:16.
See *Teeth.*

DEPARTURE
Enforced departure from Babel, Genesis 11:8.
Chosen change of direction, Genesis 13:5-13.
Romantic venture, Genesis 24:10.
Three-day journey, Genesis 30:36.
Exit from Egypt via dry land and sea, Exodus 14:1-28. (See also Ps. 105:23-38.)
Miraculous river crossing, Joshua 3:1-17.
Forward into battle, Judges 1:1-3.

Journey homeward, Ruth 1:3-7; Luke 15:13, 17-20.
Disobedient motives, 1 Samuel 15:17-19.
Travel in two directions, Jonah 1:1-3; 3:1-3.
Time to move on, Micah 2:10.
Advance notice from Jesus, John 7:33; 13:33; 14:28; 16:5; 17:11.
Beginning of the greatest journey, 2 Timothy 4:6-8.
See *Journey.*

DEPENDABILITY
Honest weights and measures, Deuteronomy 25:13-16.
God keeps His promises, Joshua 23:14-15.
False dependence on military strength, 1 Chronicles 21:17.
The Lord does what He promises to do, 2 Chronicles 6:4, 14-15.
Our Lord's enduring love, Psalm 136:1-26.
Betraying confidence, Proverbs 11:13.
Springs that fail, Jeremiah 15:18.
Do not be found sleeping when the Lord returns, Mark 13:35-37.
Need to prove faithful, 1 Corinthians 4:2.
Making most of every opportunity, Ephesians 5:15-16.
Doing good work as unto the Lord, Ephesians 6:5-8; Colossians 3:23-24.
Faithful service without pastoral supervision, Philippians 2:12-13.
Impossible for God to lie, Hebrews 6:18.
See *Honesty, Integrity.*

DEPRAVITY
Only God has consciousness of sin without guilt of sin, Genesis 3:22.
Depravity of man before Flood, Genesis 6:5.
Lifelong depravity, Genesis 8:21.
God's willingness to extend mercy, Genesis 18:16-33.
Joseph's brothers sought for guilt less than murder, Genesis 37:19-27.
People who become like animals in times of distress, Deuteronomy 28:53-57.
Quick to disobey God, Judges 2:10-13, 19; 3:7, 12; 4:1.
Son less evil than parents, 2 Kings 3:1-3.
Persistence toward doing evil, Nehemiah 9:28.
Self-condemnation, Job 9:2-3, 20.
Pure cannot come from impure, Job 14:4; 15:14-16.

Depravity of nature and man, Job 25:4-6.
World against God, Psalm 2:1-3.
Descriptive example from motherhood,
    Psalm 7:14.
Giving honor to what is vile, Psalm 12:8.
Lostness as God sees it, Psalm 14:2-3.
Conceived in sin, Psalm 51:5; 58:3.
Those who boast in evil, Psalm 52:1-4.
Sinfulness of human nature, Psalm 53:2-3.
Never a thought of kindness, Psalm 109:16.
None can stand, Psalm 130:3; Proverbs
    20:9; Ecclesiastes 7:20; Romans 3:23.
Warped minds, Proverbs 12:8.
Making mockery of sin, Proverbs 14:9.
Folly in heart of child yields to discipline,
    Proverbs 22:15.
Concealing sin, Proverbs 28:13.
Abundant guilt of Israel, Isaiah 1:4.
Calling evil good and good evil, Isaiah 5:20.
Confronted with holiness of God, Isaiah
    6:1-5.
All have become ungodly, Isaiah 9:17.
Ravages of wickedness, Isaiah 9:18.
Thinking to hide plans from the Lord,
    Isaiah 29:15.
Confident in one's own wickedness, Isaiah
    47:10.
All have gone astray, Isaiah 53:6.
Sin causes God not to hear sinner's cry,
    Isaiah 59:1-3.
Righteousness like filthy rags, Isaiah 64:6.
Proclaiming innocence when guilt is
    obvious, Jeremiah 2:34-35.
Profusion of evil, Jeremiah 3:5; Micah 7:2-
    4; Matthew 12:34-35.
Depravity of Judah made Israel seem
    righteous, Jeremiah 3:11.
Skilled in doing evil, Jeremiah 4:22.
Search for one honest person in an entire
    city, Jeremiah 5:1.
Depravity of men and clergy, Jeremiah
    8:10.
Leopard cannot change spots, Jeremiah
    13:23.
Heart is deceitful, Jeremiah 17:9.
Inevitable judgment to those who disobey
    God, Jeremiah 44:15-28.
Sheep led astray by false shepherds,
    Jeremiah 50:6.
Anger beyond measure, Lamentations
    5:21-22.
Jerusalem became more depraved than
    those from whom she learned
    depravity, Ezekiel 16:44-52.

Death to soul that sins, Ezekiel 18:4.
Enumerated depravity of an evil man,
    Ezekiel 18:10-13. (See vv. 14-17.)
Depravity of two adulterous sisters, Ezekiel
    23:1-49.
Relished wickedness, Hosea 4:8.
Three sins, even four, Amos 1:3, 6, 9, 11,
    13; 2:1, 4, 6.
Demons preferred to deliverance, Matthew
    8:28-34. (Note especially v. 34.)
Depravity of the heart, Matthew 15:19.
Faith of gross sinners compared to religion
    of Pharisees, Matthew 21:31-32.
Those who tried to prevent resurrection of
    Jesus, Matthew 27:62-66. (See also
    28:11-15.)
That which comes out, not which goes in,
    makes man unclean, Mark 7:15-23.
Men love darkness rather than light, John
    3:19-21.
Satan as spiritual father, John 8:44.
Doubt augmented by hearing truth, John
    8:45-47.
Spiritual blindness and spiritual sight, John
    9:39-41.
Those who refuse to believe in face of sure
    evidence, John 12:37-38.
Paul's confrontation with intellectual
    idolatry, Acts 17:16-34.
Description of man's depravity, Romans
    1:28-32.
Evil cannot correct evil, Romans 2:1.
Spiritual hardness, Romans 2:5.
No one righteous, Romans 3:10-18.
Depravity since time of Adam, Romans
    5:12-14; 1 Corinthians 15:22.
Sinfulness of sin, Romans 7:13.
Condition of natural man, 1 Corinthians
    2:14.
All under sin, Galatians 3:22.
Sinful nature, Galatians 5:19-21.
Without hope and without God, Ephesians
    2:12.
Enmity in mind against God, Colossians
    1:21.
Those who mistreat others as they
    themselves were once mistreated,
    1 Thessalonians 2:14-16.
Law is for those who are lost, 1 Timothy
    1:8-11.
God wants all to be saved, 1 Timothy 2:3-4.
Conduct and attitudes in last days,
    2 Timothy 3:1-5.
Life prior to regeneration, Titus 3:3.

Unintentional sin, Hebrews 9:7.
Breaking just one point of Law, James 2:10.
Rejecting destiny planned by God, 1 Peter 2:8.
Slaves of depravity, 2 Peter 2:13-22.
Provision for cleansing, 1 John 1:8-10.
Love of world, 1 John 2:15-17.
Denying that Jesus is the Christ, 1 John 2:22-23.
Whole world controlled by evil one, 1 John 5:19.
Those who refuse to repent in face of judgment, Revelation 9:20-21.
Mark of beast, Revelation 13:16-18; 14:9-10.
Agony of those who refuse to repent, Revelation 16:10-11.
Sins piled up to heaven, Revelation 18:4-5.
Evil queen refuses to admit sin, Revelation 18:7-8.
Curse forever removed, Revelation 22:3.
Continuity of evil and good, Revelation 22:11.
See *Blasphemy, Carnality, Debase, Decadent, Disobedience, Immorality, Lust.*

DEPRESSION
Anxiety out of deep waters, 2 Samuel 22:17.
Lamp of the Lord, 2 Samuel 22:29.
Facing disappointment and loss, Job 1:22.
The Lord is close to those with broken hearts and spirits, Psalm 34:18.
Desperate times, Psalm 60:3.
No song for heavy hearts, Proverbs 25:20.
One who lights deepest darkness, Isaiah 9:2.
Joy and gladness gone, Jeremiah 48:33.
Exercising hope when no basis for hope, Romans 4:18-22.
See *Anxiety, Stress.*

DESCENDANTS
No descendants in Nineveh, Nahum 1:14.

DESCRIPTION
Samson's mother described angel who came to her, Judges 13:6.
Paul's description of life of Christ, 1 Timothy 3:16.
Description of New Jerusalem, Revelation 21:15-17.

DESECRATION
Desecration of King Saul's body, 1 Samuel 31:8-10.
Touching ark of the Lord, 2 Samuel 6:6-11.
Murder in pagan temple, 2 Kings 19:37.
Setting fire to temple, 2 Kings 25:8-9.
Sin of challenging God, Isaiah 5:18-19.
Mockery of fasting, Isaiah 58:4-5.
Flesh of pigs equated with rats, Isaiah 66:17.
Heap of ruins, Jeremiah 51:37.
Pagans enter sanctuary, Lamentations 1:10.
Articles from temple in Jerusalem put into pagan temple, Daniel 1:1-2.
Misuse of goblets from temple, Daniel 5:1-4.
Priests who defiled altar, Malachi 1:6-14.
Laughing at truth spoken by Jesus, Matthew 9:23-24.
Observance of Sabbath, Matthew 12:1-13.
Misuse of temple in Jerusalem, Matthew 21:12-13.
Mixing blood of man with sacrificial blood, Luke 13:1.
See *Defamation, Defile, Iconoclastic, Irreverence, Sacrilege.*

DESERT
Forage for goat, Leviticus 16:22.
Concise description of wilderness, Deuteronomy 8:15.
Wild donkeys of desert, Job 39:5-6.
Wilderness remembered, Jeremiah 2:2-6.
Wasteland forever, Zephaniah 2:9.

DESERTERS
Soldiers who felt like grasshoppers, Numbers 13:33.
Twenty-two thousand cowards, Judges 7:3.
Terrified of Goliath, 1 Samuel 17:24.
David's fear, 2 Samuel 15:14.
Those who turned in battle, Psalm 78:9; Jeremiah 41:11-14.
No one will go into battle, Ezekiel 7:14.
Jesus deserted by disciples, Matthew 26:56.
Turning back to worldly life, 2 Timothy 4:9-10.
See *Backsliding, Coward.*

DESIGN
Distinction of species, Genesis 1:24-25.
Design in snowflake, Job 38:22.
The Lord plans far in advance, Isaiah 25:1.

Earth's design and purpose, Isaiah 45:18.
Measuring new temple area, Ezekiel 40:5-49.
See *Blueprint, Plan, Purpose.*

DESIRE
All desires granted, Psalms 37:4; 145:16.
   (Note: Not our selfish desires but
   divinely implanted desires which
   motivate us in His will!)
Desire for full obedience, Psalm 119:1-5.
Fulfilled longings, Proverbs 13:12.
Selfish request, Mark 10:35-37.
Continual lust for more, Ephesians 4:19.
Paul's supreme desire, Philippians 3:7-11.
Role of evil desire in causing one to sin,
   James 1:13-15.

DESOLATE
Fate of godless, Job 15:34.
Swept away by terror, Psalm 73:19.
Day of the Lord, Isaiah 13:9.
Destroyed overnight, Isaiah 15:1.
Haunt of jackals, Jeremiah 9:11.
Salty fate, Jeremiah 48:9.
Object of horror, Jeremiah 49:17.
The abandoned city, Lamentations 1:1.
Retribution, Ezekiel 25:12-14; Joel 3:19.
Stark terror, Nahum 2:10.
See *Abandoned, Desert, Forsaken.*

DESPAIR
Deaf to God's message, Genesis 6:2-9.
Driven to suicide, 1 Samuel 31:4;
   2 Samuel 17:23; 1 Kings 16:18; Acts
   1:18.
Desire for death, Numbers 11:10-15;
   1 Kings 19:3-5; Job 3:21; 7:15; Jeremiah
   8:3; Jonah 4:3; Revelation 9:6.
Job looked to future and saw no hope, Job
   17:11.
Troubles more numerous than hairs of
   head, Psalm 40:11-12.
Hope in time of despair, Psalm 42:5;
   Jeremiah 31:15-17.
All is darkness, Isaiah 59:9.
Harvest past, summer ended, no salvation,
   Jeremiah 8:20.
Plight of those who rebelled against the
   Lord, Ezekiel 12:19.
Joy of mankind withered away, Joel 1:12.
Agony of those who refuse to repent,
   Revelation 16:10-11.
See *Pessimism.*

DESPERATION
Help in desperate times, 2 Kings 6:24-31.
Renegade pleads for his own life from one
   he would harm, Esther 7:7.
Resorting to cannibalism, Lamentations
   2:20.

DESPISE
See *Hatred.*

DESPONDENCY
Suffering great sorrow, Genesis 37:34-35;
   2 Samuel 18:32-33.
Heartache of Moses, Numbers 11:10-15;
   17:12-13.
Description of anxiety, Deuteronomy
   28:65-67.
Frustrated leaders, Joshua 7:7.
Elijah had had enough, 1 Kings 19:3-4.
Lamenting one's existence, Job 3:1-26.
Hatred of life, Job 10:1; Jeremiah 15:10.
Hope abandoned, Job 17:13-16; Jeremiah
   18:12.
Questioning God, Psalm 77:7-9.
Glimmer of hope, Proverbs 13:12.
Joy and gladness gone, Jeremiah 48:33.
Loneliness for fellow believers,
   2 Corinthians 7:5-7.
Agony of those who refuse to repent,
   Revelation 16:10-11.
See *Anxiety, Despair, Discouragement,
   Pessimism.*

DESPOT
Egyptian oppression, Exodus 1:8-14; 5:8-9.
Rehoboam would be more oppressive than
   his father, 1 Kings 12:1-11.
People sorely mistreated, Ecclesiastes 4:1-3.
God's people in despair, Isaiah 5:7.
God uses despots, then brings them into
   judgment, Jeremiah 25:11-14; 27:1-7.
See *Dictator, Totalitarian.*

DESTINY
Chosen for greatness, Genesis 18:16-19.
Job's negative view toward meaning of life,
   Job 14:1-2.
Time for everything, Ecclesiastes 3:1-8.
Things planned long ago, Isaiah 25:1.
Future can be left safely in hands of God,
   Isaiah 46:8-11.
Destiny ordained before birth, Isaiah 49:1;
   Jeremiah 1:5.

Long durability of Jerusalem, Jeremiah
31:38-40.
Judas, who would betray, Mark 3:19.
Dual mission of Saviour, Luke 2:28-32.
Crucifixion occurred in God's time, John
7:30.
Paul confident of destiny, Acts 27:23-25.
Ultimate purpose of creation and human
life, Romans 8:18-23.
Chosen before Creation, Ephesians 1:4.
Destiny planned by God, 1 Peter 2:8.
Destiny resulting from redemption,
Revelation 1:6.
See *Fortuity, Predestination.*

DESTRUCTION
Devastation of Canaanites, Numbers 21:3.
No survivors, Deuteronomy 2:34; 3:6;
Joshua 6:21; 8:24-29.
Divine anger against nations, Isaiah 34:2.
Everlasting ruin, Jeremiah 25:9.
Ruined beyond remedy, Micah 2:10.
Stubble in furnace of judgment, Malachi
4:1.
Babylon obliterated, Revelation 18:21.
See *Judgment.*

DETAIL
Intricate detail in development of temple,
Ezekiel 40-42.
Paul did not discuss details, Hebrews 9:5.
See *Design, Plan.*

DETERGENT
Methods of washing in Job's time, Job
9:30-31.
Soda and soap, Jeremiah 2:22.

DETERIORATE
See *Death, Decay, Rust.*

DETERMINATION
No rest until task completed, Numbers
23:24.
March on with strong soul, Judges 5:21.
Moving ahead in spite of circumstances,
Psalm 44:18.
Stand firm or not at all, Isaiah 7:9.
Face set like flint, Isaiah 50:7.
Divine determination against evil,
Jeremiah 23:20.
Singleness of heart and action, Jeremiah
32:38-39.
Filled with knowledge of God's will,

Colossians 1:9-12.
See *Diligence, Resolute.*

DETERMINISM
Accidents by divine permission, Exodus
21:13.
God's plans remain firm, Job 42:2.
The Lord does what pleases Him, Psalm
135:6.
One who knows all our ways, Psalm 139:1-
16.
Time for everything, Ecclesiastes 3:1-8.
Divine plan and purpose, Isaiah 14:24.
Irreversible acts of God, Isaiah 43:13.
God knows end from beginning, Isaiah
46:8-11.
Man may not direct his own steps,
Jeremiah 10:23.
Facing grim destiny, Jeremiah 15:2-3.
What the Lord plans, Lamentations 2:17.
Prophecy about distant future, Ezekiel
12:26-27.
Acts and purposes of God, Daniel 2:19-23.
Filled with knowledge of God's will,
Colossians 1:9-12.
See *Destiny, Fortuity, Predestination.*

DETEST
See *Hatred.*

DEVELOPMENT
Boy Samuel, 1 Samuel 2:26.
Time to enlarge, Isaiah 54:2.
Nation takes time to develop, Isaiah 66:8.
Growth for those who trust in the Lord,
Jeremiah 17:7-8.
Development of Boy Jesus, Luke 2:52.
Harvest of righteousness, 2 Corinthians
9:10.
Increasing love, 1 Thessalonians 3:12.
Growing faith, 2 Thessalonians 1:3.
See *Growth, Progress.*

DEVIATE
Men of Sodom and Lot's angelic visitors,
Genesis 19:5.
Forbidden relationship between men,
Leviticus 20:13.
Example of homosexual conduct, Judges
19:22-24.
Eradication of deviates from Israel, 1 Kings
15:12. (See 14:24.)
Male prostitutes enshrined, Job 36:14.
See *Homosexual.*

DEVIOUS
Those who wanted to be part of building temple, Ezra 4:1-3.
Sanballat's scheme to hinder Nehemiah, Nehemiah 6:1-9.
Dishonestly acquitted, Micah 6:11.
See *Disruption, Hindrance.*

DEVOTIONS
Morning devotions, Psalm 5:3.
Prayer in closet, Matthew 6:5-6.
Loving God above all, Matthew 10:37-39.
Jesus at daybreak, Luke 4:42.
Jesus teaching at dawn, John 8:2.
Devout centurion, Acts 10:2.
See *Intercession, Meditation, Prayer.*

DEVOUT
He walked with God, Genesis 5:24.
A righteous man, Genesis 6:8-9.
Father's divine commendation, Genesis 18:17-19.
Father's opposition to idols, Genesis 35:2-3.
Expectant father's concern for coming son, Judges 13:8.
Doing right, being faithful, 2 Chronicles 31:20.
Blameless and upright, Job 1:1.
Man of bold prayer, Daniel 6:10.
Righteous and devout, Luke 2:25-35.
Woman fasting and praying consistently, Luke 2:36-37.
Appraisal by Jesus, John 1:47.
God-fearing centurion, Acts 10:1-2.
Full of the Holy Spirit and faith, Acts 11:22-24.
See *Commitment, Consecration, Discipleship, Holiness, Separation, Spirituality.*

DEXTERITY
Special gifts from God through Holy Spirit, Exodus 31:1-5.
Hands and feet purposely crippled, Judges 1:6.
People working together, Nehemiah 4:6.
Victory requires more than ability, Isaiah 25:11.
Skilled at art of seduction, Jeremiah 2:33.
Weakness of broken arms, Ezekiel 30:21-22.
See *Ability, Agility, Athletics.*

DIAGNOSIS
Asking prophet about son's illness, 1 Kings 14:1-14.
Hezekiah's terminal illness, Isaiah 38:1.
Great Physician, Mark 2:17.

DIARY
Stages of journey recorded by Moses, Numbers 33:1-49.

DICTATION
Prophet's certainty of voice of the Lord, Jeremiah 32:1-12.
Jeremiah dictated to Baruch the words of the Lord, Jeremiah 36:4, 15-16.
How Bible was written, 2 Peter 1:21.
See *Secretary.*

DICTATOR
People hide from evil government, Proverbs 28:28.
Unjust laws and decrees, Isaiah 10:1-2.
Those who live under non-Christian government, Isaiah 26:13.
See *Despot, Totalitarian.*

DIE
When the die is cast, Revelation 22:11.

DIET
Guests for lunch, Genesis 43:16.
Bread and meat, Exodus 16:1-12.
Edible and inedible insects, Leviticus 11:20-23.
Abstaining from all fruit of the grape, Numbers 6:2-4.
Diet of pregnant woman, Judges 13:1-5.
Refreshing breakfast, Judges 19:5-8.
Forbidden to taste food, 1 Samuel 14:24-28.
Careful of calories, Proverbs 23:1-2, 20-21.
Eating properly, Ecclesiastes 10:17.
Flesh of pigs equated with rats, Isaiah 66:17.
Daniel and his friends refused royal food, Daniel 1:8-16.
Abundant red meat, Amos 6:4.
Food of John the Baptist, Matthew 3:4.
Desiring food of pigs, Luke 15:16.
Special guest for dinner, Luke 24:29-30.
Vegetarian and nonvegetarian, Romans 14:2. (See Dan. 1:12.)
Stomach god, Philippians 3:19.
Legalistic eating, 1 Timothy 4:3. (See Heb.

13:9.)
See *Food, Gluttony, Health.*

DIFFICULTY
Thanking God in the midst of adverse
circumstances, Jeremiah 33:10-11.
Paul's bondage became a means for
ministry, Acts 28:17-28.
See *Antagonist, Enemy, Hindrance,
Obstacles.*

DIGESTION
Eating with rejoicing, Deuteronomy 27:7.
Love makes food more palatable, Proverbs
15:17.
Food from stingy man, Proverbs 23:6-8.
Meals at regular hours, Ecclesiastes 10:17.
Undigestible food, Jonah 2:10.
Attitude and food, Acts 14:17.
Wine for the stomach, 1 Timothy 5:23.
See *Appetite, Diet, Food, Health.*

DIGNITY
Bearing of a prince, Judges 8:18.
Respect at city gate, Job 29:7-10.
King bowing before his captive, Daniel
2:46.

DILEMMA
Like blind man in dark, Deuteronomy
28:29.
Walking about in darkness, Psalm 82:5.
At wit's end, Psalm 107:27.
Joseph's dilemma concerning Mary,
Matthew 1:18-19.
Pilate's dilemma, Matthew 27:19-22.
Light and darkness, John 12:35.
See *Confusion, Obstacles.*

DILIGENCE
People working with all their hearts,
Nehemiah 4:6.
Way of ant, Proverbs 6:6-8; 30:25.
Diligence brings satisfaction, Proverbs
13:4.
Hard work and fantasy, Proverbs 28:19.
Woman of high motivation, Proverbs
31:14-15.
Working with diligence, Ecclesiastes 9:10.
Found sleeping when the Lord returns,
Mark 13:35-37.
Making most of every opportunity,
Ephesians 5:15-16; Colossians 4:5.
Doing good work as unto the Lord,

Ephesians 6:5-8; Colossians 3:23-24.
Slaves to respect masters, 1 Timothy 6:1-2.
Providing for one's own needs, Titus 3:14.
Work before rest, Hebrews 4:11.
Example of those who lived by faith,
Hebrews 12:1-3.
See *Determination, Energy, Industrious,
Motivation.*

DIMENSIONS
Honest weights and measures,
Deuteronomy 25:13-16.
Given eternal viewpoint, Jeremiah 33:3.
Measuring temple area, Ezekiel 40:5-49.
Measuring width and length of Jerusalem,
Zechariah 2:1-2.
Unsearchable riches of God, Romans
11:33-36.
Dimensions of spiritual understanding,
1 Corinthians 2:9-10.
Dimensions of Christian experience,
Ephesians 3:16-19.
See *Area.*

DIRECTION
Points of compass, Genesis 13:14; Acts
27:12.
A fool does not know way to town,
Ecclesiastes 10:15.
Going in obedience toward unknown
objective, Hebrews 11:8.
See *Guidance.*

DIRECTIVE
Ultimate demands for obeying Law, Joshua
1:18.
Pagan king persuaded to permit rebuilding
of temple, Ezra 4–8.
Keeping your eyes on the Lord, Psalm
25:15.
See *Decree, Guidance, Instructions.*

DIRGE
David's lament, 2 Samuel 1:17-27.

DISAGREEMENT
Offering to make peace before battle,
Deuteronomy 20:10.
Futility of strife among brothers, 2 Samuel
2:27-28.
Good counsel when tempted to quarrel,
Proverbs 17:14, 19.
Using words with restraint, Proverbs 17:27.
Settle misunderstandings quickly, Matthew

5:25.
Disagreement between brothers, Matthew 18:15-17.
Settlement out of court, Luke 12:58.
Arguing over a point of doctrine, Acts 15:2-3.
Clash of personalities, Acts 15:36-41.
Disagreeing with doctrine and practice, 1 Corinthians 11:16.
Peter and Paul face-to-face, Galatians 2:11-21.
Basic rules for teacher in handling dispute, 2 Timothy 2:23-26.
See *Argument, Conflict, Debate, Dispute, Opinion.*

DISAPPOINTMENT
Seeing unpleasant sights, Deuteronomy 28:34.
Unharvested vineyard, Deuteronomy 28:39: Micah 6:15.
Samson more powerful and victorious in death than in life, Judges 16:30.
Facing disappointment and loss without complaining, Job 1:22.
Hope a dying gasp, Job 11:20.
No fear of bad news, Psalm 112:7-8.
Agony of waiting and joy of fulfillment, Proverbs 13:12.
Secret to relaxation, Proverbs 19:23.
Awakening to find dream untrue, Isaiah 29:8.
Frustrated hopes, Jeremiah 14:19.
Jonah became angry when God spared Nineveh, Jonah 4:1-3.
Houses unoccupied, Zephaniah 1:13.
Purpose of suffering, Romans 5:3.
Paul prayed for healing but could rejoice in negative answer, 2 Corinthians 12:7-10.
Paul's imprisonment widened sphere of influence, Philippians 1:12-14.
Sharing each other's troubles, Philippians 4:14.
Paul's attitude toward those who deserted him, 2 Timothy 4:16.
Reason for circumstances, Philemon 15-16.
Made perfect through suffering, Hebrews 2:10.
Confident now of promises fulfilled in future, Hebrews 11:13.
All tears wiped away, Revelation 21:4.
See *Discouragement, Trauma.*

DISARMAMENT
No weapons in Israel, 1 Samuel 13:19-22.
Coming world peace, Psalm 46:9; Isaiah 2:4; 11:6-9; Micah 4:3.
Break the bow, Jeremiah 49:35.
Forbidden to prepare for battle, Jeremiah 51:3.
World peace an impossibility without Christ, Matthew 24:6-8.

DISASTER
God's promise to Noah, Genesis 9:8-16.
Small town spared disaster of large city, Genesis 19:15-22.
Death caused by shock, 1 Samuel 4:12-18.
Facing disaster with confidence, Psalm 57:1.
Gentle flowing waters or mighty floodwaters, Isaiah 8:6-7.
Judgment brings righteousness, Isaiah 26:9.
Slaughter on battlefield, Isaiah 37:36.
Leaders, priests, and prophets lose heart, Jeremiah 4:9.
Punishment brought on disobedient by themselves, Jeremiah 4:18.
Fourth of earth destroyed, Revelation 6:7-8.
Disaster on all earth, Revelation 8:6-13.
Greatest earthquake of all time, Revelation 16:18-20.
Hailstones from sky, Revelation 16:21.
City burned to ground in one hour, Revelation 18:17-19.
See *Cataclysm, Defeat.*

DISCERNMENT
Detecting words of false prophet, Deuteronomy 18:21-22.
Lack of discernment, Deuteronomy 32:28.
Importance of ear to discern content, Job 12:11; 34:1-3.
Difference between mind and heart, Job 38:36.
Asking God for discernment, Psalm 119:125.
Persistent search for wisdom and insight, Proverbs 2:1-6.
Man's ways may seem right, Proverbs 21:2.
Fear and obey God, Ecclesiastes 12:13-14.
Discernment of evil, Isaiah 8:12.
Discerning false prophets, dreams, and oracles, Jeremiah 23:25-40.
Undivided heart, Ezekiel 11:19.

Priests to teach difference between holy and common, Ezekiel 44:23.

Wisdom of queen, Daniel 5:10-11.

Walking in ways of the Lord, Hosea 14:9.

Those who do not know thoughts of the Lord, Micah 4:12.

Using eyes for good or evil, Matthew 6:22-23.

Shrewd and innocent, Matthew 10:16.

Pharisees could forecast weather but not discern signs of times, Matthew 16:1-4.

Those who could not understand what Jesus said, Mark 15:29-30. (See 14:58.)

Centurion at cross understood who Jesus was, Mark 15:39.

Simeon comprehended dual mission of Saviour, Luke 2:28-32.

Herod's lack of perception, Luke 9:7-9.

Seeing and understanding what others never knew, Luke 10:23-24.

Judging mere appearances, John 7:24.

Wisdom of Gamaliel, Acts 5:34-39.

Lack of understanding what one reads, Acts 8:27-35.

Evaluating weak and strong, Romans 14:1-8.

Folly of intellectual pride, 1 Corinthians 3:18-20.

Eyes of heart, Ephesians 1:18-19.

Knowledge and insight, Philippians 1:9.

Proper understanding of the Law, 1 Timothy 1:8-11.

Distinguishing good from evil, Hebrews 5:14.

Doctrine difficult for some to understand, 2 Peter 3:15-16.

Test spirits for those that are false, 1 John 4:1-6; Revelation 2:2.

Mind with wisdom, Revelation 17:9.

See *Comprehension, Perception, Understanding, Wisdom.*

DISCIPLESHIP

Servant for life, Exodus 21:2-6.

Gifts expected from those who gave the most in battle, Numbers 31:27-31.

Material security versus God's will, Numbers 32:14-27.

Taking care of business, Deuteronomy 20:5-9.

Eagle training young to fly, Deuteronomy 32:11.

Care required in loving God, Joshua 23:11.

Loyalty of servant to king, 2 Samuel 15:19-21.

Characteristics of holy life, Psalm 15:1-5.

Key to walking with God, Psalm 18:25-26.

Those who seek find, Proverbs 8:17.

Definition of real meaning of fasting, Isaiah 58:3-7.

Sincere search for God, Jeremiah 29:10-14.

Lax in doing the Lord's work, Jeremiah 48:10.

Someone to stand in gap, Ezekiel 22:30.

Those who obey the Lord, Joel 2:11.

Those who hunger and thirst for righteousness, Matthew 5:6.

Salt and light in the world, Matthew 5:13-16.

Following Jesus, Matthew 9:9.

Marks of a disciple, Matthew 10:24-25; 16:24-25; Luke 14:26-27; John 8:31; 13:35; 14:15; 15:8.

Loving God above all, Matthew 10:37-39.

Jesus makes burden light, Matthew 11:28-30.

Jesus gave evaluation of His mother, Matthew 12:46-50.

Forsaking all to follow Christ, Matthew 19:28-30; Mark 10:28-31; Luke 18:28-30.

Parable of two sons, Matthew 21:28-31.

Attitude of servant, Matthew 23:8-12.

Calling of Simon, Andrew, James, and John, Mark 1:16-20.

Peter wanted easy way, Mark 8:31-38.

First must be last, Mark 9:35.

Disciples promoted to apostles, Luke 6:12-15.

Duty of true servant, Luke 17:7-10.

Light must be followed to avoid darkness, John 8:12.

Death of wheat kernel, John 12:24-26.

Role of hardship, Acts 14:21-22.

Paul and Barnabas visiting places of ministry, Acts 15:36.

Paul devoted time to teaching new converts, Acts 18:23.

Paul went with confidence into difficult places, Acts 20:22-24.

First a servant, then a minister, Romans 1:1.

Devotion to one another, Romans 12:10.

Testimony of Christ confirmed in convert, 1 Corinthians 1:4-6.

Paul urged converts to follow his example, 1 Corinthians 4:15-16.

Marriage for those serving the Lord,
1 Corinthians 7:32-35.
Paul's servant attitude in preaching the
Gospel, 1 Corinthians 9:19-23.
In a race, only one wins. In serving God, all
may win, 1 Corinthians 9:24-27.
Paul followed example of Christ,
1 Corinthians 11:1.
Dying daily, 1 Corinthians 15:31.
Showing love to those who cause grief,
2 Corinthians 2:5-11.
Clear marks of a disciple, 2 Corinthians
6:3-13.
Sharing concerns of leader, 2 Corinthians
8:16.
Pledged only to truth, 2 Corinthians 13:8.
Crucified with Christ, Galatians 2:20.
Serve one another in love, Galatians 5:13.
Death is gain to those who live for Christ,
Philippians 1:21.
Consider others better than yourself,
Philippians 2:3-4.
Forgetting past, pressing forward,
Philippians 3:12-16.
Filled with knowledge of God's will,
Colossians 1:9-12.
Life centered in Christ, Colossians 3:1-17.
Diligence for the Lord, Colossians 3:23-24.
Properly motivated, 1 Thessalonians 1:3.
True son in the faith, 1 Timothy 1:2.
Danger of putting money first, 1 Timothy
6:10.
Not embarrassed because of Paul's chains,
2 Timothy 1:16-18.
Paul's description of true disciple,
2 Timothy 2:1-4.
Persecution inevitable for committed
Christian, 2 Timothy 3:12.
Servant and apostle, Titus 1:1.
Enoch pleased God, Hebrews 11:5.
Faithfully running race, Hebrews 12:1-2.
Lifestyle of true disciple, James 3:17-18.
Strangers in the world, 1 Peter 1:1-2, 17.
Becoming chosen people, 1 Peter 2:9.
Walking in steps of Christ, 1 Peter 2:21-25.
Resisting Satan, 1 Peter 5:8-9.
Taking Scriptures to heart, Revelation 1:3.
Temporary suffering as reward for
faithfulness, Revelation 1:9.
Partial holiness insufficient in God's sight,
Revelation 2:1-6, 13-15, 18-20.
Holding on to faith, Revelation 2:25.
Clean in society of deceit, Revelation 3:4.
(See also v. 10.)

See *Commitment, Dedication, Followers.*

DISCIPLINE
God commanded separation in the Garden
of Eden, Genesis 2:16-17.
Poor leadership causes laxity in conduct,
Exodus 32:25.
Divine purpose for moral and physical
cleanliness, Leviticus 20:26.
Participation of group in destroying
blasphemer, Leviticus 24:14-16.
Care required in loving God, Joshua 23:11.
Whipping with thorns and briers, Judges
8:16.
Regulation of music used in worship,
1 Chronicles 6:31-32.
Better the discipline of God than judgment
of men, 1 Chronicles 21:13.
Laws and regulations, Nehemiah 9:13.
Wild ox must be tamed, Job 39:9-12.
Rejection of sin, Psalm 18:23.
God's discipline does not alter His love,
Psalm 89:32-33.
Blessing of divine discipline, Psalm 94:12-
13.
Discipline of good father, Proverbs 3:11-
12.
Those who hate discipline, Proverbs 5:12-
13.
Willingness to be disciplined and
corrected, Proverbs 10:17.
Discipline of children, Proverbs 13:24.
Folly in heart of child, Proverbs 22:15;
23:13-14; 29:15.
Eating too much honey, Proverbs 25:16.
Discipline for horse, donkey, and fool,
Proverbs 26:3.
Best meats and finest wine, Isaiah 25:6.
Sins paid back, Isaiah 65:6.
Discipline with justice, Jeremiah 30:11.
Those who will not respond, Jeremiah
32:33.
Torn but healed by the Lord, Hosea 6:1.
Those who refuse correction, Zephaniah
3:2.
Attitude of students to teachers, Matthew
10:24.
Jesus disciplined demons, Mark 1:33-34.
Cost for doubting an angel, Luke 1:18-20.
Mother's reprimand, Luke 2:48.
Branches that bear no fruit, John 15:2.
Military background of Cornelius caused
him to respect Peter, Acts 10:25-26.
Struggle against sin, Romans 6:12-13.

Incest not disciplined in Corinthian church, 1 Corinthians 5:1-2.

Runner and prize, 1 Corinthians 9:24-27.

Painfulness of good correction, 2 Corinthians 7:8-9.

Helping someone who has sinned, Galatians 6:1.

Discipline of children, Ephesians 6:4.

Avoid making enemies of those who do wrong, 2 Thessalonians 3:14-15.

Preventing teaching of false doctrine, 1 Timothy 1:3-5.

Satan as teacher, 1 Timothy 1:18-20.

Diligent in quest for spiritual maturity, 1 Timothy 4:13.

Those who sin publicly rebuked, 1 Timothy 5:20.

Power and love through self-discipline, 2 Timothy 1:7.

Enduring hardship as good soldier, 2 Timothy 2:1-4.

Athletes compete according to rules, 2 Timothy 2:5.

Gently instruct backslider, 2 Timothy 2:23-26.

Family of an elder, Titus 1:6.

How to deal with a divisive person, Titus 3:10.

Jesus Himself learned obedience, Hebrews 5:8-9.

See *Commitment, Growth, Maturity, Reproof.*

DISCONTENT

Unhappy with present leadership, Numbers 14:1-4.

People united in discontent, Joshua 9:18-19.

Beloved but barren, 1 Samuel 1:2-11.

Complaining to the Lord, Job 10:1; 23:2; Psalms 55:2; 77:3; 142:2.

Never satisfied, Proverbs 27:20; 30:15-16.

Chasing the wind, Ecclesiastes 1:17-18.

Discontent with government, Ecclesiastes 4:13-16.

Those who complain accept instruction, Isaiah 29:24.

At odds with one's Maker, Isaiah 45:9.

Plight of eunuch, Isaiah 56:3-5.

Daughters taught how to wail, Jeremiah 9:20.

Desire for more than one has, Luke 3:14.

Prodigal and his brother, Luke 15:11-31.

See *Complain, Insincerity, Insurrection,*

Mob psychology, Opposition.

DISCORD

Accusation without basis, Proverbs 3:30.

Hot-tempered man, Proverbs 15:18.

An honor to avoid strife, Proverbs 20:3.

Settle misunderstandings quickly, Matthew 5:25.

Mob incited against Paul and Silas, Acts 17:5-7.

Purposely causing trouble, Romans 16:17.

Paul and Peter face-to-face, Galatians 2:11-21.

Teachings which cause controversy, 1 Timothy 1:3-4.

Arguing terminology, 2 Timothy 2:14.

See *Abrasion, Argument, Dispute, Unrest.*

DISCOUNT

Discounting a bill, Luke 16:1-8.

DISCOURAGEMENT

Moving ahead in spite of circumstances, Psalm 44:18.

Living righteously for no seeming purpose, Psalm 73:12-13. (Note vv. 24-26.)

Faint of heart, Psalm 143:4.

Debilitating effects of poverty, Proverbs 10:15.

Discouraged because of illness, Isaiah 38:9-12.

Joy and gladness gone, Jeremiah 48:33.

No one to restore spirit, Lamentations 1:16.

Vision comes to nothing, Ezekiel 12:22-25.

Exercising hope when no basis for hope, Romans 4:18-22.

See *Complain, Despondency, Pessimism.*

DISCOURTESY

Surly and mean, 1 Samuel 25:3.

Act of kindness misinterpreted, 2 Samuel 10:1-4.

Rejecting wedding invitation, Matthew 22:1-14.

Enemy who took bread, John 13:18.

See *Rudeness.*

DISCOVERY

New and hidden things, Isaiah 48:6.

Great discoveries possible, Jeremiah 33:3.

Discovery of Jesus by His disciples, John 1:41-45.

Incredible discoveries awaiting, 1 Corinthians 2:9.

Understanding divine dimensions,
Ephesians 3:16-19.
See *Awareness, Vision.*

DISCRETION
Clean and unclean animals for food,
Leviticus 11:1-47.
Discretion in physical relationships,
Leviticus 18:1-30. (See also chap. 20.)
Foolish sins, Numbers 12:11.
Reward of persistent search for wisdom
and insight, Proverbs 2:1-6.
Lack of discretion, Proverbs 7:6-23.
Making wise choices, Proverbs 8:6-11.
Speaking what is fitting, Proverbs 10:32.
Guided by integrity, Proverbs 11:3, 6.
Judgment and understanding, Proverbs
11:12.
Conduct in king's presence, Proverbs 25:6-
7.
Discretion in neighborly visits, Proverbs
25:17.
Discreet in speech and thought,
Ecclesiastes 5:2.
Indiscreet daughters of Babylon, Isaiah
47:1-3.
Aware of false prophets, 1 John 4:1-6.
See *Perception, Tact, Wisdom.*

DISCRIMINATION
God's plan for women's rights, Genesis
3:16.
Generic name for man and woman,
Genesis 5:2.
Same rules for all, Numbers 15:15.
Census involved men 20 years or older,
Numbers 26:2.
Daughters who had no brother, Numbers
27:1-11.
Samson desired Philistine wife, Judges
14:1-2.
Abundant reward for act of kindness,
1 Samuel 30:11-18.
Daughters assisting in rebuilding of the
wall at Jerusalem, Nehemiah 3:12.
Pledge to avoid intermarriage, Nehemiah
10:30.
Wealth and prestige could not numb
Haman's resentment, Esther 5:10-14.
Faith of Canaanite woman, Matthew 15:21-
28.
Treatment given Gentiles, Matthew 20:25.
Mutual hatred of Samaritans and Jews,
Luke 9:51-56.

Deeper meaning of deliverance from
legalism, Acts 10:24-28.
One in Christ, Galatians 3:28.
Slave and owner have same Master,
Ephesians 6:9.
Wrong of discrimination, James 2:1-4.
Darkness of hatred, 1 John 2:9-11.
See *Racism, Women's rights, Xenophobia.*

DISCUSSION
Value of discussion, Proverbs 15:22.
Profuse discussion in Athens, Acts 17:21.

DISDAIN
Veteran soldier underrated abilities of boy,
1 Samuel 17:42.
Scorn for acts of humility, Psalm 69:10-11.
Scarecrow in melon patch, Jeremiah 10:5.
Object of horror, Jeremiah 49:17.
See *Demean, Dislike.*

DISEASE
Leprosy, Exodus 4:6-7; Deuteronomy 24:8;
2 Kings 5:1-14; 2 Chronicles 26:19-21.
Divine immunity, Exodus 15:26;
Deuteronomy 7:15.
Skin infection, Leviticus 13:9-17;
Deuteronomy 28:27.
Wasting diseases, Leviticus 26:15-16.
Affliction resulting from sin, Psalm 107:17;
Isaiah 3:16-17.
Suggestion of social disease, Jude 6-7. (See
Lev. 15; 22:4-5.)
See *Epidemic, Health, Medicine.*

DISFIGURE
Cutting off thumbs and big toes, Judges
1:6-7.
Gouging out eyes, Judges 16:18-21;
1 Samuel 11:1-2.
Mutilated corpses, 2 Samuel 4:12.
Self-inflicted wounds, 1 Kings 18:28; Mark
5:5.
Noses and ears cut off, Ezekiel 23:25.
See *Torment, Torture.*

DISGRACE
Causing contempt, 2 Samuel 12:14;
Nehemiah 5:9; Ezekiel 36:20; Romans
2:23-24.
Job became byword, Job 17:6.
Scattered bones of enemy, Psalm 53:5.
Fall of Moab, Jeremiah 48:16-39.
Evil in broad daylight, 2 Peter 2:13-23.

See *Shame.*

DISGUISE
Judah deceived by his daughter-in-law, Genesis 38:13-19.
Disguising true identity, Joshua 9:3-6.
David feigned madness, 1 Samuel 21:12-14.
Seance disguise, 1 Samuel 28:8.
Ahijah's perception of royal deceit, 1 Kings 14:1-18.
Prophet in disguise, 1 Kings 20:38.
Royal disguise, 1 Kings 22:30; 2 Chronicles 35:20-24.

DISGUST
Detesting display of emotion, 2 Samuel 6:14-16.
Paul's disgust with unbelieving Jews, Acts 18:5-6.

DISHARMONY
Division in communities and families, Matthew 12:25.
Meetings that do more harm than good, 1 Corinthians 11:17-18.
Those who dilute Gospel message, Galatians 1:6-9.
See *Abrasion, Complain, Unrest.*

DISHONESTY
Inaccurate weights, Leviticus 19:35-36; Deuteronomy 25:15; Proverbs 11:1; Hosea 12:7; Micah 6:11.
Dishonest report for personal gain, 2 Samuel 1:2-16. (See also 1 Sam. 31:4.)
Practicing deceit, Psalm 101:7.
Peril of lying tongue, Proverbs 12:19-22.
Fortune made by lying tongue, Proverbs 21:6.
Extortion and bribe, Ecclesiastes 7:7.
Stolen eggs like unjust riches, Jeremiah 17:11.
Despising those who tell truth, Amos 5:10.
Wealth by extortion, Habakkuk 2:6.
King Herod and magi, Matthew 2:7-8, 12.
Ananias and Sapphira, Acts 5:1-11.
Rule of integrity, Romans 12:17.
Taking advantage of others, James 5:4-5.
See *Deceit.*

DISHWASHING
Necessary ceremony, Mark 7:1-4.

DISLIKE
Dislike among family members, Genesis 4:2-9; 27:1-46; 37:1-11; Luke 15:11-32.
Saul's dislike for David, 1 Samuel 18:8-9.
Quarrelsome Christians, 1 Corinthians 1:10-17; 3:3; 2 Corinthians 12:20; Philippians 4:2.
See *Abrasion, Friction, Jealousy.*

DISLOYALTY
Those who broke faith with God, Deuteronomy 32:51.
Unwilling to follow command to do evil, 1 Samuel 22:16-17.
Servants who disobey masters, 1 Samuel 25:10.
Philistine commander feared David's loyalty, 1 Samuel 29:1-11.
Recruited to turn against their own king, 2 Kings 9:14-24.
King destroyed by associates, 2 Kings 12:19-20.
Disloyalty in battle, Jeremiah 41:11-14.

DISOBEDIENCE
First act of disobedience, Genesis 3:1-11.
Plight of Lot's wife, Genesis 19:17, 26.
Foul odor of disobedience, Exodus 16:19-20. (See also vv. 22-24.)
Unauthorized fire for worship, Leviticus 10:1.
Penalty for national disobedience, Numbers 14:22-24.
Complaint about the leadership of Moses, Numbers 16:12-14.
Disobeying the Lord, Numbers 20:11.
Disobedience of faithful, 1 Samuel 12:20.
Unwilling to follow command to do evil, 1 Samuel 22:16-17.
Better to fall into God's hands than into hands of men, 2 Samuel 24:10-14.
Incomplete faithfulness to God, 1 Kings 22:43.
Sin abounded in spite of God's mercy and judgment, Psalm 78:32.
Judgment withheld against disobedience, Psalm 78:38.
Spiritual vagabonds, Jeremiah 2:31.
Sorrow of disobedience, Jeremiah 3:21.
Obedience and disobedience, Jeremiah 7:22-26.
Birds compared to people, Jeremiah 8:7.
When God refuses to hear and answer, Jeremiah 11:14.

Stark judgment on disobedient people, Jeremiah 15:1-2; 44:1-14.
Those who trust in man, Jeremiah 17:5, 13.
The Lord turns His back on disobedient, Jeremiah 18:17.
Obedience cited as lesson, Jeremiah 35:1-16.
Disobedience negates righteousness of past, Ezekiel 18:24.
God's love for errant child, Hosea 11:1-4.
Sins cause downfall, Hosea 14:1.
Three sins, even four, Amos 1:3, 6, 9, 11, 13; 2:1, 4, 6.
Disobedient people denied materialistic possessions, Amos 5:11.
Jonah's refusal to obey the call to Nineveh, Jonah 1:3.
Those who refuse correction and do not trust in the Lord, Zephaniah 3:2.
Learning from example of disobedient forefathers, Zechariah 1:4-6.
Salt that loses its flavor, and lights that are hidden, Matthew 5:13-16.
Seeming disobedience of Boy Jesus, Luke 2:41-51.
Avoid association with those who do wrong, 2 Thessalonians 3:14-15.
Those who could not hold true to faith, 1 Timothy 1:18-20.
Sure judgment on false teaching, 2 Peter 2:1-10.
See *Rebellion.*

DISORGANIZATION

Confusion caused by disobedience, Deuteronomy 28:20.
Overabundance of shepherds, Jeremiah 12:10.
Warriors stumbling over each other, Jeremiah 46:12.
Forgetting to bring necessities, Mark 8:14.
See *Confusion.*

DISPLAY

Boasting of religious zeal, 2 Kings 10:16.
Display of wealth, Esther 1:4; Isaiah 39:2.
Status symbols, Esther 5:11.
Do not make acts of charity public, Matthew 6:1-4.
Overt fasting, Matthew 6:16.
Public performance, Matthew 23:5.
Ego displayed by teachers of Law, Mark 12:38-40.
Pomp and honor, Luke 20:46; Acts 25:23.

See *Ego, Pride.*

DISPOSITION

Danger of hot temper, Judges 18:25.
Labor and good food, Ecclesiastes 5:18-20.
Right and wrong attitudes and disposition, Ephesians 4:31-32.
Kind to everyone, 2 Timothy 2:24.
Exercise of tact in times of duress, James 1:19-20.

DISPUTE

Abram's attitude toward Lot, Genesis 13:8-9.
Futility of strife among brothers, 2 Samuel 2:27-28.
Evidence that turns against accuser, Proverbs 25:8.
Settle misunderstandings quickly, Matthew 5:25.
Bringing theological dispute into secular courtroom, Acts 18:12-17.
Paul and Peter face-to-face, Galatians 2:11-21.
Teachings which cause controversy, 1 Timothy 1:3-4.
Rules for teacher handling dispute, 2 Timothy 2:23-26.
See *Abrasion, Argument.*

DISRESPECT

Elisha's bald head, 2 Kings 2:23-24.
Disrespect for age, Job 30:1; Lamentations 5:12.
Israel turned to idols, ignoring the God who led them through wilderness, Jeremiah 2:5-8.
Jehoiakim burned scroll dictated by Jeremiah, Jeremiah 36:1-26.
Jesus accused of disrespect, John 18:19-24.
See *Demean.*

DISRUPTION

Blind men rebuked for calling out to Jesus, Matthew 20:29-34
Wrong kind of authority in congregation, 3 John 9-10

DISSATISFACTION

Fruits of bitterness, Deuteronomy 32:32.
Meaningless accomplishment, Ecclesiastes 2:11.
Those never satisfied, Haggai 1:5-6.

DISSENSION
Jealousy of Miriam and Aaron, Numbers 12:1-9.
Evidence turns against accuser, Proverbs 25:8.
Mockery of fasting, Isaiah 58:4-5.
Those not for Jesus were against Him, Luke 11:23.
Debate over doctrinal issues, Acts 15:1-2.
Clash of personalities between Paul and Barnabas, Acts 15:36-41.
Those who purposely caused trouble, Romans 16:17.
Teachings which cause controversy, 1 Timothy 1:3-4.
See *Unrest.*

DISSIPATION
End of dissolute life, 2 Kings 9:30-37.
Corrupt from birth, Psalm 58:3.
Entertainment with no thought of spiritual need, Isaiah 5:12.
From one sin to another, Jeremiah 9:3.
Continual lust for more, Ephesians 4:19.
See *Carnality, Immorality.*

DISTANCE RUNNING
Running long race, Jeremiah 12:5.

DISTINCTION
Respect at city gate, Job 29:7-10.
Honor not fitting fool, Proverbs 26:1.
Role of humility in greatness, Matthew 23:12.
Respect of Cornelius for Peter, Acts 10:25-26.
See *Attainment, Leadership, Respect, Success.*

DISTORTION
Negative and positive viewpoints, Numbers 13:17-33.
Charming but deceitful speech, Proverbs 26:24-26.
Deliberately writing falsehoods concerning Law of the Lord, Jeremiah 8:8.
Believing a lie, Jeremiah 43:1-7.
See *Apostasy, Hypocrisy.*

DISTRESS
Companion of night creatures, Job 30:29.
Desperate times, Psalm 60:3.
When God refuses to hear and answer, Jeremiah 11:14.

Remorse of king, Daniel 6:13-18.
Going without food during times of distress, Acts 27:33-36.
Agony of those who refuse to repent, Revelation 16:10-11
See *Agony, Persecution, Suffering.*

DISTURB
Purposeful disruption of progress, Ezra 4:1-5; Nehemiah 4:8.
Job's "friends," Job 2:11-13. (Note ensuing dialogue between Job and these three men.)
Disturbing the prophets, Isaiah 30:6-11; Amos 2:12.
Satanic intrusion, Zechariah 3:1-2; 1 Peter 5:8.
Silencing a disturber, Acts 13:6-12.
Enough is enough, Acts 18:5-8.
Open door in spite of opposition, 1 Corinthians 16:5-9.
Trouble from layman, 2 Timothy 4:14-15.
See *Conflict, Irritation, Opposition.*

DIVERSITY
Different kinds of gifts and service, Romans 12:6; 1 Corinthians 12:4-11.
No two alike, 1 Corinthians 4:7.
Diversity in all creation, 1 Corinthians 15:39-46.
God intends diversity to produce unity, Ephesians 4:11-13.
The Lord invites diversity in prayer, Ephesians 6:18.
See *Original.*

DIVINATION
Information by divination, Genesis 44:15.
Remunerated fortune-tellers, Numbers 22:7.
Practice of sorcery and divination, Deuteronomy 18:14.
Seeking guidance for sacred object, 1 Samuel 6:2.
False oracles and prophets, Jeremiah 23:33-40.
False encouragement, Jeremiah 27:9; Zechariah 10:2.
Certain guidance, Ezekiel 13:22-23.
Seeking omen at fork in road, Ezekiel 21:18-23.
Slave-girl fortune-teller, Acts 16:16-18.
See *Fortune-telling, Spiritism.*

DIVINITY
Pharisees could not answer Jesus, Matthew 22:41-46.
Demons recognized deity of Christ, Mark 3:11, Luke 4:41.
See *Christ, God, Trinity*.

DIVISION
Satan divided against himself, Matthew 12:22-32.
Division and dispute concerning Jesus, Luke 12:51; John 7:12, 43; 9:16; 10:19.
Disagreements among believers, 1 Corinthians 1:10-17.
Those who would alienate from truth, Galatians 4:17.
Following personal desires, Jude 17-18.
See *Abrasion, Dispute, Disruption, Factions, Jealousy*.

DIVISIVE
See *Factions*.

DIVORCE
Earliest conditions of divorce, Deuteronomy 21:10-14; 22:13-21; Ezra 10:1-16.
Remarriage of divorced persons, Deuteronomy 24:1-4; Jeremiah 3:1.
Divine attitude toward divorce, Malachi 2:14-16.
Joseph contemplated divorcing Mary, Matthew 1:19.
Cause for divorce, Matthew 5:31-32.
Teaching of Jesus concerning divorce, Matthew 19:3-9.
Bible speaks concerning remarriage, Romans 7:1-3.
Paul's view of divorce, 1 Corinthians 7:10-11.

DOCTRINE
Good teaching, Deuteronomy 32:2; Proverbs 4:2.
Practice of error, Isaiah 32:6.
Shepherds who lead sheep astray, Jeremiah 50:6.
Teaching of Pharisees, Matthew 16:12.
Response of Jesus to critics, Matthew 21:23-27.
Ability of Jesus to confound critics, Mark 11:29-33.
Doctrine of Pharisees concerning Sabbath, Luke 6:1-11.
Argument over ceremonial washing, John 3:25.
Disagreement as to ministry of Jesus, John 7:42-43.
Debate over doctrinal issues, Acts 15:1-2.
Pagans certain of erroneous belief, Acts 19:35-36.
One day more sacred than another, Romans 14:5.
Disagreements among early believers, 1 Corinthians 1:10-17.
Message of wisdom to mature Christians, 1 Corinthians 2:6.
Following teachings of good men, 1 Corinthians 3:4.
Danger of overconfidence in theology, 1 Corinthians 10:12.
Disagreeing with doctrine and practice, 1 Corinthians 11:16.
Wrong attitudes toward taking Lord's Supper, 1 Corinthians 11:20-22.
We only know in part, 1 Corinthians 13:12.
Love is the greatest biblical truth, 1 Corinthians 13:13. (Note: Faith speaks of doctrine, hope of prophecy, but love of lifestyle.)
Preaching false doctrine, 2 Corinthians 11:4-15.
Pledged only to truth, 2 Corinthians 13:8.
Paul astonished at Galatians, Galatians 1:6-9.
False disciples would dilute Gospel, Galatians 2:4-5.
Paul and Peter face-to-face, Galatians 2:11.
Bewitched Galatians, Galatians 3:1.
Persuaded by every kind of teaching, Ephesians 4:14.
Envy among those who preach Christ, Philippians 1:15-19.
Paul wanted followers to know truth, Colossians 2:2-4.
Dead to principles of world, Colossians 2:20-23.
Teachings which cause controversy, 1 Timothy 1:3-4.
Deep truths, 1 Timothy 3:9.
Theology of demons, 1 Timothy 4:1-4.
Those who take pride in false doctrine, 1 Timothy 6:3-5.
Godless chatter and opposing ideas, 1 Timothy 6:20-21.
Role of the Holy Spirit in sound doctrine, 2 Timothy 1:13-14.
Pointless dispute over words, 2 Timothy

2:14.
Those who wander from truth, 2 Timothy
2:17-18.
Avoid foolish arguments, 2 Timothy 2:23.
Those who do not want sound doctrine,
2 Timothy 4:3-4.
Faith held in common, Titus 1:4.
Student of sound doctrine, Titus 1:9.
Proper teaching for all ages, Titus 2:1-10.
Avoid foolish arguments about Law, Titus
3:9.
Depth perception in teaching and learning
doctrinal truths, Hebrews 6:1-3.
Be careful of strange teachings, Hebrews
13:9.
Doctrine difficult for some to understand,
2 Peter 3:15-16.
Bad teaching among good people,
Revelation 2:13-15.
See *Denomination, Heresy, Scripture,
Syncretism, Theology.*

DOCUMENT
Document submitted to king in opposition
to rebuilding temple, Ezra 4:12-16.
Authorization from king for travel,
Nehemiah 2:1-8.
Documents of ownership, Jeremiah 32:14.
Letter giving credentials to visiting
instructors, Acts 15:22-29.
Letters of introduction, 1 Corinthians 16:3.
See *Credentials.*

DOCUMENTATION
David documented ability to face Goliath,
1 Samuel 17:32-37.
Babylonian permission to rebuild temple,
Ezra 5:8-17; 6:1-12.
Nehemiah's authorization for travel to
Jerusalem, Nehemiah 2:1-8.
Loss of family records, Nehemiah 7:64.
Willingness to accept truth of wrongdoing,
Job 6:24.
Documentation of the ministry of Jesus,
Matthew 11:4-5.
Stephen's knowledge of Old Testament
history, Acts 7:1-60.
Paul's resumé of the Old Testament and
proclamation of the Gospel, Acts 13:16-
41.
See *Authenticity, Validity.*

DOG
No sales in sanctuary, Deuteronomy 23:18

(KJV).
Symbol of contempt, 1 Samuel 17:43;
24:14; 2 Samuel 3:8; 9:8; 16:9; 2 Kings
8:13; Proverbs 26:11; Isaiah 56:10.
Canine scavengers, 1 Kings 14:11; 21:19;
22:38.
Man's underrated friend, Job 30:1.
Prowling at night, Psalm 59:6.
Don't grasp by the ears, Proverbs 26:17.
Live dogs and dead lions, Ecclesiastes 9:4.
Children's bread given to dogs, Matthew
15:26.
Medicinal tongues, Luke 16:21.
Human "dogs," Philippians 3:2;
Revelation 22:15.

DOGMATIC
Ineptness of king's viewpoint, 1 Kings
12:1-15.
Fool airs own opinion, Proverbs 18:2.
Pagans certain of erroneous belief, Acts
19:35-36.
See *Headstrong, Opinion, Prejudice.*

DOMESTICATE
Wild ox must be tamed, Job 39:9-12.
Wild animals tamed, Isaiah 11:6-7.

DONATION
Jewelry given to God, Exodus 35:22-24.
Ample donations, Exodus 36:5.
Varied gifts, Numbers 7:3.
Personal treasures, 1 Chronicles 29:3-4.
Freely receive, freely give, Matthew 10:8.
More blessed to give, Acts 20:35.
Some to pay, others only receive,
2 Corinthians 11:7-8.
See *Contribution, Stewardship.*

DONKEY
Role of donkey in near sacrifice of Isaac,
Genesis 22:3.
Talking donkey, Numbers 22:26-34.
Incompatible ox and donkey,
Deuteronomy 22:10.
Riding white donkeys, Judges 5:10.
Thirty in a row, Judges 10:4.
Lost donkeys, 1 Samuel 9:3-4.
Divine privilege, Matthew 21:1-2.

DOOR
Door secured, Genesis 19:10.
Graffiti by divine command, Deuteronomy
11:20-21.

Golden door, 1 Kings 7:50.
Out and away, 2 Kings 9:3.
Door of hope, Hosea 2:15.
Christ the door, John 10:7-9 (KJV).
Door of opportunity, 1 Corinthians 16:8-9.

DOUBT
Abram's doubt overcome by faith, Genesis
15:1-6.
Ishmael, Abram's son of disobedience,
Genesis 16:1-16. (Note 15:1-6.)
Circumstances caused Moses to doubt
God's guidance, Exodus 5:22-23.
Doubting goodness of God in times of
confusion and disappointment, Judges
6:11-13.
Questioning ways of God, Job 10:3.
Be still and know, Psalm 46:10.
Darkness within heart prevents spiritual
sight, Matthew 6:23.
Doubt rebuked, Matthew 14:31; 17:14-20.
Potential of faith and deliverance from
doubt, Mark 9:23-24.
Apostles rebuked for doubting
Resurrection, Mark 16:14.
Zechariah and Mary could not understand
angelic announcements, Luke 1:18, 34.
Doubt can be augmented by hearing truth,
John 8:45-47.
Refusal to believe in face of sure evidence,
John 12:37-38.
Lack of faith does not alter God's
faithfulness, Romans 3:3-4.
Implications of doubting Resurrection,
1 Corinthians 15:12-19.
Sinful and unbelieving hearts, Hebrews
3:12.
Faith as sure antidote for doubt, Hebrews
11:1-3.
Helping those who doubt, Jude 22-23.

DOVE
Noah's special messenger, Genesis 8:8-
12.
Offered in sacrifice, Genesis 15:9.
Used in purification, Leviticus 12:6, 8;
14:22; Numbers 6:10.
Lament of sadness, Isaiah 38:14.
Moaning like slave girls, Nahum 2:7.
Beautiful symbol, Matthew 3:16; Luke 3:22;
John 1:32.

DOWNHEARTED
Joy and gladness gone, Jeremiah 48:33.

DRAFT DODGER
Those who sit at home, Numbers 32:6.

DRAGON
Depiction of dragon, Job 41:19-21.

DRAMA
Joseph and his brothers in Egypt, Genesis
42–45.
Crossing Red Sea, Exodus 14:21-28.
Samson's finale, Judges 16:23-30.
David and Goliath, 1 Samuel 17:1-51.
Slaves set free, again enslaved, Jeremiah
34:8-22.
Events at time of Crucifixion, Matthew
27:15-54.
Midnight prayer, Acts 16:16-34.
Paul's experience in storm and shipwreck,
Acts 27:13-44.
Silence in heaven, Revelation 8:1.
Sounding forth cry of doom, Revelation
8:13.

DREAD
Adonijah's unnecessary fear, 1 Kings 1:50-
53.
Needlessness of worry, Matthew 6:25-32.
See *Fear, Panic.*

DREAM
Thick and dreadful darkness, Genesis
15:12.
Seeking God's will, Genesis 28:11-22.
Revealing future, Genesis 37:5-10.
Divine use of visions and dreams,
Numbers 12:4-6.
Dreams as vehicles of evil, Deuteronomy
13:1-5; Jeremiah 23:25-32; Zechariah
10:2.
Symbol of unreality, Job 20:8.
Warning in dreams, Job 33:14-18.
Cause of dreams, Ecclesiastes 5:3.
Awakening to reality, Isaiah 29:8.
Pleasant sleep, Jeremiah 31:26.
Daniel could understand visions and
dreams, Daniel 1:17. (See chaps. 2; 4.)
Instructional dream, Matthew 1:20-21.
Paul's vision of Macedonian, Acts 16:9-10.
Paul assured of guidance and protection in
a vision, Acts 18:9-11.
See *Nightmare.*

DRONE
Those who do nothing, Isaiah 30:7.

DROUGHT
Famine conditions, Genesis 12:10; 26:1; Ruth 1:1; 1 Kings 17:12; 2 Kings 4:38; Nehemiah 5:3; Jeremiah 14:16.
Rain falling as dust, Deuteronomy 28:24.
No dew or rain, 1 Kings 17:1.
Land made barren, Jeremiah 14:4-6.
Scorched pastures, dried-up streams, Joel 1:19-20.
No rain during growing season, only scattered showers, Amos 4:7-8.
Widespread drought, Haggai 1:11.
See *Arid.*

DROWNING
Danger of deep water, Psalm 69:1-3.

DRUNKENNESS
Led astray by alcohol, Proverbs 20:1.
Bloodshot eyes, Proverbs 23:29-31.
Drunken spree, Isaiah 5:11; Romans 13:13.
Laid low by wine, Isaiah 28:1, 7.
Drunken watchmen, Isaiah 56:10-12.
Drunkenness fostered by the Lord, Jeremiah 13:12-14.
Truly dead drunk, Jeremiah 51:57.
Too much wine, Nahum 1:10.
See *Alcohol, Liquor, Wine.*

DUMBFOUNDED
Ezekiel overwhelmed, Ezekiel 3:15.

DUNG
Dung used for baking, Ezekiel 4:15.

DUPLICITY
Feigned madness, 1 Samuel 21:13.
Pretense of mourning, 2 Samuel 14:2.
Alleged religious loyalty, 2 Kings 10:18-19.
Friends and brothers not to be trusted,

Jeremiah 9:4-8.
King Herod and the magi, Matthew 2:7-8, 12.
Satan's use of Scripture, Matthew 4:1-11.
Pretended piety, Luke 20:20.
Camouflaged objective, Acts 23:15.
See *Hypocrisy, Sham.*

DURABILITY
See *Dedication, Determination, Endurance, Energy, Tenacity, Virility.*

DURESS
Desperate times, Psalm 60:3.
Jeremiah's anguish, Jeremiah 4:19.
Going without food during times of duress, Acts 27:33-36.
See *Anxiety, Conscience, Guilt, Stress.*

DUTY
Collecting daily manna, Exodus 16:4.
Carelessness in duty, 1 Samuel 26:7-16.
Half stood guard while other half worked, Nehemiah 4:21.
Adhering to regulations, Nehemiah 8:18.
Daily vows, Psalm 61:8.
Entrusted with secret things of God, 1 Corinthians 4:1-2.
Aim for perfection, 2 Corinthians 13:11.
Responsibility to do good, James 4:17.
See *Assignment, Responsibility.*

DYNAMIC
See *Identity, Image, Influence, Leadership, Personality.*

DYSENTERY
Violent illness, 2 Chronicles 21:12-15.
Healing for fever and dysentery, Acts 28:8.

E

EAGERNESS
David's eagerness to confront Goliath,
  1 Samuel 17:48.
So full of words, Elihu about to burst, Job
  32:17-22.
Powerful horses straining for action,
  Zechariah 6:7.
Young man eager for truth, Mark 10:17.
Early to temple, Luke 21:38.
Eager for ministry, John 4:40.
Disciple who outran Peter, John 20:4.
Ethiopian eunuch's eagerness to be
  baptized, Acts 8:36-37.
Open and receptive, Acts 10:33; 17:9.

EAGLE
Symbolic strong wings, Exodus 19:4.
Forbidden as food, Leviticus 11:13;
  Deuteronomy 14:12.
Swiftness of flight, 2 Samuel 1:23; Proverbs
  23:5.
Sky hunter, Job 9:26.
Strength, Psalm 103:5.
Renewed strength, Isaiah 40:30-31.

EAR
Pierced ear, Exodus 21:5-6.
Act of consecration, Exodus 29:20;
  Leviticus 8:23.
See *Deafness, Hearing.*

EARNESTNESS
See *Commitment, Determination, Zeal.*

EARNINGS
Earnings from prostitution unacceptable as
  a gift to God, Deuteronomy 23:18.
Protecting debtor's earning power,
  Deuteronomy 24:6.
Giving rather than receiving fee, Ezekiel
  16:32-34.

No wages, no business opportunities,
  Zechariah 8:10.
Women who helped support Jesus, Luke
  8:3.
Wages an obligation, not a gift, Romans
  4:4.
See *Honorarium, Salary, Stipend, Wages.*

EARRINGS
Earrings and foreign gods, Genesis 35:4;
  Isaiah 3:20.
From earrings to idol, Exodus 32:1-4.
Earrings offered to the Lord, Exodus 35:22;
  Numbers 31:50.
Large collection of earrings, Judges 8:22-
  27.
Wise man's rebuke likened to earring,
  Proverbs 25:12.
See *Jewelry.*

EARTH
Primordial planet, Genesis 1:2-7.
As long as earth endures, Genesis 8:22.
Earth divided, Genesis 10:25.
Sacred responsibilities for earth itself,
  Leviticus 25:1-7.
Mineral wealth, Deuteronomy 8:9.
Ancient concept of foundations, 1 Samuel
  2:8; Job 9:6.
Dust of humility, Nehemiah 9:1.
Earth as object in space, Job 26:7.
Earth's wealth belongs to God, Psalms
  24:1; 50:9-12; 95:4-5; Haggai 2:8.
Shape of earth known since antiquity,
  Isaiah 40:22.
Creator who cares for His creation, Isaiah
  42:5-7.
Design and purpose, Isaiah 45:18.
Earth's destruction, Isaiah 51:6; 2 Peter
  3:10-13; Revelation 20:11; 21:1.
Global earth indicated by varying time

activities at Christ's return, Luke 17:33-35.
See *Creation, Ecology, Natural resources, Nature.*

EARTHQUAKE
Trembling mountain, Exodus 19:17-18.
Judgment by earthquake, Numbers 16:28-34.
Mountains shaken before the Lord, Judges 5:5; 1 Kings 19:11-12.
Army in panic, 1 Samuel 14:15.
Description of an earthquake, Isaiah 24:19-20.
Between cross and empty tomb, Matthew 27:51; 28:2.
Prison doors opened, Acts 16:25-31.
Earth shaken by great earthquake, Revelation 6:12-17.
Greatest earthquake of all time, Revelation 16:18-20.

EASE
At ease in time of crisis, Numbers 32:6.
Enjoying divine goodness without serving, Nehemiah 9:35.
Faith without works, James 2:14; 4:17.
Not an easy way, 1 Peter 4:17-18.

EASTER
Prophecy of Christ riding on donkey, Zechariah 9:9.
Judas and the 30 pieces of silver, Zechariah 11:12-13.
Prophecy of the cross, Zechariah 12:10-11.
First recorded Easter observance, Acts 12:3.
Easter experienced personally, Ephesians 1:15-21.

ECLIPSE
Darkness in daytime, Job 5:14.
One cannot look at sun, Job 37:21.
Sun and moon darkened, Isaiah 13:10; Joel 2:10; Matthew 24:29.
Darkness at noon, Amos 8:9.

ECOLOGY
Man's responsibility to nature, Genesis 1:29; Deuteronomy 20:19-20.
Protection of birds, Deuteronomy 22:6.
Chemicals cause land to become unproductive, Deuteronomy 29:23.
Purifying bad water, 2 Kings 2:19-22.

Earth entrusted to humans, Psalm 115:16.
Water pollution, Proverbs 25:26.
Foul-smelling canals, Isaiah 19:6.
People defile earth, Isaiah 24:5.
Dying earth, Isaiah 51:6.
New heaven and new earth, Isaiah 65:17.
Defilement of fertile land, Jeremiah 2:7.
Land parched and wildlife gone, Jeremiah 12:4.
Too many merchants have desecrated land, Nahum 3:16.
See *Conservation, Earth, Nature.*

ECONOMY
Good times and bad, Genesis 41:35-36; Ecclesiastes 7:14.
Mortgaging property to buy food, Nehemiah 5:3. (See vv. 1-5.)
First things first, Proverbs 24:27.
Woman with economic skills, Proverbs 31:10-31.
God's great bargain, Isaiah 55:1-2.
No wages, no opportunities, Zechariah 8:10.
Treasures on earth or in heaven, Matthew 6:19-21.
Difference between human equations and power of God, John 6:1-13. (See particularly v. 7.)
Spiritual economics, Acts 3:6.
See *Finances.*

ECSTASY
Shouting and weeping, Ezra 3:10-13.
Visions of the Lord, Ezekiel 1:1.
Drunk on wine or filled with Spirit, Ephesians 5:18.
See *Emotion.*

EDIFICATION
Mutual spiritual growth, Romans 14:19; 15:2; 1 Corinthians 14:3, 26.
Knowledge versus love, 1 Corinthians 8:1.
Strengthening others, 2 Corinthians 12:19.
Body of Christ built up, Ephesians 4:10-13.

EDUCATION
Forbidden knowledge, Genesis 2:16-17; 3:1-7.
Solomon's prayer for wisdom rather than material gain, 1 Kings 3:5-15; 4:29-34.
Nationwide education for all, 2 Chronicles 17:7-9.
Teaching with parables, Psalm 78:1-8.

Stated learning objectives of Book of
  Proverbs, Proverbs 1:1-6.
Wisdom and understanding greater than
  money, Proverbs 16:16.
Properly training child, Proverbs 22:6.
Knowledge gives strength, Proverbs 24:5-
  6.
Finding wisdom like eating honey,
  Proverbs 24:13-14.
Knowledge better than wealth, Ecclesiastes
  7:12.
The sum total of knowledge, Ecclesiastes
  12:13.
Those who cannot read, Isaiah 29:11-12.
Greatest treasure, Isaiah 33:6.
Misled by incorrect knowledge, Isaiah
  47:10.
Three-year training program in Babylon,
  Daniel 1:3-5.
Prophecy of widespread education across
  world, Habakkuk 2:14.
Teaching truth, Malachi 2:6.
Attitude of students to teachers, Matthew
  10:24; Luke 6:40.
Perception of adults compared to children,
  Matthew 11:25; Luke 10:21.
Hearing but not understanding, Matthew
  13:14-15.
Mouth speaks what heart contains, Luke
  6:43-45.
Knowledge beyond classroom, John 7:14-
  15.
Holy Spirit as Teacher, John 14:26.
Simple men confound scholars, Acts 4:13.
Interest of intelligent man, Acts 13:6-7.
Intellectual pride in Athens, Acts 17:16-34.
Erudite men, Acts 22:3.
Wisdom and foolishness, 1 Corinthians
  1:18-21.
Message of wisdom to mature Christians,
  1 Corinthians 2:6.
Folly of intellectual pride, 1 Corinthians
  3:18-20; 8:1-3.
Information without eloquence,
  2 Corinthians 11:6.
Spirit of wisdom and revelation, Ephesians
  1:17.
Learning at home, Ephesians 6:4.
Both knowledge and insight, Philippians
  1:9.
Godless chatter and ideas falsely called
  knowledge, 1 Timothy 6:20-21.
Unable to acknowledge truth, 2 Timothy
  3:7.

Faith as the sure antidote for doubt,
  Hebrews 11:1-3.
When lacking wisdom, ask God, James 1:5-
  6.
See *Instruction, Students, Study, Teacher,
  Teaching.*

EFFORT
Initiative required in loving God, Joshua
  23:11.
Sow wheat but reap thorns, Jeremiah
  12:13.
Working hard for the Lord, Colossians
  3:23-24.
See *Initiative, Motivation, Performance.*

EGO
God as the only rightful display of ego,
  Genesis 1:1; Isaiah 42:8.
Captured city named after captor,
  Numbers 32:42.
Fame and honor decreed by God,
  Deuteronomy 26:19.
Appealing to king's ego, Ezra 4:14.
Requesting God's favor in response to
  one's faithfulness, Nehemiah 5:19.
Boasting of wealth and prestige, Esther
  5:11.
Contempt for unfortunate, Job 12:5.
Glory belongs only to the Lord, Psalm
  115:1.
Artist is mortal, Isaiah 44:11.
Pharaoh only loud noise, Jeremiah 46:17.
Deification of self, Ezekiel 16:23-25.
Nebuchadnezzar's ego and faith of
  Daniel's friends, Daniel 3:8-20.
Pharisees and religion of sham, Matthew
  23:5-7.
Asking for prestige rather than earning it,
  Mark 10:35-40.
Ego displayed by teachers of Law, Mark
  12:38-40.
Proud sorcerer, Acts 8:9-10.
Price paid for flagrant vanity, Acts 12:19-
  23.
Boasting of self-righteousness, Romans
  4:2.
Falsely evaluating one's self, 2 Corinthians
  10:12.
Paul's wise use of names of followers,
  Colossians 4:7-17.
One worthy of praise from all creation,
  Revelation 5:13-14.
Evil queen refused to admit sin, Revelation

18:7-8.
See *Conceit, Pride, Self-image, Status, Vanity.*

ELDER
Initial appointment of elders, Deuteronomy 1:9-15.
Chosen for church duty, Acts 14:23; 16:4; 20:28-32.
Honored for good work, 1 Timothy 5:17-19.
High standard, Titus 1:5-9; 1 Peter 5:1-5.
Healing ministry, James 5:14-15.

ELECTION
Appointment of leader, Numbers 27:16.
Elect of the Lord, Deuteronomy 4:37; 7:6; Matthew 25:34; John 15:16; Galatians 4:30; Ephesians 1:4; 1 Peter 1:2.
Choosing right leader, Deuteronomy 17:14-15.
Trees seek a king, Judges 9:7-15.
Selection by lot, Nehemiah 11:1.
Put out of office, Isaiah 22:19.
Seeking God's guidance in the choice of leadership, Hosea 8:4.
Valley of decision, Joel 3:14.
See *Politics.*

ELEPHANT
Strength of elephant, Job 40:15-24.

ELEVENTH HOUR
Turning back battle at gate, Isaiah 28:6.

ELOQUENCE
Moses lacked eloquence, Exodus 4:10.
Words aptly spoken, Proverbs 25:11.
Clever with enchanting, Isaiah 3:3.
Eloquent description of noble person, Isaiah 32:8.
Mouth like sharpened sword, Isaiah 49:2.
An instructed tongue, Isaiah 50:4.
Boldness of speech given by God, Jeremiah 1:6-10.
Wood destroyed by fire, Jeremiah 5:14.
Guided speech in times of persecution and witness, Matthew 10:19-20.
People hung onto the words of Jesus, Luke 19:48.
No one ever spoke like Jesus, John 7:46.
Spiritual truth communicated in human terms, Romans 6:19.
Love the most expressive of all,

1 Corinthians 13:1-13.
A clear sound in preaching, 1 Corinthians 14:6-12.
Paul wrote convincing letters but lacked ability in public speaking, 2 Corinthians 10:10.
Information without eloquence, 2 Corinthians 11:6.
Fine-sounding arguments, Colossians 2:4.
Successful communication requires prayer support, Colossians 4:3-4.
Letting the message ring out, 1 Thessalonians 1:8.
Magnificent conclusion of the Scripture record, Revelation 22:1-21.
See *Communication, Preaching, Speech.*

EMASCULATION
See *Eunuch.*

EMBALMING
Early Egyptian skill, Genesis 50:1-3, 26.
Spices and perfumes, 2 Chronicles 16:14; John 19:40.

EMBARRASSMENT
Fear of being killed by woman, Judges 9:54.
Samuel's disappointing sons, 1 Samuel 8:1-3.
Logic of Jesus embarrassed His opponents, Luke 13:10-17.
Coming to Jesus at night, John 3:1-2.
Paul prayed not to be ashamed, Philippians 1:20.
See *Humiliation, Shy.*

EMERGENCY
Reaction of Lot's family to emergency, Genesis 19:14-17.
Help from neighbor, Proverbs 27:10.
See *Crisis.*

EMOTION
Hagar's love for Ishmael, Genesis 21:14-16.
Isaac meeting Rebekah, Genesis 24:62-67.
Tears of Joseph, Genesis 42:24. (See also 43:29-30.)
Reunion of Joseph and his brothers, Genesis 45:1-15.
Joseph's eagerness to meet his father, Genesis 46:29.
Clever wiles of Samson's wife, Judges

14:11-19.
Profuse tears of gratitude, 1 Samuel 20:41.
King Saul's tears as he confessed his
    wrong to David, 1 Samuel 24:16-17.
Weeping until exhausted, 1 Samuel 30:4.
David's sorrow over death of Jonathan,
    2 Samuel 1:26.
David's lament for Abner, 2 Samuel 3:33-
    37.
Returning ark to Jerusalem, 2 Samuel 6:5.
David's grief over death of Absalom,
    2 Samuel 18:19-33.
Divine grief, 1 Chronicles 21:14-15.
Tears of joy as foundation laid for temple,
    Ezra 3:10-13.
Physical act of disdain, Ezra 9:3.
Tears of contrition and confession, Ezra
    10:1.
Job wept for others but was not
    remembered in his need, Job 30:25.
Excited about God and His greatness, Job
    37:1.
Difference between mind and heart, Job
    38:36.
The Lord close to those with broken hearts
    and spirits, Psalm 34:18.
Sweetness of God's promises, Psalm
    119:103.
Songs of Zion gone silent, Psalm 137:1-4.
Uplifting emotions, Proverbs 4:23.
Hotheaded fool, Proverbs 14:16-17.
Zeal without knowledge, Proverbs 19:2.
Beware hot-tempered man, Proverbs
    22:24-25.
Lacking self-control, Proverbs 25:28.
Angry man stirs up dissension, Proverbs
    29:22.
Drunk but not from wine, Isaiah 29:9;
    51:21.
Anguish of guilt, Jeremiah 4:18-19.
Jeremiah's compassion, Jeremiah 9:1.
Skilled in wailing, Jeremiah 9:17-20.
Jeremiah tried to suppress feelings,
    Jeremiah 20:9.
Power of holy words, Jeremiah 23:9.
Weeping and wailing as judgment comes,
    Jeremiah 25:34.
Weeping for joy, Jeremiah 31:9.
Joy and gladness gone, Jeremiah 48:33.
Tears of repentance, Jeremiah 50:4.
No one to comfort, Lamentations 1:16.
Ezekiel overwhelmed, Ezekiel 3:15.
Knocking knees of frightened king, Daniel
    5:6.

Daniel overwhelmed by vision, Daniel
    10:7-8.
Preaching with compassion, Joel 2:17.
Weeping and wailing, Micah 1:8.
Loss of children under Herod, Matthew
    2:18.
Grieving and misunderstanding, Matthew
    17:22-23.
Joy and fear, Matthew 28:8.
Crowd stirred up against Jesus, Mark
    15:11-15. (See 11:8-10.)
Frightened shepherds at time of Jesus'
    birth, Luke 2:8-10.
Reactions of Mary compared to those of
    shepherds, Luke 2:19-20.
Effect of music on emotions, Luke 7:31-32.
Joy experienced by Jesus, Luke 10:21.
Concern of Jesus for Jerusalem, Luke
    13:34; 19:41-44.
Rejoicing in heaven when sinner repents,
    Luke 15:3-10.
Sustaining joy of disciples, Luke 24:50-53.
Streams of living water from within, John
    7:38-39.
Tears of Jesus, John 11:35.
Too excited to open door, Acts 12:12-16.
Sorrow of parting with friends, Acts 20:36-
    38.
Sorrow of friends brought sorrow to Paul,
    Acts 21:13.
Zeal without knowledge, Romans 10:1-2.
Keep your spiritual fervor, Romans 12:11.
Anger without sin, Ephesians 4:26.
Drunk on wine or filled with the Spirit,
    Ephesians 5:18.
The kind of affection Jesus gives,
    Philippians 1:8.
Rejoice in the Lord, Philippians 4:4.
Convicting power of the Holy Spirit,
    1 Thessalonians 1:4-5.
Paul remembered tears of others,
    2 Timothy 1:3-4.
Cries of Jesus to His Heavenly Father,
    Hebrews 5:7.
Let those who are happy sing, James 5:13.
See *Excitement, Fear, Joy, Sorrow.*

EMPATHY
Remembering from experience, Exodus
    23:9.
Male pangs as of childbirth, Jeremiah 30:6.
Faith of friends resulted in a man's healing,
    Mark 2:1-12.
Troubles prepare us to help others,

2 Corinthians 1:3-4.
Paul's concern for spiritual development of followers, Colossians 2:1-5.
Paul remembered tears of others, 2 Timothy 1:3-4.
See *Involvement, Sharing.*

EMPHASIS
Reinforcing divine guidance, Joshua 23:6. (See 1:8.)
Failure to give proper emphasis, 2 Kings 13:14-19.
Jeremiah proclaimed message "again and again," Jeremiah 25:3-4.
Paul's use of hand gestures, Acts 13:16.
Paul's "punch line" conclusion to his appeal for stewardship, 2 Corinthians 9:15.
Emphasis on folly of legalism, Galatians 5:12.
Paul's insistence to followers, Ephesians 4:17.
Importance of repetition, 2 Peter 1:12-15.
Giving emphasis to former command, 1 John 2:7-8.
See *Reinforcement, Repetition.*

EMPLOYMENT
Women employed, Genesis 29:9.
Command to pay fair wages, Leviticus 19:13.
Hiring those who need employment, Deuteronomy 24:14-15.
King Solomon's fortunate officials, 1 Kings 10:8.
Sabbath duty on shifts, 2 Kings 11:4-8.
Thousands working on government project, 2 Chronicles 2:2.
Long-term employment, Proverbs 29:21.
Amos the shepherd, Amos 1:1.
Concern of centurion for servant, Matthew 8:5-13.
Workers earn their pay, Matthew 10:10; Luke 10:7; 1 Timothy 5:18.
Women who helped support Jesus from their own means, Luke 8:3.
Mutual interest between those of same occupation, Acts 18:1-3.
Evangelist seeking employment to support himself, 1 Corinthians 9:6-7.
Aim for perfection, 2 Corinthians 13:11.
Slaves and masters, Ephesians 6:5-9.
Relationship of slaves to masters, Colossians 3:22-25; 4:1.

Paul as model in daily conduct and employment, 2 Thessalonians 3:6-10.
Work more diligently for Christian employer, 1 Timothy 6:2.
Employees who can be trusted, Titus 2:9-10.
Withholding payment from those who labor, James 5:4.

EMPTINESS
Meaningless life, Ecclesiastes 1:2; 2:1.
Emptiness of mere toil, Ecclesiastes 4:7-8.
Unsatisfied dreams, Isaiah 29:7-8.
Plight of wicked compared to fulfillment of righteous, Isaiah 65:13-14.
Earth and sky under judgment, Jeremiah 4:23-26.
Stalks with no grain, Hosea 8:7.
Food and possessions that do not satisfy, Micah 6:14.
Continual lust for more, Ephesians 4:19.
Empty prayers, James 4:3.
Springs without water, 2 Peter 2:17.
Those who partake but do not possess, Jude 12-13.

EMULATION
Like father, like children, Numbers 32:14.
Jerusalem became more depraved than those from whom she learned depravity, Ezekiel 16:44-52.
Desire to be like others, Ezekiel 20:32-38.
Examples to one another, Hebrews 10:24.
Christ the perfect example, 1 Peter 2:21-25.
See *Example, Influence, Model.*

ENCOURAGEMENT
No need to fear, Genesis 26:24; 2 Kings 6:16; Isaiah 41:10; 43:1.
Skill of leadership to encourage, Exodus 14:13.
Strength of rising sun, Judges 5:31.
Do good to those who deserve it, Proverbs 3:27.
Nourishment of good speech, Proverbs 10:21.
Power of kind words, Proverbs 12:25; 15:23; 16:24.
Hope deferred, longing fulfilled, Proverbs 13:12.
Good news and cheerful looks, Proverbs 15:30.
Those who refuse encouragement,

Proverbs 25:20.
Importance of giving compliments, Isaiah 41:7.
Instructed tongue, Isaiah 50:4.
Challenge to work for divine cause, Haggai 2:4.
Divine encouragement, Matthew 9:2; 14:27; 17:7; Acts 23:11.
Surest therapy for anxious hearts, John 16:33.
Paul took time to encourage disciples, Acts 20:1-2.
Encouragement in time of storm, Acts 27:22.
Strong help weak, Romans 15:1.
Paul demonstrated skill of giving compliments, Romans 16:3-16; 1 Corinthians 11:2; 2 Corinthians 7:4-7.
Refreshing spirit of others, 1 Corinthians 16:18.
Complimenting those who had been previously rebuked, 2 Corinthians 7:14.
Encouraged by news of new convert, Galatians 1:23-24.
Paul's wise use of names of followers, Colossians 4:7-17.
Encouraging believers, 1 Thessalonians 2:11-12.
Paul encouraged by conduct of Thessalonians, 1 Thessalonians 3:6-10.
Boasting about perseverance and faith of others, 2 Thessalonians 1:4.
Strengthened by encouragement of our Lord Jesus Christ, 2 Thessalonians 2:16-17.
Not embarrassed by misfortune of friend, 2 Timothy 1:16-17.
Encouraging one another daily, Hebrews 3:13.
Remember those in prison, Hebrews 13:3.
See *Compliments, Sharing.*

ENDING
The last words of David, 2 Samuel 23:1-7.
God pronounces "the end," Ezekiel 7:2.
Last statement of great prophet, Ezekiel 48:35.
Conclusion of wrath of God, Revelation 15:1.
Scriptural finale, Revelation 22:21. (Note conclusion of Old Testament, Mal. 4:6.)
See *Conclusion, Finale.*

ENDORSEMENT
God's commendation of Job, Job 1:8.
Jesus' evaluation of John the Baptist, Matthew 11:11-14.
Empty sincerity of Pharisees, Mark 12:15-17.
See *Accreditation, Approval.*

ENDURANCE
Running long race, Jeremiah 12:5.
Strength from the Lord, Habakkuk 3:19.
Standing firm to end, Matthew 10:22.
Love endures all, 1 Corinthians 13:8-13.
Not weary in doing good, Galatians 6:9.
Standing at end of struggle, Ephesians 6:13.
Inspired by hope, 1 Thessalonians 1:3.
Enduring hardness, Hebrews 12:7.
Learning perseverance through trials and testing, James 1:2-4, 12.
See *Dedication, Determination, Energy, Tenacity, Virility.*

ENEMY
Protected from superior enemy, Exodus 14:15-31.
Kindness to enemy, Exodus 23:4-5; 2 Samuel 9:1-8. (See also Prov. 25:21-22.)
Enemies in all directions, 1 Samuel 12:11.
Prayer for guidance in confronting enemy, 2 Samuel 5:17-19.
Procedure of David with defeated Moabites, 2 Samuel 8:2.
Enemies and bandits, Ezra 8:31.
Enemy's loss of self-confidence, Nehemiah 6:16.
Rejoicing in trouble of others, Job 31:29.
Prayer for those who scorn, Job 42:10.
Facing opposition with confidence, Psalm 3:6.
Guidance in midst of one's enemies, Psalm 5:8.
Words of enemy not to be trusted, Psalm 5:9.
David became leader to strangers, Psalm 18:43-45.
Let the Lord face your enemy, Psalm 35:1-7.
Enemy falls into pit he himself designed, Psalm 57:6.
Those who hate peace, Psalm 120:6-7.
Do not rejoice in failure of enemy, Proverbs 24:17-18.

Turning back battle at gate, Isaiah 28:6.
Thousand fear one adversary, Isaiah 30:17.
Egyptians were but men, Isaiah 31:3.
Dependence on promises of God, Isaiah 37:1-38.
Persecutors put to shame, Jeremiah 17:18.
Only a loud noise, Jeremiah 46:17.
Defeat of Babylon, Jeremiah 50:46.
Giving up to enemy, Lamentations 1:5.
Plundering with glee, Ezekiel 36:5.
Nine out of 10 lost in battle, Amos 5:3.
Gates wide open to enemy, Nahum 3:13.
Love your enemy, Matthew 5:43-48.
Those who can only kill the body but not the soul, Matthew 10:28.
Silence of Jesus before accusers, Matthew 26:57-67.
Basics of Golden Rule, Luke 6:27-36.
Jesus avoided those who would take His life, John 7:1.
Hated by the world, John 15:18-21.
Forgiving spirit of martyr, Acts 7:60.
Mob incited against Paul and Silas, Acts 17:5-7.
Forgiveness for enemy, Romans 5:10.
Bless those who persecute, Romans 12:14.
Be good to your enemy, Romans 12:20.
Leave revenge in God's hands, 2 Thessalonians 1:6-7.
See *Adversary, Espionage, Opposition.*

ENERGY
Weeping until exhausted, 1 Samuel 30:4.
Too exhausted to cross ravine, 1 Samuel 30:10, 21.
Doing what you do with all your might, Ecclesiastes 9:10.
Working with dull ax, Ecclesiastes 10:10.
Feet of a deer, Habakkuk 3:19.
Creator continuing His work, John 5:17.
Holy Spirit and Resurrection, Romans 8:11. (See Eph. 1:18-21.)
Powerful energy for labor, Colossians 1:29.
Working hard for the Lord, Colossians 3:23-24.
See *Tenacity, Virility.*

ENGAGEMENT
Bride for Isaac, Genesis 24:1-58. (See 25:19-20.)
Old Testament engagement for marriage, Deuteronomy 20:7.
Fate of virgin, Deuteronomy 22:23-27.
Commitment of two lovers, Song of Songs

6:3.
Becoming like the Lord's signet ring, Haggai 2:23.
See *Romance.*

ENLISTMENT
See *Recruitment.*

ENTERPRISING
Hard work and fantasy, Proverbs 28:19.
Commercial centers in Ezekiel's time, Ezekiel 27:12-23.
Enterprising manager, Luke 16:1-8.
Making most of every opportunity, Ephesians 5:15-16.
See *Initiative.*

ENTERTAINMENT
Substituting heterosexual activity for homosexual, Judges 19:22-25.
Fighting to death for entertainment, 2 Samuel 2:12-16.
Joy of victory, Psalm 126:2.
Entertainment with no thought of spiritual need, Isaiah 5:12.
Lovers of pleasure, 2 Timothy 3:4.

ENTHUSIASM
Those who do not follow wholeheartedly, Numbers 32:11.
Failure to give proper emphasis, 2 Kings 13:14-19.
Zealous workman, Nehemiah 3:20.
So full of words he was about to burst, Job 32:17-22.
The "amen" of agreement to God's message, Jeremiah 28:5-6.
Keep your spiritual fervor, Romans 12:11.
Ready to serve and to witness, Ephesians 6:15.
Letting message ring out, 1 Thessalonians 1:8-10.
Paul's abundant pleasure over progress of Thessalonian believers, 1 Thessalonians 3:8.
Role of recent convert, 1 Timothy 3:6.

ENTICEMENT
Agents of enticement, Exodus 22:16; Judges 14:18; 2 Chronicles 18:20; Proverbs 1:10; 1 Corinthians 2:4; James 1:14.

ENTRANCE
See *Door, Gate.*

ENVIRONMENT
Choice of place to live, Genesis 13:10-13.
Influence of parents written on heart,
Proverbs 6:20-23.
Sons of sorceress, Isaiah 57:3.
Evil influence of fathers on children,
Jeremiah 16:10-12.
Mouths speak what hearts contain, Luke
6:43-45.
Influence of Scriptures since childhood,
2 Timothy 3:14-15.
Surviving in evil surroundings, 2 Peter 2:4-
9.
See *Background, Culture, Family, Heritage,*
Home, Parents.

ENVY
Examples of envy, Genesis 4:5; 37:5, 11;
Numbers 11:28-29; 12:2; 1 Samuel
18:6-9; Esther 5:13; Psalm 73:3; Mark
15:10; Acts 13:45.
Envy caused by wealth, Genesis 26:12-14.
Physical result of envy, Proverbs 14:30.
Envious of wicked, Proverbs 24:19-20.
Keeping ahead of one's neighbor,
Ecclesiastes 4:4.
Envying another's success, Daniel 6:4.
Purification of love, 1 Corinthians 13:4.
Avoid being cause of envy, Galatians 5:26.
Jealousy as cause of murder, 1 John 3:12.
See *Covet, Jealousy.*

EPIDEMIC
Outbreak of tumors, 1 Samuel 5:9.
See *Disease.*

EQUALITY
Apparel worn by members of the opposite
sex, Deuteronomy 22:5.
Jealous wife, 1 Samuel 1:3-7.
Prosperity of wicked, Jeremiah 12:1.

EQUAL RIGHTS
God's plan for women and their rights,
Genesis 3:16.
Generic name for man and woman,
Genesis 5:2.
Women employed, Genesis 29:9.
Census involved men 20 years or older,
Numbers 26:2.
Spoils for conqueror, Judges 5:30.

Fear of being killed by woman, Judges
9:54.
Daughters assisting in rebuilding wall at
Jerusalem, Nehemiah 3:12.
Without partiality, Job 34:18-19.
One upright man among a thousand but no
upright women, Ecclesiastes 7:28.
Women who command husbands, Amos
4:1.
Paul's view of woman's role in marriage,
1 Corinthians 7:4.
Paul described role of women,
1 Corinthians 11:2-16.
Wives and husbands relating to each other,
Ephesians 5:22-33.
See *Prejudice, Racism, Women, Women's*
rights.

EQUITY
Evil prosperity, Jeremiah 12:1.
Receiving what one deserves, Zechariah
1:6.
Sun rises on evil and good, Matthew 5:44-
45.
Parable of Workers in Vineyard, Matthew
20:1-16.
No divine favoritism, Acts 10:34-35;
Romans 10:12.
Eternal inheritance, 1 Peter 1:3-4.
See *Fairness, Partiality.*

EROTIC
Mixing religion with immorality, Numbers
25:1-2.
Continual lust for more, Ephesians 4:19.
See *Hedonism, Immorality, Lust.*

ERROR
Creator's grief, Genesis 6:5-8.
Youth points out mistakes of age, Job 32:6-
12.
Way of wicked, Proverbs 4:19.
Willingness to be disciplined and
corrected, Proverbs 10:17.
Misled by incorrect knowledge, Isaiah
47:10.
Believing a lie, Jeremiah 43:1-7.
Priests who gave false teaching, Malachi
2:7-9.
Light becomes darkness, Luke 11:35.
Men love darkness rather than light, John
3:19-21.
Those who do not accept truth, John 5:41-
47.

Poisoning the mind, Acts 14:2.
Pagans certain of erroneous belief, Acts
19:35-36.
False humility, Colossians 2:18.
Teachings which cause controversy,
1 Timothy 1:3-4.
Detecting presence of false prophets,
1 John 4:1-3.
See *Mistake, Wrong.*

ESCAPE
Deliverance from Great Flood, Genesis
7:7-8.
City of destruction, Genesis 19:15-30.
Delivered from mad king, 1 Samuel 19:9-
18.
Saved from death, Esther 2:21-23.
No place to escape, Job 34:21; Jeremiah
25:35; 48:44; Matthew 23:33;
1 Thessalonians 5:2-3; Hebrews 2:2-3.
Egypt as place of refuge, Jeremiah 41:16-
18.
Jonah and great fish, Jonah 1:17.
Jesus sought no escape from cross, John
12:27.
Escape from prison, Acts 5:18-20.
Safety of darkness, Acts 17:10.
Deliverance from drowning, Acts 27:30-34.
See *Pardon, Refuge.*

ESPIONAGE
Babylon surveyed Hezekiah's treasures for
subsequent thievery, Isaiah 39:1-6.
Method of false teachers, 2 Peter 2:1.
See *Enemy.*

ESTATE
Husband who did not provide for family,
2 Kings 4:1-7.
See *Inheritance.*

ESTEEM
Respect for those older, Job 32:4.
Honor of strong people, Isaiah 25:3.
Empty sincerity of Pharisees, Mark 12:15-
17.
Respect of Cornelius for Peter, Acts 10:25-
26.
See *Appreciation, Respect.*

ESTIMATION
Underestimating enemy, Deuteronomy
1:41-44.
Veteran soldier underrated abilities of boy,

1 Samuel 17:42.
Low estimation of servant, 2 Kings 8:13.
See *Evaluation.*

ESTRANGEMENT
Broken circle among the 12 tribes, Judges
21:1-6.
Separation of King Saul and Samuel,
1 Samuel 15:34-35.
Estranged from birth, Psalm 58:3.
Straying from faith, Jeremiah 2:5.
Deserting the Lord for idols, Ezekiel 14:5.
Lip service, Matthew 15:8.

ETERNAL
Habitation of God, Isaiah 57:15; Micah 5:2.
One who never changes, Hebrews 1:10-12.
Born of imperishable seed, 1 Peter 1:23.
Past, present, and future of Jesus,
Revelation 1:4, 8.
He who is and was, Revelation 11:17.
Totality of Son of God, Revelation 22:13.

ETERNAL LIFE
Life forever, Psalm 21:4; 121:8.
Old Testament concept, Daniel 12:2.
Impossible to earn, Matthew 19:16-21;
John 14:6.
All this and heaven too, Luke 18:29-30.
Key to eternal life, John 3:16; 5:24-25;
12:25.
Bread of heaven, John 6:50-58.
Eternal purpose of Scripture, John 20:30-
31.
See *Conversion, Salvation.*

ETERNITY
God predates His creation, Psalm 90:1-2;
102:25-27.
Eternal God, Isaiah 44:6.
That which God has prepared for those
who love Him, 1 Corinthians 2:9-10.
Excluded forever from presence of God,
2 Thessalonians 1:9.
God's plan from beginning of time,
2 Timothy 1:8-10.
Church promised from beginning of time,
Titus 1:1-3.
Eternal existence of God, Revelation 1:8.

EULOGY
David's lament for King Saul and
Jonathan, 2 Samuel 1:17-27.
Lament for Abner, 2 Samuel 3:33-

34.

EUNUCH
Eunuch's duties, Esther 1:10; 2:3; 4:5; Acts 8:27.
Eunuch by accident, Deuteronomy 23:1.
Like a dry tree, Isaiah 56:3.
By birth or by choice, Matthew 19:12.
Ethiopian eunuch, Acts 8:28-39.

EUPHORIC
Desires satisfied and strength renewed, Psalm 103:5.
Labor and good food, Ecclesiastes 5:18-20.

EUTHANASIA
See *Coup de grace, Despair.*

EVALUATION
Veteran soldier underrated boy's abilities, 1 Samuel 17:42.
Sanballat's ridicule of Jewish capability, Nehemiah 4:1-10.
God's commendation of Job, Job 1:8.
Job asked for honest scales, Job 31:6.
Importance of ear to discern content, Job 34:1-3.
Difference between mind and heart, Job 38:36.
Jesus' evaluation of John the Baptist, Matthew 11:11-14.
Winning converts to error, Matthew 23:15.
Weak and strong, Romans 14:1-8.
Realizing what the believer has in Christ, Ephesians 1:18-23.
Strength and weakness of church at Ephesus, Revelation 2:1-6.
See *Assessment, Estimation.*

EVANGELISM
Tent for inquirers, Exodus 33:7.
God's Word on the tongue, 2 Samuel 23:2.
Benediction for missions, Psalm 67:1-2.
Those who proclaim God's Word, Psalm 68:11.
Declare God's glory among nations, Psalm 96:3, 10; Isaiah 12:4-5.
Message for nations, Psalm 105:1.
Sow in tears, reap with joy, Psalm 126:5-6.
Alert during harvest, Proverbs 10:5.
Wise win souls, Proverbs 11:30.
Worldwide outreach, Isaiah 12:4.
Need to evangelize during night, Isaiah 21:11-12.

Lift up your voice with a shout, Isaiah 40:9.
Message to the ends of earth, Isaiah 45:22.
Beautiful feet of those who bring Good News, Isaiah 52:7.
God's Word will not return empty, Isaiah 55:10-11.
Voice like trumpet, Isaiah 58:1.
Announcing Saviour's coming, Isaiah 62:11.
Proclaiming God's glory among nations, Isaiah 66:19.
Turning deaf ear to message, Jeremiah 5:12-13.
Day coming when soul-winning not necessary, Jeremiah 31:34; Hebrews 8:10-11.
Responsibility for failing to witness, Ezekiel 3:18-19.
Some will listen, some refuse, Ezekiel 3:27.
When preacher becomes silent, Ezekiel 7:26.
Identification on forehead of those who repent, Ezekiel 9:3-11.
Shepherds who refuse to look for lost sheep, Ezekiel 34:1-31.
Coming spiritual revival in Israel, Ezekiel 39:28-29.
Courage of Daniel to point out sin of king, Daniel 5:18-26.
Ripe harvest, Joel 3:13-14.
Famine for Word of the Lord, Amos 8:11-12.
Ninevites heeded Jonah's warning, Jonah 3:3-6.
Inviting others to come, Zechariah 8:20-22.
Parable of Sower, Matthew 13:1-23; Mark 4:3-20; Luke 8:4-15.
Worth of one lost sheep, Matthew 18:12-14; Luke 15:1-7.
Some refuse, others accept, Matthew 22:1-10.
Great Commission, Matthew 28:16-20; Mark 16:15.
Fishermen become fishers of men, Luke 5:1-11.
Proclaiming Good News from town to town, Luke 8:1-2.
Praying for harvesters rather than harvest, Luke 10:1-2.
Going into streets and alleys, Luke 14:16-24.
Harvesttime is now, John 4:35-38.
Lifting up Jesus to draw men to salvation, John 12:32.

Motivating follower of Christ, Acts 1:6-8.
Resisting the Holy Spirit, Acts 7:51.
Fruit of effective witness, Acts 11:20-21.
Few converts at Athens, Acts 17:34.
Paul depended on God's will for ministry
appointments, Acts 18:20-21.
Zealous ministry of Apollos, Acts 18:24-28.
All Jews and Greeks heard message, Acts
19:10.
Places Paul needed to visit, Acts 19:21.
House evangelism, Acts 28:30-31.
Bringing message to those who have not
heard, Romans 10:14-15.
Priestly duty to proclaim Gospel, Romans
15:16.
Benediction centered on world
evangelism, Romans 16:25-27.
One plants, another waters, God gives
growth, 1 Corinthians 3:6-9.
Paul adapted himself to culture of others,
1 Corinthians 9:19-23.
Gospel message in brief, 1 Corinthians
15:1-5.
Faithfully present message whatever the
difficulties, 1 Corinthians 15:57-58.
Ministry with spiritual weapons,
2 Corinthians 10:1-5.
Rapid spread of Gospel, Colossians 1:6.
Church and its outreach, Colossians 1:24-
27.
Followers are joy and crown of those who
present the message, 1 Thessalonians
2:17-20.
Rapidly spreading message,
2 Thessalonians 3:1.
Why Paul became an evangelist,
1 Timothy 2:1-7.
Remember those in prison, Hebrews 13:3.
Turning sinner from error of his way,
James 5:20.
The Lord wants all to be saved, 2 Peter 3:9.
Helping those who doubt, Jude 22-23.
Open door, Revelation 3:8.
Those gathered from all tribes and nations,
Revelation 7:9-17.
Proclaiming angel, Revelation 14:6-7.
Combined ministry of the Holy Spirit and
church, Revelation 22:17.
See *Contextualization, Outreach,
Preaching, Soul-winning, Witness.*

EVANGELIST

Angel prophesied ministry of John the
Baptist, Luke 1:11-17.

Jesus traveled from town to town, Luke 8:1.
(See 9:6.)
Misunderstanding arising from healing of
lame man, Acts 14:8-18.
Evangelist with four daughters, Acts 21:8-
9.
Role of evangelist in bringing people to
Christ, 1 Corinthians 3:4-9.
Material payment to those who render
spiritual service, 1 Corinthians 9:9-14;
1 Timothy 5:17-18.
Making a profit from the Word of God,
2 Corinthians 2:17.
Specific calling, Ephesians 4:11.
Praying for those who minister, Ephesians
6:19-20; Colossians 4:3-4.
Paul thanked his Lord for privilege of
ministry, 1 Timothy 1:12-14.
Message Paul was called to proclaim,
1 Timothy 2:5-7.
Called to be herald, apostle, and teacher,
2 Timothy 1:11.
Paul's ministry mandate to Timothy,
2 Timothy 4:1-5.
Called to ministry of holiness, 1 Peter 1:15-
16.
See *Evangelism, Herald, Ministry.*

EVIDENCE

Dove provided evidence for Noah, Genesis
8:10-11.
Trumped-up evidence, Genesis 37:29-33.
Drama between Tamar and Judah, Genesis
38:11-26.
Circumstantial evidence against Joseph,
Genesis 39:6-20.
Guilt of murder exposed, Exodus 2:11-14.
Ninth commandment, Exodus 20:16.
Responsibility for giving evidence,
Leviticus 5:1.
Need for adequate witnesses,
Deuteronomy 17:6. (See 19:15.)
Giving false testimony, Deuteronomy
19:16, 21.
Proof of chastity, Deuteronomy 22:13-21.
David's plea for evidence of guilt,
1 Samuel 20:1.
Seeing is believing, 1 Kings 10:1-13.
Presenting evidence, 1 Kings 18:7-15.
Evidence turns against accuser, Proverbs
25:8.
Do not betray confidence, Proverbs 25:9.
Confirmed evidence, Matthew 18:16.
Those who tried to prevent resurrection of

Jesus, Matthew 27:62-66. (See also 28:11-15.)
Unable to believe in face of certain evidence, Luke 24:36-43.
Attitude of Jesus toward human testimony, John 5:34.
No condemnation without looking at facts, John 7:50-52.
Marks of cross as identity, John 20:20-29.
Case against Paul, Acts 23:23-30.
See *Certainty, Pragmatic, Proof, Validity.*

EVIL
Depravity of man before Flood, Genesis 6:5.
No curse on those who have been blessed, Numbers 22:12.
God uses evil to carry out His plans, Judges 14:1-4.
Source of demons, 1 Samuel 16:15. (See also 18:10.)
Death of infamous hero, 1 Samuel 17:51.
Evil sanctioned, 1 Kings 22:23.
God's command to destroy, 2 Kings 9:6-7.
Good and evil return to one who performs them, Job 34:7-8.
Sinful nature inherited at birth, Psalm 51:5.
Evil Assyrians led by hook in nose, Isaiah 37:29.
Those who trust in their wickedness, Isaiah 47:10-11.
Source of evil, Isaiah 54:16-17.
Backsliders, Isaiah 63:17.
Those who cling to deceit, Jeremiah 8:5.
Wicked prosperity, Jeremiah 12:1-3.
God uses despots, then brings them into judgment, Jeremiah 25:11-14.
Hosea commanded to marry evil woman, Hosea 1:2-3.
Old Testament concludes with curse, Malachi 4:6. (Compare Rev. 22:21.)
Evil influence over good, Matthew 13:24-30.
Jesus could not die before His time had come, Luke 4:28-30.
Satan entered Judas, Luke 22:3.
Approving wrong done by others, Acts 8:1.
The Law, which is good, reveals sin, which is evil, Romans 7:13-14.
Those handed over to Satan, 1 Timothy 1:18-20.
God tempts no one, James 1:13-14.
Work of devil, 1 John 3:7-8.
Test spirits for those that are false, 1 John 4:1-6.
Inevitable defeat of Satan, Revelation 12:1-9.
Mark of beast, Revelation 13:16-18; 14:9-10.
When evil serves God's purpose, Revelation 17:17.
Sins piled up to heaven, Revelation 18:4-5.
Evil queen refuses to admit sin, Revelation 18:7-8.
One angel capable of overpowering and binding Satan, Revelation 20:1-3.
See *Carnality, Depravity, Sin.*

EVOLUTION
Distinction of each species, Genesis 1:24-25.
Men and animals of different flesh, 1 Corinthians 15:39.

EXAGGERATION
City walls to sky, Deuteronomy 9:1.
Need for counting cost, Matthew 8:19-20.
Exaggeration of truth causes confusion among believers, Acts 21:17-24.
Calling dead that which has scant life, Revelation 3:1-3.
See *Hyperbole.*

EXAMINATION
Solomon could answer all questions, 1 Kings 10:3.
Self-examination, Lamentations 3:40; Matthew 7:5; 1 Corinthians 11:28; 2 Corinthians 13:5.
Daniel and friends passed oral exam, Daniel 1:18-20.
See *Scrutiny.*

EXAMPLE
Abraham's reputation in eyes of Abimelech, Genesis 21:22.
Backslidden believers a laughingstock, Exodus 32:25.
Avoid bad example, Leviticus 20:23; Deuteronomy 18:9.
Gideon provided example for success, Judges 7:17-18.
People who did not follow righteous king's example, 2 Chronicles 27:2.
Parents who provide poor example, 2 Chronicles 30:7.
Witnessing to that which has been personally experienced, Psalm 51:10-

13.
Do not disgrace others, Psalm 69:6.
Way of ant, Proverbs 6:6-8.
Giving heed to instruction, Proverbs 16:20.
Children damage reputation of parents,
Proverbs 27:11.
Recabites kept covenant with fathers,
Jeremiah 35:1-16.
Belshazzar's refusal to learn from father's
experience, Daniel 5:18-24.
Learning from example of disobedient
forefathers, Zechariah 1:4-6.
Example of prophets being persecuted,
Matthew 5:11-12.
Pharisees did not practice what they
preached, Matthew 23:1-3.
Lamp to be displayed, not hidden, Mark
4:21-22.
Jesus taught disciples to pray by His
example, Luke 11:1-4.
Spiritual light from within, Luke 11:33-36.
Warned by bad example, Luke 17:32.
Paul went with confidence into difficult
places, Acts 20:22-24.
Truly Christian lifestyle, Romans 12:9-21.
(Note v. 17.)
Paul urged converts to follow his example,
1 Corinthians 4:15-16.
Exercise of liberty in eating and drinking,
1 Corinthians 8:7-13.
Do not cause others to stumble,
1 Corinthians 10:32-33.
Paul followed example of Christ,
1 Corinthians 11:1.
Wrong attitudes in worship do more harm
than good, 1 Corinthians 11:17-32.
Good example possible only through
God's grace, 2 Corinthians 1:12.
Deserving right to be heard, 2 Corinthians
4:1-2.
Lifestyle Paul communicated by example,
2 Corinthians 6:4-10.
Supreme model of unselfishness given by
the Lord Jesus, 2 Corinthians 8:7-9.
Sharing concerns of leader, 2 Corinthians
8:16.
Right and wrong attitude and disposition,
Ephesians 4:31-32.
Life of love, Ephesians 5:1-2.
Paul's imprisonment caused others to
witness boldly, Philippians 1:12-14.
Total commitment, example of Jesus,
Philippians 2:5-11.
Worthy example to others, Philippians

3:17.
Those who became imitators of Paul,
1 Thessalonians 1:6.
Those who became model believers,
1 Thessalonians 1:7.
Paul as a model in daily conduct and
employment, 2 Thessalonians 3:6-10.
Example of God's grace to worst of
sinners, 1 Timothy 1:15-16.
Young Christians can set example,
1 Timothy 4:12.
Examples of good and bad, 1 Timothy
5:24-25.
Paul's example to Timothy, 2 Timothy
3:10-11.
Family of elder must be exemplary, Titus
1:6.
Example set by good teacher, Titus 2:6-7.
Those who show initiative, Hebrews 6:11-
12.
Service in sanctuary of ultimate High
Priest, Hebrews 8:1-6.
Example to each other, Hebrews 10:24-25.
Following example of those who lived by
faith, Hebrews 12:1-3.
Living in good relationships, Hebrews
12:14-15.
Exemplary leadership, Hebrews 13:7.
Witness of good life, 1 Peter 2:12.
Christ the perfect Example, 1 Peter 2:21-
25.
Taught by example to show love, 1 John
4:7-11.
See *Emulation, Model.*

EXASPERATION
Moses exasperated with grumbling people,
Exodus 17:4.
See *Disgust.*

EXCELLENCE
Demands within reach, Deuteronomy
30:11.
Leadership under divine guidance,
2 Chronicles 31:20-21.
Man of exemplary character, Job 1:1-8.
Selecting finest youth, Daniel 1:3-4.
Excel in grace of giving, 2 Corinthians 8:7.

EXCITEMENT
Meeting of Isaac and Rebekah, Genesis
24:62-67.
Cheer so loud it shook ground, 1 Samuel
4:5.

Harvesters see ark of God, 1 Samuel 6:13.
Returning ark to Jerusalem, 2 Samuel 6:5.
Too excited to open door, Acts 12:12-16.
See *Emotion.*

EXCLUSIVE
Only a select few permitted to travel with Jesus, Mark 5:37.
Song for an exclusive congregation, Revelation 14:1-3.

EXCUSES
Blaming another, Genesis 3:12.
Claim of inadequacy, Exodus 3:11; 4:10; Judges 6:15; Jeremiah 1:7.
Reason claimed for idolatry, Exodus 32:24.
Blaming employer, Matthew 25:24-25.
First things first in following Jesus, Luke 9:59-62.
Excuses for not attending banquet, Luke 14:16-24.
See *Blame.*

EXECUTION
No right to crucify, John 18:28-32.

EXEGESIS
Counsel darkened by words without knowledge, Job 38:2.
Speaking in language understood, Isaiah 36:11.
Mouth like sharpened sword, Isaiah 49:2.
See *Preaching.*

EXEMPLARY
Man who truly walked with God, Job 1:1.
Choice of candidates for service in government, Daniel 1:3-5.
Deserving right to be heard, 2 Corinthians 4:1-2.
Witness of good life, 1 Peter 2:12.
See *Example, Model.*

EXERCISE
Running to bring bad news, 2 Samuel 18:24-33.
Foot-racing, Jeremiah 12:5; 1 Corinthians 9:24-26.
Impetus for keeping in shape, 1 Corinthians 6:19-20.
Physical training and godliness, 1 Timothy 4:8.
See *Athletics, Physical.*

EXHIBITIONISM
Shem's attitude toward father's privacy, Genesis 9:20-27.
When David did not dress or conduct himself as king, 2 Samuel 6:17-23.
Display of wealth, Esther 1:4. (See vv. 10-12.)
Early morning religiosity can be mistaken, Proverbs 27:14.
Stripped and barefoot as sign against those who oppose the Lord, Isaiah 20:2-4.
Display of possessions, Isaiah 39:2-4.
Acts of charity not made public, Matthew 6:1-4.
Ego displayed by teachers of the Law, Mark 12:38-40; Luke 20:46-47. (See also 21:1-4.)
Proud Pharisee and humble publican, Luke 18:9-14.
Jesus challenged to display prowess, John 7:2-9.
Do not serve God to please men, Colossians 3:23-24.
See *Nudity.*

EXHILARATION
Joy beyond levity of wine, Psalm 4:7.

EXHUME
Bones exhumed from graves, Jeremiah 8:1-2.

EXORCISM
Saul expelled mediums and spiritists, 1 Samuel 28:3.
Jesus rebuked demon, Luke 4:33-36, 41.
Cured by casting out of demon, Luke 13:10-13.
Miracles in ministry of Paul, Acts 19:11-12.
Jews who tried in vain to cast out evil spirits, Acts 19:13-16.
See *Demons, Sorcery.*

EXPANSION
Need for larger building, 2 Kings 6:1-2.
Time to enlarge, Isaiah 54:2.
Time to build and extend, Micah 7:11.
See *Growth, Vision.*

EXPECTATION
Asking God for wisdom and believing it will be granted, James 1:5-7.

Our eternal inheritance, 1 Peter 1:3-4.
See *Anticipation.*

EXPEDIENT
Such a time as this, Esther 4:13-17.
God asked to hasten, Psalm 70:1.
Right time for everything, Ecclesiastes 3:1-8.
Urgent need to evangelize, Isaiah 21:11-12.
Divine time and mortal time, John 7:6.
Instant baptism, Acts 16:33.
Now is the day of salvation, 2 Corinthians 6:2.
Meaning of "today" in God's reckoning, Hebrews 4:7.
See *Urgency.*

EXPENSES
No need for expense money, Mark 6:8-11.
Some to pay, others only receive, 2 Corinthians 11:7-8.

EXPERIENCE
Knowledge that comes from wrong kind of experience, Genesis 3:6-7.
Recalling past experience, Exodus 23:9.
Learning from experience, Deuteronomy 4:32-35. (See also v. 9.)
Duty of parents to share spiritual experience with children, Deuteronomy 11:1-7.
Seeing with your own eyes, Deuteronomy 29:2-4.
An eagle trains its young to fly, Deuteronomy 32:11.
Many years of experience, Job 12:12; 32:7-8; Psalm 37:25.
Witnessing to that which has been personally experienced, Psalm 51:10-13.
Path of righteous and way of wicked, Proverbs 4:18-19.
Increasing in wisdom, Ecclesiastes 1:16.
Facing problems while young, Lamentations 3:27.
Belshazzar's refusal to learn from father's experience, Daniel 5:18-24.
Experiencing God's kingdom within, Luke 17:20-21.
Paul persecuted, thus able to encourage others, Acts 14:19-22.
Power of personal testimony, Acts 21:37–22:21; 26:1-18.
That which God has prepared exceeds human perception and experience, 1 Corinthians 2:9-10.
Troubles prepare us to help others, 2 Corinthians 1:3-4.
Experiencing reality of Christ, 1 John 1:1-4.

EXPERTISE
Sanballat's ridicule of Jewish capability, Nehemiah 4:1-10.
Proper time and procedure, Ecclesiastes 8:5-6.
Success requires more than ability, Isaiah 25:11.
Qualifications of Christ as Saviour and King, Colossians 1:15-20.
Erroneous claims to expertise, 1 Timothy 1:3-7.
Expertise in iniquity, 2 Peter 2:14.

EXPLOITATION
David refused to drink water his men had risked their lives to get, 2 Samuel 23:15-17.
Exploiting poor for personal gain, Amos 5:11.
Business profit limited by transformation of converts, Acts 19:23-28.
Paul exploited no one, 2 Corinthians 7:2.
See *Greed, Misuse.*

EXPLOITS
See *Courage, Valor.*

EXPLORATION
Searching for treasure, Job 28:1-4, 9-11.

EXPOSITION
Speaking in a language understood, Isaiah 36:11.
Exposition of parable, Matthew 13:36-43; Luke 8:11-15.
Meaning of fig tree, Matthew 24:32-34.
Parables explained, Mark 4:34.
Informal theology lesson, Luke 24:27.
See *Clarity, Exegesis, Teaching.*

EXPRESSION
See *Attitude, Countenance, Emotion, Excitement.*

EXTORTION
Usurping rights of poor, Isaiah 10:2.
Extortionists exterminated, Isaiah 16:4.

Unjust earnings at expense of others,
   Ezekiel 22:12.
Mistreatment of poor, Amos 5:11.
Greed and self-indulgence, Matthew 23:25.
Making fair collections, Luke 3:13.
See *Cheating, Dishonesty.*

EXTRAVAGANCE
Value of silver in giving, Numbers 7:13-85.
   (See also 10:2.)
God's grace lavished on us, Ephesians 1:7-
8.
See *Affluence, Luxury.*

EYES
Eli likely suffered from cataracts, 1 Samuel
   4:14-15.
Bodies full of eyes, Ezekiel 10:12.
Eye-to-eye with sorcerer, Acts 13:9-11.
Paul may have had poor eyesight,
   Galatians 6:11.
See *Sight.*

F

FABRIC
See *Clothing, Textiles.*

FABRICATION
Friends and brothers not to be trusted,
Jeremiah 9:4-8.
King Herod and magi, Matthew 2:7-8,
12.
Made-up stories to distort truth, 2 Peter
2:3.
See *Deceit, Dishonesty, Lie.*

FACADE
Ego displayed by teachers of Law, Mark
12:38-40.
False humility, Colossians 2:18.
Making the false claim of a holy life, 1 John
1:8-10.
See *Pretense.*

FACE
Transfigured, Exodus 34:29-35; Matthew
17:2; Luke 9:29.
Countenance betrays conscience, Isaiah
3:9.
Variation of facial appearance, Ezekiel
1:10.
Contrived simulation of fasting, Matthew
6:16.
Paul would not permit government
officials to save face, Acts 16:35-
40.
See *Countenance.*

FACETIOUS
Paul chided Corinthians, 2 Corinthians
11:16-21.
See *Sarcasm.*

FACIAL EXPRESSION
See *Countenance.*

FACILITY
Substitute for bridge to cross Jordan,
2 Kings 2:13-14.
Need for larger building, 2 Kings 6:1-2.
See *Provision.*

FACTIONS
Struggle between strong and weak,
2 Samuel 3:1.
Reputation as troublemaker, 2 Samuel
20:1.
Those who wanted to be part of building
temple, Ezra 4:3-5.
Christ's message caused divisions, Luke
12:51; John 7:12, 43; 10:19-21.
Those who purposely cause trouble,
Romans 16:17.
Divided by theology and personalities,
1 Corinthians 1:10-17; 3:4-9.
See *Argument, Disharmony, Disruption.*

FACTS
God's children discovering for themselves,
Numbers 13:17-20.
Stephen's knowledge of Old Testament
history, Acts 7:1-60.
See *Truth.*

FAILURE
When God terminates a project, Genesis
11:1-9.
Seed and vineyards with little harvest,
Deuteronomy 28:38-42.
Turning spiritual failure into success,
1 Kings 8:33-34.
Contempt for unfortunate, Job 12:5.
Debilitating effects of poverty, Proverbs
10:15.
Do not gloat over enemy's failure,
Proverbs 24:17-18.
Optimism versus pessimism, Jeremiah

48:47.
Enemies rejoice, Lamentations 1:21.
Ridicule of once-exalted city,
Lamentations 2:15.
Vision comes to nothing, Ezekiel 12:22-25.
Failure of Nebuchadnezzar's wisemen,
Daniel 2:1-11.
Fishermen's failure turned to success,
Luke 5:1-11.
Death to guards who permitted Peter's
escape, Acts 12:18-19.
Exercising hope when no basis for hope,
Romans 4:18-22.
Purpose of suffering, Romans 5:3.
Facing strong opposition, 1 Thessalonians
2:1-2.
See *Defeat*.

FAINT
Like wounded men, Lamentations 2:12.
Hand limp and knees weak, Ezekiel 7:17.
Totally exhausted, Daniel 8:27.

FAIRNESS
Joseph's fairness to people of Egypt,
Genesis 47:13-26.
Do not take advantage of another,
Leviticus 25:17.
Partiality to no one, Job 32:21-22.
Prosperity of wicked, Jeremiah 12:1-3.
Suffering for just and unjust, Jeremiah
49:12.
Disputing mercy and justice of God's ways,
Ezekiel 33:10-20.
Parable of Workers in Vineyard, Matthew
20:1-16.
No favoritism with God, Colossians 3:25.
See *Equity, Partiality*.

FAITH
God as first priority, Genesis 1:1.
Doubt overcome by faith, Genesis 15:1-6.
Stand still to see what God will do,
1 Samuel 12:16.
Sure of divine goodness, 2 Samuel 22:31.
Concern about army rather than promises
of God, 2 Samuel 24:10.
Opening eyes to see God's provision,
2 Kings 6:16-17.
Failure to give proper emphasis, 2 Kings
13:14-19.
The Lord is found by those who seek,
forsakes those who forsake Him,
2 Chronicles 15:2.

Evil counsel to people of faith,
2 Chronicles 32:10-15.
No need for king's protection, Ezra 8:21-
23.
Unwavering faith in time of testing, Job
1:22; 2:10.
Job would trust God though it meant death,
Job 13:15.
Advocate in heaven, Job 16:19.
Classic statement of faith, Job 19:25-26.
Sure faith, Psalm 27:1.
Proof positive, Psalm 34:8.
Letting God fulfill His purpose, Psalm 57:2.
God blesses small and great alike, Psalm
115:13.
God's eternal faithfulness, Psalm 117:2.
Confidence in the Lord better than trust in
man, Psalm 118:5-9.
Trusting now and in future, Psalm 131:3.
Certainty of God's promises, Psalm 145:13.
Faith greater than physical strength, Psalm
147:10-11.
Faith formula, Proverbs 3:5-6.
Humility and faith key to success, Proverbs
22:4.
Promised security, Proverbs 29:25; Nahum
1:7.
Stand firm or not at all, Isaiah 7:9.
Poised faith, Isaiah 26:3.
Confidence in fiery furnace, Daniel 3:16-
18.
Calling on God because of His great mercy,
Daniel 9:18.
Fear because of stolen idol, Hosea 10:5.
Righteous live by faith, Habakkuk 2:4.
Faith in God the greatest strength,
Zechariah 12:5.
Faith touches God's willingness to
respond, Matthew 8:2-4.
Faith rewarded in measure of its content,
Matthew 8:13.
Confidence in power of Jesus, Matthew
9:18-25.
Peter's attempt to walk on water, Matthew
14:22-31.
Jesus overlooked racist tradition, Matthew
15:21-28.
Faith to remove mountains, Matthew
17:20; 21:21-22.
Faith of friends resulted in man's healing,
Mark 2:1-5.
In the presence of the One who bestows
faith, disciples lacked faith, Mark 4:36-
41.

Faith of others required for healing, Mark 6:4-6.
Unlimited potential of faith and deliverance from doubt, Mark 9:23-24.
Attitude of Jesus to little children, Mark 10:13-16.
Active faith of blind Bartimaeus, Mark 10:46-52.
Certainty of answered prayer, Mark 11:24.
Small faith in the great God, Luke 11:20.
Power of small faith, Luke 17:5-6.
Frailty of human faith, Luke 22:31-38.
Taking Jesus at His word, John 4:50.
Assurance at time of death, John 11:25-26.
Living by faith, Romans 1:17.
Faith of Abraham, Romans 4:1-3.
Justified by faith, Romans 5:1.
Conflict between faith and works, Romans 9:30-33.
Faith given, not generated, Romans 10:17.
Faith the only standard of conduct, Romans 14:23; Hebrews 11:6.
Joy and peace in believing, Romans 15:13.
Faith is ultimate intelligence, 1 Corinthians 3:18-23.
Confidence in unseen, 2 Corinthians 4:18.
Living by faith, not by sight, 2 Corinthians 5:1-7.
Self-examination, 2 Corinthians 13:5.
Difference between faith and works, Galatians 3:2-5.
Righteous live by faith, Galatians 3:11.
Love validates faith, Galatians 5:6.
Faith as a shield, Ephesians 6:16.
Spiritual need totally fulfilled in Christ, Colossians 1:15-23.
Faith and love together, 1 Thessalonians 5:8.
Fight the good fight, 1 Timothy 6:12.
Absolute confidence in the One whom we believe, 2 Timothy 1:12.
Failure to combine hearing with believing, Hebrews 4:1-3.
Righteous live by faith, Hebrews 10:38.
The faith chapter, Hebrews 11:1-40.
Faith beyond doubt, James 1:6.
Faith and works, James 2:17.
Kept through faith, 1 Peter 1:5.
Believing without seeing, 1 Peter 1:8-9.
Overcoming world through faith, 1 John 5:4.

FAITHFULNESS
Divine faithfulness, Deuteronomy 7:9;

1 Corinthians 1:9.
Reward to those who are faithful, 2 Samuel 22:26-27.
Trustworthy promises, 1 Kings 8:56.
An undivided heart, Psalm 86:11.
Proclaiming divine faithfulness, Psalm 89:1.
Trustworthy messenger, Proverbs 25:13.
Jeremiah beaten for proclaiming truth, Jeremiah 20:1-2.
Faithful proclamation of God's Word for nearly a quarter century, Jeremiah 25:1-3.
Message of Jeremiah brings threat of death, Jeremiah 26:1-16.
Jeremiah, faithful to God's words, put in prison, Jeremiah 37:1-21.
Faithfulness and compassion new every morning, Lamentations 3:22-26.
The Heavenly Father acknowledges those who acknowledge Him, Matthew 10:32-33.
Do not be found sleeping when the Lord returns, Mark 13:35-37.
Paul faithful in duty to God, Acts 23:1-5.
Faithful service without pastoral supervision, Philippians 2:12-13.
Be faithful until Christ returns, 1 Timothy 6:11-16.
Temporary suffering as a reward for faithfulness, Revelation 1:9.
Partial holiness insufficient in God's sight, Revelation 2:1-6, 13-15, 18, 20.
Holding on to the faith, Revelation 2:25.
Faithful in society of deceit, Revelation 3:4, 10.
Those beheaded for their faithfulness and testimony, Revelation 20:4.
See *Commitment, Discipleship.*

FALL
Adam's fall, Genesis 3:6-7.
Image of God and image of man, Genesis 5:1-3.
Sin of first parent, Isaiah 43:27.
Entry of sin into world, Romans 5:12.
Death came by Adam, 1 Corinthians 15:21.
Guilt of first woman, 1 Timothy 2:14.
See *Carnality, Debauchery, Disobedience, Sin.*

FALSE
Friends and brothers not to be trusted, Jeremiah 9:4-8.

Despising those who tell the truth, Amos 5:10.

False brothers, Galatians 2:3-4.

False humility, Colossians 2:18.

False teachers and prophets, 2 Peter 2:1; 1 John 4:1.

Counterfeit anointing, 1 John 2:27.

Detecting presence of false prophets, 1 John 4:1-3.

Feigning life when spiritually dead, Revelation 3:1.

See *Counterfeit, Deceit.*

FALSEHOOD

Primordial falsehood, Genesis 3:4-5.

The deceit of Abram concerning Sarai, his wife, in Egypt, Genesis 12:10-13.

Open honesty, Leviticus 19:11-12.

Rahab lied to protect spies, Joshua 2:1-6.

David used falsehood to protect his life, 1 Samuel 20:5-7.

Misrepresenting people's motives, Ezra 4:11-16.

Inviting test of integrity, Job 31:5-6.

Inborn deceitfulness, Psalms 10:7; 52:2-4.

Flattering lips, Psalm 12:2.

Guarded tongue, Psalm 34:13.

Mouth given to deceit, Psalm 50:19.

Smooth as butter, Psalm 55:21.

Deceit disallowed, Psalm 101:7.

Hand and mouth given to err, Psalm 144:8.

Lying lips, Proverbs 12:22.

Bread of deceit, Proverbs 20:17.

Believing a lie, Jeremiah 43:1-7.

See *Deceit, Lie.*

FAME

Heroes of old, Genesis 6:4.

Greatness of Moses, Deuteronomy 34:10-12.

Joshua's fame, Joshua 6:27.

Little-known sons and daughters of King Saul, 1 Samuel 14:49.

David's name made great, 2 Samuel 7:9; 1 Chronicles 14:17.

How David became famous, 2 Samuel 8:13.

Worldwide acclaim, 1 Kings 4:31; 10:1.

Local celebrities, 1 Chronicles 12:30.

Given great name by the Lord, 1 Chronicles 17:21.

Fame of Jesus, Matthew 4:24; 9:31; Luke 5:15.

Servant mode, key to greatness, Matthew 20:26; 23:11.

Role of humility in greatness, Matthew 23:12.

Fame of Jesus because of miracles, Mark 1:35-45.

First last and last first, Mark 10:31.

Respect of Cornelius for Peter, Acts 10:25-26.

See *Celebrity, Image, Self-image.*

FAMILIARITY

The Lord knew Moses face-to-face, Deuteronomy 34:10.

Familiarity breeds contempt, Mark 6:4; John 4:44.

Becoming too familiar, 1 Timothy 6:2.

FAMILY

Family musical tradition, Genesis 4:21.

Childless Abram's promise of offspring, Genesis 15:1-6.

Ishmael, Abram's son of disobedience, Genesis 16:1-16. (Note 15:1-6.)

Bearing children at advanced age, Genesis 16:16; 17:1-21; 21:1-5.

Family forecast, Genesis 18:17-19.

Preserving family line through incest, Genesis 19:30-38.

Time of severe testing, Genesis 22:1-14.

Parents unhappy with daughters-in law, Genesis 26:34-35.

Bond between relatives, Genesis 29:1-14.

Father as spiritual leader, Genesis 35:1-5.

Taking leave to check on family welfare, Exodus 4:18.

Family ties broken, Exodus 21:2-4.

Joshua frequently identified by his family name, Exodus 33:11; Numbers 11:28; 13:16; 14:6, 30; Joshua 1:1; 2:1; Judges 2:8; 1 Kings 16:34.

Respect within family, Deuteronomy 5:16; Ephesians 6:2.

Turning away from wrong family influence, Deuteronomy 13:6-10.

Adopted into God's family, Deuteronomy 14:1-2; Isaiah 63:16; Hosea 11:1; John 1:12; Romans 8:15; 2 Corinthians 6:18; Galatians 4:4-6

Large family of Ibzan, Judges 12:8-9.

Childless Hannah and her subsequent child and children, 1 Samuel 1:5, 20; 2:21.

Three deaths in one family, 1 Samuel 4:12-20.

Little-known sons and daughters of King Saul, 1 Samuel 14:49.

Futility of strife among brothers, 2 Samuel 2:27-28.

David's many wives, 2 Samuel 5:13.

Strength of family ties, 2 Samuel 16:5-8.

Adonijah sought to take over David's throne, 1 Kings 1:1-27.

Heathen worship for Solomon's wives, 1 Kings 11:8.

Famous family, 1 Chronicles 12:30.

Together in worship, 2 Chronicles 20:13; Nehemiah 12:43.

Assisting in rebuilding wall at Jerusalem, Nehemiah 3:12.

Job's concern over festivity in family, Job 1:4-5.

Ostrich shows little care for family, Job 39:13-17.

Slander against relatives, Psalm 50:20.

Warning to highborn, Psalm 62:9.

Stranger to one's family, Psalm 69:8.

God's faithfulness intended for generation after generation, Psalms 100:5; 103:17-18; 119:90.

Father's righteousness blesses family, Psalm 112:1-3.

Children a blessing from the Lord, Psalms 127:3-5; 128:3-6.

Living together in unity, Psalm 133:1-3.

Conveying God's message from generation to generation, Psalm 145:4-7; Isaiah 59:21; Joel 1:3.

Simple food with peace and quiet, Proverbs 17:1.

Having 100 children, Ecclesiastes 6:3.

Parents and their God-given children, Isaiah 8:18.

Sad plight of obstinate children, Isaiah 30:1-5.

Enemies within one's family, Jeremiah 12:6; Micah 7:6.

Evil influence of fathers on children, Jeremiah 16:10-12.

Disgrace of childlessness, Jeremiah 22:30.

Parents and children responsible for their own sin, Ezekiel 18:4-20.

Gospel divides the world and households, Matthew 10:32-36; Luke 12:49-53.

Division in communities and families, Matthew 12:25.

Parable of Two Sons, Matthew 21:28-31.

Earthly relationships not same in heaven, Matthew 22:23-30; Mark 12:18-25.

Members of Jesus' own family thought Him deranged, Mark 3:20-21. (Note v. 31.)

Attitude of Jesus toward earthly relationships, Mark 3:31-35; Luke 8:19-21.

Leaving all to follow Jesus, Mark 10:28-31.

Rebellion within family, Mark 13:12.

Obedience of the Child Jesus to His parents, Luke 2:41-52.

Genealogy of Jesus, Luke 3:23-38.

Family rejection a high cost of discipleship, Luke 14:26-27.

Christ rejected by His own people, John 1:11.

Unbelieving brothers of Jesus, John 7:5.

Satan as spiritual father, John 8:44.

Grief-stricken family, John 11:17-44.

Cornelius and his devout family, Acts 10:1-2. (See also vv. 7, 22.)

Mother and children together in faith, Acts 16:13-15.

Father and family together in faith, Acts 16:25-34.

Financial responsibility of children, 2 Corinthians 12:14-15.

Relationship of parents and children, Ephesians 6:1-4; Colossians 3:18-21.

Welfare should begin within family, 1 Timothy 5:3-8.

Disobedience to parents, 2 Timothy 3:2.

Influence of Scriptures since childhood, 2 Timothy 3:14-15.

Family of elder must be exemplary, Titus 1:6.

Melchizedek had neither father nor mother, Hebrews 7:1-3.

Moses refused to be known as son of Pharaoh's daughter, Hebrews 11:23-24.

Esau sold his birthright, Hebrews 12:16-17.

God's grace among those of all ages, 1 John 2:12-14.

Becoming children of God, 1 John 3:1-3.

Only some of the children walking in truth, 2 John 4.

Joy of Christian children, 3 John 4.

See *Children, Daughter, Daughter-in-law, Home, Parents, Son.*

FAMINE

Turning to cannibalism, Deuteronomy 28:53; 2 Kings 6:28.

Example of famine, Isaiah 5:13; 9:18-21; Jeremiah 14:1-6.

Israel turned away from Living Water, Jeremiah 2:13, 18.
People in search of bread, Lamentations 1:11.
Children dying in mothers' arms, Lamentations 2:12.
Bread secured at risk of death, Lamentations 5:9.
Failure of harvest, Hosea 9:2; Joel 1:11.
Seeds that will not sprout, cattle and sheep without pasture, Joel 1:17-18.
Call to turn to the Lord, Amos 4:6.
See *Hunger, Thirst.*

FANATICISM
Prophets of Baal, 1 Kings 18:28.
Ezra and the people wept bitterly, Ezra 10:1.
Zeal without knowledge, Proverbs 19:2; Romans 10:2.
Members of Jesus' family thought Him deranged, Mark 3:20-21. (Note v. 31.)
Religious mob violence, Acts 7:51-60; 21:36; 22:23.
Murderous threats, Acts 9:1-5.

FANTASY
Hard work and fantasy, Proverbs 28:19.

FARMER
Mankind's first occupation, Genesis 2:15; 3:23.
Famous farmers, Genesis 4:2; 9:20; 1 Chronicles 27:26.
Seedtime and harvest, Genesis 8:22.
Hundredfold harvest, Genesis 26:12.
Farm tasks, Genesis 37:7; Leviticus 19:9; Deuteronomy 11:10; Judges 6:11; Ruth 3:2; 1 Kings 19:19; Psalm 72:6; Proverbs 31:16.
Year-long holiday for farmers, Leviticus 25:1-4.
Ready market for product, 2 Kings 3:4.
Livestock struck by lightning, Psalm 78:48.
How to farm successfully, Proverbs 3:9-10.
Farmers apparently living in villages, Jeremiah 31:24.
Lamenting farmers, Amos 5:16.
Livelihood from land, Zechariah 13:5.
Patient with weather, James 5:7.
See *Agriculture.*

FASHION
When silver was out of style, 1 Kings 10:21.

Discussing latest intellectual subjects, Acts 17:21.
Approved head covering and hairstyle, 1 Corinthians 11:13-16.

FAST FOOD
Abraham knew how to prepare fast food, Genesis 18:6-7.

FASTING
Moses fasted for 80 days, Deuteronomy 9:11-18.
In time of sorrow, 1 Samuel 31:13; 1 Chronicles 10:12.
During national crisis, 2 Samuel 1:12.
Fasting Elijah, 1 Kings 19:7-8.
In need of courage, Esther 4:16.
Scorn for acts of humility, Psalm 69:10-11.
Weakness from fasting, Psalm 109:24.
Real meaning of fasting, Isaiah 58:3-7.
Prayer and fasting, Daniel 9:3.
Fasting for repentance, Joel 1:13-14.
Animals and men fast together, Jonah 3:7.
Insincere fasting and repentance, Zechariah 7:1-6.
Joy in fasting, Zechariah 8:19.
Pretense of fasting, Matthew 6:16.
Disciples did not fast, Matthew 9:14-15; Mark 2:18-20; Luke 5:33-35.
Four thousand had not eaten for three days, Mark 8:1-3.
Jesus in desert, Luke 4:1-2.
Way of guidance, Acts 13:2-3.
Fasting with evil intent, Acts 23:12-13.
Little value in itself, 1 Corinthians 8:8.

FATE
The death of king by random arrow, 2 Chronicles 18:33-34.
If I perish, I perish, Esther 4:16.
All days preordained, Psalm 139:16.
Time for everything, Ecclesiastes 3:1-8.
Things planned long ago, Isaiah 25:1.
Filled with knowledge of God's will, Colossians 1:9-12.
See *Chance, Fortuity, Predestination.*

FATHER
Musical father, Genesis 4:21.
Regret of Creator, Genesis 6:6.
Forefathers of all mankind, Genesis 9:18-19.
Exemplary fathers, Genesis 17:18; 35:1-5; 2 Samuel 12:15-16; 1 Chronicles 29:19;

Matthew 17:14-16.
Test of father's love for God and his son,
Genesis 22:1-14.
Father's sorrow and joy, Genesis 45:25-28.
(See Gen. 37–45.)
Children penalized for father's sin, Exodus
20:5-7; 34:6-7; Numbers 14:18.
Father's authority over daughter, Numbers
30:3-5.
Father prays for guidance in teaching son,
Judges 13:8.
Attitude toward affections of daughters,
Judges 15:1-2.
Salary for father from children, Judges
17:7-13.
Known because of famous son, 1 Samuel
1:1-20.
Father's shame for immoral sons,
1 Samuel 2:22-23.
Eli's grief for ark of God greater than for
deaths of sons, 1 Samuel 4:16-18.
Son's influence over father, 1 Samuel
19:1-6.
Father and son together in death,
2 Samuel 1:23.
Rivalry between father and son, 2 Samuel
15:1-37.
Attitude of David toward rebellious son,
2 Samuel 18:5.
Father would have died in place of son,
2 Samuel 18:32-33.
King David's joy at seeing son, Solomon,
become king, 1 Kings 1:47-48.
Aged father's counsel to son, 1 Kings 2:1-
9.
King Solomon succeeded by son, 1 Kings
11:41-43.
Sacrifice of son, 2 Kings 16:3; 2 Chronicles
28:3.
Killed by his own sons, 2 Chronicles 32:21.
Repentance of unrepentant son,
2 Chronicles 33:1-13.
Fate of father, fate of sons, Esther 9:12-14.
Job's concern over festivity in family, Job
1:4-5.
Compassion for children, Psalm 103:13-14.
Discipline of good father, Proverbs 3:11-
12; 4:1-10.
Leaving inheritance to children, Proverbs
13:22.
Like father, like children, Jeremiah 16:10-
13.
Fathers unable to help children, Jeremiah
47:3.

Neither good nor evil transmitted from
father to son, Ezekiel 18:3-20.
Belshazzar's refusal to learn from father's
experience, Daniel 5:18-24.
Father and son to same prostitute, Amos
2:7.
God's total approval of His Son, Matthew
3:17.
Concern for only child, Luke 9:38.
Father's compassion for lost son, Luke
15:11-32.
How father should deal with children,
1 Thessalonians 2:11-12.
Timothy, spiritual son of Paul, 1 Timothy
1:2, 18; 2 Timothy 1:2; 2:1.
The Lord's children taken by hand,
Hebrews 8:9.

FAULT
All have sinned, Proverbs 20:9.
Those who look for something to criticize,
Mark 3:2.
Only God can judge, Romans 8:33.
Avoid making enemies of those who do
wrong, 2 Thessalonians 3:14-15.
Love that overlooks faults, 1 Peter 4:8.
Commendation before reproof, Revelation
2:2-6, 13-16, 19-20.
See *Error, Mistake.*

FAULT FINDING
See *Complain, Criticism, Gossip, Slander.*

FAVORITISM
Parents who have favorites, Genesis 25:27;
37:3.
Preference of one person for another,
Genesis 27:6-17; 29:30, 34; 43:34;
Deuteronomy 21:15-17; 1 Samuel 1:4-
5.
Jealousy of younger brother, Genesis 37:1-
36.
Fate of favorite daughter, only child,
Judges 11:29-39.
Boaz left extra grain for Ruth to glean, Ruth
2:15-16.
Partiality to no one, Job 32:21-22; 34:18-
19.
Prosperity of evil, Jeremiah 12:1.
Good favor used to glorify God, Daniel 1:9-
10.
Jerusalem, apple of God's eye, Zechariah
2:8.
Sun rises on all men, Matthew 5:43-48.

No racial boundaries for the Lord, Acts 10:34-35; Romans 10:12.

Favoring one against another, 1 Corinthians 4:6.

No favoritism with God, Colossians 3:25.

Avoid any kind of partiality, 1 Timothy 5:21.

See *Nepotism, Partiality, Preference.*

FEAR

Frightened by fallen leaf, Leviticus 26:36.

Guilty people afraid of worship, Numbers 17:12-13.

Poor example of cowardice, Deuteronomy 20:8.

Ten thousand cowards on the run, Deuteronomy 32:30.

David not sure God would protect him, 1 Samuel 27:1-2.

Touching ark of the Lord, 2 Samuel 6:6-11.

David's fear of Absalom's popularity, 2 Samuel 15:13-14.

Solomon's mercy to Adonijah, 1 Kings 1:43-53.

Unnecessary fear, 1 Kings 1:50-53.

Fearful of opposition, 1 Kings 19:1-5.

Turning to the Lord in fear, 2 Chronicles 20:2-12, 29.

Surrounded by terror, Job 15:24.

Fear of future, Psalm 55:4-5.

No fear of bad news, Psalm 112:7.

Fear of man, Psalm 118:6-9; Proverbs 29:25; 2 Timothy 4:16.

Phantom fears, Proverbs 28:1.

One who lights deepest darkness, Isaiah 9:2.

Thousand flee from one enemy, Isaiah 30:17.

Strength and repose from the Lord, Isaiah 35:3-4.

Fear of death, Isaiah 38:1-6.

Sufficiency of our Lord, Isaiah 41:10.

Fear of speaking to those who are older, Jeremiah 1:6-7.

Given boldness to proclaim God's message, Jeremiah 1:8-10.

Snorting of enemy horses, Jeremiah 8:16.

Courage and cowardice, Jeremiah 26:13-15, 20-24.

Hand limp and knee weak, Ezekiel 7:17.

Reaction to prophet's message, Ezekiel 21:7.

Knocking knees of frightened king, Daniel 5:6.

Confident though sitting in darkness, Micah 7:8.

Futility of worry, Matthew 6:25-32.

Needless fear, Matthew 14:30; 17:6; Mark 5:33.

Needless fear in time of storm, Mark 4:35-41.

Frightened mother of James, Mark 16:1-8.

Sight of an angel, Luke 1:11-12.

Fear at night, Luke 2:8-14.

Circumstances and confidence of faith, Luke 8:22-25.

No need to fear in presence of Jesus, John 6:20.

Parents of man born blind, John 9:18-23.

Peace only Christ can give, John 14:27.

Standing firm whatever circumstances, Philippians 1:27-30.

God's peace available at all times, 2 Thessalonians 3:16.

Holy fear as motivating factor, Hebrews 11:7.

Reverent fear of God, 1 Peter 1:17.

Fear causes people to give glory to God, Revelation 11:13.

See *Apprehension, Worry.*

FEAST

Historic wedding feasts, Genesis 29:22; Esther 2:18; John 2:1-11.

Food and revelry, Exodus 32:6; Judges 9:27; 1 Samuel 25:36.

Eating and rejoicing, Deuteronomy 27:7; Song of Songs 2:4.

Banquet for a thousand, Daniel 5:1.

Eating to complete satisfaction, Joel 2:26.

Guests at banquet, Luke 14:8-24.

See *Banquet, Celebration, Festivity, Marriage.*

FEATURES

Radiant face of Moses, Exodus 34:30; 2 Corinthians 3:7-8.

Wisdom alters facial features, Ecclesiastes 8:1.

Variation of facial appearance, Ezekiel 1:10.

Face of Jesus at Transfiguration, Matthew 17:2.

Features like lightning, Matthew 28:3.

Evidence of having been with Jesus, Acts 4:13.

Influence of persecution, Acts 6:15.

Personal features forgotten, James 1:23-

25.
See *Countenance.*

FEET
Taking care of one's feet, 2 Samuel 19:24.
Trampled by a hungry mob, 2 Kings 7:17-20.
Boots worn in battle, Isaiah 9:5.
Beautiful feet of those who bring good news, Isaiah 52:7.
Feet strengthened for conquest, Micah 4:13.
At feet of Jesus, Matthew 15:30; Mark 5:22-23; Luke 7:37-38; 10:39; John 11:32; Revelation 1:17.
See *Foot-washing, Running, Walk.*

FELLOWSHIP
Food and fellowship, Deuteronomy 14:23; 15:20.
Fellowship offerings, 1 Samuel 11:15.
Two people becoming one in spirit, 1 Samuel 18:1-4.
Friendship centered in the name of the Lord, 1 Samuel 20:42.
Companions in danger, 1 Samuel 22:23.
Undependable friends, Job 6:15-17.
Glorifying God together, Psalm 34:3.
Living together in unity, Psalm 133:1-3.
Two better than one, Ecclesiastes 4:9-12.
Shelter from wind, Isaiah 32:2.
Saviour left with no one to help Him, Isaiah 63:5.
Agreement necessary for two to walk together, Amos 3:3.
Neighbors sitting in shade, Zechariah 3:10.
Jesus ate with "sinners," Mark 2:15-17.
People at peace with each other, Mark 9:50.
Those of varying styles of ministry, Luke 9:1-62.
The Lord who is always at hand, Acts 2:25-28.
Those who experience fellowship, Acts 2:42; 1 Corinthians 1:9; Philippians 2:1; 1 John 1:3, 7.
Closely knit group of believers, Acts 5:12-13.
Sharing insights into Scriptures, Acts 18:24-26.
Loving fellowship between Paul and followers, Acts 20:36-38.
Consistent prayer for other Christians, Romans 1:8-10; 1 Corinthians 1:4-9;

Ephesians 1:11-23; Philippians 1:3-6; Colossians 1:3-14.
Mutual encouragement among Christians, Romans 1:11-12.
Honor others above yourself, Romans 12:10.
Share blessing and mourning, Romans 12:15.
Accepting one another, Romans 15:7.
Refreshed together, Romans 15:32.
Greetings to friends, Romans 16:3-16.
United in mind and thought, 1 Corinthians 1:10. (Note: Some translate "mind and attitude.")
Relationship of men and women in ministry, 1 Corinthians 11:11.
Putting food above things more important, 1 Corinthians 11:20-22.
Different kinds of gifts and service, 1 Corinthians 12:4-11.
Participation of all in times of worship, 1 Corinthians 14:26.
Greet with holy kiss, 1 Corinthians 16:20; 1 Peter 5:14
Sharing both suffering and comfort, 2 Corinthians 1:7.
Freedom in the Spirit, 2 Corinthians 3:17.
Hearts opening to each other, 2 Corinthians 6:11-13.
Paul's visit with Peter, Galatians 1:18.
Right hand of fellowship, Galatians 2:9-10.
Do good to all, especially believers, Galatians 6:10.
Members of God's family, Ephesians 2:19-22.
Imitators of God expressing love to others, Ephesians 5:1-2.
Keeping in touch concerning activity and welfare, Ephesians 6:21-22.
Channel of much blessing, Philippians 1:25-26.
Like-minded people serving God in love, Philippians 2:1-2.
Instruction on unity in church, Philippians 4:1-9.
Sharing each other's troubles, Philippians 4:14.
Greetings from Rome to Philippi, Philippians 4:21-23.
Thanking God for blessing and fellowship of others, Colossians 1:3-6.
Concern for spiritual development of followers, Colossians 2:1-5.
Love and fellowship in ministry,

1 Thessalonians 2:7-9.
Christians missing each other,
1 Thessalonians 2:17-20; 3:1-5.
Overflowing love among believers,
1 Thessalonians 3:12.
Brotherly love comes from God,
1 Thessalonians 4:9.
Encouraging each other, 1 Thessalonians
5:11.
Thanking God for others when we pray,
2 Thessalonians 1:3.
Timothy, spiritual son of Paul, 1 Timothy
1:2, 18; 2 Timothy 1:2; 2:1.
Praying together without dispute,
1 Timothy 2:8.
Christian community like family,
1 Timothy 5:1-2.
Those not embarrassed by friend's
misfortune, 2 Timothy 1:16-17.
Avoid foolish arguments, 2 Timothy 2:23.
Paul desired fellowship with Timothy,
2 Timothy 4:9-10.
Slave who became brother, Philemon 16.
Use of guest room, Philemon 22.
Need for mutual encouragement, Hebrews
3:13.
Example to each other, in fellowship with
each other, Hebrews 10:24-25.
Living in good relationships, Hebrews
12:14-15.
Love each other as brothers, Hebrews 13:1.
Confessing sins one to another, James
5:16.
Love that results from holiness, 1 Peter
1:22.
Living stones built on the Living Stone,
1 Peter 2:4-8.
Darkness of hatred, 1 John 2:9-11.
Love one another, 1 John 4:7-11.
Love in truth, 3 John 1.
Brothers and companions at all times,
Revelation 1:9.
Fellowship with the Lord Himself,
Revelation 3:20.
When God comes to live with men,
Revelation 21:1-4.
See *Companionship, Camaraderie,
Rapport, Unanimity.*

FEMINIST
Generic name for man and woman,
Genesis 5:2.
Women at historic events, Matthew 28:8;
Mark 15:47; Luke 2:37-38; John 20:1;

Acts 16:13-14.
See *Women's rights.*

FERMENTATION
Bread without yeast, Genesis 19:3.
Fermentation of wine, Mark 2:22.
See *Alcohol, Leaven.*

FEROCITY
Women's hair and lions' teeth, Revelation
9:8.

FERTILITY
Bearing children at advanced age, Genesis
16:16; 17:1-21; 21:1-5.
Infertility in household of Abimelech,
Genesis 20:17-18.
Pregnancy in answer to prayer, Genesis
25:21.
Old Testament morality, Genesis 30:1-24.
Beyond age of childbearing, Ruth 1:11.
Childless Hannah and her child and
children, 1 Samuel 1:5, 20; 2:21.
Blessing of producing children, Psalm
127:5.
Barren land made fertile, Isaiah 41:18-20.
Meadow grass and thriving trees, Isaiah
44:4.

FESTIVITY
Time to rejoice and not weep, Nehemiah
8:9-10.
Celebration after rebuilding the wall,
Nehemiah 8:16-18.
Calamity at family gathering, Job 1:18-19.
Entertainment with no thought of spiritual
need, Isaiah 5:12.
Revelry of Tyre and Sidon, Isaiah 23:6-12.
Banquet for Jesus, Luke 5:27-35.

FETISH
Religious works involved in idolatry, Isaiah
46:1.
Use of magic charms, Ezekiel 13:18.

FETTERS
Strength of Samson tested, Judges 16:21-
30.
Shackles and hook in nose, 2 Chronicles
33:11. (See also Ps. 149:6-9.)
Young king humiliated, 2 Chronicles 36:5-
6.
Prophet in chains, Jeremiah 40:1-5.
Chained between two soldiers, Acts 12:1-

19.
Extra chains for prize prisoner, Acts 21:33.
See *Prison.*

FETUS
Desiring prenatal death, Job 3:11.
Destiny of unborn, Psalm 139:15-16.
Divine call to unborn, Isaiah 49:1.
God's prenatal plan for Jeremiah,
    Jeremiah 1:4-5; 20:17.
See *Abortion, Pregnancy.*

FEVER
Debilitating, crippling fever, Leviticus
    26:14-16.
Fever unto death, Deuteronomy 28:22.
Burning fever, Job 30:30.
Ailing mother-in-law, Matthew 8:14.
Fever and dysentery, Acts 28:8.

FICKLE
Love like morning mist, Hosea 6:4.
Changeable Galatians, Galatians 1:6-9.

FICTION
World's shortest short story, Ecclesiastes
    9:14-15. (Note "surprise" ending.)
Cleverly invented stories, 2 Peter 1:16; 2:3.
See *Literature.*

FIDELITY
Joseph's integrity, Genesis 39:6.
Honest expense accounts, 2 Kings 12:13-
    15.
Faithful workmen, 2 Chronicles 34:12.
Responsible warehousing, Nehemiah
    13:13.
Looking for one honest person in
    Jerusalem, Jeremiah 5:1.
Free from corruption or negligence, Daniel
    6:4.
Requirement for service, 1 Corinthians
    4:2.
See *Character, Dependability, Integrity.*

FIFTH COLUMN
Disruptive people among believers, Jude
    3-4.

FIGS
Leaves for garments, Genesis 3:7.
Symbol of abundance, Numbers 13:23;
    Deuteronomy 8:7-9.
Medicinal, 2 Kings 20:7; Isaiah 38:21.

Commercialize, Nehemiah 13:15.

FIGURE OF SPEECH
Blood cries out, Genesis 4:10.
Earth's nausea, Leviticus 18:25.
Furnace of persecution, Deuteronomy
    4:20; Jeremiah 11:4.
Intoxicated arrows, Deuteronomy 32:42.
Stones with ears, Joshua 24:27. (Also see
    Ps. 77:16.)
Walking heart led by eyes, Job 31:7.
Animated bronze and iron, Job 40:18.
Pregnant with evil, Psalm 7:14.
Broken heart, Psalm 69:20.
Tongues rule earth, Psalm 73:9.
Amnesia of hand, Psalm 137:5.
Food for eyes, Psalm 145:15.
Lamp of the Lord, Proverbs 20:27.
Secrets between hands, Matthew 6:3.
Misunderstanding figure-of-speech,
    Matthew 16:5-12.
Body communication, 1 Corinthians
    12:15-16.

FILTH
Soda and soap, Jeremiah 2:22.
New garments for Joshua, Zechariah 3:1-7.

FILTHY LUCRE
Tainted money paid to Judas, Matthew
    27:3-10.
See *Bribery.*

FINALE
Last words of David, 2 Samuel 23:1-7.
Last verse of Psalms, Psalm 150:6.
Ezekiel's prophecy of "the end," Ezekiel
    7:2.
Last statement of great prophet, Ezekiel
    48:35.
Fulfillment of times, Ephesians 1:9-10.
Christ suffered once for all, Hebrews 9:24-
    28.
End is near, 1 Peter 4:7.
Conclusion of Bible, Revelation 22:20-21.
See *Ending.*

FINANCES
Treasures on earth or in heaven, Matthew
    6:19-21.
Estimating cost before starting to build,
    Luke 14:28-30.
Human equations and power of God, John
    6:1-13. (See particularly v. 7.)

Importance of paying debts, Romans 13:8.
Sharing ministry expense, Philippians 4:15-19.
Paul worked to provide income, 1 Thessalonians 1:9.
Paul as model in daily conduct and employment, 2 Thessalonians 3:6-10.
Receiving no help from pagans, 3 John 7.

FINISH
See *Completion, Conclusion, Ending, Termination.*

FIRE
Purified by fire, Numbers 21:28; Ezekiel 22:20-22; Zechariah 13:9; Malachi 3:2; 1 Corinthians 3:13; 1 Peter 1:7.
Angel ascending in flame of fire, Judges 13:20.
Excrement used as fuel, Ezekiel 4:9-15.
Lake of fire, Revelation 19:19-21.
See *Kindling.*

FISHERMAN
Waters stocked with abundance, Genesis 1:20-21.
A song to fish by, Isaiah 42:10.
Agents of judgment, Jeremiah 16:16-18.
Fisherman's paradise, Ezekiel 47:9-10.
Fisherman and catch, Habakkuk 1:14-15.
Burning incense to fishing net, Habakkuk 1:16.
Fishermen become fishers of men, Matthew 4:19; Mark 1:17; Luke 5:1-11.
Coin in a fish's mouth, Matthew 17:27.
Miraculous catch, John 21:1-12.

FITNESS
Hindrance to worship, Leviticus 21:16-23.
Death of healthy person, Job 5:26.
Candidates for service in Babylonian government, Daniel 1:3-5.
Qualifications for following Jesus, Luke 9:23-26.
See *Athletics, Health.*

FLAG
Tribal and family banners, Numbers 2:2.
Raise the flag, Psalm 20:5.
Enemy flags, Psalm 74:4.
Banner of love, Song of Songs 2:4.
Divine banner summons earth's nations, Isaiah 5:26.
Messiah likened to a banner, Isaiah 11:10, 12.
Frightened by military flags, Isaiah 31:9.
Flag of proclamation, Jeremiah 50:2.
Summons to action, Jeremiah 51:12.

FLASHBACK
Literary technique of flashback used concerning Herod and John the Baptist, Mark 6:14-29.

FLATTERY
Jacob's sincere flattery to his brother, Genesis 33:10.
Likening king to angel, 2 Samuel 14:17.
Evil use of flattery, Psalms 36:1-4; 78:36; Proverbs 2:16; 24:24; Romans 16:18.
Speech smoother than oil, Proverbs 5:3.
Avoid those given to flattery, Proverbs 20:19.
Rebuke better than flattery, Proverbs 28:23.
Flattering one's neighbor, Proverbs 29:5.
Empty sincerity of Pharisees, Mark 12:15-17.
Dishonest compliments, Luke 20:21.
Glory belongs to God alone, 1 Corinthians 3:7.
Complimenting those who had been previously rebuked, 2 Corinthians 7:14.
Paul avoided flattery, 1 Thessalonians 2:5.
See *Exaggeration, Obsequious, Sham.*

FLAVOR
Food with good flavor, Genesis 27:4-31.
Sweet water, Exodus 15:25.
Gourmet manna, Exodus 16:31.
Unable to detect flavors, 2 Samuel 19:35.
Tasteless egg white, Job 6:6.
Avoid craving for delicacies, Proverbs 23:3.
Hunger improves flavor, Proverbs 27:7.
Bitter flavor, Matthew 27:34.
Sweet in mouth, sour in stomach, Revelation 10:9-11.
See *Delicacy, Food, Gourmet, Taste.*

FLEDGLING
Eagle training young to fly, Deuteronomy 32:11.

FLEECE
Gideon's procedure, Judges 6:36-40.
Refusing to put God to test, Isaiah 6:10-12.

FLESH
Unsatisfied dreams of hunger and thirst,
Isaiah 29:7-8.
Put out offending eye, Matthew 5:29.
Self-crucified, Romans 6:6.
Struggle between flesh and spirit, Romans
7:15-18.
Put on Christ, Romans 13:14.
Secret to subduing flesh, Galatians 5:16;
Colossians 3:5.
Continual lust for more, Ephesians 4:19.
Role of desire in causing one to sin, James
1:13-15.
See *Carnality, Worldliness.*

FLIGHT
Possible allusion to airplanes, Isaiah 60:8.
Ezekiel lifted up between earth and
heaven, Ezekiel 8:3.
Flying scroll, Zechariah 5:1-2.

FLIRTATION
Haughty women of Zion, Isaiah 3:16-17;
4:4.
Worst of women, Jeremiah 2:33.
Adulterous look, Hosea 2:2.

FLOOD
Noah's escape, Genesis 7:1-24.
Evil men destroyed, Job 22:16.
Divine promise, Isaiah 54:9.
Rising waters, Jeremiah 47:2.
Authenticity of Flood attested by Jesus,
Matthew 24:36-39.
Apostolic validation, 1 Peter 3:18-22;
2 Peter 2:4-5.
Water spewed from serpent's mouth,
Revelation 12:15-16.

FLUENT
Tip of tongue, Job 33:2.
Lips speak with deception, Psalm 12:1-2.
Mouth like sharpened sword, Isaiah 49:2.
See *Eloquence, Speech.*

FOLLOWERS
Choosing mighty and brave for service,
1 Samuel 14:52.
David's army of chosen men, 2 Samuel
6:1; 23:8-39.
Light must be followed to avoid darkness,
John 8:12.
Sheep and shepherd, John 10:27; 12:26.
In His steps, 1 Peter 2:21.

See *Discipleship.*

FOLLOW-UP
Shepherding new converts, Acts 15:36.
(Note disagreement concerning
methods, vv. 37-40.)
Teaching new converts, Acts 18:23.
Paul eager for proper counsel with
Thessalonians, 1 Thessalonians 3:1-5.
Paul's constant prayer for Timothy,
2 Timothy 1:3.
Looking after needs of new congregation,
Titus 1:5-9.
See *Convert.*

FOLLY
Nations fall into the pit they have dug,
Psalm 9:15.
Overconfidence, Psalm 49:13.
Discerning heart, Proverbs 15:14.
Foolish repetition, Proverbs 26:11.
Folly of not listening to the Lord's
commands, Isaiah 48:17-18.
Hatching another's eggs, Jeremiah 17:11.

FOMENT
See *Controversy, Devious, Jealousy,
Scheme.*

FOOD
Let land produce, Genesis 1:11-12.
Man and animals originally vegetarian,
Genesis 1:29-30.
First use of meat as food, Genesis 9:3.
Food as item of hospitality, Genesis 18:1-8.
Offering mortal amenities to angels,
Genesis 19:1-4.
How taste for game influenced Isaac's
feelings toward Esau, Genesis 25:27-28.
(See also 27:2-4.)
Edible and inedible insects, Leviticus
11:20-23.
Craving for meat, Deuteronomy 12:20.
Early instance of food and fellowship,
Deuteronomy 14:23; 15:20.
Vitality of bread, Judges 7:13-15.
Temporal food not eaten by immortals,
Judges 13:16.
Sampling food offered for sacrifice,
1 Samuel 2:13-14.
Food containing blood, 1 Samuel 14:31-
33.
Unpalatable food, 2 Kings 4:40.
Eating that which grows on its own,

2 Kings 19:29.
Blessing better than richest food, Psalm 63:5.
Manna called bread of angels, Psalm 78:25.
Hunger makes man work harder, Proverbs 16:26.
Avoid overeating, Proverbs 23:1-3.
Wisdom like eating honey, Proverbs 24:13-14.
Too lazy to eat, Proverbs 26:15.
Lion eating straw, Isaiah 11:7.
From harvest to making bread, Isaiah 28:28.
Meat not to be eaten, Isaiah 66:17.
Those who once ate delicacies, Lamentations 4:5.
Bread secured at risk of death, Lamentations 5:9.
Food defiled by unclean fuel, Ezekiel 4:12-15.
Priests given best food, Ezekiel 44:28-31.
Failure of harvest, Hosea 9:2.
Plenty to eat, Joel 2:26.
Forbidden food denied, Zechariah 9:7.
Cooking pots in the Lord's house, Zechariah 14:20-21.
Food of John the Baptist, Matthew 3:4.
Food supplied to those who trust, Matthew 6:31.
Pharisees criticized Jesus for picking grain on Sabbath, Matthew 12:1-8.
Feeding 5,000, Matthew 14:13-21; Mark 6:30-44; Luke 9:10-17; John 6:1-13.
Eating or not eating on Sabbath, Mark 2:23-27.
Even Jesus became hungry, Luke 4:1-2.
Celebrating commitment with banquet, Luke 5:27-32.
Food for dead girl, Luke 8:55.
Too much concern for food and drink, Luke 12:29.
Food considered more important than spiritual results, John 6:26-40.
Dinner in Jesus' honor, John 12:2.
Time to express love, John 13:1-2.
Morsel of bread to implicate Judas, John 13:21-27.
Hunger caused Peter to fall into trance, Acts 10:10.
No food unclean, Romans 14:14.
Limited spiritual diet, 1 Corinthians 3:1-2.
Unmuzzled ox, 1 Corinthians 9:9-14.
Physical hunger and spiritual sustenance, 1 Corinthians 11:34.

Stomach as god, Philippians 3:19.
Sweet in mouth, sour to stomach, Revelation 10:9-10.
Wedding supper in heaven, Revelation 19:9.
See *Diet, Feast, Gourmet.*

FOOL
Fool's perception, 1 Samuel 26:21; Proverbs 12:15.
Blind atheism, Psalms 14:1; 53:1.
Foolish woman, Proverbs 9:13-16.
Gullibility, Proverbs 14:15.
Repetitive folly, Proverbs 26:11.
End result for materialist, Luke 12:16-21.
Fools for Christ's sake, 1 Corinthians 4:10.
Pauline sarcasm, 2 Corinthians 11:16-29.

FOOLISH
Wild donkey's colt, Job 11:12.
Careless about danger, Proverbs 22:3.
Parables to a fool, Proverbs 26:1-12.
Our own foolish past, Titus 3:3.

FOOT-WASHING
Courtesy to guests, Genesis 18:4.
Wife's duty, 1 Samuel 25:40-41.
Act of love, Luke 7:44; John 13:5; 1 Timothy 5:10.

FORBEARANCE
Divine wrath delayed, Isaiah 48:9.
Tolerance toward bad reports, 1 Corinthians 11:18-19.
Showing love to those who cause grief, 2 Corinthians 2:5-11.
Humble, gentle, patient, Ephesians 4:2.
Forgive as the Lord forgave, Colossians 3:13.
See *Forgiveness, Pardon.*

FORBIDDEN
Forbidden fruit, Genesis 2:17.
Sweetness of stolen things, Proverbs 9:17.
Sacred mountain that could not be touched, Hebrews 12:18-21.

FORBODING
Potential snare, Exodus 34:2.
Prayer in view of forboding danger, Nehemiah 4:7-9.
Impending persecutions, Mark 13:9.
Wolves among the sheep, Acts 20:28-31.
Satan's relentless pursuit, 1 Peter 5:8.

See *Danger, Peril.*

FORECLOSURE
Clothing not usable as equity, Exodus 22:25.
Protecting debtor's earning power, Deuteronomy 24:6.
See *Mortgage.*

FOREFATHERS
Three forefathers of mankind, Genesis 9:18-19.
Genealogy of Jesus, Matthew 1:1-16; Luke 3:23-38.

FOREIGNER
Forbidding marriage between foreigners, Genesis 24:3.
Foreword to Golden Rule, Exodus 22:21; 23:9.
Passage denied by Edom to Israel, Numbers 20:14-21.
Aliens who succeed above local citizenry, Deuteronomy 28:43-44.
Foreigners seeking help, 2 Samuel 22:45-46.
Census of aliens, 2 Chronicles 2:17-18.
Influx of immigrants, 2 Chronicles 15:9.
Queen Esther's secret nationality, Esther 2:20.
Centurion named Cornelius, Acts 10:1-33.
See *Xenophobia.*

FOREKNOWLEDGE
Father's foreknowledge of sons' futures, Genesis 49:1-27.
Destiny set for rebellious people, Numbers 14:35.
Future accomplishment assured, Numbers 21:34.
Moses told where to go for his death, Deuteronomy 32:48-50.
Informed prophet, 1 Kings 14:1-5.
Prophet knew what fate had been decreed, 2 Kings 6:31-32.
Words of prophet fulfilled, 2 Kings 7:17-20.
Chosen to build temple, 1 Chronicles 28:2-10.
God's plans remain firm, Job 42:2.
The Lord does what pleases Him, Psalm 135:6.
One who knows all our ways, Psalm 139:1-16.

Righteous path, wicked way, Proverbs 4:18-19.
Steps directed by the Lord, Proverbs 20:24.
Unknown tomorrow, Proverbs 27:1.
Meaningless future, Ecclesiastes 2:15-16.
Roundelay of life, Ecclesiastes 6:10.
No one knows, Ecclesiastes 10:14.
Not putting the Lord to the test, Isaiah 7:10-12.
Divine plan and purpose, Isaiah 14:24.
Ordained, planned, brought to pass, Isaiah 37:26.
Foretelling a nation's future, Isaiah 42:9; 44:7; Daniel 2:28-29.
One who knows future, Isaiah 45:11-13; Acts 15:18.
Future left in hands of God, Isaiah 46:8-11.
Called before birth, Isaiah 49:1; Jeremiah 1:5.
Fortune and destiny, Isaiah 65:11.
Distant future, Ezekiel 12:26-27.
Divine plan revealed to prophets, Amos 3:7.
Our future needs known to God, Matthew 6:8.
Sacred secret, Matthew 24:36.
Unknown hour of Christ's return, Mark 13:26-33.
Father's prophecy of son, Luke 1:67-79.
Confirmation of Isaiah's prophecy, Luke 4:17-22.
Advance preparation for Passover, Luke 22:7-13.
Gospel anticipated in advance, Galatians 3:6-9.
Coming of the Lord as a thief, 1 Thessalonians 5:1-2.
See *Predestination.*

FORERUNNER
Those who went ahead of the chariot, 2 Samuel 15:1.
John the Baptist, Malachi 3:1; Mark 1:2-8; Luke 3:1-20.
Jesus has made advance preparations, Hebrews 6:19-20.

FORESTRY
All kinds of trees, Genesis 2:9.
Living among trees, Genesis 13:18. (See 14:13; 18:1.)
Abraham's planting of tree, Genesis 21:33.
Saving trees in conquered city, Deuteronomy 20:19.

Trees seek king, Judges 9:7-15.
Finest trees felled, 2 Kings 19:23.
Forest ranger, Nehemiah 2:8.
Tree lies where it falls, Ecclesiastes 11:3.
Reforestation, Isaiah 44:14.
Lumber for idols, Jeremiah 10:2-5.
Garden of Gethsemane, John 18:1.
See *Ecology, Trees.*

FOREWORD
Introduction to world history, Genesis 1:1-2.
Foreword to Book of Proverbs, Proverbs 1:1-6.

FORGERY
Forged signature, 1 Kings 21:1-16.
See *Counterfeit.*

FORGIVENESS
Demonstrating forgiving spirit, Exodus 23:4-5; Proverbs 24:17; 25:21-22.
Parable used to convince need to forgive, 2 Samuel 14:1-21.
Job prayed for unwise friends, Job 42:7-10.
God's forgiveness and punishment, Psalm 99:8.
Depth of mercy and grace, Psalm 145:8-9.
Power of love, Proverbs 10:12.
Controlled anger, Proverbs 19:11.
God's great love to faithless Israel, Jeremiah 3:12-13.
God's total forgiveness, Jeremiah 50:20.
Greatness of God's mercy, Hosea 14:4.
Gracious and compassionate Lord to those who repent, Joel 2:12-13.
Given a second chance, Jonah 1:1-3; 3:1-3.
Forgiving grace and mercy of God, Micah 7:18.
Giving must be in forgiving spirit, Matthew 5:23-24.
Power in forgiving others, Matthew 6:14-15.
Principles of forgiveness, Matthew 18:21-22; Mark 11:25-26; Luke 6:37; 17:3-4; James 5:15-16.
Gratitude for great forgiveness, Luke 7:39-50.
Forgiving spirit of martyr, Acts 7:60.
Forgiveness for enemy, Romans 5:10.
Showing love to those who cause grief, 2 Corinthians 2:5-11.
Forgive one another and be patient, Colossians 3:13.

Sins of ignorance, 1 Timothy 1:12-14.
Paul's attitude toward those who deserted him, 2 Timothy 4:16.
Mercy of salvation, Hebrews 10:17.
Power of love to forgive, 1 Peter 4:8.
Our advocate with Heavenly Father, 1 John 2:1-2.

FORGOTTEN
Forgiven and forgotten sin, Psalm 103:12.
Former things not brought to mind, Isaiah 65:17.
Forgotten Sabbath, Lamentations 2:6.
Divine memory, Luke 12:6.

FORMALITY
Unaware of the Lord's presence, Genesis 28:16.
Something more than religious performance, Psalms 51:16-17; 69:30-31.
God's voice more important than ours, Ecclesiastes 5:1; Hosea 6:6; Micah 6:6-7.
Meaningless religious procedures, Isaiah 1:13.
Rules taught by men, Isaiah 29:13.
Garments worn by priests in temple, Ezekiel 42:14.
Divine detestation of mere formalism, Amos 5:21-23.
Clothing of kings and prophets, Matthew 11:7-9.
Washing hands before eating, Matthew 15:1-2.
Formality without reality, Matthew 23:23; Galatians 4:9-11; Colossians 2:20; 2 Timothy 3:1-5.
Mere performance of religion, Romans 2:17-29; 1 Corinthians 7:19.
Paul's prior formalism, Philippians 3:4-7.
See *Liturgy.*

FORMIDABLE
City walls to sky, Deuteronomy 9:1.
One plus God equals majority, 1 Samuel 14:6-14.

FORMULA
God's formula for success, Joshua 1:8.

FORSAKEN
Prophecy of Golgotha outcry, Psalm 22:1.
Wondering if God has forgotten, Psalm 77:8; Isaiah 49:14.

Briefly abandoned, Isaiah 54:7.
Weeping with no one to comfort,
    Lamentations 1:16.
See *Abandoned, Loneliness.*

FORTUITY
No chance accident, Exodus 21:12-13.
Death by measurement, 2 Samuel 8:2.
Random arrow, 2 Chronicles 18:33-
    34.
Time for everything, Ecclesiastes 3:1-8.
God's perfect timing, Isaiah 49:8.
See *Chance, Happenstance.*

FORTUNES
Dramatic reversal of fortunes, Esther
    5:9–7:10.
Poor people of Judah discovered true
    wealth, Jeremiah 39:10; 40:11-12.

FORTUNE-TELLING
Joseph pretended to believe in divination,
    Genesis 44:5.
Divination arts outlawed, Deuteronomy
    18:9-13.
Man cannot discover his future,
    Ecclesiastes 7:14.
Tools of the fortune-teller, Isaiah 65:11.
Men of wisdom in Nebuchadnezzar's
    court, Daniel 2:1-4.
Daniel interpreted Nebuchadnezzar's
    dream, Daniel 2:24-49.
Conversion of fortune-teller, Acts 16:16-
    19.
See *Divination, Sorcery.*

FORTY
Duration of flood, Genesis 7:17.
Spying in Canaan, Numbers 13:25.
Years of wandering, Numbers 32:13.
Arrogant giant, 1 Samuel 17:16.
Reign of David and Solomon, 1 Kings 2:11;
    11:42.
Probation for Nineveh, Jonah 3:4.
Temptation of Jesus, Luke 4:1-2.
Ministry after Resurrection, Acts 1:3.

FOSSILS
Waters that formerly covered earth, Psalm
    104:7-9.

FOSTER PARENTS
Mordecai foster father of Esther, Esther
    2:7.

FOUNDATION
Weak as spider's web, Job 8:14.
Building on rock or sand, Matthew 7:24-27.
Laying good foundation, 1 Corinthians
    3:10.

FOUNDER
Building first city, Genesis 4:17.
Father of history, Genesis 12:1-3.
Author of our faith, Hebrews 12:2.

FOUNTAIN
Fountain of life, Psalm 36:9.
Water pollution, Proverbs 25:26.
Forsaken springs of living water, Jeremiah
    2:13.
Fountain from the temple, Joel 3:18;
    Zechariah 13:1.
Supreme guidance of Shepherd,
    Revelation 7:17.
See *Water.*

FRAGRANCE
Aroma of good sacrifice, Genesis 8:20-21.
    (See Lev. 23:18; 2 Cor. 2:15; Eph. 5:1-
    2.)
Fragrance for worship, not personal
    enjoyment, Exodus 30:34-38.
No fragrance permitted in sin offering,
    Leviticus 5:11.
David's use of lotion, 2 Samuel 12:20.
Multiple spices, Song of Songs 3:6.
Expensive perfume on feet of Jesus, John
    12:1-8.
Modern commerce in luxuries, Revelation
    18:11-13.
See *Cosmetics, Perfume.*

FRAME OF REFERENCE
Bible-centered mentality, Psalm 1:2.
Pleasant boundary lines, Psalm 16:6.
Developing a truly spiritual frame-of-
    reference, Psalms 19:14; 139:23-24.
Warped minds and men of wisdom,
    Proverbs 12:8.
Learning to think clean, Isaiah 1:16-20.
God of Israel spoken of as "god" by pagan
    king, Isaiah 37:10.
God's perspective and man's perspective,
    Isaiah 55:8-9.
Inability to understand and explain,
    Jeremiah 9:12.
To those who call, unsearchable truth
    awaits, Jeremiah 33:3.

Knowing who is the Lord, Ezekiel 6:10, 14; 7:4, 9, 27; 12:16, 20; 13:9, 23; 14:11.
People without understanding, Hosea 4:14.
Communicating God's message to children, Joel 1:1-3.
Truly good life, Micah 6:8.
Sin committed in heart, Matthew 5:27-28.
Inner mark of outer spirituality, Matthew 12:34-37.
Unable to understand scriptural teaching, Matthew 16:5-12.
Revealing thoughts of heart, Luke 2:34-35.
Good out of good heart, evil from evil, Luke 6:45.
Followers of Jesus unable to understand coming Crucifixion, Luke 9:44-45; 18:31-34.
Preferring darkness to light, John 3:19-21.
Sin and rebellion as basis for thought and action, Romans 1:21-32.
Mind centered on natural desires, Romans 8:5-8. (Note also vv. 9-11.)
Renewing mind, Romans 12:2.
Paul and Peter face-to-face, Galatians 2:11.
Spirit of wisdom and revelation, Ephesians 1:17.
Thinking as believer, Ephesians 3:16-19.
Darkened understanding, Ephesians 4:18.
Filled with knowledge of God's will, Colossians 1:9-14. (See 2:2-3.)
Enmity in mind against God, Colossians 1:21.
Taken captive by wrong thinking, Colossians 2:8.
Enriching one's own thought process, Colossians 3:1-2.
Fix thoughts on Jesus, Hebrews 3:1.
Eternal frame-of-reference, Hebrews 10:34.
Mentality of success, 1 Peter 1:15.
Clear mind of negative thoughts, 1 Peter 2:1.
Virtues added to grace, 2 Peter 1:5-9.
Viewpoint of world, 1 John 4:5.
See *Mind.*

FRANKINCENSE
Used in holy oil, Exodus 30:34-38.
Meal offerings and showbread, Leviticus 2:1-2, 15; 24:7.
Excluded from some offerings, Leviticus 5:11.
Product of Arabia, Isaiah 60:6.

FRANKNESS
See *Candor.*

FRAUD
Do not defraud neighbor, Leviticus 19:13.
Despising those who tell the truth, Amos 5:10.
Acquittal of dishonesty, Micah 6:11.
Disciples doubted Saul's conversion, Acts 9:26-27.
Believers in litigation, 1 Corinthians 6:3-8.
Gaining benefit by taking advantage, James 5:4-5.
Method of false teachers, 2 Peter 2:1.
See *Deceit, Dishonesty.*

FREEDOM
Freedom of choice, Genesis 13:10-13.
King imprisoned and set free, 2 Kings 24:15; 25:27-29.
Wild donkeys of desert, Job 39:5-6.
Shattered yoke, Isaiah 9:4; 10:27.
Yoke removed, Isaiah 14:25.
Proclaiming freedom, Isaiah 61:1.
Slaves set free, enslaved again, Jeremiah 34:8-22.
Liberty for Jeremiah after capture of Jerusalem, Jeremiah 40:1-4.
Free men ruled over by slaves, Lamentations 5:8.
Truth sets free, John 8:31-32, 36.
Deeper meaning of deliverance from legalism, Acts 10:24-28.
Peter's vision of clean and unclean, Acts 11:4-10.
Freedom from mastery of sin, Romans 6:14.
Set free from legality, Romans 7:1-6.
Deliverance from sin through Christ alone, Romans 7:24-25.
Unmuzzled ox, 1 Corinthians 9:9-14.
Freedom in the Spirit, 2 Corinthians 3:17.
Called to be free, Galatians 5:13.
Filled with knowledge of God's will, Colossians 1:9-12.
Rescued from dominion of darkness, Colossians 1:13-14.
Freedom lifestyle, 1 Peter 2:16.
See *Liberty.*

FREELOADING
Some pay, others only receive, 2 Corinthians 11:7-8.

FREEWILL
Freewill offerings, Leviticus 22:21-23; 23:38; Numbers 15:3; Deuteronomy 12:6, 17; 16:10; 23:23; 2 Chronicles 31:14; Ezra 1:4; 3:5; 7:16; 8:28; Psalm 119:108.
Valley of decision, Joel 3:14.

FRICTION
Those who wanted to be part of building the temple, Ezra 4:1-3.
Those who purposely cause trouble, Romans 16:17.
See *Abrasion, Conflict.*

FRIENDLESS
No one to comfort, Lamentations 1:2.

FRIENDSHIP
Wrong influence of friends, Deuteronomy 13:6-9.
Two people becoming one in spirit, 1 Samuel 18:1-4.
Loyalty torn between father and close friend, 1 Samuel 19:1-2.
Friendship at cutting edge, 1 Samuel 20:1-4.
Friendship centered in name of the Lord, 1 Samuel 20:42.
Marks of true friendship, 2 Samuel 1:23; John 15:13-15.
False friends, 2 Samuel 16:16-23.
Governments on friendly terms, 1 Kings 5:1.
Elijah and Elisha, 2 Kings 2:2.
Friends became adversaries, Job 2:11-13.
Reaching out to friend in need, Job 6:14.
Undependable friends, Job 6:15-17.
Man who turned against his friends, Job 17:5.
Alienating another's friends, Job 19:13-22.
Betrayal of friendship, Psalms 41:9; 55:12-14.
Loss of closest friends, Psalm 88:8.
Consistent relationship, Proverbs 17:17.
Closer than a brother, Proverbs 18:24.
Purchasing friends with money, Proverbs 19:4.
Friendship can be overdone, Proverbs 25:17.
Wounds of friend, Proverbs 27:6.
Rebuke better than flattery, Proverbs 27:6.
Two better than one, Ecclesiastes 4:9-12.
Shelter from wind, Isaiah 32:2.

No help from wrong friends, Jeremiah 2:37.
Friends and brothers who cannot be trusted, Jeremiah 9:4-5.
Friends become enemies, Jeremiah 13:20-22.
Waiting for another friend to fail, Jeremiah 20:10.
Betrayed by friends, Lamentations 1:2, 19.
Friends of paralytic man, Mark 2:1-12; Luke 5:17-26.
Strange friendship of Herod and Pilate, Luke 23:12.
True meaning of friend, John 15:12-17.
Barnabas true friend to Saul, Acts 9:26-27.
Friends of Paul, the prisoner, Acts 27:3.
Paul's many greetings to friends, Romans 16:3-16.
Conduct of true friend, 2 Timothy 1:16-18.
Friend forsakes, 2 Timothy 4:10-17.
Timothy released from prison, Hebrews 13:23.
Worldly friends, James 4:4.
See *Camaraderie, Fellowship.*

FRIVOLOUS
Beautiful but dumb, Proverbs 11:22.

FRUGALITY
Food supply gathered, Genesis 41:35-36.
Careful frugality, Proverbs 13:11.
Choice food and oil, Proverbs 21:20.
Frugal with time, Proverbs 31:27.
No food wasted, Matthew 14:20; 15:37; John 6:12.
Unnecessary frugality, Mark 14:4-5.

FRUIT
Creation of fruits, Genesis 1:11-12.
Aaron's staff, Numbers 17:8.
Care of fruit trees, Deuteronomy 20:19-20.
Apple of God's eye, Deuteronomy 32:10; Psalm 17:8.
Eating wild fruit, Isaiah 37:30.
Beautiful tree destroyed in judgment, Jeremiah 11:16.
Verdant growth for those who trust in the Lord, Jeremiah 17:7-8.
Tree known by fruit, Matthew 12:33-35.
Degrees of spiritual fruit, Mark 4:20.
Good land and unproductive land, Hebrews 6:7-8.
Harvest every month of year, Revelation 22:2.

FRUITLESS
Those who do nothing, Isaiah 30:7.
Harvest past, summer ended, no salvation, Jeremiah 8:20.
Stalks with no grain, Hosea 8:7.
See *Reward.*

FRUSTRATION
See *Confusion, Disappointment, Emptiness, Futility.*

FRYING PAN
Use of frying pan, Leviticus 2:7.
From frying pan to fire, Amos 5:19.

FUEL
Twigs gathered for fires, Isaiah 27:11.
Scarcity of firewood, Lamentations 5:4.
Dung used for baking, Ezekiel 4:12-15.
See *Fire.*

FUGITIVE
Flight of Moses, Exodus 2:11-15.
Sheltering a slave, Deuteronomy 23:15-16.
David's flight from Saul, 1 Samuel 21:10-11.
Absalom's flight from revenge murder, 2 Samuel 13:30-38.
Two escaped slaves, 1 Kings 2:39-40.
Flight to Egypt, 1 Kings 11:26-40.
Holy family's flight to Egypt, Matthew 2:13-15.
Return of a fugitive, Philemon 1-25.
See *Refuge.*

FULFILLMENT
True joy comes only from the Lord, Psalm 84:11.
Desires satisfied, strength renewed, Psalm 103:5.
Satisfaction from the Lord, Psalm 107:8-9.
Agony of waiting, joy of fulfillment, Proverbs 13:12.
Emptiness of mere success and affluence, Ecclesiastes 2:4-11.
Something more than eating and drinking, Ecclesiastes 2:24-26.
Labor and good food, Ecclesiastes 5:18-20.
Enjoying years of life, Ecclesiastes 11:8.
Reward for obedience, Isaiah 48:17-18.
Plight of wicked, fulfillment of the righteous, Isaiah 65:13-14.
Ancient paths, good way, Jeremiah 6:16.
Unsatisfied sword, Jeremiah 46:10.

Promise of fulfillment to beleaguered Israel, Jeremiah 50:19.
Eating to complete satisfaction, Joel 2:26.
Aged Simeon saw promised Saviour, Luke 2:25-32.
Those who hunger, Luke 6:21.
Satisfied by miracle food, Luke 9:17.
Living water from within, John 7:37-39.
Christ gives full life, John 10:10.
Joy complete, John 15:11.
Good things God gives daily, Acts 14:17.
Overflowing with hope through Holy Spirit, Romans 15:13.
God's grace lavished on us, Ephesians 1:7-8.
Paul's pleasure over progress of Thessalonian believers, 1 Thessalonians 3:8.
Oil of joy, Hebrews 1:9.
Discipline produces righteousness and peace, Hebrews 12:11.
Inexpressible and glorious joy, 1 Peter 1:8-9.
Peace that is in Christ, 1 Peter 5:14.
Joy of good reputation, 3 John 3-4.
Certainty of success in Christian life, Jude 24-25.
Totality of Son of God, Revelation 22:13.
Invitation to those who are thirsty, Revelation 22:17.
See *Contentment, Maturity, Satisfaction.*

FUMIGATION
Purifying rooms of temple, Nehemiah 13:9.

FUNCTION
One threshes grain, one grinds flour, Isaiah 28:28.
Salt and light in the world, Matthew 5:13-16.
Function of gifts in body of Christ, 1 Corinthians 12:27-30.
Proper understanding of the Law, 1 Timothy 1:8-11.

FUND-RAISING
Sources of funds for temple, 2 Kings 12:4-5.
Using temple for business purposes, Mark 11:15-17.
Paul's refusal to depend on people for material support, 1 Corinthians 9:7-18.
Divine example for Christian giving, 2 Corinthians 8:9.

Receiving no help from pagans, 3 John 7.
See *Stewardship.*

FUNERAL
Importance of place of burial, Genesis
23:1-20. (See 25:8-10.)
Embalming in Egypt done by physicians,
Genesis 50:2-3.
All Israel assembled to mourn Samuel,
1 Samuel 25:1.
The body of King Saul, 1 Samuel 31:11-13.
(See also 2 Sam. 2:4-6.)
Delegation sent to express condolence,
2 Samuel 10:1-2.
Respect for bodies of dead, 2 Samuel
21:13-14.
Body of evil woman, 2 Kings 9:34-37.
Grave cannot praise God, Isaiah 38:18.
Peaceful and honorable death, Jeremiah
34:4-5.
Flute an instrument for mourning,
Matthew 9:23-24.
Jesus buried without ceremony, Matthew
27:57-60; Mark 15:42-47; Luke 23:50-
54; John 19:38-42.
Grief at burial of Stephen, Acts 8:2.
See *Burial, Death, Grave, Tomb.*

FURNITURE
Lampstand of pure gold, Exodus 25:31.
Furnishing good home, Proverbs 24:3-4.

FUTILITY
Wishing for given day not to exist, Job 3:6.
Chasing wind, Ecclesiastes 2:11.
Emptiness of mere toil, Ecclesiastes 4:7-8.
Wood for making gods and cooking fires,
Isaiah 44:14-20.
Stain soda and soap will not cleanse,
Jeremiah 2:22.
Those who feed on wind, Hosea 12:1.
Shriveled seeds, Joel 1:17.
Too little and too late, Amos 3:12.
Possible and impossible, Luke 18:27.
Futility of no resurrection message,
1 Corinthians 15:13-19.
See *Emptiness.*

FUTURE
Fruit contained seed for future, Genesis
1:12.
God's promise to Abraham, Genesis 13:14-
17; 15:2-5. (Note some see the "dust of
the earth" as Jewish or earthly family,

"the stars" as the future church or
heavenly family.)
Joseph's prediction of deliverance from
Egypt, Genesis 50:24-25.
God's promise to David, 2 Samuel 7:12.
God's plan and purpose cannot be
thwarted, Job 42:2.
Inevitable fate of world governments,
Psalm 2:7-9.
Special guidance for those who fear the
Lord, Psalm 25:14.
Hope in time of despair, Psalm 42:5.
Fear of future, Psalm 55:4-5.
Wicked lack eternal perspective, Psalm
92:6-7.
God's message for unborn, Psalm 102:18.
Bright path of righteous, Proverbs 4:18.
Do not boast about tomorrow, Proverbs
27:1.
Man does not know what others will do
with his projects, Ecclesiastes 3:22.
As God plans, so it will be, Isaiah 14:24.
Evangelize during the night, with morning
coming, Isaiah 21:11-12.
God makes new thing, Isaiah 43:19.
Future left safely in God's hands, Isaiah
46:8-11.
Destiny ordained before birth, Isaiah 49:1.
Tools of fortune-teller, Isaiah 65:11.
Good news and bad news, Jeremiah 34:1-
7.
In desperation, Zedekiah listened to
Jeremiah, Jeremiah 38:14-28.
Meaning of his own prophecy withheld
from Daniel, Daniel 12:8-9. (Note
v. 13.)
Time to build and extend, Micah 7:11.
Nineveh to have no descendants, Nahum
1:14.
God's revelation will come to pass,
Habakkuk 2:3.
Jesus foretold death and resurrection,
Matthew 16:21; 20:17-19.
An angel prophesied ministry of John the
Baptist, Luke 1:11-17.
That which God has prepared for those
who love Him, 1 Corinthians 2:9-10.
Confidence in unseen, 2 Corinthians 4:18.
Fulfillment of times, Ephesians 1:9-10.
Citizenship in heaven, Philippians 3:20-21.
Son in body of ancestor, Hebrews 7:9-10.
Unsure of tomorrow, James 4:13-16.
Inheritance that can never perish, 1 Peter
1:4.

Unlimited future for children of God, 1 John 3:1-3.

Sure word of prophecy, Revelation 22:10. See *Promise, Prophecy, Tomorrow.*

G

GARDEN
Let the land produce, Genesis 1:9-12.
Earth as fruitful garden, Genesis 1:29.
Planting separate seeds in given areas,
  Deuteronomy 22:9.
Changing vineyard into vegetable garden,
  1 Kings 21:2.
The garden slug, Psalm 58:8.
Gardener, Jeremiah 29:5; John 20:15.
Well-watered garden, Jeremiah 31:12.
Flowers that wither, seeds that perish,
  1 Peter 1:23-25.
See *Agriculture, Fruit, Vegetable.*

GARMENT
Garments of salvation, Isaiah 61:10.
Not dressed for the wedding, Matthew
  22:9.
A building as a garment, 2 Corinthians 5:3-
  4.
Wearing white clothes, Revelation 3:18.
Robes washed white, Revelation 7:14.
Clothes ready for quick departure,
  Revelation 16:15.
Bright, clean linen, Revelation 19:8.
See *Clothing, Wardrobe.*

GATE
Place of meeting, Genesis 19:1; 23:10;
  34:20; Psalm 69:12.
City gates, Deuteronomy 3:5; Joshua 6:26;
  1 Samuel 23:7; 2 Samuel 18:24.
Wooden gate, Nehemiah 1:3.
Bronze gate, Isaiah 45:2.
Iron gate, Acts 12:10.

GEMS
Precious stones imported, 1 Kings 10:2.
Gems in royal crown, 1 Chronicles 20:2.
Temple gems, 1 Chronicles 29:2.
Adornment for pagan king, Daniel 11:38.

Precious stones likened to spiritual value,
  1 Corinthians 3:11-15.
See *Jewelry.*

GENEALOGY
Loss of family records, Nehemiah 7:64.
Genealogy of Jesus, Matthew 1:1-17; Luke
  3:22-38.
Davidic lineage of Christ, Romans 1:3.
See *Ancestors, Heritage.*

GENEROSITY
Abimelech's generosity to Abraham,
  Genesis 20:14-15.
Giving with willing heart, Exodus 25:2.
Blessing on generous, Psalm 112:5.
Giving to poor is lending to the Lord,
  Proverbs 19:17.
Blessing for generous man, Proverbs 22:9.
Give to those who ask, Matthew 5:42.
Secret acts of charity, Matthew 6:1-4.
Parable of Workers in Vineyard, Matthew
  20:1-16.
Excel in grace of giving, 2 Corinthians 8:7.
Much to those who give much, less to those
  who give less, 2 Corinthians 9:6-11.
God's grace lavished on us, Ephesians 1:7-
  8.
See *Giving, Philanthropy, Stewardship.*

GENETICS
Like father, like son, Genesis 5:1-3.
Jacob's experiment with his flocks,
  Genesis 30:37-39.

GENOCIDE
The Arab race nearly destroyed at
  inception, Genesis 21:9-21.
Threat of population reduction,
  Deuteronomy 28:62.
Destroying entire population, 1 Samuel

15:3.
Scarcity of people, Isaiah 13:12.
Total destruction of community, Jeremiah
51:20-23.
One-fourth of earth's population
destroyed, Revelation 6:8.

GENTILE
All nations included, Genesis 22:17-18.
Gentile who loved God, Job 1:1-3.
Light for Gentiles, Isaiah 9:6; 60:3.
A centurion named Cornelius, Acts 10:1-
33.
Gentile conversions, Acts 11:1; 13:48; 15:7.

GENTLENESS
One brother's attitude toward another,
Genesis 33:1-11.
Gentleness of Boaz to Ruth, Ruth 3:7-15.
Gentle shepherd, Isaiah 40:11.
Lambs among wolves, Luke 10:3.
Jesus and little children, Luke 18:15-17.
Like mother of little children,
1 Thessalonians 2:7.
Lifestyle of disciple, 2 Timothy 2:24; Titus
3:1-2.
Heaven's wisdom, James 3:17.
See *Kindness, Meekness.*

GENUFLECT
Bowing in respect, Genesis 33:6-7.
Bowing down before king, 1 Samuel 24:8.
Bowing before the Lord, Nehemiah 8:3-6.
Obeisance in new creation, Isaiah 66:23.
King bowing before his captive, Daniel
2:46.
Command not to worship angels,
Revelation 19:10.
See *Awe.*

GENUINE
Building on rock or sand, Matthew 7:24-27.
John the Baptist looked for authentic
Messiah, Matthew 11:1-5.
Wisdom of Gamaliel, Acts 5:33-39.
Barnabas a true friend to Saul, Acts 9:26-
27.
Holy Spirit our seal of ownership,
2 Corinthians 1:21-22.
Validity of faith, 1 Thessalonians 1:8-10.
True son in faith, 1 Timothy 1:2.
Hypocrisy of profession without
obedience, 1 John 2:4-6.
See *Authenticity, Validity.*

GEOGRAPHY
Division of earth into continents, Genesis
10:25.
Two nations unborn, Genesis 25:23.
Lord of hills and valleys, 1 Kings 20:28.
River of city of God, Psalm 46:4.
Seeking high rock, Psalm 61:1-2; 62:2, 6-7.
Praise of the Lord in all earth, Psalm 113:3.
Lifting up one's eyes to hills, Psalm 121:1.
Wisdom came before all creation, Proverbs
8:24-31.
Man comes and goes, earth remains
constant, Ecclesiastes 1:4.
Divine evaluation of nations, Isaiah 40:15-
17.
Commercial centers in Ezekiel's time,
Ezekiel 27:12-23.
Mountains an object of divine affection,
Ezekiel 36:1-12.
Mountains crumble but God's ways
eternal, Habakkuk 3:6.
Right foot on sea, left foot on land,
Revelation 10:2.
No longer any sea, Revelation 21:1.
See *Earth.*

GEOLOGY
Establishment of earth's surface, Genesis
1:9-10; Psalms 18:15; 24:1-2; 104:5-13.
Wealth in earth, Genesis 2:11-12.
Hot center of earth, Job 28:5-6.
Creator at work, Job 28:9-11.
Earth round like seal, Job 38:14.
Mountains crumble but God's truth
endures, Habakkuk 3:6.
See *Mountains, Rock.*

GEOMETRY
Traveling by straight line, Psalm 107:7.
Geometric depth of spiritual experience,
Ephesians 3:16-19.

GERIATRICS
Age of man before Flood, Genesis 6:3.
Old Testament fathers, Genesis 11:10-26.
Bearing children at advanced age, Genesis
16:16; 21:1-7.
Description of Abraham's old age, Genesis
25:8.
Jacob spoke of life as pilgrimage, Genesis
47:9.
Loss of physical sensitivities with age,
2 Samuel 19:35.
Keeping warm in old age, 1 Kings 1:1-4.

Old man and revenge, 1 Kings 2:5-9.
Solomon's wayward old age, 1 Kings 11:4-6.
Death of healthy, vigorous person, Job 5:26.
Wisdom and understanding come with years, Job 12:12.
End of life, Job 16:22.
Wicked who lived to ripe old age, Job 21:7.
Job longed for happiness of younger years, Job 29:4-6.
Youth defers to age, Job 32:4-9.
Job's longevity, Job 42:16-17.
Old age looks back on God's faithfulness, Psalm 37:25.
End of life comes quickly, Psalm 39:4-6.
Concern for faith in old age, Psalm 71:9, 17-18.
Satisfying long life, Psalm 91:16
Fruitful in old age, Psalm 92:14-15.
Wineskin withered in heat of fire, Psalm 119:83.
Guidance of Scripture for all of life, Psalm 119:111-112.
Years added to life, Proverbs 10:27.
Splendor of gray hair, Proverbs 16:31.
Youth and old age, Proverbs 20:29.
Care of aged parents, Proverbs 23:22-25.
Good old days, Ecclesiastes 7:10.
Enjoy life but with reservation, Ecclesiastes 11:8.
Sustained to old age, Isaiah 46:4.
Heavy yoke on aged, Isaiah 47:6.
God's wrath on young and old alike, Jeremiah 6:11.
Process of aging, Lamentations 3:4.
Darius made king at 62, Daniel 5:30-31.
Not noticing coming of gray hair, Hosea 7:9.
Young prophesy, old dream dreams, Joel 2:28.
Ripe old age, Zechariah 8:4.
Aged Simeon saw promised Saviour, Luke 2:25-32.
Ministry of elderly widow, Luke 2:36-38.
Marks of old age, John 21:18.
Ravages of age need not hinder inner growth, 2 Corinthians 4:16.
How to rebuke older man, 1 Timothy 5:1.
Conduct of older men and women, Titus 2:2-3.
Paul as an old man, Philemon 9.
Abraham as good as dead, Hebrews 11:12.
Busy for the Lord in advancing years,

2 Peter 1:13-14.
See *Birthday, Old age.*

GERMANY
Some believe Gomer an ancient tribe in geographical area of Germany, Ezekiel 38:6.

GERMS
See *Disease, Health, Sanitation.*

GESTATION
Destiny of unborn, Psalm 139:15-16.
God's prenatal plan for Jeremiah, Jeremiah 1:4-5.
Baby that leaped in mother's womb, Luke 1:39-44.
See *Pregnancy.*

GESTURE
Clapping and foot-stamping, Ezekiel 25:6.
Paul's use of hand gestures, Acts 13:16.

GIANT
Seeing each other as giants, Numbers 13:33.
Tall Anakites, Deuteronomy 2:11, 21.
Goliath, 1 Samuel 17:4-6.
Six-fingered giant, 2 Samuel 21:16, 20.
Mighty angel, Revelation 10:1-3.

GIDDY
Beautiful but dumb, Proverbs 11:22.

GIFT
Betrothal gifts, Genesis 24:53.
Joseph's gifts to brothers, Genesis 45:21-23.
Gift from plunder, 1 Samuel 30:26.
Exchange of gifts between Solomon and Queen of Sheba, 1 Kings 10:10; 2 Chronicles 9:12.
Gifts to celebrate Job's prosperity, Job 42:10-11.
Divine promise, Psalm 84:11.
Gift for departing visitor, Jeremiah 40:5.
Given a new spirit, Ezekiel 11:19.
Gifts of magi, Matthew 2:11.
Gift of rest, Matthew 11:28.
Gift of tongues, Acts 2:1-4.
Free gift of salvation, Romans 5:16-18; 6:23; 12:6-8.
Many gifts of the Spirit to the body of Christ, 1 Corinthians 12:1-31.

God intends diversity to produce unity, Ephesians 4:11-13.
Holy Spirit designates distribution of gifts, Hebrews 2:4.
Equipped by God of peace, Hebrews 13:20-21.
See *Grace.*

GIVING
Challenge to tithe, Malachi 3:10.
Giving only for God's glory, Matthew 6:1-4.
Widow's mite, Mark 12:42; Luke 21:2.
First day of week, 1 Corinthians 16:2.
Providing for those in need, 2 Corinthians 8:12-14.
Sowing and reaping, 2 Corinthians 9:6-7.
See *Benevolence, Philanthropy, Stewardship.*

GLEANERS
Providing for strangers and poor, Leviticus 19:9-10; 23:22; Deuteronomy 24:19-20.
Setting for romance, Ruth 2:2, 8, 23.
Leaving a few grapes on vine, Jeremiah 49:9.
See *Harvest.*

GLOOM
Joy and gladness gone, Jeremiah 48:33.
See *Pessimism.*

GLORIFY
Nature and people praise the Lord, Psalm 148:1-14.
Lights shining, Matthew 5:16.
Fruit of unity, Romans 15:5-6.
Gratitude for redemption, 1 Corinthians 6:19-20.
See *Praise.*

GLORY
Mountain of Transfiguration, Matthew 17:1-8.
Contemplating resurrection and exaltation of Christ, Ephesians 1:18-23.
See *Awe.*

GLOSSOLALIA
Gift of tongues, Acts 19:1-7.
Words beyond normal vocabulary, Romans 8:16, 26-27.
Omission of gift of tongues, Romans 12:4-8. (See 15:17-19.)
See *Gift, Tongues.*

GLUTTONY
Mistrust of the manna supply, Exodus 16:18-27.
Eyes bigger than stomach, Numbers 11:32.
Craving for meat, Deuteronomy 12:20.
Knife to throat, Proverbs 23:1-3.
Sure road to poverty, Proverbs 23:21.
Too much honey, Proverbs 25:16.
Overstuffed fool, Proverbs 30:21-22.
Best of meats and finest wine, Isaiah 25:6.
Dogs with big appetites, Isaiah 56:11.
Nebuchadnezzar's exploitation of conquered people, Jeremiah 51:34.
Eating to excess, Amos 6:4-7.
Rich fool, Luke 12:19-20.
Putting food above things more important, 1 Corinthians 11:20-22.
Physical hunger and spiritual sustenance, 1 Corinthians 11:34.
Continual lust for more, Ephesians 4:19.
Stomach as god, Philippians 3:19.
See *Food, Undisciplined.*

GOAL
Desire for full obedience, Psalm 119:1-5.
Look straight ahead, Proverbs 4:25-27.
Man's plans and God's purposes, Proverbs 19:21.
Noble man makes noble plans, Isaiah 32:8.
Enlarge your vision, Isaiah 54:2-3.
Singleness of heart and action, Jeremiah 32:38-39.
Seeking great things in rebellion against God, Jeremiah 45:4-5.
See *Ambition, Objective.*

GOD
Appearances of God, Exodus 24:9-12; 40:34-38; 1 Kings 8:10-11; Isaiah 6:1-9.
Death to those who see Him, Judges 13:21-23.
The God who destroys His enemies, 1 Samuel 15:1-10.
Great, mighty, and awesome God, Nehemiah 9:32.
Elihu declared the greatness of God, Job 36:22-26.
Divine role in Creation, Job 38–39.
Contrast between God's anger and love, Psalm 30:5.
All of space cannot contain God's love, Psalm 108:4-5.
Consciousness of God in hearts of men, Ecclesiastes 3:11.

Omniscience of God, Isaiah 40:13-14.
The first and the last, Isaiah 44:6.
God never forgets, Isaiah 49:15.
God's thoughts not man's thoughts, Isaiah 55:8-9; Hosea 11:9.
The God without precedent, Isaiah 64:4.
Near and far away, Jeremiah 23:23.
God's glory seen but not God Himself, Ezekiel 43:1-5.
Enduring personality of God, Micah 7:18-19.
Those who see God apart from human affairs, Zephaniah 1:12.
God incarnate in Christ, John 10:30; 14:9-14.
All-encompassing goodness of God, Romans 4:16.
Both kind and stern, Romans 11:22.
Mediator between God and men, 1 Timothy 2:5.
God's great love, 1 John 3:1-3.
See *Christ, Trinity.*

GODDESS
Worship of Queen of Heaven, Jeremiah 7:18.
Goddess Diana (Artemis), Acts 19:24, 28, 35.

GOLD
First record of gold, Genesis 2:11-12.
Ornaments, Genesis 24:22; Exodus 3:22; 11:2.
Solomon's annual take, 1 Kings 10:14-17. (Note: 666 talents equal to about 25 tons!)
Royal splendors, 2 Chronicles 9:17-24.
More precious than gold, Psalms 19:10; 119:127; Proverbs 3:14.
Apples of gold, Proverbs 25:11.
See *Treasure, Value.*

GOLDEN RULE
First statement of Golden Rule, Leviticus 19:18.
Returning neighbor's lost property, Deuteronomy 22:1-3.
Memories of Egypt, Deuteronomy 24:17-18.
Remembering lack of integrity in others, Deuteronomy 25:17-18.
Golden Rule reversed, Proverbs 21:13.
When not to do as others have done, Proverbs 24:29.

Old Testament version, Obadiah 15.
Mercy to those who show mercy, Matthew 5:7.
Golden Rule defined, Matthew 7:12.
Seeking mercy but mistreating another, Matthew 18:23-35.
Basics of Golden Rule, Luke 6:27-36.
Seeking good of others above one's self, 1 Corinthians 10:24.
Showing love to those who cause grief, 2 Corinthians 2:5-11.
Those who mistreat others as they themselves were once mistreated, 1 Thessalonians 2:14-16.
Do not pay back wrong for wrong, 1 Thessalonians 5:15.
Golden Rule stated negatively, Revelation 18:6.
See *Reciprocation.*

GOODNESS
Some juice left in grapes, Isaiah 65:8.
Dependable goodness of God, Matthew 7:7-11.
Always right time to do good, Mark 3:1-6.
Do not be judged by observance of legalism, Colossians 2:16.

GOOD WORKS
Exemplary life does not bring salvation, Matthew 19:16-26.
As unto the Lord, Matthew 25:35-36.
Conduct toward enemies, Luke 6:35.
Good words for the centurion, Luke 7:4-5.
Reward for good works, Romans 2:5-11.
Faith in action, 1 Thessalonians 1:3; James 2:17-18.
Rich in good deeds, 1 Timothy 6:18.
Sin of not doing good, James 4:17.
See *Conduct.*

GOSPEL
Unique parable of redemption, Ecclesiastes 9:14-15.
Followers of Jesus unable to understand coming Crucifixion, Luke 9:44-45.
Message of Christ brings life and destruction, Luke 20:17-18.
Lifting up Jesus to draw men to salvation, John 12:32.
Theme of post-Resurrection apostles, Acts 4:2.
Power of Gospel in life of sorcerer, Acts 8:9-13.

Gospel known as "the Way," Acts 19:9, 23; 22:4; 24:22.
Message of Cross foolishness to lost, 1 Corinthians 1:18.
Gospel message in brief, 1 Corinthians 15:1-5.
Message of salvation came through Abraham, Galatians 3:6-9.
To be carefully heeded, Hebrews 2:1-3.
Eternal life given to us, 1 John 5:11-12.

GOSSIP

Speak neither good nor evil, Genesis 31:24.
Circumstantial evidence against Joseph, Genesis 39:6-20.
Gossip condemned, Leviticus 19:16.
Need for adequate witnesses, Deuteronomy 17:6. (See also 19:15.)
Giving false testimony, Deuteronomy 19:16-21.
Hired to intimidate God's servant, Nehemiah 6:12-13.
Protection from lash of tongue, Job 5:21.
Job became byword to those about him, Job 17:6; 30:9.
Not concerned for error of others, Job 19:4.
Scorn consumed like water, Job 34:7.
Praying for those who scoff, Job 42:10.
Only God knows how many foes, Psalm 3:1-2.
The way of righteous, Psalm 15:1-3.
When others speak evil, Psalm 17:2.
Resolving not to sin with one's mouth, Psalm 17:3.
Blessing of honest speech, Psalm 34:12-13.
Enjoying misfortune of others, Psalm 35:15, 26-28.
Keeping tongue from speaking wrong, Psalm 39:1.
Slander spread to others, Psalm 41:6-9.
Slandering one's relatives, Psalm 50:20.
Attack against those who have done no wrong, Psalm 59:4.
Sins of mouth and lips, Psalm 59:12.
Devastation of words, Psalm 64:3.
Retribution for evil tongue, Psalm 64:8.
Hatred without reason, Psalm 69:4.
Danger of neighborhood slander, Psalm 101:5.
Object of scorn, Psalm 109:25, 29, 31.
Finding confidence in Scripture when others speak lies, Psalm 119:69-70, 78.
Prayer when one becomes object of gossip, Psalms 120:3; 123:3-4.

Let the Lord vindicate, Psalm 135:14.
Our words known before we speak them, Psalm 139:4.
Tongues of serpents, Psalm 140:3.
How to avoid taking part in gossip, Psalm 141:3.
Protect mouth and lips, Proverbs 4:24.
Corrupt mouth, Proverbs 6:12-14.
Pride, evil behavior, and perverse speech, Proverbs 8:13.
Speech of righteous, of wicked, Proverbs 10:11.
Destruction of mouth, Proverbs 11:9.
Betraying confidence, Proverbs 11:13.
Healing tongue and deceitful tongue, Proverbs 15:4.
Gossip separates close friends, Proverbs 16:28.
Evil of listening to gossip, Proverbs 17:4.
Destructive to friendship, Proverbs 17:9.
Choice morsels, Proverbs 18:8; 26:22.
Gossip by man who talks too much, Proverbs 20:19.
Guarding tongue, Proverbs 21:23.
Keeping another person's confidence, Proverbs 25:9.
Like wood for fire, Proverbs 26:20.
Vocabulary of hatred, Proverbs 26:28.
Beware who hears words of criticism, Ecclesiastes 10:20.
Power of words, Isaiah 29:20-21.
Fear not reproach of men, Isaiah 51:7.
Deceitful tongue, Jeremiah 9:3.
Speaking cordially with deceitful heart, Jeremiah 9:8.
Leave enemy's works in God's hands, Lamentations 3:55-66.
Bloody tales, Ezekiel 22:9.
Quiet in times of evil, Amos 5:13.
Song of ridicule, Micah 2:4.
Tongues that speak deceitfully, Micah 6:12.
Plotting people's ruin, Habakkuk 2:10.
Punishment for those who mock the Lord's people, Zephaniah 2:9-10.
Satan's role as accuser, Zechariah 3:1-2.
Joseph did not want to make Mary subject of public disgrace, Matthew 1:19.
Rejoice when people speak falsely of you, Matthew 5:11-12.
Judging and criticizing others, Matthew 7:1-5.
Jesus criticized for fellowship with sinners, Matthew 9:10-12.
Slander spoken against Jesus Himself,

Matthew 11:18-19.
Words condemn or acquit us, Matthew
12:37.
Not what goes into mouth but what comes
out, Matthew 15:10-20.
Silence of Jesus before His accusers,
Matthew 27:12-14.
Those who look for something to criticize,
Mark 3:1-6.
False witness against Jesus, Mark 14:53-59.
Rejoice when criticized for faith, Luke
6:22-23.
Ultimate measure, Luke 6:37.
Gossip about Jesus, John 7:12.
Judging mere appearances, John 7:24.
No condemnation without looking at facts,
John 7:50-52.
Woman caught in adultery, John 8:3-11.
Gossip classified with vilest of sins,
Romans 1:29-30.
Wrong of judging others, Romans 2:1.
Tongues that speak deceit, Romans 3:13.
Bless those who persecute, Romans 12:14.
Criticizing conduct of another Christian,
1 Corinthians 10:27-33.
Love has no part in gossip, 1 Corinthians
13:6.
Danger of hurting others, Galatians 5:15.
Avoid unwholesome talk, Ephesians 4:29.
Conversation full of grace, Colossians 4:6.
Mind your own business, 1 Thessalonians
4:11.
Root cause of gossip, 2 Thessalonians 3:11.
Deacons not double-tongued, 1 Timothy
3:8 (KJV).
Going from house to house, 1 Timothy
5:13.
Avoid godless chatter, 2 Timothy 2:16.
Living above criticism, Titus 2:8.
Slander no one, Titus 3:2; James 4:11-12.
Deceit of unruly tongue, James 1:26.
Guard tongue well, James 3:3-6.
Do not repay evil with evil or insult with
insult, 1 Peter 3:9.
Putting those to shame who gossip, 1 Peter
3:16.
Pride leads to gossip, 3 John 9-10.
See *Character assassination, Slander,
Tongue.*

GOURMET
Broiled meat, Exodus 12:8.
Honey-flavored manna, Exodus 16:31.
Good, special, and holy, Numbers 18:8-13.

Food with pleasant aroma, Numbers 28:2.
Deceptive delicacies, Proverbs 23:3.
Delicacies taken away, Lamentations 4:5.
Priests given best food, Ezekiel 44:28-31.
Daniel refused Babylon's royal food,
Daniel 1:8-16.
Choice meat, Amos 6:4.
Craving early figs, Micah 7:1.
See *Delicacy, Food.*

GOVERNMENT
Patriarchal, theocratic, and monarchial,
Genesis 27:29-39; Exodus 18:13-26;
1 Samuel 8:5-22.
Government for the people, Genesis 41:25-
57.
Scriptural attitude toward government,
Genesis 42:6; Matthew 22:18-21; Acts
5:29; Romans 13:1-7; 1 Timothy 2:1-3.
Fairness in time of famine, Genesis 47:13-
26.
Show respect to church and court,
Deuteronomy 17:12.
Gideon's definition of theocracy, Judges
8:22-23.
Most powerful government at God's
mercy, 1 Samuel 12:25.
Immorality in politics, 2 Samuel 3:6-11.
Departments in government, 2 Samuel
8:15-18; 20:23-26; 1 Kings 4:1-7.
Solomon's prayer for wisdom and
discernment, 1 Kings 3:1-15.
Solomon's cabinet, 1 Kings 4:1-7.
Solomon's good and large reign, 1 Kings
4:20-21.
Corruption in government, 1 Kings 21:5-
13.
Rejecting righteous king's example,
2 Chronicles 27:2.
Pagan king persuaded to permit rebuilding
of temple, Ezra 4–8.
Obey God and king, Ezra 7:26; Ecclesiastes
8:12.
Nehemiah's authorization for travel to
Jerusalem, Nehemiah 2:1-8.
Rights of citizen, Nehemiah 5:5.
Looking out for people's welfare, Esther
10:3.
God over nations, Job 34:29-30.
Inevitable fate of world governments,
Psalm 2:7-9.
The Lord reigns forever, Psalm 9:7-8.
Nations fall into pit they have dug, Psalm
9:15.

Limited help earthly leaders can give, Psalm 146:3.

Blessing of righteousness in nation, Proverbs 14:34.

Love secures king's throne, Proverbs 20:28.

Detestable prayers of lawbreakers, Proverbs 28:9.

Hiding from evil government, Proverbs 28:28.

Sobriety necessary for good government, Proverbs 31:4-7.

Discontent with government, Ecclesiastes 4:13-16.

Evils of bureaucracy, Ecclesiastes 5:8-9.

Government in hands of children, Isaiah 3:4.

Unjust laws and oppressive decrees, Isaiah 10:1-4.

Community in turmoil, Isaiah 22:2.

National righteousness, Isaiah 26:2.

Exiles subject to government for their own good, Jeremiah 29:4-7.

Establishment of local government, Jeremiah 30:20.

King and priest forsaken, Lamentations 2:6.

Misguided by evil government, Ezekiel 11:1-4.

Wicked officials, Ezekiel 22:27.

Government-sponsored education, Daniel 1:3-20.

Daniel given high position in Babylon, Daniel 2:48-49.

King at age 62, Daniel 5:30-31.

Seeking God's guidance in choice of leadership, Hosea 8:4.

For continued sinning, certain judgment, Amos 1:3, 6, 9, 11, 13; 2:1, 4, 6. (Note nature of sin in each of these judgments.)

Iniquity of evil leadership, Malachi 3:5.

Paying taxes to government, Matthew 22:15-22; Luke 20:21-25.

Census at time of Jesus' birth, Luke 2:1-5.

Embarrassment of government officials, Acts 16:35-40.

No complaint legislated, Acts 18:12-17.

Pagan official rebuked those who disputed Christianity, Acts 19:35-41.

Asking for bribe, Acts 24:26.

Government leaders serve divine purposes, Romans 9:17-18.

Submission to authorities, Romans 13:1-7.

City director of public works, Romans 16:23.

Privileged citizenship, Ephesians 2:19-20.

Praying for those in authority, 1 Timothy 2:1-4.

Be subject to rulers and authorities, Titus 3:1; Hebrews 13:17; 1 Peter 2:13-17.

Role of demons in world politics, Revelation 16:13-14.

One-hour reign of ten kings, Revelation 17:12.

See *Bureaucracy, Leadership, Politics.*

GRACE

Old Testament definition of God's grace, Exodus 34:6-7.

Forgiving, gracious, and compassionate God, Nehemiah 9:17.

Again and again God withheld judgment, Psalm 78:38.

God does not deal with us according to what we deserve, Psalm 103:9-10.

God's goodness innate to His person, Psalm 109:21.

Depth of God's mercy and grace, Psalm 145:8-9.

The Lord's hand remains upraised, Isaiah 5:25; 9:21; 10:4.

Hands skilled in doing evil, Micah 7:3.

Wealthy by extortion, Habakkuk 2:6.

GRACE BEFORE MEALS

Blessing before eating, 1 Samuel 9:13.

Our Lord gave thanks before eating, Matthew 14:19; 15:36; 1 Corinthians 11:24.

Apostolic blessing, Acts 27:35.

GRAFFITI

Graffiti by divine command, Deuteronomy 11:20-21.

GRAFT

See *Bribery, Bureaucracy, Corruption, Deceit, Dishonesty.*

GRANDCHILDREN

No descendants in Nineveh, Nahum 1:14.

GRANDPARENTS

Frustrated grandfather, Genesis 31:22-29.

Joy of seeing grandchildren, Genesis 48:11.

Grandmother important enough to be

mentioned by name, 1 Kings 15:10.
Confessing sins of ancestors, Nehemiah 9:2.
Job's longevity, Job 42:16-17.
Living to see children's children, Psalm 128:5-6.
Conveying God's message from generation to generation, Psalm 145:4-7; Joel 1:3.
Inheritance for grandchildren, Proverbs 13:22.
Blessing of grandchildren to aged, Proverbs 17:6.
Illustration of obedience to parents and grandparents, Jeremiah 35:1-16.
Zephaniah's lineage, Zephaniah 1:1.
Forefathers gone, Zechariah 1:5.
Healing of Peter's mother-in-law, Matthew 8:14-15.
Grandmother's faith transmitted to daughter and grandson, 2 Timothy 1:5.
Responsibility of grandmother to next generation, Titus 2:3-5.
See *Forefathers.*

GRAPHOLOGY
Identified by handwriting, 2 Thessalonians 3:17. (See Col. 4:18.)

GRATIFICATION
See *Gluttony, Hedonism, Immorality, Lust.*

GRATIS
Divine bargain, Isaiah 55:1-2.

GRATITUDE
Joseph's need forgotten by cupbearer, Genesis 40:1-23. (See 41:9.)
Offering of thanksgiving, Leviticus 7:12.
Bowing in appreciation, Ruth 2:10.
Profuse tears of gratitude, 1 Samuel 20:41.
Seeking recipient of thanks, 2 Samuel 9:1.
Reciprocation of kindness, 2 Samuel 10:2; 2 Kings 4:13.
David's song of praise, 2 Samuel 22:1-51.
King Solomon's gratitude for God's faithfulness and goodness, 1 Kings 8:14-21.
Thank and praise the Lord morning and evening, 1 Chronicles 23:30.
Value of sacrifice and offering, Psalm 50:23.
Thanking God for enduring love, Psalm 106:1.

Thanksgiving leads to witnessing, Psalm 107:1-3.
Hymn of thanks to the Lord, Psalm 136:1-26.
Thanking God in midst of adverse circumstances, Jeremiah 33:10-11.
Daniel's gratitude to God for wisdom he needed, Daniel 2:19-23.
Sinful woman who washed feet of Jesus with her tears, Luke 7:36-50.
One of 10 expressed gratitude, Luke 17:12-19.
Jesus gave thanks, John 6:11.
Joyful gratitude, Colossians 1:11-12.
Overflowing with thankfulness, Colossians 2:6-7.
Praise to God for success in ministry, 1 Thessalonians 3:8-10.
Gratitude for privilege of ministry, 1 Timothy 1:12-14.
See *Thanksgiving.*

GRATUITY
Offering a gratuity for directions, 1 Samuel 9:1-9.
Daniel refused king's gratuities, Daniel 5:17.
See *Honorarium.*

GRAVE
Not to be touched, Numbers 19:16-18.
Wishing to be buried near parents' grave, 2 Samuel 19:37.
Respect for dead bodies, 2 Samuel 21:13-14.
Preferred to earthly home, Job 17:13.
Zero activity in grave, Ecclesiastes 9:10.
Graves hewn of rock, Isaiah 22:16.
Burial in ignominy, Jeremiah 22:19.
Grave robbed of victory, 1 Corinthians 15:55.
See *Burial, Tomb.*

GREATNESS
Greatness of Moses, Deuteronomy 34:10-12.
Naaman's conditional greatness, 2 Kings 5:1.
Assured greatness in heaven, Matthew 5:19.
Jesus not recognized in His hometown, Matthew 13:55-58.
Role of humility in greatness, Matthew 20:26; 23:11-12.

Greatness of Jesus beyond enumeration, John 21:25.

Contemplating Christ's resurrection and exaltation, Ephesians 1:18-23.

Qualifications of Saviour and King, Colossians 1:15-20.

See *Fame.*

GREED

Scarcity of land, Genesis 13:5-7.

Dispute over water rights, Genesis 26:19-22.

To each what is needed and nothing more, Exodus 16:16-18.

God's warning against greed for property, Deuteronomy 2:5.

Elisha's servant requested payment for master's ministry, 2 Kings 5:20-27.

Growing rich at expense and harm of others, Psalm 52:7.

Selfish prayer, Psalm 106:14-15.

Never a thought of kindness, Psalm 109:16.

Three things never satisfied, Proverbs 30:15-16.

Money alone never satisfies, Ecclesiastes 5:10.

Dishonest gain, Jeremiah 22:17.

Thinking to prosper because of another's failure, Ezekiel 26:1-3.

Shepherds who care more for themselves than their flocks, Ezekiel 34:2.

Those who hoard plunder, Amos 3:10.

Grape pickers leave a few grapes, Obadiah 5.

Wealth by extortion, Habakkuk 2:6.

Evening wolves, Zephaniah 3:3.

Betrayal of Jesus for 30 silver coins, Matthew 26:14-16, 47-50.

Folly of material greed, Luke 12:13-21.

Continual lust for more, Ephesians 4:19.

Trapped by desire for riches, 1 Timothy 6:9-10.

Unsatisfied inner desires, James 4:1-2.

Corrosion of gold and silver, James 5:1-3.

See *Selfishness.*

GREETING

Hearty, healthful greeting, 1 Samuel 25:6.

Cordial greeting of angel, Luke 1:28-31.

Paul's greetings to his many friends, Romans 16:3-16.

Paul's greeting to church at Corinth, 1 Corinthians 1:1-3.

Greet with a kiss, 1 Corinthians 16:20;

1 Peter 5:14.

Greetings from Rome to Philippi, Philippians 4:21-23.

Friends greeted by name, 3 John 14.

GRIEF

Jacob's sorrow over loss of Joseph, Genesis 37:33-35.

Time of mourning concluded, Genesis 50:4.

Shaving head of mourner, Deuteronomy 14:1-2.

Eli's grief for ark greater than for deaths of sons, 1 Samuel 4:16-18.

Husband's death brings death to wife, 1 Samuel 4:19-20.

Personal grief put aside to lead others, 2 Samuel 19:1-8.

No song for heavy heart, Proverbs 25:20.

Grieving the Holy Spirit, Isaiah 63:10; Ephesians 4:30.

Women skilled in wailing, Jeremiah 9:17-20.

Grief-stricken city, Lamentations 1:4.

Grief of Jesus over need of Jerusalem, Luke 19:41-44.

Paul remembered tears of others, 2 Timothy 1:3-4.

Agony of those who refuse to repent, Revelation 16:10-11.

See *Mourning, Sorrow.*

GROWTH

Growth in spirit and character, 1 Samuel 2:26.

Multiplying troops, 2 Samuel 24:3.

From strength to strength, Psalm 84:7.

Sure road to maturity, Proverbs 9:1-6.

Enlarge your plans, Isaiah 54:2-3; Micah 7:11.

The Lord guides and corrects those who seek Him, Jeremiah 10:23-24.

Growth for those who trust the Lord, Jeremiah 17:7-8.

Shriveled seeds, Joel 1:17.

Tiny seed becomes great tree, Matthew 13:31-32; Mark 4:30-32.

Seedtime to harvest, Mark 4:26-29.

Balanced life of Jesus, Luke 2:52.

Growth of early church, Acts 9:31.

Growth through suffering, Romans 5:3-4.

Good work will be completed, Philippians 1:6.

Forgetting past, pressing forward to goal,

Philippians 3:12-16.
Filled with knowledge of God's will,
Colossians 1:9-12.
Receiving Christ and growing in Him,
Colossians 2:6-7.
Hearts that become strong and blameless,
1 Thessalonians 3:13.
Growing in faith and love, 2 Thessalonians
1:3.
Diligent in quest for spiritual maturity,
1 Timothy 4:13.
Not spirit of timidity but of power and love
through discipline, 2 Timothy 1:7.
Those slow to grow in spiritual perception,
Hebrews 5:11-14.
Confident of growth in followers, Hebrews
6:9.
Taking initiative to be rid of evil traits,
1 Peter 2:1.
Spiritual milk for growth, 1 Peter 2:2-3.
Additions to faith, 2 Peter 1:5-9.
Growing in grace, 2 Peter 3:18.
Good health and spiritual growth, 3 John
3.
Development of faith, Jude 20.

GRUDGE
Do not seek revenge, Leviticus 19:18;
Proverbs 20:22; 24:29; Romans 12:17;
1 Peter 3:9.
See *Retribution.*

GRUESOME
See *Sadistic, Torture.*

GRUMBLING
See *Complain.*

GUARANTEE
God's promise to Noah, Genesis 9:8-16.
Reuben's guarantee to his father, Genesis
42:37.
Certainty of eternal life, 1 John 5:11-12.
See *Assurance.*

GUARDIAN
Specific enumeration of trained men,
Genesis 14:14.
Looking out for the welfare of the people,
Esther 10:3.
Shielded by God's power, 1 Peter 1:5.

GUESTS
Formal greeting, Genesis 18:2.

Mistreatment of guests, 2 Samuel 10:1-5.
Various kinds of guests, 1 Kings 1:41, 49;
Proverbs 9:18; 25:17; Matthew 22:11;
Luke 7:39-50; Acts 18:1-3;
1 Corinthians 10:27; Hebrews 13:2.
Queen of Sheba and King Solomon,
1 Kings 10:1-13.
Room for prophet, 2 Kings 4:8-10.
Departure of unwelcome guests, Psalm
105:38.
One thousand guests at Belshazzar's
banquet, Daniel 5:1.
Hospitality for apostles, Matthew 10:9-15.
Paul would come to stay awhile,
1 Corinthians 16:5-6.

GUIDANCE
Provision of light, Genesis 1:3, 14-19.
Obedience of Abram, Genesis 12:1-14.
Abimelech guided by the Lord in conduct
toward Sarah, Genesis 20:1-18.
Asking God for specific guidance, Genesis
24:11-15.
Angelic guidance, Genesis 24:40.
Seeking God's will by divination, Genesis
30:27.
Jacob reassured by God to enter Egypt,
Genesis 46:1-4.
Circumstances caused Moses to doubt
God's guidance, Exodus 5:22-23.
Trusting God in face of insurmountable
opposition, Exodus 14:5-14.
Strange test of guidance, Exodus 16:2-5.
Guardian angel, Exodus 23:20.
Knowing way across desert, Numbers
10:29-33.
Confidence in face of danger, Numbers
14:8-9.
Seeking God's guidance in choosing
leader, Deuteronomy 17:14-15.
Specific orders, Joshua 8:8.
Gideon's fleece, Judges 6:36-40.
God reveals Himself through His Word,
1 Samuel 3:21.
Difference between personal decision and
divine guidance, 1 Samuel 14:36-41.
David inquired of the Lord, 2 Samuel 2:1-
4; 5:12, 17-19.
Guidance in life of David, 2 Samuel 7:1-16.
Prayer after assurance of divine guidance,
2 Samuel 7:18-29.
Lamp of the Lord, 2 Samuel 22:29.
Strength from God, 2 Samuel 22:33.
Work of Spirit within man, Job 32:8.

God speaks in different ways, Job 33:14.
Ministry of angels, Job 33:23-25.
Guidance in midst of enemies, Psalm 4:8.
Role of Scripture, Psalm 19:7-11.
Special guidance for those who fear the
Lord, Psalm 25:14.
Not our desires but desires the Lord places
in our hearts, Psalm 37:3-5. (See also
20:4-5.)
Sure success a delight to the Lord, Psalm
37:23-24.
Let God make the plan, Psalm 40:5.
Prayer for undivided heart, Psalm 86:11.
Light promised upright, Psalm 97:11.
Scriptural precepts, Psalm 119:4.
Prayer for perception in study of Scripture,
Psalm 119:18.
Scriptures become one's counselor, Psalm
119:24.
Scripture a lamp and light, Psalm 119:105.
Asking God for discernment, Psalm
119:125.
The Lord fulfills His purposes, Psalm 138:8.
Prayer for inner peace and righteousness,
Psalm 139:23-24.
Prayer for instruction and confidence,
Psalm 143:10.
Ultimate request for guidance, Proverbs
3:5-6.
Bright path of righteous, Proverbs 4:18.
Those who seek, find, Proverbs 8:17.
Wise listen to good counsel, Proverbs 9:9.
Divine wisdom and human motives,
Proverbs 19:21.
Steps directed by the Lord, Proverbs 20:24.
Letting God teach His ways, Isaiah 2:3.
Stop trusting in man, Isaiah 2:22.
Refusing to test God, Isaiah 7:10-12.
Perfect faithfulness of God, Isaiah 25:1.
Guidance for farmer, Isaiah 28:24-26.
In time of adversity, Isaiah 30:19-21
The Lord our King, Isaiah 33:22.
Way of holiness, Isaiah 35:8.
Doors opened that will not be shut, Isaiah
45:1-5.
God knows end from beginning, Isaiah
46:10-11.
The God who knows what is best, Isaiah
48:17-18.
Certain supply of need and guidance,
Isaiah 49:10.
Walking in dark with confidence, Isaiah
50:10.
Information from the Lord, Isaiah 52:13.

The Lord will always guide, Isaiah 58:11.
Those who stumble without guidance,
Isaiah 59:10
Ask for the ancient paths, good way,
Jeremiah 6:16.
Only the sovereign God can correctly
direct man's steps, Jeremiah 10:23.
Road signs and guideposts, Jeremiah
31:21.
Seeking omen at fork in road, Ezekiel
21:18-23.
Guidance of Holy Spirit, Ezekiel 36:26-27.
Key to divine guidance, Hosea 12:6.
God's way is right way, Hosea 14:9.
Prophet conveys revelation of the Lord,
Amos 3:7.
Creator's thoughts revealed to man, Amos
4:13.
Famine for words of the Lord, Amos 8:11-
12.
Taught the way of the Lord, Micah 4:2.
Those who do not know the Lord's
thoughts, Micah 4:12.
Broken staff, Zechariah 11:10.
Joseph and Mary led into and out of Egypt,
Matthew 2:13-21.
Instructions to 12 apostles, Matthew 10:5-
42. (See also 11:1.)
God of the living, Matthew 22:32.
Two-word command, Mark 2:14.
Leadership of Holy Spirit and leadership of
Satan, Luke 4:1, 5, 9.
Night of prayer before important decision,
Luke 6:12-16.
Light must be followed to avoid darkness,
John 8:12.
Shepherd and sheep, John 10:1-6.
Walking in light, John 12:35-36.
Certain way, truth, and life, John 14:6.
Promised Counselor, John 14:16-17.
Jesus took care to instruct His apostles,
Acts 1:1-2.
Asking for guidance but depending on
earthly procedure to obtain result, Acts
1:24-26.
Guided by angel, Acts 8:26.
Ananias guided to Saul, Acts 9:10-17.
Guidance from Holy Spirit, Acts 13:1-3.
Preaching hindered by Holy Spirit, Acts
16:6-7.
Paul's Macedonian vision, Acts 16:9-10.
Assured of guidance and protection in a
vision, Acts 18:9-11.
God's will for ministry appointments, Acts

18:20-21.
The Lord Himself commissioned Paul to minister, Acts 23:11.
All things work for good, Romans 8:28.
Concluding ministry in area, Romans 15:23-24.
The Lord opens door, 2 Corinthians 2:12.
Paul guided by revelation, Galatians 2:2.
Illness caused Paul to preach Gospel in Galatia, Galatians 4:13-14.
God works out everything according to His will, Ephesians 1:11-12.
Foolishness of missing God's will, Ephesians 5:17.
Promise to believers concerning knowing God's will, Colossians 1:9-14.
How a father should deal with children, 1 Thessalonians 2:11-12.
Communication in person and by writing, 1 Timothy 3:14-15.
Ministering spirits to those who believe, Hebrews 1:14.
The Lord takes His children by the hand, Hebrews 8:9.
By faith, Noah and Abraham obeyed God, Hebrews 11:7-12.
Going in obedience toward unknown objective, Hebrews 11:8.
If you lack wisdom, ask God, James 1:5-6.
Horses and ships, James 3:3-4.
Eyes of the Lord on the righteous, 1 Peter 3:12.
God is light, totally apart from darkness, 1 John 1:5-7.
Living by truth, 1 John 1:9-10.
Springs of living water, Revelation 7:16-17.
See *Direction.*

GUILE
Sanballat's scheme to hinder Nehemiah, Nehemiah 6:1-9.
Deceit brings hurt, Proverbs 26:28.
Friends and brothers not to be trusted, Jeremiah 9:4-8.
King Herod and the magi, Matthew 2:7-8, 12.
See *Deceit.*

GUILT
Passing blame to others, Genesis 3:8-13, 17-19.
Cain's denial of guilt, Genesis 4:8-10.
Joseph's brothers sought for guilt less than murder, Genesis 37:19-27.

Circumstantial evidence against Joseph, Genesis 39:6-20.
Feigned guilt of Joseph's brothers, Genesis 44:1-34.
Murder exposed, Exodus 2:11-14.
Function of Old Testament scapegoat, Leviticus 16:20-22.
One man brings guilt on entire assembly, Numbers 16:22.
Frightened of place of worship, Numbers 17:12-13.
Minute but debilitating guilt of leadership, Numbers 20:12.
Identification of evil act, Numbers 25:14.
Death caused by accident, Numbers 35:22-25; Deuteronomy 19:4-7.
Strange sacrifice when murderer cannot be found, Deuteronomy 21:1-9.
Degrees of sin against man and God, 1 Samuel 2:22-25.
Plea for evidence of guilt, 1 Samuel 20:1.
Accused of murder for abetting suicide, 2 Samuel 1:1-16.
David's claim of righteousness and innocence, 2 Samuel 22:21-25.
Conscience-stricken David, 2 Samuel 24:10-17.
Executing fathers but sparing sons, 2 Kings 14:5-6.
Agony of guilt, Psalm 38:4; Proverbs 28:17.
Awareness of sin and guilt, Psalm 51:3.
God's forgiveness and multitude of our sins, Psalm 130:3-4.
Stealing food, Proverbs 6:30-31.
Evil attitude toward guilt, Proverbs 17:15.
Blessed are those who convict guilty, Proverbs 24:24-25.
Abundant guilt of Israel, Isaiah 1:4.
Guilt atoned by fire, Isaiah 6:6-7.
Do not dwell on the past, Isaiah 43:18.
Unable to wash away stain of guilt, Jeremiah 2:22.
Disgrace of getting caught, Jeremiah 2:26.
Proclaiming innocence when guilt is obvious, Jeremiah 2:34-35.
Sincere disgrace of those who realize sinfulness, Jeremiah 3:24-25.
God's total forgiveness, Jeremiah 50:20.
Ezekiel bearing sin of people, Ezekiel 4:4-6.
Degrees of sin in God's sight, Ezekiel 16:48-52.
Parents and children responsible for their own sin, Ezekiel 18:4-20.

Pardon for bloodguilt of nation, Joel 3:21.
Casting lots to determine guilt, Jonah 1:7.
Admitting guilt, Jonah 1:10.
Pondering what it will take to please the Lord as a sacrifice for sin, Micah 6:7.
Dishonesty cannot be overlooked, Micah 6:11.
Unpardonable sin, Matthew 12:31-32.
Hypocrisy akin to murder, Matthew 23:29-32.
Judas as accomplice to murder, Matthew 26:14-16; 27:3.
Guilty of much, guilty of less, Luke 7:36-50.
Indictment of Pharisees, Luke 11:45-54.
Bearing scorn of sin, John 3:14-15.
Morsel of bread to implicate Judas, John 13:21-27.
Sin done in ignorance, Acts 3:17.
Approving wrong done by others, Acts 8:1.
Paul bitten by snake, Acts 28:1-6.

Guilt of self-righteousness, Romans 2:1-16.
Sins of ignorance, 1 Timothy 1:12-14.
Blame for evil placed on women, 1 Timothy 2:14.
Breaking just one point of Law, James 2:10.
Those who turn backs, 2 Peter 2:20-22.
See *Conscience.*

GULF STREAM
Paths in sea, Isaiah 43:16.

GULLIBLE
Believing anything, Proverbs 14:15.
Easily turned from truth, Galatians 1:6; 3:1-5.
Wind-tossed, James 1:6.

GYPSY
Cain, first wanderer, Genesis 4:13-14.

H

HABITS
Habitual evil, Jeremiah 13:23; 22:21; Micah 2:1.
Man a slave to whatever masters him, 2 Peter 2:19.

HAIR
Aged prophet, 1 Samuel 12:2.
Samson's uncut hair, Judges 13:4-5.
Rapport with old men, Job 15:10.
Crown of splendor, Proverbs 16:31; 20:29.
Haughty women of Zion become bald, Isaiah 3:16-17; 4:4.
Priests instructed to keep hair neatly trimmed, Ezekiel 44:20.
Not noticing coming of gray hair, Hosea 7:9.
Paul's haircut in response to vow, Acts 18:18.
Paul's instruction relative to cutting hair, 1 Corinthians 11:14-15.
See *Barber.*

HALLOWED
See *Sacred.*

HANDICAP
Hindrance to worship, Leviticus 21:16-23.
Cutting off thumbs and big toes, Judges 1:7.
Crippled son of Jonathan shown kindness by David, 2 Samuel 9:1-13.
Helping blind and lame, Job 29:15.
Even lame plunder, Isaiah 33:23.
Blind see, deaf hear, Isaiah 35:5.
Father of John the Baptist stricken with muteness, Luke 1:11-22.
Speaking with signing, Luke 1:62.
Mute demon, Luke 11:14.
Crippled body caused by demon, Luke 13:10-13.

Sin as cause of blindness, John 9:1-12.
Antidote for vanity, 2 Corinthians 11:30. (See 12:7-10.)
Paul may have had poor eyesight, Galatians 6:11.
Paul's chains increased his ministry, Philippians 1:12-14.

HANDS
Right hand as more prestigious, Genesis 48:14; Exodus 15:6; Psalms 16:8; 48:10; Isaiah 62:8.
Holding hands in time of danger, Genesis 19:16.
Left-handed, Judges 3:15.
Right-handed murder, Judges 5:26.
Seven hundred left-handed soldiers, Judges 20:16.
Helping hand, 2 Kings 10:15.
Secrets between hands, Matthew 6:3.
Healing hand, Matthew 9:25; Acts 3:7; 9:41.
Speaking with signing, Luke 1:62.
See *Ambidextrous.*

HANDSOME
Boy David, 1 Samuel 16:12.
Handsome Absalom, 2 Samuel 14:25.
Outstanding among 10,000, Song of Songs 5:10.
Attractive young men, Zechariah 9:17.
See *Physique.*

HANDWRITING
Identified by handwriting, 2 Thessalonians 3:17.

HAPPENSTANCE
Death of king by random arrow, 2 Chronicles 18:33-34.
See *Chance, Fortuity.*

HAPPINESS
Eating with rejoicing, Deuteronomy 27:7.
Joy of the Lord your strength, Nehemiah
8:10.
Daily reading Scriptures, Nehemiah 8:17-
18.
God offers "river of delights," Psalm 36:8.
Heart's desire, Psalm 37:4.
Anointed with oil of joy, Psalm 45:7;
Hebrews 1:9.
Light and joy promised upright, Psalm
97:11.
Desires satisfied and strength renewed,
Psalm 103:5.
Delight in Bible study, Psalm 119:24.
Enjoying fruit of labor, Psalm 128:2.
Banquet for Jesus, Luke 5:27-35.
Living water from within, John 7:37-39.
Joy complete, John 15:11.
Sharing comfort through experience,
2 Corinthians 1:3-5.
Rejoice in the Lord, Philippians 4:4.
Joy of problems and testing, James 1:2-4.
Inexpressible and glorious joy, 1 Peter 1:8-
9.
Joy of good reputation, 3 John 3-4.
Source of great joy, Jude 24-25.
See *Attitude, Emotion, Joy.*

HARBINGER
Prophecy of boiling pot, Jeremiah 1:13-15.

HARDHEADED
Ineptness of king's viewpoint, 1 Kings
12:1-15.
Motivated by hook and bit, 2 Kings 19:28.
Fool airs his own opinion, Proverbs 18:2.
See *Stubborn.*

HARDNESS
Brazen look of prostitute, Jeremiah 3:3.
Caring neither for God nor man, Luke
18:1-5.
Refusal to repent in face of judgment,
Revelation 9:20-21; 16:10-11.

HARDSHIP
Trusting in all circumstances, Job 13:15.
Gentle flowing waters or mighty flood
waters, Isaiah 8:6-7.
Persecution implements spread of Gospel,
Acts 8:3-4.
Purpose of testing, 2 Corinthians 1:2-11.
The Lord disciplines those He loves,

Hebrews 12:5-11.
See *Persecution.*

HARDWARE
Maker of tools, Genesis 4:22.
Murderous hammer, Judges 4:21.
Variety of hardware, 2 Samuel 12:31.
Made without hammer, 1 Kings 6:7.
Nail manufacture, 1 Chronicles 22:3.

HARLOT
See *Prostitute.*

HARMONY
Loving neighbor as yourself, 1 Samuel
18:1.
Two in agreement, Amos 3:3.
People at peace with each other, Mark
9:50.
United in mind and thought, 1 Corinthians
1:10.
Diversity to produce unity, Ephesians 4:11-
16.
Those who sow in peace, James 3:18.
See *Rapport, Unanimity.*

HARVEST
Perpetual seasons, Genesis 8:22.
Abundance of grain, Genesis 41:49.
Feast of Harvest, Exodus 23:16.
Harvest gleaning, Leviticus 19:9;
Deuteronomy 24:19; Ruth 2:3.
Giving firstfruit to the Lord, Deuteronomy
26:1-4.
Stolen crops, Deuteronomy 28:33.
Unwanted rain, 1 Samuel 12:17.
Asleep during harvest, Proverbs 10:5.
Bad weather in harvest, Proverbs 26:1.
Bad harvest, Isaiah 5:10.
Joy of harvest stilled, Isaiah 16:9-10.
The Lord watches over fruitful vineyard,
Isaiah 27:2-3.
From harvest to making bread, Isaiah
28:28.
Twofold purpose of harvest yield, Isaiah
55:10.
Eating one's own harvest, Isaiah 62:8-9.
Refusing to glorify God for harvest,
Jeremiah 5:24.
Harvest denied disobedient, Jeremiah
8:13.
Sow wheat, reap thorns, Jeremiah 12:13.
Leaving a few grapes on vine, Jeremiah
49:9.

Failure of harvest, Hosea 9:2.
Farmers weeping for lost harvest, Joel 1:11.
Abundant rain, abundant harvest, Joel 2:23-24.
Planting but not harvesting, Micah 6:15.
Good crops withheld, Haggai 1:10-11.
Promised blessing on harvest, Haggai 2:19.
Manually separating chaff from grain, Luke 6:1.
Farmer receives first share of crop, 2 Timothy 2:6.
Good crops and weeds, Hebrews 6:7-8.
Those gathered from all tribes and nations, Revelation 7:9-10.
Great harvest of earth in final days, Revelation 14:14-20.
Crop to harvest every month of year, Revelation 22:2.
See *Agriculture, Gleaners.*

HASTE
On urgent business, 1 Samuel 21:8.
Urgent instructions, 2 Kings 4:29.
News on the run, Habakkuk 2:2.
Good news to tell, Matthew 28:7.
Making haste to reach Jesus, Mark 5:2-6.
Food is ready, Luke 14:15-23.
Prodigal's father, Luke 15:20.
See *Hurry.*

HATRED
Avoid hatred, Leviticus 19:17; Proverbs 15:17.
Hated prophet, 1 Kings 22:8.
Wealth and prestige could not numb Haman's resentment, Esther 5:10-14.
Psychological effects of resentment and envy, Job 5:2.
Cure for hatred, Proverbs 10:12.
Love for enemies, Matthew 5:43-44.
Basic cause of hatred, John 15:18-24.
Darkness of hatred, 1 John 2:9-11.
Hatred same as murder, 1 John 3:15.
Cannot love God and hate a brother, 1 John 4:20-21.

HEADSTRONG
Fool airs own opinion, Proverbs 18:2.
See *Stubborn.*

HEALING
God the great healer, Psalm 103:3.
Healing blind, deaf, and dumb, Isaiah 35:5-6.
Isaiah's prophecy concerning healing, Isaiah 53:4.
No balm in Gilead, Jeremiah 8:22.
False remedies, Jeremiah 46:11.
Healing ministry of Jesus, Matthew 8:14-17.
Relationship of illness to sin, Matthew 9:1-7.
Double healing, Matthew 9:18-25.
Power and authority over evil spirits and illness, Matthew 10:1-8.
Epilepsy caused by demon, Matthew 17:14-20.
Healing increased popularity of Jesus, Mark 3:7-10.
Faith of others required for healing, Mark 6:4-6.
Jesus rebuked fever, Luke 4:38-39.
Danger of emphasizing healing above Healer, Luke 7:21-23.
Illness caused by spirit, Luke 13:10-16.
Thirty-eight year wait for healing, John 5:1-8.
Purpose for sickness, John 11:4.
Authority of Christians to heal sick, Acts 3:11-16.
Misunderstanding arising from healing lame man, Acts 14:8-18.
Miracles in Paul's ministry, Acts 19:11-12.
Paul omitted healing in enumerating gifts, Romans 12:4-6. (See 15:17-19.)
Priority of healing ministry, 1 Corinthians 12:28-31.
Paul prayed for healing but could rejoice in a negative answer to his prayer, 2 Corinthians 12:7-10.
Praying for sick, James 5:13-15.
See *Medicine.*

HEALTH
Role of disease in judgment for sin, Leviticus 26:14-16.
Moses retained virility until death, Deuteronomy 34:7.
Evil spirits and poor health, 1 Samuel 16:16.
Hearty, healthful greeting, 1 Samuel 25:6.
Satan challenged God for Job's physical well-being, Job 2:3-6.
Psychological effects of resentment and envy, Job 5:2.
Death of healthy, vigorous person, Job 5:26.
Worthless physicians, Job 13:4.

Job's bad breath, Job 19:17.
Wicked who lived to ripe old age, Job 21:7.
Long life in answer to prayer, Psalm 21:4.
Ill and in great pain, Psalm 38:1-22.
Freedom from human illness, Psalm 73:5.
Fearfully and wonderfully made, Psalm 139:14.
Dying before one's time, Ecclesiastes 7:17.
Fifteen years added to life, Isaiah 38:1-6.
Young men of excellent health chosen for royal service, Daniel 1:3-6.
Daniel refused royal food and wine, Daniel 1:8-16.
Years of medical expense, Mark 5:25-26.
Better to be impaired physically than spiritually, Mark 9:43-48.
Crippled body caused by demon, Luke 13:10-13.
Sin as cause of ill health, John 5:14.
Responsibility for health of child, John 9:1-12.
Illness caused Paul to preach Gospel in Galatia, Galatians 4:13-14.
Paul may have had poor eyesight, Galatians 6:11.
Physical training and godliness, 1 Timothy 4:8.
Keeping soul in good health, 3 John 2.
Health and wealth plus spiritual vitality, 3 John 2-4.
See *Medicine, Rheumatism, Sickness, Therapy.*

HEARING
Making sure someone is listening, 2 Samuel 20:17.
Ears of wise, Proverbs 18:15.
Words worth hearing, Proverbs 25:12.
Hearing messenger but ignoring message, Ezekiel 33:32.
Hearing in vain, Matthew 7:26; James 1:23-24.
See *Ear.*

HEART
Inner heart known to God, 1 Samuel 16:7; 1 Chronicles 28:9; Matthew 9:4.
Center of emotion and affection, Psalm 26:2-3; Proverbs 4:23; Ezekiel 11:19; 36:26; Colossians 3:15-17.
Prayer for a clean heart, Psalm 51:10.
Attitudes, Proverbs 15:13-15; Matthew 15:18-20.
See *Motivation.*

HEARTACHE
See *Disappointment, Grief, Sorrow, Trauma.*

HEARTBEAT
Brevity of life, Job 7:6; 9:25; Psalms 39:5; 103:15-16; James 4:14.

HEARTLESS
Murderer's calloused response, Genesis 4:9.
Those who pass by, Lamentations 1:12.
When God acts without pity, Ezekiel 7:4, 9.
Heartless piety, Luke 10:31.
Caring neither for God nor man, Luke 18:1-5.
Empty words of comfort, James 2:16.
See *Calloused.*

HEAT
Cold and heat, Genesis 8:22.
Heat of the day, Genesis 18:1.
Furnace of testing, Daniel 3:21-23.
Heat of south wind, Luke 12:55.
Scorching heat of sun, James 1:11.
Lake of fire, Revelation 19:19-21.
See *Fire.*

HEATHEN
Divine message to heathen, Genesis 20:3-7; 41:1-24; Daniel 4:1-18; 5:24-29.
Defiled and detestable, Leviticus 18:24-30.
Heathen nations, 2 Kings 16:3; 17:8; Psalms 2:1; 9:15; 126:2; 135:15; Ezekiel 39:21.
Seeking magi, Matthew 2:1-12.
Centurion who reached out to Jesus, Matthew 8:5-13; Luke 7:2-9.
Those who do not have scriptural guidance, Romans 2:14-15.
God revealed to those who did not seek, Romans 10:20.
Pagan idols actually demons, 1 Corinthians 10:20.
Those gathered from all tribes and nations, Revelation 7:9-10.
See *Pagan.*

HEAVEN
Holy dwelling place, Deuteronomy 26:15; 1 Kings 8:30; John 14:2.
Joy in heaven and earth, 1 Chronicles 16:31.
Job's confusion as to eternal future, Job

10:19-22.
Beyond highest stars, Job 22:12.
More desirable than earth, Psalm 73:25.
Heaven throne, earth footstool, Isaiah 66:1.
Treasure site, Matthew 6:19-20.
View at death, Acts 7:55-56.
That which God has prepared for those
   who love Him, 1 Corinthians 2:9-10.

HEDONISM
Wiles of wicked woman, Genesis 39:6-19.
Defiant sin, Numbers 15:30-31.
Blatant display of immorality, Numbers
   25:6-9.
Lust toward young virgins, Deuteronomy
   22:23-29.
Lack of discernment, Deuteronomy 32:28.
Strong man and sex, Judges 15:1-2.
Attraction of prostitute, Judges 16:1.
Homosexual activity, Judges 19:22.
Enjoying plunder taken in battle, 1 Samuel
   30:16.
Solomon's many loves, 1 Kings 11:1-6.
Lavish display of wealth, Esther 1:4-8.
Replacing queen, Esther 2:1-4.
Covenant to avoid lust, Job 31:1.
Vivid portrayal of moral seduction,
   Proverbs 7:6-23.
He who loves pleasure, Proverbs 21:17.
Seeking right kind of pleasure, Proverbs
   24:13-14.
Meaningless laughter and pleasure,
   Ecclesiastes 2:1-3, 10.
Preference for laziness, Ecclesiastes 4:7-8.
Search for pleasure, Ecclesiastes 8:15.
Materialistic view of pleasure, Ecclesiastes
   10:19.
Pleasure-seeking youth, Ecclesiastes 11:9.
Fear and obey God, Ecclesiastes 12:13.
Arrogance of man brought low, Isaiah
   2:12-18.
Revelry brought to halt, Isaiah 24:8-9.
Unsatisfied dreams, Isaiah 29:7-8.
Dissatisfaction of purposeless existence,
   Isaiah 56:10-12.
Those who burn with lust, Isaiah 57:5.
Feet that rush into sin, Isaiah 59:7.
Skilled at art of seduction, Jeremiah 2:33.
Description of lustful men, Jeremiah 5:8.
Refusal to go God's way, Jeremiah 11:7-8.
Detestable acts in public places, Jeremiah
   13:26-27.
Feet that love to wander, Jeremiah 14:10.
Evil feasting avoided, Jeremiah 16:8-9.

Stubbornness of evil hearts, Jeremiah
   16:12.
Looking to flesh for strength, Jeremiah
   17:5.
Lifetime of evil, Jeremiah 32:30.
Judgment on arrogance, Jeremiah 50:31-
   32.
An end to luxury, Jeremiah 51:13.
Good life gone, Lamentations 4:1-5.
Beauty misused, Ezekiel 16:15.
Lust and promiscuity of two sisters, Ezekiel
   23:1-49.
End to noisy songs, Ezekiel 26:13.
Carnal pursuits of priests, Hosea 4:7.
Relished wickedness, Hosea 4:8.
Those who love shameful ways, Hosea
   4:18.
Morning after, Joel 1:5.
Women who command husbands, Amos
   4:1.
Personal desire above need of others,
   Amos 6:6.
Clergyman for pleasure seekers, Micah
   2:11.
Depending on physical strength,
   Habakkuk 1:11.
Alcohol and nudity, Habakkuk 2:15.
Self-made idols, Habakkuk 2:18-19.
Wealth plundered, houses demolished,
   wine unused, Zephaniah 1:13.
Fate of carefree city, Zephaniah 2:15.
Fruit of selfishness and neglect for the
   Lord's house, Haggai 1:2-5.
Emptiness of physical conduct and
   gratification, Haggai 1:6.
High cost for dance, Mark 6:21-29.
Desire for more than one has, Luke 3:14.
Like children in marketplace, Luke 7:31-
   32.
Desire for recognition in congregation,
   Luke 11:43.
All kinds of greed, Luke 12:15-21.
Disillusioned with wild life, Luke 15:13-16.
Friends purchased with worldly wealth,
   Luke 16:9.
Influencing others to sin, Luke 17:1.
As in days of Noah, Luke 17:26-27.
Temporal concepts contrasted to
   relationships in heaven, Luke 20:27-39.
Preferring darkness to light, John 3:19-21.
Primary concern for physical gratification,
   John 6:26.
Body as instrument of sin, Romans 6:12-
   13.

Living according to sinful nature, Romans 8:5-8.
Attainment of temporal, 1 Corinthians 4:8.
Hedonism within body of Christ, 1 Corinthians 5:9-13.
Those whose god is their stomach, Philippians 3:19.
Disintegration of earth's glories, James 1:11.
Favoritism toward wealth, James 2:1-4.
Love of world, 1 John 2:15-17.
Physical pollution, Jude 8
Those who follow natural instincts, Jude 19.
See *Carnality, Flesh, Pleasure.*

HEED
Be careful, Matthew 6:1.
Beware of deceivers, Matthew 24:4.
Be on guard, Mark 13:9, 33.
Build with care, 1 Corinthians 3:10.
Avoid fake confidence, 1 Corinthians 10:12.
Paying attention to Scripture, Hebrews 2:1-3.
See *Attention, Response.*

HEIGHT
Tower of Babel, Genesis 11:1-9.
Stature of King Saul, 1 Samuel 10:23-24.
Goliath the giant, 1 Samuel 17:4; 2 Samuel 21:19; 1 Chronicles 20:5.
Lofty stars, Job 22:12.
Towering tree brought low, Ezekiel 31:3-18.
Tree of great height, Daniel 4:10-12.
Man of short stature, Luke 19:1-6.
See *Size.*

HEIR
Substitute heir, Genesis 15:3; 21:10.
Beneficiary receives all, Genesis 25:5.
Daughter as full heir, Numbers 27:8; 36:9.
Rights of the oldest son, Deuteronomy 21:15-17.
Resistant to leaving legacy, Ecclesiastes 2:18.
Conditions for exercising will, Hebrews 9:16-17.
See *Inheritance.*

HELL
Job's confusion as to eternal future, Job 10:19-22.

Fires of Tophet prepared, Isaiah 30:33.
Fiery furnace of judgment, Matthew 13:37-42, 49-50.
Excluded forever from presence of God, 2 Thessalonians 1:9.
Lake of fire, Revelation 19:19-21.
Those not in Book of Life, Revelation 20:7-15.

HELP
Divine helper, Deuteronomy 33:29; 2 Chronicles 25:8; Psalm 27:9.
Strength and shield, Psalm 28:7.
Deliverer, Psalm 40:17.
Antidote to fear, Isaiah 41:10; Hebrews 13:6.
See *Assistance.*

HERALD
Prophecy of John the Baptist, Isaiah 40:3. (See Matt. 3:1-3.)
Pagan proclamation, Daniel 3:1-6.
Herald angels, Luke 2:8-14.
Mark of evangelist, 1 Timothy 2:7; 2 Timothy 1:11.
See *Evangelist, Messenger.*

HERBAL
Leaves of a tree used for healing, Revelation 22:2.

HERDSMAN
See *Shepherd.*

HERESY
Prophecy of the imagination, Ezekiel 13:1-23.
Those who do not know the Scriptures, Matthew 22:29.
Jesus criticized for healing paralytic man, Mark 2:6-12.
Light that becomes darkness, Luke 11:35.
Wisdom of Gamaliel, Acts 5:33-39.
Exorcists at work, Acts 19:13-16.
Preaching false doctrine, 2 Corinthians 11:4-15.
Paul astonished at the Galatians, Galatians 1:6-9.
False disciples who would dilute the Gospel, Galatians 2:4-5.
Bewitched Galatians, Galatians 3:1.
Penalty for misleading others, Galatians 5:10.
Paul wanted followers to know truth,

Colossians 2:2-4.
Danger of deceptive philosophy,
Colossians 2:8.
Preventing teaching of false doctrine,
1 Timothy 1:3-5.
Godless chatter and opposing ideas,
1 Timothy 6:20-21.
Be careful of strange teachings, Hebrews
13:9.
False teachers and destructive heresies,
2 Peter 2:1-3.
Detecting presence of false prophets,
1 John 4:1-3.
False teaching and wrong conduct, Jude 3-
4.
Bad teaching among good people,
Revelation 2:13-15.
See *Cult, Syncretism.*

HERO
No prophet like Moses, Deuteronomy
34:10-12.
How David became famous, 2 Samuel
8:13.
Anonymous heroes of faith, Hebrews
11:35-39.
See *Fame.*

HERITAGE
Value of musical father, Genesis 4:21.
Image of God and image of man, Genesis
5:1-3.
Birthright offered at bargain, Genesis
25:27-34.
Forefather's obedience brings blessing to
succeeding generations, Numbers
14:24.
God's covenant through many
generations, Deuteronomy 5:2-3.
Solomon's inheritance of righteousness
from father, 1 Kings 11:9-13.
Benefiting from promise given to David,
2 Kings 8:16-19.
Children and grandchildren in continuing
disobedience, 2 Kings 17:41.
Confessing sins of ancestors, Nehemiah
9:2.
Ancestral property, Nehemiah 11:20.
Blessing of God from generation to
generation, Psalm 44:1-3.
Heritage for children, Proverbs 20:7.
Ancient boundary stone, Proverbs 22:28;
23:10-11.
Ancestral rock, Isaiah 51:1.

Ruins rebuilt, Isaiah 58:12.
Ignoring God who led them through
wilderness, Jeremiah 2:5-8.
Ark of covenant forgotten, Jeremiah
3:16.
Ancient paths, good way, Jeremiah 6:16.
Obedience to parents and grandparents,
Jeremiah 35:1-16.
Telling message to children's children,
Joel 1:3.
The Lord's anger toward forefathers,
Zechariah 1:2.
Genealogy of Jesus, Matthew 1:1-17; Luke
3:23-38.
Honoring those who murdered prophets,
Matthew 23:29-32.
Comparing old and new, Luke 5:36-39.
Satan as spiritual father, John 8:44.
Stephen's knowledge of Old Testament
history, Acts 7:1-60.
Paul used history of Israel as means to
witness, Acts 13:13-52.
Laying good foundation, 1 Corinthians
3:10.
Lessons to be learned from Israel's history,
1 Corinthians 10:1-13.
Grandmother's faith passed on to progeny,
2 Timothy 1:5.
Influence of Scriptures since childhood,
2 Timothy 3:14-15.
Responsibility to next generation, Titus
2:3-5.
See *Background, Family, Grandparents,
Parents.*

HERMENEUTICS
Bible study applied to righteous lifestyle,
Psalm 119:9-11.
Purpose of searching Scriptures, Proverbs
1:1-3.
Persistent study abundantly rewarded,
Proverbs 2:1-6.
Proper student attitude, Proverbs 19:20.
Learn and apply, Proverbs 22:17.
Role of emotion in learning, Proverbs
23:12.
Beyond monetary value, Proverbs 23:23.
Analytical study and research, Ecclesiastes
7:25.
Function of wisdom in decision-making,
Ecclesiastes 8:5.
Divine pedagogy, Isaiah 28:26.
Supreme challenge for Bible student,
2 Timothy 3:16.

HESITATION
At tomb of Jesus, John 20:5, 8.
Timid and bold, 2 Corinthians 10:1.
See *Reluctance.*

HETERODOXY
Wrong interpretation of Scripture,
    Jeremiah 8:8.
Shepherds who lead sheep astray,
    Jeremiah 50:6.
See *Cult, Heresy, Syncretism.*

HIDING
In Garden of Eden, Genesis 3:10.
Seclusion of baby Moses, Exodus 2:2-3.
Concealed spies, Joshua 6:17, 25.

HIDING PLACE
Shadow of divine wings, Psalm 17:8.
Sheltering tabernacle, Psalm 27:5; 31:20.
Musical refuge, Psalm 32:7.
Refuge of Scripture, Psalm 119:114.
Shelter in time of storm, Isaiah 32:2.
See *Protection, Refuge, Shelter.*

HIGHWAY
Public thoroughfare, Numbers 20:19.
Need for building roads, Deuteronomy
    19:1-3.
Roads abandoned for paths, Judges 5:6.
Way of Holiness, Isaiah 35:8.
Way through desert, Isaiah 40:3-4; 43:19.
Road signs and guideposts, Jeremiah 31:21.
Broad and narrow way, Matthew 7:13-14.
Used by robber, Luke 10:30-33.

HIKING
Too exhausted to cross ravine, 1 Samuel
    30:10, 21.

HILLS
Ancient hills, Genesis 49:26.
Land of hills and valleys, Deuteronomy
    11:11.
Hills sacred to heathen, 1 Kings 20:23.
When hills melt, Psalm 97:5.
Joyful hills, Psalm 98:8.
Hills of hope, Psalm 121:1.
Ancient mountains, Habakkuk 3:6.
Level place in hilly area, Luke 6:17.
See *Geology.*

HINDRANCE
Prayer unanswered when sin cherished,

Psalm 66:18-19.
Those who said it was not time to rebuild
    temple, Haggai 1:3-4.
Hindering others from entering kingdom
    of heaven, Matthew 23:13-15.
Rich receive less blessing than poor, Luke
    6:20, 24-25.
Mob incited against Paul and Silas, Acts
    17:5-7.
Hindered from running good race,
    Galatians 5:7.
Wrong kind of authority in congregation,
    3 John 9-10.
See *Obstacles.*

HISTORY
Joseph, the unknown, Exodus 1:8.
Stages of journey recorded by Moses,
    Numbers 33:1-49.
Asking about former days, Deuteronomy
    4:32-35.
Reading history book to induce sleep,
    Esther 6:1.
Fate of nations in God's hands, Job 12:23;
    34:29-30; Psalms 2:1-6; 113:4.
Basic apostasy of nations, Psalm 2:1-3.
Inevitable fate of world governments,
    Psalm 2:7-9.
God will have last word in history, Psalm
    9:5.
Evil brings about its own retribution, Psalm
    9:15.
Blessing of God from generation to
    generation, Psalm 44:1-3.
Promise of God to Israel, Psalm 45:16.
Time when peace will cover earth, Psalm
    46:8-10.
Resumé in song of Israel's history, Psalms
    78:1-72; 106:1-48.
Ponder the works of the Lord, Psalm 111:2-
    4.
History repeats itself, Ecclesiastes 1:9; 3:15.
Evil deeds inscribed on scroll, Isaiah 30:8.
Divine evaluation of nations, Isaiah 40:15-
    17.
God knows end from beginning, Isaiah
    46:10-11.
Ruins rebuilt, Isaiah 58:12.
A nation takes time to develop, Isaiah 66:8.
Ark of covenant forgotten, Jeremiah 3:16.
The Lord of history revealed, Ezekiel 20:42
Image depicting world history, Daniel 2:29-
    45.
Nebuchadnezzar's view of predestination,

Daniel 4:15.

Divine goodness in Israel's history, Micah 6:3-5.

Words of Jesus concerning end times, Mark 13:1-37.

Many writers attempted to record New Testament events, Luke 1:1-2.

Orderly account of happenings, Luke 1:3-4.

Purpose of sacred history, John 20:30-31.

Books of world could not contain full story of Jesus, John 21:25.

Stephen resorted to history for his defense, Acts 7:1-60.

Resumé of Old Testament and proclamation of the Gospel, Acts 13:16-41.

Concise resumé of God's plan through ages, Romans 1:1-6.

Ultimate purpose of Creation and human life, Romans 8:18-23.

Certain judgment coming on earth, Romans 9:28.

Fulfillment of times, Ephesians 1:9-10.

Paul's unique description of life of Christ, 1 Timothy 3:16.

Influence of demons over world leaders, Revelation 16:13-14.

When evil serves God's purpose, Revelation 17:17.

HOBBY

David kept weapons of Goliath, 1 Samuel 17:54.

David frequently played harp, 1 Samuel 18:10. (See 19:9.)

HOLIDAY

Sabbatical year, Leviticus 25:1-7.

Instructions for sacred feasts, Numbers 28:16-31. (See also chap. 29.)

Loss of summer house, Amos 3:15.

See *Rest.*

HOLINESS

Righteous man without blame, Genesis 6:9.

Call to perfection, Genesis 17:1.

God's radiance on countenance, Exodus 34:29-35.

Drinking does not mix with worship, Leviticus 10:8-10.

Prime impetus to holiness, Leviticus 11:44-45.

Separated unto holiness, Leviticus 20:26; Deuteronomy 14:2.

Holiness by virtue of occupation, Leviticus 21:8.

Personal responsibility in resisting temptation, Deuteronomy 13:4.

Abounding with God's favor, Deuteronomy 33:23.

Blameless before the Lord, 2 Samuel 22:24.

Man who truly walked with God, Job 1:1.

Pure cannot come from impure, Job 14:4.

Characteristics of holy life, Psalm 15:1-5.

Qualification for worship, Psalm 24:3-5.

Holiness of God reveals personal sinfulness, Isaiah 6:1-5.

Yearning for the Lord, Isaiah 26:9.

Highway of holiness, Isaiah 35:8.

Those who pursue righteousness, Isaiah 51:1.

Coming to the Lord with clean vessels, Isaiah 66:20.

Absolute holiness of God, Daniel 9:14.

Walking in ways of the Lord, Hosea 14:9.

Lips must first be purified, Zephaniah 3:9.

Realization of sin in presence of Jesus, Luke 5:8.

Sanctifying truth, John 17:17.

Righteousness comes from God by faith, Romans 1:17.

Holiness from within, Romans 2:28-29.

Boasting of self-righteousness, Romans 4:2.

Righteousness not obtained through observing sacraments, Romans 4:9-12.

New life in Christ, Romans 6:4.

Freedom from mastery of sin, Romans 6:14.

Hate evil, cling to good, Romans 12:9.

Christian lifestyle, Romans 13:12-14.

True measure of spirituality, Romans 14:17-18.

Wise about good, innocent about evil, Romans 16:19.

Believer's body Holy Spirit's temple, 1 Corinthians 3:16-17; 6:19-20.

Presence of Holy Spirit in life of commitment, 2 Corinthians 3:7-8.

Impetus to holiness, 2 Corinthians 7:1.

Fruit of the Spirit, Galatians 5:22.

Attitude of mind determines conduct in life, Philippians 4:8-9.

Description of life centered in Christ, Colossians 3:1-17.

Life that pleases God, 1 Thessalonians 4:1-8.

Holy Spirit and the impact of Scripture, 2 Thessalonians 2:13.

Resisting ungodliness and passions of world, Titus 2:11-12.

Made perfect through suffering, Hebrews 2:10.

Law makes nothing perfect, Hebrews 7:18-19.

Discipline that produces righteousness and peace, Hebrews 12:11.

Lifestyle of true disciple, James 3:17-18.

Personal initiative in holy living, James 4:7-10.

Sanctifying work of the Spirit, 1 Peter 1:1-2.

Call to holiness, 1 Peter 1:13-16.

Made holy by obeying truth, 1 Peter 1:22.

Taking initiative to be rid of evil traits, 1 Peter 2:1.

True scope of holiness, 1 Peter 3:9.

Christ's return an impetus for holy living, 1 Peter 4:7-8.

Everything needed for spiritual and material welfare, 2 Peter 1:3.

Attributes of mature Christian life, 2 Peter 1:5-9.

Sin and provision for cleansing, 1 John 1:8-10.

Purifying privilege, 1 John 3:1-3.

Deliverance from continual sin, 1 John 3:4-6.

Devil's work destroyed, 1 John 3:8.

Seen in God's sight, 1 John 5:18.

Keeping soul in good health, 3 John 2.

Partial holiness insufficient in God's sight, Revelation 2:1-6, 13-15, 18-20.

Continuity of evil and good, Revelation 22:11.

See *Sanctification, Separation.*

HOLISTIC

Total involvement in loving God, Deuteronomy 6:5.

Enslaved bodies, Nehemiah 9:37.

Fearfully and wonderfully made, Psalm 139:13-16.

Total protection in fiery furnace, Daniel 3:27.

All-out love for God, Mark 12:30; Luke 10:27.

Fourfold life of Jesus, Luke 2:52.

Light for the whole body, Luke 11:36.

Thomas' need for holistic proof, John 20:24-28.

Instruments of sin, Romans 6:13; 8:13.

Living sacrifice, Romans 12:1-2.

All-out righteousness, Romans 13:14.

Bodies members of Christ, 1 Corinthians 6:14-15.

Honoring God with one's body, 1 Corinthians 6:19-20.

Body control, 1 Corinthians 9:27; Galatians 5:16.

Related parts of body, 1 Corinthians 12:12-26.

Christ revealed in our bodies, 2 Corinthians 4:10.

Role of body in marriage, Ephesians 5:33.

HOLY SPIRIT

Role of the Holy Spirit in Creation, Genesis 1:2.

Special gifts through Holy Spirit, Exodus 31:1-5.

Changed into different person by the Holy Spirit, 1 Samuel 10:6-9.

Words given by the Holy Spirit, 2 Samuel 23:2.

Temple building plans given by the Holy Spirit, 1 Chronicles 28:12.

Source of guidance to inner mind, Job 32:8; 33:4.

Removal of Holy Spirit, Psalm 51:11.

Lamp of the Lord, Proverbs 20:27.

Standard against evil, Isaiah 59:19-21.

Anointing to preach, Isaiah 61:1.

Grieving the Holy Spirit, Isaiah 63:10.

Ezekiel's commission to minister, Ezekiel 2:1-5.

Clean hearts, changed and guided lives, Ezekiel 36:25-27.

Teacher for righteousness, Joel 2:23.

Young prophesy, old dream dreams, Joel 2:28.

Filled with the Spirit of the Lord, Micah 3:8.

Not by might nor by power, Zechariah 4:6.

Birth of Jesus, Matthew 1:18.

Like descending dove, Mark 1:10-11.

Jesus experienced power of the Spirit, Luke 4:14.

Living water from within, John 7:37-39.

Promised Counselor, John 14:16-17.

Ministry of the Holy Spirit, John 16:5-14.

Role of Holy Spirit in salvation and righteous living, Romans 8:6-11.

Prayer guided by the Holy Spirit, Romans

8:26-27.
Hope, joy, and peace, Romans 15:13.
Guidance in Bible study, 1 Corinthians 2:6-16.
Holy Spirit's temple, 1 Corinthians 3:16-17; 6:19-20.
Act of God's power, 1 Corinthians 6:14.
Guidance of the Holy Spirit in marriage, 1 Corinthians 7:40.
Satisfying drink, 1 Corinthians 12:13.
Seal of ownership, 2 Corinthians 1:21-22.
Letter kills but the Spirit gives life, 2 Corinthians 3:6; Ephesians 1:13.
Presence of Holy Spirit in a life of commitment, 2 Corinthians 3:7-8.
Purity through the Holy Spirit, Galatians 5:16.
Spirit of wisdom and revelation, Ephesians 1:17.
Christ raised from dead by the Holy Spirit, Ephesians 1:18-21; 1 Peter 3:18.
Access to God through the Holy Spirit, Ephesians 2:18-22.
Holy Spirit's power working within, Ephesians 3:20-21.
Do not grieve the Holy Spirit, Ephesians 4:30.
Convicting power of the Holy Spirit, 1 Thessalonians 1:4-5.
Antichrist restrained until return of the Lord, 2 Thessalonians 2:7-8.
Work of the Holy Spirit and impact of Scripture, 2 Thessalonians 2:13; 1 Peter 1:1-2.
Soundness of faith, 2 Timothy 1:13-14.
Function and distribution of gifts, Hebrews 2:4.
Author of Scripture, 2 Peter 1:20-21.
Anointed with truth, 1 John 2:20, 27.
Confident of salvation, 1 John 3:24.
Witness of Holy Spirit contrasted to false spirits, 1 John 4:1-3.
Christ in believer's life, 1 John 5:6.
Praying in the Holy Spirit, Jude 20.
The Holy Spirit speaking to the churches, Revelation 2:29.
See *Trinity.*

HOME
Living in cave, Genesis 19:30.
Love for childhood home, Genesis 31:30; Psalm 137:1-6.
Dedicating one's house to the Lord, Leviticus 27:14.

Newlyweds establishing home, Deuteronomy 24:5.
Best drinking water, 2 Samuel 23:15.
Hospitality for prophet, 2 Kings 4:8-10.
Desiring to die in one's home, Job 29:18.
Stones and dust of Jerusalem, Psalm 102:14.
Building in vain unless the Lord is the builder, Psalm 127:1.
Establishment of good home, Proverbs 24:3-4.
Tent or cottage, Isaiah 38:12; Hebrews 11:9-10.
Residence by sea, Acts 10:6.
Education at home, Ephesians 6:4.
Use of guest room, Philemon 22.
See *Family.*

HOMESICK
Homesick for Egypt, Numbers 11:1-6.
No song in homesick heart, Psalm 137:4.
Homesick delinquent, Luke 15:11-32.

HOMOSEXUAL
Men of Sodom and Lot's angelic visitors, Genesis 19:5.
Forbidden relationship between men, Leviticus 20:13.
Male prostitutes, Deuteronomy 23:17.
Example of homosexual conduct, Judges 19:22-24.
Eradication of deviates from Israel, 1 Kings 15:12. (See 14:24.)
Unnatural passion and desire, Romans 1:24-27.
Condemnation of homosexual activity, 1 Corinthians 6:9-10.

HONESTY
Integrity of leadership, Numbers 16:15; 1 Samuel 12:4.
Refusal of bribe, 2 Samuel 18:12; 1 Kings 13:8.
No need for expense vouchers, 2 Kings 12:15.
Elihu's forthright introduction to Job, Job 33:1-5.
Necessity for approaching the Lord, Psalm 24:3-4.
No place for deceit in God's house, Psalm 101:7.
Honest answer like a kiss, Proverbs 24:26.
Value of open rebuke, Proverbs 27:5.
Hatred of those with integrity, Proverbs

29:10; Amos 5:10.
Happiness from honesty and God's
provision, Proverbs 30:7-9.
Use of accurate scales, Ezekiel 45:9-10.
Advice to tax collectors, Luke 3:12-13.
Testimony of man and testimony of God,
1 John 5:9.
See *Integrity.*

HONEY
Sweet flavor of manna, Exodus 16:31.
Not to be used for sacrifices, Leviticus 2:11.
Avoid excessive sweets, Proverbs 25:27.
Taste of bridal lips, Song of Songs 4:11.

HONOR
Sister's disgrace avenged, 2 Samuel 13:23-29.
Divine gift of wealth and prestige, 1 Kings
3:13; Ecclesiastes 6:2.
Honor and respect for prominent man, Job
29:7-10.
Nature and people praise the Lord, Psalm
148:1-14.
Humility before honor, Proverbs 18:12.
Eloquent description of noble person,
Isaiah 32:8.
Honor among thieves, Jeremiah 49:9.
Special mention for great prophet,
Zechariah 3:1-9.
Role of humility in greatness, Matthew
23:12.
Asking for prestige rather than earning it,
Mark 10:35-45.
Respect of Cornelius for Peter, Acts 10:25-26.
Whatever measure of success, glory
belongs to God alone, 1 Corinthians
3:7.
See *Citation, Commendation, Prestige.*

HONORARIUM
Offering required to obtain divine
leadership, 1 Samuel 9:1-9.
Requesting payment for spiritual ministry,
2 Kings 5:20-27.
Money, food, and drink for temple
workers, Ezra 3:7.
Payment to choir members, Nehemiah
12:47.
Prostitute giving rather than receiving a
fee, Ezekiel 16:32-34.
Refusing king's gratuities, Daniel 5:17.
Murderous payment to daughter of

Herodias, Matthew 14:1-12.
Payment to those who minister, Luke 9:1-6; 1 Corinthians 9:7-14; 1 Timothy
5:17-18.
Spiritual wages, John 4:36.
Not making profit of the Gospel,
2 Corinthians 2:17.
Proof of love to visitors, 2 Corinthians 8:24.
(See 9:5.)
Concern for pastor, Philippians 4:10-19.
Paul avoided greed, 1 Thessalonians 2:5.
Paul worked to provide needed income,
1 Thessalonians 2:9; 2 Thessalonians
3:6-10.
Godliness and financial gain, 1 Timothy
6:5.
Danger of greed in ministry, 1 Peter 5:2-3.

HOPE
Classic statement of faith, Job 19:25-26.
Optimism for poor and needy, Psalm 9:18.
Be encouraged, Psalm 31:24.
Antidote for despair, Psalm 42:5; Jeremiah
31:15-17.
Continuity of hope, Psalm 71:5.
Deferred hope, Proverbs 13:12.
Hope for righteous, Proverbs 14:32.
Light shining in darkness, Isaiah 60:1-2.
Safety in times of trouble and persecution,
Jeremiah 42:1-22.
Optimism in time of pessimism, Jeremiah
48:47.
Behind devastation, ahead anticipation,
Joel 2:3.
Hope against all hope, Romans 8:24.
Assurance of eternal encouragement,
2 Thessalonians 2:16-17.
Blessed hope, Titus 2:11-14.
Anchor of soul, Hebrews 6:19.
Living hope, 1 Peter 1:3.
Tent of human body to be put aside,
2 Peter 1:13-14.
See *Faith, Trust.*

HORIZONS
God promises unsearchable horizons,
Jeremiah 33:3.
Looking forward to spiritual horizons,
Philippians 3:12-14.
See *Anticipation, Future.*

HORROR
Aftermath of battle, Psalm 79:3.
Day of the Lord, Isaiah 13:16.

Brothers and neighbors in conflict, Isaiah 19:2.

Those who wish to die but cannot, Revelation 9:4-6.

See *Disaster, Trauma.*

HORSE

War animal, Exodus 14:9; 15:19.

Egyptian horses forbidden, Deuteronomy 17:16; Isaiah 31:1.

Bit and bridle, Psalm 32:9.

No assurance of safety, Psalm 33:17; Proverbs 21:31.

Swifter than eagles, Jeremiah 4:13.

Fearful neighing of stallions, Jeremiah 8:16.

Four beautiful horses, Zechariah 6:2-3; Revelation 6:2-8.

Divine steed, Revelation 19:11.

HORTICULTURE

First animals ate only plants for food, Genesis 1:30.

Earth's first and foremost garden, Genesis 2:8.

Forbidden fruit, Genesis 2:16-17; Leviticus 19:23.

Care of fruit trees, Deuteronomy 20:19-20.

Solomon's knowledge of botany, 1 Kings 4:33.

Vegetable garden, 1 Kings 21:2.

Palatial gardens, 2 Kings 21:18; Esther 7:7.

Beauty of growing things, Luke 12:27-28.

Caring for tree that did not bear fruit, Luke 13:6-9.

Flowers of field, 1 Peter 1:24.

See *Agriculture, Farmer, Garden.*

HOSPITALITY

Abram in Egypt, Genesis 12:10-20.

Abraham's hospitality to three visitors, Genesis 18:1-8.

Offering mortal amenities to angels, Genesis 19:1-4.

Hospitality extended to Abraham's servant, Genesis 24:12-33.

Hospitality to one who has befriended, Exodus 2:16-20.

Kindness to strangers, Exodus 23:9; Leviticus 24:22; Deuteronomy 10:19.

Passage denied by Edom to Israel, Numbers 20:14-21.

Refusing to give bread to Gideon's 300, Judges 8:4-6.

Delayed departure, Judges 19:1-10.

Example of those who do and do not show hospitality, Judges 19:12-21.

Mistreatment of guests, 2 Samuel 10:1-5.

Queen of Sheba's visit with King Solomon, 1 Kings 10:1-13.

Room for prophet, 2 Kings 4:8-10.

Job's consideration of strangers, Job 31:32.

When to refuse hospitality, Proverbs 23:6.

Gift for departing visitor, Jeremiah 40:5.

One thousand guests at Belshazzar's banquet, Daniel 5:1.

Influencing neighbors to alcoholism, Habakkuk 2:15.

Sacred cooking pots, Zechariah 14:20.

Hospitality for apostles in their ministry, Matthew 10:9-10; Luke 10:5-8.

Rude refusal of hospitality, Matthew 22:2-10.

Divine reciprocation of hospitality, Matthew 25:34-45.

Concern for hungry guests, Mark 8:1-3.

Ready at the Lord's command, Mark 14:13-15.

Guest who remained three months, Luke 1:56.

Putting first things first, Luke 10:38-42.

Hospitality to those who cannot repay, Luke 14:12-14.

Tax collectors and "sinners" made welcome at Jesus' table, Luke 15:1-7.

Host for Last Supper, Luke 22:7-12.

Enemy who took bread, John 13:18-27.

Ample rooms in Father's house, John 14:2.

Peter, though a guest of Cornelius, felt free to invite others, Acts 10:21-23.

From jail to jailer's home, Acts 16:34.

Jason persecuted for having Paul and Silas in his home, Acts 17:5-7.

Using the home for discipleship training, Acts 18:26.

Hospitality on Island of Malta, Acts 28:1-2.

Hospitality of Publius to Paul, Acts 28:7.

Practice hospitality, Romans 12:13.

Paul would come to stay awhile, 1 Corinthians 16:5-6.

Hospitality to recommended stranger, 1 Corinthians 16:10-11.

Double visit, 2 Corinthians 1:16.

Peter and Paul in Jerusalem, Galatians 1:18.

Welcome Paul received from Galatians, Galatians 4:14.

Messengers given good reception,

1 Thessalonians 1:8-10.
Required in church leadership, Titus 1:7-8.
Use of guest room, Philemon 22.
Entertaining angels without knowing it,
Hebrews 13:2.
Being sincerely hospitable, 1 Peter 4:9.
Denying hospitality to those of false
teaching, 2 John 10-11.
Strangers who are Christians, 3 John 5-8.
Fellowship with the Lord Himself,
Revelation 3:20.
See *Guests*.

HOSTAGE
Held hostage in sealed cave, Joshua 10:16-
18.
Hostages taken from Jerusalem, 2 Kings
14:14; 2 Chronicles 25:24.
See *Captive, Prison*.

HOSTESS
Prompt gathering together of food,
1 Samuel 25:18.
Food for unexpected guest, 1 Kings 17:7-
16.

HOSTILITY
Unanimous complaint, Exodus 16:2.
Putting end to envious conflict, 2 Samuel
2:26-29.
Daring to burn prophecy of Jeremiah,
Jeremiah 36:20-24.
Mob of bad characters incited against Paul
and Silas, Acts 17:5-7.
See *Resentment*.

HOUSE
Brick house, Genesis 11:3.
Household gods stolen, Genesis 31:19, 34;
Judges 18:20.
Stone house, Leviticus 14:40-45.
Part of city wall, Joshua 2:15.
Too lazy to repair house, Ecclesiastes
10:18.
Paul's rented house, Acts 28:30.
Living in tent en route to city of God,
Hebrews 11:9-10.

HOUSE ARREST
House made into prison, Jeremiah 37:15.
Paul under house arrest, Acts 28:16.

HOUSE CHURCH
Special greeting to house church, Romans

16:5.

HOUSEKEEPER
Hospitable Sarah, Genesis 18:6.
Happy mother at home, Psalm 113:9.
Ideal woman, Proverbs 31:10-31.
Too busy with many things, Luke 10:40-41.

HUMANE
Helping fallen animal, Exodus 23:5.
Leave revenge to God's timing, 1 Samuel
26:1-11.
Consideration shown to Paul, the prisoner,
Acts 27:3.

HUMANITARIAN
Good Samaritan, Luke 10:30-37.
Christian duty, Galatians 6:10;
1 Thessalonians 5:15.

HUMANITY
Distinction between animal life and human
life, Leviticus 24:21; 1 Corinthians
15:39.
Lacking strength of stone, Job 6:12.
God remembers we are but flesh, Psalm
78:38-39.
Jesus became hungry, Matthew 21:18.
Human provision and divine provision,
Mark 6:35-44.
Dual nature of man, Romans 7:21-25.
Humanity of Jesus whereby humans share
His divine life, Hebrews 2:14-18.
High priests men of weakness, Hebrews
7:28.
Role of evil desire in causing one to sin,
James 1:13-15.
See *Flesh, Weakness*.

HUMAN RELATIONS
Successful handling of people, Exodus
18:14-27.
Courtesy to foreigners, Exodus 23:9.
Deceiving one's neighbor, Leviticus 6:2.
Talk about spiritual matters, Deuteronomy
6:4-7.
Debt cancelled every seven years,
Deuteronomy 15:1.
Attitude toward poor, Deuteronomy 15:7-
11.
Protection of escaped slave, Deuteronomy
23:15-16.
Identification by manner of speech, Judges
12:5-6.

Art of careful negotiation, Ruth 4:1-8.
Loyalty to parents in conflict with loyalty to friend, 1 Samuel 20:1-3.
Praising subject above king, 1 Samuel 21:11.
Warm salutation, 1 Samuel 25:6.
Showing favor for personal interest, 1 Samuel 27:12.
Commendation of king, 1 Samuel 29:6-7.
Share and share alike, 1 Samuel 30:24.
Misunderstanding gesture of goodwill, 2 Samuel 10:1-4.
Solomon's alliance with king of Egypt, 1 Kings 3:1.
Wisdom of Solomon, 1 Kings 4:29-34.
Ineptness of king's viewpoint, 1 Kings 12:1-15.
Winning favor of an enemy, 2 Kings 6:8-23.
Men of bad circumstances share good fortune with others, 2 Kings 7:3-9.
Inequity among citizens, Nehemiah 5:1-5.
Wisdom in appealing to king, Esther 7:3-4.
Renegade pleads for his life, Esther 7:7.
Abandoned by friends in time of trouble, Job 6:14-17.
Caring for those in need, Proverbs 3:27-28.
Judging poor with fairness, Proverbs 29:14.
Role of revelation in society, Proverbs 29:18.
Human inequity, Proverbs 30:21-23.
Government based on love and faithfulness, Isaiah 16:5.
Beauty for ashes, Isaiah 61:1-3.
Daily administration of justice, Jeremiah 21:12.
Making and breaking promise to slaves, Jeremiah 34:8-22.
Cords of human kindness, Hosea 11:4.
Pity for those experiencing misfortune, Obadiah 12.
Justice, mercy, and compassion, Zechariah 7:8-10.
Complaining about another man's generosity, Matthew 20:1-16.
Prophet without honor among his own people, Mark 6:4-6.
Like teacher, like student, Luke 6:40.
Greatest in kingdom, Luke 9:46-48.
Relationship between strangers, Luke 10:5-12.
Frankness of Jesus to Pharisees, Luke 11:37-54.
Sharing with others, Luke 12:48.

Settling disputes out of court, Luke 12:58-59.
Honor for some above another, Luke 14:7-11.
Reaching out for those in need, Luke 14:12-14.
Go to war or negotiate peace, Luke 14:31-32.
Hospitality toward unbelievers, Luke 15:1-2.
Attitude of father and resentful brother, Luke 15:11-32.
Role of wealth in earthly friendships, Luke 16:9.
Great guilt of wrongly influencing others, Luke 17:1.
Attitudes between owners and workers, Luke 17:7-10.
Gratitude of foreigner, Luke 17:11-19.
Kindness to Paul, the prisoner, Acts 24:23
Interest in other people, Colossians 4:7.
Relating mother's gentleness to others, 1 Thessalonians 2:7-8.
Mind your own business, 1 Thessalonians 4:11.
See *Courtesy, Hospitality, Psychology.*

HUMILIATION
Feigned guilt of Joseph's brothers, Genesis 44:1-34.
Aliens who succeed above local citizenry, Deuteronomy 28:43-44.
Cutting off thumbs and big toes, Judges 1:7.
Saul's thousands and David's tens of thousands, 1 Samuel 18:7. (See 21:11; 29:5.)
Act of kindness misinterpreted, 2 Samuel 10:1-4.
Stripped of one's honor, Job 19:9.
Fortified city made desolate, Isaiah 27:10.
Into silence and darkness, Isaiah 47:5.
Fall of Moab, Jeremiah 48:16-39.
Description of Jerusalem destroyed, Lamentations 1:1.
Satan and his fall likened to king of Tyre, Ezekiel 28:11-19.
Jesus criticized on cross, Matthew 27:39-44.
Pilate's question to King of kings, Mark 15:2.
Humiliation of Jesus before Crucifixion, John 19:1-3.
See *Embarrassment, Ignominy.*

HUMILITY
Humble beginning from dust, Genesis 2:7.
Prayer of humility, Genesis 32:9-10.
Unaware of God's radiance on
countenance, Exodus 34:29-35.
Saul's humility concerning his anointing,
1 Samuel 10:13-22.
David's prayer after receiving assurance of
divine guidance, 2 Samuel 7:18-29.
Unworthy of being in presence of the king,
2 Samuel 19:24-28.
God's attitude toward humility and pride,
2 Samuel 22:28.
Pathway to honor and wealth, 1 Kings
3:11-14; Proverbs 22:4.
Great things and small things, 2 Kings
5:13.
David's self-evaluation, 1 Chronicles
17:16-19.
Ezra's attitude in prayer, Ezra 9:6.
Job sensed his utter depravity, Job 9:20.
All men alike before God, Job 33:6-7.
Serve the Lord with fear and trembling,
Psalm 2:11.
Key to doing what is right, Psalm 25:9.
Sacrifice God blesses, Psalm 51:15-17.
Doorkeeper in God's house, Psalm 84:10.
Praise and glory belong only to God, Psalm
115:1.
Giving God glory for success, Psalm
118:21.
God's Word gives understanding to
simple, Psalm 119:130.
Prayer of humility, Psalm 123:1-2.
Humble attitude before the Lord, Psalm
131:1.
God's attitude to proud and humble, Psalm
138:6.
Understanding for those of simple ways,
Proverbs 9:6.
Wise listen to good counsel, Proverbs 9:9.
Lowly in spirit, Proverbs 16:19.
Humility should come before honor,
Proverbs 18:12.
Praise as test of humility, Proverbs 27:21.
Limited understanding of ignorant man,
Proverbs 30:2-4.
Humility and meekness bring joy, Isaiah
29:19.
Humility caused by anguish of soul, Isaiah
38:15.
Lowly in spirit, Isaiah 57:15.
Jeremiah's fear and reluctance of
proclaiming God's message, Jeremiah
1:6-10.
Boasting only in the Lord, Jeremiah 9:23-
24.
Physical act of humility in worship,
Jeremiah 41:4-5.
Do not seek personal greatness, Jeremiah
45:5.
Daniel took care to give God glory for
wisdom, Daniel 2:30.
Seek righteousness and humility,
Zephaniah 2:3.
God's blessing on meek and humble,
Zephaniah 3:12.
Blessed are the meek, Matthew 5:5.
Centurion felt unworthy to have Jesus
enter his home, Matthew 8:5-10; Luke
7:6-7.
Jesus asked that His miracles be kept
private, Matthew 9:29-31.
Students and servants beneath teachers
and masters, Matthew 10:24.
Example of Jesus, Matthew 12:15-21.
As a little child, Matthew 18:2-4.
Spiritual greatness through humility and
servitude, Matthew 20:20-28.
Donkey chosen to serve Jesus, Matthew
21:1-7.
Servant attitude in spiritual service,
Matthew 23:8-12.
First must be last, Mark 9:35.
Message conveyed through little children,
Mark 10:13-16.
Prophet and one widow, Luke 4:23-26.
Qualifications for following Jesus, Luke
9:23-26.
Greatest in Christ's kingdom, Luke 9:46-
48.
Excited about wrong phenomena, Luke
10:17-20.
Choosing place of honor, Luke 14:7-11.
Prodigal's opinion of himself, Luke 15:21.
Vain man and humble man at worship,
Luke 18:9-14.
Humbled before the Lord, John 1:27.
Becoming less that Christ may become
greater, John 3:30.
Example set by Jesus toward His Heavenly
Father, John 5:30.
Jesus washed feet of disciples, John 13:1-
17.
First a servant, then a minister, Romans
1:1.
Not thinking of one's self too highly,
Romans 12:3.

Honor first to others, Romans 12:10.
Associate with people of low position,
Romans 12:16.
Whatever measure of success, glory
belongs to God alone, 1 Corinthians
3:7.
Education must be humbling experience,
1 Corinthians 8:1-2.
Adapting to culture of others,
1 Corinthians 9:19-23.
Total function of body of Christ,
1 Corinthians 12:14-20.
Illustration of human body, 1 Corinthians
12:21-25.
Gift of love, 1 Corinthians 13:4.
Paul considered himself least of apostles,
1 Corinthians 15:9.
Antidote for vanity, 2 Corinthians 11:30.
(See 12:7-10.)
Paul's thorn in flesh, 2 Corinthians 12:7.
Paul recognized his weakness,
2 Corinthians 13:9.
Humbling experience of salvation,
Ephesians 2:8-10.
Less than least, Ephesians 3:8-9.
Consider others better than yourself,
Philippians 2:3-4.
Paul considered himself worst of sinners,
1 Timothy 1:15.
Attitude toward those who desert,
2 Timothy 4:16.
Humility toward all, Titus 3:2.
Son of God became flesh, Hebrews 2:5-9.
In His own words, Christ defined His
incarnation, Hebrews 10:5-7.
Humble circumstances are high position,
James 1:9.
Lifestyle of true disciple, James 3:17-18.
Humble before the Lord, James 4:10.
Way up is down, 1 Peter 5:6.
See *Meekness.*

HUMOR

Waters stocked with abundance, Genesis
1:20-21.
Strange names of kings, Genesis 14:1-9.
Tar pits of Siddim, Genesis 14:10.
Angel's description of unborn Ishmael,
Genesis 16:11-12.
Abraham knew how to prepare fast food,
Genesis 18:6-7.
When laughter is out of place, Genesis
18:10-15.
Warning of angels taken as joke, Genesis

19:14.
Isaac's name means "he laughs," Genesis
21:3, 6.
One-upmanship among magicians,
Exodus 7:8-12.
Consecrated big toe, Exodus 29:20.
Perceptive, reasoning donkey, Numbers
22:21-34.
Plan that backfired, Numbers 23:11-12.
Specific about definition, Deuteronomy
2:5.
New clergy comes in all earnestness,
Deuteronomy 18:6-7.
Ox and donkey cannot plow together,
Deuteronomy 22:10.
Damage to knees hinders prayer,
Deuteronomy 28:35.
Melting because of fear, Joshua 2:24.
Pagan god protected by those he is to
protect, Judges 6:31.
Reckless adventurers, Judges 9:4.
Trees seek king, Judges 9:7-15.
Big mouths, Judges 9:38.
Fear of being killed by woman, Judges
9:54.
Thirty sons and 30 daughters, Judges 12:9.
(See v. 14.)
Cheer so loud it shook ground, 1 Samuel
4:5.
Bizarre offering, 1 Samuel 6:4-5.
Two things to worry about, 1 Samuel 9:5.
Saul, shy concerning his anointing, hid
among baggage, 1 Samuel 10:22.
David's confident response to taunts of
Goliath, 1 Samuel 17:42-47.
Hearty, healthful greeting, 1 Samuel 25:6.
Grasping man by beard, 2 Samuel 20:9.
Public relations approach, 1 Kings 1:42.
Imported apes and baboons, 1 Kings
10:22.
Injury by freak accident, 2 Kings 1:2.
Respect for a prophet born by fear, 2 Kings
1:1-15.
Well-situated city with poor water, 2 Kings
2:19-22.
Wait until your beards grow long,
1 Chronicles 19:5.
Humorous verse, 1 Chronicles 26:18 (KJV).
Gold, silver, apes, and baboons,
2 Chronicles 9:21.
Confusion between joy and sorrow, Ezra
3:12-13.
Head of house by royal edict, Esther 1:22.
Haman plotted death of Mordecai but was

commanded by king to be part of rewarding Mordecai, Esther 5:14; 6:10-11.
Mistaken identity, Esther 6:6-9.
Definition of witless man, Job 11:12.
God chided Job in time of trouble, Job 38:1–40:2; 40:7–41:34.
Freedom of donkey from civilization's din, Job 39:5-7.
Short on innate wisdom, Job 39:13-17.
God chided Job about elephant's strength, Job 40:24.
One cannot make a pet of leviathan (crocodile), Job 41:5.
God as pugilist, Psalm 3:7.
Cobra refuses to listen, Psalm 58:4-5.
Frogs in bedrooms of Egypt, Psalm 105:30.
Departure of unwelcome guests, Psalm 105:38.
Grumbling in tents, Psalm 106:25.
Mouths filled with laughter, Psalm 126:2.
Beauty only skin deep, Proverbs 11:22.
Glory of large population, Proverbs 14:28.
Love makes food more palatable, Proverbs 15:17.
Good news and cheerful looks, Proverbs 15:30.
Hunger makes man work harder, Proverbs 16:26.
Wisdom of silence elevates fool, Proverbs 17:28.
Answering before listening, Proverbs 18:13.
Getting best price, Proverbs 20:14.
Quarrelsome wife, Proverbs 21:9, 19; 25:24; 27:15-16.
Avoid overeating, Proverbs 23:1-3.
Food of stingy man, Proverbs 23:6-8.
Confusion of drunkenness, Proverbs 23:30-35.
Honest answer is like kiss, Proverbs 24:26.
Too much sleep, Proverbs 24:33.
Honor does not fit fool, Proverbs 26:1.
How to control fool and comprehend his ways, Proverbs 26:3-12.
Too lazy to eat, Proverbs 26:15.
Meddling in affairs of others, Proverbs 26:17.
Bitterness tastes sweet when hungry, Proverbs 27:7.
Early morning religiosity can be mistaken, Proverbs 27:14.
Tilling land or chasing fantasies, Proverbs 28:19.

Lizards found in kings' palaces, Proverbs 30:28.
Stirring up anger, Proverbs 30:33.
Ignorance is bliss, Ecclesiastes 1:18.
Politicians keeping eyes on each other, Ecclesiastes 5:8.
Profuse words confuse meaning, Ecclesiastes 6:11.
Good old days, Ecclesiastes 7:10.
Fool does not know way to town, Ecclesiastes 10:15.
Carpentry of lazy man, Ecclesiastes 10:18.
Money answer for everything, Ecclesiastes 10:19.
Beware who hears words of criticism, Ecclesiastes 10:20.
Crops not planted and harvested by looking at sky, Ecclesiastes 11:4.
Much study wearies body, Ecclesiastes 12:12.
God whistles, Isaiah 5:26; 7:18.
No protest when judgment comes, Isaiah 10:14.
Small beds for tall people, Isaiah 28:20.
Led by hook in nose, Isaiah 37:29.
Dogs with big appetites, Isaiah 56:11.
Dandled on knees of Jerusalem, Isaiah 66:12.
Males easily find wild donkey, Jeremiah 2:24.
As many gods as towns, Jeremiah 2:28.
Description of profligate men, Jeremiah 5:8.
Scarecrow in melon patch, Jeremiah 10:5.
Men on foot cannot compete with horses, Jeremiah 12:5.
Stolen eggs like unjust riches, Jeremiah 17:11.
Eating sour grapes, Jeremiah 31:29.
Pharaoh only loud noise, Jeremiah 46:17.
Beautiful heifer and gadfly, Jeremiah 46:20.
Examining liver for guidance, Ezekiel 21:21.
Knocking knees of frightened king, Daniel 5:6.
Women who command husbands, Amos 4:1.
From frying pan to fire, Amos 5:19.
Seaweed around Jonah's head, Jonah 2:5.
Indigestion for fish that swallowed Jonah, Jonah 2:10.
To swallow a camel, Matthew 23:24.
Jesus scolding evil spirit, Mark 1:23-26.

Jesus, taking serious subject, gave touch of humor to delight His listeners, Mark 12:35-37.

Ego displayed by teachers of Law, Mark 12:38-40.

Speck in brother's eye, plank in your own, Luke 6:41-42.

Jesus called Herod a fox, Luke 13:31-32.

Tact of man once blind, John 9:24-34.

Number of fish caught, John 21:11.

Hunger caused Peter to fall into trance, Acts 10:10.

Paul embarrassed those who had wrongly persecuted him, Acts 16:35-39.

Jews who sought in vain to use name of Paul in casting out demons, Acts 19:13-16.

Sleeping during sermon, Acts 20:7-12.

Marriage counsel from bachelor, 1 Corinthians 7:27-28.

Putting up with a little foolishness, 2 Corinthians 11:1.

Willing to be accepted as fool, 2 Corinthians 11:16-19.

Super-apostles in Corinth, 2 Corinthians 12:11.

Crafty fellow, 2 Corinthians 12:16.

Devouring each other, Galatians 5:15.

Foolish talk and coarse joking, Ephesians 5:4.

Train wild animals but not the tongue, James 3:7-8.

Sweet in mouth, sour to stomach, Revelation 10:9-10.

HUNGER

Remembering Egypt instead of trusting God, Exodus 16:2-3.

Craving for meat, Deuteronomy 12:20.

Stealing food, Proverbs 6:30-31.

Motivated by good appetite, Proverbs 16:26.

Awakening to reality, Isaiah 29:8.

Food at no cost, Isaiah 55:1-2.

People in search of bread, Lamentations 1:11.

Children without food and drink, Lamentations 4:4.

Better die by sword than famine, Lamentations 4:9.

Food and water cut off from Jerusalem, Ezekiel 4:15-17.

Call to turn to the Lord, Amos 4:6.

Spiritual hunger, Amos 8:11-13; Matthew

5:6; 1 Peter 2:2.

Pharisees criticized Jesus for picking grain on Sabbath, Matthew 12:1-8.

Physical hunger and spiritual sustenance, 1 Corinthians 11:34.

See *Famine.*

HUNTING

God created both domestic and wild animals, Genesis 1:24-25.

Mighty hunter, Genesis 10:8-9.

Ishmael, the archer, Genesis 21:20.

Esau, the hunter, Genesis 25:27.

Rules of hunt, Leviticus 17:13.

Strange and sadistic hunting expedition, 1 Samuel 18:24-27.

Flea hunt, 1 Samuel 26:20.

Man who killed lion in snowfall, 2 Samuel 23:20.

Lion hunt, Job 10:16.

Job, in his misery, likens himself to creatures, Job 30:29.

Mountains rich with game, Psalm 76:4.

Use of snares, Psalm 141:9-10; Proverbs 1:17; Ecclesiastes 9:12; Amos 3:5.

Worship of fishing, Habakkuk 1:16.

See *Sportsman.*

HURRY

God asked to hasten, Psalm 70:1.

See *Haste, Impatience.*

HURT

Partial blindness inflicted as disgrace, 1 Samuel 11:2-11.

Wounds deep as sea, Lamentations 2:13.

How to respond when others hurt you, Luke 17:3-4.

See *Injury.*

HUSBAND

Woman taken from husband, Genesis 2:23-24.

Involvement in contracts made by wife, Numbers 30:10-15.

King Xerxes decreed man should rule house, Esther 1:22.

Young couple, Proverbs 5:18.

Fury of betrayed husband, Proverbs 6:27-35.

Companionship with wife, Ecclesiastes 9:9.

Duty of husband, 1 Corinthians 7:3; Ephesians 5:25; 1 Peter 3:7.

Husband head of home, 1 Corinthians

11:3.
Unsaved husband won to Christ by
example, 1 Peter 3:1-2.

HYBRID
Jacob's experiment with flocks, Genesis
30:37-39.

HYGIENE
Divine preservation of food, Exodus 16:19-
24.
Meat clean and unclean for food, Leviticus
11:1-47.
Cleanliness following pregnancy and birth,
Leviticus 12:1-8.
Preventing infection from spreading,
Leviticus 13:45-46.
Keeping camp free of infection, Numbers
5:1-4.
Turning bad food into good, 2 Kings 4:38-
41.
Bad breath, Job 19:17.
Unhealthy and unclean, Isaiah 65:4.
Stain that soda and soap will not cleanse,
Jeremiah 2:22.
Danger of deadly disease, Jeremiah 16:1-9.
Excrement used as fuel, Ezekiel 4:9-15.
Salt that loses its saltiness, Luke 14:34-35.
Desiring food of pigs, Luke 15:16.
See *Health, Sanitation.*

HYMN
Song of Moses, Exodus 15:1-18, 21.
Witness of song, Deuteronomy 31:19. (See
song of Moses in chap. 32.)
Song of Deborah, Judges 5:1-31.
Preview of David's songs, 2 Samuel 22:1-
51.
Song of gratitude to the Lord, 1 Chronicles
16:7-36.
Stanza of two lines, 2 Chronicles 5:13; Ezra
3:11.
Contrast of hearts, Isaiah 65:14.
Unheeded lyrics, Ezekiel 33:32.
See *Choir, Music.*

HYPERBOLE
Numerous as sand and stars, Genesis
13:16; 22:17; 28:14; 1 Samuel 13:5;
1 Kings 4:20; 2 Chronicles 1:9;
Hebrews 11:12.
Walls to sky, Deuteronomy 9:1.
Numerous as locusts, camels beyond
counting, Judges 7:12.

Daughter worth seven sons, Ruth 4:15.
Praising a subject above a king, 1 Samuel
21:11.
Angelic likeness of king, 2 Samuel 14:17.
Measureless wisdom of Solomon, 1 Kings
4:29.
Big feet, 2 Kings 19:24.
Anticipation of long life, Job 29:18.
Meat like rain, Psalm 78:27.
Vast judgment, Isaiah 34:3-7.
Many widows, Jeremiah 15:8.
Contrasting superlatives, Lamentations
4:7-8.
Wine dripping from mountains, Amos
9:13.
Greedy as grave, Habakkuk 2:5.
Breaking Paul's heart, Acts 21:13.
Speaking as though God could know
foolishness and weakness,
1 Corinthians 1:25.
Eyes torn out, Galatians 4:15.
Folly of legalism, Galatians 5:12.
Seeming exaggeration which, in fact, is
basic spiritual reality, Ephesians 1:18-
22.
Less than least, Ephesians 3:8.
Emotional battle lines, James 4:1.
See *Exaggeration.*

HYPNOSIS
See *Mob psychology.*

HYPOCRISY
Pharaoh's insincere repentance, Exodus
9:27.
Turning to rejected brother in time of
need, Judges 11:1-10.
Doing right but not wholeheartedly,
2 Chronicles 25:2.
Job accused of hypocrisy, Job 4:1-3; 11:4-6.
Undependable friends, Job 6:15-17.
Condemned by one's own words, Job 15:6.
He whose motives are different from his
speech, Psalms 55:21; 62:4.
Prayers which incite God's anger, Psalm
80:4.
Double-minded men, Psalm 119:113.
Disguising true self by false speech,
Proverbs 26:24-26.
Early morning religiosity can be mistaken,
Proverbs 27:14.
Detestable prayers of lawbreakers,
Proverbs 28:9.
Meaningless oaths, Isaiah 48:1-2.

Mockery of fasting, Isaiah 58:4-5.
Those who witness dishonestly, Jeremiah 5:1-2.
Disparity between creed and conduct, Jeremiah 7:9-11.
Those who speak well of you but betray you, Jeremiah 12:6.
Some think King Zedekiah's request for prayer insincere, Jeremiah 37:3.
Coming to prophet without true faith in the heart, Ezekiel 14:4.
Scorning those who have done wrong, Ezekiel 16:56-57.
Not practicing what is preached, Ezekiel 33:31.
Vanity over wealth and self-righteousness, Hosea 12:8.
Those who misuse God's blessing, Hosea 13:6.
Spiritual pride of disobedient people, Amos 4:5.
Jonah's willingness to witness in midst of disobedience, Jonah 1:9.
Leaders and priests perform services primarily for money, Micah 3:11.
Those who recognize the Lord and Molech, Zephaniah 1:5.
Defiled offerings from defiled people, Haggai 2:13-14.
Insincere fasting and repentance, Zechariah 7:1-6.
Tears of false repentance, Malachi 2:13.
King Herod and the magi, Matthew 2:7-8, 12.
Satan's use of Scripture, Matthew 4:1-11.
Righteousness of the Pharisees, Matthew 5:20.
Performing righteousness in view of others, Matthew 6:1.
Avoid hyper-piety, Matthew 6:16-18.
Those who simply say, "Lord, Lord," Matthew 7:21-23.
Hypocrisy of Pharisees, Matthew 15:7-9.
Seeking mercy while mistreating another, Matthew 18:23-35.
Faith of gross sinners compared to religion of Pharisees, Matthew 21:31-32.
Man without wedding clothes, Matthew 22:11-13.
Pharisees did not practice what they preached, Matthew 23:1-3; Luke 11:45-54.
Clean outside, filthy inside, Matthew 23:25-28.

Hypocrisy akin to murder, Matthew 23:29-32.
Faithful and unfaithful service, Matthew 24:45-51.
Those who do miracles in Jesus' name, Mark 9:38-41.
Practice what you preach, Luke 3:7-8.
Identification of hypocrite, Luke 13:23-27, 31.
Pretending to be honest, Luke 20:20.
Jesus could see into hearts of men, John 5:41-42.
Seeking salvation by devious route, John 10:1.
Accusing others of sins we ourselves commit, Romans 2:1.
Those who cause divisions, Romans 16:17-18.
Pretending to be what one is not, Galatians 6:12-15.
False humility, Colossians 2:18.
Faith plus good conscience, 1 Timothy 1:19.
Only a form of godliness, 2 Timothy 3:5.
Profession versus possession, Titus 1:16; 1 John 2:4-6; Jude 12-13.
Unbridled tongue, James 1:26.
Those who walk in darkness, 1 John 1:5-7.
Methods of disruptive hypocrite, 3 John 9-10.
Misuse of Christian liberty, Jude 4.
Feigning life when spiritually dead, Revelation 3:1.
See *Deceit, Sham.*

HYPOTHESIS
Grinding a fool, Proverbs 27:22.
Nest among stars, Obadiah 4.
Gain world, lose soul, Mark 8:36; Luke 9:25.
Ten thousand guardians, 1 Corinthians 4:15.
Resounding gong, clanging cymbal, 1 Corinthians 13:1-3.
Preaching angel, Galatians 1:8.
See *Figure of speech.*

HYSSOP
Used for sprinkling blood, Exodus 12:22.
Grows from walls, 1 Kings 4:33.
Instrument of cleansing, Psalm 51:7.
Vinegar for Jesus on the cross, John 19:28-29.

I

ICON
Unique illustration of religious works involved in idolatry, Isaiah 46:1.

ICONOCLASTIC
Destroy foreign gods, Genesis 35:2.
Moses and golden calf, Exodus 32:19-20.
God supreme above idols, Leviticus 26:1.
Destroy carved images and idols, Numbers 33:51-52.
Avoid architecture which detracts from worship, Deuteronomy 16:21-22.
Impotent gods, Deuteronomy 32:37-38.
Pledge to forsake foreign gods, Joshua 24:19-27.
Let gods protect themselves, Judges 6:25-32.
Silver idol for true God, Judges 17:4.
Ignominy for an idol, 1 Samuel 5:1-5.
Pagan prophets, ministers, and priests destroyed, 2 Kings 10:18-29.
Time for reformation, 2 Kings 23:12-25.
Defilement in sanctuary, 2 Chronicles 29:1-11.
Removal of all idols, 2 Chronicles 34:33.
Punish idols, Jeremiah 51:47.
Altars demolished, Ezekiel 6:4.
Rid of gods forever, Hosea 14:3.
Destruction of evil properties, places, and practices, Micah 5:10-15.
Destroying items of sorcery, Acts 19:18-20.

IDENTITY
Identification of farm animals, Genesis 30:37-43.
Joseph the unknown, Exodus 1:8.
Desert named Sin, Exodus 17:1.
Presence of God the ultimate identity, Exodus 33:15-16.
Holiness by virtue of occupation, Leviticus 21:8.

Dedicating one's house to the Lord, Leviticus 27:14.
Name on each staff, Numbers 17:1-2.
Identification of evil act, Numbers 25:14.
Known as the Lord's treasure, Deuteronomy 26:18.
Total loss of personal worth, Deuteronomy 28:68.
God can single out individual, Deuteronomy 29:21.
Friend or enemy, Joshua 5:13.
Manner of speech, Judges 12:5-6.
Angel unrecognized, Judges 13:16.
Known because of famous son, 1 Samuel 1:1-20.
Prophet of God called seer, 1 Samuel 9:8-9.
Who qualifies as a prophet, 1 Samuel 10:12.
Wisdom and spiritual identity, 1 Kings 10:1.
Mistaken identity, Esther 6:1-13.
Majestic name, Psalm 8:9.
Recognized as one who follows the Lord, Psalm 119:74.
Like idol, like follower, Psalm 135:15-18.
Each star given name, Psalm 147:4.
Women in need of name, Isaiah 4:1.
Known by name before birth, Isaiah 49:1.
The God without precedent, Isaiah 64:4.
Worthless idols, worthless people, Jeremiah 2:5.
Relationship of God to His people, Jeremiah 32:38.
Bearing mark of repentance, Ezekiel 9:3-6.
New names given Hebrew students in Babylon, Daniel 1:6-7.
Daniel's pagan name but king's acknowledgment of Daniel's faith, Daniel 4:8.
Jonah made known his identity, Jonah 1:5-

11.
Becoming like the Lord's signet ring,
Haggai 2:23.
Prophet denying true identity, Zechariah
13:4-5.
Disciples did not identify Jesus as Creator,
Matthew 8:23-27.
Jesus identified, Matthew 16:13-20.
Demons have names, Mark 5:8-9.
Jesus mistaken for Elijah or John the
Baptist, Mark 6:14-16.
Mistaken identity of Jesus, Mark 6:45-51;
John 7:27.
Identity of stranger, Mark 14:13-15.
Identity of Jesus affirmed, Mark 15:1-2.
Registered in town of one's initial identity,
Luke 2:1-4.
Those who thought John the Baptist might
be the Messiah, Luke 3:15.
Demon recognized identity of Jesus, Luke
4:33-34.
Confused identity of Jesus, Luke 9:18-20.
Demons recognized identity of believers,
Luke 10:17-20.
Those for and those against, Luke 11:23.
Ultimate identification of hypocrite, Luke
13:23-27.
Jesus not recognized on road to Emmaus,
Luke 24:13-35.
Identity of John the Baptist, John 1:19-27.
Jesus and man healed at Bethesda, John
5:12-15.
Identity of Jesus leads to faith, John 9:35-
41.
Shepherd and his sheep, John 10:1-6.
Jesus challenged to prove divinity, John
10:22-39.
Love as supreme identity of relationship,
John 13:34.
Those who follow Christ, John 15:18-21.
Pilate and the King of the Jews, John
19:19-22.
Jesus mistaken for gardener, John 20:10-
18.
Disciples first called Christians, Acts 11:26.
Saul's name changed to Paul, Acts 13:9, 13.
Paul and Barnabas thought to be gods, Acts
14:8-12.
Paul accused of being terrorist, Acts 21:38.
Penetrating discovery of personal identity,
Romans 7:17-25.
Identified by the Holy Spirit, Romans 8:16;
2 Corinthians 1:21-22.
Living identification, 2 Corinthians 3:1-3.

Mark of an apostle, 2 Corinthians 12:12.
Identified in Christ, Ephesians 1:11-12.
Marked by the Holy Spirit, Ephesians 1:13.
(Note the "seal" is an official
identification, as on a document.)
Love, the identification mark of early
Christians, Ephesians 1:15; Philippians
1:9; Colossians 1:3-4; 1 Thessalonians
1:3; 2:8; 3:12; 4:9-10; 2 Thessalonians
1:3; 1 Timothy 1:5; 2 Timothy 1:7;
Philemon 4-7; 1 John 1:5-6.
Membership in God's household,
Ephesians 2:19-20.
Recorded in Book of Life, Philippians 4:3.
Christ in you, Colossians 1:27.
Christ the fullness of deity, Colossians 2:9-
10.
Conduct of those who have died with
Christ, Colossians 2:20-23.
Paul's wise use of names of followers,
Colossians 4:7-17.
Giving glory to the name of Jesus,
2 Thessalonians 1:12.
Identified by handwriting, 2 Thessalonians
3:17.
Gold and silver, wood and earth,
2 Timothy 2:19-20. (Note also v. 21.)
God's Son superior to angels, Hebrews
1:3-4.
How Jesus identified with mankind,
Hebrews 2:17-18.
Moses chose to identify with God's people,
Hebrews 11:24-25.
David and Samuel given small mention in
Hebrews, Hebrews 11:32.
Christ the Living Stone; believers lesser
stones, 1 Peter 2:4-5.
Chosen people, royal priesthood, 1 Peter
2:9.
Identified as children of God, 1 John 3:1-3.
Mark of the Christian, 1 John 3:11, 14.
Friends greeted by name, 3 John 14.
Believers as priests, Revelation 1:6.
Identified with name of God, Revelation
3:12.
Servants of God marked with seal,
Revelation 7:3.
Those not having seal of God on foreheads,
Revelation 9:4.
Mark of the beast, Revelation 13:16-18;
14:9-10.
Covered with blasphemous names,
Revelation 17:3.
Names not written in Book of Life,

Revelation 17:8.
Unknown name, Revelation 19:12.
God's name on forehead, Revelation 22:4.
See *Self-image*.

IDEOLOGY
Avoiding ways of heathen, Deuteronomy
18:9.
Certain of erroneous belief, Acts 19:35-36.

IDLENESS
Learn from diligent ant, Proverbs 6:3-11.
Sleeping in harvest, Proverbs 10:5.
Too lazy to repair house, Ecclesiastes
10:18.
Jobless, Matthew 20:6-7.
Talking instead of working, Acts 17:21.
No work, no food, 2 Thessalonians 3:10.
See *Laziness*.

IDOLATRY
Making idols forbidden, Exodus 20:4.
Not to speak an idol's name, Exodus 23:13.
Food for idols not to be eaten, Exodus
34:15; Acts 21:25; 1 Corinthians 8:1-6.
God never appears as an image,
Deuteronomy 4:15-16.
Secret idols, Deuteronomy 27:15.
Making idol to please the Lord, Judges
17:3.
Priests who engaged in idol worship,
Judges 18:30-31.
Strange function of idol in David's home,
1 Samuel 19:13.
Abandoned idols, 2 Samuel 5:21.
Idolatrous king, 2 Chronicles 28:1-4.
Repentant idolator, 2 Chronicles 33:1-17.
Idolatry put away, 2 Chronicles 34:1-7.
Difference between the Creator and idols,
Psalm 96:5.
Graphic description of idols, Psalm 115:2-
8.
Gods made by men's hands, Psalm 135:15-
18; Jeremiah 16:20.
Superstitions of Israel, Isaiah 2:6-8.
God spoken of as one of many, Isaiah
37:10. (See vv. 6, 23.)
Wood for making gods and cooking fires,
Isaiah 44:14-20.
Idol-makers put to shame, Isaiah 45:16.
Ignorance of worshiping idols, Isaiah
45:20.
Impotence of gods made by men, Isaiah
46:6-7.

As many gods as towns, Jeremiah 2:28.
Worship of Queen of Heaven, Jeremiah
7:18.
Idols compared to scarecrows, Jeremiah
10:5.
Futility of idols, Ezekiel 6:13.
Idols in the heart, Ezekiel 14:1-11.
Children sacrificed to idols, Ezekiel 23:37.
Decorative images in temple, Ezekiel
41:17-20.
Worship of image built by
Nebuchadnezzar, Daniel 3:1-6.
Fear because of stolen idol, Hosea 10:5.
Worship of what hands have made, Hosea
14:3.
False security of man-made idols,
Habakkuk 2:18-19.
Those who recognize the Lord and
Molech, Zephaniah 1:5.
Marriage to daughter of a god, Malachi
2:11.
Worship of men, Acts 14:8-18.
Paul's confrontation with idolatry in
Athens, Acts 17:16-34.
Preaching of Gospel hindered business of
idol-makers, Acts 19:20-41.
Worshiping created rather than the
Creator, Romans 1:25.
Pagan idols actually demons,
1 Corinthians 10:20.
Led astray to dumb idols, 1 Corinthians
12:2.
Keep yourself from idols, 1 John 5:21.
Those cast into lake of fire, Revelation 21:8.

IGNOMINY
Cutting off thumbs and big toes, Judges
1:7.
Ignominy to an idol, 1 Samuel 5:1-5.
Desecration of King Saul's body, 1 Samuel
31:8-10.
How the mighty have fallen, 2 Samuel
1:27.
David's delegation put to shame, 2 Samuel
10:4-5.
David's willingness to accept rebuke,
2 Samuel 16:5-12.
Job became byword, Job 30:9-10.
Food for jackals, Psalm 63:10.
Fortified city made desolate, Isaiah 27:10.
Into silence and darkness, Isaiah 47:5.
God's prophet lowered into mud,
Jeremiah 38:6.
Burial in ignominy, Jeremiah 41:9.

Heap of ruins, Jeremiah 51:37.
Joseph did not want to make presumed sin
of Mary public, Matthew 1:19.
Mockery against Jesus, Mark 14:65; 15:16-
20, 29-32.
Humiliation of Jesus before Crucifixion,
John 19:1-3.
Paul would not permit government
officials to save face, Acts 16:35-40.
See *Embarrassment.*

IGNORANCE
Sins of ignorance, Leviticus 22:14;
Numbers 15:22-26; Hosea 4:6; Luke
23:34; John 16:2.
Innate ignorance, Job 11:7-8; 28:12-13;
Psalm 139:6.
Ignorance of future, Proverbs 27:1;
Jeremiah 10:23.
Ignorance is bliss, Ecclesiastes 1:18.
Those who cannot read, Isaiah 29:11-12.
Priests unaware of blemished sacrifices,
Malachi 1:6-14.
Pretended ignorance of Peter, Luke 22:57-
60.
Altar to unknown god, Acts 17:23.
Ignorance overlooked, Acts 17:30.
Inexcusable guilt, Romans 1:19-25.
Spiritual ignorance, 1 Corinthians 2:7-10.
Partial ignorance, 1 Corinthians 13:12.
Ignorance with complete confidence,
Hebrews 11:8.
That which is not understood, Jude 10.
See *Blindness.*

ILLEGITIMACY
Born of forbidden marriage, Deuteronomy
23:2.

ILLICIT
Motherhood by incest, Genesis 19:30-38.
Illicit relationship between those in
spiritual service, 1 Samuel 2:22.
Utterly defiled, Jeremiah 3:1-3.
Lust and promiscuity of two sisters, Ezekiel
23:1-49.
See *Degradation, Immorality, Lust.*

ILLITERACY
Meaningless writing, Isaiah 29:11-12.

ILLNESS
Role of disease in judgment for sin,
Leviticus 26:14-16.

Illness deeper than physical, 1 Kings 14:1-
14.
Miraculous sign for Hezekiah,
2 Chronicles 32:24-26.
Illness caused by Satan, Job 2:6-7.
God speaks through suffering, Job 33:14,
19-21.
Afflicted since youth, Psalm 88:15.
Judgment brings righteousness, Isaiah
26:9.
Relationship of illness to sin, Matthew 9:1-
7; John 5:14.
Years of medical expense, Mark 5:25-26.
Jesus rebuked fever, Luke 4:38-39.
Illness caused by spirit, Luke 13:10-16.
Invalid for 38 years, John 5:1-9.
Present suffering not to be compared with
coming glory, Romans 8:18.
Purpose of trouble, 2 Corinthians 4:17-18.
Concern for those who are ill, Philippians
2:26-27.
Made perfect through suffering, Hebrews
2:10.
Value of testing, trials, and problems,
James 1:2-4, 12; 1 Peter 1:6-7.
Praying for sick, James 5:13-15.
Benefit of bodily suffering, 1 Peter 4:1-2.
See *Disease, Hygiene.*

ILLUMINATION
God's provision of light, Genesis 1:3, 14-
19.
Abundance of light, Isaiah 30:26; 60:19.
Profuse use of lamps, Acts 20:8.
Light makes everything visible, Ephesians
5:14.
Earth illuminated by angelic splendor,
Revelation 18:1.
See *Light, Visibility.*

ILLUSTRATION
Likening Samson's strength to fire and
thread, Judges 16:7-12.
Teaching with parables, Psalm 78:1-8.
Little city illustrates world, sin, redemption,
Ecclesiastes 9:14-15.
Object lesson of clay jar, Jeremiah 19:1-12.
Good figs and bad figs, Jeremiah 24:1-10.
Immeasurable grace of God, Jeremiah
31:37.
Illustration to Israelites of broken promises
to God, Jeremiah 35:1-16.
Parable of vine branch, Ezekiel 15:1-7.
Parable of two eagles and vine, Ezekiel

17:1-24.
Israel as lioness and fruitful vine, Ezekiel 19:1-14.
Valley of dry bones, Ezekiel 37:1-14.
Basket of ripe fruit, Amos 8:1-2.
Likening Babylon to fisherman, Habakkuk 1:14-17.
Measuring basket, Zechariah 5:5-11.
Why Jesus used parables, Matthew 13:10-13; Luke 8:9-10.
Paul quoted poets of Athens, Acts 17:28.
Using visual to illustrate point, Acts 21:10-11.
Spiritual truth communicated in human terms, Romans 6:19.
Unmuzzled ox, 1 Corinthians 9:9-14.
Lifestyle communicated by example, 2 Corinthians 6:4-10.
Example from life, Galatians 3:15.
Hagar and Sarah, Galatians 4:21-31.
See *Object lesson, Visual.*

IMAGE
Wicked life not to be forgotten, Isaiah 23:16.
Lost self-esteem, Lamentations 4:2.
Haggai called the Lord's messenger, Haggai 1:13.
Joseph did not want to blight Mary's personal image, Matthew 1:19.
Ego displayed by teachers of the Law, Mark 12:38-40.
Danger of falsely evaluating one's self, 2 Corinthians 10:12.
Paul willing to be accepted as fool, 2 Corinthians 11:16-19.
Identified in Christ, Ephesians 1:11-12.
Imprisonment widened sphere of influence, Philippians 1:12-14.
Qualifications of Christ as Saviour and King, Colossians 1:15-20.
God's Son superior to angels, Hebrews 1:3-4.
David and Samuel given small mention in Hebrews, Hebrews 11:32.
See *Reputation.*

IMAGINATION
Mind of man given to evil, Genesis 6:5.
Power of mortal imagination, Genesis 11:6.
Prophets who see nothing, Ezekiel 13:1-3.
Idols in the heart, Ezekiel 14:1-11.
Sins of imagination, Matthew 5:28.
Foolish heart darkened, Romans 1:21.

IMITATION
Imitating heathen, 1 Samuel 8:19-20; 2 Kings 17:15.
Digging their own cisterns, Jeremiah 2:13.
Disciples could not believe Saul's conversion genuine, Acts 9:26-27.
Paul invited imitators, 1 Corinthians 4:16; Philippians 4:9.
Providing model for new believers, 2 Thessalonians 3:9.

IMMATURITY
Easily deceived, Hosea 7:11.
Immaturity of new convert, Acts 8:13-24.
New convert given instruction in effective witness, Acts 18:24-26.
Those who had only initially believed, Acts 19:1-7.
Milk and solid food, 1 Corinthians 3:1-2.
No longer infants, Ephesians 4:14.
Those who make spectacular prophecies, 2 Thessalonians 2:1-2.
Those with little strength, Revelation 3:8.
See *Growth.*

IMMENSITY
Given the eternal viewpoint, Jeremiah 33:3.
Holy Spirit's power working within us, Ephesians 3:20-21.

IMMIGRATION
Development of earth's population after Flood, Genesis 10:32.
Abram in Egypt, Genesis 12:10-20.
Aliens who succeed above local citizenry, Deuteronomy 28:43-44.

IMMINENT
Day close at hand, Joel 2:1-2; Obadiah 15; Zephaniah 1:14.
Death more certain than wealth, Luke 12:16-21.
Our Lord's nearness, Philippians 4:5.
Justice at hand, James 5:9.
End of age, 1 Peter 4:7.
No more delay, Revelation 10:6; 22:10.

IMMOBILIZE
Laying land completely waste, 2 Kings 3:19.

IMMODEST
Pagan religion and immorality, Numbers

25:1-2.
Utterly defiled, Jeremiah 3:1-3.
Wrong and right boasting, Jeremiah 9:23-
24.
Lust and promiscuity of two sisters, Ezekiel
23:1-49.
Alcohol and nudity, Habakkuk 2:15.
See *Discretion, Immorality, Shame.*

IMMOLATION
Sacrifice of son, 2 Kings 16:3.

IMMORALITY
Son born of disobedience, Genesis 16:1-
16. (Note 15:1-6.)
Lot's virgin daughters, Genesis 19:4-8, 30-
38.
Male covetousness, Exodus 20:17;
Proverbs 6:24.
Wanton woman becomes unfaithful to
husband, Judges 19:1-3.
Immorality in sacred places, 1 Samuel
2:22.
Immorality in politics, 2 Samuel 3:6-11.
Leisure leads to lust, 2 Samuel 11:1-5.
Immorality used for vengeance, 2 Samuel
16:20-23.
Immorality reduces personal value,
Proverbs 6:25-26.
Please God, escape immorality,
Ecclesiastes 7:26.
Worst of women, Jeremiah 2:33.
Life of prostitute, Jeremiah 3:1-2; Micah
1:7.
Lust among neighbors, Jeremiah 5:8.
Ministration of evil prophets, Jeremiah
23:10-14.
Deeds done in the dark, Ezekiel 8:12.
Merchandising feminine beauty, Ezekiel
16:15.
Wickedness of Nineveh likened to
prostitution, Nahum 3:3-4.
Adultery in a man's heart and mind,
Matthew 5:27-28.
Conduct of Herod, Luke 3:19-20.
Condemnation of immorality,
1 Corinthians 6:9-10.
A man's conquest of immorality,
1 Corinthians 9:27.
Avoid unwholesome talk, Ephesians 4:29.
Evil conduct and speech put to death,
Colossians 3:5-10.
Evil desires of youth, 2 Timothy 2:22.
Guilt in a man's heart, James 1:14-15.

Sin in broad daylight, 2 Peter 2:13-22.
Clothing of those engaged in immorality,
Jude 23.
Immorality in body of Christ, Revelation
2:20.
Babylon, mother of prostitutes, Revelation
17:1-6.
Those cast into lake of fire, Revelation 21:8.
See *Degradation, Lust, Vice.*

IMMORTALITY
Divine gift, Genesis 1:26-27; 2:9.
Death makes possible deliverance from
sinful nature, Genesis 3:22.
Enoch's walk with God, Genesis 5:24.
Eating temporal food, Judges 13:16.
Rejoining lost loved ones, 2 Samuel 12:23.
Elijah to heaven in chariot, 2 Kings 2:11.
Job's confusion as to eternal future, Job
10:19-22; 14:7-14.
Classic statement of faith, Job 19:25-26.
Eternal inheritance, Psalm 37:18.
David's confidence in resurrection, Psalm
49:15.
Eternity in hearts of men, Ecclesiastes 3:11.
Spirits of mortals and beasts, Ecclesiastes
3:21.
Resurrection of all mankind, Daniel 12:2-3.
Eternal life, John 3:14-16.
True immortality, John 8:51.
Jesus could not die before God's time,
John 19:11.
Beautiful death of martyr, Acts 7:54-56.
Spiritual body different from earthly body,
1 Corinthians 15:42-55.
That which is earthly and that which is
eternal, 2 Corinthians 5:1.
One who never changes, Hebrews 1:10-12.
Melchizedek had neither birth nor death,
Hebrews 7:1-3.
Born of imperishable seed, 1 Peter 1:23.
Tent of this body to be put aside, 2 Peter
1:13-14.
Brief immortality of those who long for
death, Revelation 9:6.
Those over whom second death has no
power, Revelation 20:4-6.

IMMUNITY
Spared from Egyptian plagues, Exodus
8:22-23.
Cities of refuge, Numbers 35:6-15.
Immunity from every disease,
Deuteronomy 7:15.

Freedom from human illness, Psalm 73:5.

IMPACT
Ezekiel overwhelmed, Ezekiel 3:15.
Like teacher, like student, Luke 6:40.
Paul's witness to Agrippa, Acts 26:28-29.
Faith reported worldwide, Romans 1:8.
Work of God reported widely,
    1 Thessalonians 1:8-10.

IMPATIENCE
Unwilling to wait for God's timing, Genesis
    16:1-4.
Impatient community, Exodus 16:2.
Murmuring people, Numbers 20:1-10.
Giving vent to anger, Proverbs 29:11.
Daring to ask God to hurry, Isaiah 5:18-19.
At odds with one's Maker, Isaiah 45:9.
Jonah's impatience, Jonah 4:8-9.
Seeming impatience of Jesus, Mark 9:19;
    Luke 12:50.
Inhospitable treatment, Luke 9:54.
Two sisters, Luke 10:40.
Paul changed audience from Jews to
    Gentiles, Acts 18:4-6.

IMPENITENCE
Warning against disobedience, Leviticus
    26:21.
Gross example of impenitent heart,
    Deuteronomy 29:19-21.
One sin as great as another, 1 Samuel
    15:23. (See James 2:10.)
Rebelling against light, Job 24:13.
Proud of wrongdoing, Psalm 52:1.
Hardened hearts, Psalm 95:8; Mark 3:5;
    Hebrews 3:7-8.
Ignoring reproof, Proverbs 29:1.
Stubborn iron necks, Isaiah 48:4.
Willful disobedience, Jeremiah 44:15-19.
Unwilling to be convinced, Luke 16:31.
Hardness of heart, John 12:37-40.
Rebellion against truth, 1 Thessalonians
    2:15-16.
See *Rebellion, Rejection.*

IMPERATIVE
Imperative to witness, Ezekiel 3:18-19.
Entrusted with secret things of God,
    1 Corinthians 4:1-2.
See *Urgency.*

IMPERFECTION
None can boast, Proverbs 20:9.

Cheating and polluting, Amos 8:5-6.
Salt that looses saltiness, Luke 14:34-35.
One blemish among 12, John 6:70-71.
Need for new covenant, Hebrews 8:7.
See *Blemish.*

IMPERTINENCE
Destiny set for rebellious people, Numbers
    14:35.
Pride and arrogance, 1 Samuel 2:3.
Elisha's bald head, 2 Kings 2:23-24.
Lack of respect, Esther 5:9-10.
Wisdom of sluggard, Proverbs 26:16.
Daring to scoff at name of the Lord, Isaiah
    36:18-21; 37:6.
God of Israel spoken of as "god" by pagan
    king, Isaiah 37:10.
Refusal to go God's way, Jeremiah 11:7-8.
Accusing the Lord of deceit, Jeremiah 20:7.

IMPETUOUS
Peter in garden, John 18:10-11.

IMPETUS
King's business urgent, 1 Samuel 21:8.
Motivated by hook and bit, 2 Kings 19:28.
Good things stored in heart, Luke 6:45.
See *Motivation.*

IMPIETY
Scoffing at God, Exodus 5:2; 2 Chronicles
    32:16-17.
Seeking to ignore the Lord, Job 21:14;
    Romans 1:28.
Sin of challenging God, Isaiah 5:18-19.
Laughing at truth spoken by Jesus,
    Matthew 9:23-24.
Misuse of temple, Matthew 21:12-13.
See *Blasphemy.*

IMPOLITE
See *Discourtesy, Rudeness.*

IMPORTANCE
Comparing sun and moon with stars,
    Genesis 1:16.
Desire for recognition in congregation,
    Luke 11:43.
Paul's wise use of names of followers,
    Colossians 4:7-17.
See *Identity.*

IMPOSTOR
Sin of only one person, Numbers 16:22.

Vindication by earthquake, Numbers 16:28-34.
Manner of speech, Judges 12:5-6.
Dishonest report for personal gain, 2 Samuel 1:2-16. (See also 1 Sam. 31:4.)
Deceitful, malicious man, Proverbs 26:24-26.
God the Creator and gods who perish, Jeremiah 10:11-12.
Riches gained unjustly, Jeremiah 17:11.
False prophets, Jeremiah 23:16-18.
Dreams versus Word of the Lord, Jeremiah 23:33-40.
Prophets who see nothing, Ezekiel 13:1-3.
Thieves and robbers among sheep, John 10:1, 7-10.
Disciples could not believe Saul's conversion genuine, Acts 9:26-27.
Method of false teachers, 2 Peter 2:1.
See *Deceit.*

IMPOTENCE
King David advanced in years, 1 Kings 1:1-4.
Desire no longer stirred, Ecclesiastes 12:5.
See *Geriatrics.*

IMPRECATION
Self-judgment, Ruth 1:17.
Eli's warning to Samuel, 1 Samuel 3:17.
David's claim of innocence, 2 Samuel 3:28-29.

IMPRESSIVE
Queen of Sheba overwhelmed by Solomon's grandeur, 2 Chronicles 9:3.
Humor, Acts 16:37.
Paul's imprisonment widened sphere of influence, Philippians 1:12-14.
See *Display.*

IMPRISONMENT
Placed with king's prisoners, Genesis 39:20.
King imprisoned rebuking seer, 2 Chronicles 16:7-10.
Deterrent to crime, Ecclesiastes 8:11.
House made into prison, Jeremiah 37:15-16.
Set free by angels, Acts 5:17-19.
Peter's escape from prison, Acts 12:1-10.
Set free by earthquake, Acts 16:16-40.
Paul arrested in Jerusalem, Acts 21:30-33.

Paul in prison aboard ship, Acts 27:1-2.
Prison epistles, Ephesians 6:20; Philippians 1:7, 13-14, 16; Colossians 4:3, 18; 2 Timothy 2:9; Philemon 10, 13.
Satan imprisoned thousand years, Revelation 20:1-3, 7-8.
See *Prison.*

IMPROVEMENT
Tear down old, build new, Judges 6:25-26.

IMPROVISATION
Improvised ceremony for new king, 2 Kings 9:11-13.
Improvised prophecies, Ezekiel 13:1-3.

INACCURACY
Negative and positive viewpoints, Numbers 13:17-33.
Fortunate missing of target, 1 Samuel 19:9-10.
Speaking to inanimate object, 1 Kings 13:2.
Deliberately written falsehoods, Jeremiah 8:8-9.

INAUGURATION
Moses turned control over to Joshua, Deuteronomy 31:1-8.
Secret anointing of king, 2 Kings 9:1-13.
See *Politics.*

INCARNATION
Incarnation prophesied, Genesis 3:15; Deuteronomy 18:15-18; Psalm 2:7; Isaiah 11:1.
Virgin Birth predicted, Isaiah 7:14; 9:6.
Place of Jesus' birth, Micah 5:2-3.
Pharisees could not answer question Jesus gave them, Matthew 22:41-46.
Word made flesh, John 1:14.
God on earth seen only in presence of Christ, John 6:46; 14:8-13; Colossians 1:15.
God in mortal flesh, Romans 8:3.
He who was rich became poor, 2 Corinthians 8:9.
Christ's physical body, Colossians 1:22; 2:9.
Paul's unique description of life of Christ, 1 Timothy 3:16.
Son of God who became flesh, Hebrews 2:5-9.
In His own words, Christ defined Incarnation, Hebrews 10:5-7.

Redemption planned before the Creation of world, 1 Peter 1:18-20.
Test of orthodoxy, 1 John 4:2.
Birth of Christ reviewed, Revelation 12:1-5.
See *Nativity, Redemption.*

INCENSE
Ingredients for making incense, Exodus 30:34-35; Song of Songs 3:6.
No incense with sin offering, Leviticus 5:11.
Incense and jealous husband, Numbers 5:11-15.
Prayer like incense, Psalm 141:2.
Used in worship of idols, Ezekiel 8:11.
Gift to Jesus, Matthew 2:11.
Life a type of incense, Ephesians 5:1-2.
See *Fragrance.*

INCENTIVE
Incentive for underprivileged, Leviticus 23:22.
King's business urgent, 1 Samuel 21:8.
Offerings to repair temple, 2 Kings 12:9-15.
Motivated by hook and bit, 2 Kings 19:28.
Divine incentive for king, 2 Chronicles 1:7-10.
Pharisees not truly concerned for safety of Jesus, Luke 13:31.
Compelling motivation of hunger, Luke 15:13-20.
Ultimate in being properly motivated, 1 Thessalonians 1:3.
See *Motivation.*

INCEST
Lot and his two daughters, Genesis 19:30-38.
Abraham's relationship to wife and stepsister Sarah, Genesis 20:12.
Clearly forbidden in Levitical law, Leviticus 18:6-18; 20:11-12, 17-21.
Sleeping with sister, Deuteronomy 27:22-23.
Amnon and Tamar, 2 Samuel 13:1-14.
Violation of family members, Ezekiel 22:11.
Man takes father's wife, 1 Corinthians 5:1-2.
See *Intermarriage.*

INCIDENTAL
Comparing sun and moon with stars, Genesis 1:16.
Paul avoided details, Hebrews 9:5.

INCOME
Earnings from prostitution unacceptable gift to God, Deuteronomy 23:18.
Protecting debtor's earning power, Deuteronomy 24:6.
Giving on first day of week, 1 Corinthians 16:2.
Paul worked to provide needed income, 1 Thessalonians 2:9.
See *Finances, Honorarium, Wages.*

INCOMPETENCE
Sanballat's ridicule of Jewish capability, Nehemiah 4:1-10.
Regret of poor student, Proverbs 5:12-13.
House left untended, Ecclesiastes 10:18.
God the Creator and gods who perish, Jeremiah 10:11-12.
Prophets who see nothing, Ezekiel 13:1-3.
Weakness of broken arms, Ezekiel 30:21-22.
See *Weakness.*

INCONSISTENT
Silver idol for the true God, Judges 17:4.
Jehu's hypocrisy, 2 Kings 10:16-31.
Seeing faults of others but ignoring one's own, Matthew 7:3-5.
Not practicing what is preached, Matthew 23:3-4.
Pious and hypocritical attitudes toward Jesus, Luke 6:1-11.
Profession without performance, Luke 6:46; Titus 1:16.
Judging others, Romans 2:1, 21-23.
Paul chided Corinthians, 2 Corinthians 11:16-21.
Changeable Galatians, Galatians 1:6-9.
See *Hypocrisy.*

INCORRIGIBLE
Those who do not know how to blush, Jeremiah 6:15.
Anger beyond measure, Lamentations 5:21-22.
For continued sinning, certain judgment, Amos 1:3, 6, 9, 11, 13; 2:1, 4, 6. (Note nature of sin in each of these judgments.)
Paul an example of God's grace to worst of sinners, 1 Timothy 1:15-16.

Those who refuse to repent in face of judgment, Revelation 9:20-21.
See *Carnality, Depravity.*

INCUMBENT
Put out of office, Isaiah 22:19.
See *Politics.*

INDECISION
Reluctance of Lot to leave Sodom, Genesis 19:15-16.
Delayed departure, Judges 19:1-10.
Between two opinions, 1 Kings 18:21.
Easily deceived, Hosea 7:11.
Cannot serve two masters, Matthew 6:24.
Turning away from commitment, Luke 9:62.
Double-minded, James 1:8.
See *Reluctance.*

INDEPENDENCE
Defiant sin, Numbers 15:30-31.
Greatest freedom, Psalm 119:45.
Refusal to go God's way, Jeremiah 11:7-8.
Truth sets free, John 8:31-32, 36.
Body as unit, 1 Corinthians 12:12-30.
See *Freedom.*

INDIA
Extent of Xerxes' kingdom, Esther 1:1; 8:9.

INDICTMENT
Indictment for blasphemy, 1 Kings 21:13.
Treasonable prophecy, Jeremiah 26:1-24.
Daniel and friends, Daniel 3:12; 6:13.
Courage to point out sin of king, Daniel 5:18-28.
Indictments of Jesus, Matthew 26:61-65; Mark 15:3, 26; Luke 23:2-3, 38; John 18:30, 33; 19:12, 19-22.
Guilt of Judas, Matthew 27:3.
Those who look for something to criticize, Mark 3:2.
Indictment of Pharisees, Luke 11:45-54.
Stephen's indictment, Acts 6:11, 13.
Paul and Silas, Acts 16:20-21.
Accusations against Paul, Acts 17:7; 18:13; 24:5; 25:18-19, 26-27.
See *Arrest.*

INDIFFERENCE
Warning of angels taken as joke, Genesis 19:14.
Complacent women, Isaiah 32:9.

Those who pass by, Lamentations 1:12.
Relegating prophetic judgment to distant future, Ezekiel 12:26-28.
Slumbering Jonah, Jonah 1:5-6.
Those who neither seek the Lord nor ask about Him, Zephaniah 1:6.
Fate of carefree people, Zephaniah 2:15.
Priests unaware of blemished sacrifices, Malachi 1:6-14.
Rejecting wedding invitation, Matthew 22:1-14.
Slumbering disciples, Mark 14:32-41.
See *Calloused, Insensitive, Lethargy.*

INDIGESTION
Love makes food more palatable, Proverbs 15:17.
Indigestion for fish that swallowed Jonah, Jonah 2:10.
Sweet in mouth, sour to stomach, Revelation 10:9-10.
See *Food.*

INDIVIDUAL
God singles out individual, Deuteronomy 29:21.
Without precedent, Isaiah 64:4.
Individual repentance, Jeremiah 36:1-3.
Individual salvation, Romans 10:13.

INDOLENCE
Slumbering sluggard, Proverbs 6:9-10.
Sleep and success, Proverbs 20:13.
Characteristics of a sluggard, Proverbs 26:12-16.
Do-nothing people, Isaiah 30:6-7.
At time of their Lord's greatest need, disciples slept, Matthew 26:36-45.
See *Laziness, Lethargy.*

INDULGENCE
Too much food and drink, Proverbs 23:20.
From one sin to another, Jeremiah 9:3.
Jesus accused of luxury, Matthew 26:6-13.
Continual lust for more, Ephesians 4:19.
See *Hedonism.*

INDUSTRIOUS
Energy and efficiency, 1 Kings 11:28.
Making most of time and opportunity, Psalm 90:12; Ecclesiastes 12:1; 1 Corinthians 7:29; Ephesians 5:16; Colossians 4:5.
Take example from ant, Proverbs 6:6.

Hard work and fantasy, Proverbs 28:19.
Doing what you do with all your might,
Ecclesiastes 9:10.
Creator continuing at work, John 5:17.
Never lacking in zeal, Romans 12:11.
Paul worked to support his ministry,
2 Thessalonians 3:6-10.
See *Initiative, Motivation.*

INDUSTRY
Too many merchants desecrate land,
Nahum 3:16.
See *Ecology.*

INEPT
Wild donkey's colt, Job 11:12.
Parables to a fool, Proverbs 26:1-12.

INEQUITY
Forced to make bricks without straw,
Exodus 5:6-18.
Sin of only one person, Numbers 16:22.
Honest weights and measurements,
Deuteronomy 25:13-16.
Share and share alike, 1 Samuel 30:24.
Inequity among citizens, Nehemiah 5:1-5.
Security for wicked, Job 12:6.
Joys of wicked, Job 21:6-16.
Wrong made right, Proverbs 28:8.
Human inequity, Proverbs 30:21-23.
Pessimistic Jew, Ecclesiastes 1:15.
Politics and needs of poor people,
Ecclesiastes 5:8-9.
Confusing rewards for righteous and
wicked, Ecclesiastes 8:14.
Common destiny, Ecclesiastes 9:1-2.
Fools in high positions, Ecclesiastes 10:5-7.
Grain and wine to enemy, Isaiah 62:8-9.
Evil prosper, Jeremiah 12:1.
Seeming inequity of testing, Jeremiah
15:15-18.
Power used unjustly, Jeremiah 23:10.
Denial of rights and justice, Lamentations
3:34-36.
Enemies without cause, Lamentations
3:52.
Those who should live die and those who
should die live, Ezekiel 13:19.
God permits evil government to punish His
people, Habakkuk 1:5-11.
Honesty in tax collection, Luke 3:12-13.
Attitude between owners and workers,
Luke 17:7-10.
See *Cheating, Unfairness.*

INEVITABLE
Time for everything, Ecclesiastes 3:1-8.
Certain judgment, Jeremiah 44:15-28.
Divine decisions irrevocable, Romans
11:29.
See *Predestination.*

INEXPERIENCE
Foolish sins, Numbers 12:11.
Father assisting inexperienced son,
1 Chronicles 22:5; 29:1.
See *Novice.*

INFALLIBLE
When God has not spoken, Deuteronomy
18:21-22.
Unfailing promises, Joshua 23:4.
No lie comes from truth, 1 John 2:20-21.

INFAMY
Defiant sin, Numbers 15:30-31.
Infamy to daughter of king, 2 Kings 9:30-
37.
Bodies lying unburied, Jeremiah 9:22.
Burial of donkey, Jeremiah 22:19.
Royalty put to shame, Lamentations 5:12.
Treasures of the Lord in pagan temple,
Daniel 1:2.
Crucifixion of Jesus, Matthew 27:35-44;
Mark 15:22-32; Luke 23:33-43; John
19:18-27.
Demeaning the Son of God, Hebrews
13:12-13.
Sin in broad daylight, 2 Peter 2:13-22.
See *Degradation, Iniquity.*

INFANTICIDE
Instructed to kill male infants, Exodus 1:16;
Matthew 2:16; Acts 7:19.
Sacrifice of son, 2 Kings 16:3.
See *Abortion.*

INFANT MORTALITY
Future end of infant mortality, Isaiah 65:20.
Improper care of newborn, Ezekiel 16:4-5.

INFATUATION
Samson's infatuation for Philistine
woman, Judges 14:1-3.
True love mistaken for infatuation,
1 Samuel 18:20-29.
David and Bathsheba, 2 Samuel 11:2-5.
Love like morning mist, Hosea 6:4.
See *Courtship.*

INFERTILITY
Unwillingness to wait for God's timing, Genesis 16:1-4.
Beloved but barren, 1 Samuel 1:2-7.
Land made productive, 2 Kings 2:19-22.
Land that produces sparingly, Isaiah 5:10.
Plight of eunuch, Isaiah 56:3-5.
Scatter salt on condemned land, Jeremiah 48:9.
Wombs that miscarry, Hosea 9:14.
Place of saltpits, Zephaniah 2:9.
See *Barren, Childless.*

INFINITE
Job's concept of space/time, Job 26:7-14.
Outer space has limits, Psalm 147:4.
Contemplating resurrection and exaltation of Christ, Ephesians 1:18-23.
Sovereignty of Jesus over earth, Revelation 1:5.
See *Eternity, Space/time.*

INFLUENCE
Benefit of musical father, Genesis 4:21.
Like father, like son, Genesis 5:1-3.
Following wrong crowd, Exodus 23:2.
Resist wrong influence, Deuteronomy 12:4.
Way of unbeliever not to be followed in worship, Deuteronomy 12:29-32.
Turning away from wrong family influence, Deuteronomy 13:6-10.
Role of Rachel and Leah, Ruth 4:11.
Son's influence over his father, 1 Samuel 19:1-6.
Solomon's great wisdom, 1 Kings 4:29-34.
Wisdom and spiritual identity, 1 Kings 10:1.
Children and grandchildren in continuing disobedience, 2 Kings 17:41.
Historical mention of mothers, not fathers, in record of young kings, 2 Kings 23:31, 36; 24:8, 18.
Victim of bad influence, 2 Chronicles 13:7.
Influence of evil woman, 2 Chronicles 21:6.
Refusal to obey king's command, Esther 1:10-18.
Esther challenged to use influence with king, Esther 4:12-14; 9:12.
Mordecai used influence for good of Jews, Esther 10:3.
Like idol, like follower, Psalm 135:15-18.
Written on tablet of heart, Proverbs 3:1-4.

Influence of parents, Proverbs 6:20-23.
Terminal impact of death, Proverbs 11:7.
Good news and cheerful looks, Proverbs 15:30.
Children proud of parents, Proverbs 17:6.
Seeking political favors, Proverbs 19:6; 29:26.
Properly training a child, Proverbs 22:6.
Even Moses and Samuel could not intercede, Jeremiah 15:1.
Evil influence of fathers on children, Jeremiah 16:10-12.
Prophets who aid evildoers, Jeremiah 23:14.
Like mother, like daughter, Ezekiel 16:44.
Desire to be like others, Ezekiel 20:32-38.
Influence of clergy on people, Hosea 4:9.
Father and son to same prostitute, Amos 2:7.
Responsible for nation's sin, Micah 1:13.
Influencing neighbors to alcoholism, Habakkuk 2:15.
Salt of earth, Matthew 5:13.
Let your light shine, Matthew 5:14-16; Philippians 2:15.
Evil influence over good, Matthew 13:24-30.
Danger of wrong influence over children, Matthew 18:6; Mark 9:42.
Mother's desire for favors for her sons, Matthew 20:20-24.
Like teacher, like student, Luke 6:40.
Spiritual light from within, Luke 11:33-36.
Peril of influencing others to sin, Luke 17:1-3.
Plot to kill Lazarus because of his influence, John 12:9-11.
Relatives and friends of Cornelius, Acts 10:24-27.
People with influence turned against Paul and Barnabas, Acts 13:50.
Poisoning minds, Acts 14:2.
Prominent women chose to follow Christ, Acts 17:4.
Faith of Christians at Rome known across world, Romans 1:8.
Result of Adam's disobedience, Romans 5:12.
Yeast of malice and wickedness, 1 Corinthians 5:8.
Exercise of liberty in eating and drinking, 1 Corinthians 8:7-13.
Do not cause others to stumble, 1 Corinthians 10:32-33.

Led astray to dumb idols, 1 Corinthians 12:2.
Bad company and good character, 1 Corinthians 15:33.
Those who refresh the spirit, 1 Corinthians 16:18.
Differing reactions to Christian personality, 2 Corinthians 2:15-16.
Report of Paul's new faith encouraged others, Galatians 1:23-24.
Abraham blessed and became a blessing, Galatians 3:9.
Paul's imprisonment widened sphere of influence, Philippians 1:12-14.
Channel of much blessing, Philippians 1:25-26.
Be above criticism, Philippians 2:15-16. (See also 1 Cor. 8:10-13.)
Model to other believers, 1 Thessalonians 1:7-8.
How father should deal with children, 1 Thessalonians 2:11-12.
Avoid idle brothers, 2 Thessalonians 3:6.
Desire to be overseer, 1 Timothy 3:1.
Do not share sins of others, 1 Timothy 5:22.
Grandmother's faith passed on, 2 Timothy 1:5.
Influence of Scriptures since childhood, 2 Timothy 3:14-15.
Do not show favoritism, James 2:1.
Strategic control of speech, James 3:2-6.
Influence unto salvation, 1 Peter 3:1-2.
Surviving in evil surroundings, 2 Peter 2:4-9.
Children of good parents, 2 John 4.
Wrong kind of authority in congregation, 3 John 9-10.
See *Reputation.*

INFORMATION
Rahab lied to protect spies, Joshua 2:1-6.
Captive gives information about enemy, Judges 8:13-14.
Failure to evaluate bad counsel, Ezra 4:11-22.
Speaking in language understood, Isaiah 36:11.
Watchman's responsibility as danger approaches, Ezekiel 33:1-9.
Attention to important information, Ezekiel 40:4.
Knowledge increased, Daniel 12:4.
Word-of-mouth publicity concerning Jesus, Matthew 4:24.
Ways of communicating God's message, Hebrews 1:1-2.
Taking Scriptures to heart, Revelation 1:3.
See *Instruction, Research, Statistics, Study.*

INGRATITUDE
Definitive guidance soon forgotten, Genesis 40:16-23.
Not recognizing divine favor, Numbers 16:9-10.
Material blessing and spiritual blessing, Deuteronomy 8:12-14.
Corrupt reaction to Creator's goodness, Deuteronomy 32:5-7; Judges 10:11-14.
New generation forgot the Lord, Judges 2:10-12.
National backsliding, Judges 8:33-35.
Saul's short memory, 1 Samuel 15:17-19.
Useless concern for another's property, 1 Samuel 25:21.
Negative attitude to gifts from a king, 1 Kings 9:10-13.
Murder in place of gratitude, 2 Chronicles 24:22.
Danger of success, 2 Chronicles 26:15-16; Hosea 4:7.
Blasphemy and assassination instead of praise, Nehemiah 9:26.
Divine provision ignored, Psalms 78:16-31; 106:7.
Deliverer of city forgotten, Ecclesiastes 9:14-15.
Forgetting God's mercy and love, Ezekiel 16:4-22.
Only 1 of 10 returned to thank Jesus, Luke 17:11-19.
Ingratitude prophesied, 2 Timothy 3:2.
See *Rudeness.*

INHABIT
Earth and other planets, Isaiah 45:18.

INHERITANCE
Abraham's possessions to Isaac, Genesis 25:5.
Birthright offered at bargain, Genesis 25:27-34.
Provision for inheritance, Genesis 38:7-11; Deuteronomy 25:5-10.
Determined by casting lots, Numbers 26:55.
Relatives concerned about intermarriage, Numbers 36:1-4.

Right of first son, Deuteronomy 21:15-17.

Inheritance and purchase, Ruth 4:6; Jeremiah 32:8.

King David's joy at seeing son become king, 1 Kings 1:47-48.

Son's inheritance of righteousness from father, 1 Kings 11:9-13.

Asking for double portion of prophet's spirit, 2 Kings 2:9.

Husband who did not provide for family, 2 Kings 4:1-7.

Ancestral property, Nehemiah 11:20.

Doing good with ill-gained wealth, Proverbs 28:8.

Neither good nor evil transmitted from father to son, Ezekiel 18:3-20.

Early request for inheritance, Luke 15:12.

Probate of will, Hebrews 9:16-17.

Esau sold birthright, Hebrews 12:16-17.

Inheritance that can never perish, 1 Peter 1:4.

See *Legacy.*

INIQUITY

Evil as in a sponge, Job 15:16.

Seeming unbalance between good and bad, Job 21:7-26.

Blatant ungodliness, Psalm 53:1-3.

Sin on a leash, Isaiah 5:18.

Isaiah's conviction of sin, Isaiah 6:5. (Note: Scripture nowhere shows Isaiah as an evil person.)

Seeming inequity in death of righteous, Isaiah 57:1-2.

Those who do not know how to blush, Jeremiah 6:15.

Suffering for great guilt, Jeremiah 30:12-14.

Injustice and bloodshed, Ezekiel 9:9.

Sins cause downfall, Hosea 14:1.

For continued sinning, certain judgment, Amos 1:3, 6, 9, 11, 13; 2:1, 4, 6. (Note the nature of sin in each of these judgments.)

Insomnia and evil plans, Micah 2:1.

Old Testament concludes with a curse, Malachi 4:6.

Overt hypocrisy, Matthew 23:28.

Cause of backsliding, Matthew 24:12.

Sins piled up to heaven, Revelation 18:4-5.

Commitment to sin or to righteousness, Romans 6:19.

See *Carnality, Depravity, Evil, Sin.*

INITIATIVE

Man who built city, Genesis 10:11-12.

Moved of heart to do God's work, Exodus 35:20-21, 25-26, 29.

Providing for underprivileged while giving incentive, Leviticus 23:22.

No rest until task accomplished, Numbers 23:24.

Urgent business, 1 Samuel 21:8.

Prompt gathering together of food, 1 Samuel 25:18.

People working with all their heart, Nehemiah 4:6.

Conscious rejection of sin, Psalm 18:23.

Initiative rewarded, Proverbs 12:11; 22:29; 24:27.

Similarity of slackness to destruction, Proverbs 18:9.

Hard work and fantasy, Proverbs 28:19.

Learn from ants, Proverbs 30:25.

Initiative in action, Ecclesiastes 9:10.

Lazy hands and leaking roof, Ecclesiastes 10:18.

Parable of Talents, Matthew 25:14-30.

Paralytic let down from roof, Luke 5:17-26.

Divine initiative in soul-winning, Luke 19:10.

Resisting temptation, Luke 22:40.

Put knowledge into action, John 13:17.

Making room in heart for acceptance of others, 2 Corinthians 7:2.

Making most of opportunities, Ephesians 5:15-16; Colossians 4:5.

Do not become lazy, Hebrews 6:11-12.

Scriptural teaching put into action, James 1:22-25.

Personal initiative in holy living, James 4:7-10.

See *Diligence.*

INJURY

Perilous activities, Ecclesiastes 10:9.

See *Wounds.*

INJUSTICE

Justice toward strangers and widows, Exodus 22:21.

Avoid injustice, Exodus 23:1-7.

Practice Golden Rule, Deuteronomy 24:17-18.

Ways of men with rights of others, Job 24:2-3.

Divine values, Proverbs 17:15.

Enforced justice, Proverbs 28:8.

Unjust laws and oppressive decrees, Isaiah 10:1-4.
Injustice rewarded, Amos 5:11-12.
Evil government to punish God's people, Habakkuk 1:1-6.
Shameless injustice, Zephaniah 3:5.
Injustice in depth, Luke 16:10; Revelation 22:11.
Hated without reason, John 15:25.
Imprisoned for conversion of fortune-teller, Acts 16:16-40.
Injustice avenged, 1 Thessalonians 4:7.
See *Inequity*.

INNOCENCE
Joseph falsely accused, Genesis 39:11-20.
Feigned guilt of Joseph's brothers, Genesis 44:1-34.
Strange sacrifice when guilty murderer cannot be found, Deuteronomy 21:1-9.
King Saul's accusation and Abimelech's innocence, 1 Samuel 22:11-15.
David's innocence in murder of Abner, 2 Samuel 3:22-37.
David's claim of righteousness and innocence, 2 Samuel 22:21-25.
Prayer for blameless life, Psalm 19:13.
Cleansed for worship, Psalm 26:6.
Condemning innocent, Proverbs 17:15.
Beauty with innocence, Song of Songs 4:7.
Pilate's claim of innocence, Matthew 27:24.
Suffering and innocence of Jesus, Luke 23:15-16.
Jesus flogged before Crucifixion, John 19:1-6.
Redemptive cleansing, Ephesians 5:26-27.
Blameless before the Lord, Revelation 14:5.
See *Guilt*.

INNOVATION
New way to Jesus, Luke 5:17-20.
New replaces old, Hebrews 8:13.

INQUEST
Inquest following murder, Deuteronomy 21:1-9.

INQUIRY ROOM
Tent for inquirers, Exodus 33:7.

INQUISITIVE
Mother-in-law's inquiry, Ruth 3:16-17.

Curiosity of angels, 1 Peter 1:12.
See *Curiosity*.

INSANITY
Seeing unpleasant sights, Deuteronomy 28:34.
David feigned madness, 1 Samuel 21:12-14.
Mentally ill understand, Isaiah 32:4.
King becomes like animal, Daniel 4:31-34.
Jesus' family thought Him insane, Mark 3:20-21. (Note v. 31.)
Accused of demon-possession, John 10:20.
See *Mental health*.

INSECT
Land free of flies, Exodus 8:21.
Besieged by locusts, Exodus 10:4; Judges 6:5.
Insects listed in Bible, Exodus 16:20; Leviticus 11:22; Deuteronomy 7:20; Judges 14:8; 1 Samuel 24:14; Psalms 78:46; 105:31; Proverbs 6:6; 30:15; Ecclesiastes 10:1; Isaiah 50:9; Joel 1:4; Amos 4:9; Matthew 23:24.
Advance platoon of hornets, Exodus 23:28; Joshua 24:12.
Clean and unclean, Leviticus 11:21-25; Deuteronomy 14:9.
Enemy like swarm of bees, Deuteronomy 1:44; Psalm 118:12.
Moth-eaten garment, Job 13:28.
Carnivorous flies, Psalm 78:45.
Ants succeed little by little, Proverbs 30:25.
Swarms of locusts, Isaiah 33:4.
Spinning spider's web, Isaiah 59:5.
Locusts who attack only people, Revelation 9:3-6.

INSECURITY
Insecurity of wicked, Psalm 37:1-2, 10.
Insecure eagle's nest, Jeremiah 49:16.
Babylon's wall leveled, Jeremiah 51:58.
Foolish trusting in oneself, Luke 12:16-21.
Insecurity of wealth, 1 Timothy 6:17.

INSENSITIVE
People like animals in times of distress, Deuteronomy 28:53-57.
As one under anesthesia, Proverbs 23:34-35.
Burning truth not understood, Isaiah 42:25.
Wealth numbs conscience, Hosea 12:8.

Witnessing miracles with hard hearts, Matthew 11:20.
Caring neither for God nor man, Luke 18:1-5.
Calloused hearts, closed ears and eyes, Acts 28:27.
Seared conscience, 1 Timothy 4:1-2.
See *Calloused, Heartless.*

INSIGHT
Donkey who saw angel, Numbers 22:23-28. (Note v. 31.)
Shrewd and innocent, Matthew 10:16.
Misunderstanding figure-of-speech, Matthew 16:5-12.
Unaware of divine purpose and presence, Luke 24:13-27.
Hard teaching, John 6:60.
Wisdom of Gamaliel, Acts 5:34-40.
Eyes of the heart, Ephesians 1:18-19.
Reward of careful reflection, 2 Timothy 2:7.
See *Perception, Sensitivity.*

INSIGNIFICANT
House of clay, Job 4:19.
Mortals as worms, Job 25:6.
Minuteness of man, Psalm 8:3-4.
Grasshopper compared to God, Isaiah 40:22.
Small town with great destiny, Micah 5:2.
Day of small things, Zechariah 4:10.
Tiny mustard seed, Matthew 13:31-32.
Illustration of human body, 1 Corinthians 12:21-25.

INSINCERITY
Pharaoh's insincere repentance, Exodus 9:27.
Worship and play, Exodus 32:6.
Doing right but not wholeheartedly, 2 Chronicles 25:2.
Backslider's call to God in time of trouble, Jeremiah 2:27.
Friends and brothers not to be trusted, Jeremiah 9:4-8.
Lacking true faith in the heart, Ezekiel 14:4.
Love like morning mist, Hosea 6:4.
Insincere fasting and repentance, Zechariah 7:1-6.
King Herod and magi, Matthew 2:7-8, 12.
Hypocrisy of Pharisees, Matthew 15:7-9; Mark 12:15-17.

Praising Jesus, then condemning Him, Matthew 21:6-11; 27:20-23.
Ego displayed by teachers of the Law, Mark 12:38-40.
See *Hypocrisy.*

INSOMNIA
Keeping awake, Nehemiah 2:11-16.
Reading at night, Esther 6:1.
Job's sleepless nights, Job 7:4.
Companion of night creatures, Job 30:29.
Frogs in bedrooms of Egypt, Psalm 105:30.
Awake at night for a purpose, Psalm 119:148.
Good sleep induced by hard day's work, Ecclesiastes 5:12.
Wandering streets at night, Song of Songs 3:1-2.
Time remaining until morning, Isaiah 21:11-12.
Troubled dreams, Daniel 2:1.
King who could not sleep, Daniel 6:16-23.

INSPIRATION
Prophecy to sound of music, 2 Kings 3:15-16.
Temple building plans given by Holy Spirit, 1 Chronicles 28:12.
Absolute dependability of God's Word, Psalm 12:6.
Dwelling on heights, Isaiah 33:16.
Many attempts to record New Testament events, Luke 1:1-4.
Guidance of Holy Spirit in attitude toward marriage, 1 Corinthians 7:40.
Paul's recognition of writings as authentic Scripture, 1 Corinthians 14:37-38.
Encouraging believer, 1 Thessalonians 2:11-12.
All Scripture God-breathed, 2 Timothy 3:16-17.
Inspired by Holy Spirit, 2 Peter 1:20-21.
Message conveyed by angel, Revelation 1:1-3.
Example of verbal inspiration in Scriptures, Revelation 1:11.
See *Creativity.*

INSTABILITY
Description of sinful Israel, 1 Kings 14:15.
Too much food and drink, Proverbs 23:20.
Spiritual vagabonds, Jeremiah 2:31.
Love like morning mist, Hosea 6:4.
Changeable Galatians, Galatians 1:6-9.

Tossed by waves, Ephesians 4:14; James 1:6.
Carried away by strange teachings, Hebrews 13:9.

INSTALLATION
Moses turned control over to Joshua, Deuteronomy 31:1-8.
Ceremony for new king, 2 Kings 9:11-13.

INSTIGATE
See *Cause, Guilt.*

INSTINCT
Birds avoid nets, Proverbs 1:17.
Preparing for cold weather, Proverbs 30:25; 31:21.
Birds know when to migrate, Jeremiah 8:7.
See *Nature.*

INSTRUCTION
Giving specific orders, Joshua 8:8.
Assigned teachers, 2 Chronicles 17:7-9.
Willingness to accept truth of wrongdoing, Job 6:24.
Important instruction for children, Psalm 78:2-8; Daniel 1:3-20.
Those who hate discipline, Proverbs 5:12-13.
Taught by the Lord, Jeremiah 16:21.
Design, measurement, and arrangements for erecting temple, Ezekiel 43:10-12.
Two-word command, Mark 2:14.
The Law a schoolmaster, Galatians 4:1.
See *Children, Learning objectives, Teaching.*

INSTRUMENT
Writing with ordinary pen, Isaiah 8:1.
Chosen like signet ring, Haggai 2:23.
God's instruments in bringing people to Christ, 1 Corinthians 3:5-9.
See *Tool.*

INSUBORDINATION
Unwilling to follow king's command to do evil, 1 Samuel 22:16-17.
Servants disobey masters, 1 Samuel 25:10.
Refusal to obey royal command, Esther 1:10-18.
See *Disobedience, Stubborn.*

INSULT
Men of Sodom and Lot's angelic visitors, Genesis 19:5.
Silent toward those who insult, 1 Samuel 10:27.
Elisha's bald head, 2 Kings 2:23-24.
Upset by criticism, Job 20:2-3.
Deriding someone's hometown, John 1:46.
Insult to Cretans, Titus 1:12.
See *Criticism, Scoff, Scorn.*

INSURANCE
Built-in safety devices, Deuteronomy 22:8.
Husband who did not provide for family, 2 Kings 4:1-7.
Eternal inheritance, 1 Peter 1:3-4.

INSURRECTION
God's command to destroy, 2 Kings 9:6-7.
King assassinated by associates, 2 Kings 12:19-20.
Killing in one political party, then another, 2 Kings 21:23-24.
Father killed by sons, 2 Chronicles 32:21.
See *Rebellion, Traitors.*

INTEGRATION
Ways of the heathen, Deuteronomy 18:9.
Dark and lovely, Song of Songs 1:5-6.
The Jews and the centurion, Acts 10:22, 28, 34-35.
See *Racism.*

INTEGRITY
Men of integrity, Exodus 18:21.
Making vow, oath, or pledge, Numbers 30:1-2.
Example of honest dealings, 1 Samuel 12:4.
Bribe refused, 2 Samuel 18:12; 1 Kings 13:8.
No need for expense accounts, 2 Kings 12:15.
Some good in Judah, 2 Chronicles 12:12.
Job's integrity, Job 27:4-6; 29:14; 31:1-40.
The Lord judges integrity, Psalm 7:8.
In-depth character, Psalms 15:1-5; 18:20; Philippians 4:8.
Practicing deceit, Psalm 101:7.
He who is generous and exercises justice, Psalm 112:5.
Mercy and truth, Proverbs 3:3-4.
Motivated by integrity, Proverbs 11:3; 20:7.
Honesty is of the Lord, Proverbs 16:11.
Wealth of honesty, Proverbs 19:1.

Honest answer like kiss, Proverbs 24:26.
Hatred of those with integrity, Proverbs 29:10; Amos 5:10.
Noble plans bring success, Isaiah 32:8.
Truth nowhere to be found, Isaiah 59:15.
Looking for one honest person in Jerusalem, Jeremiah 5:1.
Daniel's integrity in government affairs, Daniel 6:1-4.
Two kings lie to each other, Daniel 11:27.
Dishonest scales, Hosea 12:7.
Speak truth to each other, Zechariah 8:16-17.
Fullest integrity, Luke 16:10.
Jesus knew what was in men, John 2:24-25.
Always do what is right, Romans 12:17.
Importance of paying debts, Romans 13:8.
Living life worthy of calling, Ephesians 4:1.
Speak truthfully to neighbors, Ephesians 4:25.
Do not lie, Colossians 3:9-10.
Faith plus good conscience, 1 Timothy 1:19.
The God who does not lie, Titus 1:2.
Demonstrating integrity in Christian living, Titus 2:7-8.
Truth and love united, 2 John 3, 5-6.
No lie in mouths of multitude in heaven, Revelation 14:5.
Those cast into lake of fire, Revelation 21:8.
City of total integrity, Revelation 21:27.
See *Character, Honesty.*

INTELLECTUAL
Humility concerning great matters, Psalm 131:1.
Religion without reality, Proverbs 14:12.
Grecian Jews, Acts 9:29.
Profuse discussion of ideas, Acts 17:21.
Intellectuals and message of Cross, 1 Corinthians 1:18-24.
Message of wisdom to mature Christians, 1 Corinthians 2:6.
Wisdom of world, 1 Corinthians 3:18-23.
Eyes of heart, Ephesians 1:18-19.
Godless chatter and opposing ideas falsely called knowledge, 1 Timothy 6:20-21.
God cannot lie, Titus 1:2.
Lacking wisdom, ask God, James 1:5-6.
See *Knowledge, Wisdom.*

INTELLECTUAL PRIDE
Boast only about the Lord, Jeremiah 9:23-24.

Destruction of wise men of Edom, Obadiah 8.
Intellectual pride in Athens, Acts 17:16-34.
Folly of intellectual pride, 1 Corinthians 3:18-20; 8:1-2.
See *Pride, Vanity.*

INTELLIGENCE
Solomon's great wisdom, 1 Kings 4:29-34.
Wild donkey's colt, Job 11:12.
Search for wisdom and understanding, Job 28:12, 20-28.
Fear of the Lord, Psalm 111:10.
Understanding to simple, Psalm 119:130.
God's greatness beyond comprehension, Psalm 145:3.
Knowledge, rarest of jewels, Proverbs 20:15.
Those wise in their own eyes, Isaiah 5:21.
Boasting only in the Lord, Jeremiah 9:23-24.
Daniel and his friends superior to best of king's court, Daniel 1:3-20.
Gift from God, Daniel 1:17.
Daniel looked to God for knowledge, Daniel 2:14-28.
Prophecy of widespread knowledge across world, Habakkuk 2:14.
Adults like children, Matthew 11:16-17.
Greater wisdom than Solomon's, Matthew 12:42.
Folly of intellectual pride, 1 Corinthians 3:18-20.
Faith the ultimate intelligence, 1 Corinthians 3:18-23.
Eyes of heart, Ephesians 1:18-19.
Gift of understanding, 1 John 5:20.
Mind with wisdom, Revelation 17:9.
See *Mind.*

INTEMPERANCE
Wine a mocker, Proverbs 20:1.
Too much food and drink, Proverbs 23:20.
Wine sampling, Proverbs 23:29-31.
Overt alcoholism, Isaiah 5:11.
Laid low by wine, Isaiah 28:1, 7.
Social drinking, Habakkuk 2:15.
Drinking to drown troubles, Luke 21:34.
Continual lust for more, Ephesians 4:19.
See *Alcohol.*

INTENSITY
Nehemiah's total commitment, Nehemiah 5:14-16.

Path of righteous, Proverbs 4:18.
See *Concentration.*

INTENTION
Consciously doing what is right, Leviticus
22:29.
Life's highest intent, Joshua 24:15.
Hiding true intentions, 1 Samuel 16:1-5.
Act of violence, Matthew 26:51-52; Mark
14:46-47; Luke 22:49-51; John 18:10-
11. (Some have suggested Peter
intended to kill, not simply sever an
ear!)
Priority motivation, Matthew 6:33; John
4:34; Acts 20:24.
See *Motivation.*

INTERCESSION
Abraham's intercession for Sodom,
Genesis 18:20-33.
Reuben's intercession for Joseph, Genesis
37:21-22.
The young man who defended Paul, Acts
23:16-22.
Paul's appeal on behalf of Onesimus,
Philemon 10-11.
See *Mediator.*

INTEREST
Loans without interest, Exodus 22:25.
Earn no profit from brothers, Leviticus
25:36-37; Deuteronomy 23:19-20.
Lending money without interest, Psalm
15:5.
Money sharks, Proverbs 28:8.
See *Mortgage.*

INTERIOR DECORATING
Jeweled walls, Isaiah 54:12.
Palatial decor, Jeremiah 22:14.

INTERMARRIAGE
Request to marry heathen, 1 Kings 2:13-
25.
Intermarriage with heathen people, Ezra
9:1-4; 10:18-44.
Pledge to not intermarry with heathen,
Nehemiah 10:30.
Intermarriage between Jew and Greek,
Acts 16:1.
See *Alien.*

INTERMEDIARY
Looking out for welfare of people, Esther
10:3.
Speak up for those who cannot help
themselves, Proverbs 31:8-9.

INTERNSHIP
National internship, Deuteronomy 8:2.
Eagle trains fledglings to fly, Deuteronomy
32:11.
Refining process, Job 23:10; Zechariah
13:9; James 1:2-3.

INTERPRETATION
Speaking in language understood, Isaiah
36:11.
Failure of Nebuchadnezzar's wise men,
Daniel 2:1-11.
Daniel interpreted Nebuchadnezzar's
dream, Daniel 2:24-49.
Interpretation of tongues, 1 Corinthians
14:26-28.

INTERVENTION
Meddling in affairs of others, Proverbs
26:17.
Faith of friends resulted in man's healing,
Mark 2:1-5.

INTIMACY
The God who is ever near, Deuteronomy
4:7.
The Lord knew Moses face-to-face,
Deuteronomy 34:10.

INTIMIDATION
Song of ruthless made silent, Isaiah 25:5.
Needlessness of worry, Matthew 6:25-27.
Endeavoring to silence Peter and John,
Acts 4:16-20.
Activity of Saul against the church, Acts
8:3.
See *Opposition.*

INTRIGUE
Joseph and his brothers, Genesis 37:18-20.
Drama between Tamar and Judah, Genesis
38:11-26.
Leave revenge to God's timing, 1 Samuel
26:11.
Gallows for his own neck, Esther 5:11-14;
9:25.
See *Drama.*

INTRODUCTION
Prelude to history, Genesis 1:1-2.

Public relations approach, 1 Kings 1:42.
Forthright introduction to one criticized,
Job 33:1-5.
Foreword to Book of Proverbs, Proverbs
1:1-6.
Terse introduction to birth of Jesus,
Matthew 1:18.
Jesus related parable as crowd gathered,
Luke 8:4-15.
Jesus introduced Himself to three of His
disciples, John 1:35-42.
Credentials to visiting instructors, Acts
15:22-31.
Paul's wise reintroduction of Onesimus to
Colossians, Colossians 4:9. (See Phile.
10-11.)

INTROSPECTION
Inviting inner analysis, Psalm 139:23-24.
Need for self-evaluation, Romans 2:17-28.
See *Self-examination.*

INTRUDER
Aliens who succeed above local citizenry,
Deuteronomy 28:43-44.
Meddling in affairs of others, Proverbs
26:17.
See *Foreigner.*

INVENTION
Inventor of harp and flute, Genesis 4:21.
Manufacture of tools, Genesis 4:22.
Maker of musical instruments,
2 Chronicles 7:6; 29:26.
Development of new machinery,
2 Chronicles 26:15.
Schemes of men, Ecclesiastes 7:29.
Wonder on wonder, Isaiah 29:14.
Prophecy of mere imagination, Ezekiel
13:1-3.
Beyond inventive genius, 1 Corinthians
2:9.

INVENTORY
Negative and positive viewpoints,
Numbers 13:17-33.
Debt canceled every seven years,
Deuteronomy 15:1.
Making much of little, 2 Kings 4:1-7.
Finding no stock missing, Job 5:24.
Greedy for gain, Jeremiah 8:10.
Inventory of personal conduct, Haggai 1:5.
Paul's evaluation of his own ministry, Acts
20:17-38.

See *Assessment.*

INVESTIGATION
The Lord investigated situation at Sodom
and Gomorrah, Genesis 18:20-21.
Purpose of research project, 1 Kings 10:6-
7.
Glory of kings, Proverbs 25:2.
Ask for ancient paths, Jeremiah 6:16.
See *Survey.*

INVESTMENT
Owning share of king, 2 Samuel 19:43.
Giving to poor is lending to the Lord,
Proverbs 19:17.
Treasures on earth and treasures in
heaven, Matthew 6:19-21.
Purchase of sure investment, Matthew
13:44.
False economy of materialism, Mark 8:36.
Wise and unwise use of money, Luke
19:11-27.

INVIGORATE
Strength for weary, Isaiah 40:29-31.

INVISIBLE
Reality of unseen, 1 Peter 1:8-9.
Kingdom of God within you, Luke 17:20-
21.
Intangible made tangible, Hebrews 11:1-3,
6.
See *Unseen.*

INVITATION
Hezekiah's letter of invitation to once
wayward Israel, 2 Chronicles 30:6-9.
Call to reason, Isaiah 1:18.
Buy without money, Isaiah 55:1.
Seek the Lord while He may be found,
Isaiah 55:6-7.
God's great invitation to call on Him,
Jeremiah 33:3.
Come and rest, Matthew 11:28.
Rejecting wedding invitation, Matthew
22:1-14.
Follow Jesus, Mark 1:17.
Take up the cross, Mark 10:21.
Invitation to banquet, Luke 14:17.
Paul, asked to remain in Ephesus,
promised to return, Acts 18:19-21.
Those invited to wedding supper in
heaven, Revelation 19:9.
Combined ministry of Holy Spirit and

church in evangelism, Revelation 22:17.

INVOICE
Discounting the bill, Luke 16:1-8.

INVOLVEMENT
Egyptian compassion to Hebrew child, Exodus 2:1-10.
Those who do not follow wholeheartedly, Numbers 32:11.
Foolish involvement with one's neighbor, Proverbs 6:1-5.
Faith of friends resulted in a man's healing, Mark 2:1-12.
Involvement in need of others, Mark 6:35-43.
Good Samaritan, Luke 10:30-37.
Poured out like drink offering, Philippians 2:17; 2 Timothy 4:6.
Paul's concern for spiritual development of followers, Colossians 2:1-5.
See *Caring.*

IRON
Initial use, Genesis 4:22.
Iron bed, Deuteronomy 3:11.
Floating axhead, 2 Kings 6:4-7.
Ore from the earth, Job 28:2.
Iron shackles, Psalm 105:18.
Smelting various metals, Ezekiel 22:20.
Iron gate, Acts 12:10.

IRONY
A wife's biting tongue, 2 Samuel 6:20.
Elijah and Baal, 1 Kings 18:27.
Job and his accusers, Job 12:2.
Ironic declaration of "freedom," Jeremiah 34:17.
Paul's ironic evaluation of weak Christians, 1 Corinthians 4:8-18.
See *Satire.*

IRRATIONAL
Job accused of not speaking sensibly, Job 18:2.
Sick drunk, Isaiah 28:7.
Members of Jesus' own family thought Him insane, Mark 3:20-21. (Note v. 31.)
See *Insanity.*

IRRELIGIOUS
Breaking Sabbath, Exodus 31:12-17.
Generation in spiritual ignorance, Judges 2:10.

Work of the Lord in decline, 1 Samuel 3:1.
Defying message of prophet, Jeremiah 43:1-3.
Pagan beyond redemption, Jeremiah 51:9.
Disrespect for sanctuary, Ezekiel 25:1-4.
Hindered from worship by evil deeds, Hosea 5:4.
Laughing at truth spoken by Jesus, Matthew 9:23-24.
See *Apostasy, Rebellion.*

IRRESPONSIBLE
Thoughtlessly taking oath, Leviticus 5:4.
House left untended, Ecclesiastes 10:18.
Deliberately writing falsehoods, Jeremiah 8:8.
False prophets, Jeremiah 23:16-18.
Prophets who see nothing, Ezekiel 13:1-3.
Forgetting to bring necessities, Mark 8:14.
See *Careless, Lethargy.*

IRREVERENCE
Worship and play, Exodus 32:6.
Destroying blasphemer, Leviticus 24:14-16.
Immorality in sacred places, 1 Samuel 2:22.
No God, no priest, no Law, 2 Chronicles 15:3.
Insulting the Lord, 2 Chronicles 32:17.
Sin of challenging God, Isaiah 5:18-19.
Mockery of fasting, Isaiah 58:4-5.
Divine integrity questioned, Jeremiah 21:7.
Laughing at truth spoken by Jesus, Matthew 9:23-24.
Misuse of temple in Jerusalem, Matthew 21:12-13.
Temple court defiled, Revelation 11:1-2.
See *Blasphemy.*

IRRIGATION
Earth before rainfall, Genesis 2:4-6, 10.
Dispute over water rights, Genesis 26:19-22.
Irrigation unnecessary as in Egypt, Deuteronomy 11:10.
Good land but bad water, 2 Kings 2:19-22.
Hezekiah's project, 2 Chronicles 32:30.
Controlled watercourse, Proverbs 21:1.
Reservoirs for irrigation, Ecclesiastes 2:6.
Abundance of water, Isaiah 41:18-20.
Thirsty land, Isaiah 44:3; 58:11.
Well-watered garden, Jeremiah 31:12.
See *Agriculture, Water.*

IRRITATION
Thorns in side, Judges 2:3.
Giving heed to instruction, Proverbs 16:20.
Quarrelsome person, Proverbs 19:13.
See *Abrasion.*

ISLAM
First example of tension between Arabs and Israel, Genesis 21:8-10. (Note in v. 16 the near destruction of Arab race.)
Muslims look to Ishmael as their father, Genesis 21:13; 25:12-18.
Syrian king hostile to Israel, 1 Kings 11:25; 2 Kings 13:22.
First instance of Arab opposing Israel, Nehemiah 2:19-20.
Sanballat's ridicule of Jewish capability, Nehemiah 4:1-10.
Highway for Arab world, Isaiah 19:23.
Lebanon and Israel, Isaiah 35:1-2.
Fate of those who oppose Israel, Isaiah 60:12.
Libya and Arabia, Ezekiel 30:5.
Folly of *jihad,* John 16:2.

ISRAEL
Divine covenant with Abram, Genesis 15:1-5.
First instance of Arab opposing Israel, Nehemiah 2:19-20.
Sanballat's ridicule of Jewish capability, Nehemiah 4:1-10.
Promise of God to nation of Israel, Psalm 45:16.
God's command to pray for peace of Jerusalem, Psalm 122:6.
Prophecy of abundance, Isaiah 32:2.
Gathering of Jews to Israel, Isaiah 43:5-7.
Nation recipient of blessing, Isaiah 60:10-11.
Fate of those who oppose Israel, Isaiah 60:12.
Land promised to dispersed Israelites, Jeremiah 16:14-15.
Restoration of Israel as nation, Jeremiah 30:8-17; 33:23-26.
People, once scattered, regathered, Jeremiah 31:10.
Barren Israel to become fruitful, Jeremiah 32:42-44.

The Lord who will make Himself known in history, Ezekiel 20:42.
Nugget description of Jews making Israel their nation, Ezekiel 28:25.
Valley of dry bones, Ezekiel 37:1-14.
Modern Israel is developed with unwalled villages, Ezekiel 38:1–39:29.
God's promise to bless Israel, Hosea 14:4-7.
Early example of dispersal, Joel 3:6.
Permanent home and certain future for Jews, Amos 9:15.
People of Israel brought to homeland, Zephaniah 3:20.
Lesson of fig tree, which many believe depicts Jewish awakening and return to Israel, Mark 13:28-31.
Spiritual blindness of early religious leaders, Acts 5:30-33.
Paul changed audience from Jews to Gentiles, Acts 18:4-6.
Coming blessing through Israel, Romans 11:13-15.
Salvation of Israel, Romans 11:25-27.
See *Messiah.*

ITINERARY
Stages of journey recorded by Moses, Numbers 33:1-49.
Journey with the Lord's approval, Judges 18:6.
No need for expense money, Mark 6:8-11.
Itinerary of Jesus, Luke 4:42-44; 8:1; 9:6.
Places Paul needed to visit, Acts 19:21.
Paul changed itinerary to avoid conflict, Acts 20:2-3.
Paul's detailed listing of itinerary, Acts 21:1-8.
Ports visited by Paul en route to Rome, Acts 27:1-8.
Hospitality to a minister on itinerary, 1 Corinthians 16:10-11.
See *Journey, Travel.*

IVORY
Palatial splendor, 1 Kings 10:18; 22:39.
Imported luxury, 1 Kings 10:22; Ezekiel 27:6, 15.
Luxurious sleep, Amos 6:4.

J

JAIL
House arrest, Jeremiah 37:15.
Adventure in Philippian jail, Acts 16:23-34.
See *Prison.*

JEALOUSY
Negative attitude of Cain, Genesis 4:3-7.
Greed over scarcity of land, Genesis 13:5-7.
Attitude of Ishmael toward Isaac, Genesis 21:8-10.
Envy caused by wealth, Genesis 26:12-14.
Resentment of Joseph's brothers, Genesis 37:3-4.
Divine jealousy, Exodus 20:5; Deuteronomy 32:16, 21; Psalm 78:58; Isaiah 30:1-2.
Only God has the right to be jealous, Exodus 34:14.
Legal specifications for jealous husband, Numbers 5:12-31.
Jealousy of Miriam and Aaron, Numbers 12:1-9.
Sharing honors in military victory, Judges 12:1-3.
Facing competition, 1 Samuel 17:55-58.
King's jealousy of subject, 1 Samuel 18:8.
Possessiveness of those who would claim David as their king, 2 Samuel 19:43.
Saul's daughter Michal angered by David's dancing, 1 Chronicles 15:29.
Poison to soul, Job 5:2.
Furious husband, Proverbs 6:34.
Do not covet sinners, Proverbs 23:17.
Jealousy more cruel than anger, Proverbs 27:4.
Neighborhood envy, Ecclesiastes 4:4.
Jealous love, Song of Songs 8:6.
Idol of jealousy, Ezekiel 8:5.
Divine jealousy subsided, Ezekiel 16:42.
Burning with jealousy, Zechariah 8:1.
Parable of Workers in Vineyard, Matthew 20:1-16.
Jealousy within family, Luke 15:11-32.
Dissension and jealousy in church, Acts 6:1.
Rejection of Gospel caused by religious jealousy, Acts 13:45.
Religious leaders jealous of Paul's audience, Acts 13:45.
Opposition caused by jealousy, Acts 17:5.
Spiritual envy, Romans 10:19; 11:11.
Do not compare yourself with others, Galatians 6:4-5.
Envy among those who preach Christ, Philippians 1:15.
Jealousy cause of murder, 1 John 3:12.
See *Covet.*

JESUS
Bread of Life, John 6:35.
Light of the world, John 8:12.
The gate, John 10:9.
Way, truth, and life, John 14:6.
True Vine, John 15:1-7.
Jesus Christ Himself, the Word of life, 1 John 1:1-4. (See John 1:1-3.)
Our advocate with the Heavenly Father, 1 John 2:1-2 (KJV).
Unique name for Jesus, Revelation 3:14.
Rider on white horse, Revelation 19:11-16.
Totality of the Son of God, Revelation 22:13.
See *Messiah, Redeemer.*

JEWELRY
Betrothal gifts, Genesis 24:52-53.
Hindrance to righteousness, Genesis 35:2-4.
Rings on fingers, Genesis 41:42; Exodus 35:32; Esther 8:8; Luke 15:22.
Items of plunder, Exodus 3:22; 11:2; 12:35; Isaiah 3:18-23.

Jewelry removed during mourning, Exodus 33:4-6.
Given to the Lord, Exodus 35:22; Numbers 31:50-52.
Maiden and bride, Jeremiah 2:32.
Silver, gold, jewelry lose value, Ezekiel 7:19-20.
Becoming like the Lord's signet ring, Haggai 2:23.
Pearl of great value, Matthew 13:45-46.
Hairstyles and jewelry, 1 Timothy 2:9-10.
Inner beauty, 1 Peter 3:3-4.
Jewels adorning evil woman, Revelation 17:4.
See *Cosmetics, Ring.*

JOGGING
Running long race, Jeremiah 12:5.

JOKE
Folly of practical joking, Proverbs 26:18-19.
See *Humor.*

JOURNALISM
Dishonest writing, Jeremiah 8:8.
Write message plainly, Habakkuk 2:2.
News spread of miracles performed by Jesus, Matthew 9:26.
See *Literature.*

JOURNEY
Journey of discontented people, Exodus 16:1-3; 17:1-2.
Travel by divine directive, Numbers 9:23.
Destiny set for rebellious people, Numbers 14:35.
Brief listing of itinerary, Numbers 21:10-19.
Mountains turned into roads, Isaiah 49:11.
See *Itinerary.*

JOY
Enjoyment of salvation, 1 Samuel 2:1; Ezra 6:22; Psalms 13:5; 16:5-11; 20:5; 64:10; Habakkuk 3:18.
Divine attribute, 1 Samuel 2:21.
Time to rejoice and not weep, Nehemiah 8:9.
Joy of the Lord your strength, Nehemiah 8:10.
Day after day devoted to reading Scriptures, Nehemiah 8:17-18.
Spiritual joy superior to material blessing,

Psalm 4:7.
River of delight, Psalm 46:4.
True joy comes only from the Lord, Psalm 84:11.
Joy of revival, Psalm 85:6.
All fountains in the Lord, Psalm 87:6-7.
Serve the Lord with gladness, Psalm 100:1-2.
Sorrow of death brings joy to the Lord, Psalm 116:15.
Delight in Bible study, Psalm 119:24.
Joy from reading Bible, Psalm 126:5-6; Jeremiah 15:16.
Joy of salvation, Isaiah 12:2.
Universal rejoicing, Isaiah 44:23.
Nature rejoicing, Isaiah 55:12.
Weeping for joy in Israel, Jeremiah 31:9.
False joy of drunkenness, Jeremiah 51:39.
Clapping hands at fate of Nineveh, Nahum 3:19.
Jewels in crown, Zechariah 9:16.
Rewarded with joy, Matthew 25:21.
Christmas joy, Luke 2:10-11.
Joy in heaven over a soul's salvation, Luke 15:3-10.
Sharing comfort through experience of trouble, 2 Corinthians 1:3-5.
Radiant face of Moses, 2 Corinthians 3:7-8.
Oil of joy, Hebrews 1:9.
Joy in suffering, 1 Peter 4:13.

JUDGE
Righteous judgment, Genesis 18:25; Deuteronomy 1:12-17.
Spiritual quality of a judge, Exodus 18:21; Ezra 7:25.
Priests and judges work together, Deuteronomy 17:8-11.
Judge's sentencing of criminal, Deuteronomy 25:1-3.
Judging temporal and spiritual wrongs, 1 Samuel 2:25.
Dishonest courts, 1 Samuel 8:3.
Judges as servants of God, 2 Chronicles 19:5-10.
God as Judge, Ecclesiastes 3:17; Jeremiah 11:20.
See *Judgment, Justice, Litigation.*

JUDGMENT
Judgment inflicted by angels, Genesis 19:11.
Death by fire during worship, Numbers 16:35.

Mood of Old Testament justice, 2 Samuel 1:1-16.
Cause of famine, 2 Samuel 21:1.
Better fall into God's hands than hands of men, 2 Samuel 24:13-14.
Symbol of judgment and forgiveness, 1 Chronicles 21:27-30.
Self-concern for error, Job 19:4.
Let God be judge, Job 32:13.
Reward for one's deeds, Psalm 62:12.
When God withheld His judgment, Psalm 78:38.
God judges with equity, Psalm 98:8-9.
The Lord sees all, Proverbs 15:3.
Guilty and innocent, Proverbs 17:15.
Coming day of judgment, Isaiah 2:12-21.
Babylon, as prophesied, Isaiah 13:19-22.
Judgment likened to storm, Isaiah 28:2.
Those who trust in their wickedness, Isaiah 47:10-11.
Sins paid back, Isaiah 65:6.
Plight of wicked compared to fulfillment of righteous, Isaiah 65:13-14.
Destruction of wealth and security, Jeremiah 5:17.
Harvest taken away from disobedient, Jeremiah 8:13.
The Lord's mercy follows His judgment, Jeremiah 12:14-17.
Friends become enemies, Jeremiah 13:20-22.
Judgment on disobedient people, Jeremiah 15:1-2.
Peril of forsaking the Lord, Jeremiah 17:13.
Breaking potter's jar, Jeremiah 19:1-13.
Absence of joy and productive activity, Jeremiah 25:10.
Cup of God's wrath, Jeremiah 25:15-29.
Ironic declaration of "freedom," Jeremiah 34:17. (See vv. 8-22.)
Second judgment on evil king, Jeremiah 36:27-32.
Certainty of judgment, Jeremiah 37:9-10.
Multiple judgment on disobedient, Jeremiah 44:1-14.
Inevitable judgment to those who disobey God, Jeremiah 44:15-28.
Sword that cannot rest, Jeremiah 47:6-7.
The Lord judges like an enemy, Lamentations 2:2, 5.
Four kinds of judgment, Ezekiel 14:21.
Tyre, city of luxury, brought down, Ezekiel 27:1-36. (See also 28:1-19.)
Books opened, Daniel 7:10.

Certain judgment for unfaithfulness, Hosea 9:7.
Coming Day of the Lord, Joel 2:1-2.
For continued sinning, certain judgment, Amos 1:3, 6, 9, 11, 13; 2:1, 4, 6. (Note nature of sin in each of these judgments.)
Divine response to those who repent, Jonah 3:10.
The Lord slow to anger, Nahum 1:3.
Silver and gold of no value when judgment falls, Zephaniah 1:18.
God of judgment becomes God of mercy, Zechariah 8:14-15.
Old Testament concludes with curse, Malachi 4:6.
The Saviour who brought a sword, Matthew 10:34-35.
Parables concerning final judgment, Matthew 13:36-43, 47-50.
Separating sheep from goats, Matthew 25:31-33.
Jesus eager for judgment to come, Luke 12:49.
As in days of Noah, Luke 17:26-30.
Redeemer and Judge, John 5:22-23.
Graves give up both good and evil, John 5:25-26.
No condemnation without looking at facts, John 7:50-52.
Jesus came to save the world, not judge it, John 12:47.
Wisdom of Gamaliel, Acts 5:35-40.
Accusing others of sins we ourselves commit, Romans 2:1.
Each person to be judged according to his record, Romans 2:5-11.
No condemnation in Christ, Romans 8:1-2.
Only God can judge, Romans 8:33.
Certain judgment coming on earth, Romans 9:28.
Need for discipline within congregation, 1 Corinthians 5:1-13.
Importance of judging one's self, 1 Corinthians 11:28-32.
Importance of conduct on earth, 2 Corinthians 5:10.
No favoritism with God, Colossians 3:25.
Excluded forever from presence of God, 2 Thessalonians 1:9.
Those who cause difficulty among believers, Titus 3:10-11.
Penalty paid for everyone, Hebrews 2:9.
Those forbidden God's rest, Hebrews 3:11.

Like double-edged sword, Hebrews 4:12.
Nothing kept secret from God, Hebrews 4:13.
Falling into hands of living God, Hebrews 10:31.
Christ will return to reward faithful, Hebrews 10:35-38.
All must give account to God, 1 Peter 4:4-6.
Sure judgment on false teaching, 2 Peter 2:1-10.
Facing our Lord unashamed, 1 John 2:28.
Bed of suffering, Revelation 2:20-22.
Like a thief, Revelation 3:3.
Only the One who redeemed is qualified to judge, Revelation 5:1-9.
Four horsemen, Revelation 6:1-8.
Earth shaken by great earthquake, Revelation 6:10-17.
Sounding forth cry of doom, Revelation 8:13.
Peril to those not having seal of God on foreheads, Revelation 9:4.
Judgment and rewards, Revelation 11:18.
Conclusion of God's wrath, Revelation 15:1.
Beverage of judgment, Revelation 16:5-6.
Agony of those who refuse to repent, Revelation 16:10-11.
Binding of Satan, Revelation 20:1-3.
Satan, false prophet, and those not in Book of Life, Revelation 20:7-15.
Cast into lake of fire, Revelation 20:10; 21:8.
When the die is cast, Revelation 22:11.
Reward for what one has done, Revelation 22:12.
See *Condemnation.*

JURY
Ten man jury of elders, Ruth 4:1-4.
Infamous "trial" of Jesus, Matthew 27:11-26; Mark 15:1-15; Luke 23:1-25; John 18:28-40.

JUSTICE
Mood of Old Testament justice, 2 Samuel 1:1-16.
David saw he should be punished, not his followers, 2 Samuel 24:12-17.
King Jehoash did not assassinate sons for

murder committed by fathers, 2 Kings 14:5-6.
Haman hung on gallows prepared for Mordecai, Esther 7:1-10.
God will judge with equity, Psalm 98:8-9.
The Lord defends the poor, Proverbs 22:22-23.
Those who convict the guilty, Proverbs 24:24-25.
Fate of good and evil, Isaiah 65:13-14.
Disputing mercy and justice of God's ways, Ezekiel 33:10-20.
Books opened, Daniel 7:10.
Unfairness in condemning Jesus, John 7:50-52.
Ultimate end for Judas, Acts 1:18-20.
Case against Paul, Acts 23:23-30.
God judges impartially, 1 Peter 1:17.
Awesome judgment of God on evil, Revelation 16:5-7.
See *Judge, Judgment, Litigation.*

JUSTIFICATION
Faith credited to righteousness, Genesis 15:6.
Mortal righteousness before God, Job 2:9; 25:4.
The Lord vindicated beleaguered Job, Job 42:7-10.
No one righteous, Psalm 143:2.
One who made justification possible, Isaiah 53:4-6.
The One who justifies, Jeremiah 23:6.
Mode of justification, John 5:24; Acts 13:39; Romans 1:16-17.
Faith as synonym for righteousness, Romans 4:5-25.
Justification by faith, Romans 5:1; Galatians 2:16; 3:24.
See *Redemption.*

JUVENILE DELINQUENT
Old Testament procedure with juvenile delinquent, Deuteronomy 21:18-21.
David's grief over death of Absalom, 2 Samuel 18:19-33.
Delinquent teenager became king, 2 Kings 24:8-9.
Peril to those who cause little ones to sin, Luke 17:1-2.
Evil desires of youth, 2 Timothy 2:22.

K

KIDNAPPING
Kidnap and rescue of Lot, Genesis 14:12-16.
Capital punishment imposed, Exodus 21:16; Deuteronomy 24:7.
Abduction of girls of Shiloh, Judges 21:15-23.
David's family kidnapped from Ziklag, 1 Samuel 30:3-5.

KINDLING
Twigs gathered for fires, Isaiah 27:11.
Twigs set ablaze, Isaiah 64:1-2.
See *Fire.*

KINDNESS
Returning good for evil, Genesis 50:15-21.
Kindness to man and daughters, Exodus 2:16-21.
Kindness to strangers, Leviticus 19:34.
Reward for act of kindness, 1 Samuel 30:11-18.
Kindness of pagan king, 2 Kings 25:27-30.
Outreach to others, Proverbs 14:21.
Ebed-Melech rewarded for kindness to Jeremiah, Jeremiah 38:7-13; 39:15-18.
Name with evil meaning but king who did good deeds, Jeremiah 52:31-34.
Joseph did not want to make Mary subject of public disgrace, Matthew 1:19.
Kindness as spiritual service, Matthew 25:34-36; Luke 6:34-35.
Kindness in action, Romans 12:10, 15.
Showing love to those who cause grief, 2 Corinthians 2:5-11.
Christian lifestyle, Ephesians 4:32; Colossians 3:12; 2 Peter 2:5-7.
See *Benevolence, Charity, Philanthropy.*

KINGDOM
Reign of Xerxes from India to Nile, Esther 1:1.
Purpose of God's eternal reign, Psalm 9:7-8.
Coming kingdom of God, Daniel 2:44; Revelation 17:14.
Not of this world, John 18:36.

KISS
First recorded kiss involved deceit, Genesis 27:22-27.
Emotional kiss, Genesis 29:11; 45:15.
Man kissing man, Exodus 18:7; 1 Samuel 20:41; 2 Samuel 14:33.
Parting kiss, Ruth 1:14.
Kiss of death, 2 Samuel 20:9-10.
Departure from parents, 1 Kings 19:20.
Taste of bridal lips, Song of Songs 4:11.
Betraying kiss, Matthew 26:48-49; Luke 22:47-48.
Kiss of contrition, Luke 7:38.
Farewell kiss, Acts 20:37-38.
Holy kiss, Romans 16:16.
See *Affection.*

KITCHEN
Meat cooked in sacred place, Exodus 29:31.
Ancient dishwashing, 2 Kings 21:13.
Cooking pots in the Lord's house, Zechariah 14:20-21.

KNEELING
Royal humility before the Lord, 1 Kings 8:54; 2 Chronicles 6:13.
Kneeling in self-abasement, Ezra 9:5.
Humility in the Lord's presence, Psalm 95:6.
Every knee will bow, Isaiah 45:23; Romans 14:11.
Courageous prayer, Daniel 6:10.
Divine example, Luke 22:41.

Martyr's posture, Acts 7:59-60.
Kneeling together, Acts 20:36.
Prayer meeting on beach, Acts 21:5.
See *Genuflect.*

KNOWLEDGE
Innate knowledge, Genesis 2:9, 17.
Inception of secular knowledge, Genesis 3:5-6, 22-23.
Holistic knowledge, Exodus 23:9; John 9:25; 2 Corinthians 1:3-4.
Secret things belong to God, Deuteronomy 29:29.

Source of knowledge and wisdom, Proverbs 2:3-5.
Divine performance, Proverbs 3:19-20.
Quest for knowledge, Proverbs 15:14.
Gift from God, Daniel 1:17.
Knowledge increased, Daniel 12:4.
Unable to comprehend information, Luke 9:44-45.
Putting knowledge into action, John 13:17.
Coming fullness, 1 Corinthians 13:9-12.
Knowing the Lord, Philippians 3:8.
See *Education, Teaching.*

L

LABOR
Task of producing food, Genesis 3:17-19.
People more valuable than material things, Genesis 14:21.
Women employed, Genesis 29:9.
Attitude of management toward labor, Exodus 5:2-5.
Day of rest, Exodus 20:9-11.
Honest pay for honest work, Leviticus 19:13; Luke 10:7.
Earnings from prostitution unacceptable as gift to God, Deuteronomy 23:18.
Wages paid when due, Deuteronomy 24:14-15.
Prayer for those who labor, Deuteronomy 33:11.
Woodcutters and water carriers, Joshua 9:26-27.
Labor unrest incited, Ezra 4:1-6.
Working from morning to night, Nehemiah 4:21.
Blessing of hard work, Proverbs 14:23.
Meaningless toil, Ecclesiastes 4:8.
Hard work brings sound sleep, Ecclesiastes 5:12.
Doing what you do with all your might, Ecclesiastes 9:10.
Using foreign workers, Isaiah 60:10.
Unjust treatment of laborers, Jeremiah 22:13.
Concern of centurion for servant, Matthew 8:5-13.
Students and servants beneath teachers and masters, Matthew 10:24.
Only a carpenter's Son, Matthew 13:55; Mark 6:1-3.
Labor relations, Matthew 20:9-16; 21:33-41.
Good service rewarded, Luke 12:35-40.
Paul the tentmaker, Acts 18:3.
Trade unions, Acts 19:23-27.

Wages an obligation, not a gift, Romans 4:4.
Fruit of labor, 1 Corinthians 9:7.
Aim for perfection, 2 Corinthians 13:10.
Working with one's hands, Ephesians 4:28.
Doing good work as unto the Lord, Ephesians 6:5-8.
Slave and masters, Ephesians 6:9; Colossians 3:22-25; 4:1.
Paul worked to support ministry, 2 Thessalonians 3:6-10.
Slaves subject to masters, 1 Timothy 6:1-2; Titus 2:9-10.
Dignity of labor, Titus 3:14.
Slave who became brother, Philemon 8-21.
Work before rest, Hebrews 4:11.
Failing to pay workman's wages, James 5:4.
See *Employment, Wages.*

LAITY
Those assigned as gatekeepers, 1 Chronicles 9:22-27.
Amos the shepherd, Amos 1:1.
Ministry of aged widow, Luke 2:36-38.
Many at Antioch taught and preached, Acts 15:35.
City director of public works, Romans 16:23.
Paul worked to support ministry, 2 Thessalonians 3:6-10.
Priesthood for believers, 1 Peter 2:5.

LAMB
See *Sheep, Shepherd.*

LAMPS
Miracle light, Genesis 15:17.
Night light, Exodus 27:20-21; Leviticus 24:2-4.
Lamp of wicked put out, Job 18:6; 21:17.

Keep lamp burning, Psalm 18:28.
Lamp of the Lord, Proverbs 20:27.
Lamp not hidden, Matthew 5:15.
Profuse use of lamps at Troas, Acts 20:8.
See *Illumination, Light.*

LAND
Original proprietor, Genesis 13:14-17.
Gift of land for burial, Genesis 23:1-6.
Widow's rights, Ruth 4:3-9.
Mortgaging land to buy food, Nehemiah
 5:3.
Misappropriated product, Ecclesiastes 5:9.
Rented vineyard, Luke 20:9-16.
See *Property.*

LAND REFORM
Distribution of land, Numbers 26:53-56.

LANGUAGE
Language confounded, Genesis 11:5-9.
Aramaic used instead of Hebrew, Isaiah
 36:11.
The Lord's use of literary device
 concerning freedom, Jeremiah 34:17.
Multilingual information, John 19:20.
Divine linguistics, Acts 2:8.
Effect of speaking in people's language,
 Acts 22:2.
See *Linguistics.*

LARCENY
See *Robbery, Stealing, Thieves.*

LARGE
Army of locusts, Joel 2:1-9.

LASCIVIOUSNESS
Perils to consider, Proverbs 5:3-13.
Lure of evil, Proverbs 7:6-27.
Overt perversion, Romans 1:27;
 1 Corinthians 5:1.
Clear warning of Scripture, 1 Corinthians
 6:9-18.
Disciplined body, 1 Corinthians 9:27;
 Colossians 3:5.
Unrepentant impurity, 2 Corinthians
 12:21.
Lost sensitivity, Ephesians 4:19.
Sodom and Gomorrah, Jude 7.
See *Debauchery, Immorality, Lust.*

LAUD
Avoiding partiality and flattery, Job 31:21-

22.
Jesus' evaluation of John the Baptist,
 Matthew 11:11-14.
Complimenting those who had been
 previously rebuked, 2 Corinthians 7:14.

LAUGHTER
When laughter is out of place, Genesis
 18:10-15.
Laughter with an aching heart, Proverbs
 14:13.
Meaningless laughter, Ecclesiastes 2:2.
Sorrow better than laughter, Ecclesiastes
 7:3.
Laughter of fools, Ecclesiastes 7:6.
Scornful laughter, Ezekiel 25:1-4.
Laughter today, tears tomorrow, Luke 6:25;
 James 4:9.
See *Humor.*

LAW
Respect to church and court,
 Deuteronomy 17:12.
Priests as judges, Ezekiel 44:24.
Law points to Christ, Galatians 3:23-25;
 Hebrews 10:1.

LAWYER
Avoid hasty litigation, Proverbs 25:8;
 Matthew 5:25.
Carnal lawyers, Luke 10:25; 11:46.
Lawyers consulted to impugn Jesus, Luke
 14:3.
Christian versus Christian, 1 Corinthians
 6:1.
Zenas the lawyer, Titus 3:13.
See *Litigation.*

LAZINESS
Too much sleep, Proverbs 6:10-11; 20:13;
 24:33.
Blessing of hard work, Proverbs 14:23.
Similarity of slackness to destruction,
 Proverbs 18:9.
Those who do nothing, Isaiah 30:7.
Lax in the Lord's work, Jeremiah 48:10.
Disciples sleeping while Jesus prayed,
 Mark 14:32-41.
Those who are busybodies,
 2 Thessalonians 3:11-12.
See *Lethargy.*

LEADERSHIP
Authority of Creator's command, Genesis

Qualifications of Christ as Saviour and King, Colossians 1:15-20.
Paul considered himself servant to church, Colossians 1:24-26.
Paul's relentless effort on behalf of his followers, Colossians 1:28-29.
Christ as Head over all, Colossians 2:9-10.
Paul's use of names of followers, Colossians 4:7-17.
Example of Paul's leadership, 1 Thessalonians 2:1-16.
Desire to be overseer, 1 Timothy 3:1.
Communication in person and by writing, 1 Timothy 3:14-15.
Servant and apostle, Titus 1:1.
Paul's followers given responsibility for their own affairs, Titus 1:5.
Credentials of elder, Titus 1:6-9.
Leadership with authority, Titus 2:15.
Request instead of command, Philemon 8-10.
High priest selected from among people, Hebrews 5:1.
Gentleness as mark of good leadership, Hebrews 5:2-3.
Leaders who are example, Hebrews 13:7.
Submit to authority, Hebrews 13:17.
If you lack wisdom, ask God, James 1:5-6.
Exercising wisdom that comes from heaven, James 3:17-18.
Joy of good report about followers, 3 John 3-4.
Wrong kind of authority in congregation, 3 John 9-10.
Delegation of satanic authority, Revelation 13:2.
Temporary authority of beast, Revelation 13:5.
Role of demons and their influence over world leaders, Revelation 16:13-14.
One-hour reign of 10 kings, Revelation 17:12.
See *Administration.*

LEARNING
Eagle training young to fly, Deuteronomy 32:11.
God-given ability to understand Scripture, Psalm 119:125.
Eye and ear never satisfied, Ecclesiastes 1:8.
The Lord guides and corrects those who seek Him, Jeremiah 10:23-24.
God-given intelligence, Daniel 1:17.

Fluent and intelligent, Acts 7:22.
Sharing together insights into Scriptures, Acts 18:24-26.
Trained under famous teacher, Acts 22:3.
Pointless quarreling over words, 2 Timothy 2:14.
See *Students, Teaching.*

LEARNING OBJECTIVES
The Lord's demands are within reach, Deuteronomy 30:11.
Purpose of research project, 1 Kings 10:6-7.
Stated learning objectives of Book of Proverbs, Proverbs 1:1-6.
Objective of divine instruction understood, Isaiah 2:3; 54:13.
Deliberately writing falsehoods concerning the Law, Jeremiah 8:8.
Daughters taught how to wail, Jeremiah 9:20.
Training for Daniel and young friends, Daniel 1:3-4.
Communicating God's message to children, Joel 1:1-3.
Like teacher, like student, Luke 6:40.
Good teaching put into action, John 13:17.
Teaching the most excellent way, 1 Corinthians 12:31.
Making joy complete, 1 John 1:1-4.

LEATHER
Rejected hide, Exodus 29:14.
Retained by priest, Leviticus 7:8.
Leather belt, 2 Kings 1:8; Mark 1:6.
Simon the tanner, Acts 10:6.

LEAVEN
Procedure for making bread, Exodus 12:34.
Unleavened bread of necessity, Exodus 12:39.
Suitable for offering to the Lord, Leviticus 7:13.
No yeast with meat, Leviticus 10:12.
Boasting about bread, Amos 4:5.
Leaven as a type of sin, 1 Corinthians 5:6-8.
See *Fermentation.*

LECHEROUS
Perverted justice, 1 Samuel 8:3.
Premeditated lechery, Proverbs 1:10-13.
Unrequited appetites, Isaiah 56:11.

Greedy for gain, Jeremiah 8:10.
Hatching unlaid eggs, Jeremiah 17:11.
Trampling on others, Amos 2:7.
Cheating and polluting, Amos 8:5-6.
Lecherous piety, Micah 3:11.
Greed of Judas, Matthew 26:15-16.
Misused slave girl, Acts 16:19.
Some pay and others only receive,
    2 Corinthians 11:7-8.
See *Greed, Selfishness.*

LEGACY
Inheritance of a spirit, 2 Kings 2:9-10.
Ask for ancient paths, Jeremiah 6:16.
Communicating God's message to
    children, Joel 1:1-3.
Probate of a will, Hebrews 9:16-17.
See *Inheritance.*

LEGAL
Loss of family records, Nehemiah 7:64.
See *Lawyer.*

LEGALISM
Circumcision at advanced age, Genesis
    17:10-27.
Abstaining from both wine and fruit of
    grape, Numbers 6:2-4.
Gathering wood on Sabbath, Numbers
    15:32-36.
Ultimate in demands for obeying Law,
    Joshua 1:18.
Good laws and regulations, Nehemiah
    9:13.
Preventing merchandising on Sabbath,
    Nehemiah 13:15-19.
Profusion of rules, Isaiah 28:10.
Taking the Bible as legalistic, Isaiah 28:13.
Worship based on rules, Isaiah 29:13.
Illustration of religious works involved in
    idolatry, Isaiah 46:1.
Digging cisterns, Jeremiah 2:13.
Pharisees criticized Jesus for picking grain
    on Sabbath, Matthew 12:1-8; Mark 2:23-
    27; Luke 6:1-5.
Not what goes into mouth, but what comes
    out, Matthew 15:10-20; Mark 7:15-23.
Fullest measure of the Law, Matthew
    23:23.
Those who fast while others do not, Mark
    2:18-20.
Rich young man who kept the Law, Mark
    10:17-27.
Fulfilling requirements of the Law, Luke

2:39.
Legalism versus Christian virtue, Luke
    10:25-37.
Burden of legality, Luke 11:45-46.
Spiritual growth hindered, Luke 11:52.
Jesus carefully watched by Pharisees, Luke
    14:1.
Arguing over ceremonial washing, John
    3:25.
Serving God seven days a week, John 5:16-
    17.
Those who professed to keep the Law,
    John 7:19.
Peter's vision of clean and unclean, Acts
    10:9-16; 11:4-10.
Deeper meaning of deliverance from
    legalism, Acts 10:24-28.
Effort to bring Old Testament doctrine into
    New Testament experience, Acts 15:1-
    11.
Conversion of ruler of synagogue, Acts
    18:8.
Paul's preaching contrary to law, Acts
    18:13.
Paul urged to appease legalists, Acts 21:17-
    26.
Case against Paul, Acts 23:23-30.
Those circumcised who do not keep the
    Law, Romans 2:25-27.
Faith upholds the Law, Romans 3:31.
Faith of Abraham, Romans 4:1-3.
The Law aroused sinful passions, Romans
    7:5.
Purpose of the Law in revealing sin,
    Romans 7:7-12, 14.
Conflict between faith and works, Romans
    9:30-33.
Trying to establish one's own
    righteousness, Romans 10:3.
No food unclean, Romans 14:14.
Liberty without license, 1 Corinthians 6:12.
Legalism versus courtesy, 1 Corinthians
    10:27-30.
Letter kills but Spirit gives life,
    2 Corinthians 3:6.
Avoid being stumbling block,
    2 Corinthians 6:3.
Paul's avoidance of legality, Galatians 2:3,
    11-21.
Difference between faith and works,
    Galatians 3:2-5.
Law points to Christ, Galatians 3:23-25.
Paul's emphasis on folly of legalism,
    Galatians 5:12.

Salvation by faith, not works, Ephesians
2:8-9.
Paul had reason for confidence in flesh,
Philippians 3:2-11.
Let not others judge, Colossians 2:16.
Dead to principles of this world, Colossians
2:20-23.
Handling conflict in church with firmness
and love, 1 Timothy 1:3-7.
Proper understanding of Law, 1 Timothy
1:8-11.
Theology of demons, 1 Timothy 4:1-4.
Talkers and deceivers, Titus 1:10-14.
Avoid foolish arguments about Law, Titus
3:9.
Salvation not possible through Law,
Hebrews 7:11.
Law makes nothing perfect, Hebrews 7:18-
19.
Need for New Covenant, Hebrews 8:7.
Regulations for worship, Hebrews 9:1.
Role of Law in pointing to coming
perfection in Christ, Hebrews 10:1.
Physical act in worship cannot bring
spiritual result, Hebrews 10:2-4.
Legalism of old, liberty of new, Hebrews
12:18-24.
Not redeemed with silver and gold, 1 Peter
1:18-19.
See *Work (Spiritual)*.

LEISURE
Leisure leads to lust, 2 Samuel 11:1-5.
No time to rest, Mark 6:31.

LEPROSY
Enforced isolation, Leviticus 13:4;
Numbers 5:1-3.
Suddenly leprous, Numbers 12:10.
Religious therapy for leprosy,
Deuteronomy 24:8; Matthew 8:2-4.
Experience and healing of Naaman,
2 Kings 5:1-14.
King afflicted, 2 Chronicles 26:19, 21.
Ten healed, 1 expressed gratitude, Luke
17:12-19.

LESBIANS
Women having lust for each other,
Romans 1:26.
See *Homosexual.*

LETHARGY
Those who lag behind, Deuteronomy

25:17-19.
Those who do nothing, Isaiah 30:7.
Complacent women, Isaiah 32:9.
Slumbering Jonah, Jonah 1:5-6.
Those who said it was not time to rebuild
temple, Haggai 1:3-4.
Slumbering disciples in Gethsemane,
Matthew 26:40-45.
Those who sleep during worship hour,
Mark 14:37-38.
Wake up from slumber, Romans 13:11.

LETTER-WRITING
Letter with murderous motive, 2 Samuel
11:14.
Letter to wrong address, 2 Kings 5:1-8.
Placing disturbing letter before the Lord,
2 Kings 19:14-19.
Letters for safe conduct, Nehemiah 2:7-9.
Unsealed open letter, Nehemiah 6:1-13.
Letter of defense for Paul, Acts 23:23-34.
Our lives communicate Christ's message,
2 Corinthians 3:1-3.
Beautiful letter on behalf of converted
slave, Philemon 1-25.
See *Correspondence*.

LEWDNESS
See *Depravity, Immorality, Nudity*.

LIABILITY
Liability for treacherous animal, Exodus
21:28-32.
Cities of refuge, Numbers 35:6-15.
Need for two or three witnesses,
Deuteronomy 19:15.
See *Litigation*.

LIBERAL ARTS
Solomon's liberal arts education, 1 Kings
4:29-34.
Thorough knowledge, 1 Kings 10:1-9.
Variety of subjects learned, Daniel 1:3-4.
See *College, Education*.

LIBERALISM
Wayward community, Deuteronomy
13:12-18.
Detecting words of false prophet,
Deuteronomy 18:21-22.
Book of Law lost in temple, 2 Chronicles
34:14-15.
Difference between man's way and right
way, Proverbs 14:12; 16:25.

People ask for pleasant sermons, Isaiah 30:10.

God overthrows learning of wise, Isaiah 44:25.

People love dishonest prophets and priests, Jeremiah 5:31; 6:13.

Beware of deceptive words, Jeremiah 7:4-8.

Wrong interpretation of Scripture, Jeremiah 8:8.

Error of preaching what God does not promise, Jeremiah 14:11-16.

Wicked priests who persecuted Jeremiah, Jeremiah 20:1-2.

Ministration of evil prophets, Jeremiah 23:10-14.

Words of man and words of God, Jeremiah 23:16-18.

Prophets who proclaimed lies, Jeremiah 27:14-15; Ezekiel 22:28.

Lost sheep led astray by false shepherds, Jeremiah 50:6; Micah 3:5-7.

Those who speak out of their own imagination, Ezekiel 13:2-16.

Those who recognize the Lord and Molech, Zephaniah 1:5.

Arrogant prophets and profane priests, Zephaniah 3:4.

Priests who gave false teaching, Malachi 2:7-9.

Do not make acts of charity public, Matthew 6:1-4.

Those who simply say "Lord, Lord," Matthew 7:21-23.

Blind leaders of blind, Matthew 15:14; Luke 6:39.

Missing real purpose of worship, Matthew 23:23-24.

Those who tried to prevent resurrection of Jesus, Matthew 27:62-66. (See also 28:11-15.)

Message taught by men instead of by God, Mark 7:6-9.

Persecuted for proclaiming Resurrection, Acts 4:1-4.

Modified use of the name of Jesus, Acts 19:13.

God's lavished grace, Ephesians 1:7-8.

Role of pride in false teaching, 1 Timothy 6:3-5.

Godless chatter and opposing ideas, 1 Timothy 6:20-21.

Only a form of godliness, 2 Timothy 3:5.

Those who deceive others are themselves deceived, 2 Timothy 3:13.

Those who do not want sound doctrine, 2 Timothy 4:3-4.

See *Apostasy, Cult, Modernism, Syncretism.*

LIBERTY

King imprisoned and set free, 2 Kings 24:15; 25:27-29.

Greatest freedom, Psalm 119:45.

Proclaim freedom, Isaiah 61:1.

Conditional freedom, Jeremiah 34:8-11.

Truth sets us free, John 8:31-32, 36.

The deeper meaning of deliverance from legalism, Acts 10:24-28.

Peter's vision of clean and unclean, Acts 10:9-16; 11:4-10.

Liberty no excuse for sin, Romans 6:1-2.

Freedom from mastery of sin, Romans 6:14.

Once slaves to sin, now slaves to righteousness, Romans 6:18.

Christ's death and resurrection set us free from legality, Romans 7:1-6.

Liberty without license, 1 Corinthians 6:12.

Exercise of liberty in eating and drinking, 1 Corinthians 8:7-13.

Unmuzzled ox, 1 Corinthians 9:9-14.

Freedom of believer in matters of conduct, 1 Corinthians 10:23-33.

Freedom in the Spirit of the Lord, 2 Corinthians 3:17.

From Law to grace, Galatians 4:1-7. (See chap. 3.)

Called to be free, Galatians 5:13.

Filled with knowledge of God's will, Colossians 1:9-12.

Rescued from dominion of darkness, Colossians 1:13-14.

Word of God not chained, 2 Timothy 2:9.

Legalism of old, liberty of new, Hebrews 12:18-24.

Timothy released from prison, Hebrews 13:23.

The law that gives freedom, James 2:12-13.

Misuse of liberty, 1 Peter 2:16.

Those who misuse Christian liberty, Jude 4.

See *Freedom.*

LICENSE

Example of carrying rules too far, Mark 2:23-27.

Liberty without license, 1 Corinthians 6:12.

LICENTIOUS
Wiles and treachery, Genesis 39:6-18.
Playing with fire, Proverbs 6:27-29.
Haughty women, Isaiah 3:16.
Adultery committed in profusion,
Jeremiah 3:6.
Lust and promiscuity of two sisters, Ezekiel
23:1-49.
Continual lust for more, Ephesians 4:19.
See *Adultery, Immorality, Lasciviousness.*

LIE
David used falsehood to protect his life,
1 Samuel 20:5-7.
Condemned by one's own words, Job 15:6.
Punishment for false witness, Proverbs
19:5.
Prophets who proclaimed lies, Jeremiah
27:14-15.
Jeremiah gave initially positive response to
false prophecy, Jeremiah 28:1-17. (Note
vv. 5-9.)
Jeremiah commanded to lie by King
Zedekiah, Jeremiah 38:24-27.
Believing lie, Jeremiah 43:1-7.
Two kings lie to each other, Daniel 11:27.
Tongues that speak deceitfully, Micah 6:12.
False witness against Jesus, Mark 14:53-59.
See *Deceit.*

LIFE
Life as pilgrimage, Genesis 47:9.
Distinction between animal life and human
life, Leviticus 24:21.
Value established by person's age,
Leviticus 27:1-8.
Quick passing of our days, Job 9:25-26.
Negative view toward meaning of life, Job
14:1-2.
Length of life determined, Job 14:5.
Brevity of life, Job 16:22.
Quick passing of lifetime, Psalms 39:4-6;
89:47; 90:1-6, 10, 12.
Experiencing divine wonders before death,
Psalm 88:10-12.
Living, not dead, praise the Lord, Psalm
115:17.
Motivation for praising God through all of
life, Psalms 119:175; 150:6.
Fragility of existence, Psalm 144:3-4.
Chasing wind, Ecclesiastes 1:17-18.
Time for everything, Ecclesiastes 3:1-8.
Dying before one's time, Ecclesiastes 7:17.
Sweetness of life, Ecclesiastes 9:4.

Enjoy life but with reservation, Ecclesiastes
11:8.
Death in early years of life, Isaiah 38:10.
Grave cannot praise God, Isaiah 38:18.
Earth and other planets, Isaiah 45:18.
Lamenting fact of one's birth, Jeremiah
15:10.
Those who should live die, and those who
should die live, Ezekiel 13:19.
Prophesy to breath, Ezekiel 37:9.
True immortality, John 8:51.
Building on good foundation,
1 Corinthians 3:10-15.
Rapid deterioration of human body,
2 Corinthians 4:16-18.
Flowers and grass wither, 1 Peter 1:24-25.
Body but a tent, 2 Peter 1:13.
See *Longevity, Mortality, Old age.*

LIFESTYLE
What God asks of us, Deuteronomy 10:12-
13.
Citizens of darkness, Job 24:13-17.
Walk of believer in contrast to unbeliever,
Psalm 1:1-6.
The way of the righteous, Psalm 15:1-3.
Path of righteous and way of wicked,
Proverbs 4:18-19.
Recommended lifestyle, Ecclesiastes 8:15.
Description of righteous man, Ezekiel
18:5-9.
Practice what you preach, Ezekiel 33:31.
Walking in ways of the Lord, Hosea 14:9.
Amos the shepherd, Amos 1:1.
Ideal lifestyle, Micah 6:8.
Guidelines for holy and purposeful
ministries, Luke 6:12-49.
Seeking pleasure from those things which
cause spiritual death, Romans 6:21.
Christian lifestyle, Romans 12:9-21; 13:12-
14; Ephesians 4:1-3.
Life characterized by love, 1 Corinthians
13:1-13.
Peter and Paul face-to-face, Galatians 2:11-
21.
Fruit of the Spirit, Galatians 5:22-23.
Living life worthy of calling, Ephesians 4:1-
2.
New lifestyle in Christ, Ephesians 4:22-24.
Imitators of God expressing love to others,
Ephesians 5:1-2.
Enemies of the cross, Philippians 3:18-21.
Attitude of mind dictates conduct in life,
Philippians 4:8-9.

Filled with knowledge of God's will,
Colossians 1:9-12.
Lifestyle of those risen with Christ,
Colossians 3:1-17.
Prepared for return of Christ,
1 Thessalonians 3:13.
Motivated to truly Christian lifestyle,
1 Thessalonians 4:11-12.
Faith plus good conscience, 1 Timothy
1:19.
Young Christians can set example,
1 Timothy 4:12.
Conduct and attitudes in last days,
2 Timothy 3:1-5.
Marks of Christian lifestyle, Titus 3:1-2.
Enoch pleased God, Hebrews 11:5.
Instructions for living Christian life,
Hebrews 13:1-9.
Living by Scriptures, James 2:8-10.
Demonstration of true faith, James 3:13.
Attributes of mature Christian life, 2 Peter
1:5-9.
Live for what is eternal, 2 Peter 3:11-14.
Living by truth, 1 John 1:9-10.
Doing what is right, 1 John 2:29.
Love results from obedience to Scripture,
2 John 6.
Evil conduct as negative witness, Jude 7.
See *Conduct, Frame of reference.*

LIGHT
Strength of rising sun, Judges 5:31.
Light as source of audible sound, Job 38:7;
Psalm 19:2-4.
Divine light for mortals, Psalm 27:1; John
8:12.
Light of Scriptures, Psalm 119:105.
One who lights deepest darkness, Isaiah
9:2.
Abundance of light, Isaiah 30:26.
No need for sun and moon, Isaiah 60:19-
20.
Believers as light, Matthew 5:14;
Philippians 2:15.
Parable of Ten Virgins, Matthew 25:1-13.
Light to be displayed, not hidden, Mark
4:21-22.
Follow light, avoid darkness, John 8:12.
Profuse use of lamps at Troas, Acts 20:8.
Light makes everything visible, Ephesians
5:14.
Rescued from dominion of darkness,
Colossians 1:13-14.
Danger of seeing light but walking in

darkness, 2 Peter 2:21.
Emphasis to former command, 1 John 2:7-
8.
Earth illuminated by angelic splendor,
Revelation 18:1.

LIGHTNING
Mountain drama, Exodus 19:16; 20:18.
Enemy dispersed, 2 Samuel 22:15; Psalm
18:14.
Beyond mortal authority, Job 38:35.
Livestock struck by lightning, Psalm 78:48.
Luminous stabs, Psalm 97:4.
Lightning as weapon of war, Psalm 144:6.
Speed of light, Ezekiel 1:13-14.
Likened to Second Coming, Matthew
24:27.

LIKE-MINDED
Like idol, like follower, Psalm 135:15-18.
Two in agreement, Amos 3:3.
Like teacher, like student, Luke 6:40.
Thinking as Jesus thought, Philippians 2:5-
8.

LIKENESS
See *Profile, Similarity.*

LIMITATION
Testing of divine patience, Numbers 14:18.
Naaman's conditional greatness, 2 Kings
5:1.
Evaluating military logistics, Luke 14:31-
32.

LINEAGE
No son to carry on Absalom's name,
2 Samuel 18:18.
Protection for future king, 2 Kings 11:1-3.
Zephaniah recorded lineage, Zephaniah
1:1.

LINEN
Royal cloth, Genesis 41:42.
Weaving with other fabrics forbidden,
Leviticus 19:19; Deuteronomy 22:11.
Bed sheets, Proverbs 7:16.
Aramean product, Ezekiel 27:16.
Burial cloth for Jesus, Mark 15:46; John
20:5.

LINGUISTICS
One common speech, Genesis 11:1.
Aramaic instead of Hebrew, Isaiah 36:11.

Those of strange language, Jeremiah 5:15.
Those unwilling and those willing to listen,
Ezekiel 3:4-6.
Language and literature of Babylon, Daniel
1:3-4.
Day of Pentecost, Acts 2:1-12.
Effect of message spoken in one's own
language, Acts 22:1-2.
See *Language.*

LIQUOR
Drink stronger than wine, Leviticus 10:9;
Deuteronomy 14:26.
Other fermented drink, Deuteronomy
29:6.
Alcohol and pregnancy, Judges 13:4.
Wine and beer, Proverbs 20:1; 31:4, 6.
Beer with bad taste, Isaiah 24:9.
Drunken priests and prophets, Isaiah 28:7.
No strong drink for John the Baptist, Luke
1:15.

LISTENING
Importance of ear to discern content, Job
34:1-3.
Giving heed to instruction, Proverbs 16:20.
Those who do not want to hear truth, Isaiah
30:10-11.
Importance of welcoming message,
1 Thessalonians 1:6.
Listening to Holy Spirit speak to churches,
Revelation 2:29.
See *Attention, Learning.*

LITERACY
Lack of understanding what one reads,
Acts 8:27-35.
See *Comprehension, Reading.*

LITERATURE
What poets say, Numbers 21:27-30.
A place for words, Deuteronomy 27:2-3.
Setting murder to verse, Judges 5:24-27.
Job wanted written record of his agony, Job
19:23-24.
Descriptive use of words, Psalm 7:14.
Pen of skillful writer, Psalm 45:1.
Playing harp while presenting a proverb,
Psalm 49:4.
Foreword to Book of Proverbs, Proverbs
1:1-6.
Profuse words confuse meaning,
Ecclesiastes 6:11.
Shortest short story ever written,

Ecclesiastes 9:14-15.
No end to making books, Ecclesiastes
12:12.
Unique figure of speech, Isaiah 14:23.
Figure of speech concerning birth and
death, Isaiah 26:19.
Description of judgment, Isaiah 30:14.
Deceitful theology, Jeremiah 8:8.
Description of judgment bringing absence
of joy and productive activity, Jeremiah
25:10.
Instructions to write book, Jeremiah 30:2.
Use of literary device concerning freedom,
Jeremiah 34:17.
Scroll eaten by Ezekiel, Ezekiel 3:1-3.
Language and literature of Babylon, Daniel
1:3-4.
Message written with clarity, Habakkuk
2:2.
Gigantic scroll, Zechariah 5:1-2.
Jesus' use of figures of speech, Mark 8:14-
21.
Books of world could not contain full story
of Jesus, John 21:25.
Author of life itself, Acts 3:15.
Paul quoted poets of Athens, Acts 17:28.
Preferring not to write, 2 John 12. (See
3 John 13-14.)
Small book, Revelation 10:2.
Book which cannot be revised, Revelation
22:18.
See *Author, Fiction, Writing.*

LITIGATION
Moses seated as judge, Exodus 18:13.
Demand and decree, Exodus 21:22.
Ruthless witnesses in court, Psalm 35:11.
Do not come hastily to court against
neighbors, Proverbs 25:8.
Priests served as judges, Ezekiel 44:24.
Legal conflicts resulting from false oaths,
Hosea 10:4.
Sound judgment in courtroom, Zechariah
8:16.
Settle matters out of court, Matthew 5:25.
Give more than amount sued, Matthew
5:40; Luke 12:58.
Bringing theological dispute into secular
courtroom, Acts 18:12-17.
Paul appealed to higher court, Acts 25:9-
12.
Lawsuits among believers, 1 Corinthians
6:1-8.
See *Judge, Justice, Lawyer.*

LITURGY
Woman's purification, Numbers 5:11-31.
Prayer for protection, Numbers 10:35.
Lifeless worship, Isaiah 29:13.
Actions and motivations, Jeremiah 4:4.
Covering head in worship, 1 Corinthians 11:5-10.
Regulations for worship, Hebrews 9:1.

LOAN
See *Borrowing, Credit, Finances, Mortgage.*

LOCAL
Those native born, Numbers 15:13.
Acceptance of hometown person, Matthew 13:57; Mark 6:4; John 4:44.

LOGIC
People who refuse to listen to reason, 1 Samuel 8:4-21.
Strategy of Jesus in facing accusers, Matthew 21:25-27; Mark 11:29-33.
Pharisees could not answer question Jesus gave them, Matthew 22:41-46.
Jesus and Pharisees, Luke 14:1-6.
Wisdom of Gamaliel, Acts 5:34-40.

LONELINESS
Job's deep sense of being alone, Job 19:13-14.
Companion of night creatures, Job 30:29.
Fair-weather friends, Psalm 31:11.
Loss of closest friends, Psalm 88:8.
Insomnia, Psalm 102:7.
Songs of Zion gone silent, Psalm 137:1-4.
No one cares, Psalm 142:4.
Neither son nor brother, Ecclesiastes 4:8.
Deserted by everyone, Mark 14:48-50.
Utter loneliness of Jesus on the cross, Mark 15:34.
Memories of better days, Luke 15:14-17.
Alone in time of need, John 5:7.
Loneliness of Epaphroditus, Philippians 2:25-30.
Christians missing each other, 1 Thessalonians 2:17–3:5.
Timothy's tears, 2 Timothy 1:4.
Paul's desire for fellowship of Timothy, 2 Timothy 4:9-10.
Those who deserted Paul when he needed them, 2 Timothy 4:16-17.
Wanting to see friends face-to-face, 3 John 14.
See *Abandoned, Forsaken.*

LONGEVITY
Oldest man, Genesis 5:27.
Age of man before Flood, Genesis 6:3.
Jacob spoke of life as pilgrimage, Genesis 47:9.
Honesty and longevity, Deuteronomy 25:15.
Desire for long life, 1 Kings 1:31; Psalm 34:11-13; 1 Peter 3:10-11.
Way of all earth, 1 Kings 2:2.
Reward of obedience, 1 Kings 3:14; Proverbs 10:27.
Fifteen years added to Hezekiah's life, 2 Kings 20:5-6.
Death in full vigor, Job 5:26.
Long life given in answer to prayer, Psalm 21:4.
Age 70 to 80, Psalm 90:10.
Satisfying long life, Psalm 91:16.
Enjoying years of life, Ecclesiastes 11:8.
People live to age of trees, Isaiah 65:20-22
Forefathers gone, Zechariah 1:5.
Cane in hand, Zechariah 8:4.
Our body but a tent, 2 Peter 1:13.
See *Geriatrics, Old age.*

LONG-WINDED
Arrogant speech, 1 Samuel 2:3.
Words like a blustering wind, Job 8:2.
Long-winded speeches, Job 16:3.
Apt speech, Proverbs 25:11.
Wise speech, Ecclesiastes 12:11.
Instructed tongue, Isaiah 50:4.
Need for disciplined tongue, James 1:26.
See *Loquacious.*

LOOTING
Crops and animals taken by enemy, Judges 6:3-6.
Robbing dead after battle, 1 Samuel 31:8-10; 2 Samuel 23:10.
Making frolic of plunder, Jeremiah 50:11-12.

LOQUACIOUS
Words like blustering wind, Job 8:2.
Wisdom of silence, Job 13:5.
Pharaoh only loud noise, Jeremiah 46:17.
Paul's long sermon, Acts 20:7.

LORD'S DAY
Setting aside day for rest, Genesis 2:2-3.
Not doing business on Sabbath, Nehemiah 10:31.

Merchandising on Sabbath, Nehemiah
13:15-18.
Avoiding work on Sabbath, Jeremiah
17:21-27.
Eating or not eating on Sabbath, Mark
2:23-27; Luke 6:1-5.
See *Sunday.*

LORD'S TABLE
See *Passover.*

LOST
Depravity of man before Flood, Genesis
6:5.
Those far from the Lord, Ezekiel 11:15.
Without hope and without God, Ephesians
2:12.
God's grace to worst of sinners, 1 Timothy
1:15-16.
God wants all to be saved, 1 Timothy 2:3-4.
Life prior to regeneration, Titus 3:3.
Failure to combine hearing with believing,
Hebrews 4:1-3.
Names not written in Book of Life,
Revelation 17:8; 20:11-15.
See *Depravity.*

LOTS
The Lord involved in casting lots, Leviticus
16:8.
Inheritance by lot, Numbers 26:55.
Maps made by casting lots, Joshua 18:8-10.
Prayer and chance, 1 Samuel 14:41-42.
Death by measurement, 2 Samuel 8:2.
Day of doom, Esther 3:2-7.
Divine control over chance, Proverbs
16:33.
Settling disputes, Proverbs 18:18.
Chosen for service, Luke 1:8-9.
See *Chance.*

LOVE
Intensity and integrity of love between two
men, 2 Samuel 1:26.
Solomon's test in determining identity of
true mother, 1 Kings 3:16-28.
Our Lord's enduring love, Psalm 136:1-26.
True love cannot be quenched, Song of
Songs 8:7.
God's love never lessens, Isaiah 54:10.
How God loves, Malachi 1:2.
Marriage on earth compared to
relationship in heaven, Mark 12:18-27.
Greatest act of love, John 3:16.

Mark of true discipleship, John 13:34-35.
Forgiving spirit of martyr, Acts 7:60.
Be always in debt to love, fulfillment of the
Law, Romans 13:8-10.
Seeking good of others above one's self,
1 Corinthians 10:24.
Imitators of God expressing love to others,
Ephesians 5:1-2.
Christians keeping in touch concerning
activity and welfare, Ephesians 6:21-22.
Undying love, Ephesians 6:24.
The kind of affection Jesus gives,
Philippians 1:8.
Ministry of love among Christians,
Colossians 3:12-14; 1 Thessalonians
3:12.
Power of love to forgive, 1 Peter 4:8.
God's great love, 1 John 3:1-3.
Mark of Christian, 1 John 3:11, 14.
Actions speak louder than words, 1 John
3:18.
Truth and love united, 2 John 3, 5-6.
Love in the truth, 3 John 1.
See *Affection, Camaraderie, Marriage,
Rapport, Romance.*

LOWLINESS
Unworthy of being in presence of king,
2 Samuel 19:24-28.
Supreme example of lowliness, Matthew
8:20.
See *Humility.*

LOYALTY
Test of father's love to God and son,
Genesis 22:1-14.
Those who do not follow wholeheartedly,
Numbers 32:11.
Turning away from wrong family influence,
Deuteronomy 13:6-10.
Turning to rejected brother in time of
need, Judges 11:1-10.
Jonathan's loyalty torn between his father
and close friend, 1 Samuel 19:1-2.
Friendship of David and Jonathan at
cutting edge, 1 Samuel 20:1-4.
Philistine commander feared David's
loyalty, 1 Samuel 29:1-11.
Loyalty of servant to king, 2 Samuel 15:19-
21.
Loyalty of King David doubted by his men,
2 Samuel 19:1-8.
Neglecting personal appearance until sure
of king's safety, 2 Samuel 19:24.

Protection for future king, 2 Kings 11:1-3.
Those of dubious loyalty, 1 Chronicles
12:19.
Laws of land must be obeyed, Ezra 7:26;
Ecclesiastes 8:2; Romans 13:1; Titus 3:1;
1 Peter 2:13.
Those who turned from Ishmael to
Johanan in battle, Jeremiah 41:11-14.
Loving God above all, Matthew 10:37-39.
You cannot serve two masters, Luke 16:13.
Obeying Christ's commands, John 14:21-
24.
Jesus and Simon Peter, John 21:15-17.
Daily death of true commitment,
1 Corinthians 15:30-31.

LUCID
Message spoken and written, Exodus
31:18; 32:16; Deuteronomy 10:4.
Writing guided by divine hand,
1 Chronicles 28:19.
Divine inspiration, 2 Chronicles 36:22.
Message written with clarity, Habakkuk
2:2.
See *Eloquence.*

LUCK
Death by measurement, 2 Samuel 8:2.
Death of king by random arrow,
2 Chronicles 18:33-34.
Date-setting, Esther 3:7.
Divine control of chance events, Proverbs
16:33.
Settling disputes, Proverbs 18:18.
Use of magic charms, Ezekiel 13:18.
From frying pan to fire, Amos 5:19.
Guilt by casting lot, Jonah 1:7.
Casting lots for Jesus' garments, Matthew
27:35.
Choice of replacement for Judas, Acts
1:18-26.
See *Chance, Lots.*

LUGGAGE
Recovered goods, Genesis 14:14-16.
Smuggled baggage, Genesis 44:1-12.
Queen's luggage, 1 Kings 10:2.
Plundered baggage, Proverbs 1:10-15.
Belongings packed for exile, Ezekiel 12:1-
7.
Traveling light, Luke 10:4.

LUMBER
Chest of acacia wood, Exodus 25:10.

Protection for trees, Deuteronomy 20:19.
Leader among trees, Judges 9:7-15.
Wood for building temple, 1 Kings 5:3-11.
Selecting choice timber, 2 Kings 19:23.
Lumber from royal forest, Nehemiah 2:8.
See *Carpenter, Forestry, Trees.*

LUST
Lot's offer of virgin daughters, Genesis
19:4-8.
Lust that seemingly turned to love, Genesis
34:1-4.
Mixing immorality with worship, Numbers
25:1-2.
David and Bathsheba, 2 Samuel 11:1-27.
Immorality used for vengeance, 2 Samuel
16:20-23.
Weakness of King Solomon, 1 Kings 11:1-
13.
Avoiding lust requires discipline, Job 31:1.
Lost value through lust, Proverbs 6:25-26.
Description of profligate men, Jeremiah
5:8.
Unsatisfied sword, Jeremiah 46:10.
Adultery and lust in heart and mind,
Ezekiel 6:9.
Merchandising feminine beauty, Ezekiel
16:15.
Violation of family members, Ezekiel
22:11.
Depravity of two adulterous sisters, Ezekiel
23:1-49.
Father and son to same prostitute, Amos
2:7.
Adultery in heart and mind, Matthew 5:27-
28.
Sexual impurity, Romans 1:24.
Continual lust for more, Ephesians 4:19.
Those who keep themselves pure,
Revelation 14:4.
See *Adultery, Depravity, Immorality,
Promiscuity.*

LUXURY
King Solomon's diet, 1 Kings 4:22-23.
Solid gold table setting, 1 Kings 10:21-22.
Week-long banquet, Esther 1:5-6.
Sumptuous bed and board, Amos 6:4.
People in fine homes while temple in
ruins, Haggai 1:1-4.
Jesus accused of luxury, Matthew 26:6-13;
Mark 14:3-9.
Hairstyles and jewelry, 1 Timothy 2:9-
10.

See *Affluence, Hedonism.*

LYNCHING
Hanging of king, Joshua 8:29.
Jews had no right to crucify, John 18:28-32.

LYRICS
Songs of joy, Psalm 126:2.
Meaningless lyrics of love song sung with
beautiful voice, Ezekiel 33:32.
See *Hymn.*

M

MACHINERY
Protecting debtor's earning power,
   Deuteronomy 24:6.
New inventions, 2 Chronicles 26:15.

MACHO
See *Conceit, Hedonism.*

MAGGOTS
Worms in dead bodies, Isaiah 66:24.

MAGIC
Seeking God's will by divination, Genesis
   30:27.
Wise men of Egypt, Genesis 41:1-24.
Joseph pretended to believe in divination,
   Genesis 44:5.
Competing with professionals, Exodus 7:8-
   12; 8:1-19.
Superstitions of Israel, Isaiah 2:6-8.
False oracles and prophets, Jeremiah
   23:33-40.
Baffled magicians, Daniel 1:20; 2:1-13; 4:4-
   7.
Sorcerer's vanity, Acts 8:9-11.
Those cast into lake of fire, Revelation
   20:10; 21:8.

MAGISTRATE
See *Authority, Government, Leadership.*

MAGNITUDE
Scope of God's presence, 1 Kings
   8:27.
Eternal viewpoint, Jeremiah 33:3.
Army of locusts, Joel 2:1-9.
Contemplating resurrection and exaltation
   of Christ, Ephesians 1:18-23.
Geometric dimensions of spiritual
   experience, Ephesians 3:17-18.
Right foot on sea, left foot on land,

Revelation 10:2.
See *Dimensions, Large.*

MAIM
Cutting off thumbs and big toes, Judges
   1:7.
Crippled from fall in childhood, 2 Samuel
   4:4.
Wounds and welts from beating, Isaiah 1:5-
   6.
King's arm broken, Ezekiel 30:21.
See *Handicap, Injury.*

MAINTENANCE
Repairing the temple, 2 Kings 12:4-5.
Lazy man's house, Ecclesiastes 10:18.
Oil as protection against rust, Isaiah 21:5.

MAJESTY
Divine glory, majesty, splendor,
   1 Chronicles 29:11.
Likened to majesty of sun, Job 37:21-24.
Voice of the Lord, Psalm 29:3-9.
Garments of eternal majesty, Psalm
   93:1-2.
High and exalted, Isaiah 6:1.
Prophecy of Christ, Micah 5:4. (Note
   fulfillment in such passages as Mark
   16:19; Luke 22:69; Acts 2:36; 5:31; Phil.
   2:9; Heb. 1:9; 1 Peter 3:22; Rev. 5:12.)
See *Royalty, Splendor.*

MAJORITY
Following wrong crowd, Exodus 23:2.
Putting confidence in numerical strength,
   Judges 7:2. (See v. 12.)
One plus God equals majority, 1 Samuel
   14:6-14.
Human strength of little value, Psalm
   33:16.
The wide and narrow, Matthew 7:13-14.

MALCONTENT
Unanimous complaint of community,
Exodus 16:2.
Putting God to test, Exodus 17:1-4.
Chasing wind, Ecclesiastes 1:17-18.
Money never satisfies, Ecclesiastes 5:10.
Those who complain accept instruction,
Isaiah 29:24.
Blaming the Lord for problems, Habakkuk
1:1-4.
Attitude of Prodigal Son's brother, Luke
15:25-32.
Peril of grumbling, 1 Corinthians 10:10.
Admonition for good attitude, Philippians
2:14; 1 Timothy 6:6-8.
Content with what you have, Hebrews 13:5.
See *Contentment, Discontent, Murmuring.*

MALICE
Bear no grudge, Leviticus 19:18.
Blighted personalities, Deuteronomy
32:32-33; Psalm 10:7-14; Proverbs 6:14-
19; Romans 1:29-32.
Compassion versus malice, 2 Kings 6:21-
22.
Wealth and prestige could not numb
Haman's resentment, Esther 5:10-14.
Discipline against malice, Job 31:29-30.
Lurking enemies, Psalms 56:5-6; 57:4-6;
59:3-7.
Malicious speech, Psalm 140:3; Proverbs
30:14.
Evil insomnia, Proverbs 4:16-17; Micah
2:1.
Folly of taking revenge, Ezekiel 25:15-17.
Malice in practice, Matthew 5:38-41; Acts
23:12-14.
Divine condemnation, 1 John 2:9-11; 3:14-
15.
See *Envy, Hatred.*

MAN
Measure of a man, 1 Kings 2:2-3.
Low estimation of man's worth, Job 25:5-6.
Clay in Potter's hands, Isaiah 29:16; 45:9;
64:8; Jeremiah 18:6.
Setting traps for men, Jeremiah 5:26.
No man to be found, Ezekiel 22:30.
See *Humanity, Morality.*

MANAGEMENT
Attitude of management toward labor,
Exodus 5:2-5.
Young kings of Israel, 2 Kings 23:31, 36;
24:8, 18.
Giving job assignments, Nehemiah 13:30.
Those who treat laborers unjustly,
Jeremiah 22:13.
Concern of centurion for servant, Matthew
8:5-13; Luke 7:3.
Labor relations, Matthew 20:9-16; 21:33-
41.
Trade unions, Acts 19:23-27.
Payment to laborers, Romans 4:4.
Avoiding harsh use of authority,
2 Corinthians 13:10.
Withholding payment from those who
labor, James 5:4.
See *Leadership, Organization.*

MANDATE
Giving specific orders, Joshua 8:8.
God's promise of blessing but warning
against disobedience, 1 Kings 9:1-9.
Pagan king persuaded to permit rebuilding
of temple, Ezra 4-7.
Clear directive to Jeremiah, Jeremiah 11:6.
Imperative to witness, Ezekiel 3:18-19.
Two-word command, Mark 2:14.
Entrusted with secret things of God,
1 Corinthians 4:1-2.
Paul's ministry mandate to Timothy,
2 Timothy 4:1-5.
See *Decree, Ultimatum.*

MANIPULATE
Manipulated wealth, Proverbs 21:6.
Political manipulation, Ecclesiastes 5:8-9.
Inequity between friends, Jeremiah 9:5.
Riches gained unjustly, Jeremiah 17:11.
Exploiting poor for personal gain, Amos
5:11.
Cheating and polluting, Amos 8:5-6.
Doing good without expecting
reciprocation, Luke 6:27-36.
Relationship to neighbors, Ephesians 4:25.

MANNERS
Courtesy to visitors, Genesis 18:1-7. (Note
v. 8, Abraham standing as guests ate.)
Visiting angels, Genesis 19:1-2.
Biological expediency, Genesis 31:35.
Bad manners toward Great Provider,
Exodus 16:1-18.
Courtesy to senior citizens, Leviticus 19:32;
Job 29:7-8.
Examples of bad manners, Judges 8:35,
1 Samuel 25:21.

Elisha's bald head, 2 Kings 2:23-24.
Wisdom of silence, Job 13:5.
Legalism versus courtesy, 1 Corinthians
10:27-30.
Love's exemplary deportment,
1 Corinthians 13:5.
Conduct among strangers, Colossians 4:5-
6.
Avoid misuse of another's hospitality,
2 Thessalonians 3:7-10.
See *Courtesy, Guests, Hospitality.*

MANPOWER
Taking care of business, Deuteronomy
20:5-9.
Seven men plus one additional, Micah 5:5.
See *Labor.*

MANUFACTURE
Maker of tools, Genesis 4:22.
Shortage of materials, Exodus 5:6-9.
Commercial centers in Ezekiel's time,
Ezekiel 27:2-23.
See *Machinery, Tool.*

MAP
Road signs and guideposts, Jeremiah
31:21.

MARATHON
Running long race, Jeremiah 12:5.

MARCHING
Parade to the sea, Exodus 13:17–14:31.
Encircling Jericho, Joshua 6:2-20.
Stormy marching, Judges 5:4.
Atop Jerusalem's wall, Nehemiah 12:27-
39.
Trembling earth, Psalm 68:7-8.
Soldiers like serpents, Jeremiah 46:22.
Precision marching, Joel 2:8. (See also
v. 11.)

MARKS
Needless bruises, Proverbs 23:29.
Wounds and welts, Isaiah 1:6.
Marks of sin on countenance, Isaiah 3:9.
Incurable wound, Jeremiah 30:12; Micah
1:9.
Mark of beast, Revelation 19:20.

MARKETING
Commerical centers, Ezekiel 27:2-23.
Idle in marketplace, Matthew 20:3.

Temple as marketplace, Luke 19:45-48.
Dealing in human merchandise, Acts
16:16-23.
See *Barter, Commerce.*

MARRIAGE
First arranged marriage, Genesis 2:18-24.
Abraham's deceitfulness concerning
Sarah, Genesis 20:1-18. (See 12:10-20.)
Abraham's marriage to Keturah after
death of Sarah, Genesis 23:1-20; 25:1-2.
Search for bride for Isaac, Genesis 24:1-58.
(See 25:19-20.)
Respect for status of married woman,
Genesis 26:7-11. (See also 20:1-18.)
Esau's two wives, Genesis 26:34-35.
Marriage between relatives, Genesis 29:12,
23, 28; 2 Chronicles 11:18.
Relationship strengthened after birth of
son, Genesis 29:35.
Responsibility after illicit relationship,
Exodus 22:16.
Incest and impropriety, Leviticus 20:14-21.
Special rules for clergy, Leviticus 21:1-15.
Husband's involvement in contracts made
by wife, Numbers 30:10-15.
Father's attitude toward affections of
daughters, Judges 15:1-2.
Shortage of wives, Judges 21:14.
Kidnapping wives, Judges 21:20-21.
Age variable between Boaz and Ruth, Ruth
3:10-13.
David demanded that Michal be taken
from her husband, 2 Samuel 3:12-16.
David's many wives, 2 Samuel 5:13.
Hatred of wife for husband, 2 Samuel 6:16-
23.
Solomon born from bad marriage,
2 Samuel 12:24-25.
Ill-fated request for wife, 1 Kings 2:13-25.
Strengthening one's position through
marriage, 2 Chronicles 18:1.
Beautiful queen refused to be put on
display, Esther 1:9-21.
Strategic verse for marriage, Psalm 34:3.
Counsel on marriage relationship,
Proverbs 5:15-19.
Fury of betrayed husband, Proverbs 6:27-
35.
Blessing of good wife, Proverbs 12:4.
Favor of the Lord, Proverbs 18:22.
Good marriages made in heaven, Proverbs
19:14.
Quarrelsome wife, Proverbs 21:9, 19;

25:24.
Two better than one, Ecclesiastes 4:9-12.
Enjoy life together, Ecclesiastes 9:9.
Taste of bridal lips, Song of Songs 4:11.
True love cannot be quenched, Song of
Songs 8:7.
Culminated joy of bride and bridegroom,
Jeremiah 7:34.
Forbidden in time of judgment, Jeremiah
16:1-4.
Wife who preferred strangers to husband,
Ezekiel 16:32.
Lesson for wicked Israel, Ezekiel 24:15-24.
Restrictions on marriage for priests,
Ezekiel 44:22.
Hosea commanded to marry evil woman,
Hosea 1:2-3.
Unable to have children, Hosea 9:11.
Youthful marriage terminated, Joel 1:8.
Agreement necessary for walking together,
Amos 3:3.
Women who command their husbands,
Amos 4:1.
Marriage to daughter of god, Malachi 2:11.
Vows of youth, Malachi 2:15.
Cause for divorce, Matthew 5:31-32.
Healing of Peter's mother-in-law, Matthew
8:14-15.
Teaching of Jesus concerning divorce,
Matthew 19:3-9; Mark 10:1-12.
Relationship in heaven of those who have
married and remarried, Mark 12:18-25.
Brief marriage of prophetess, Luke 2:36-
37.
Dominant husband, John 1:13.
Woman with many husbands, John 4:17-
18.
Relationship of husband and wife,
1 Corinthians 7:1-7.
Marriage between unbelievers and
believers, 1 Corinthians 7:10-16.
Troubles of married life, 1 Corinthians
7:25-28.
Wife traveling with husband, 1 Corinthians
9:5.
Paul described role of women,
1 Corinthians 11:2-16.
Wives and husbands relating to each other,
Ephesians 5:22-33: Colossians 3:18-19;
1 Peter 3:1-2, 7.
Elder must have but one wife, Titus 1:6.
Responsibility of young wives in home,
Titus 2:3-5.
Honorable and pure, Hebrews 13:4.

No fear in love, 1 John 4:18.
No more bride and bridegroom in Babylon,
Revelation 18:24.
Garments of bride, Revelation 19:7-8; 21:2.
Bride of Christ, Revelation 21:9.
See *Divorce, Remarriage, Romance.*

MARTYR
Sword of the Lord bathed in blood, Isaiah
34:6.
Those who are persecuted, Matthew 5:10.
Death of John the Baptist, Matthew 14:1-
12.
Those who only destroy body, Luke 12:4-5.
Stoning of Stephen, Acts 6:8–7:60.
James slain with sword, Acts 12:2.
Living martyrdom, Romans 8:36.
Willing to lay down one's life for others,
1 John 3:16.
Faithful in persecution, Revelation 2:13.
Put to death for witness, Revelation 6:9.
Drunk with blood of saints, Revelation
17:6.
Beheaded for faithfulness and testimony,
Revelation 20:4.
See *Persecution.*

MASCULINE
See *Athletics, Virility.*

MASON
Use of specific materials for building,
Genesis 11:3.
Large stones covered with plaster,
Deuteronomy 27:2.
Palace construction, 2 Samuel 5:11.
Salaried workmen, 2 Kings 12:11-12.
Temple builders, 1 Chronicles 22:2;
2 Chronicles 24:12.
Mortar and brickwork, Nahum 3:14.
See *Construction.*

MASQUERADE
False prophets, Jeremiah 23:16-18.
Ego displayed by teachers of Law, Mark
12:38-40.
Satan as angel of light, 2 Corinthians 11:14.
Method of false teachers, 2 Peter 2:1.
See *Pretense.*

MASTERPIECES
Skilled in one's work, Proverbs 22:29.
Artist is mortal, Isaiah 44:11.
See *Skill, Talent.*

MATERIALISM
Exchanging what you have for that which is far better, Genesis 45:20.
Foul odor of disobedience, Exodus 16:19-20. (See also vv. 22-24.)
Monetary value of human being, Leviticus 27:1-8.
Material security versus God's will, Numbers 32:14-27.
Plunder permitted at Ai, Joshua 8:1-2.
Gold a snare to good man, Judges 8:24-27.
Making idol to please the Lord, Judges 17:3.
Solomon's prayer for wisdom rather than material gain, 1 Kings 3:5-15. (See 4:29-34.)
Solomon took less time to build temple than to build palace, 1 Kings 6:37-38; 7:1.
Materialism versus obedience, 1 Kings 13:7-10.
David's sin in depending on number of fighting men, 1 Chronicles 21:17.
Experiences of Job in loss of material possessions, Job 1:13-21.
Nauseating affluence, Job 20:15.
Wicked often prosper, Job 21:7.
Folly of trusting in wealth, Job 31:24-28.
Riches and bribes, Job 36:18-19.
Everything belongs to God, Job 41:11; Psalms 24:1-2; 50:9-12.
Wealth can numb thoughts of God, Psalm 10:3-6.
Trusting solely in the Lord, Psalm 20:7.
Better little with righteousness than wealth with wickedness, Psalm 37:16-17.
Short-lived prosperity of wicked, Psalm 37:35-36.
Folly of trusting in wealth, Psalm 49:5-12.
Stones and dust of Jerusalem, Psalm 102:14.
Eternal God and temporal creation, Psalm 102:25-27.
Creditors seize all, Psalm 109:11.
Finding greatest values in life, Psalm 119:36-37.
Greater value found only in Scripture, Psalm 119:72.
Treasure in God's promises, Psalm 119:162.
Heathen gods made by the hands of men, Psalm 135:15-18.
Total end of all for wicked man, Proverbs 11:7.

Riches not to be trusted, Proverbs 11:28.
Value of little with faith over much with turmoil, Proverbs 15:16.
Purchase of prestige, Proverbs 18:16.
Value of good name, Proverbs 22:1.
Money alone never satisfies, Ecclesiastes 5:10.
Man born naked and so departs, Ecclesiastes 5:15.
Dangers of national wealth, Isaiah 2:7-8.
Ruins of rich, Isaiah 5:17.
Trust in the Lord, not horses and chariots, Isaiah 31:1-3.
Rejecting one's idols of silver and gold, Isaiah 31:7.
Wood for making gods and cooking fires, Isaiah 44:14-20.
Impotence of man-made gods, Isaiah 46:6-7.
That which money cannot buy, Isaiah 55:1-2.
Destruction of wealth and security, Jeremiah 5:17.
Wealth given away in judgment, Jeremiah 17:3.
People of Jerusalem obeyed God, then coveted old ways, Jeremiah 34:8-22.
Foolishness of seeking great things in rebellion against God, Jeremiah 45:4-5.
Sons and daughters sacrificed to idols, Ezekiel 16:20.
Priests to own no property, Ezekiel 44:28.
Wealth numbs conscience, Hosea 12:8.
Worship of what hands have made, Hosea 14:3.
Those who hoard plunder become insensitive to right, Amos 3:10.
Food and possessions do not satisfy, Micah 6:14.
Too many merchants desecrated land, Nahum 3:16.
Those whose own strength is their god, Habakkuk 1:11.
Those who recognize the Lord and Molech, Zephaniah 1:5.
Silver and gold of no value when judgment falls, Zephaniah 1:18.
Those never satisfied, Haggai 1:5-6.
Silver and gold like dust and dirt, Zechariah 9:3.
Reward of good stewardship, Malachi 3:8-10.
Kingdoms of the world, Matthew 4:8-9.
Treasures on earth and treasures in

heaven, Matthew 6:19-21.
God provides for nature, takes care of His children, Matthew 6:25-34.
Jesus had no place of residence, Matthew 8:20.
Clothes describe man, Matthew 11:7-9.
Gain the world, forfeit soul, Matthew 16:25-26.
Money changers in temple, Matthew 21:12-13.
Deceitfulness of wealth, Mark 4:19.
Eternal value of soul, temporal values of life, Mark 8:35-37.
Rich young man who kept the Law, Mark 10:17-27.
Sharing with others, Luke 3:11.
Folly of greed over material things, Luke 12:13-21.
Those who must see signs and wonders to believe, John 4:48.
Purchasing power of wages, John 6:7.
Disciples wanted earthly kingdom restored, Acts 1:4-8.
Early Christians had all things in common, Acts 4:32.
Scrolls of value destroyed by converted sorcerers, Acts 19:19.
Wood, hay, and straw instead of gold, silver, costly stones, 1 Corinthians 3:12-13.
Enemies and attitudes in last days, 2 Timothy 3:1-5.
Love of money, Hebrews 13:5.
Poor can be rich in faith, James 2:5.
Danger of greed in ministry, 1 Peter 5:2-3.
Fragile realities of earth and sky, 2 Peter 3:5-13.
Sharing material possessions with others, 1 John 3:17.
Merchants of earth lament destruction of Babylon, Revelation 18:11-19.
Earth and sky flee from the eternal, Revelation 20:11.
Description of New Jerusalem, Revelation 21:15-27.
See *Affluence, Secular.*

MATHEMATICS
Quantity beyond numbering, Genesis 15:5; 32:12.
Balance in generations through periods of Bible history, Matthew 1:17.
Groups of 50 for 5 miracle loaves, Luke 9:14-15.

Difference between human equations and power of God, John 6:1-13. (See particularly v. 7.)
Geometric dimensions of Christ's love, Ephesians 3:14-19.
Measurement of temple, Revelation 11:1-2.
Measurement of New Jerusalem, Revelation 21:16-17.

MATURITY
Ways of wisdom, Proverbs 2:13-20.
Sure road to maturity, Proverbs 9:1-6.
Depths of spiritual truth, John 6:60-69.
Purpose of suffering, Romans 5:3.
Freedom from mastery of sin, Romans 6:14.
Filled with hope, joy, and peace, Romans 15:13.
Milk and solid food, 1 Corinthians 3:1-2; Hebrews 5:11-14; 6:1-3; 1 Peter 2:2-3.
No longer a child, 1 Corinthians 13:11; 14:20; Ephesians 4:14.
Willing to be accepted as fool, 2 Corinthians 11:16-19.
Spirit of wisdom and revelation, Ephesians 1:17.
Geometric dimensions of spiritual experience, Ephesians 3:17-18.
Becoming mature Christians, Ephesians 4:13.
Standing at end of struggle, Ephesians 6:13.
Good work begun will be completed, Philippians 1:6.
Standing firm whatever the circumstances, Philippians 1:27-30.
Forgetting past, pressing forward to goal, Philippians 3:12-16.
Content in all situations, Philippians 4:12.
Marks of Christian maturity, Colossians 1:3-8.
Filled with knowledge of God's will, Colossians 1:9-12.
Spiritual need fulfilled in Christ, Colossians 1:15-23.
Receiving Christ and growing in Him, Colossians 2:6-7.
Ultimate in being properly motivated, 1 Thessalonians 1:3.
Hearts that become strong and blameless, 1 Thessalonians 3:13.
Motivated to truly Christian lifestyle, 1 Thessalonians 4:11-12.
Growing in faith and love, 2 Thessalonians

1:3.
Mature attitude toward teaching on
Christ's return, 2 Thessalonians 2:1-2.
Diligent in quest for spiritual maturity,
1 Timothy 4:13.
Calm in all situations, 2 Timothy 4:5.
Made perfect through suffering, Hebrews
2:10.
Scriptural maturity, Hebrews 5:11-14.
Discipline of testing, Hebrews 12:7.
Role of testing in maturing one's faith,
James 1:2-4.
Listen before speaking, James 1:19.
Strategic control of speech, James 3:2.
Sharing weakness with each other, James
5:16.
Strong, firm, and steadfast, 1 Peter 5:10.
All we need to live life of godliness, 2 Peter
1:3.
Distinct element of spiritual maturity,
2 Peter 1:5-9.
Growing in grace, 2 Peter 3:18.
Deliverance from practicing sin, 1 John
3:8-10.
Health and wealth plus spiritual vitality,
3 John 2-4.
Temporal wealth and spiritual wealth,
Revelation 3:15-18.
See *Discipleship, Growth.*

MAXIM
Deeds reveal person, 1 Samuel 24:13.

MEALS
Dinner, Genesis 24:33; Luke 24:29-30.
Lunch, Genesis 43:16; John 4:6, 31.
Breakfast, Judges 19:5; John 21:9.
See *Cooking.*

MEASUREMENT
Honest scales, Job 31:6.
Use of measuring device, Jeremiah 31:39;
Ezekiel 40:3; 42:16; Zechariah 2:1.
Measuring new temple area, Ezekiel 40:5-
49.
Measurement of New Jerusalem,
Revelation 21:15-21.
See *Dimensions, Mathematics.*

MEAT
Man and animals originally vegetarian,
Genesis 1:29-30; 2:9.
Beginning of meat as food, Genesis 9:3.
Utensil for meat, Exodus 27:3; 38:3;

Numbers 4:14.
Food containing blood, 1 Samuel 14:31-
33.
Meat which is not to be eaten, Isaiah 66:17.
Spiritual food, 1 Corinthians 3:1-3;
Hebrews 5:11-14.

MEDDLE
False reports and malicious witness,
Exodus 23:1.
Meddling in affairs of others, Proverbs
26:17.
Busybodies, 2 Thessalonians 3:11.
From house to house, 1 Timothy 5:13.
Suffering as meddler, 1 Peter 4:15.
See *Busybody.*

MEDIA
Let others praise you, Proverbs 27:2.
Secret thoughts conveyed to others,
Ecclesiastes 10:20.
Engraved with iron tool, Jeremiah 17:1.
Man with writing kit, Ezekiel 9:11.
Publishing message plainly, Habakkuk 2:2.
Flying scroll, Zechariah 5:1-4.
Decision to communicate by writing, Luke
1:1-4.
Angelic announcement of Good News,
Luke 2:10.
See *Communication, Writing.*

MEDIATOR
People in need of mediator, Exodus 20:19;
Deuteronomy 5:27.
Standing between living and dead,
Numbers 16:48.
Burdened leadership, Deuteronomy 9:18.
Job's cry for someone to mediate between
him and God, Job 9:33-35.
Even Moses and Samuel could not
intercede, Jeremiah 15:1.
People's dependence on a prophet's
prayers, Jeremiah 42:1-4.
Message came through prophet, Haggai
1:1.
Faith of friends resulted in man's healing,
Mark 2:1-5.
God only known through Christ, Luke
10:22; 1 Timothy 2:5; Hebrews 8:6;
9:15, 24; 12:24; 1 John 2:1.
Jesus our guarantee, Hebrews 7:22.

MEDICINE
Embalming in Egypt, Genesis 50:2-3.

Worthless physicians, Job 13:4.
Attitude and health, Proverbs 17:22.
Beyond medical help, Isaiah 1:6.
Practical prescription, Isaiah 38:21.
Careless attention to wound, Jeremiah 8:11.
No balm in Gilead, Jeremiah 8:22.
Medicinal leaves, Ezekiel 47:12; Revelation 22:2.
Divine approval of doctors, Matthew 9:12.
Years of medical expense, Mark 5:25-26.
Good Samaritan, Luke 10:33-34.
See *Health, Remedies.*

MEDITATION
Daily meditation, Joshua 1:8.
Constant meditation, Psalm 1:2.
Night thoughts, Psalm 4:4.
Time for reflection, Psalm 16:7.
Heart meditation, Psalm 19:14.
Thirst for the living God, Psalm 42:1-2.
Deep calling unto deep, Psalm 42:7-8.
Meditation in temple, Psalm 48:9.
Meditation through the night, Psalm 63:6.
Geriatric reflections, Psalms 77:10-12; 143:5.
Day-long experience, Psalm 119:97.
True wisdom obtained from Scriptures, Psalm 119:98-100.
Prayer for inner peace and righteousness, Psalm 139:23-24.
Delight in God's Word, Jeremiah 15:16.
Go out to the plain, Ezekiel 3:22-23.
Silent before the Lord, Zephaniah 1:7; Zechariah 2:13.
Prayer in the closet, Matthew 6:5-6.
Solitude at daybreak, Luke 4:42.
Jesus withdrew from crowd to pray, Luke 5:16.
Ultimate "holy of holies," 1 Corinthians 3:16.
Alone in Athens, 1 Thessalonians 3:1.
In-depth reflection, 1 Timothy 4:13-15.
Reward of careful reflection, 2 Timothy 2:7.
Fix thoughts on Jesus, Hebrews 3:1.
Those who take Scriptures to heart, Revelation 1:3.
See *Quiet time.*

MEEKNESS
Quality of life, Psalms 22:26; 37:11; 2 Timothy 2:24.
Soft response to anger, Proverbs 15:1; 16:32.
Quiet joy of contentment, Proverbs 30:7-8.
Humility in seeking the Lord, Zephaniah 2:3.
Day of small things, Zechariah 4:10.
Blessed are the meek, Matthew 5:5.
Divine example, Matthew 11:29; 27:13-14.
Right spirit in victory over evil, Luke 10:17-20.
Response to mistreatment, Romans 12:14.
Dimensions of love, 1 Corinthians 13:4-7; Ephesians 4:1-2.
Paul timid in presence of Corinthians, 2 Corinthians 10:1.
Fruit of Spirit, Galatians 5:22-23.
Relating to others with gentleness, 1 Thessalonians 2:7-8.
See *Humility.*

MELANCHOLY
Restless mind, Ecclesiastes 2:23.
Daughters taught to wail, Jeremiah 9:20.
Joy and gladness gone, Jeremiah 48:33.
Pouting Jonah, Jonah 4:5.
Heavy hearts, Luke 21:34.
See *Pessimism.*

MEMBERSHIP
Membership in God's household, Ephesians 2:19-20.
Recorded in Book of Life, Philippians 4:3.
See *Congregation.*

MEMORIAL
Memorial to site of dream, Genesis 28:18-19.
Covenant monument, Genesis 31:45.
Experience at Bethel, Genesis 35:9-15.
Passover memorial, Exodus 12:14.
Living memorial, Exodus 13:12-16.
Harvest festival, Leviticus 23:39-44.
Captured city named after captor, Numbers 32:42.
Monument to the Lord's help, 1 Samuel 7:12.
Absalom's memorial to himself, 2 Samuel 18:18.
Lord's Supper, Luke 22:19-20; 1 Corinthians 11:24-26.

MEMORIZATION
Memorized promises, Joshua 23:14.
Solomon's songs and proverbs, 1 Kings 4:32.

Meditation of heart, Psalm 19:14.
Deliverance and guidance, Psalm 119:11,
105, 129-130.
Written on tablet of heart, Proverbs 7:2-3.
Knowing and obeying the Lord's
commands, Isaiah 48:17-18.
God's Law in the heart, Isaiah 51:7.
Certain function of God's Word, Isaiah
55:10-11.
Delectable Word of God, Jeremiah 15:16.
God's Law in mind and on heart, Jeremiah
31:33. (See Heb. 10:16.)
Communicating God's message to
children, Joel 1:1-3.
Coming need for memorized Scripture,
Amos 8:11-12.
Value of memorized Scripture, Micah 2:7.
Function of Scripture within believer, John
17:14-17.
See *Frame of reference, Scripture.*

MEMORY
Remembering and implementing divine
teaching, Deuteronomy 4:9.
Things known in the heart, 1 Kings 2:44.
Memories of old temple caused tears of joy
as new temple begun, Ezra 3:10-13.
Wishing for remembered day not to exist,
Job 3:6.
Longing for remembered happiness of
younger years, Job 29:4-6.
Gratitude for God's goodness, Psalm
143:5.
Good old days, Ecclesiastes 7:10.
God never forgets, Isaiah 49:15.
Former things not brought to mind, Isaiah
65:17.
Greater blessing causes lesser blessing to
be forgotten, Jeremiah 16:14-15.
Bitterly remembering old days,
Lamentations 1:7.
Eating scroll, Ezekiel 3:1-4.
Daniel made notes, did not trust memory,
Daniel 7:1.
Remembering glory of better days, Haggai
2:3.
Paul's limited recall, 1 Corinthians 1:16.
Remembering those absent,
1 Thessalonians 2:17.
See *Recollect, Reminiscence.*

MENACE
Wicked bend their bows, Psalm 11:2.
Song of ruthless made silent, Isaiah 25:5.

Pharaoh only loud noise, Jeremiah 46:17.
See *Danger, Threat.*

MENOPAUSE
Beyond years of childbearing, Genesis
18:11.

MENSTRUATION
Modified social procedures, Genesis 31:33-
35.
Levitical requirements, Leviticus 15:19-30;
20:18.
Defilement of idols, Isaiah 30:22.
Ezekiel's description of puberty, Ezekiel
16:5-9.
Intimacy forbidden, Ezekiel 18:6.
Women violated, Ezekiel 22:10.
Type of uncleanness, Ezekiel 36:17.

MENTAL HEALTH
David feigned madness, 1 Samuel 21:12-
14.
Renewed by Scripture, Psalm 119:93.
Like idol, like follower, Psalm 135:15-18.
Outer and inner feelings, Proverbs 14:13.
Cheerful heart, Proverbs 17:22. (See
18:14.)
Daughters taught how to wail, Jeremiah
9:20.
Becoming like animal, Daniel 4:31-34.
Members of Jesus' own family thought
Him insane, Mark 3:20-21. (Note v. 31.)
See *Depression, Insanity.*

MENTALITY
Definition of witless man, Job 11:12.
Bible-centered mentality, Psalm 1:2.
Understanding to simple, Psalm 119:130.
Parables to a fool, Proverbs 26:1-12.
Easily deceived, Hosea 7:11.
Adults like children, Matthew 11:16-17.
Folly of intellectual pride, 1 Corinthians
3:18-20; 8:1-3.
Spirit of wisdom and revelation, Ephesians
1:17.
Enmity in mind against God, Colossians
1:21.
Fix thoughts on Jesus, Hebrews 3:1.
Mentality of success, 1 Peter 1:15.
Mind clear of negative thoughts, 1 Peter
2:1.
Stimulated to wholesome thought, 2 Peter
3:1.
See *Comprehension, Intelligence.*

MENU
Same food for 40 years, Exodus 16:35.
Wickedness and violence, Proverbs 4:17.
Cheap food causes illness, Proverbs 23:6-8.
See *Cooking.*

MERCENARIES
Reckless adventurers, Judges 9:4. (See 11:3.)
Hiring of foot soldiers, 2 Samuel 10:6.
Requesting payment for spiritual ministry, 2 Kings 5:20-27.
Hired chariots, 1 Chronicles 19:7.
Israelite soldiers for hire, 2 Chronicles 25:6.
Cowardly mercenaries, Jeremiah 46:21.
See *Army.*

MERCHANDISE
Prostitute who paid instead of being paid, Ezekiel 16:33-34.
Use of accurate scales, Ezekiel 45:9-10.
Cargo loses value in storm, Jonah 1:5.
See *Commerce.*

MERCILESS
Partial blindness threatened, 1 Samuel 11:2-11.
Destroying entire population, 1 Samuel 15:3.
Death of Absalom, 2 Samuel 18:9-15.
See *Brutality, Sadistic, Torture.*

MERCY
Divine willingness to extend mercy, Genesis 18:16-33.
Mercy in action, Genesis 39:21-23.
David and Saul, 1 Samuel 24:10-17.
Mercy to the merciful, 2 Samuel 22:26; Psalm 18:25.
Solomon's mercy to Adonijah, 1 Kings 1:43-53.
Imprisoned and set free, 2 Kings 24:15; 25:27-29.
"Mercy" rendered as "love" in new translations, Psalm 23:6.
Contrast between God's anger and love, Psalm 30:5.
Recollections of long life, Psalm 37:25-26.
God's forgiveness and punishment, Psalm 99:8.
Undeserved mercy, Psalm 103:9-10.
God's goodness innate in His person, Psalms 109:21; 145:8-9.

Benevolence of heart, Proverbs 14:21-22, 31.
In midst of judgment, the Lord's hand upraised, Isaiah 5:25; 9:21; 10:4.
Mercy to the coward, Isaiah 30:17-18.
God's great love to faithless Israel, Jeremiah 3:12-13.
The Lord's mercy follows His judgment, Jeremiah 12:14-17.
Immeasurable grace of God, Jeremiah 31:37.
Mercy of Ebed-Melech to suffering Jeremiah, Jeremiah 38:6-13.
In desperation, Zedekiah listened to Jeremiah, Jeremiah 38:14-28.
Babylonian mercy to poor, Jeremiah 39:10.
Optimism in time of bleak pessimism, Jeremiah 48:47.
Mercy of God in time of judgment, Lamentations 3:31-33.
Divine patience with rebellious Israel, Ezekiel 20:1-44.
Greatness of God's mercy, Hosea 14:4.
Pardon for bloodguilt of nation, Joel 3:21.
Pagan sailors reluctant to cast Jonah overboard, Jonah 1:11-15.
Forgiving grace and mercy of God, Micah 7:18.
The Lord slow to anger, Nahum 1:3.
God of judgment becomes God of mercy, Zechariah 8:14-15.
Willingness of Jesus to fulfill physical need, Luke 5:12-13.
Admonition of Jesus, Luke 6:36.
God's love for the unlovely, Ephesians 2:1-5.
Mercy and grace unto salvation, Ephesians 2:6-10.
Christ-centered conduct, Colossians 3:12-13.
The Lord wants all to be saved, 2 Peter 3:9.

MERRYMAKING
Tragedy at Job's home, Job 1:13-19.
Deep inner feelings, Proverbs 14:13.
Entertainment with no thought of spiritual need, Isaiah 5:12.
High price for dance, Mark 6:21-29.
See *Frivolous.*

MESSAGE
Refusing to hear God's message, Judges 6:10.
Words given by Holy Spirit, 2 Samuel 23:2.

King's edict for sparing Jews, Esther 8:14.
Those who do not want to hear truth, Isaiah 30:10-11.
Speaking in understood language, Isaiah 36:11.
Fingers writing on wall, Daniel 5:5.
Mourning over a message, Daniel 10:1-3.
One-chapter book, Obadiah 1-21.
Spectacular communication from heaven, Luke 2:8-14.
Sufficient communication to convey message, John 20:30-31.
Theme of post-Resurrection apostles, Acts 4:2.
Paul's resumé of Old Testament and proclamation of Gospel, Acts 13:16-41.
Gospel known as "the Way," Acts 19:9, 23; 22:4; 24:22.
Gospel message in brief, 1 Corinthians 15:1-8.
Power of Gospel in whatever manner proclaimed, Philippians 1:15-18; 1 Thessalonians 1:4-5.
Word of God in its fullness, Colossians 1:25-26.
Message Paul was called to proclaim, 1 Timothy 2:5-7.
Various ways of communicating God's message, Hebrews 1:1-2.
Faith as credibility to what is heard, Hebrews 4:2.
Message for all ages, 1 John 2:12-14.
Message conveyed by angel, Revelation 1:1-3.

MESSENGER
Angel who came to Samson's mother, Judges 13:6.
Unheeded messengers, Jeremiah 25:4; Matthew 22:3.
Bearer of bad news, Ezekiel 33:21.
Peter and crowing rooster, Mark 14:29-31, 66-72.
Angelic communication, Luke 1:19; Revelation 1:1.
By divine appointment, John 1:6.
Young man who protected Paul, Acts 23:16-22.
See *Ministry, Missionary, Preaching.*

MESSIAH
David's reign same length of time as life of Christ, 2 Samuel 5:5.
Solomon's concept of Jesus, Proverbs

30:4.
Prophecy of Virgin Birth, Isaiah 7:14.
Birth and coming of Messiah, Isaiah 9:1-7.
Tested stone in Zion, Isaiah 28:16.
Prophecy of John the Baptist and Christ, Isaiah 40:1-5.
Prophetic description of Jesus, Isaiah 53:1-12.
Coming of Christ and proclamation of Gospel, Isaiah 61:1-3.
Redeemer and King, Isaiah 63:1.
Birth in Bethlehem, Micah 5:2.
Desired of all ages, Haggai 2:6-7.
Triumphal Entry into Jerusalem, Zechariah 9:9.
Prophecy of Judas and 30 pieces of silver, Zechariah 11:12-13.
Prophecy of the cross, Zechariah 12:10-11.
Conquering Lord of lords, Zechariah 14:3-4.
Authentic Messiah, Matthew 11:1-5.
Death of David, death of Christ, and messianic implications, Acts 2:29-35.
Abraham anticipated salvation of Jew and Gentile, Galatians 3:6-9.
Sovereignty of Jesus over all earth, Revelation 1:5.
Unique name for Jesus, Revelation 3:14.
Rider on white horse, Revelation 19:11-16.
Totality of the Son of God, Revelation 22:13.
See *Jesus, Second Coming.*

METAL
Metalworkers, Exodus 31:1-5; 1 Chronicles 22:15-16; Isaiah 40:19.
Silver not precious metal, 1 Kings 10:21, 27.
Strength of iron, Jeremiah 15:12.
Gold and silver belong to God, Haggai 2:8.
See *Ore.*

METAPHOR
Rising like the sun, Judges 5:31.
Lord and shepherd, Psalm 23:1.
Sun and shield, Psalm 84:11.
Shield and rampart, Psalm 91:4.
Sow and reap, Hosea 10:12.
Wickedness in the flesh, Zechariah 5:7-8.
Salt of earth, Matthew 5:13.
Seed and soil, Matthew 13:19-23, 37-43.
Bread and body, Matthew 26:26.
Lamp of witness, John 5:35.
Bread of Life, John 6:35.

Light of world, John 8:12.
Jesus as the gate, John 10:9.
True Vine, John 15:5.
Sorrow turned to joy, John 16:20.
Speaking plainly, John 16:25.
Lampstands and stars, Revelation 1:20.
Incense and prayers, Revelation 5:8.

METEOROLOGIST
Divine control of weather, Job 28:24-27;
    36:27-33; 37:6-21; Psalm 135:7.
Divine meteorologist, Jeremiah 14:22.
Rain in spotted areas, Amos 4:7-8.
Formation of clouds and rainfall, Amos 9:6.
Weather on request, Zechariah 10:1.
Forecasting weather, Matthew 16:2; Luke
    12:54-56.
See *Weather.*

METEORS
Stars falling to earth, Revelation 6:13.
Huge hailstones, Revelation 16:21.
See *Astronomy.*

MIDNIGHT
Peril at midnight, Exodus 11:4.
Ten virgins, Matthew 25:6.
Midnight song and prayer, Acts 16:25.
Preaching until midnight, Acts 20:7.

MIGRATION
Aliens succeed above local citizenry,
    Deuteronomy 28:43-44.
Building population by statistics,
    Nehemiah 11:1.
Hawk flies south, Job 39:26.
Birds know when to migrate, Jeremiah 8:7.

MILDEW
Cleaning a house of mildew, Leviticus
    14:33-53.
Terminal disorder, Deuteronomy 28:22.
Blight and mildew, Amos 4:9; Haggai 2:17.

MILITARY
Threat of iron chariots, Judges 1:19.
God as militarist, Judges 3:1-2.
David's concern about army above
    promises of God, 2 Samuel 24:10.
Complete devastation, 2 Kings 3:19.
Men trained for service, 1 Chronicles 5:18.
Strength of God's army, Psalm 68:17.
Angel in military, Isaiah 37:36.
Cornelius and devout family, Acts 10:1-2.

(See also vv. 7, 22.)
Good soldiers of Christ Jesus, 2 Timothy
    2:1-4.
See *Mercenaries.*

MILK
Curds and milk for visitors, Genesis 18:8.
Milk and honey, Deuteronomy 32:13-14;
    Isaiah 7:22.
Water requested, milk served, Judges 4:19.
Dairy product in desert, 2 Samuel 17:29.
Milk to butter, Proverbs 30:33.
Spiritual food, 1 Corinthians 3:1-3;
    Hebrews 5:11-14.

MILLENNIUM
See *Second Coming.*

MIND
The Lord knows our thoughts, Psalms
    94:11; 139:1-4.
Danger of evil thoughts, Jeremiah 4:14.
Revealing thoughts of heart, Luke 2:34-35.
Depraved minds, Romans 1:28.
Natural mind and Spirit-controlled mind,
    Romans 8:6-8.
Futility of thinking, Ephesians 4:17.
Attitude of mind dictates conduct in life,
    Philippians 4:8-9.
Egotistical mind, Colossians 2:18.
Corrupt mind and conscience, Titus 1:15.
Thoughts fixed on Jesus, Hebrews 3:1.
Minds prepared for action, 1 Peter 1:13.
See *Frame of reference, Thinking, Thought.*

MINERALS
Wealth of earth, Genesis 2:11-12.
Listed in Scripture, Genesis 11:3; Numbers
    21:9; 31:22; Deuteronomy 8:9; 29:23;
    Job 19:24; 28:18.
Silver not precious metal, 1 Kings 10:21,
    27.
Mining deep into earth, Job 28:1-4.
Gold and silver belong to God, Haggai 2:8.

MINISTRY
Work begun by God, impaired by
    disobedience, Jeremiah 11:17.
Teaching, preaching, healing, Matthew
    4:23; 9:18-25.
No chance for rest in busy ministry, Mark
    6:30-34.
Ministry of aged widow, Luke 2:36-38.
Varying styles of ministry, Luke 9.

Joy of serving Christ, Luke 10:17.

Misunderstanding role of Jesus in ministry, Luke 12:13-14.

Barnabas and Saul, Acts 11:22-26.

Many at Antioch taught and preached, Acts 15:35.

Holy Spirit hinders preaching in area, Acts 16:6-7.

Giving up on those who refuse to accept truth, Acts 18:5-6.

New convert given instruction for effective witness, Acts 18:24-26.

Paul's evaluation of his own ministry, Acts 20:17-38.

Paul's bondage a means for ministry, Acts 28:17-28.

First a servant, then a minister, Romans 1:1.

Importance of prayer in ministry, Romans 1:8-10; 15:31-32.

Service of mutual benefit, Romans 1:11.

Concluding ministry in an area, Romans 15:24-25.

Entrusted with secret things of God, 1 Corinthians 4:1-2.

In a race, only one wins. In serving God, all may win, 1 Corinthians 9:24-27.

Relationship of men and women in ministry, 1 Corinthians 11:11.

Ministry of prayer, Ephesians 6:18.

Paul a channel of much blessing to Philippians, Philippians 1:25-26.

Church and its outreach, Colossians 1:24-29.

Praying for those who minister, Colossians 4:3.

Faith, love, and hope, 1 Thessalonians 1:3.

Preaching and teaching with more than words, 1 Thessalonians 1:4-5.

Paul's clear motivation in preaching and teaching, 1 Thessalonians 2:1-6.

Faithful until Christ returns, 1 Timothy 6:11-16.

Power and love through discipline, 2 Timothy 1:7.

God's plan for perpetuation of Gospel, 2 Timothy 2:1-4.

Ministry mandate to Timothy, 2 Timothy 4:1-5.

Crown of righteousness for faithful ministry, 2 Timothy 4:6-8.

Tools through whom God ministers, Titus 1:1-3.

Called to ministry of holiness, 1 Peter 1:15-16.

Holy priesthood for believers, 1 Peter 2:5.

Continuing zeal of aging worker, 2 Peter 1:13-14.

Ministering in name of the Lord, 3 John 7.

Helping those who doubt, Jude 22-23.

Poor performance in service to God, Revelation 3:2.

See *Clergy, Missionary, Preaching.*

MINORITY

Minority of righteousness, Genesis 6:6-8.

Smallest and weakest, Judges 6:14-16.

Gleaning of one vineyard better than harvest of another, Judges 8:2.

King chosen from smallest tribe, 1 Samuel 9:21.

One plus God against many, 1 Samuel 14:9-14.

Human strength of little value, Psalm 33:16.

Little tribe of Benjamin led all others, Psalm 68:27.

God blesses small and great alike, Psalm 115:13.

Victory not necessarily to swift and strong, Ecclesiastes 9:11.

Least becomes great, Isaiah 60:22.

Tiny grains of sand hold back ocean, Jeremiah 5:22.

Babylonian mercy to poor, Jeremiah 39:10.

Not one upright man remaining, Micah 7:2.

God's blessing on meek and humble, Zephaniah 3:12.

Day of small things, Zechariah 4:10.

Wide and narrow, Matthew 7:13-14.

Faith small as mustard seed, Matthew 13:31-32; 17:20; Mark 4:30-32.

First last, last first, Matthew 19:30; Mark 10:31.

Many invited, few chosen, Matthew 22:1-14.

Prophet and one widow, Luke 4:23-26.

Facing adversary with limited troops, Luke 14:31-32.

Remnant of Israel, Romans 11:1-5.

Those of humble backgrounds and abilities, 1 Corinthians 1:26.

Illustration of human body, 1 Corinthians 12:21-25.

See *Racism.*

MIRACLES

Miracles performed by false prophet,

Deuteronomy 13:1-5.
Dearth of miracles, Psalm 74:9.
Reward of selfish prayer, Psalm 106:14-15.
Not putting God to the test, Isaiah 7:11-12.
Blind see, deaf hear, Isaiah 35:5.
Hezekiah's illness and healing, Isaiah 38:1-6.
Reversal of sun's shadow, Isaiah 38:7.
Protection of Daniel's friends in fiery furnace, Daniel 3:22-27.
Futile attempt to prevent miracle, Matthew 27:62-66. (See also 28:11-15.)
Emphasizing healing above Healer, Luke 7:21-23.
Those who must see signs and wonders to believe, John 4:48.
Purpose of miracles in Jesus' ministry, John 10:22-39; 20:30-31.
Conversion of Roman leader influenced by sorcerer, Acts 13:6-12.
Miracles in Paul's ministry, Acts 19:11-12.
Holy Spirit brought Christ back from the dead, Romans 8:11; Ephesians 1:18-21.
Function of gifts of Spirit, Hebrews 2:4.

MIRROR
Israelite women's contribution for making worship basin, Exodus 38:1-8.
Mirror-like skies, Job 37:17-18.
Water as mirror, Proverbs 27:19.
Poor reflection, 1 Corinthians 13:12.
Our faces as mirrors, 2 Corinthians 3:18.
Mirrors never lie, James 1:22-25.

MISANTHROPE
See *Deceit, Mistrust.*

MISCEGENATION
Distinction of each species, Genesis 1:24-25.
Avoiding marriage to foreigner, Genesis 24:1-4.
Danger of marriage to pagans, Exodus 34:12-16; Deuteronomy 7:1-4.

MISCHIEF
Scheming to cause harm, Nehemiah 6:1-2.
Preventive care for children, Job 1:1-5.
Satanic view of man's motivations, Job 2:1-10.
In-depth mischief, Job 15:35.
Lurking in secret, Psalm 10:8.
Lying awake to scheme, Psalm 36:4; Proverbs 4:16.

Minds busy with evil, Isaiah 32:6.
See *Devious.*

MISER
Poverty caused by hoarding, Proverbs 11:24; Ecclesiastes 5:13.
Cold heart today, needy heart tomorrow, Proverbs 21:13.
Food of stingy man, Proverbs 23:6-8.
Greed a form of idolatry, Colossians 3:5.
See *Stingy.*

MISERY.
See *Agony, Pain, Suffering, Torture.*

MISFORTUNE
Men of bad circumstances share good fortune with others, 2 Kings 7:3-9.
Satanic view of man's motivations, Job 2:1-10.
Judgment brings righteousness, Isaiah 26:9.
From frying pan to fire, Amos 5:19.
Trouble will not happen twice, Nahum 1:9.
See *Accident.*

MISREPRESENTATION
Deceiving one's neighbor, Leviticus 6:1-2.
Negative and positive viewpoints, Numbers 13:17-33.
Discerning the prophets, Deuteronomy 18:21-22; Jeremiah 23:16-18.
Twisting words, Psalm 56:5.
Writing falsehoods concerning God's Law, Jeremiah 8:8.
Riches gained unjustly, Jeremiah 17:11.
Cheating and polluting, Amos 8:5-6.
See *Deceit, Falsehood, Lie.*

MISSIONARY
Love for foreigners, Deuteronomy 10:19.
Journey with the Lord's approval, Judges 18:6.
Solomon's attitude toward foreigners, 1 Kings 8:41-43.
Missionary assignment, 2 Kings 17:27-28.
Outreach to heathen, 1 Chronicles 16:23-24.
Bible reference used by missionaries, Psalm 2:8.
Benediction for missions, Psalm 67:1-2.
Those who proclaim God's Word, Psalm 68:11.
Declare God's glory among nations, Psalm

96:3, 10; 105:1.
Sow in tears, reap with joy, Psalm 126:5-6.
Singing to the Lord in foreign land, Psalm 137:4.
Alert during harvest, Proverbs 10:5.
God reaches out to heathen, Isaiah 5:25-26.
Isaiah's call to convey message, Isaiah 6:8-10; 12:4-5; 45:22.
Evangelize during night, with morning coming, Isaiah 21:11-12.
Light for Gentiles, Isaiah 49:6; 60:3.
Beautiful feet of those who bring good news, Isaiah 52:7; Nahum 1:15.
Those who did not ask for God's message, Isaiah 65:1-5.
Harvest past, summer ended, no salvation, Jeremiah 8:20.
Responsibility for failure to witness, Ezekiel 3:18-19.
Someone to stand in gap, Ezekiel 22:30.
Responsibility of watchman to warn wicked, Ezekiel 33:7-9.
Those who witness shine like stars, Daniel 12:3.
Ripe harvest, Joel 3:13-14.
Famine for words of the Lord, Amos 8:11-12.
Jonah's call to missionary assignment, Jonah 3:1-9.
Teaching, preaching, healing, Matthew 4:23.
Plentiful harvest, few workers, Matthew 9:37-38.
Great Commission, Matthew 28:16-20; Mark 16:15.
Gospel must be preached to all nations, Mark 13:10.
Biblical models, Luke 19:10; John 3:2; Acts 8:4-5; 15:7; 18:24; 2 Peter 2:5.
Greatest model for mission, John 3:16.
Harvesttime, John 4:35-38.
Lifting up Jesus to draw men to salvation, John 12:32.
Spiritual conquest, not earthly possession, should motivate follower of Christ, Acts 1:6-8.
Message to entire world, Acts 10:9-20.
Missionary commissioning, Acts 13:2-4.
Paul's vision of Macedonia, Acts 16:9-10.
Faith reported all over world, Romans 1:8.
Bringing message to those who have not heard, Romans 10:14-15; 15:21.
Benediction concerning world

evangelization, Romans 16:25-27.
Material payment to those who render spiritual service, 1 Corinthians 9:9-14; 1 Timothy 5:17-18.
Adapting to culture of others for effective preaching, 1 Corinthians 9:19-23.
Faithfully present message whatever difficulties, 1 Corinthians 15:57-58.
Open door of opportunity, 1 Corinthians 16:9.
Christ's ambassadors in the world, 2 Corinthians 5:18-21.
Clear marks of serving disciple, 2 Corinthians 6:3-13.
Abraham anticipated salvation of Jew and Gentile, Galatians 3:6-9.
Less than least, Ephesians 3:8-9.
Praying for those who minister, Ephesians 6:19-20; Colossians 4:3-4.
Rapid spread of Gospel message, Colossians 1:6.
Church and its outreach, Colossians 1:24-27.
Paul thanked his Lord for privilege of ministry, 1 Timothy 1:12-14.
Message Paul was called to proclaim, 1 Timothy 2:5-7.
Called to be a herald, apostle, and teacher, 2 Timothy 1:11.
Divine plan for perpetuation of Gospel, 2 Timothy 2:1-4.
Paul's ministry mandate to Timothy, 2 Timothy 4:1-5.
Paul's credentials in ministry, Titus 1:1-3.
Called to a ministry of holiness, 1 Peter 1:15-16.
Willing to lay down one's life for others, 1 John 3:16.
Proclaiming angel, Revelation 14:6-7.
See *Contextualization, Evangelism.*

MISTAKE
Divine regret, Genesis 6:5-8.
Righteous man rises again and again, Proverbs 24:15-16.
Remorse of Judas, Matthew 27:3.
See *Error, Guilt, Wrong.*

MISTAKEN IDENTITY
Case of mistaken identity, Esther 6:1-13.
Jesus a stranger to His own followers, Mark 4:35-41.
Jesus mistaken for Elijah and John the Baptist, Mark 6:14-16; John 8:27-29.

MISTREATMENT
Complaining of mistreatment, Exodus
17:1-3.
Partial blindness threatened as disgrace,
1 Samuel 11:2-11.
House left untended, Ecclesiastes 10:18.
Making and breaking promise to slaves,
Jeremiah 34:8-22.
Exploiting poor for personal gain, Amos
5:11.
See *Persecution.*

MISTRUST
Act of kindness misinterpreted, 2 Samuel
10:1-4.
Friends and brothers not to be trusted,
Jeremiah 9:4-8.
Those who refused to believe Jeremiah's
prophecy of protection, Jeremiah 43:1-
3.
Neighbors and friends who cannot be
trusted, Micah 7:5.
See *Deceit.*

MISUNDERSTANDING
Making wrong right, Numbers 5:6-7.
When others speak evil of you, Psalm 17:2.
Twisting of words, Psalm 56:5.
Some things better spoken than written,
2 John 12; 3 John 13-14.
See *Communication.*

MISUSE
Sacrifice misused, 1 Samuel 2:12-17.
David refused to drink water which had
endangered the lives of his men,
2 Samuel 23:15-17.
Taking advantage of others, James 5:4-5.

MOB PSYCHOLOGY
Complaining community, Exodus 16:2.
Following crowd, Exodus 23:2.
People prone to idolatry, Exodus 32:19-28.
Wrong kind of unanimity, Numbers 11:4-
10.
Community-wide discontent, Numbers
14:1-4.
Lack of discernment, Deuteronomy 32:28.
Trampled by hungry mob, 2 Kings 7:17-20.
(See entire chapter.)
Mob psychology at trial of Jesus, Matthew
27:15-26. (See 21:1-11.)
Potential mob violence during Passover,
Mark 14:1-2.

People of synagogue versus Jesus, Luke
4:28-30.
People trampling over each other, Luke
12:1.
Persuasive power of mob, Luke 23:13-25.
Following Jesus out of curiosity, John 12:9-
11, 17-18.
Poisoning minds of others, Acts 14:2.
Worshiping Paul and Barnabas because of
their spiritual power, Acts 14:8-18.
Bad characters incited against Paul and
Silas, Acts 17:5-7.
People confused in riotous crowd, Acts
19:32.
Crowd incensed against Paul, Acts 22:22;
23:10.

MOCKERY
Defiant sin, Numbers 15:30-31.
Putting blame on God, 2 Kings 6:33.
Scorn for acts of humility, Psalm 69:10-11.
Making mockery of fasting, Isaiah 58:4-5.
Disrespect for sanctuary, Ezekiel 25:1-4.
Laughing at truth spoken by Jesus,
Matthew 9:23-24.
Mixing human blood with sacrifices, Luke
13:1.
See *Disdain, Scoff.*

MODEL
Righteous man without blame, Genesis
6:9.
Abraham's reputation in eyes of
Abimelech, Genesis 21:22.
Backslidden believers a laughingstock,
Exodus 32:25.
King who put aside personal grief to lead
people, 2 Samuel 19:1-8.
Man who truly walked with God, Job 1:1.
Practice what you preach, Psalm 51:10-13.
Do not disgrace others, Psalm 69:6.
Example of persecuted prophets, Matthew
5:11-12.
Like teacher, like student, Luke 6:40.
Supreme model of love and outreach, John
3:16-17.
Paul urged converts to follow his example,
1 Corinthians 4:15-16; 11:1;
2 Thessalonians 3:6-10.
Deserving right to be heard, 2 Corinthians
4:1-2.
Lifestyle Paul communicated by example,
2 Corinthians 6:4-10.
Supreme model of unselfishness,

2 Corinthians 8:7-9.
Sharing concerns of leader, 2 Corinthians 8:16.
Ultimate career, life of love, Ephesians 5:1-2.
Standing firm whatever circumstances, Philippians 1:27-30.
Paul's commendation of Timothy, Philippians 2:19-23.
Those who became model believers, 1 Thessalonians 1:7.
Example of God's grace to worst of sinners, 1 Timothy 1:15-16.
Paul's model of good teaching, 2 Timothy 1:13-14.
Paul's example to Timothy, 2 Timothy 3:10-11.
Elder's family must be exemplary, Titus 1:6.
Example set by good teacher, Titus 2:6-7.
Those who show initiative, Hebrews 6:11-12.
Service in sanctuary of ultimate High Priest, Hebrews 8:1-6.
Those who lived by faith, Hebrews 12:1-3.
Christ's example teaches us to show love, 1 John 4:7-11.
See *Example, Exemplary.*

MODERATION
Casting off restraint, Proverbs 29:18.
Balanced wisdom and piety, Ecclesiastes 7:16.
Relationship of husband and wife, 1 Corinthians 7:1-7.
The continual lust for more, Ephesians 4:19.
See *Restraint.*

MODERNISM
Those who turn away, Judges 2:17; 1 John 2:19.
Pharisees and religion of sham, Matthew 23:5-7.
Shipwrecked faith, 1 Timothy 1:18.
Turning to myths, 2 Timothy 4:4.
See *Apostasy, Liberalism, Syncretism.*

MODESTY
First awareness of nudity, Genesis 3:7. (See 2:25.)
Nakedness of Noah, Genesis 9:20-27.
Demure maiden, Genesis 24:61-65.
Unworthy of being in presence of king,

2 Samuel 19:24-28.
Clothes torn off, Jeremiah 13:22.
Act of shame, Jeremiah 13:26.
Jesus asked that His miracles be kept private, Matthew 9:29-31.
Special modesty in regard to body organs, 1 Corinthians 12:22-25.
Modesty in dress, 1 Timothy 2:9-10.
See *Discretion.*

MOLDING
Clay molds used for artifacts, 2 Chronicles 4:17.
Potter and clay, Isaiah 45:9; Jeremiah 18:1-4.

MOMENTO
David kept weapons of Goliath, 1 Samuel 17:54.

MONEY
Currency by weight, Genesis 23:16; Ezra 8:24-27; Jeremiah 32:9.
Animals, land, and people used in place of money, Genesis 47:16-21.
Monetary value of human being, Leviticus 27:1-8.
Value of silver in stewardship, Numbers 7:13-85; 10:2.
Services to be paid for in cash, Deuteronomy 2:6.
Lending money without interest, Psalm 15:5.
Prostitute giving rather than receiving fee, Ezekiel 16:32-34.
Value and designation of currency, Ezekiel 45:12.
Silver and gold belong to God, Haggai 2:8.
Reward of good stewardship, Malachi 3:8-10.
Tainted money paid for betraying Jesus, Matthew 27:3-10.
No need for expense money, Mark 6:8-11.
Estimating cost before starting to build, Luke 14:28-30.
Human equations and power of God, John 6:1-13. (See particularly v. 7.)
Spiritual economics, Acts 3:6.
Power of God not for sale, Acts 8:18-24.
Owners of slave girl angered by loss of income, Acts 16:16-24.
Business profit limited by transformation of converts, Acts 19:23-28.
Evangelist seeking employment to support

himself, 1 Corinthians 9:6-7.
Unmuzzled ox, 1 Corinthians 9:9-14.
Root of evil, 1 Timothy 6:10.
See *Barter.*

MONOLOGUE
Reciting proverbs to musical
   accompaniment, Psalm 49:4.
See *Eloquence.*

MONOTHEISM
Silver idol for true God, Judges 17:4.
Nebuchadnezzar confused between
   admission of one true God and belief in
   many gods, Daniel 3:28-30; 4:18.
No god but the Lord, Hosea 13:4.

MONOTONY
Same food for 40 years, Exodus 16:35.

MONUMENT
See *Memorial.*

MOOD
See *Attitude, Disposition, Frame of
   reference.*

MOON
Not to be worshiped, Deuteronomy 4:19.
Abundant blessings of nature,
   Deuteronomy 33:13-16.
Inert sun and moon, Joshua 10:12-14.
Moon-gazing, Job 31:26.
Moon designates seasons, Psalm 104:19.
Romantic likeness, Song of Songs 6:10.
Humiliated moon, Isaiah 24:23.
Moon turned to blood, Joel 2:31.
See *Astronomy.*

MORALE
Taking care of business, Deuteronomy
   20:5-9.
Leadership for those in trouble, 1 Samuel
   22:2.
Ineptness of king's viewpoint, 1 Kings
   12:1-15.
People working diligently together,
   Nehemiah 4:6.
Inequity among citizens, Nehemiah 5:1-5.
Security in the Lord, Psalm 127:1-2.
Jeremiah persecuted for destroying morale
   of soldiers, Jeremiah 38:1-6.
Joy and gladness gone, Jeremiah 48:33.
Demoralizing influence of hunger, Luke

15:13-20.
See *Optimism, Pessimism.*

MORALITY
Abram, Sarai, and the Egyptians, Genesis
   12:10-20.
Abimelech guided by the Lord in conduct
   toward Sarah, Genesis 20:1-18.
Law concerning remarriage of divorced
   persons, Deuteronomy 24:1-4.
Moral conduct of Boaz, Ruth 3:7-14.
David's respect for concubines, 2 Samuel
   20:3.
David advanced in years, 1 Kings 1:1-4.
Eunuchs looked after queen, Esther 1:10;
   2:3.
Avoiding lust requires discipline, Job 31:1.
Morality vital part of spirituality, Jeremiah
   3:1-5.
Ezekiel's description of puberty, Ezekiel
   16:5-9.
Exemplary life does not bring salvation,
   Matthew 19:16-26; Mark 10:17-20.
Those who need Great Physician, Mark
   2:17.
As in the days of Noah, Luke 17:26-30.
Function of conscience, Romans 2:14-15.
Special modesty toward body organs,
   1 Corinthians 12:22-25.
Result of new birth, 2 Corinthians 5:17.
Fruit of the heart, Hebrews 8:10.
Those who keep themselves pure,
   Revelation 14:4.
See *Chastity, Purity, Virgin.*

MORNING
Arising early to stand before the Lord,
   Genesis 19:27; Exodus 34:4-5.
Early morning bath, Exodus 8:20.
Action around Jericho at daybreak, Joshua
   6:12-20.
Strength of rising sun, Judges 5:31.
Early morning dew on fleece, Judges 6:38.
Early morning spectacle, 1 Samuel 5:4.
Early morning admonition, 2 Chronicles
   20:20.
Dawn greeted with music, Psalm 57:8.
Mother's work never finished, Proverbs
   31:15.
End of sleepless night, Daniel 6:18-23.
Dawn to darkness, Amos 4:13.
Morning of all mornings, Matthew 28:1-10;
   Mark 16:1-8; Luke 24:1-12; John 20:1-9.
Crowing rooster and Peter, Mark 14:29-31,

66-72.
Jesus at daybreak, Luke 4:42.
Jesus teaching at dawn, John 8:2.
Given the morning star, Revelation 2:28.

MORNING STAR
Dawn in your heart, 2 Peter 1:19.
Divine property, Revelation 2:28.
Bright morning star, Revelation 22:16.
See *Astronomy*.

MORTALITY
Death makes possible deliverance from
    sinful nature, Genesis 3:22.
Desire to live forever, 1 Kings 1:31.
Way of all earth, 1 Kings 2:2.
Lacking strength of stone, Job 6:12.
Life and breath in God's hands, Job 12:10.
Length of life determined, Job 14:5.
Pessimistic view of mortality, Job 14:7-11.
    (See also v. 14.)
We are but men, Psalm 9:20.
God, not man, can help us in time of
    trouble, Psalm 60:11-12.
Experiencing divine wonders before death,
    Psalm 88:10-12.
Limited perfection for mortals, unlimited
    for God, Psalm 119:96.
Fragility of existence, Psalm 144:3-4.
Wise man and fool soon forgotten,
    Ecclesiastes 2:16.
No power over day of one's death,
    Ecclesiastes 8:8.
Stop trusting in man, Isaiah 2:22.
Egyptians were but men, Isaiah 31:3.
People drained of power, Isaiah 37:27.
Death in early years of life, Isaiah 38:10.
Wide contrast between temporal and
    spiritual, Isaiah 40:7-8.
People to live to age of trees, Isaiah 65:20-
    22.
Foolishness of depending on mortal flesh,
    Jeremiah 17:5.
Those who should live die, those who
    should die live, Ezekiel 13:19.
Dual nature of man, Romans 7:21-25.
That which God has prepared exceeds
    human perception and experience,
    1 Corinthians 2:9-10.
Rapid deterioration of human body,
    2 Corinthians 4:16-18.
Paul experienced anxiety, Philippians 2:28.
Our body but a tent, 2 Peter 1:13.
Limited authority of the beast, Revelation

13:1-18.
Blood of dead man, Revelation 16:3.
See *Death, Humanity, Life, Longevity*.

MORTGAGE
Mortgaging property to buy food,
    Nehemiah 5:3.

MOTHER
Motherhood by incest, Genesis 19:30-38.
Love of Hagar for Ishmael, Genesis 21:14-
    16.
Death in childbirth, Genesis 35:16-20.
Wisdom of Moses' mother, Exodus 2:1-10.
Mother to be honored, Exodus 20:12.
Parental discretion, Leviticus 18:7.
Role of Rachel and Leah in strengthening
    house of Israel, Ruth 4:11.
Dedicating child given to praying woman,
    1 Samuel 1:25-28.
Michal had no children, 2 Samuel 6:23.
Bathsheba's intercession on behalf of her
    son, Solomon, 1 Kings 1:11-21.
Adonijah's ill-fated request for wife,
    1 Kings 2:13-25.
Solomon's wise test in determining
    identity of true mother, 1 Kings 3:16-
    28.
Historical mention of mothers in record of
    young kings, 2 Kings 23:31, 36; 24:8, 18.
Animals of nature born in secret, Job 39:1.
Ostrich knows little of motherhood, Job
    39:13-17.
Descriptive example from motherhood,
    Psalm 7:14.
Barren woman becomes happy mother,
    Psalm 113:9.
Mother's law, Proverbs 1:8; 6:20.
Care of aged parents, Proverbs 23:22-25.
Mother's shame, Proverbs 29:15.
Woman of noble character, Proverbs
    31:10-31.
Sons of sorceress, Isaiah 57:3.
Surrogate mother among birds, Jeremiah
    17:11.
Like mother, like daughter, Ezekiel 16:44.
Desecrated mother, Ezekiel 19:10-14.
Anger of bear robbed of cubs, Hosea 13:8.
Mother of Jesus at cross, Mark 15:40.
Reactions of Mary compared to that of
    shepherds, Luke 2:19-20.
Mother's reprimand, Luke 2:41-50.
Jesus' own mother and brothers unable to
    get through crowd, Luke 8:19-21.

Pain of childbirth brings joy, John 16:21.
Woman like mother to Paul, Romans 16:13.
Kept safe in childbirth, 1 Timothy 2:15.
Those who bring up children, 1 Timothy 5:10.
Woman in heaven who gave birth, Revelation 12:1-6.
See *Childbirth, Childless, Pregnancy.*

MOTHER-IN-LAW
Exemplary relationship, Ruth 1:8-18.
Faith brings family conflict, Matthew 10:34-36.
Wife's mother ill, Mark 1:30.

MOTIVATION
Doing what is right, Genesis 4:7.
Joseph's brothers sought for guilt less than murder, Genesis 37:19-27.
Moved of heart to do God's work, Exodus 35:20-21, 25-26, 29.
Consciously doing what is right, Leviticus 22:29.
Questionable sincerity of repentance, 1 Samuel 15:13-35.
Respect for prophet born by fear, 2 Kings 1:1-15.
Zealous workman, Nehemiah 3:20.
Submitting to God's tests of motive and thought, Psalm 26:2.
Highest motive life can know, Psalm 27:4.
Desires the Lord places in our hearts, Psalm 37:3-5. (See also 20:4-5.)
Knowledge of God's Word leads to desire for His will, Psalm 40:8.
Letting God fulfill His purpose, Psalm 57:2.
The Lord knows our very thoughts, Psalm 94:11.
No place for deceit in God's house, Psalm 101:7.
Choosing to follow way of truth, Psalm 119:30.
Finding life's greatest values, Psalm 119:36-37.
Seeking, considering, hastening to obey Scripture, Psalm 119:57-64.
Build in vain unless the Lord builds, Psalm 127:1.
David's determination to fulfill destiny, Psalm 132:1-5.
Our thoughts and motives, Psalm 139:1-4.
Guard your heart, Proverbs 4:23.
The lazy and the diligent, Proverbs 10:4.

Man's plans and God's decree, Proverbs 16:1.
Motivated by good appetite, Proverbs 16:26.
Love of pleasure, Proverbs 21:17.
Overt effort to become rich, Proverbs 23:4-5; 28:20.
Working with diligence, Ecclesiastes 9:10.
Nothing hidden from God, Isaiah 29:15-16.
Noble man makes noble plans, Isaiah 32:8.
Knowing what is right, Isaiah 51:7.
God tests heart and mind, Jeremiah 11:20; 17:10.
Sincere search for God, Jeremiah 29:10-14.
God's Law in the mind and on the heart, Jeremiah 31:33.
God, who sees all, rewards good, Jeremiah 32:19.
Singleness of heart and action, Jeremiah 32:38-39.
Examine one's ways and return to the Lord, Lamentations 3:40.
Undivided heart, Ezekiel 11:19.
God never acts without cause, Ezekiel 14:23.
Plundering with glee, Ezekiel 36:5.
Seek good, not evil, Amos 5:14.
Righteous live by faith, Habakkuk 2:4.
Challenge to work for divine cause, Haggai 2:4.
King Herod and magi, Matthew 2:7-8, 12.
Disciples immediately left occupations to follow Jesus, Matthew 4:20-22.
Anger a form of murder, Matthew 5:21-22.
Motivations of men and motivations of Jesus, Matthew 8:1-3.
Thoughts of heart, Luke 2:34-35.
Mouth speaks what heart contains, Luke 6:43-45.
Jesus could not be diverted from the cross, Luke 23:35-39.
Love of the Lord involves outreach to others, John 21:15-18.
Persistence in witnessing, Acts 5:42.
David's motivation, Acts 13:22.
Paul went with confidence into difficult places, Acts 20:22-24.
Motivation comes from within, Romans 2:28-29.
Motivated by the Spirit instead of the Law, Romans 7:6.
Struggle between flesh and spirit, Romans 7:15-18.

Wood, hay, and straw instead of gold, silver, costly stones, 1 Corinthians 3:12-13.

Hidden motives brought to light, 1 Corinthians 4:5.

Paul's motives for preaching Gospel, 1 Corinthians 9:16-18.

Doing all for glory of God, 1 Corinthians 10:31.

Motivated by message, 1 Corinthians 15:10.

Faithfully present message despite difficulties, 1 Corinthians 15:57-58.

Do everything in love, 1 Corinthians 16:13-14.

Compelled by love of Christ, 2 Corinthians 5:14.

Paul exploited no one, 2 Corinthians 7:2.

Giving from continuity of desire, 2 Corinthians 9:10.

Life of love, Ephesians 5:1-2.

Doing good work unto the Lord, Ephesians 6:5-8.

Power of Gospel in whatever manner proclaimed, Philippians 1:15-18.

Forgetting past, pressing forward, Philippians 3:12-16.

True value of giving, Philippians 4:17.

Whatever you say or do, Colossians 3:17.

Do not serve God to please men, Colossians 3:23-24.

Properly motivated, 1 Thessalonians 1:3.

Love and fellowship in ministry, 1 Thessalonians 2:7-9.

Motivated to Christian lifestyle, 1 Thessalonians 4:11-12.

Good purpose fulfilled, 2 Thessalonians 1:11. (See Ps. 37:4.)

Desire to be overseer, 1 Timothy 3:1.

Motivation toward wealth, 1 Timothy 6:9-10.

Evil desires of youth, 2 Timothy 2:22.

Those who preach and teach for dishonest gain, Titus 1:10-16.

Favors extended with proper motivation, Philemon 14.

Fear as motivating factor, Hebrews 11:7.

Faithfully running race, Hebrews 12:1-2.

Love of money, Hebrews 13:5.

Role of evil desire in causing one to sin, James 1:13-15.

Scriptural teaching in action, James 1:22-25.

Minds prepared for action, 1 Peter 1:13.

Actions speak louder than words, 1 John 3:18.

Ministering in name of the Lord, 3 John 7.

God searches mind and heart, Revelation 2:23.

Role of demons in world politics, Revelation 16:14.

When evil serves God's purpose, Revelation 17:17.

See *Initiative, Objective.*

MOTIVE

King Saul's selfish motive in offering daughter to David, 1 Samuel 18:20-23.

Moving straight ahead, Proverbs 4:25-27.

God sees all of man's ways, Proverbs 5:21.

The Lord blamed for our misdeeds, Isaiah 63:17.

Seek good, not evil, Amos 5:14.

Sin committed in heart, Matthew 5:27-28.

Decision to communicate by writing, Luke 1:1-4.

Emphasizing healing above the Healer, Luke 7:21-23.

Motivated by hunger, Luke 15:13-20.

Jesus could see into hearts of men, John 5:41-42.

See *Objective.*

MOUNTAINS

Ark rested on Ararat, Genesis 8:4.

Abraham offered Isaac on Moriah, Genesis 22:2.

Law given on Sinai, Exodus 19:11.

Moving mountains, Job 9:5; Ezekiel 38:20.

Prehistoric landscape, Psalm 90:1-2.

Melting mountains, Psalm 97:5.

Object of divine affection, Ezekiel 36:1-12.

Ascension from Olivet, Acts 1:12.

MOURNING

Strange rite at time of death, Deuteronomy 14:1-2.

All Israel assembled to mourn Samuel, 1 Samuel 25:1.

King who put aside personal grief to continue leading his people, 2 Samuel 19:1-8.

Weeping and wailing, Micah 1:8.

Shaving head in mourning, Micah 1:16.

Flute as instrument for mourning, Matthew 9:23-24.

Mourning death of Dorcas, Acts 9:39.

See *Death, Grief, Sorrow.*

MUGGING
Fear of walking in public places, Jeremiah 6:25.

MULTILINGUAL
Tower of Babel, Genesis 11:1-9.
Language confused by intermarriage, Nehemiah 13:23-27.
Language best understood, Isaiah 36:11.
Learning new language, Daniel 1:3-4.
Multilingual information, John 19:20.
Day of Pentecost, Acts 2:6.
See *Language*.

MULTITUDE
Entire community in rebellion, Exodus 16:2.
Power in numbers, Numbers 22:2-4.
Multitudes followed Jesus, Matthew 4:25; 13:2; 15:30; 19:2; Mark 1:33; 2:13; 3:20; Luke 12:1.
Multitude of demons, Luke 8:26-31.
See *Mob psychology*.

MUMBLING
See *Murmuring*.

MUNDANE
Great things and small things, 2 Kings 5:13.
Mundane activity leads to miraculous event, 2 Kings 6:1-7.
Writing with ordinary pen, Isaiah 8:1.
Day of small things, Zechariah 4:10.
See *Boredom*.

MURDER
First murder, Genesis 4:1-16.
Institution of capital punishment, Genesis 9:6.
Premeditated murder, Genesis 27:41-45; 2 Samuel 13:28-29.
Murder forbidden, Exodus 20:13; Matthew 19:18; Romans 13:9; 1 Peter 4:15; 1 John 3:15.
Accused of murder for abetting suicide, 2 Samuel 1:1-16.
Killing in self-defense, 2 Samuel 2:22-23.
David's plot against Uriah, 2 Samuel 11:14-17.
Absalom's murder of Amnon for disgracing his sister, 2 Samuel 13:23-29.
Total depravity throughout land, Micah 7:2.

Herod's slaughter of male babies, Matthew 2:13-18.
Death of John the Baptist, Matthew 14:1-12.
Judas as an accomplice to murderers, Matthew 26:14-16.
Murder thwarted by Jesus, Luke 4:28-30.
Deceitful plan to destroy Paul, Acts 23:12-22.
Jealousy the cause of murder, 1 John 3:12.
Desire to kill, Revelation 6:4.

MURMURING
Complaining against leadership, Exodus 5:15-21; 15:22-24; 16:2-3; Numbers 16:1-41; 20:1-4.
Testing divine patience, Numbers 14:26-37.
Job reprimanded for murmuring, Job 15:11-13; 34:34-37.
Counsel not to complain, Psalm 37:1.
David's lament, Psalm 44:1-26.
Temper flares against the Lord, Proverbs 19:3.
Lamenting one's birth, Jeremiah 15:10.
Doubting God's goodness, Malachi 3:14.
Martha's questioning, Luke 10:40.
Danger of faulting the Lord, Romans 9:19-20.
Avoid murmuring, Philippians 2:14 (KJV).
See *Complain, Discontent*.

MUSEUM
Ruins rebuilt, Isaiah 58:12.
Historical items kept in earthly tabernacle, Hebrews 9:3-4.

MUSIC
Musical instruments a family tradition, Genesis 4:21.
Musical send-off, Genesis 31:27.
Song of Moses, Exodus 15:1-18, 21.
Song to well in desert, Numbers 21:17-18.
Singing at watering places, Judges 5:11.
David frequently played harp, 1 Samuel 18:10. (See 19:9.)
Singer of psalms, 2 Samuel 23:1.
Prophecy to sound of music, 2 Kings 3:15-16.
Payment to choir members, Nehemiah 12:47.
Musicians required to work to support themselves, Nehemiah 13:10-11.
In time of sorrow, Job 30:31.

Using harp as instrument of praise, Psalm 43:4.
Reciting proverbs to musical accompaniment, Psalm 49:4.
Singing with steadfast heart, Psalm 57:7.
The cobra and the tune, Psalm 58:4-5.
Procession of singers into sanctuary, Psalm 68:24-25.
Resumé in song of Israel's history, Psalms 78:1-72; 106:1-48.
Overture of worship, Psalm 81:2.
Fountains in the Lord, Psalm 87:6-7.
Praising the Lord with voice and instrument, Psalm 98:4-6.
Making Scripture the theme of song, Psalm 119:54.
Laughter and music go together, Psalm 126:2.
Walking through city with harp and sad song, Isaiah 23:16.
Song of ruthless made silent, Isaiah 25:5.
Meaningless lyrics, beautiful voice, Ezekiel 33:32.
Variety of instruments, Daniel 3:5.
When God turns a deaf ear to praise, Amos 5:22. (See 8:3, 10.)
Flute as instrument for mourning, Matthew 9:23-24.
Angels praising God, Luke 2:13-14. (Notice, however, that the Bible uses "saying" and not "singing." Some believe angels will not sing until the work of redemption has been completed. Also, Mary's "song" is recorded in Scripture as "Mary said," 1:46.)
Effect of music on emotions, Luke 7:31-32.
Potential singing stones, Luke 19:37-40.
Hymns and spiritual songs, Colossians 3:16.
Congregational singing, Hebrews 2:12.
Great choir of angels, Revelation 5:11-12.
Song for exclusive congregation, Revelation 14:1-3.
Harps for redeemed in heaven, Revelation 15:2-4.
Musicians put to silence, Revelation 18:22.

See *Choir, Hymn, Orchestra, Solo.*

MUSLIM
See *Islam.*

MOUSTACHE
Trimmed moustache, 2 Samuel 19:24.

MUTE
Loss of speech, Ezekiel 3:26.
Ashamed and silent before the Lord, Ezekiel 16:63.
Father of John the Baptist stricken, Luke 1:11-22.
Mute demon, Luke 11:14.
Silence in heaven, Revelation 8:1.
See *Signing.*

MUTINY
Threat of mutiny, Numbers 14:1-4.
Guards unwilling to follow command to evil, 1 Samuel 22:16-17.
God's command to destroy, 2 Kings 10:6-7.
King destroyed by associates, 2 Kings 12:19-20.
Slaves turn against masters, Zechariah 2:9.
See *Anarchy.*

MYRRH
Commercial commodity, Genesis 37:25.
Father's unknowing gift to long lost son, Genesis 43:11.
Used in compounding anointing oil, Exodus 30:23.
Royal cosmetic, Esther 2:12.
Royal fragrance, Psalm 45:8.
Perfume for romance, Song of Songs 3:6.
Fragrant lips, Song of Songs 5:13.
Nativity gift, Matthew 2:11.
Embalming ingredient, John 19:39.

MYSTICAL
Prophet of God called seer, 1 Samuel 9:9.
Strange movement of shadow, 2 Kings 20:8-11.
Putting end to mediums and spiritists, 2 Kings 23:24.

N

NAGGING
Fathers should not exasperate children,
Ephesians 6:4.

NAIVE
Easily deceived, Hosea 7:11.
The validity of young faith, 1 Timothy 4:12.

NAKEDNESS
Initial awareness of nudity, Genesis 3:7.
(See 2:25.)
Noah's nakedness, Genesis 9:20-25.
Act of shame, Jeremiah 13:26.
See *Nudity*.

NAME
Giving meaning to name, Genesis 3:20.
Names of children, Genesis 4:1-2, 25-26;
5:28-29, 32; 21:3; 30:8; 41:51; Exodus
2:10; Ruth 4:17; 1 Samuel 4:21;
1 Chronicles 2:9; 4:9; Hosea 1:4; Luke
1:60; 2:21.
Strange names of kings, Genesis 14:1-9.
Abram changed to Abraham, Genesis 17:5.
(Note Abram means "exalted father"
and Abraham means "father of
many.")
Others given new names, Genesis 17:15;
32:28; 41:45; Judges 6:32; 2 Samuel
12:25; Acts 13:9.
Joshua frequently identified by family
name, Exodus 33:11; Numbers 11:28;
13:16; 14:6, 30; Joshua 1:1; 2:1; Judges
2:8; 1 Kings 16:34.
Two names of Gideon, Judges 7:1. (He was
called Gideon during his prowess, but
Jerub-Baal when speaking of his
polygamy, 8:28-30.)
Meaning of name, Judges 13:17-18;
1 Samuel 25:25.
Naomi changed name to Mara, Ruth 1:20.

Similarity of names of prophets and
disciples, 1 Kings 19:19-21.
Forgetting God's name, Psalm 44:20.
Value of good name, Proverbs 22:1.
Beauty of name, Song of Songs 1:3.
Name above all names, Isaiah 9:6.
Meaning of a name, Isaiah 62:4; Matthew
1:21.
Similar names of father and son, Jeremiah
22:24.
Variation of name for father and son,
Jeremiah 24:1.
Name with an evil meaning but king who
did good deeds, Jeremiah 52:31-34.
New names given Hebrew students in
Babylon, Daniel 1:6-7.
Daniel's pagan name but king's
acknowledgment of Daniel's faith,
Daniel 4:8.
Angel names newborn son, Luke 1:13.
Choice of name for John the Baptist, Luke
1:57-65.
Saul's name changed to Paul, Acts 13:9.
Paul's wise use of names of followers,
Colossians 4:7-17.
Eternal name of God, Hebrews 1:8.
Christ called "the Name," 3 John 7.
Friends greeted by name, 3 John 14.
Unique name for Jesus, Revelation 3:14.
Name of temple in heaven, Revelation
15:5.
Covered with blasphemous names,
Revelation 17:3.
Unknown name, Revelation 19:12.

NARCISSISM
Personal needs ahead of divine guidance,
Exodus 16:1-18.
Using sacred offering for personal gain,
1 Samuel 2:29.
Skilled at art of seduction, Jeremiah 2:33.

Greedy for gain, Jeremiah 8:10.
Good life gone, Lamentations 4:1-5.
Women of Sodom, Ezekiel 16:49.
Personal desire above need of others,
Amos 6:6.
Fate of carefree city, Zephaniah 2:15.
Fruit of selfishness, Haggai 1:2-5.
Concern for oneself more than for the
Lord, Zechariah 7:4-6.
Value of serving God, Malachi 3:14-15.
Golden Rule reversed, Matthew 18:21-25.
Love for others grows cold, Matthew 24:12.
Doing good without expecting
reciprocation, Luke 6:27-36.
Who to be greatest in kingdom, Luke 9:46-
48.
Desire for recognition in congregation,
Luke 11:43.
All kinds of greed, Luke 12:15-21.
Desiring place of honor at table, Luke 14:7-
11.
Backlash of selfishness, Luke 15:11-32.
Attitude between owners and workers,
Luke 17:7-10.
Pharisees desired visible kingdom, Luke
17:20-21.
Hindrance of selfishness in seeking
salvation, Luke 18:18-25.
Temple as marketplace, Luke 19:45-48.
Christian attitude toward others, Romans
12:10.
Valid functioning of self-interest,
2 Corinthians 9:6-11.
Those whose god is their stomach,
Philippians 3:19.
See *Hedonism, Self-interest, Selfishness.*

NATIONALISM
Establishment of clans, Genesis 10:32.
Nation's originator, Genesis 19:37-38.
Hagar's choice of wife for Ishmael, Genesis
21:21. (See v. 9, and 16:1-2.)
Abraham's concern for wife for Isaac,
Genesis 24:1-4.
Jacob commanded not to marry Canaanite,
Genesis 28:1. (See 26:34.)
Right to purchase slaves, Leviticus 25:44.
Love for foreigners, Deuteronomy 10:19.
Samson desired Philistine wife, Judges
14:1-2.
Keeping bloodline pure, Nehemiah 10:30.
Country born in a day, Isaiah 66:8.
Gospel to all nations, Matthew 24:14.
Jews and the centurion, Acts 10:22, 28, 34-

35.
Intermarriage between Jew and Greek,
Acts 16:1.
Respect for citizen of one's own country,
Acts 22:25-29.
See *Foreigner, Miscegenation, Xenophobia.*

NATIONS
Native born, Numbers 15:13.
Most powerful government at God's
mercy, 1 Samuel 12:25.
The Lord listed for Jeremiah nations He
would judge, Jeremiah 25:15-29.
Tyre, city of luxury, brought down, Ezekiel
27:1-36. (See also 28:1-19.)
For continued sinning, certain judgment,
Amos 1:3, 6, 9, 11, 13; 2:1, 4, 6. (Note
the nature of sin in each of these
judgments.)
See *Government.*

NATIVITY
Star of Bethlehem prophesied, Numbers
24:17.
Birth of Jesus prophesied, Isaiah 7:10-14.
Bethlehem prophecy, Micah 5:2.
The Christmas story, Matthew 1:18-25;
Luke 2:1-20.
Birth of Christ reviewed, Revelation 12:1-5.
See *Christmas.*

NATURAL RESOURCES
Metals mined on earth, Numbers 31:22.
Oil from rock, Deuteronomy 32:13.
Purifying bad water, 2 Kings 2:19-22.
Excrement used as fuel, Ezekiel 4:9-15.
Commercial centers in Ezekiel's time,
Ezekiel 27:12-23.
Gold and silver belong to God, Haggai 2:8.
Salt loses saltiness, Luke 14:34-35.

NATURE
God created both domestic and wild
animals, Genesis 1:24-25.
Intelligence of serpent, Genesis 3:1.
Supremacy of humans over beasts and
birds, Genesis 9:1-3.
Worship among trees, Genesis 13:18. (See
14:13; 18:1.)
Abraham planted a tree, Genesis 21:33.
Divine use of nature, Exodus 19:9.
Worshiping God in nature, Deuteronomy
4:15-20.
Protection of birds, Deuteronomy 22:6.

Song about the sun, Judges 5:31.
Jotham's parable about choice of king,
Judges 9:7-15.
Solomon's extensive knowledge of nature,
1 Kings 4:29-34.
All nature praises Creator, 1 Chronicles
16:31-33.
Power and authority of Creator, Job 9:1-10.
Nature as teacher, Job 12:7-8; Psalm 8:3-4;
Mark 4:28; 13:28.
Path for wind and storm, Job 28:25-27.
Homage to sun and moon, Job 31:26-28.
Procedure of rainfall, Job 36:27-30; 37:6,
15-16.
God spoke to Job of Creation, Job 38:1-14,
31-33.
God speaks through nature and through
His Word, Psalm 19:1-14; Romans 1:18-
20.
River of city of God, Psalm 46:4.
All nature praises God, Psalms 69:34;
96:11-12.
Bird nest near altar, Psalm 84:3.
Divine law governing nature, Psalm 89:8-
13.
Poem to God of nature, Psalm 104:1-26.
Earth entrusted to man, Psalm 115:16.
Nature and people praise the Lord, Psalm
148:1-14.
Earth and sky show wisdom of God,
Proverbs 3:19-20.
Danger of angry bear, Proverbs 17:12.
Future harmony in nature, Isaiah 11:6-9.
People defile earth, Isaiah 24:5.
Divine glory revealed, Isaiah 35:1-2.
Eating wild fruit, Isaiah 37:30.
Dying earth, Isaiah 51:6.
People to live to age of trees, Isaiah 65:20-
22.
Birds know God's way for them, Jeremiah
8:7.
Birds and animals gone in wake of
desolation, Jeremiah 9:10.
Earth and sky reflect wisdom of God,
Jeremiah 10:12-13.
Parched land and wildlife gone, Jeremiah
12:4.
God of all nature, Jeremiah 31:35.
Divine judgment against mountains and
hills, Ezekiel 6:1-5.
Worship of sun, Ezekiel 8:16.
Wild animals' fear of God, Joel 2:22.
Creative functions, Amos 4:13.
Lord of earth, Amos 9:5-6.

Symbol of divine provision, Matthew 6:28-
30.
Value of one sparrow in God's sight, Luke
12:6.
Men and animals of different flesh,
1 Corinthians 15:39.
Christ the Creator, Colossians 1:15-17.
See *Animals, Animism, Forestry.*

NAVIGATION
Ships built by King Solomon, 1 Kings 9:26-
28.
Fleet of ships that never set sail, 1 Kings
22:48.
Wonders of the waters, Psalm 107:23-24.
Paths in the sea, Isaiah 43:16.
Tyre, power on the sea, Ezekiel 26:15-18.
Soundings to determine position at sea,
Acts 27:27-29.
See *Ocean.*

NAVY
Solomon's ships, 1 Kings 9:26.
Jehoshaphat's fleet, 1 Kings 22:48.
See *Ocean.*

NEED
God provided exactly what each Israelite
needed, Exodus 16:17-20.
Turning to a rejected brother in time of
need, Judges 11:1-10.
Help from God alone, 2 Kings 6:26-27.
Wealth numbs conscience, Hosea 12:8.
Call to turn to the Lord, Amos 4:6.
Meeting need for cup of cold water,
Matthew 10:42.
Involvement in need of others, Mark 6:35-
43.
Jesus knew when He had been touched,
Luke 8:43-48.
Reaching out to help others, Acts 11:27-30.
Macedonian call, Acts 16:9.
Christ met our greatest need, Romans 5:6-
8.
Lord invites diversity in prayer, Ephesians
6:18.
Families should take care of those in need,
1 Timothy 5:3-8.
See *Weakness.*

NEGATIVE
Negative report of spies, Numbers 13:26-
33.
Old Testament concludes with curse,

Malachi 4:6.
Letter kills but Spirit gives life,
2 Corinthians 3:6.
See *Positive.*

NEGLECT

No evidence of neglect, Exodus 21:28.
Responsibility for negligence, Exodus
21:36.
Livestock grazing in another man's
pasture, Exodus 22:5.
Neglecting the Word of the Lord, 1 Samuel
3:1.
Neglect of duty, Nehemiah 9:35; Luke
12:47.
Lazy man's house, Ecclesiastes 10:18.
Some said it was not time to rebuild
temple, Haggai 1:3-4.
Foolish response to divine message,
Matthew 7:26.
Refusing to do good works, James 2:14;
4:17.
See *Careless.*

NEGOTIATION

Abraham's bargaining with God on behalf
of Lot, Genesis 18:20-33.
Offering to make peace before battle,
Deuteronomy 20:10.
Life for life, Joshua 2:14.
Strategy for facing superior enemy, Luke
14:31-32.

NEIGHBOR

Men's responsibility toward each other,
Genesis 9:5.
Integrity between neighbors, Exodus
20:16; Leviticus 19:13-18.
Liability for treacherous animal, Exodus
21:28-32.
Animal injury to neighbor's property,
Exodus 22:5.
Criminal act to hate one's neighbor,
Deuteronomy 19:11-13.
Demonstrated neighborliness,
Deuteronomy 22:1-4.
Loving neighbor as yourself, 1 Samuel
18:1.
Help of good neighbors, Ezra 1:6.
Doing good to others, Proverbs 3:27-28.
Seldom visit neighbor, Proverbs 25:17.
Neighborhood integrity, Proverbs 26:18-
19.
Nearby neighbor better than distant

relative, Proverbs 27:10.
Loudly blessing neighbor, Proverbs 27:14.
Keeping ahead of one's neighbor,
Ecclesiastes 4:4.
Lust among neighbors, Jeremiah 5:8.
Speaking cordially with deceitful heart,
Jeremiah 9:8.
Neighbors sitting in shade, Zechariah 3:10.
Neighbors of Jesus unaware of His
greatness, Matthew 13:53-58; Mark 6:1-
6; Luke 4:22-24.
Christian attitude toward neighbors,
Matthew 22:34-40.
Importance of loving your neighbor, Mark
12:28-34.
Good news shared among neighbors, Luke
1:57-58.
Effective witness to one's neighbor, John
4:39.
Live in harmony with others, Romans
12:16-18.
Love your neighbor, Romans 13:9-10.
Those who speak truthfully to their
neighbors, Ephesians 4:25.
Care in one's conduct toward unbelievers,
Colossians 4:5.
Royal law of Scripture, James 2:8.

NEIGHBORHOOD

Choice of place to live, Genesis 13:10-13.
Dislike of wealthy neighbors, Genesis
26:12-17.
When God establishes a community,
Jeremiah 30:20.
Fountain flowing from the Lord's house,
Joel 3:18.
Judgment on evil community, Zephaniah
3:1.
Living in peace, Zechariah 8:16-17.
Salt and light in the world, Matthew 5:13-
16.
Division in communities and families,
Matthew 12:25.
Being example to unbelievers, 1 Peter
2:12.
City of total integrity, Revelation 21:27.
See *Community.*

NEOPHYTE

Father assists inexperienced son,
1 Chronicles 22:5; 29:1.

NEPOTISM

Rights of oldest son, Deuteronomy 21:15-

17.
Special favor to daughter, Judges 1:12-15.
Political aspirations of family man, Judges 9:1-2.
Sons appointed to succeed fathers, 1 Samuel 8:1-3.
Army appointment for king's cousin, 1 Samuel 14:50.
Share and share alike, 1 Samuel 30:24.
Government jobs for sons, 2 Samuel 8:16.
Mother's wiles, 1 Kings 1:11-31.
Chosen to build temple, 1 Chronicles 28:10.
Son fulfills father's dream, 2 Chronicles 6:3-11.
Brother appointed mayor, Nehemiah 7:2.
Fools in high places, Ecclesiastes 10:5-7.
Family of David always on throne, Jeremiah 33:17.
End to noisy songs, Ezekiel 26:13.
Avoid partiality, 1 Timothy 5:21; James 2:1.
See *Family, Favoritism, Politics.*

NEST
Nest in rock, Numbers 24:21.
Eagle stirs nest, Deuteronomy 32:11.
Lofty nest of eagle, Job 39:27; Jeremiah 49:16.
Sparrows and swallows nesting at temple, Psalm 84:3.
Wandering from nest, Proverbs 27:8.
Nest for owls, Isaiah 34:15.
Security for doves, Jeremiah 48:28.
More comfort for birds than for the Son of man, Luke 9:58.

NET
See *Snare, Trap.*

NETWORKING
Putting in a good word for someone else, Genesis 40:14.
Using a mother's influence, 1 Kings 2:13.
Influence of others, Nehemiah 6:1-19.
Cultivating materialistic friendships, Proverbs 19:6.
Primary rule for successful networking, Matthew 7:12; Luke 6:31; Romans 14:19.
A mother's request, Matthew 19:20-24.
Judas misused relationship with Jesus, Matthew 26:47-52; Mark 14:43-46; Luke 22:47; John 18:1-4.
Saul recommended by Barnabas, Acts 9:27.
It's whom you know, Acts 12:20.
Phoebe recommended by Paul, Romans 16:2.
Developing rapport, 1 Corinthians 9:20-23.
Providing inspiration for others, 2 Corinthians 9:2; 1 Thessalonians 1:8.
Making most of every opportunity, Ephesians 5:15-16.
See *Influence.*

NEUTRALITY
Angel of the Lord, Joshua 5:13-15.
Cannot be spiritually neutral, Matthew 12:30; Mark 9:39-40; Luke 11:23; 16:13.

NEW
New song, Psalms 33:3; 40:3; 149:1; Isaiah 42:10; Revelation 14:3.
Given new name, Isaiah 56:4-5; 62:2; Acts 11:26; Revelation 3:12.
New things, Isaiah 42:9; 43:19; 48:6; Revelation 21:5.
Made new by faith, Ezekiel 11:19; 36:26; John 3:3; 2 Corinthians 5:17; Galatians 6:15; Ephesians 2:14-15; 1 Peter 1:23.

NEWS
Death of King Saul, 2 Samuel 1:1-12.
Good news from distant land, Proverbs 25:25.
Concurrent messages of bad news, Jeremiah 51:31-32.
Bearer of bad news, Ezekiel 33:21.
See *Media.*

NIGHT
Not traveling after sunset, Genesis 28:11.
Night watches, 1 Samuel 11:11; Psalm 119:148; Lamentations 2:19; Matthew 14:25; Luke 12:38.
Canopy for the Lord, 2 Samuel 22:12.
Time for heart searching, Psalms 4:4; 16:7.
Plotting evil while falling asleep, Psalm 36:4.
Meditation at night, Psalm 63:6.
Night songs, Psalm 77:6.
Calling to the Lord day and night, Psalm 88:1-2.
Moon designates seasons, Psalm 104:19.
Conclusion of day's work, Psalm 104:23.
Giving thanks at midnight, Psalm 119:62, 148.
Dawn to darkness, Amos 4:13.

Cry of owl, Zephaniah 2:14.
No night in heaven, Zechariah 14:7.
Night divided into time zones, Mark 13:35.
Fear in the night, Luke 2:8-14.
Night of prayer, Luke 6:12.
Nicodemus came to Jesus at night, John
    3:2, 19:39.
Night hours, Acts 23:23.
See *Darkness*.

NIGHTMARE
Thick and dreadful darkness, Genesis
    15:12.
Troubled dream of future, Genesis 41:1-8.
Foreboding loaf of bread, Judges 7:13-14.
Frightening dreams, Job 7:13-15; Daniel
    2:1; 4:5.
Many cares cause dreams, Ecclesiastes 5:3.
See *Dream*.

NOISE
Rebellious revelry, Exodus 32:17-20.
Solomon's arrangement for absence of
    noise during building of temple,
    1 Kings 6:7.
Laughter and joy, Psalm 126:2.
End to noisy songs, Ezekiel 26:13.

NOMAD
Cain, the first wanderer, Genesis 4:13-14.
Those who love to wander, Jeremiah 14:10.

NOMINAL
Nominal piety of King Zedekiah, Jeremiah
    37:1-3.
Neither cold nor hot, Revelation 3:16.

NONPROFIT
Priests tax free, Ezra 7:24.
Paying taxes to government, Matthew
    22:15-22.

NONVERBAL COMMUNICATION
Putting foot to the neck, Joshua 10:24.
Visible evidence of sorrow, Isaiah 15:2-3.

NONVIOLENCE
Trusting God for deliverance, 2 Chronicles
    32:1-21.
Evaluating military logistics, Luke 14:31-
    32.

NOON
Time for lunch, Genesis 43:16, 25.

Groping at midday, Deuteronomy 28:29.
Midday rest, 2 Samuel 4:5.
Noontime drinking spree, 1 Kings 20:16.
Death at noon, 2 Kings 4:20.
Noonday brightness, Job 11:17.
Prayer at noon, Psalm 55:17.
Midday plague, Psalm 91:6.
Noonday at night, Isaiah 58:10.
High noon adventure, Acts 22:6.

NORTH AMERICA
Prophecy some conjecture as referring to
    North America, Isaiah 18:1-2, 7.

NOSTALGIA
Looking back on "better" days, Exodus
    16:2-3.
Those who remembered glory of temple,
    Haggai 2:3.
Prodigal son, Luke 15:17.
Rich man in torment, Luke 16:25-27.
See *Memory*.

NOTES
Eating scroll, Ezekiel 3:1-4.
Daniel did not trust memory, Daniel 7:1.

NOTORIETY
How David became famous, 2 Samuel
    8:13.
Role of humility in greatness, Matthew
    23:12.
Respect of Cornelius for Peter, Acts 10:25-
    26.
See *Fame*.

NOVICE
Father and inexperienced son,
    1 Chronicles 22:5; 29:1.
Training Daniel and friends, Daniel 1:3-4.
A king's favor, Daniel 2:49.
Validity of young faith, 1 Timothy 4:12.

NOW
Living for today in God's favor,
    Ecclesiastes 9:7.
Best time for salvation, 2 Corinthians 6:2.

NUCLEAR
Sky and earth destroyed by fire, 2 Peter
    3:7, 10-12.

NUDITY
First awareness of nudity, Genesis 3:7. (See

2:25.)
Shem's attitude toward father's privacy, Genesis 9:20-27.
Shame of exposed nakedness, Isaiah 47:2-3.
Act of shame, Jeremiah 13:26-27.
Nudity as a form of shame, Ezekiel 16:35-38.
Brave warriors flee naked, Amos 2:16.
Drunken neighbor, Habakkuk 2:15.
Sinful exposure, Revelation 16:15.
See *Immodest, Nakedness.*

NUISANCE
Thorns in the side, Judges 2:3.
Disturbing privacy of others, Proverbs 25:17.

NUMBERS
Moabites intimidated by Israelites coming out of Egypt, Numbers 22:4-6.
Balance in generations through periods of Bible history, Matthew 1:17.
Evaluating military logistics, Luke 14:31-32.

NURSES
Nurse named Deborah, Genesis 35:8.
Nurse for baby Moses, Exodus 2:7.
Mother-in-law as nurse, Ruth 4:16.
Nurse and child flee for safety, 2 Samuel 4:4.
Hidden nurse and child, 2 Kings 11:2.

NUTRITION
Food in wilderness, Exodus 16:2-35.
Egyptian delicacies, Numbers 11:5.
Abigail's balanced diet, 1 Samuel 25:18.
Bread and fruit, 2 Samuel 16:1-2.
Mother's milk, Isaiah 66:11.
Polluting wheat, Amos 8:6.
Salt that loses saltiness, Luke 14:34-35.
Desiring food of pigs, Luke 15:13-16.
See *Diet, Health.*

O

OATH
Solemn covenant, Genesis 14:22-23;
26:26-29.
Avoid oaths with wicked people, Exodus
23:1.
Fake oaths, Leviticus 6:2-5; Jeremiah 7:8-9.
Good men and sinners taking oaths,
Ecclesiastes 9:2.
Taking false oath, Jeremiah 5:2.
The Lord almighty has sworn by Himself,
Jeremiah 51:14.
Do not swear falsely, Zechariah 8:17.
Simply yes or no, Matthew 5:33-37; James
5:12.
Profane, murderous oath, Acts 23:12-14.
Oath of an angel, Revelation 10:5-7.
See *Pledge, Vow.*

OBEDIENT
Obedience of Abram, Genesis 12:1-4.
Circumcision at advanced age, Genesis
17:10-27.
Predicted result of obedience, Genesis
18:19.
Exercising complete obedience, Exodus
7:6.
Prior to his time of leadership, Joshua's
obedience to commands of Moses,
Exodus 17:10.
Promised reward for obedience, Exodus
19:5.
Pledge of congregation, Exodus 24:1-7.
Promise of answered prayer, Exodus
33:17.
Journey by divine directive, Numbers 9:23.
Reward for father's obedience, Numbers
14:24.
Complete reading of the Law, Joshua 8:35.
Divine obedience to mortal request,
Joshua 10:13-14.
God's command to obedience, 1 Samuel

15:13-23.
Bringing ark to Jerusalem, 2 Samuel 6:1-
15.
Reward of long life, 1 Kings 3:14.
Warning against disobedience, 1 Kings
9:1-9.
Materialism versus obedience, 1 Kings
13:7-10.
Great things and small things, 2 Kings
5:13.
Obedience brings security, 2 Kings 21:8.
Reward for obeying God, Job 36:11.
Scripture meaningful to those who obey it,
Psalms 25:10; 103:17-21.
Beautiful prayer for undivided heart, Psalm
86:11.
Fulfilling vows to the Lord, Psalm 116:14,
18-19.
Following guidance of Scripture, Psalm
119:1-16, 57-64.
Once astray, now obedient, Psalm 119:67.
Guidance of Scripture for all of life, Psalm
119:111-112.
Obedience by divine instruction, Psalm
143:10.
Thoroughly keeping divine commands,
Proverbs 7:2.
Disobedient children, Isaiah 1:1-4.
Man's plans and God's will, Isaiah 30:1.
Reward for obedience, Isaiah 48:17-18;
Jeremiah 7:22-23.
Penalty for disobeying, Jeremiah 11:1-5.
Obedience even though threatened with
death, Jeremiah 26:1-16.
Obedience to parents and grandparents,
Jeremiah 35:1-16.
Walking in ways of the Lord, Hosea 14:9.
Mighty are those who obey the Lord, Joel
2:11.
Jonah learned to obey, Jonah 3:3.
Cannot obey two masters, Matthew 6:24.

Parable of Two Sons, Matthew 21:28-31.
Divine kinship, Mark 3:35.
Fulfilling requirements of the Law, Luke
2:39.
Obedience of the Child Jesus to His
parents, Luke 2:41-52.
Wisdom from doing God's will, John 7:17.
Obedience of Jesus to His Father, John
12:50; Romans 5:19; Hebrews 5:8-9.
Doing what Christ commands, John 14:15.
Obeying God rather than men, Acts 4:18-
20; 5:29.
Obedience resulting from faith, Romans
1:5.
Obedience brings righteousness, Romans
2:13.
Reputation for obedience, Romans 16:19.
Athletes compete according to rules,
2 Timothy 2:5.
Turn away from wickedness, 2 Timothy
2:19.
Following the will of God, Titus 2:9-10.
By faith Noah and Abraham obeyed God,
Hebrews 11:7-12. (Note travel to
unknown destination, v. 8.)
Those who do not obey the Gospel, 1 Peter
4:17.
Hypocrisy of profession without
obedience, 1 John 2:4-6.
Obedience to God's commands attests to
love of God, 1 John 5:1-3.
Love results from obedience to Scripture,
2 John 6.
Promised blessing for those who read and
obey, Revelation 1:3.
Clean in society of deceit, Revelation 3:4.
(See also v. 10.)
See *Discipleship.*

OBEISANCE
See *Genuflect.*

OBESITY
Eating of fat prohibited, Leviticus 3:17;
7:24.
Old and obese, 1 Samuel 4:18.
Knife to the throat, Proverbs 23:1-3.
Too much food and drink, Proverbs 23:20.
Responsibility to care for our bodies,
1 Corinthians 6:19-20.
See *Health.*

OBITUARY
Obituary of six words, Numbers 20:1.

OBJECTIVE
Keeping eyes on the Lord, Psalm 25:15.
Desire for full obedience, Psalm 119:1-5.
Look straight ahead, Proverbs 4:25-27.
Description of noble person, Isaiah 32:8.
Using faulty bow, Hosea 7:16.
Worldly objectives and spiritual objectives,
Luke 12:29-31.
Aim for perfection, 2 Corinthians 13:11.
See *Goal, Motivation, Vision.*

OBJECT LESSON
Old Testament object lesson, Jeremiah
13:1-11.
Potter and clay, Jeremiah 18:1-8.
Message of a coin, Matthew 22:17-22; Mark
12:13-17; Luke 20:20-26.
Illustration with belt, Acts 21:10-11.
See *Illustration, Teaching, Visual.*

OBLIGATION
Abram refused to be obligated to king of
Sodom, Genesis 14:22-24.
Blessings bring obligation, Deuteronomy
4:32-40.
Recognized obligation, Psalm 116:12-17.
Paul reminded Philemon of obligations
owed, Philemon 17-19.
Responsibility to do good, James 4:17.
See *Debt, Responsibility.*

OBLIVION
Name blotted out, Deuteronomy 9:14;
29:20; Psalm 109:13; Isaiah 14:22.
Memory of life erased from earth,
Deuteronomy 32:26; Job 18:17.
Sins removed by God's grace, Psalm 103:3;
Acts 3:19.
Stillborn child, Ecclesiastes 6:3-4.
Fortified city made desolate, Isaiah 27:10.
Into silence and darkness, Isaiah 47:5.
Judgment across face of the earth,
Zephaniah 1:2-3.

OBSCENITY
Obscenity committed in anger,
Deuteronomy 25:11-12.
Covenant to avoid lust, Job 31:1.
Depravity of two adulterous sisters, Ezekiel
23:1-49.
See *Degradation, Depravity, Immorality.*

OBSCURE
Some of Paul's writing difficult to

understand, 2 Peter 3:15-16.

OBSEQUIOUS
Perfume for lady, Ruth 3:3.
Overt obsequiousness, 1 Samuel 25:23-41; 2 Samuel 9:6; 14:4-20.
Pleasing the king, Esther 2:15.
Avoid partiality and flattery, Job 31:21-22.
Folly of flattery, Proverbs 28:23.
King paid honor to slave, Daniel 2:46-49.
Loyalty exaggerated, Mark 14:31.
Pharisees alleged concern for safety of Jesus, Luke 13:31.

OBSOLETE
Haunt of jackals, Jeremiah 9:11.
Built-in obsolescence, Matthew 6:19.
Even the temple was temporary, Matthew 24:1-2.
Old Covenant obsolete, Hebrews 8:13.

OBSTACLES
The God who levels mountains, Isaiah 45:1-3.
Face set like flint, Isaiah 50:7.
Men on foot cannot compete with horses, Jeremiah 12:5.
Faith small as mustard seed can move mountain, Matthew 17:20; 21:21-22.
Roll away stone, Mark 16:3-4.
Hindered from running good race, Galatians 5:7.
See *Hindrance.*

OBSTINATE
Wrong kind of unanimity, Numbers 11:4-10.
No success outside God's will, Numbers 14:41-45.
Advice rejected, 1 Kings 12:12-15.
Persistent sins, 2 Chronicles 28:22-23.
Ignoring the word of the Lord, Jeremiah 7:13; 25:3.
Deliberate falsehood concerning Law of the Lord, Jeremiah 8:8.
Daring to burn prophecy, Jeremiah 36:20-24.
Sinful stubbornness, Jeremiah 44:15-27.
Reluctance of demon to leave one possessed, Mark 1:21-26.
See *Rebellion.*

OBSTRUCTION
Those who said it was not time to rebuild

temple, Haggai 1:3-4.
Separated by great chasm, Luke 16:26.
See *Opposition.*

OCCUPATION
Holiness by virtue of occupation, Leviticus 21:8.
Role of priest, Deuteronomy 18:1-2.
Tentmakers, Paul and Aquila, Acts 18:1-3.
Zenas, the lawyer, Titus 3:13.
See *Employment.*

OCEAN
Valley of sea, 2 Samuel 22:16.
Waters assigned to boundaries, Job 38:8-11; Psalm 104:6-9.
Wonders of deep waters, Psalm 107:23-24.
Sleeping on the high seas, Proverbs 23:34.
Paths in sea, Isaiah 43:16.
Tiny grains of sand hold back ocean, Jeremiah 5:22.
The God of all nature, Jeremiah 31:35.
No longer any sea, Revelation 21:1.
See *Nature, Navigation.*

OFFENSE
Zophar upset by criticism, Job 20:2-3.
Differing reactions to truly Christian personality, 2 Corinthians 2:15-16.
See *Reaction.*

OFFERING
Presented at door, Leviticus 1:3.
Use of salt, Leviticus 2:13.
Persistent sacrifices offered in temple, Ezekiel 43:18-27.
Priests who defiled altar, Malachi 1:6-14.
Refined gold and silver, Malachi 3:2-4.
Giving on first day of week, 1 Corinthians 16:2.
See *Stewardship.*

OFFSPRING
See *Barren, Children, Pregnancy.*

OIL
Oil from rock, Deuteronomy 32:13.

OLD AGE
Promise of many years, Genesis 15:15.
Failing eyesight, Genesis 27:1; 48:10; 1 Samuel 3:2; 4:15.
Swift and difficult passage of time, Genesis 47:9.

Stand up when old person appears,
Leviticus 19:32.
Time for retirement, Deuteronomy 31:2.
Loss of physical sensitivities, 2 Samuel
19:35.
Feebleness, 1 Kings 1:1; Psalm 71:9;
Zechariah 8:4.
Full of days, 1 Chronicles 29:28.
Timidity of youth to those older, Job 32:6.
Recollections of long life, Psalm 37:25-26.
Dread of old age, Psalm 71:9; Ecclesiastes
12:1.
Crowned with gray hair, Proverbs 16:31.
Respect for older parents, Proverbs 23:22.
Bitter attitude, Ecclesiastes 6:3-6.
Good old days, Ecclesiastes 7:10. (See not
so good old days, Lam. 1:7.)
No security in old age, Jeremiah 6:11-12.
Wrinkled skin, Lamentations 3:4.
Do not mistreat old people, 1 Timothy 5:1-
2.
See *Geriatrics, Longevity.*

OMEN
The prophecy of the boiling pot, Jeremiah
1:13-15.
Seeking omen at fork in road, Ezekiel
21:18-23.

OMINOUS
See *Danger, Fear, Threat.*

OMNIPOTENCE
No dwelling large enough for God, 1 Kings
8:27.
Beyond highest stars, Job 22:12.
Omnipotent God touches weak, Job 36:5.
Sure of God's plan and purpose, Job 42:2.
Exalting God above heavens, Psalm 57:5.
Divine versatility, Psalms 115:3; 135:6;
Isaiah 43:13; Matthew 19:26.
Source of everlasting strength, Isaiah 26:4.
Heavens and hand of God, Isaiah 40:12.
The One who never wearies, Isaiah 40:28.
Immeasurable grace of God, Jeremiah
31:37.
Nothing too hard for the Lord, Jeremiah
32:17, 27.
Resurrection power innate with God, Acts
26:8.
All power, Romans 4:17-24.
Unsearchable riches, Romans 11:33-36.
Limiting God's perfection, 1 Corinthians
1:25.

Scope of God's greatness in Christ, Jude
24-25.
Sovereignty of Jesus over earth, Revelation
1:5.
Reign of omnipotent God, Revelation 19:6.
See *Sovereignty.*

OMNIPRESENCE
Undetected presence of the Lord, Genesis
28:16.
Present in heaven and on earth,
Deuteronomy 4:39; Isaiah 66:1.
Scope of God's presence, 1 Kings 8:27.
The Lord is everywhere, Psalm 139:5-12;
Jeremiah 23:23-24.
Divine periphery of vision, Proverbs 15:3.
One always nearby, Acts 17:27.
The One who fills the universe, Ephesians
4:10.

OMNISCIENCE
God sees every action, Job 31:4; 34:21.
Unlimited understanding, Psalm 147:5.
Omniscience of God, Isaiah 40:13-14.
The Heavenly Father knows each sparrow,
numbers the hairs on one's head,
Matthew 10:28-30.
Greater wisdom than Solomon's, Matthew
12:42.
Time of Christ's coming held secret,
Matthew 24:36.
Knowledge of all mankind, John 2:24.
Validity of Christ's deity, John 16:30.
Limiting the wisdom of God, 1 Corinthians
1:25.

OPENNESS
See *Receptive.*

OPINION
Rebekah permitted to make her own
decision, Genesis 24:54-58.
Negative and positive viewpoints,
Numbers 13:17-33.
Influenced by popular opinion, 1 Samuel
14:45; 15:24; 2 Chronicles 20:21;
Jeremiah 38:19.
Veteran soldier underrates abilities of boy,
1 Samuel 17:42.
Divided into factions, 1 Kings 16:21-22.
Pagan king persuaded to permit rebuilding
of temple, Ezra 4-8.
Opinions of fool, Proverbs 18:2.
He who answers before listening, Proverbs

18:13.

Wise in his own eyes, Proverbs 26:16.

Wrong and right boasting, Jeremiah 9:23-24.

Pilate's reticence, Matthew 27:23-26; Luke 23:13-25; John 19:4-16.

Demons refused permission to speak, Mark 1:33-34.

Ego of Pharisees, Luke 11:45-46.

Attitude of Pharisees toward helping others on Sabbath, Luke 13:10-17.

Different opinions concerning Jesus, John 7:12-13.

Reluctant Pharisees, John 12:42-43.

Paul and Peter face-to-face, Galatians 2:11-21.

Scripture not matter of personal opinion, 2 Peter 1:20-21.

See *Viewpoint.*

OPINIONATED

See *Prejudice.*

OPPONENT

Successfully facing formidable opponent, Numbers 21:21-26.

Future accomplishment assured, Numbers 21:34.

Son sought to impress father, 1 Samuel 14:1-14.

Revenge left to God's timing, 1 Samuel 26:1-11.

Trying to intimidate, Ezra 4:4.

Stirring up trouble, Nehemiah 4:8.

Opposition to prophets, Isaiah 30:10; Jeremiah 11:21; Amos 2:12-13; Micah 2:6.

Facing enemy eye-to-eye, Jeremiah 34:3.

Total conquest of enemy, Jeremiah 50:35-40.

Satan, foremost opponent, Zechariah 3:1-2.

Multitude of demons, Luke 8:26-31.

Abusive opposition, Acts 18:6.

Opposition to ministry, 1 Corinthians 16:9; 2 Timothy 3:8.

See *Adversary, Opposition.*

OPPORTUNIST

Discerning the prophets, Deuteronomy 18:21-22.

Rejecting sure opportunity, 1 Samuel 24:1-8.

Dishonest report for personal gain,

2 Samuel 1:2-16. (See also 1 Sam. 31:4.)

Mother's wiles, 1 Kings 1:11-31.

Those who wanted to be part of building temple, Ezra 4:3-5.

Time for everything, Ecclesiastes 3:1-8.

Seeking right time, Isaiah 55:6.

Looking to flesh for strength, Jeremiah 17:5.

Riches gained unjustly, Jeremiah 17:11.

See *Insincerity.*

OPPORTUNITY

Opportunity withdrawn, Proverbs 1:24-33; Hosea 5:6.

Doors opened that will not be shut, Isaiah 45:1.

Seek the Lord while He may be found, Isaiah 55:6-7.

Give glory to God before darkness comes, Jeremiah 13:16; John 12:35-36.

Given a second chance, Jonah 1:1-3; 3:1-3.

Privilege of hearing Christ's message, Matthew 13:17.

Closed door of opportunity for repentance, Luke 13:25-28.

Excuses for not attending a banquet, Luke 14:16-24.

Greatest opportunity of all time, John 3:16-17.

Seizing the opportunity, John 9:4; Acts 3:12; 21:40.

Those scattered by persecution, Acts 11:19-21.

Opportunity rejected by Jews became choice for Gentiles, Acts 13:46.

Paul, arrested by soldiers, asked for opportunity to witness, Acts 21:37.

Open door for Gospel, 1 Corinthians 16:8-9.

Divinely opened door, 2 Corinthians 2:12; Revelation 3:8.

Opportunity still stands, Hebrews 4:1.

OPPOSITION

Let God confuse and deal with opposition, Exodus 23:27-33.

Underestimating the enemy, Deuteronomy 1:41-44.

Mutual respect between enemies, Deuteronomy 2:4-5.

The God who overcomes great enemies, Deuteronomy 20:1.

Threat of iron chariots, Judges 1:19.

Fighting the Lord's battles, 1 Samuel 25:28.

David lamented King Saul's death, 2 Samuel 1:1-27.

Confrontation between David's men and Abner's men, 2 Samuel 2:12-17.

David's attitude toward murder of King Saul's son, 2 Samuel 4:1-12.

Prayer for guidance in confronting enemy, 2 Samuel 5:17-19.

Overcoming obstacles with God's help, 2 Samuel 22:30.

Destroying opposition, 1 Kings 2:13-46.

Killing in one political party, then another, 2 Kings 21:23-24.

Opposition to rebuilding temple, Ezra 4:5, 12-16.

Sanballat's scheme to hinder Nehemiah, Nehemiah 6:1-9.

Enemy's loss of self-confidence, Nehemiah 6:16.

Only God knows how many foes, Psalm 3:1-2.

Facing opposition with confidence, Psalm 3:6.

Enemies turned back in disgrace, Psalm 6:10.

Divine presence in times of trouble, Psalm 14:4-5.

Hatred without reason, Psalm 69:4.

Plans and desires of wicked, Psalm 140:6-8.

At peace with one's enemies, Proverbs 16:7.

Provocation by fool, Proverbs 27:3.

Angry man stirs up dissension, Proverbs 29:22.

Great strength of enemy, Isaiah 5:26-30.

Protection against evil strategy, Isaiah 8:10.

Turning back enemy at gate, Isaiah 28:6.

Egyptians were but men, Isaiah 31:3.

Opposition to reproclamation of God's message, Isaiah 36:13-21.

King Hezekiah's dependence on promises of God, Isaiah 37:1-38.

The God who can level mountains, Isaiah 45:1-3.

The Lord despised and rejected, Isaiah 53:3.

Fate of those who oppose Israel, Isaiah 60:12.

Jeremiah given strength to declare God's message, Jeremiah 1:6-10, 17-19.

Persecutors put to shame, Jeremiah 17:18.

The Lord like a mighty warrior, Jeremiah 20:11.

Giving up to enemy, Lamentations 1:5.

Courage to face adverse circumstances, Ezekiel 2:6-7.

Love your enemy, Matthew 5:43-48.

Parable of Tenants, Matthew 21:33-44.

Those who tried to prevent Resurrection, Matthew 27:62-66. (See also 28:11-15.)

Prayers answered when all is well, Mark 11:25.

Ability of Jesus to confound critics, Mark 11:29-33.

Trying to catch Jesus in His own words, Mark 12:13-17.

Jesus kept silent when criticized, spoke to declare Himself the Christ, Mark 14:53-62.

Folly of unfounded criticism, Luke 8:49-56.

Rejecting those who speak truth about Christ, Luke 10:16.

Strategy for facing superior enemy, Luke 14:31-32.

Opponents of Jesus applauded His logic, Luke 20:39.

Debate between Jesus and teachers of darkness, John 8:13-59.

Plot to kill Lazarus because of his influence, John 12:9-11.

Prayer in time of stress, Acts 4:23-26.

Saul as enemy of church, Acts 8:1-3.

Opposition of sorcerer, Acts 13:6-8.

Jealous Jewish leaders, Acts 13:45-51.

Poisoning minds, Acts 14:2.

Imprisoned for conversion of fortune-teller, Acts 16:16-40.

Mob incited against Paul and Silas, Acts 17:5-7.

Persistent opposition from Thessalonica, Acts 17:13.

Those who sneered at resurrection message, Acts 17:32.

Paul's disgust with unbelieving Jews, Acts 18:5-6.

Those who sought publicly to refute Paul's preaching and teaching, Acts 19:8-9.

Physical harm caused by demons, Acts 19:13-16.

Entire city in uproar, Acts 19:23-41.

Itinerary changed to avoid conflict, Acts 20:2-3.

Accusations which could not be proved, Acts 25:7.

When God is for us, Romans 8:31.

Be good to your enemy, Romans 12:20.
Overcome evil with good, Romans 12:21.
Conflict from unbelievers, Romans 15:31-32.
Those who cause divisions, Romans 16:17.
Purpose of testing, 2 Corinthians 1:2-11.
Pleasing God rather than men, Galatians 1:10.
Standing at end of struggle, Ephesians 6:13.
Paul's attitude toward those who opposed him, Philippians 1:15-18.
Privilege of suffering, Philippians 1:29-30.
Enemies of the Cross, Philippians 3:18-21.
Rising above opposition in proclaiming Gospel, 1 Thessalonians 2:1-2.
Hindered by Satan, 1 Thessalonians 2:18.
Anticipating persecution in advance, 1 Thessalonians 3:4.
Leave revenge in God's hands, 2 Thessalonians 1:6-7.
Persecution inevitable for committed Christian, 2 Timothy 3:12.
Those who oppose message, 2 Timothy 4:14-15.
Not to point of shedding blood, Hebrews 12:4.
Fear not what man may do, Hebrews 13:6.
Resisting Satan, 1 Peter 5:8-9.
Witnessing in face of judgment, Revelation 11:3-12.
See *Adversary, Hindrance.*

OPPRESSION
Unfairness to laborers in Egypt, Exodus 5:6-18.
Successfully facing formidable opponent, Numbers 21:21-26.
Oppression of poor people, Deuteronomy 24:14-15; Proverbs 14:31; Ezekiel 22:29; Amos 5:11-12; 8:4-6.
Rehoboam would be more oppressive than father, 1 Kings 12:1-11.
Divine refuge, Psalm 9:9.
Desperate times, Psalm 60:3.
Exemplary alternative, Isaiah 33:15-16.
Palace built by unrighteousness, Jeremiah 22:13-15.
Assurance to Israel in Egypt, Jeremiah 46:27.
No chance for escape, Jeremiah 48:44.
Enemies without cause, Lamentations 3:52.
Binding heavy burdens, Matthew 23:2-4.

Mixing human blood with sacrifices, Luke 13:1.
See *Persecution.*

OPTIMISM
Boy brings hope to army of Israel, 1 Samuel 17:32.
Good news expected from good man, 2 Samuel 18:27.
Laughter and joy can return, Job 8:21.
Certainty of deliverance in trouble, Psalm 34:19.
Hope in time of despair, Psalm 42:5.
Pessimism turns to optimism, Psalm 73:12-28.
Light dawns in darkness, Psalm 112:4.
No fear of bad news, Psalm 112:7-8.
Rejoicing in day the Lord has made, Psalm 118:24.
Lifting one's eyes to hills, Psalm 121:1.
Blessing of cheerful heart, Proverbs 17:22.
Light shining in darkness, Isaiah 60:1-2.
God fulfills His promises, Jeremiah 29:10-11.
Optimism in time of pessimism, Jeremiah 48:47.
Behind devastation, ahead anticipation, Joel 2:3.
Prayer with joy of confidence, Philippians 1:3-6.
Motivated by joy given by Holy Spirit, 1 Thessalonians 1:6.
Assurance of eternal encouragement, 2 Thessalonians 2:16-17.
See *Encouragement, Positive.*

OPTION
Three choices of punishment, 1 Chronicles 21:8-13.
Better option than scarlet sins, Isaiah 1:18.
Boldness of speech, Jeremiah 1:6-10.
Valley of decision, Joel 3:14.
Choice of Jesus or Barabbas, Matthew 27:15-26.
Only one spiritual option, John 6:66-69.
Choice of two extremes, Acts 3:14.
Paul and Barnabas turn to Gentiles, Acts 13:46-48.
See *Choice.*

ORCHARD
Almond trees, Numbers 17:8; Ecclesiastes 12:5; Jeremiah 1:11.
Fig tree for everyone, 1 Kings 4:25.

Cultivation necessary to produce fruit,
Proverbs 27:18.
Shade of an apple tree, Song of Songs 8:5.
Procedure for fertilizing tree, Luke 13:8.
See *Fruit, Horticulture, Trees.*

ORCHESTRA
Skill with musical instruments a family
tradition, Genesis 4:21.
Instrumental ensemble, 2 Samuel 6:5.
Four-thousand-piece orchestra,
1 Chronicles 23:5.
Exact number of musicians, 1 Chronicles
25:7.
Voices and instruments celebrating rebuilt
wall of Jerusalem, Nehemiah 12:27-43.
Voice and instrument praising the Lord,
Psalm 98:4-6.
See *Music.*

ORDER
Confusion caused by disobedience,
Deuteronomy 28:20.
Avoiding confusion in worship,
1 Corinthians 14:29-33, 40.

ORDINANCE
Lasting ordinance, Exodus 12:14.
Same ordinance for alien and native,
Numbers 9:14.
Preventing merchandising on Sabbath,
Nehemiah 13:15-19.
Vain and valid, Isaiah 1:10-17.
Ordinances broken, Isaiah 24:5.
Decrees to be remembered, Malachi 4:4.
Ordinances insufficient for salvation,
Ephesians 2:15; Colossians 2:14-23;
Hebrews 9:1-10.
See *Legalism.*

ORDINARY
Mundane activity leads to miraculous
event, 2 Kings 6:1-7.
Those of simple ways can have
understanding, Proverbs 9:6.

ORDINATION
Consecrated for service, Numbers 8:10;
27:18; Deuteronomy 34:9.
Commission with encouragement,
Deuteronomy 3:28.
Laying on of hands, Acts 6:5-6; 13:1-3.
Paul's credentials as apostle, Galatians 1:1.
Do not be hasty in laying on hands,

1 Timothy 5:22.
Called to be herald, apostle, teacher,
2 Timothy 1:11.
Christ Himself ordained by His Father,
Hebrews 5:4-6.
Called to ministry of holiness, 1 Peter 1:15-
16.
See *Call.*

ORE
Gold and silver of earth belong to God,
Haggai 2:8.
See *Natural resources.*

ORGANIZATION
David's army of chosen men, 2 Samuel
6:1; 23:8-39.
Solomon's organization for building
temple, 1 Kings 5:12-18.
Foremen and laborers, 2 Chronicles 2:2.
Need for counsel, Proverbs 15:22.
Fate of man's effort after death,
Ecclesiastes 3:22.
Two functions of priest, Ezekiel 40:44-46.
Appointing 12 Apostles, Mark 3:13-19.
Groups of 50 for 5 miracle loaves, Luke
9:14-15.
Delegating distribution of welfare to
widows, Acts 6:1-4.
Need for proper credentials, Acts 15:22-31.
Serving the Lord in unity, Romans 15:5-6;
1 Corinthians 1:10.
Rank and responsibility in church,
1 Corinthians 12:28-31.
Good organization, 1 Corinthians 14:33-
40.
Building fitted together unto the Lord,
Ephesians 2:21.
God intends diversity to produce unity,
Ephesians 4:11-13.
Orderliness of Colossians commended,
Colossians 2:5.
Appointing elders and expediting details,
Titus 1:6-9.
Paul operated through proper channels,
Philemon 12-14.
Submit to authority, Hebrews 13:17.

ORGY
From one sin to another, Jeremiah 9:3.
Overt lust of two prostitute sisters, Ezekiel
23:1-31.
Continual lust for more, Ephesians 4:19.
Evil men who commit sin in broad

daylight, 2 Peter 2:13-22.
See *Lust.*

ORIGINAL
The God without precedent, Isaiah 64:4.

ORNITHOLOGY
Birds unclean for food, Leviticus 11:13-18.
Protection of birds, Deuteronomy 22:6.
Birds know seasons of migration, Jeremiah
8:7.
See *Birds.*

ORPHAN
Divine love for orphans, Exodus 22:22-24.
Tithe given to fatherless, Deuteronomy
26:12.
Background of Queen Esther, Esther 2:7.
God looks after fatherless, Psalms 10:14;
68:5.
Protect orphan property, Proverbs 23:10;
Isaiah 1:17.

ORTHODOXY
Way of unbeliever not to be followed in
worship, Deuteronomy 12:29-32.
Salvation through faith apart from
legalism, Acts 15:1-11.
Persevere in life and doctrine, 1 Timothy
4:16.
Holy Spirit promotes soundness of faith,
2 Timothy 1:13-14.
No lie comes from truth, 1 John 2:20-21.
See *Doctrine, Truth.*

OSTENTATIOUS
Boasting of pious zeal, 2 Kings 10:16.
Queen of Sheba overwhelmed by
Solomon's grandeur, 2 Chronicles 9:3.
Six-month display of wealth, Esther 1:4.
Pious pretense, Proverbs 25:14; 27:2.
Early morning religiosity can be mistaken,
Proverbs 27:14.
Boast only about the Lord, Jeremiah 9:23-
24.
Do not make acts of charity public,
Matthew 6:1-4.
Nonverbal piety, Matthew 23:5.
Jesus accused of luxury, Matthew 26:6-13.

OUTER SPACE
Immeasurable scope of divine greatness,
2 Chronicles 6:12-19.
Wheels of Ezckiel's vision, Ezekiel 1:15-21.

See *Astronomy, Space/time.*

OUTREACH
Solomon's attitude toward foreigners,
1 Kings 8:41-43.
Fountain flowing from sanctuary, Joel 3:18.
Rescue too late at lion's mouth, Amos 3:12.
Inviting others to seek the Lord, Zechariah
8:20-22.
Giving cup of cold water, Matthew 10:42.
Reward for looking after needs of others,
Matthew 25:34-40.
Faith reported all over world, Romans 1:8.
Care in one's conduct toward unbelievers,
Colossians 4:5.
Remember those in prison, Hebrews 13:3.
See *Charity.*

OUTWARD APPEARANCE
God looks at heart, not outward
appearance, 1 Samuel 16:7.
No need to fear giant, 1 Samuel 17:32.
Laughter with an aching heart, Proverbs
14:13.
Whitewashed tombs, Matthew 23:27.
Need for proper appraisal, John 7:24.
See *Display.*

OVERBEARING
Disturbing privacy of others, Proverbs
25:17.

OVERCONFIDENCE
Thinking it easy to face an enemy,
Deuteronomy 1:41-42.
Putting confidence in numerical strength,
Judges 7:2. (See v. 12.)

OVERTIME
People who served double duty, Nehemiah
4:22.
See *Labor.*

OWL
Unclean bird, Leviticus 11:13-17.
Desert creature, Psalm 102:6.
Screech owl, Isaiah 34:11.

OWNERSHIP
Mistreatment to slaves, Exodus 21:20-21.
Delay of ownership, Leviticus 25:29.
Name on each staff, Numbers 17:1-2.
Property involved in inheritance, Numbers
36:1-9.

Permanent ownership of property,
Deuteronomy 4:40.
Respecting neighbor's boundary,
Deuteronomy 19:14.
Ancestral property, Nehemiah 11:20.
Property of angry man, Esther 8:1. (See
5:9–7:10.)
Eating one's own harvest, Isaiah 62:8-9.

Jeremiah's purchase of field, Jeremiah
32:6-15.
Priests to own no property, Ezekiel 44:28.
Silver and gold belong to God, Haggai
2:8.
Deposit on our final redemption,
Ephesians 1:14.
See *Possessions, Property.*

P

PACIFISM
Unworthy to build house of God,
1 Chronicles 28:2-3.
Seek peace, Psalm 34:14.
Warmongers, Psalm 120:6-7.
Wisdom versus weapons, Ecclesiastes
9:18.
Coming world peace, Isaiah 2:4; Hosea
2:18.
See *Peace, War.*

PACK ANIMALS
Beasts of burden, 1 Chronicles 12:40.

PAGAN
A god of stone shows reverence for ark of
God, 1 Samuel 5:1-5.
Sacrifice of son, 2 Kings 16:3.
Pagan king speaks of Israel's "god,"
Isaiah 37:10.
Nebuchadnezzar confused between one
true God and many gods, Daniel 3:28-
30; 4:18.
Pagans certain of erroneous belief, Acts
19:35-36.
Gathered from all tribes and nations,
Revelation 7:9-10.
See *Heathen.*

PAIN
Suffering to the depths, Job 14:22.
Incessant pain, Job 30:17; 33:19; Isaiah
21:3.
Men suffering pains of childbirth, Jeremiah
30:6.
Thoughtfulness of Ebed-Melech in
rescuing Jeremiah, Jeremiah 38:7-13.
Wounds deep as sea, Lamentations 2:13.
Response of Jesus to intense pain,
Matthew 8:5-7.
Wine at Crucifixion, Mark 15:23-24, 36.

Those who wish to die but cannot,
Revelation 9:4-6.
See *Suffering.*

PALACE
David embarrassed by palatial affluence,
2 Samuel 7:2.
Solomon spent more time building palace
than temple, 1 Kings 6:37-38; 7:1.
Assassination site, 2 Kings 15:25.
Archives kept in palace, Ezra 6:2.
Affluent display, Esther 1:2-8.
Palace garden, Esther 7:7.

PANIC
Faith as antidote for fear, Exodus 14:13.
Enemy thrown into confusion, Exodus
23:27-30.
Flight from imaginary enemy, Leviticus
26:17.
Enemies flee in seven directions,
Deuteronomy 28:7.
One person frightens 1,000, Deuteronomy
32:30; Joshua 23:10.
Loss of 30,000 soldiers, 1 Samuel 4:10.
Melting in all directions, 1 Samuel 14:16.
Death of hero routs army, 1 Samuel 17:51.
Hearts melt with fear, 2 Samuel 17:10.
Abandon camp, 2 Kings 7:7.
Chaff in the wind, Psalm 35:5.
Warriors stumbling over each other,
Jeremiah 46:12.
Peril outside and plague inside, Ezekiel
7:15-17.
Knocking knees of frightened king, Daniel
5:6.
Nations in anguish, Joel 2:6.
Bravest warriors flee, Amos 2:16.
From one fear to another, Amos 5:18-19.
Terrified by glory of the Lord, Luke 2:9.
Fear of drowning, Luke 8:22-25.

See *Fear.*

PARABLE
Parable of trees, Judges 9:8-15.
David subject of convicting parable,
2 Samuel 12:1-10.
Parable used to convince King David to
forgive Absalom, 2 Samuel 14:1-21.
Vine of Egypt, Psalm 80:8-16.
Old Testament object lesson, Jeremiah
13:1-11.
Potter and clay, Jeremiah 18:1-4.
Two baskets of figs, Jeremiah 24:1-10.
Parable of vine branch, Ezekiel 15:1-7.
Two eagles and a vine, Ezekiel 17:1-24.
Valley of dry bones, Ezekiel 37:1-14.

PARADE
Migration of Joseph's family with their
possessions, Genesis 46:5-7.
Procession around wall, Nehemiah 12:31-
43.
Marching in line, Joel 2:7-8.

PARADIGM
A man who truly walked with God,
Job 1:1.
Example of prophets being persecuted,
Matthew 5:11-12.

PARADOX
Wealth is poverty, Proverbs 13:7.
Noonday darkness, Isaiah 58:10. (See Matt.
6:23.)
Saving and losing, losing and saving,
Matthew 10:39; 16:25.
Principles of self-interest, Luke 9:23-25.
Divine foolishness and mortal wisdom,
1 Corinthians 1:25.
Seen and unseen, 2 Corinthians 4:18.
Contrasting circumstances and realities,
2 Corinthians 6:4, 8-10.
Strength from weakness, 2 Corinthians
12:10-11.
To know what cannot be known,
Ephesians 3:16-19.
The law that gives freedom, James
2:12-13.
See *Contrast.*

PARASITE
In pursuit of a flea, 1 Samuel 24:14.
Garden slug, Psalm 58:8.
See *Insect.*

PARDON
Testing divine patience, Numbers 14:18.
God's total forgiveness, Jeremiah 50:20.
Anger beyond measure, Lamentations
5:21-22.
Forgiveness for an enemy, Romans 5:10.
See *Forgiveness.*

PARENTS
Relationship between Adam and Eve,
Genesis 4:1-2, 25.
Like father, like son, Genesis 5:1-3.
Age of Old Testament fathers, Genesis
11:10-26.
Bearing children at advanced age, Genesis
16:16; 17:1-21; 21:1-5. (See Rom. 4:18-
21.)
Father as head of house, Genesis 18:19.
Test of Abraham's love to God and his son,
Genesis 22:1-14.
Witness to offspring, Exodus 10:2.
Teaching children to understand spiritual
functions, Exodus 12:26-27;
Deuteronomy 6:20-24.
Physical harm to parents forbidden,
Exodus 21:15.
Cursing parents, Exodus 21:17; Proverbs
20:20; 30:11.
Observing the Lord's Day, Leviticus 23:3.
Father's authority over daughter, Numbers
30:3-5.
Remembering and following divine
teaching, Deuteronomy 4:9.
Duty of parents to share spiritual
experience with children,
Deuteronomy 11:1-7.
Father prays for guidance in teaching son,
Judges 13:8.
Loyalty torn between father and close
friend, 1 Samuel 19:1-2.
Father and son together in death,
2 Samuel 1:23.
Rivalry between father and son, 2 Samuel
15:1-37.
Son less evil than parents, 2 Kings 3:1-3.
Confessing sins of ancestors, Nehemiah
9:2.
When forsaken by parents, God may be
trusted, Psalm 27:10.
Blessing of God from generation to
generation, Psalms 44:1-3; 78:1-7.
Spiritual confidence since birth, Psalm
71:5-6, 17-18.
Children special blessing from the Lord,

Psalm 127:3-5.

Advice of King Solomon to son, Proverbs 1:8-19.

Discipline of good father, Proverbs 3:11-12; 4:1-10.

Influence of parents written on heart, Proverbs 6:20-23.

Proper discipline of children, Proverbs 13:24.

Children should be proud of parents, Proverbs 17:6; Zechariah 10:7.

Grief caused by foolish son, Proverbs 17:25.

Children who rob parents, Proverbs 19:26; 28:24.

Heritage for children, Proverbs 20:7.

Properly training child, Proverbs 22:6.

Child's heart yields to discipline, Proverbs 22:15.

Care of aged parents, Proverbs 23:22-25.

Father conveying God's truth to children, Isaiah 38:18-19.

Abraham and Sarah, Isaiah 51:2.

Evil influence of fathers, Jeremiah 16:10-12.

When it is better not to have had children, Jeremiah 22:30.

Obedience to father's command regarding wine, Jeremiah 35:1-14.

Obedience to parents and grandparents, Jeremiah 35:1-16.

Fathers unable to help children, Jeremiah 47:3.

Sons and daughters sacrificed to idols, Ezekiel 16:20.

Message conveyed to children's children, Joel 1:3.

Joseph and Mary led into and out of Egypt, Matthew 2:13-21.

Gospel can turn children against parents, Matthew 10:32-36.

Causing child to go astray, Mark 9:42.

Parents given son in declining years, Luke 1:5-25.

Mary and Joseph did not fully realize significance of their Son, Luke 2:25-35.

Obedience of Jesus to His parents, Luke 2:41-52.

Parents surprised by answer to their prayers, Luke 8:56.

Concern for only child, Luke 9:38.

Responsibility for health of child, John 9:1-12.

How father should deal with children,

1 Thessalonians 2:11-12.

Influence of Scriptures since childhood, 2 Timothy 3:14-15.

Family of elder must be exemplary, Titus 1:6.

King without father or mother, Hebrews 7:1-3.

When the Lord takes His children by the hand, Hebrews 8:9.

Importance of discipline, Hebrews 12:5-11.

Message for all ages, 1 John 2:12-14.

Children of good parents, 2 John 4.

Joy of believer's children, 3 John 4.

See *Family, Father, Mother.*

PARITY

Questioning why evil prosper, Jeremiah 12:1.

PAROLE

King imprisoned and set free, 2 Kings 24:15; 25:27-29.

Satan released from prison, Revelation 20:1-3, 7-10.

PARSIMONIOUS

Cheap food served by stingy man causes illness, Proverbs 23:6-8.

Attitude of disciples, Matthew 26:8-9; John 12:4-5.

See *Stingy.*

PARSONAGE

House next door to synagogue, Acts 18:7.

PARTIALITY

Parental preference, Genesis 25:28; 27:6-17; 33:2; 37:3; 42:4.

Partiality to no one, Job 32:21-22.

Questioning why evil prosper, Jeremiah 12:1.

Accusing God of partiality, Ezekiel 33:20.

Hatred between Samaritans and Jews, Luke 9:51-56.

Favoring one man against another, 1 Corinthians 4:6.

Forbidden among believers, 1 Timothy 5:21.

See *Favoritism.*

PARTICIPATION

Ox and donkey cannot plow together, Deuteronomy 22:10.

Iron sharpens iron, Proverbs 27:17.

Two in agreement, Amos 3:3.
Faith of friends resulted in man's healing,
Mark 2:1-5.
Participation of all in times of worship,
1 Corinthians 14:26.
Carrying one's own load, Galatians 6:5.
Philippians shared ministry expense when
others did not, Philippians 4:15-19.
See *Cooperation, Teamwork, Unity.*

PARTING
Purposeful separation from loved ones,
John 14:28.
Jesus went away so Holy Spirit could come,
John 16:5-7.
Paul's emotional parting with Christians of
Ephesus, Acts 20:17-38.
See *Separation.*

PARTNERSHIP
As iron sharpens iron, Proverbs 27:17.
Two better than one, Ecclesiastes 4:9-12.
Two in agreement, Amos 3:3.
Jesus called those He wanted, Mark 3:13.
Disciples sent out two-by-two, Mark 6:7.
Barnabas and Saul, Acts 11:22-26.

PARTY
Entertainment with no thought of spiritual
need, Isaiah 5:12.
Noise of carefree crowd, Ezekiel 23:42.
See *Revelry.*

PASSION
Romance of Boaz and Ruth, Ruth 3:7-18.
Unrequited sexual desire, Ezekiel 16:23-
30.
Intense passion, Hosea 7:6.
Marriage on earth compared to
relationship in heaven, Mark 12:18-27.
Continual lust for more, Ephesians 4:19.
See *Romance.*

PASSOVER
Establishment of Passover, Exodus 12:3-
49.
Special Passover sites, Deuteronomy 16:5-
7.
Observed by Jesus, Matthew 26:17-20.
Adapted to body of Christ, 1 Corinthians
5:7; 11:23-26.

PASSPORT
Nehemiah's authorization for travel,
Nehemiah 2:1-8.
See *Credentials.*

PAST
Former things not brought to mind, Isaiah
65:17.

PASTOR
Uniting behind new leader, Joshua 1:16-
18.
The weakness of people left without
spiritual guidance, Judges 2:18-19.
Shepherd and ruler, 1 Chronicles 11:1-2.
Two functions of priest, Ezekiel 40:44-46.
Faithful service without pastoral
supervision, Philippians 2:12-13.
Marks of successful pastor,
1 Thessalonians 2:7-12.
Pastoral function, 1 Thessalonians 5:12;
2 Timothy 2:2-6; 4:1-5.
See *Clergy.*

PATIENCE
Testing divine patience, Numbers 14:18;
Psalm 86:15; Nahum 1:3.
Stand still to see what God will do,
1 Samuel 12:16; Psalm 37:7.
Accepting divine correction, Job 5:17;
Psalm 4:4; Proverbs 3:11.
Patience rewarded, Psalm 40:1; Isaiah 25:9.
Waiting patiently for the Lord, Psalm
130:5-6.
Agony of waiting and joy of fulfillment,
Proverbs 13:12.
Those who speak in haste, Proverbs 29:20.
Conclusion worth waiting for, Ecclesiastes
7:8.
Proper time for every procedure,
Ecclesiastes 8:6.
Year-by-year maturing of vines, Isaiah
37:30.
Delay in answered prayer, Isaiah 49:8.
Silence of the Saviour in time of suffering,
Isaiah 53:7.
Divine patience with rebellious Israel,
Ezekiel 20:1-44.
Divine patience tested to breaking point,
Amos 1:3, 6, 9, 13; 2:1, 4, 6.
Certainty that God's revelation will come
to pass, Habakkuk 2:3.
Growth takes time, Mark 4:28.
Full measure of forgiveness, Luke 17:3-4.
Invalid who waited 38 years for healing,
John 5:1-8.

Giving up on those who refuse message,
Acts 18:5-6.

Accepting affliction patiently, Romans
12:12.

Paul showed tolerance toward bad reports,
1 Corinthians 11:18-19.

Avoid complaint or argument, Philippians
2:14-15.

Accepting all circumstances and situations,
Philippians 4:11-13.

Forgive one another and be patient,
Colossians 3:13.

Good soldiers, 2 Timothy 2:3-5.

Kind to everyone, 2 Timothy 2:24.

Eternal perspective, Hebrews 10:34.

Faith to believe what has not been
received, Hebrews 11:13.

Learning perseverance through trials and
testing, James 1:2-4.

Submission to divine wisdom, James 4:7.

Farmer's patience as he waits for harvest,
James 5:7.

Job's patience rewarded, James 5:11.

Disappointment accepted as God's will,
1 Peter 4:12-13, 19.

Patience of the Lord toward the lost,
2 Peter 3:9.

Seated one day on the throne, Revelation
3:21.

PATRIOTISM

Those who sit at home, Numbers 32:6.

Duty of citizens to new leadership, Joshua
1:16-17.

Defense of one's country, 1 Samuel 17:26-
51.

Loyalty to national leaders, 2 Samuel 1:18-
27; 2:10.

Spiritual burden, Nehemiah 1:2-11.

Concern for national survival, Esther 4:13-
17.

Prayer for community, Psalm 122:6.

Daniel's prayer of repentance for himself
and his nation, Daniel 9:1-19.

Good words for centurion, Luke 7:4-5.

Submission to authorities, Romans 13:1-7.

See *Citizenship.*

PAWN

Clothing not to be held overnight, Exodus
22:26-27.

Rules for operating pawn service,
Deuteronomy 24:10-17.

Inhumane conduct, Job 22:6.

Conduct of money lender, Ezekiel 18:7-16.

PAYMENT

Abram refused payment from king of
Sodom, Genesis 14:22-24.

Requesting payment for spiritual ministry,
2 Kings 5:20-27.

Money, food, and drink for temple
workers, Ezra 3:7.

Prostitute giving rather than receiving,
Ezekiel 16:32-34.

Wages an obligation, not gift, Romans 4:4.

Divine deposit on our final redemption,
Ephesians 1:14.

See *Barter, Honorarium, Stipend, Wages.*

PEACE

Desire for peace and security, 2 Kings
20:19.

Living under shadow of the Almighty,
Psalm 91:1-2.

An honor to avoid strife, Proverbs 20:3.

The Peacemaker, Isaiah 53:5.

Proclaiming peace when there is no peace,
Jeremiah 6:14; 8:11.

Break the bow, Jeremiah 49:35.

Israel today consists of unwalled villages,
Ezekiel 38:10-12.

Swords beaten into plowshares, Micah 4:3.

Blessed are the peacemakers, Matthew 5:9.

World peace an impossibility without
Christ, Matthew 24:6-8.

Jesus predicted no peace on earth, Mark
13:6-8.

See *Pacifism.*

PEERS

Following wrong crowd, Exodus 23:2.

PENALTY

Destiny set for rebellious people, Numbers
14:35.

Paying penalty for subversion, Esther 7:1-
10.

Like idol, like follower, Psalm 135:15-18.

Cost for doubting an angel, Luke 1:18-20.

PENITENCE

Disaster delayed, 1 Kings 21:29.

Respect for prophet, 2 Kings 1:1-15.

Tears of contrition and confession, Ezra
10:1.

Acknowledgment of sin, Psalm 32:5-6.

Conditions for forgiveness, Ezekiel 18:21-

23.
Guilt of Judas, yet he did not repent,
Matthew 27:3.
Role of grief in repentance, 1 Corinthians
5:1-2.
See *Repentance.*

PENMANSHIP
Writing with clarity, Deuteronomy 27:8;
Habakkuk 2:2.

PERCEPTION
Unaware of the Lord's presence, Genesis
28:16.
Donkey who saw an angel, Numbers
22:23-28. (Note v. 31.)
Eyes that see, ears that hear, Deuteronomy
29:2-4.
Opening eyes to see God's provision,
2 Kings 6:16-17.
Fear tests words, Job 12:11.
Work of the spirit within man, Job 32:8.
Prayer for perception in study of
Scriptures, Psalm 119:18.
Sovereign God correctly directs man's
steps, Jeremiah 10:23.
Understanding visions and dreams, Daniel
1:17.
Wisdom of queen, Daniel 5:10-11.
Shrewd and innocent, Matthew 10:16.
Perception of adults as compared to
children, Matthew 11:25.
Hearing but not understanding, Matthew
13:14-15.
Partial, then full vision for blind man, Mark
8:22-25.
Saviour's dual mission comprehended,
Luke 2:28-32.
Jesus knew when He had been touched,
Luke 8:43-48.
Herod's lack of perception, Luke 9:7-9.
Followers of Jesus unable to understand,
Luke 9:44-45.
Divine perception of man, John 2:25.
Samaritan woman perceived who Jesus is,
John 4:27-30.
Lack of spiritual perception, John 8:47.
Spiritual blindness and spiritual sight, John
9:39-41.
Some heard thunder, others an angel's
voice, John 12:29.
Misunderstanding words of Jesus, John
16:17-18.
Wisdom of Gamaliel, Acts 5:34-39.

Beyond human perception and
experience, 1 Corinthians 2:9-10.
Spirit of wisdom and revelation, Ephesians
1:17.
Eyes of heart, Ephesians 1:18-19.
Depth of insight, Philippians 1:9.
Proper understanding of the Law,
1 Timothy 1:8-11.
Reward of careful reflection, 2 Timothy
2:7.
Pointless quarreling over words,
2 Timothy 2:14.
Proceeding from "milk" to "solid food,"
Hebrews 5:11-14. (See also 6:1-3.)
Wisdom of the mind, Revelation 17:9.
See *Comprehension, Understanding.*

PERFECTION
Challenge to blameless conduct, Genesis
17:1.
Divine perfection and faithfulness,
Deuteronomy 32:4.
Made pure through testing, Job 23:10.
A perfect way, Psalm 18:32.
Impossibility of perfection, Ecclesiastes
7:20.
High cost of perfection, Matthew 19:21.
Evaluation of Nathanael by Jesus, John
1:47.
Aim for perfection, 2 Corinthians 13:11.
Our perfect High Priest, Hebrews 4:15;
7:26.
Sinless Saviour, 1 Peter 1:18-19; 2:22.
Those who claim they have not sinned,
1 John 1:8-10.
See *Exemplary.*

PERFORMANCE
God does what He says He will do,
Numbers 23:19.
Jesus challenged to display prowess, John
7:2-9.
Do not serve God to please men,
Colossians 3:23-24.
Poor performance in service to God,
Revelation 3:2.
See *Conduct.*

PERFUME
Fragrant incense, Exodus 30:7.
Temple fragrance not for personal
enjoyment, Exodus 30:34-38.
Purposeful use of perfume, Ruth 3:3.
Fragrant clothing, Psalm 45:8.

Many fragrances, Song of Songs 4:10-14.
Anointing of Jesus, Matthew 26:6-13; Mark
14:3-9.
See *Cosmetics, Myrrh.*

PERIL
Successfully facing formidable opponent,
Numbers 21:21-26.
David's lack of confidence, 1 Samuel 27:1.
Go to neighbor for help, Proverbs 27:10.
Facing grim destiny, Jeremiah 15:2-3.
Peril outside, plague inside, Ezekiel 7:15-
17.
Responsibility of watchman as danger
approaches, Ezekiel 33:1-9.
See *Danger.*

PERJURY
Thoughtlessly taking an oath, Leviticus 5:4.
Giving false testimony, Leviticus 6:3;
Deuteronomy 19:16, 21.
Falsehood concerning Law of the Lord,
Jeremiah 8:8.
False prophets, Jeremiah 23:16-18.

PERMISSION
Qualifications for coming into God's
presence, Psalm 24:3-4. (See Eph.
2:18.)
Gates open, Isaiah 26:2. (See John 10:9.)
Opportunity for anyone, Isaiah 55:1-3.
Come, Matthew 11:28-29.
Bold admittance, Hebrews 4:14-16.
See *Approval, Credentials.*

PERPETUAL
Unending faithfulness, Joshua 24:14.
One who never changes, Hebrews 1:10-12.

PERPLEXITY
Sacrifice of daughter, Judges 11:30-40.
Lamp of the Lord, 2 Samuel 22:29.
Waters up to neck, Psalm 69:1.
Security in the Lord, Psalm 127:1-2.
Those who confuse others, Galatians 1:6-9.
Some of Paul's writing difficult to
understand, 2 Peter 3:15-16.
See *Confusion.*

PERSECUTION
Satanic challenge, Job 2:4-5.
Lurking enemies, Psalms 11:2; 56:5;
Proverbs 29:10.
Desperate times, Psalm 60:3.

Scorn endured for God's glory, Psalm 69:7.
Wishing for persecutor to be persecuted,
Psalm 119:84-88.
Let the Lord vindicate, Psalm 135:14.
Songs of Zion gone silent, Psalm 137:1-4.
Sword of the Lord bathed in blood, Isaiah
34:6.
Prayer for deliverance from persecutors,
Jeremiah 15:15.
Let persecutors be put to shame, Jeremiah
17:18.
Jeremiah beaten for proclaiming truth,
Jeremiah 20:1-2.
Jeremiah persecuted for prophesying
truth, Jeremiah 37–38.
Swift pursuit of enemy, Lamentations 4:19.
Saved from trouble and in trouble, Daniel
3:16-18.
Opportunity to witness, Matthew 10:16-20.
Fear not those who only kill body, Matthew
10:28.
Peter wanted easy way to discipleship,
Mark 8:31-38.
Son of proprietor killed by tenants, Mark
12:1-12.
Scoffing at Jesus on the cross, Mark 15:29-
32.
Rejoice when criticized for faith, Luke
6:22-23.
Secret believers, John 12:42-43.
World first hated our Lord, John 15:18-19.
Jesus warned of persecution, John 16:1-4.
Persecuted for proclaiming resurrection,
Acts 4:1-4.
Rejoicing in persecution, Acts 5:41.
Death of Stephen, Acts 6:8–7:60.
Persecution implemented spread of
Gospel, Acts 8:3-4.
Early church in time of peace, Acts 9:31.
Those scattered by persecution witnessed
wherever they went, Acts 11:19-21.
Jealous Jewish leaders, Acts 13:45-51.
Paul's persecution enabled him to
encourage others, Acts 14:19-22.
Paul and Silas imprisoned for conversion
of fortune-teller, Acts 16:16-40.
Persistent opposition, Acts 17:13.
Paul knew he would face persecution, Acts
20:17-24; 21:10-14.
Paul's former role in persecution of
Christians, Acts 22:19-20.
Imprisonment made possible Paul's visit to
Rome, Romans 1:13.
Rejoice in suffering, Romans 5:3-4.

Present suffering not to be compared with coming glory, Romans 8:18.
When God is for us, Romans 8:31.
Be joyful and patient, Romans 12:12.
Bless those who persecute, Romans 12:14.
Strengthened by faithful Lord, 1 Corinthians 1:8-9.
Persecution brought overflowing joy and generosity, 2 Corinthians 8:1-5.
Paul's rank in Judaism, Galatians 1:13-14.
Bearing marks of Jesus, Galatians 6:17.
Work of church enhanced, Philippians 1:14.
Privilege of suffering, Philippians 1:29-30.
Sharing in sufferings of Christ, Philippians 3:10-11.
Paul asked friends to remember his bondage, Colossians 4:18.
Motivated by joy given by Holy Spirit, 1 Thessalonians 1:6.
Anticipating persecution in advance, 1 Thessalonians 3:4.
Growth in spite of persecution and trials, 2 Thessalonians 1:3-4.
Leave revenge with God, 2 Thessalonians 1:6-10.
Suffering for sake of Gospel, 2 Timothy 1:12.
Persecution inevitable for committed Christian, 2 Timothy 3:12.
Safety in the Lord, 2 Timothy 4:18.
Made perfect through suffering, Hebrews 2:10.
Persecution of new converts, Hebrews 10:32-34.
Moses chose persecution rather than pleasures of sin, Hebrews 11:25.
Recognizing persecution as avenue of blessing, Hebrews 11:35.
Fear not what man may do, Hebrews 13:6.
Willingness to suffer, Hebrews 13:11-14.
Maturing value of testing, James 1:2-4, 12.
Purpose of trials and grief, 1 Peter 1:6-7.
Bearing pain of unjust suffering, 1 Peter 2:19-21.
Suffering for what is right, 1 Peter 3:13, 17.
Suffering in the name of Christ, 1 Peter 4:12-16.
Sure rescue in the Lord, 2 Peter 2:7-9.
Brothers and companions at all times, Revelation 1:9.
Do not fear suffering, Revelation 2:10.
Faithful in face of persecution, Revelation 2:13.

The Lord disciplines those He loves, Revelation 3:19.
Put to death for faithful witness, Revelation 6:9.
Witnessing in face of judgment, Revelation 11:3-12.
Satan given temporary power to persecute believers, Revelation 13:5-7.
Test of endurance and faithfulness, Revelation 13:10; 14:12.
Drunk with blood of saints, Revelation 17:6.
All tears wiped away, Revelation 21:4.
See *Oppression.*

PERSEVERANCE
Fortunes restored, Deuteronomy 30:1-3.
Unending faithfulness, Joshua 24:14.
Not giving in to weariness, Judges 8:4.
Working diligently together, Nehemiah 4:6.
Made pure through testing, Job 23:10.
Path of the just, Proverbs 4:18.
Keeping self under control, Proverbs 29:11.
Doing what you do with all your might, Ecclesiastes 9:10.
Enduring faith, Matthew 24:13.
Facing tough times, 2 Timothy 2:1-3.
Learning perseverance through trials and testing, James 1:2-4.
Reward for Job's patience, James 5:11.
Holding on to faith, Revelation 2:25.
See *Diligence.*

PERSISTENCE
Unending faithfulness, Joshua 24:14.
Persistence toward doing evil, Nehemiah 9:28.
Faithful in daily prayer, Psalm 5:3.
Searching for wisdom and insight, Proverbs 2:1-6.
Activity with full energy, Ecclesiastes 9:10.
For continued sinning, certain judgment, Amos 1:3, 6, 9, 11, 13; 2:1, 4, 6. (Note nature of sin in each of these judgments.)
Enduring to the end, Mark 13:13.
New way to get to Jesus, Luke 5:17-20.
Climbing tree to see Jesus, Luke 19:1-9.
Invalid who waited 38 years, John 5:1-8.
Persistence in witnessing, Acts 5:42.
Persistent opposition, Acts 17:13.
Example of those who lived by faith,

Hebrews 12:1-3.
Reward for Job's patience, James 5:11.
See *Relentless, Tireless.*

PERSONAL

Each responsible for personal guilt only,
Deuteronomy 24:16; Job 19:4; Jeremiah
31:29-30; Ezekiel 18:20.
Individual touch of Jesus, Matthew 9:25;
Mark 9:27.
Whosoever, John 3:16; Romans 10:13.
See *Individual.*

PERSONALITY

Angel's description of unborn Ishmael,
Genesis 16:11-12.
Contrasting personalities of Jacob and
Esau, Genesis 25:27.
Blighted personality, Deuteronomy 32:32-
33.
Quarrelsome personality, Proverbs 27:15-
16.
Faces reflect hearts, Proverbs 27:19.
Clash of personalities between Paul and
Barnabas, Acts 15:36-41.
Struggle between flesh and spirit, Romans
7:15-18, 21-25.
Differing reactions to truly Christian
personality, 2 Corinthians 2:15-16.
Paul and Peter face-to-face, Galatians 2:11.
Fruit of Spirit, Galatians 5:22-23.
Motivated by joy given by Holy Spirit,
1 Thessalonians 1:6.
Inner beauty, 1 Peter 3:3-4.
Additions to faith, 2 Peter 1:5-9.
See *Identity.*

PERSONNEL

People more valuable than material things,
Genesis 14:21.
Seven men plus one additional, Micah 5:5.

PERSPECTIVE

God's point of view and man's, Job 10:3-7;
Isaiah 55:8-9.
Learning what cannot be seen, Job 34:32.
Short duration of life, Psalm 39:4.
Wicked lack eternal perspective, Psalm
92:6-7.
Ezekiel lifted up between earth and
heaven, Ezekiel 8:3.
Wide and narrow, Matthew 7:13-14.
Looking only on surface, 2 Corinthians
10:7.

Filled with knowledge of God's will,
Colossians 1:9-12.
Word of God in its fullness, Colossians
1:25-26.
A day like a thousand years, 2 Peter 3:8.
See *Viewpoint.*

PERSUASION

Moses' plea for guide through desert,
Numbers 10:29-33.
Vindication by earthquake, Numbers
16:28-34.
Asking for special favor, Judges 1:13-15.
Wiles of Samson's wife in solving his
riddle, Judges 14:11-19.
Hearts of people won through clever
manipulation, 2 Samuel 15:1-6.
Motivated by hook and bit, 2 Kings 19:23.
Pagan king persuaded to permit rebuilding
of temple, Ezra 4–8.
Let the Lord make your cause valid, Psalm
37:6.
Speaking with gentle tongue, Proverbs
25:15.
Deceitful, malicious man, Proverbs 26:24-
26.
Haughty women of Zion, Isaiah 3:16-
17.
Believe the Good News, Mark 1:14-15.
Like teacher, like student, Luke 6:40.
Influencing others to sin, Luke 17:1.
Basis for persuasion and teaching, Acts
17:2-4.
Paul's preaching and teaching, Acts 19:8.
King Agrippa would not be persuaded,
Acts 26:28.
Imprisonment widened Paul's sphere of
influence, Philippians 1:12-14.
Fine-sounding arguments, Colossians 2:4.
Ultimate in being properly motivated,
1 Thessalonians 1:3.
Gospel communicated with words and
power, 1 Thessalonians 1:4-5.
See *Convincing, Eloquence.*

PERVERSION

Suggestion of social disease, Jude 7-8.

PERVERT

Mixing religion with immorality, Numbers
25:1-2.
Silver to dross, wine to water, Isaiah 1:22.
Deliberately falsifying, Jeremiah 8:8.
See *Defile.*

PESSIMISM
Fate of spies who brought bad report from Canaan, Numbers 14:36-38.
Pessimism of unbelief, 2 Kings 18:29-35.
Persistent calamity, Job 18:12.
Pessimism turns to optimism, Psalm 73:12-28.
All seems meaningless, Ecclesiastes 1:2.
Negative view of existence, Ecclesiastes 4:1-3.
Going from one trouble to another, Amos 5:19.
Old Testament ends with curse, Malachi 4:6.
Hope when no basis for hope, Romans 4:18-22.
Circumstances do not necessarily indicate reality, Hebrews 11:11-12.
See *Attitude, Despair, Frame of reference.*

PESTILENCE
Price of disobedience, Deuteronomy 28:15-24; Psalm 78:50.
Haunt of jackals, Jeremiah 9:11.
Locusts who attack people, Revelation 9:3-6.

PETITION
Document submitted to king in opposition to rebuilding temple, Ezra 4:12-16.

PETROLEUM
Source of oil, Deuteronomy 32:13.

PETS
Noah and dove, Genesis 8:9.
One little lamb, 2 Samuel 12:1-3.
See *Animals.*

PHARISEE
Mockery of fasting, Isaiah 58:4-5.
Beware of false praise, Jeremiah 12:6.
Hypocrisy, Matthew 15:9.
Religion of sham, Matthew 23:5-7.
View of the resurrection, Acts 23:6-8.
Methods of disruptive hypocrite, 2 John 9-10.

PHILANTHROPY
God, who sees all, rewards, Jeremiah 32:19.
Do not make acts of charity public, Matthew 6:1-4.
Woman who helped poor, Acts 9:36-42.

Sharing with those in need, 1 John 3:17.
See *Benevolence.*

PHILOSOPHY
Human viewpoint, Ecclesiastes 1:2.
Fragile wisdom of man, Isaiah 29:14.
Philosophers at Athens called Paul a babbler, Acts 17:18.
Not wise but fools, Romans 1:22.
Man's wisdom versus God's, 1 Corinthians 1:20; 3:19-20.
Deceptive philosophy, Colossians 2:8.
See *Intellectual.*

PHONY
Hyper-piety, Matthew 6:16-18.
Religion of sham, Matthew 23:5-7.
Clean outside, filthy inside, Matthew 23:25-28.
Ego displayed by teachers of Law, Mark 12:38-40.
Disciples could not believe Saul's conversion genuine, Acts 9:26-27.
False humility, Colossians 2:18.
See *Artificial, False, Sham.*

PHYSICAL
Prayer for physical strength, Nehemiah 6:9.
Fearfully and wonderfully made, Psalm 139:14.
Race not to swift or strong, Ecclesiastes 9:11.
Examining liver for guidance, Ezekiel 21:21.
Healing increased popularity of Jesus, Mark 3:7-10.
Better to be limited physically than lost, Mark 9:43-48.
Man of short stature, Luke 19:1-6.
Body is the Holy Spirit's temple, 1 Corinthians 6:19-20.
Rapid deterioration of human body, 2 Corinthians 4:16-18.
Good health and spiritual growth, 3 John 3.
See *Mortality.*

PHYSICIAN
Physicians as morticians, Genesis 50:2.
Seeking only medical help, 2 Chronicles 16:12.
Careless attention to wound, Jeremiah 8:11.
Doctor needed in Gilead, Jeremiah 8:22.

Only sick people need doctor, Matthew
9:12; Luke 5:31.
Greetings from Doctor Luke, Colossians
4:14.
See *Health, Medicine, Therapy.*

PHYSIQUE
Bearing of prince, Judges 8:18.
Samson's mother described angel who
came to her, Judges 13:6.
Stature of King Saul, 1 Samuel 10:23-24.
Appearance of boy David, 1 Samuel 16:12.
Handsome Absalom, 2 Samuel 14:25.
Man short of stature, Luke 19:1-10.
See *Athletics.*

PIETY
Piety caused by fear, 2 Chronicles 20:29.
Scorn for acts of humility, Psalm 69:10-11.
Early morning religiosity, Proverbs 27:14.
Real meaning of fasting, Isaiah 58:3-7.
Pious speech from wayward hearts,
Jeremiah 5:1-2.
Those who offer false praise, Jeremiah
12:6.
Scorning those who have done wrong,
Ezekiel 16:56-57.
Satan's use of Scripture, Matthew 4:1-11.
Those truly pious, Matthew 5:1-29.
Performing righteousness in view of
others, Matthew 6:1.
Sabbath observance, Matthew 12:1-13.
Faith of gross sinners compared to religion
of Pharisees, Matthew 21:31-32.
Ultimate test, Matthew 22:36-40.
Missing real purpose of worship, Matthew
23:23-24.
Morality and materialism, Mark 10:17-25.
Pious and hypocritical attitudes toward
Jesus, Luke 6:1-11.
Face of angel, Acts 6:15.
Personal righteousness not obtained
through observing sacraments, Romans
4:9-12.
Victory over carnal nature, Romans 8:1-17.
Love chapter, 1 Corinthians 13:1-13.
Showing love to those who cause grief,
2 Corinthians 2:5-11.
Spirit's presence in life of commitment,
2 Corinthians 3:7-8.
Seeking righteousness by human effort,
Galatians 3:3.
Fruit of the Spirit, Galatians 5:22-23.
True religion, James 1:27.

Lifestyle of true disciple, James 3:17-18.
Call to holiness, 1 Peter 1:13-16.
Spiritual growth, 2 Peter 1:5-9.
Partial holiness insufficient, Revelation
2:1-6, 13-15, 18, 20.
See *Commitment, Spirituality.*

PILGRIM
Life seen as pilgrimage, Genesis 47:9.
Aliens and strangers, 1 Chronicles 29:15;
Psalms 39:12; 119:19; Hebrews 11:8-10,
13; 1 Peter 1:1-2, 17.
Pilgrims because of disobedience, Hosea
9:17.

PILLAR
Lot's wife, Genesis 19:26; Luke 17:32.
Anointing object, Genesis 28:18-22.
Historic markers, Exodus 24:1-4.
Boundary marker, Joshua 15:6.
Death of Samson, Judges 16:25-30.
Temple adornment, 1 Kings 7:13-22.
See *Architecture.*

PITFALL
Tar pits of Siddim, Genesis 14:10.
Danger of pride in conquest of demons,
Luke 10:16-20.
See *Snare, Trap.*

PITY
Concern of Pharaoh's daughter for baby
Moses, Exodus 2:5-6.
No pity in judgment, Lamentations 2:2.
Joseph did not want to make Mary subject
of public disgrace, Matthew 1:19.
Refusal of Jesus to accept pity, Luke 23:27-
28.
See *Compassion.*

PLAN
Journey with the Lord's approval, Judges
18:6.
Hiding of true intentions, 1 Samuel 16:1-5.
Man's plans and God's purpose, Proverbs
19:21.
Patience needed to persuade, Proverbs
25:15.
Drawing plan for battle, Ezekiel 4:1-3.
Design, measurement, and arrangements
to be carefully followed, Ezekiel 43:10-
12.
Estimate cost before starting to build, Luke
14:28-30.

Paul took care in planning journey,
2 Corinthians 1:15-17.
No certainty of tomorrow, James 4:13-16.
Redemption planned before Creation,
1 Peter 1:18-20.
See *Design, Map.*

PLATITUDES
Making promises to curry loyalty,
1 Samuel 22:6-8.
Flattering lips speak with deception, Psalm
12:1-2.
Those who do not want to hear truth, Isaiah
30:10-11.
Fine-sounding arguments, Colossians 2:4.
See *Hyperbole.*

PLAY
Carnality in action, Exodus 32:6.
Playing rough, 2 Samuel 2:14.
National celebration, 2 Samuel 6:5.
Frolicking animals, Job 40:20.
Child and cobra, Isaiah 11:8.

PLAYBOY
Carousing soldiers, 1 Samuel 30:8.
Playing with fire, Proverbs 6:27-28.
Lack of discretion, Proverbs 7:6-23.
Deep inner feelings, Proverbs 14:13.
He who loves pleasure, Proverbs 21:17.
Preferring play to work, Ecclesiastes 4:7-8.
End to noisy songs, Ezekiel 26:13.
Influencing others to sin, Luke 17:1.
Those who carouse, 2 Peter 2:13-16.
See *Hedonism, Narcissism.*

PLAY-ON-WORDS
Use of a literary device concerning
freedom, Jeremiah 34:17.
See *Figure of speech, Literature.*

PLEASURE
Time to rejoice and not weep, Nehemiah
8:9-10.
Nauseating pleasure, Job 20:12-16.
Man's value to God, Job 22:2-3.
Joy beyond levity of wine, Psalm 4:7.
True joy comes only from the Lord, Psalm
84:11.
Covert pleasures, Proverbs 9:17.
Love of pleasure, Proverbs 21:17.
Meaningless activity, Ecclesiastes 2:1-11.
Alcoholism, Isaiah 5:11-12.
Wages of sin, Lamentations 1:14.

Peril of ease, Amos 6:1.
Fisherman burns incense to net, Habakkuk
1:16.
Deathly conduct, 1 Timothy 5:6.
Lovers of pleasure, 2 Timothy 3:4.
Moses' choice to refuse pleasures of Egypt,
Hebrews 11:24-25.
Joy of problems and testing, James 1:2-4.
Those who carouse, 2 Peter 2:13-16.
Joy of good reputation, 3 John 3-4.
See *Comfort, Hedonism, Narcissism, Play.*

PLEBISCITE
Uncalled but unanimous vote, Exodus
16:2.
Agreement with the will of God,
1 Chronicles 13:2.
The choice of Jesus or Barabbas, Matthew
27:15-26.
See *Vote.*

PLEDGE
Pledge of unified congregation, Exodus
24:1-7.
Making and paying pledge, Deuteronomy
23:21.
Keeping vow to God, Psalm 65:1.
Better not to vow than fail to fulfill,
Ecclesiastes 5:5.
Taking false oath, Jeremiah 5:2.
See *Covenant, Promise.*

PLENTY
Promised abundance, Leviticus 26:5;
Deuteronomy 30:9; Psalm 132:15;
Isaiah 30:23; Amos 9:13.
Abundant life in Christ, John 10:10.
Abounding in God's grace, 2 Corinthians
9:8.
God's grace lavished on us, Ephesians 1:7-
8.
Good land and unproductive land,
Hebrews 6:7-8.
Ample provision for life of godliness,
2 Peter 1:3.
See *Abundance.*

PLUNDER
Crops and animals taken by enemy, Judges
6:3-6.
Fate of dead after battle, 1 Samuel 31:8-10.
Making frolic of plunder, Jeremiah 50:11-
12.
Plundering with glee, Ezekiel 36:5.

POETRY
Song of Moses, Exodus 15:1-18.
Verse about deliverance, Numbers 21:27-30.
Setting murder to verse, Judges 5:24-27.
Hannah's song, 1 Samuel 2:1-10.
Elegy, 2 Samuel 1:19-27; 3:33-34.
Elizabeth's song, Luke 1:42-45.
See *Literature, Lyrics.*

POISE
See *Assurance, Confidence.*

POISON
Deliverance from snakebite, Numbers 21:4-9.
Venom of vipers, Deuteronomy 32:24.
Fangs of an adder, Job 20:16.
Deaf cobra, Psalm 58:4.
Poison speech, Psalm 140:3; James 3:8.
Pestilence of locusts in judgment, Revelation 9:7-11.
See *Venom.*

POLICE
Security at entrance to Garden of Eden, Genesis 3:24.
Security for Sabbath duty, 2 Kings 11:4-12.
Day and night protection, Nehemiah 4:9.
Guard at our Lord's tomb, Matthew 27:65-66.
Satan under arrest, Revelation 20:1-3.

POLITENESS
See *Courtesy, Guests, Hospitality, Manners.*

POLITICS
Building first city, Genesis 4:17.
Esau married non-Canaanite to please his father, Genesis 28:6-9.
Choosing right leader, Deuteronomy 17:14-15.
Short, concise speech, Judges 9:1-2.
David and Saul, 1 Samuel 17:32-37; 2 Samuel 2:8-32.
Immorality in politics, 2 Samuel 3:6-11.
Winning people's favor, 2 Samuel 15:1-6.
Owning share of king, 2 Samuel 19:43.
Adonijah sought to take over David's throne, 1 Kings 1:1-27.
Alliance confirmed by marriage, 1 Kings 3:1.
Secret anointing of king, 2 Kings 9:1-13.
The priest and the king, 2 Kings 11:15-18.

Ages of young kings, 2 Kings 21:1, 19; 22:1; 23:36; 24:8, 18; 2 Chronicles 33:1, 21; 34:1; 36:2, 5, 9, 11.
Killing in one political party, then another, 2 Kings 21:23-24.
Inevitable fate of world governments, Psalm 2:7-9.
Death ends influence of secular leadership, Psalm 146:3-4.
Favor of a ruler, Proverbs 19:6.
Good and bad leadership, Proverbs 28:12.
Politicians keep their eyes on each other, Ecclesiastes 5:8-9.
Right and left, Ecclesiastes 10:2.
Governed by children, Isaiah 3:4.
Put out of office, Isaiah 22:19.
Man who refused bribes and related evil, Isaiah 33:15-16.
Reward of evil politics, Jeremiah 22:13.
King in respectable exile, Jeremiah 52:31-34.
Wicked officials in city, Ezekiel 22:27.
Daniel and friends given high positions, Daniel 2:48-49.
Darius became king at age 62, Daniel 5:30-31.
Daniel's integrity in government affairs, Daniel 6:1-4.
Importance of divine guidance in choice of leaders, Hosea 8:4.
Future of world political systems, Micah 7:16-17.
Establishing government by evil methods, Habakkuk 2:12.
Pharisees feared Roman reaction to ministry of Jesus, John 11:48.
King Herod killed to gain favor with those who opposed Christians, Acts 12:1-4.
Paul kept in prison to please Jews, Acts 24:27.
Praying for those in authority, 1 Timothy 2:1-4.
Do not show favoritism, James 2:1.
Role of demons in world politics, Revelation 16:14.
One-hour reign of 10 kings, Revelation 17:12.
See *Bureaucracy.*

POLLUTION
Silver to dross, wine to water, Isaiah 1:22.
Foul-smelling canals, Isaiah 19:6.
Bodies unburied, Jeremiah 9:22.
Defiled with blood, Lamentations 4:14.

Polluting wheat, Amos 8:6.
Evil influence over good, Matthew 13:24-30.
Salt loses saltiness, Luke 14:34-35.
See *Defile*.

POLYGAMY
First examples of bigamy, Genesis 4:19; 16:3; 26:34-35.
First record of polygamy, Genesis 28:9.
Second wife after beautiful drama of monogamy, Genesis 29:16-30.
Consideration for first wife, Exodus 21:10.
Forbidden, Leviticus 18:18; Deuteronomy 17:17.
Spoils of war, Deuteronomy 20:10-15.
David's many wives, 1 Samuel 25:39-44.
Solomon's many wives, 1 Kings 11:1-3.
Elder must have but one wife, Titus 1:6.

POOR
Harvest gleaning for poor, Leviticus 19:9-10.
Poor and rich, 1 Samuel 2:7.
Benevolent spirit, Job 29:11-15; 30:25; 31:15-22.
Sense of true value, Psalm 37:16; Proverbs 13:7; 28:6.
Call to altruism, Psalm 82:3-4.
Divine opportunity, Proverbs 19:17; Matthew 25:42-45.
Penalty for selfishness, Proverbs 21:13.
See *Poverty*.

POPULARITY
King Saul's lack of popularity with some subjects, 1 Samuel 10:26-27.
David's pleased subjects, 2 Samuel 3:36.
Winning favor of people, 2 Samuel 15:1-6.
David's fear of Absalom's popularity, 2 Samuel 15:13-14.
Many seek Job's favor, Job 11:19.
The wide and the narrow, Matthew 7:13-14.
Pharisees' fear of crowd, Matthew 21:45-46; John 4:1-3.
Healing increased popularity of Jesus, Mark 3:7-10.
Jesus' own mother and brothers unable to get through crowd, Luke 8:19-21.
Seeking praise of men, John 12:42-43.
Respect of Cornelius for Peter, Acts 10:25-26.
King Herod killed to gain favor with those who opposed Christians, Acts 12:1-4.
Favor resulting from dependability, Colossians 3:22.

POPULATION
God's plan for increase, Genesis 9:1.
Rapid population growth after Flood, Genesis 10:1-32.
Census involved men 20 years or older, Numbers 26:2.
Threat of population reduction, Deuteronomy 28:62.
Population of Israel reduced, 2 Kings 10:32.
Building population by statistics, Nehemiah 11:1.
Scarcity of people, Isaiah 13:12.
God's command to increase population, Jeremiah 29:4-6.
People taken into exile, Jeremiah 52:28-30.
Population decimated by divine judgment, Ezekiel 5:12.
Nineveh considered large city, Jonah 3:3.
Census of entire Roman world, Luke 2:1-3.
Many demons living in one man, Luke 8:30.

PORK
Meat not to be eaten, Leviticus 11:7; Isaiah 65:4; 66:17.
Jewelry not for pigs, Matthew 7:6.
Habitat for demons, Matthew 8:30.
Mud dwellers, 2 Peter 2:22.

POSITION
Asking for prestige rather than earning it, Mark 10:35-45.
Paul's rank in Judaism, Galatians 1:13-14.
Blessed in heavenly realms, Ephesians 1:3.
Those who demand first place, 3 John 9.
See *Prestige*.

POSITIVE
God's attitude toward Creation, Genesis 1:4, 10, 12, 18, 21, 25, 31.
Message not yes or no, 2 Corinthians 1:18-20.
Letter kills but Spirit gives life, 2 Corinthians 3:6.
Taking positive view to problems, 2 Corinthians 4:17-18.
See *Negative*.

POSSESSIONS
Exchanging what you have for that which is far better, Genesis 45:20.
Permanent ownership of Israel, Deuteronomy 4:40.
Earth is God's property, Psalm 95:4-5.
Stones and dust of Jerusalem, Psalm 102:14.
Eating one's own harvest, Isaiah 62:8-9.
Kingdoms of the world, Matthew 4:8-9.
Ananias and Sapphira, Acts 5:1-11.
See *Affluence, Property*.

POSSESSIVE
Misuse of sacrifice to the Lord, 1 Samuel 2:12-17.
Owning share of king, 2 Samuel 19:43.
Requesting payment for spiritual ministry, 2 Kings 5:20-27.
Greedy for gain, Jeremiah 8:10.
See *Greed*.

POSTERITY
Witness to future generations, Exodus 16:32-34.
Father's preventive care for children, Job 1:1-5.
Life of Jesus recorded for continuing generations, Luke 1:1-4.

POSTHUMOUS
Memories of woman's kindness perpetuated, Matthew 26:6-13.
Dead yet continuing to speak, Hebrews 11:4.
Good deeds follow good people, Revelation 14:13.

POSTPONE
Those who said it was not time to rebuild temple, Haggai 1:3-4.
See *Delay*.

POSTURE
Bearing of prince, Judges 8:18.
Reclining at mealtime, Luke 22:14.
Sitting down and standing up, Acts 13:14, 16.

POTENTIAL
Like idol, like follower, Psalm 135:15-18.
Potential capability of the child Jeremiah, Jeremiah 1:7.
Potential of blessing lost to idols, Hosea 9:10.
Evaluating military logistics, Luke 14:31-32.
Unlimited future for children of God, 1 John 3:1-3.
See *Capability, Future*.

POVERTY
Pet lamb of poor family, 2 Samuel 12:1-6.
Poor people spared captivity, 2 Kings 24:14.
Function of evil, Psalm 14:6.
Better little with righteousness than wealth with wickedness, Psalm 37:16-17.
Value of little with faith over much with turmoil, Proverbs 15:16.
Simple food with peace and quiet, Proverbs 17:1.
Pain of being poor, Proverbs 19:7.
Poverty better than dishonesty, Proverbs 19:22.
Rich and poor have common origin, Proverbs 22:2.
The Lord defends the poor, Proverbs 22:22-23.
Speak up for those who cannot help themselves, Proverbs 31:8-9.
Babylonian mercy to poor, Jeremiah 39:10; 40:7-9.
Prosperity forgotten, Lamentations 3:17.
Exploiting poor for personal gain, Amos 5:11.
Poverty's deepest dimensions, Haggai 2:16-17.
Poor in spirit, Matthew 5:3.
Jesus and earthly possessions, Matthew 8:19-20.
Disciples traveled humbly with humble equipment, Mark 6:8-11.
Poor can inherit kingdom, Luke 6:20.
No place for Jesus to lay His head, Luke 9:58.
Concern of early Christians for poor, Galatians 2:9-10.
Living in tent en route to city of God, Hebrews 11:9-10.
Those who endure poverty to glory of God, Hebrews 11:37-38.
Poor can be rich in faith, James 2:5.
True wealth, Revelation 2:9.

POWER
Nothing too hard for God, Jeremiah 32:27.
Power of divine message, Luke 4:32.

Power to witness, Acts 1:8.
Holy Spirit brought Christ back from dead, Romans 8:11. (See Eph. 1:18-21.)
Strength from weakness, 2 Corinthians 12:9.
Means by which the Lord Jesus will overthrow man of sin, 2 Thessalonians 2:8.
See *Omnipotence.*

POWERLESS
Unable to face enemy, Leviticus 26:37; Deuteronomy 28:32; Joshua 7:12.
Unable to drive out invader, Judges 1:21.
Admitting lack of strength, 2 Chronicles 20:12.
Men become like women, Isaiah 19:16; Jeremiah 50:37; 51:30; Nahum 3:13.
See *Weakness.*

PRACTICAL JOKE
Folly of practical joking, Proverbs 26:18-19.

PRACTICE
Practice what you preach, Psalm 51:10-13; Ezekiel 33:31.

PRAGMATIC
Evil men recognize God's power, Exodus 8:1-19.
Medical proof of virginity, Deuteronomy 22:13-19.
Showing favor for personal interest, 1 Samuel 27:12.
Afraid of ark of the Lord, 2 Samuel 6:9-11.
Death by measurement, 2 Samuel 8:2.
Three choices for punishment, 1 Chronicles 21:8-13.
Father's preventive care for children, Job 1:1-5.
Contentment with daily bread, Proverbs 30:8.
Stark evaluation of life, Ecclesiastes 5:15; 7:1-5.
Looking frankly at emptiness of life, Isaiah 55:2.
Presumed proof of power of a goddess, Jeremiah 44:11-19.
Test and compare, Daniel 1:12-15.
Man who measured Jerusalem, Zechariah 2:1-2.
Proving the Lord by tithing, Malachi 3:10.
Wisdom of serving God, Malachi 3:14-15.

View of Jesus toward Sabbath, Matthew 12:1-13.
New way to get to Jesus, Luke 5:17-20.
Receiving good for doing good, Luke 6:37-38.
Good things from good heart, evil from evil, Luke 6:45.
Centurion's view of Jesus, Luke 7:1-10.
Pharisee's evaluation of Jesus, Luke 7:36-50.
Looking at circumstances instead of Jesus, Luke 9:10-17.
Letter of Law made practical in spirit, Luke 10:35-37.
Pharisees desired visible kingdom, Luke 17:20-21.
When curiosity led to blessing, Luke 18:35-43.
Believing visible evidence, John 4:39-42.
Making judgments by appearance, John 7:20-24.
Seeing is believing, John 9:35-38.
Believing the key to seeing, John 11:40.
Doubting Thomas, John 20:24-29.
Sufficient evidence to make decision, John 20:30-31.
Realizing God's work cannot be stopped, Acts 5:38-39.
Those who demand visible and rational evidence, 1 Corinthians 1:22-25.
Pragmatic aspects of faith, Hebrews 11:1-3.
Eyewitness to reality, 1 John 1:1-4.
See *Tangible.*

PRAISE
Song of Moses, Exodus 15:1-18.
Woman lauded for murder, Judges 5:24-27.
Avoiding partiality and flattery, Job 32:21-22.
Harp as instrument of praise, Psalm 43:4.
Giving praise to God's Word, Psalm 56:10.
Singing with steadfast heart, Psalm 57:7.
Cry of praise to the Lord, Psalm 89:8.
Giving the Lord glory due Him, Psalm 96:8.
David's song of praise, Psalm 103:1-22.
Praise and glory belong only to God, Psalm 115:1; Acts 12:21-23; 1 Corinthians 3:7.
Nature and people praise the Lord, Psalm 148:1-14.
Last verse of Psalms, Psalm 150:6.
Let another praise you, Proverbs 27:2.
Praise, test of humility, Proverbs 27:21.
Folly of flattery, Proverbs 28:23.

Talented people encouraging each other,
Isaiah 41:7.
Joy and gladness, Jeremiah 33:11.
Daniel's gratitude to God for needed
wisdom, Daniel 2:19-23.
Praise from pagan lips, Daniel 4:37.
When God turns deaf ear to praise, Amos
5:22. (See 8:3, 10.)
Jesus' evaluation of John the Baptist,
Matthew 11:11-14.
Crowd praised Jesus prior to crying out,
"Crucify Him!" Matthew 21:6-11.
(Note 27:20-23.)
Danger of being well spoken of, Luke 6:26.
Duty of true servant, Luke 17:7-10.
Receive praise from God, 1 Corinthians
4:5.
Compliments expressed to others,
2 Corinthians 7:14.
Let the Lord commend, 2 Corinthians
10:17-18.
Trying to please others, Galatians 1:10.
Paul's clear motivation in preaching and
teaching, 1 Thessalonians 2:1-6.
Praise to God for success in ministry,
1 Thessalonians 3:8-10.
Good deeds will be made known,
1 Timothy 5:25.
One worthy of praise from all creation,
Revelation 5:13-14.
Outcry of praise to God, Revelation 7:11-
12.
Fear causes people to give glory to God,
Revelation 11:13.
Concluding proclamation of faith in God,
Revelation 15:3-4.
See *Worship*.

PRAYER
Pregnancy in answer to prayer, Genesis
25:21.
Prayer of humility, Genesis 32:9-10.
God's answer to grumbling community,
Exodus 16:3-5.
Promise of answered prayer to those who
please the Lord, Exodus 33:17.
Prayer for protection, Numbers 10:35.
Persistent prayer in time of need, 1 Samuel
7:8.
Praying for rain, 1 Samuel 12:18.
Difference between personal decision and
seeking divine guidance, 1 Samuel
14:36-41.
Prayer through night, 1 Samuel 15:11.

Unanswered prayer and spiritism,
1 Samuel 28:5-20.
David's prayer for guidance, 2 Samuel
5:17-19.
Receiving assurance of divine guidance,
2 Samuel 7:18-29.
Solomon's prayer for wisdom and
discernment, 1 Kings 3:1-15; 4:29-34.
God listens when people pray, 1 Kings
8:52; Psalm 6:9.
Prayer of national repentance,
2 Chronicles 7:14.
Prayer for physical strength, Nehemiah 6:9.
Cry of anguish in time of suffering, Job 6:8-
10.
Job knew his Advocate was in heaven, Job
16:19.
Job's critics spoke of a God removed from
man's affairs, Job 22:12-14.
Unanswered prayers, Job 30:20.
Vitality of answered prayer, Job 33:26.
Persistent daily prayer, Psalm 5:3.
Confidence that God will answer, Psalms
17:6; 138:1-3.
Importance of praise with prayer, Psalm
18:3.
God hears prayer in time of trouble, Psalm
18:6.
Highest motive life can know, Psalm 27:4.
Prayer in response to divine command,
Psalm 27:8.
Prayer answered in times of trouble, Psalm
34:17.
The desires the Lord places in our hearts
assure blessing and guidance, Psalm
37:3-5. (See also 20:4-5.)
Prayer in time of suffering and
disappointment, Psalm 38:9.
Thirst for the living God, Psalm 42:1-2.
Deep calling unto deep, Psalm 42:7-8.
God has the means for answering prayer,
Psalms 50:9-15; 65:2.
Seeking high rock, Psalm 61:1-2.
Prayer unanswered when sin is cherished,
Psalm 66:18-19.
In time of desperation, Psalm 69:1-3.
Danger of putting God to the test, Psalm
78:18-22.
Prayers which incite God's anger, Psalm
80:4.
Prayer for revival, Psalm 85:1-7.
Prayer for undivided heart, Psalm 86:11.
Calling to the Lord day and night, Psalm
88:1-2.

Qualification for answered prayer, Psalm 91:14-16.
Reward of selfish prayer, Psalm 106:14-15.
David known as man of prayer, Psalm 109:4.
Calling out to God in time of deep depression, Psalm 116:1-4.
Release from anguish, Psalm 118:5.
Giving thanks at midnight, Psalm 119:62.
Asking God only for that which His Word teaches, Psalm 119:65.
Prayer of humility, Psalm 123:1-2.
Prayer for inner peace and righteousness, Psalm 139:23-24.
Altar of prayer, Psalm 141:2.
Desires of righteous fulfilled, Psalm 145:17-19; Proverbs 10:24. (See also Ps. 37:4.)
Prayer unanswered, Proverbs 1:29-31.
Ultimate request for guidance, Proverbs 3:5-6.
Agony of waiting and joy of fulfillment, Proverbs 13:12.
Detestable prayers of lawbreakers, Proverbs 28:9.
Cautious words in God's presence, Ecclesiastes 5:2.
Meaningless offerings, Isaiah 1:11-17.
The Lord is quick to answer, Isaiah 30:19.
Hezekiah's prayer put God's glory first in time of trouble, Isaiah 37:14-20.
Certainty of answered prayer, Isaiah 49:8; Mark 11:24.
Relentless prayer until answer comes, Isaiah 62:6-7.
Answer before request, Isaiah 65:24.
Backslider calls to God in time of trouble, Jeremiah 2:27.
When God refuses to hear and answer, Jeremiah 11:14.
Unanswered prayers of disobedient, Jeremiah 14:11.
Sincere search for God, Jeremiah 29:10-14.
Great and mighty things, Jeremiah 33:3.
People's dependence on a prophet's prayers, Jeremiah 42:1-4.
An answer in 10 days, Jeremiah 42:7.
Prayer God does not hear, Lamentations 3:8; Micah 3:4.
Prayer unanswered though seekers shout in God's ears, Ezekiel 8:18.
Answered prayer of wayward people, Ezekiel 36:37-38.

Desperate prayer in time of emergency, Daniel 2:18. (See vv. 14-23.)
Faith ahead of loyalty to king, Daniel 6:5-11.
Awe of talking to God, Daniel 10:15-21.
Praying inside fish, Jonah 2:1.
Lips must first be purified, Zephaniah 3:9.
The Lord listens to those who listen to Him, Zechariah 7:13.
Praying for rain, Zechariah 10:1.
Privacy of prayer, Matthew 6:5-13.
Asking, seeking, knocking, Matthew 7:7-8.
Faith touches God's willingness to respond, Matthew 8:2-4.
Prayer for harvest, Matthew 9:37-38.
Faith to remove mountains, Matthew 21:21-22.
Example of Jesus in early morning, Mark 1:35.
Power of prayer in times of crisis, Mark 9:14-29.
Blind man's simple request, Mark 10:46-52.
Ministry of aged widow, Luke 2:36-38.
Willingness of Jesus to answer cry of need, Luke 5:12-13.
Jesus withdrew from crowd to pray, Luke 5:16.
Night of prayer, Luke 6:12.
Those who asked Jesus for help surprised at answer, Luke 8:56.
Praying for harvesters rather than the harvest, Luke 10:1-2.
God's goodness in answer to prayer, Luke 11:5-13.
Persistent prayer, Luke 18:1-8.
Proud Pharisee and humble publican, Luke 18:9-14.
Promised answer to prayer, John 14:13-14; 16:23-24.
Chosen for guidance and blessing, John 15:16.
Prayer of Jesus before going to cross, John 17:1-26.
Disciples wanted earthly blessing but Jesus promised spiritual opportunity, Acts 1:6-7.
Disciples asked God for guidance but resorted to earthly procedure, Acts 1:24-26.
Interesting form of prayer in time of stress, Acts 4:23-26.
Prayer for personal advantage only, Acts 8:24.

Power of prayer in time of need, Acts 12:5.
Paul's consistent prayer for other
    Christians, Romans 1:8-10;
    1 Corinthians 1:4-9; Ephesians 1:11-23;
    Philippians 1:3-6; Colossians 1:3-14;
    1 Thessalonians 1:2-3; 2 Thessalonians
    1:3.
Words beyond normal vocabulary,
    Romans 8:15-16.
Prayer guided by Holy Spirit, Romans 8:26-
    27.
Paul asked for prayer that his service
    would be acceptable, Romans 15:31-32.
Praying aloud in presence of others,
    1 Corinthians 14:15-17.
Paul prayed for healing but could rejoice in
    getting negative answer, 2 Corinthians
    12:7-10.
Access to God through the Holy Spirit,
    Ephesians 2:18.
Coming to God with confidence, Ephesians
    3:12.
Prayer with spiritual depth for other
    Christians, Ephesians 3:14-21.
Praying in the Spirit, Ephesians 6:18.
Praying for those who minister, Ephesians
    6:19-20; Colossians 4:3-4.
God can do more than we ask or imagine,
    Philippians 1:9.
Prayer that brings peace, Philippians 4:6-7.
High priority to ministry of prayer,
    Colossians 4:2.
Prayer warrior, Colossians 4:12.
Praise to God for success in ministry,
    1 Thessalonians 3:8-9.
Paul's persistent prayer for Thessalonians,
    1 Thessalonians 3:10.
Subjects for prayer, 1 Timothy 2:1-4.
Paul's constant prayer for Timothy,
    2 Timothy 1:3.
Coming to our High Priest, Hebrews 4:14-
    16.
Cries of Jesus to His Heavenly Father,
    Hebrews 5:7.
Abraham waited patiently for God's
    promise, Hebrews 6:13-15.
Our High Priest in heaven, Hebrews 8:1-2.
Coming to God in full assurance, Hebrews
    10:9-23.
Confident now of God's fulfillment of His
    promises in future, Hebrews 11:13.
Asking God for wisdom and believing it
    will be granted, James 1:5-7.
Praying with wrong motives, James 4:3.

Prayer of righteous man, James 5:16.
Power of Elijah's prayer, James 5:17-18.
Prayers hindered in bad marriage, 1 Peter
    3:7.
The Lord attentive to prayer, 1 Peter 3:12.
Cast all cares on the Lord, 1 Peter 5:7.
Confidence and conditions, 1 John 3:21-
    22.
Assurance of answered prayer, 1 John
    5:14-15.
Pray in the Holy Spirit, Jude 20.
Incense and the prayers of saints,
    Revelation 8:3-4.
Concluding proclamation of faith in God,
    Revelation 15:3-4.
We are not to pray to or worship angels,
    Revelation 22:8-9.

PRAYER MEETING
Appointed time for prayer in temple, Acts
    3:1.
Prayer meeting on beach, Acts 21:5.

PREACHING
Time of little preaching, 1 Samuel 3:1.
God revealed Himself through His word,
    1 Samuel 3:21.
God's Word on the tongue, 2 Samuel 23:2.
Mocking God's messengers, 2 Chronicles
    36:16.
People ask for pleasant sermons, Isaiah
    30:10.
Opposition to God's message, Isaiah
    36:13-21.
Mouth like sharpened sword, Isaiah 49:2.
Instructed tongue, Isaiah 50:4.
Voice like trumpet, Isaiah 58:1.
Anointed to proclaim coming of Christ and
    proclamation of Gospel, Isaiah 61:1-3.
Portray the Lord's goodness, Isaiah 63:7.
Boldness of speech given by God,
    Jeremiah 1:6-10.
Turning deaf ear to message, Jeremiah
    5:12-13.
Words destroyed by fire, Jeremiah 5:14.
Offensive words to those who will not hear,
    Jeremiah 6:10.
Beware of deceptive words, Jeremiah 7:4-
    8.
Rejection of message, Jeremiah 7:25-26.
False cry for peace, Jeremiah 8:11.
Directive from the Lord to Jeremiah,
    Jeremiah 11:6.
Attempt to silence prophets, Jeremiah

11:21; Amos 2:12.

Error of preaching what God does not promise, Jeremiah 14:11-16.

Jeremiah beaten for proclaiming truth, Jeremiah 20:1-2, 7-8.

Crying out to those who reject God's Word, Jeremiah 22:29.

Words of man and words of God, Jeremiah 23:16-18.

Those whom the Lord did not call, Jeremiah 23:21.

Dreams, visions, and the Word of God, Jeremiah 23:25-32.

Faithful proclamation of God's Word, Jeremiah 25:1-4.

Message of Jeremiah brings threat of death, Jeremiah 26:1-16.

Prophets who proclaimed lies, Jeremiah 27:14-15; Ezekiel 22:28.

Jeremiah gave initially positive response to false prophecy of Hananiah, Jeremiah 28:1-17. (Note "amen" of agreement in vv. 5-6.)

Jeremiah, faithful to God's Word, put in prison, Jeremiah 37:1-21.

Message of Jeremiah rejected, Jeremiah 43:1-7. (See 44:15-19.)

Courage to minister under any circumstances, Ezekiel 2:6-7.

Some will listen, some refuse, Ezekiel 3:27; Matthew 22:1-10.

Ezekiel's message to mountains, Ezekiel 6:1-4.

When the preacher becomes silent, Ezekiel 7:26.

Those who speak out of their own imagination, Ezekiel 13:2-16.

Proclaiming only what people want to hear, Ezekiel 14:4-10.

Those who disbelieved message Ezekiel proclaimed, Ezekiel 20:49.

Reaction to prophet's message, Ezekiel 21:7.

God's message proclaimed with boldness, Ezekiel 33:21-33.

Trampled grass and muddied water, Ezekiel 34:18-19.

Courage of Daniel to point out sin of king, Daniel 5:18-26.

Preaching with compassion, Joel 2:17.

Preaching did not mix with politics, Amos 7:13.

People who did not want to face truth, Micah 2:6.

Given words to speak, Matthew 10:19-20.

Simplicity of profound truth, Matthew 11:25-26; 1 Corinthians 1:17-29.

Living Word pierces heart, Luke 2:34-35.

Commission to preach and teach, Luke 4:14-21.

Preaching with authority, Luke 4:32.

Jesus and His disciples proclaiming Good News, Luke 8:1-2.

Jesus proclaimed depths of spiritual truth, John 6:60-69.

Theme of post-Resurrection apostles, Acts 4:2.

Message rejected, Acts 7:1-60.

Paul's resumé of Old Testament and proclamation of Gospel, Acts 13:16-41.

Speaking effectively, Acts 14:1.

Holy Spirit hindered preaching in an area, Acts 16:6-7.

Basis for persuasion and teaching, Acts 17:2-4.

Resurrection message in opposition to idolatry, Acts 17:16-18.

Paul's great sermon at Athens, Acts 17:19-33.

Places Paul needed to visit, Acts 19:21.

Falling asleep during long sermon, Acts 20:7-12.

Spiritual truth communicated in human terms, Romans 6:19.

Speaking only of what Christ has done in us, Romans 15:18-19.

Paul asked for prayer that his ministry would be acceptable, Romans 15:31-32.

Speaking and knowledge enriched in Christ, 1 Corinthians 1:5-6.

Simplicity of Paul's message, 1 Corinthians 2:1-5.

Importance of gift of prophecy, 1 Corinthians 14:1-5.

Spreading fragrance of Christ, 2 Corinthians 2:14.

Making profit from Word of God, 2 Corinthians 2:17.

Plainness of speech, 2 Corinthians 3:12-13.

Paul wrote convincing letters but lacked ability in public speaking, 2 Corinthians 10:10.

Information without eloquence, 2 Corinthians 11:6.

Repetition for emphasis, Philippians 3:1; 2 Peter 1:12-15.

Word of God in its fullness, Colossians

1:25-26.
Effective preaching demands involvement, 1 Thessalonians 1:4-5.
Letting message ring out, 1 Thessalonians 1:8.
Rising above opposition in proclaiming Gospel, 1 Thessalonians 2:1-2.
Abundant praise to God for success in ministry, 1 Thessalonians 3:8-10.
Those who make spectacular prophecies, 2 Thessalonians 2:1-2.
Proper understanding of the Law, 1 Timothy 1:8-11.
Message Paul was called to proclaim, 1 Timothy 2:5-7.
Giving caution concerning false teaching, 1 Timothy 4:1-6.
Those who oppose message, 2 Timothy 4:14-15.
Paul's responsibility to proclaim message God had given him, Titus 1:1-3.
Proclaiming the Word of God, 1 Peter 4:11.
Temporary suffering as a reward for faithfulness, Revelation 1:9.
See *Exegesis, Receptive, Sermon.*

PREDESTINATION
Chosen for greatness, Genesis 18:16-19.
Birth of nation, Genesis 21:12-13.
Destined purpose, Exodus 9:16.
Future accomplishment assured, Numbers 21:34.
Predestined city, 2 Chronicles 6:6.
Chosen people, Psalm 33:12.
Chosen person, Psalm 65:4; Jeremiah 1:4-5.
All things ordained, Psalm 139:15-16.
Time for everything, Ecclesiastes 3:1-8.
Things planned long ago, Isaiah 25:1.
The Lord will do what He has said, Isaiah 46:11.
God's perfect timing, Isaiah 49:8.
Jeremiah appointed prophet before birth, Jeremiah 1:5.
Destined for death and peril, Jeremiah 15:2.
Nebuchadnezzar's view of predestination, Daniel 4:15.
Jesus knew what He would do, John 6:6, 37-45.
Jesus prayed for those given to Him by the Father, John 17:1-12.
History predestined, Acts 17:26.

Predestined goodness, Romans 8:28-33.
Divine decisions irrevocable, Romans 11:29.
Paul set apart from birth, Galatians 1:15-17.
Chosen before Creation, Ephesians 1:4-6, 11-12.
Filled with knowledge of God's will, Colossians 1:9-12.
Paul destined for persecution and trials, 1 Thessalonians 3:1-5.
Rejecting destiny planned by God, 1 Peter 2:8.
Determined number of martyrs, Revelation 6:9-11.
See *Destiny, Foreknowledge.*

PREDICTABLE
Joseph's prediction of deliverance from Egypt, Genesis 50:24-25.
People quick to disobey God, Judges 2:10-13, 19; 3:7, 12; 4:1.
Future can be left safely in God's hands, Isaiah 46:8-11.
Good news and bad news, Jeremiah 34:1-7.
Prophecy of imagination, Ezekiel 13:1-23.
Angel prophesied ministry of John the Baptist, Luke 1:11-17.
Forecasting weather, Luke 12:54-56.

PREEMINENCE
God as first priority, Genesis 1:1.
The God who is greater than numbers, Deuteronomy 20:1.
No other God like the Lord, Isaiah 46:9.
Knowing who is the Lord, Ezekiel 6:10, 14; 7:4, 9, 27; 12:16, 20; 13:9, 23; 14:11.
Earth filled with the Lord's glory, Habakkuk 2:14.
Danger of pride in conquest of demons, Luke 10:16-20.
Qualifications of Christ as Saviour and King, Colossians 1:15-20.
God's Son superior to angels, Hebrews 1:3-4.
See *Supremacy.*

PREFERENCE
Same rules for all, Numbers 15:15.
Gifts expected from those who gave most in battle, Numbers 31:27-31.
Right of first son, Deuteronomy 21:15-17.
Better option than sins as scarlet, Isaiah

1:18.
Jerusalem, apple of God's eye, Zechariah
2:8.
See *Favoritism*.

PREGNANCY
Infertility in household of Abimelech,
Genesis 20:17-18.
Children born in old age, Genesis 21:1-7.
Pregnancy in answer to prayer, Genesis
25:21.
Onan's procedure toward command of
Judah, Genesis 38:8-10.
Rights of pregnant woman, Exodus 21:22.
Beyond age of childbearing, Ruth 1:11.
Wonder of body being formed,
Ecclesiastes 11:5.
Time of birth, Isaiah 26:17; 66:9.
God's prenatal plan for Jeremiah,
Jeremiah 1:4-5.
Elizabeth and Zechariah given son in their
declining years, Luke 1:5-25.
Baby that leaped in his mother's womb,
Luke 1:39-44.
Woman's joy in giving birth, John 16:21.
See *Fertility*.

PREJUDICE
Hagar's choice of wife for Ishmael, Genesis
21:21.
Abraham's concern for wife for Isaac,
Genesis 24:1-4.
Wealth and prestige could not numb
Haman's resentment, Esther 5:10-14.
Opinions of fool, Proverbs 18:2.
One upright man but no upright woman,
Ecclesiastes 7:28.
Attitudes cause hearing without
understanding, Matthew 13:14-15.
Jesus overlooked racist tradition, Matthew
15:21-28.
Mutual hatred of Samaritans and Jews,
Luke 9:51-56.
Faith in Christ can bring family division,
Luke 12:49-53.
Refusing to believe revealed truth, John
9:39-41.
Disciples slow to accept converted Saul,
Acts 9:26.
Deliverance from legalism, Acts 10:24-28.
No racial prejudice in God's heart, Acts
10:34-35; 15:5-9.
Poisoning the mind, Acts 14:2.
Making room in heart for acceptance of

others, 2 Corinthians 7:2.
Proper attitude toward poor, James 2:1-8.
Darkness of hatred, 1 John 2:9-11.
Viewpoint of world, 1 John 4:5.
See *Opinion*.

PRELIMINARY
Jesus recited parable as crowd gathered to
hear Him preach, Luke 8:4-15.

PREMEDITATED
Judas under contract to betray Jesus,
Matthew 26:14-16.

PRENATAL
Destiny of unborn, Psalm 139:15-16.
God's prenatal plan for Jeremiah,
Jeremiah 1:4-5.
See *Predestination*.

PREPARATION
Spiritual preparation for future victory,
Joshua 3:5.
Dig ditches for water, 2 Kings 3:15-17.
Extra containers needed, 2 Kings 4:3-4.
Divine plans made far in advance, Isaiah
25:1.
Preparing way of the Lord, Isaiah 40:3.
Break up unplowed ground, Hosea 10:12.
Preaching of John the Baptist, Matthew
3:1-3; Mark 1:2-8; Luke 3:1-20.
Parable of Ten Virgins, Matthew 25:1-13.
Night of prayer before important decision,
Luke 6:12-16.
Prepared in advance for persecution, Luke
21:12-15.

PRESSURE
Delegating work to others, Exodus 18:17-
27.
Waters up to neck, Psalm 69:1.
King Herod yielded to pressure, Matthew
14:6-11.
Divine pressure to fulfill destiny, Luke
12:50.
Night coming, work to do, John 9:4.
Paul in a hurry to reach Jerusalem, Acts
20:16.
Keep your head in all situations, 2 Timothy
4:5.
See *Duress, Stress*.

PRESTIGE
Heroes of old, Genesis 6:4.

People followed Simon, the sorcerer, Acts 8:9-11.

Respect of Cornelius for Peter, Acts 10:25-26.

Prominent women chose to follow Christ, Acts 17:4.

Insulting someone of high rank, Acts 23:4-5.

God calls those of humble backgrounds and abilities, 1 Corinthians 1:26.

Paul's rank in Judaism, Galatians 1:13-14.

Those who only seem to be important, Galatians 2:6.

Blessed in heavenly realms, Ephesians 1:3.

Life's highest prestige, Ephesians 3:12.

Paul could have boasted of former status, Philippians 3:2-11.

Qualifications of Christ as Saviour and King, Colossians 1:15-20.

Purpose and means of spiritual success, 2 Thessalonians 1:11-12.

Desire to be overseer, 1 Timothy 3:1.

Paul's credentials in ministry, Titus 1:1-3.

Position in life subordinate to following the will of God, Titus 2:9-10.

God's Son superior to angels, Hebrews 1:3-4.

Greatest of all high priests, Hebrews 7:26.

David and Samuel given small mention, Hebrews 11:32.

Take pride in humble circumstances, James 1:9.

Clothes do not necessarily make the man, James 2:1-5.

Identified as children of God, 1 John 3:1-3.

Those who demand first place, 3 John 9-10.

Believers as priests, Revelation 1:6.

Seated with the Lord on His throne, Revelation 3:21.

Illumination of a great angel's presence, Revelation 18:1.

See *Acclaim, Fame.*

PRESUMPTION

Motivation for Tower of Babel, Genesis 11:4.

Disobeying the Lord's command, Numbers 14:41-44.

Attitude toward divine specifications, Numbers 20:8-12.

Ignoring divine promises, Numbers 21:5.

Speaking other than the Lord's message, Deuteronomy 18:20.

Entering forbidden area, 2 Chronicles 26:16.

Presumptuous sins, Psalm 19:13.

Presumption about future, Proverbs 27:1; Isaiah 56:12; James 4:13-14.

Taking prosperity and life for granted, Luke 12:19.

Presuming God's grace available at man's convenience, Acts 24:25.

PRETENSE

Pretending to be wealthy, Proverbs 13:7.

Those who boast of giving but do not give, Proverbs 25:14.

Early morning religiosity, Proverbs 27:14.

Strutting rooster, Proverbs 30:31.

Boast only about the Lord, Jeremiah 9:23-24.

Pharaoh only loud noise, Jeremiah 46:17.

King Herod and the magi, Matthew 2:7-8, 12.

Do not make acts of charity public, Matthew 6:1-4.

Empty sincerity of Pharisees, Mark 12:15-17.

Those who perform only for pretense, Mark 12:38-40.

Pretending to be what one is not, Galatians 6:12-15.

False humility, Colossians 2:18.

Making false claim of holy life, 1 John 1:8-10.

Feigning life when spiritually dead, Revelation 3:1.

See *Counterfeit, Sham.*

PREVARICATE

A God who cannot lie, Numbers 23:19.

Honest weights and measurements, Deuteronomy 25:13-16.

Dishonest report for personal gain, 2 Samuel 1:2-16. (See also 1 Sam. 31:4.)

Deliberately writing falsehoods concerning Law of the Lord, Jeremiah 8:8.

Friends and brothers not to be trusted, Jeremiah 9:4-8.

Believing a lie, Jeremiah 43:1-7.

See *Deceit, Dishonesty, False, Lie.*

PREVENTION

Approval of parents, Numbers 30:3-5.

Elimination of blacksmiths, 1 Samuel 13:19.

The Lord on our side, Psalm 124:1-5.
Ounce of prevention, Luke 12:39.

PREVIEW
Moses saw but did not experience
Promised Land, Numbers 27:12-14.
Transfiguration a preview of glory to come,
Luke 9:28-36.

PRICE
Practice of barter in Ezekiel's time, Ezekiel
27:12-23.
Cheating on weight and cost, Amos 8:5-6.
High price for dance, Mark 6:21-29.
Warning of persecution given by Jesus,
John 16:1-4.
See *Cost.*

PRIDE
Danger of material possessions,
Deuteronomy 8:11-20; Psalm 52:7;
Proverbs 18:11-12; Jeremiah 48:7.
Small leader demanded humility from
strong constituents, Judges 9:14-15.
Those who want to share honors in military
victory, Judges 12:1-3.
Improper time for boasting, 1 Samuel 2:1-
3.
Divine attitude toward humility and pride,
2 Samuel 22:28; Psalm 138:6.
Boastful attitude of King Rehoboam,
1 Kings 12:10-11.
Job's sarcasm to proud accusers, Job 12:2-
3.
Elihu accused Job of self-righteousness,
Job 34:1-9; 36:4.
Pride numbs spirituality and goodness,
Psalm 10:2-11.
Vanity numbs realization of sin, Psalm
36:2.
Making one's boast in the Lord, Psalm
44:8.
Possessive pride, Psalm 49:11; Proverbs
28:11.
The Lord hates pride, evil behavior,
perverse speech, Proverbs 8:13.
Pride brings destruction, Proverbs 16:18.
Proud and arrogant man, Proverbs 21:24.
Satanic origination, Isaiah 14:13-15.
God does not yield His glory to another,
Isaiah 42:8; 48:11.
Pride and arrogance, Jeremiah 48:29.
Nebuchadnezzar's ego offended by faith of
Daniel's friends, Daniel 3:8-20.

Vain ambition, Daniel 5:20-23.
Vanity over wealth and self-righteousness,
Hosea 12:8.
Spiritual pride of disobedient people,
Amos 4:5.
Fate of carefree people, Zephaniah 2:15.
Vanity denounced by Jesus, Matthew 23:6-
12; Mark 12:38-39.
Fruit of the heart, Mark 7:21-23.
Parental pride of Joseph and Mary, Luke
2:33.
Desire to be greatest in Christ's kingdom,
Luke 9:46-48.
Pride concerning wrong things, Luke
10:17-20.
Vain man and humble man at worship,
Luke 18:9-14. (Note self-righteousness,
vv. 11-12.)
Simon, the proud sorcerer, Acts 8:9-10.
Price paid for flagrant vanity, Acts 12:19-
23.
Intellectual pride in Athens, Acts 17:16-34.
No place for boasting in Christian
experience, Romans 3:27.
Boasting of self-righteousness before men
not valid before God, Romans 4:2.
Associate with people of low position,
Romans 12:16.
Many simple people brought to Christ,
1 Corinthians 1:26-31.
Paul's description of those who thought
they had attained spiritual success,
1 Corinthians 4:1-21.
Proud of immorality, 1 Corinthians 5:1-2.
Intellectual pride, 1 Corinthians 8:1-3;
2 Timothy 3:7.
Paul could boast about his converts,
2 Corinthians 10:8.
Falsely evaluating oneself, 2 Corinthians
10:12.
Antidote for vanity, 2 Corinthians 11:30.
(See 12:7-10.)
Danger of conceit, Galatians 5:26.
False estimation of greatness, Galatians
6:3.
Do nothing in vanity, Philippians 2:3.
Boasting about perseverance and faith of
others, 2 Thessalonians 1:4.
Role of conceit in false doctrine, 1 Timothy
6:3-5.
Take pride in humble circumstances,
James 1:9.
God resists proud people, James 4:6.
God gives grace to the humble, 1 Peter 5:5-

6.
Empty, boastful words, 2 Peter 2:18.
Those who demand first place, 3 John 9.
Blind materialism, Revelation 3:17-18.
Evil queen refuses to admit sin, Revelation
18:7-8.
See *Arrogance, Vanity.*

PRIEST
First recorded priesthood, Genesis 14:18.
(See Heb. 5:6-11.)
Father-in-law of Moses, Exodus 18:1.
Predating giving of Law, Exodus 19:22-24.
Neophyte priests, Exodus 24:5.
Lineage, Exodus 27:21; 28:43; 29:9.
Marriage of priests, Leviticus 21:7-15.
Without blemish, Leviticus 21:17-23.
Priests as leaders, Joshua 3:15;
2 Chronicles 11:13.
Priests paid no tax, Ezra 7:24.
Celibacy evaluated by Jesus, Matthew
19:12.
See *Clergy.*

PRIORITY
God as first priority, Genesis 1:1.
Comparing sun and moon with stars,
Genesis 1:16.
Placing God as supreme above idols,
Leviticus 26:1.
Only the best to be given to the Lord,
Numbers 18:29.
Material security versus God's will,
Numbers 32:14-27.
Eli's grief for ark of God greater than for
death of sons, 1 Samuel 4:16-18.
Solomon took less time to build temple
than to build his palace, 1 Kings 6:37-
38; 7:1.
Time best spent, Psalm 84:10.
Importance of first things first, Proverbs
24:27; Haggai 1:3-4; Matthew 6:33;
Luke 9:59-62; 10:38-42.
Time for everything, Ecclesiastes 3:1-8.
Priorities change with progress, Isaiah
28:28.
Missionary and evangelistic priority, Isaiah
52:7.
Imperative to witness, Ezekiel 3:18-19.
Treasures on earth or in heaven, Matthew
6:19-21.
Purchasing pearl of great value, Matthew
13:45-46.
Forsaking all to follow Christ, Matthew

19:28-30.
Last act of Jesus before Crucifixion was to
show compassion, Matthew 20:29-34.
Morality and materialism, Mark 10:17-25.
First last and last first, Mark 10:31.
Two most important commandments,
Mark 12:28-34.
Great Commission, highest priority
following Resurrection, Mark 16:15.
Disciples excited about wrong
phenomena, Luke 10:17-20.
Greed over one's possessions, Luke 12:14-
15.
Greatest of all priorities, Luke 12:29-31.
That which is highly valued, Luke 16:14-15.
Disciples wanted earthly blessing but Jesus
promised spiritual opportunity, Acts
1:6-8.
Priority in obedience, Acts 5:29.
Danger of putting money first, 1 Timothy
6:10.
Priority delivery of God's message,
Hebrews 1:1-2.
Moses regarded disgrace for Christ greater
than treasures of Egypt, Hebrews 11:26.
See *Motivation, Value.*

PRISON
Egyptian, Genesis 40:2-3.
Held in custody for Sabbath-breaking,
Numbers 15:34.
Mighty Samson in prison, Judges 16:21.
King imprisoned and set free, 2 Kings
24:15; 25:27-29.
Kindness to prisoners, Jeremiah 38:7-28;
Acts 16:33; 24:23; 27:1-3.
Life imprisonment, Jeremiah 52:11.
Visiting hours, Matthew 11:2; 25:35-46.
Prison evangelism, Acts 16:22-34.
Paul under house arrest, Acts 28:16.
Timothy released from prison, Hebrews
13:23.
Binding of Satan, Revelation 20:1-3.
See *Jail.*

PRIVACY
Disturbing privacy of others, Proverbs
25:17.
Keep your stewardship private, Matthew
6:2-4.
Prayer in the closet, Matthew 6:5-6.
Fasting in secret, Matthew 6:16-18.
Futile attempt to hold a retreat, Luke 9:10-
11.

Deeds of darkness, Ephesians 5:8-14.
Paul found Athens a suitable place to be left alone, 1 Thessalonians 3:1.
See *Meditation*.

PRIVILEGE
Daniel used his good favor to glorify God, Daniel 1:9-10.
Privilege brings responsibility, Amos 3:2.
Knowing divine secrets, Matthew 13:11.
Privilege of hearing Christ's message, Matthew 13:17.
Only a select few permitted to travel with Jesus, Mark 5:37.
Much required of those given much, Luke 12:48.
Privileged information, 1 Corinthians 2:9-10; Colossians 1:25-27; 1 John 2:20.
Greatest of all privileges, 1 John 3:1-2. (See Eph. 3:12.)
Seated with the Lord on His throne, Revelation 3:21.
Those invited to wedding supper in heaven, Revelation 19:9.
See *Opportunity*.

PROBATE
Probate of a will, Hebrews 9:16-17.

PROBING
Mining deep into the earth, Job 28:1-4.
Glory of kings, Proverbs 25:2.

PROBLEMS
David ran to confront Goliath, 1 Samuel 17:48.
Overcoming obstacles with divine help, 2 Samuel 22:30.
Experiencing suffering and reversal without blaming God, Job 1:22.
Trouble inherent to mortality, Job 5:7.
Troubles more numerous than hairs of head, Psalm 40:11-12.
The Lord does as He pleases, Psalm 135:6.
Test of true friend in times of trouble, Proverbs 17:9.
Secret to true relaxation, Proverbs 19:23.
Certainty of answered prayer, Isaiah 49:8.
Thanking God during adverse circumstances, Jeremiah 33:10-11.
Disciples feared storm while Jesus slept, Matthew 8:23-27.
Worries of life, Mark 4:19.
The God of all comfort, 2 Corinthians 1:3-4.

Clear marks of disciple, 2 Corinthians 6:3-13.
God works out everything according to His will, Ephesians 1:11-12.
Still standing at end of struggle, Ephesians 6:13.
Value of sharing each other's troubles, Philippians 4:14.
Promise of deliverance in Christ, Hebrews 7:23-28.
Maturing value of testing, trials, and problems, James 1:2-4, 12.

PROCEDURE
Prayer for protection, Numbers 10:35.
Proper marking of boundaries, Numbers 34:1-12.
Avoid ways of heathen, Deuteronomy 18:9.
First estimating cost before starting to build, Luke 14:28-30.

PROCESSION
Migration of Joseph's family with all their possessions, Genesis 46:5-7.
Encircling Jericho, Joshua 6:1-20.
Triumphal entry of Jesus, Matthew 21:1-11.

PROCLAMATION
Destiny set for rebellious people, Numbers 14:35.
Nationwide communication, 2 Chronicles 30:1-10; Esther 1:22.
False prophets, Jeremiah 23:16-18; Ezekiel 13:1-3.
Heralding command, Daniel 3:4-7.
Message written with clarity, Habakkuk 2:2.
Angelic proclamation, Luke 2:9-12.
Oath of an angel, Revelation 10:5-7.
Concluding proclamation of faith in God, Revelation 15:3-4.
See *Decree*.

PROCRASTINATION
Prompt offering, Exodus 22:29.
Delayed departure, Judges 19:1-10.
King's business urgent, 1 Samuel 21:8.
Putting family first, 1 Kings 19:20-21.
Royal delay, Esther 5:8.
Do not wait another day, Proverbs 27:1.
Ignoring word of the Lord, Jeremiah 7:13.
Days not prolonged, Ezekiel 12:22-28.

No delay in the Lord's timing, Habakkuk
2:3; Matthew 24:48-51.
Those who said it was not time to rebuild
temple, Haggai 1:3-4.
Attempting to delay God's call, Matthew
8:21; Luke 9:59-62.
Five unprepared virgins, Matthew 25:2-13.
Making excuses, Luke 14:16-21.
Rich man and Lazarus, Luke 16:19-31.
No time like present, Acts 24:25.
Now is the day of salvation, 2 Corinthians
6:2.
No more delay, Revelation 10:6.
See *Delay.*

PROCREATION
God's command to His creation, Genesis
1:22, 27-28.
Dominant husband, John 1:13.
See *Pregnancy.*

PRODUCT
Shortage of materials for manufacturing
product, Exodus 5:6-9.
See *Manufacture.*

PRODUCTIVITY
Land that produces sparingly, Isaiah 5:10.
Time to enlarge, Isaiah 54:2.
Good land and unproductive land,
Hebrews 6:7-8.
See *Agriculture, Horticulture, Prolific.*

PROFANITY
Speaking against the Lord, 2 Chronicles
32:16.
Sin of challenging God, Isaiah 5:18-19.
Laughing at truth spoken by Jesus,
Matthew 9:23-24.
Attributing work of God to demons,
Matthew 9:34.
Satan as instructor, 1 Timothy 1:20.
Slandering the Lord's name, James 2:7.
Swearing by heaven or earth, James 5:12.
See *Blasphemy.*

PROFESSIONAL
Counselors hired to frustrate plans for
building temple, Ezra 4:5.
Women skilled in wailing, Jeremiah 9:17-
20.

PROFILE
Variation of facial appearance, Ezekiel

1:10.

PROFLIGATE
Males easily find wild donkey, Jeremiah
2:24.
Worst of women, Jeremiah 2:33.
Those who do not know how to blush,
Jeremiah 6:15.
Sow the wind, Hosea 8:7.
See *Lust.*

PROGENY
Three forefathers of mankind, Genesis
9:18-19.
Like father, like children, Numbers 32:14.
God's promise to David, 2 Samuel 7:12.
No son to carry on Absalom's name,
2 Samuel 18:18.
Father's greatness and son's greater fame,
1 Kings 1:47-48.
Children and grandchildren in continuing
disobedience, 2 Kings 17:41.
Disgrace of not having children, Jeremiah
22:30.
No descendants in Nineveh, Nahum 1:14.
Son yet in body of ancestor, Hebrews 7:9-
10.
See *Children.*

PROGRESS
Avoiding staying too long in one place,
Deuteronomy 1:6-8.
March on with strong soul, Judges 5:21.
From shepherd boy to king, 1 Chronicles
17:7.
Priorities change with progress, Isaiah
28:28.
Country born in a day, Isaiah 66:8.
The Lord guides and corrects those who
seek Him, Jeremiah 10:23-24.
Growth takes time, Mark 4:28.
Comparing old and new, Luke 5:36-39.
Buying up opportunities, Ephesians 5:15-
16.
Progress in living Christian life, 2 Peter
1:5-9.
See *Accomplishment.*

PROJECT
God saw His Creation as good, Genesis
1:10, 12, 18, 21, 25.
When God terminates project, Genesis
11:1-9.
Praising God as foundations are laid for

temple, Ezra 3:10-13.
Nehemiah's total commitment to
rebuilding wall, Nehemiah 5:14-16.
Building in vain unless the Lord is the
Builder, Psalm 127:1.
David's determination to fulfill destiny,
Psalm 132:1-5.
Patience needed to persuade, Proverbs
25:15.
The Lord plans far in advance, Isaiah 25:1.
By faith Noah built ark, Hebrews 11:7.

PROLIFIC
Thirty sons and 30 daughters, Judges 12:9.

PROMINENCE
Death of great man, 2 Samuel 3:38.
Respect at city gate, Job 29:7-10.
City on hill, Matthew 5:14.
First will be last, last first, Matthew 19:30.
See *Fame, Prestige.*

PROMISCUITY
Discretion in physical relationships,
Leviticus 18:30. (See also chap. 20.)
Defiant sin, Numbers 15:30-31.
Blatant display of immorality, Numbers
25:6-9.
Illicit relationships between those in
spiritual service, 1 Samuel 2:22.
Short story with moral for disobedient
man, 2 Samuel 12:1-4. (See also vv. 5-
13.)
Solomon's many loves, 1 Kings 11:1-13.
Unrequited sexual desire, Ezekiel 16:23-
30.
Lust and promiscuity of two sisters, Ezekiel
23:1-49.
See *Immorality, Lust, Shame.*

PROMISE
God's promise to Noah, Genesis 9:8-16.
God's promise to Abram, Genesis 12:2-3;
13:14-17; 15:2-5. (Note: Some see
"dust of the earth" as Jewish or earthly
family and "the stars" as future church
or heavenly family.)
Bearing children at advanced age, Genesis
16:16; 21:1-5.
God tested Abraham concerning covenant
of promise, Genesis 22:1-18. (See
13:16; 15:5.)
The Lord's guidance in life of David,
2 Samuel 7:1-16.

Fate of favorite daughter, only child,
Judges 11:29-39.
God remembers His covenant forever,
Psalm 111:5; Jeremiah 29:10-11.
Certainty of national restoration, Jeremiah
33:23-26.
God will do what He promises, Romans
4:18-25.
Abraham waited patiently for God's
promise, Hebrews 6:13-14.
Jesus, our guarantee, Hebrews 7:22.

PROMOTION
Let others praise you, Proverbs 27:2.
Daniel and friends given high positions in
Babylon, Daniel 2:48-49.
News of miracles performed by Jesus
spread quickly in spite of low-profile
approach, Luke 5:12-15.
Disciples became apostles, Luke 6:12-15.
See *Citation.*

PROOF
Seeing with one's own eyes, 1 Kings 10:7.
Evidence turns against accuser, Proverbs
25:8.
Do not betray another's confidence,
Proverbs 25:9.
Failure of Nebuchadnezzar's wise men,
Daniel 2:1-11.
Divine revelation does not require external
evidence, Mark 8:11-12.
Testimony of man born blind, John 9:25.
Jesus challenged to prove His divinity,
John 10:22-39.
Seeing is believing, John 20:8.
Seeing marks of the cross as identity, John
20:20-29.
See *Apologetics, Pragmatic.*

PROPAGANDA
Making promises to curry loyalty,
1 Samuel 22:6-8.
Let others praise you, Proverbs 27:2.
Poisoning minds of others, Acts 14:2.

PROPAGATION
Creator's plan and command, Genesis
1:11-28.
After the Flood, Genesis 9:1-7.
See *Reproduction.*

PROPERTY
Wealthy Abram, Genesis 13:2.

Greed over scarcity of land, Genesis 13:5-11.
Dispute over property rights, Genesis 21:22-31.
Mistreatment of slaves, Exodus 21:20-21.
Animals cause damage to neighbor's property, Exodus 22:5.
Delay of ownership, Leviticus 25:29.
Dedicating one's house to the Lord, Leviticus 27:14.
Name on each staff, Numbers 17:1-2.
Priests owned no property, Numbers 18:20.
Distribution of land, Numbers 26:53-56.
Material security versus God's will, Numbers 32:14-27.
Marked boundaries, Numbers 34:1-12.
Property involved in inheritance, Numbers 36:1-9.
Divine warning against greed, Deuteronomy 2:5.
Permanent ownership, Deuteronomy 4:40.
Respecting neighbor's boundary, Deuteronomy 19:14.
Town and country, Deuteronomy 28:3.
Enjoying benefits developed by others, Joshua 24:13.
Ancestral property, Nehemiah 11:20.
Property of angry man, Esther 8:1. (See 5:9–7:10.)
Threshing floor became site for altar, 2 Samuel 24:18-25.
Well-situated city with poor water, 2 Kings 2:19-22.
Repairing the temple, 2 Kings 12:4-5.
All earth belongs to the Lord, Psalm 24:1-2.
Stones and dust of Jerusalem, Psalm 102:14.
Ancient boundary stone, Proverbs 22:28; 23:10-11.
Lazy man's house, Ecclesiastes 10:18.
Jeremiah's purchase of field, Jeremiah 32:6-15.
Barren Israel to become fruitful, Jeremiah 32:42-44.
Boasting and trusting in wealth, Jeremiah 49:4.
Land given to Levites not to be sold, Ezekiel 48:13-14.
Kingdoms of the world, Matthew 4:8-9.
Jesus had no place of residence, Matthew 8:20; Luke 9:58.
Rich man provided tomb for Jesus, Matthew 27:57-61.

Residence by sea, Acts 10:6.
Probate of will, Hebrews 9:16-17.
See *Real estate.*

PROPHECY
Women prophets, Exodus 15:20; Judges 4:4; 2 Kings 22:14; Nehemiah 6:14; Isaiah 8:3; Luke 2:36-38; Acts 21:9; Revelation 2:20.
Qualification as a prophet, 1 Samuel 10:12.
Time when peace will cover earth, Psalm 46:8-10.
Command to pray for peace of Jerusalem, Psalm 122:6.
God fulfills prophet's message, Isaiah 44:26.
God knows end from beginning, Isaiah 46:10-11.
Prophecy of boiling pot, Jeremiah 1:13-15.
Certainty of God's word, Ezekiel 12:26-28.
Prophecy of imagination, Ezekiel 13:1-23.
Prophecy to breath, Ezekiel 37:9.
Meaning of his own prophecy withheld from Daniel, Daniel 12:8-9. (Note v. 13.)
Pharisees asked Jesus for miraculous sign, Matthew 12:38-40.
Pharisees could forecast weather but not discern signs of times, Matthew 16:1-4.
Revelation of Jesus by Isaiah, John 12:37-41.
Predicting severe famine, Acts 11:28-30.
Resurrection as fulfillment of prophecy, Acts 13:32-39.
Message of salvation came through Abraham, Galatians 3:6-9.
Folly of date-setting, 2 Thessalonians 2:1-3.
Scoffers in last days concerning return of Christ, 2 Peter 3:3-4.
Sure word of prophecy, Revelation 22:10.

PROPITIOUS
Seeking at right time, Isaiah 55:6.
New every morning, Lamentations 3:22-24.

PROPRIETY
Act of shame, Jeremiah 13:26.
Always right time to do good, Mark 3:1-6.
See *Tact.*

PROSELYTE
Alien celebrating Passover, Exodus 12:48.

Illustration of stolen harvest, Deuteronomy 28:33.
Converts to Judaism, Acts 6:5; 13:43; 17:4.

PROSPERITY
Joseph prospered in Egypt, Genesis 39:2.
Fortunes restored, Deuteronomy 30:1-3.
Wicked often prosper, Job 21:7.
Reward of obeying God, Job 36:11.
Wealth of Job's remaining years, Job 42:12.
Stealing from poor and giving to rich, Proverbs 22:16.
Abundance of silver and chariots, Isaiah 2:7.
Promise of land "flowing with milk and honey," Jeremiah 11:5.
Prosperous wicked, Jeremiah 12:1-3.
National prosperity, Ezekiel 16:13-14.
King's prosperity linked to conduct, Daniel 4:27.
Stewardship based on personal income, 1 Corinthians 16:2.
Health and wealth plus spiritual vitality, 3 John 2-4.
See *Affluence.*

PROSTITUTE
Judah deceived by daughter-in-law, Genesis 38:13-19.
Shameless, Proverbs 2:16.
Way of harlot, Proverbs 5:1-10; 7:6-27; 9:14-17; Isaiah 23:15-16.
Merchandising feminine beauty, Ezekiel 16:15.
Wickedness of Nineveh likened to prostitution, Nahum 3:3-4.
See *Debauchery, Degradation, Wiles.*

PROTECTION
God's blessing and protection for Ishmael, Genesis 21:9-21.
Prayer for protection, Numbers 10:35.
No curse on those who have been blessed, Numbers 22:12.
City walls to sky, Deuteronomy 9:1.
Threat of iron chariots, Judges 1:19.
Strong tower in besieged city, Judges 9:51.
Safety in fields of Boaz, Ruth 2:4-22.
Companions in danger, 1 Samuel 22:23.
David not sure God would protect him, 1 Samuel 27:1-2.
Killing in self-defense, 2 Samuel 2:22-23.
Building city around fortress, 1 Chronicles 11:7-9.
God our refuge and strength, Psalm 46:1-3.
Protection against evil strategy, Isaiah 8:10.
Angel of the Lord destroys enemy soldiers, Isaiah 37:36.
Those called by His name need fear no danger, Isaiah 43:1-2.
Message of boldness, conduct of coward, Jeremiah 26:13-15, 20-24.
Safest place to be in times of trouble and persecution, Jeremiah 42:1-22.
Wise dove, Jeremiah 48:28.
Safety in midst of peril, Ezekiel 34:25.
Protection of Daniel's friends in fiery furnace, Daniel 3:22-27.
Daniel in lions' den, Daniel 6:13-24.
Gates wide open to enemy, Nahum 3:13.
Jerusalem, city without walls, Zechariah 2:3-5.
Escape to Egypt, Matthew 2:13-15.
Value of sparrow and value of soul, Matthew 10:28-30.
Jesus could not die before His time had come, Luke 4:28-30; John 7:30.
Ounce of prevention, Luke 12:39.
Trusting the Lord and trusting in weapons, Luke 22:35-38.
Protection from evil one, John 17:15; 1 John 5:18-19.
Protection of night, Acts 17:10.
Paul assured divine protection, Acts 18:9-11.
Shield of faith, Ephesians 6:16.
Ministering spirits to those who believe, Hebrews 1:14.
Shielded by God's power, 1 Peter 1:5.
Hiding in caves and crying out to mountains, Revelation 6:15-17.
See *Refuge, Safety.*

PROTEST
Stripped and barefoot as sign against those who oppose the Lord, Isaiah 20:2-4.
Entire city in uproar, Acts 19:23-41.
See *Rebellion.*

PROTOCOL
Nocturnal conduct of Boaz and Ruth, Ruth 3:7-15.
Lack of respect, Esther 5:9-10.
Importance of Passover to enemies of Jesus, Mark 14:1-2.
Paul operated through proper channels, Philemon 12-14.

See *Discretion.*

PROTOTYPE
Example of the prophets being persecuted, Matthew 5:11-12.
The perfect prayer, Matthew 6:9-13.
Deserving right to be heard, 2 Corinthians 4:1-2.
Supreme model of unselfishness, 2 Corinthians 8:7-9.
See *Example, Original.*

PROVERBS
Origin of a saying, 1 Samuel 10:11-12.
Deeds reveal person, 1 Samuel 24:13.
Three thousand proverbs, 1 Kings 4:32.
Purpose of proverbs, Proverbs 1:1-6.
Research into proverbs, Ecclesiastes 12:9.
Example outside Book of Proverbs, Ezekiel 16:44.
Censored proverb, Ezekiel 18:2-4.

PROVISION
Role of Holy Spirit in darkness of Creation, Genesis 1:2.
God speaks and events occur, Genesis 1:9, 11, 15.
God's provision for loyal Abraham, Genesis 22:1-14.
Carts provided for Joseph's brothers, Genesis 45:16-20.
Springs and palm trees, Exodus 15:27.
To each what is needed and nothing more, Exodus 16:16-18.
God's presence, ultimate provision, Exodus 33:15.
No help from king, 2 Kings 6:26-27.
Bread from heaven, Nehemiah 9:15.
Strength comes from God, Psalm 18:32.
In old age, true believer looks back on God's faithfulness, Psalm 37:25.
Wealth of earth belongs to God, Psalm 50:9-15.
God's love and God's strength, Psalm 62:11-12.
God provides rain for crops and pastures, Psalm 65:9-13.
God's blessing on those who praise Him, Psalm 67:5-6.
Help comes from the Lord's hand, Psalm 109:26-27.
Eternal faithfulness, Psalms 117:2; 118:29.
Barns filled and flocks abundant, Psalm 144:13.

Food for righteous, Proverbs 10:3.
Happiness from honesty and God's provision, Proverbs 30:7-9.
The Lord our strength each morning, Isaiah 33:2; Zephaniah 3:5.
Certain supply of need and guidance, Isaiah 49:10.
Dying earth, Isaiah 51:6.
God's righteousness lasts forever, Isaiah 51:8.
The Lord will guide always, Isaiah 58:11.
Fate of good and evil, Isaiah 65:13-14.
Israel turned away from living water, Jeremiah 2:13-18.
Nothing too hard for the Lord, Jeremiah 32:17, 27.
Protection of Daniel's friends in fiery furnace, Daniel 3:22-27.
Daniel in lions' den, Daniel 6:13-24.
Grapes in desert, Hosea 9:10.
Jonah and great fish, Jonah 1:17.
Not by might nor by power, Zechariah 4:6.
God who provides for all nature takes care of His children, Matthew 6:25-34; Luke 12:22-31.
Provision of income for 12 Apostles, Matthew 10:9-10.
Feeding 5,000, Matthew 14:13-21; Mark 6:35-44; Luke 9:12-17; John 6:5-13.
Coin in mouth of fish, Matthew 17:24-27.
Jesus teaches lesson on God's goodness in answer to prayer, Luke 11:5-13.
Given words to speak, Luke 21:15.
Special food Jesus had to sustain Him, John 4:31-34.
Promised answer to prayer, John 14:13-14.
Christ met our greatest need, Romans 5:6-8.
Right of an apostle to receive material support, 1 Corinthians 9:7-14; 1 Timothy 5:17-18.
We are promised same power which brought Jesus back from grave, Ephesians 1:18-21.
Profound truth presented briefly, Ephesians 3:1-3.
Holy Spirit's power working within us, Ephesians 3:20-21.
Concern for pastor, Philippians 4:10-19.
Spiritual need totally fulfilled in Christ, Colossians 1:15-23.
Powerful energy for labor, Colossians 1:29.
We bring nothing into the world, take

nothing out, 1 Timothy 6:6-8.
Confidence in the One whom we believe, 2 Timothy 1:12.
When friends deserted him, the Lord met Paul's need, 2 Timothy 4:16-18.
Equipped by the God of peace, Hebrews 13:20-21.
Every good gift from above, James 1:16-17.
Cast all cares on the Lord, 1 Peter 5:7.
Everything we need for spiritual and material welfare, 2 Peter 1:3.
Divine purpose in giving Scriptures, 2 Peter 1:15.
God's best in abundance, Jude 2.
Never again hunger or thirst, Revelation 7:16.
See *Abundance, Need, Supply.*

PROVOCATION
Trouble caused by carelessness, Exodus 21:35-36.
Prayer for protection, Numbers 10:35.
Foolish sins, Numbers 12:11.
Successfully facing formidable opponent, Numbers 21:21-26.
Zophar upset by criticism, Job 20:2-3.
Giving heed to instruction, Proverbs 16:20.
Daring to scoff at the name of the Lord, Isaiah 36:18-21. (See 37:6.)
At odds with one's Maker, Isaiah 45:9.
Ignoring the word of the Lord, Jeremiah 7:13.
Daughters taught how to wail, Jeremiah 9:20.
Mixing human blood with sacrifices, Luke 13:1.
Attitude of prodigal son's brother, Luke 15:25-32.
See *Aggressive, Dispute, Trouble.*

PRUDENCE
Joseph in Potiphar's house, Genesis 39:4-10.
Disciplined conduct, Psalms 39:1; 112:1.
Circumspect, Proverbs 14:8-18; Luke 14:28-32.
Open to counsel, Proverbs 24:6.
Wisdom of Gamaliel, Acts 5:34-40.

PSALMS
Preview of David's songs, 2 Samuel 22:1-51.
Singer of psalms, 2 Samuel 23:1.
David quoted, Luke 20:42-43; Acts 13:33,

35.
Communicating with Psalms, Ephesians 5:19; Colossians 3:16.
Book of happiness, James 5:13.

PSYCHIATRY
Renewed by Scripture, Psalm 119:93.
Renewing of mind, Romans 12:1-2.

PSYCHOLOGY
Public relations approach, 1 Kings 1:42.
Appealing to king's ego in protesting, Ezra 4:14.
Mob psychology at trial of Jesus, Matthew 27:15-26; Mark 15:11-15. (See Matt. 21:1-11; Mark 11:8-10.)
Crowd psychology, John 6:1-2.
See *Mob psychology.*

PUBERTY
Ezekiel's description of puberty, Ezekiel 16:5-9.
See *Adolescence.*

PUBLICANS
Reputation of tax collectors, Matthew 5:46; 9:11; 11:19; 18:15-17.
Calling of Matthew, Matthew 9:9-13; Mark 2:14; Luke 5:27.
Ideal conversion examples, Matthew 21:32.
Change of values, Luke 3:12-14.
Two kinds of sinners, Luke 18:9-14.
Jesus and Zaccheus, Luke 19:1-10.

PUBLICATION
Endless supply of books, Ecclesiastes 12:12.

PUBLICITY
Let others praise you, Proverbs 27:2.
Word-of-mouth publicity concerning Jesus, Matthew 4:24; 9:26; Luke 5:12-15.
Jesus pressured to gain prominence among men, John 7:1-5.
See *Media.*

PUBLIC OPINION
Life spared, 1 Samuel 14:45.
Lost kingdom, 1 Samuel 15:23.
Majority procedure, Matthew 7:13-14.
Danger of public reaction, Matthew 14:5.
Jesus before Pilate, Matthew 27:19-26;

Mark 15:1-15.
Minority fears, John 7:13.
Innocent man made political ploy, Acts 12:3.
See *Consensus, Plebiscite.*

PUBLIC RELATIONS
Public relations approach, 1 Kings 1:42.
Affairs of people, Nehemiah 11:24.

PULPIT
Ezra standing above people, Nehemiah 8:5.

PUNISHMENT
Death penalty, Genesis 9:5-6; Numbers 35:16-21.
Whipping with thorns and briers, Judges 8:16.
Murder of Amnon for disgracing Absalom's sister, 2 Samuel 13:23-29.
Better to fall into God's hands than into hands of men, 2 Samuel 24:13-14.
God has right to judge, Psalm 51:4.
Divine forgiveness and punishment, Psalm 99:8.
God's arm coming down in punishment, Isaiah 30:30.
Sins paid back, Isaiah 65:6.
God uses despots, then brings them into judgment, Jeremiah 25:11-14.
Sword that cannot rest, Jeremiah 47:6-7.
Cost for doubting an angel, Luke 1:18-20.
Ananias and Sapphira, Acts 5:1-11.
Guards who failed to hold Peter in prison, Acts 12:18-19.
See *Discipline.*

PURCHASE
Practice of barter, Ezekiel 27:12-23.
Deposit made on our final redemption, Ephesians 1:14.
See *Barter.*

PURGE
Jehu and reformation in Israel, 2 Kings 9–10.

PURITY
Circumcision at advanced age, Genesis 17:10-27.
Abimelech guided by the Lord in conduct toward Sarah, Genesis 20:1-18.
Clear oil used in tabernacle, Exodus 27:20.
Pure cannot come from impure, Job 14:4.
Personal righteousness a means to God's blessing, Psalm 18:20-21.
Whiter than snow, Psalm 51:7.
Purity of heart, a gift from God, Psalm 51:10.
Adolescence depicted, Ezekiel 16:5-13.
Women violated, Ezekiel 22:10.
The Lord has first right to the body, 1 Corinthians 6:13-16.
Purity through Holy Spirit, Galatians 5:16.
Mark of true Christian, Ephesians 5:1-3.
Purified by blessed hope, Titus 2:11-14.
Call to holiness, 1 Peter 1:13-16.
Purified by obeying truth, 1 Peter 1:22.
Garments worn by angels in heaven, Revelation 15:6.
Garments of bride in heaven, Revelation 19:7-8.
See *Chastity, Virtue.*

PURPOSE
Hiding of true intentions, 1 Samuel 16:1-5.
Nehemiah's total commitment to rebuilding wall, Nehemiah 5:14-16.
Eloquent description of noble person, Isaiah 32:8.
Divine purpose in creating, Isaiah 45:18.
God never acts without cause, Ezekiel 14:23.
Salt and light in world, Matthew 5:13-16.
Filled with knowledge of God's will, Colossians 1:9-12.
Ultimate in being properly motivated, 1 Thessalonians 1:3.

PURSE
Sharing common purse, Proverbs 1:14.
Expense money for long journey, Proverbs 7:19-20.
Bags of gold, Isaiah 46:6.
Journey by faith, Matthew 10:9-10; Luke 10:4; 22:35.
Keeper of money bag, John 12:6.
See *Money.*

PUTRID
Divine preservation of food, Exodus 16:19-

24.
Ultimate end of man, Job 13:28.
Flies and perfume, Ecclesiastes 10:1.
Worms in dead bodies, Isaiah 66:24.
Drunkenness and vomit, Jeremiah 48:26.
Place for vultures, Luke 17:37.

See *Decay*.

PYRAMID
Monument in Egypt, Isaiah 19:19-20.
   (Note: Some think this verse refers to
   the Great Pyramid.)

Q

QUALIFICATION
Witnessing to that which has been personally experienced, Psalm 51:10-13.
Qualification for answered prayer, Psalm 91:14-16.
Worthy things to say, Proverbs 8:6.
What God requires, He provides, Isaiah 2:3.
Qualifications for following Jesus, Luke 9:23-26.
Certification of Christ as Saviour and King, Colossians 1:15-20.
Prepared by God to succeed as believer, Hebrews 13:20-21.
Only the One who redeemed us is qualified to be our Judge, Revelation 5:1-9.
See *Ability*.

QUALITY
Clear oil used in tabernacle, Exodus 27:20.
Gleaning of one vineyard better than harvest of another, Judges 8:2.
Display of good talent, Psalm 45:1.
New every day, Lamentations 3:22-24.
Salt loses saltiness, Luke 14:34-35.
See *Value*.

QUALMS
Needlessness of worry, Matthew 6:25-27.
Paul could be timid and bold, 2 Corinthians 10:1.
See *Apprehension, Worry*.

QUANTITY
Putting confidence in numerical strength, Judges 7:2. (See v. 12.)
Thirty sons and 30 daughters, Judges 12:9.
Sins piled up to heaven, Revelation 18:4-5.

QUARANTINE
Preventing infection from spreading in community, Leviticus 13:45-46.
King afflicted with leprosy, 2 Kings 15:5.
King who desecrated temple, 2 Chronicles 26:16-21.
See *Disease, Health*.

QUARREL
Futility of strife among brothers, 2 Samuel 2:27-28.
Evidence that turns against accuser, Proverbs 25:8.
Settle misunderstandings quickly, Matthew 5:25.
How to solve disagreement between brothers, Matthew 18:15-17.
Whether to contest enemy or seek peace terms, Luke 14:31-32.
Forgiveness for enemy, Romans 5:10.
Those teachings which cause controversy, 1 Timothy 1:3-4.
See *Strife*.

QUESTIONS
Questions for spies sent to Canaan, Numbers 13:18-20.
When God Himself asks questions, Numbers 14:11.
Questions for subversion, Judges 16:6-18.
Mother-in-law's inquiry, Ruth 3:16-17.
Questioning actions of the Lord, 2 Kings 6:33.
Most ignorant of men, Proverbs 30:2-4.
Wise put to shame, Jeremiah 8:9.
Jeremiah questioned God's way, Jeremiah 12:1.
Inquiring about divine love, Malachi 1:2.
Zechariah and Mary could not understand the angelic announcements, Luke 1:18, 34.

Paul accused of being terrorist, Acts 21:38.

QUIET
Solomon's arrangement for absence of
noise during building of temple,
1 Kings 6:7.
Importance of quietness in rest, Mark 6:31.

QUIET TIME
Predawn prayer in time of trouble, Psalm
119:147.

Strength every morning, Isaiah 33:2.
Go out to plain, Ezekiel 3:22-23.
Prayer in closet, Matthew 6:5-6.
Jesus retired to hills, Matthew 14:23; 15:29.
Example of Jesus in early morning, Mark
1:35; Luke 4:42.
Finding a quiet place, Mark 6:31; 7:24.
Jesus often went to lonely places for
prayer, Luke 5:16.
Spending night in prayer, Luke 6:12.
Alone for prayer, Luke 22:41.

R

RACE
Hagar's choice of wife for Ishmael, Genesis 21:21.
Abraham's concern for a wife for Isaac, Genesis 24:1-4.
Beauty of dark skin, Song of Songs 1:5-6.

RACISM
First example of tension between Arabs and Israel, Genesis 21:8-10. (Note near destruction of Arab race.)
Request to marry heathen, 1 Kings 2:13-25.
Pledge to avoid intermarriage, Nehemiah 10:30.
Revenge against those who did not assist Israelites, Nehemiah 13:1-3.
Wealth and prestige could not numb Haman's resentment, Esther 5:10-14.
Dark and lovely, Song of Songs 1:6.
Uproar of foreigners, Isaiah 25:5.
Skin color by Creator's choice, Jeremiah 13:23.
Jesus overlooked racist tradition, Matthew 15:21-28.
Treatment given to Gentiles, Matthew 20:25.
Black man helped Jesus carry cross, Mark 15:21. (Note: Cyrene was a city in North Africa.)
Prophet from Galilee, John 7:41-52.
Deeper meaning of deliverance from legalism, Acts 10:24-28.
No racial prejudice with the Lord, Acts 10:34-35; 15:5-8.
All are one in Christ, Galatians 3:28.
Wrong of discrimination, James 2:1-4.
See *Prejudice*.

RAIN
First rainfall, Genesis 7:11-12. (See 2:4-6.)
Plague of hail and rain, Exodus 9:22-34.
Rainless sky and parched earth, Leviticus 26:19-20.
Rain denied, Deuteronomy 11:17; 28:24.
Abundant blessings of nature, Deuteronomy 33:13-16.
Thunder and rain, 1 Samuel 12:18.
Heavy rain, 1 Kings 18:41.
Activity hindered, Ezra 10:9.
Rainy season, Ezra 10:13.
Gift of north wind, Proverbs 25:23.
Storage for rain, Ecclesiastes 1:7.
Accurate meteorological information, Ecclesiastes 11:3.
Rain like Scripture, Isaiah 55:10.
Autumn and spring rains, Joel 2:23; Acts 14:17.
Formation of clouds and rainfall, Amos 9:6.
Dew from heavens, Zechariah 8:12.
Rain no respecter of persons, Matthew 5:45.
Patient farmer awaiting rain, James 5:7.
See *Meteorologist, Weather*.

RALLY
Vast assembly, 1 Kings 8:65.

RANK
Least and greatest, Jeremiah 42:1-3.
Asking for prestige rather than earning it, Mark 10:35-40.
Those who demand first place, 3 John 9.
See *Position, Prestige*.

RAPE
Girl who did not call for help, Deuteronomy 22:25-27.
Amnon and Tamar, 2 Samuel 13:1-14.
Accusation of king against Haman, Esther 7:8.
Mistreated captives, Isaiah 13:16;

Zechariah 14:2.
Women and virgins ravished,
Lamentations 5:11.

RAPPORT
Friend or enemy, Joshua 5:13.
Samson and Philistine woman, Judges
14:7.
Rapport between old man and boy,
1 Samuel 3:1-18.
Two people becoming one in spirit,
1 Samuel 18:1-4.
Absalom won hearts of people, 2 Samuel
15:1-6.
David's rapport with men of Judah,
2 Samuel 19:14.
King's rapport with his people,
2 Chronicles 1:1.
Rapport between father and son, Proverbs
4:3-4.
No rapport between righteous and wicked,
Proverbs 29:27.
Friends and brothers cannot be trusted,
Jeremiah 9:4-5.
Divinely given rapport, Daniel 1:9.
Jesus criticized for fellowship with sinners,
Matthew 9:10-12.
Rapport among Christians, avenue of
witness, John 13:34-35.
Friends instead of servants, John 15:14-15.
Early Christian community, Acts 2:46-47.
Paul asked to speak in synagogue, Acts
13:13-15.
Mutual interest between those of same
occupation, Acts 18:1-3.
Grief of friends at time of separation, Acts
20:36-38.
Effect of speaking in people's language,
Acts 22:2.
Paul's reputation as former Pharisee, Acts
23:6.
Greeted by friends in faraway place, Acts
28:15.
Paul asked for prayer that his service
would be acceptable, Romans 15:31-32.
Need for unity among believers,
1 Corinthians 1:10-17.
Differing reactions to truly Christian
personality, 2 Corinthians 2:15-16.
Hearts opening to each other,
2 Corinthians 6:11-13.
Making room in heart for acceptance of
others, 2 Corinthians 7:2.
Rapport between ministers of Gospel,

2 Corinthians 8:16-18.
Paul's visit with Peter in Jerusalem,
Galatians 1:18.
Paul and Barnabas given right hand of
fellowship, Galatians 2:9-10.
Paul's concern for spiritual development
of followers, Colossians 2:1-5.
Actions toward others, Colossians 4:5.
Paul's wise use of names of followers,
Colossians 4:7-17.
Gentle like mother, 1 Thessalonians
2:7.
Overflowing love among believers,
1 Thessalonians 3:12.
Enriching fellowship, 2 Thessalonians 1:3-
4.
No place for arguments and quarrels,
2 Timothy 2:23-24.
How Jesus identified with mankind,
Hebrews 2:17-18.
Gentleness as mark of good leadership,
Hebrews 5:1-2.
Loving as brothers, Hebrews 13:1.
Known as God's friend, James 2:21-23.
Confessing sins one to another, James
5:16.
Loving deeply from heart, 1 Peter 1:22.
Love that overlooks faults, 1 Peter 4:8.
Fellowship in difficult times, Revelation
1:9.
See *Unanimity.*

RAPTURE
Time of Christ's return kept secret, Mark
13:32.
Watching for the Lord to come, Luke
12:35-40.
Promise of Christ's return, John 14:3.
Mistaken information as to return of Christ,
John 21:20-23.
Resurrection at coming of Christ,
1 Corinthians 15:51-55.
Waiting for Christ's return,
1 Thessalonians 1:10.
Those prepared for return,
1 Thessalonians 3:13.
Folly of date setting, 2 Thessalonians
2:1-3.
Purified by blessed hope, Titus 2:11-14.
Returning as Lord and King, Hebrews 9:24-
28.
Living hope, 1 Peter 1:3-5.
Scoffers in last days, 2 Peter 3:3-4.
See *Second Coming.*

RATIONAL
Prodigal came to his senses, Luke 15:17.
Wisdom of Gamaliel, Acts 5:34-39.
Keep your head in all situations, 2 Timothy 4:5.

RATIONALIZE
Questioning misfortune, Judges 6:13.
Misunderstanding gesture of goodwill, 2 Samuel 10:1-4.
Putting blame on God, 2 Kings 6:33.
Disputing mercy and justice of God's ways, Ezekiel 33:10-20.
See *Pragmatic.*

RAW MATERIAL
Wealth in the earth, Genesis 2:11-12.
Wood for making gods and cooking fires, Isaiah 44:14-20.
Wood fit for a king, Ezekiel 19:11.
Cheating on weight and cost, Amos 8:5-6.
See *Natural resources.*

REACTION
Negative attitude of Cain, Genesis 4:3-7.
Reactions of Mary compared to that of shepherds, Luke 2:19-20.
Differing reactions to truly Christian personality, 2 Corinthians 2:15-16.

READING
Message to read, Deuteronomy 6:9.
Literacy program, Deuteronomy 11:19-21.
Many books cause weariness, Ecclesiastes 12:12.
Scroll eaten by Ezekiel and sweet as honey, Ezekiel 3:1-3.
Posted sign, John 19:19-20.
Purposeful reading, John 20:30-31.
See *Literacy.*

REAL ESTATE
Purchase of plot to pitch tent, Genesis 33:19.
Government purchasing agent, Genesis 47:20.
Delay of ownership, Leviticus 25:29.
Israel's permanent deed, Deuteronomy 4:40.
Widow's land for sale, Ruth 4:3.
Purchase of land for altar, 2 Samuel 24:24.
Exchanging one property for another, 1 Kings 21:1-16.
Woman involved in land purchase,
Proverbs 31:16.
Greed for property, Isaiah 5:8.
Jeremiah's purchase of field, Jeremiah 32:6-15.
Seller unable to recover land, Ezekiel 7:13.
Leased land, Matthew 21:33-41; Mark 12:1-9.
Residence by the sea, Acts 10:6.
Living in rented house, Acts 28:30.
See *Property.*

REALISM
Negative and positive viewpoints, Numbers 13:17-33.
The Lord's demands within reach, Deuteronomy 30:11.

REALITY
Scripture contains both blessings and curses, Joshua 8:34.
Witnessing to that which has been personally experienced, Psalm 51:10-13.
Awakening to find dream untrue, Isaiah 29:8.
Disciples had no need for fasting when Jesus was with them, Mark 2:18-20.
Experiencing God's kingdom within, Luke 17:20-21.
Promise of life in Christ Jesus, 2 Timothy 1:1.
Faith without works, James 2:14-18.
Reality of unseen, 1 Peter 1:8-9.
Experiencing reality of Christ, 1 John 1:1-4.

REAP
Joy at harvesttime, 1 Samuel 6:13.
Reap what is sown, Job 4:8; Galatians 6:7.
Sow in tears, reap with joy, Psalm 126:5.
Lazy at harvesttime, Proverbs 10:5.
Plant wickedness, reap evil, Hosea 10:13-14.
Reap what is sown, Obadiah 15.
Size of harvest, 2 Corinthians 9:6.
See *Harvest.*

REASON
Folly of listening to Satan's reasoning, Genesis 3:1-5.
People who refuse to listen to reason, 1 Samuel 8:4-21.
Questioning why wicked prosper, Jeremiah 12:1-3.

Disputing mercy and justice of God's ways, Ezekiel 33:10-20.
Wisdom of Gamaliel, Acts 5:34-39.
Use of reasoning in teaching, Acts 17:1-3.

REBELLION
No success outside God's will, Numbers 14:41-45.
Those who refuse to hear God's message, Judges 6:10.
Rebellion of prosperous wicked against God, Job 21:7-16.
Police intervention, Proverbs 17:11.
Trying patience of God, Isaiah 7:13.
Vow to Babylonian Queen of Heaven, Jeremiah 44:24-30.
Those far from the Lord, Ezekiel 11:15.
Hearts hard as flint, Zechariah 7:11-12.
Stephen resorted to history for his defense, Acts 7:1-60.
Enmity in mind against God, Colossians 1:21.
Avoid association with those who do wrong, 2 Thessalonians 3:14-15.
Agony of those who refuse to repent, Revelation 16:10-11.
See *Discontent, Disobedience.*

REBUKE
David's willingness to accept rebuke, 2 Samuel 16:5-12.
Youth points out mistake of age, Job 32:6-12.
Willingness to take correction, Proverbs 25:12.
Value of open rebuke, Proverbs 27:5.
Wounds of friend, Proverbs 27:6.
Jesus rebuked demon, Luke 4:33-36.
Unable to accept rebuke, Acts 7:51-58.
Paul rebuked and struck by high priest, Acts 23:1-5.
Unregretted sorrow for causing hurt, 2 Corinthians 7:8-9.
Paul recognized his weakness, 2 Corinthians 13:9.
Christian method of rebuke, 2 Thessalonians 3:14-15.
Those who sin are to be rebuked publicly, 1 Timothy 5:20.
See *Reprimand, Scolding.*

RECEPTIVE
Defying message of prophet, Jeremiah 43:1-3.

Communicating to those who ought to be eager to listen, Ezekiel 3:4-9.
Bereans listened with eagerness, Acts 17:11-12.

RECIPROCATION
Blessing to those who bless, injury to those who injure, Genesis 12:3.
Exchange of gifts between Solomon and queen of Sheba, 2 Chronicles 9:12.
When not to do as others have done, Proverbs 24:29.
God returns to those who return to Him, Zechariah 1:3.
Divine reciprocation, Matthew 25:34-45.
Doing good without expecting returned favors, Luke 6:27-36.
Returning an invitation, Luke 14:12-14.
Boomerang effect of immorality, 1 Corinthians 6:18-20.
Abraham was blessed and became a blessing, Galatians 3:9.

RECITATION
Reciting proverbs to musical accompaniment, Psalm 49:4.
See *Eloquence.*

RECKLESS
Driving like madman, 2 Kings 9:20.
Careless about danger, Proverbs 22:3.

RECOGNITION
Honor not fitting for fool, Proverbs 26:1.
Paul's wise use of names of followers, Colossians 4:7-17.
David and Samuel given small mention in Hebrews, Hebrews 11:32.
Song of Moses sung in heaven, Revelation 15:2-4.

RECOLLECT
Former things not brought to mind, Isaiah 65:17.
Remembering glory of better days, Haggai 2:3.
See *Memory.*

RECOMMENDATION
God's commendation of Job, Job 1:8.
Jesus' evaluation of John the Baptist, Matthew 11:11-14.
Jesus had no need for human credentials, John 5:31-40.

Barnabas, true friend to Saul, Acts 9:26-27.
Letters of introduction, 1 Corinthians 16:3.
Those of whom one can speak well, 3 John
12.

RECOMPENSE
Salary arrangement for priest,
Deuteronomy 18:1-2.
Rewards of obedience, Deuteronomy 28:1-
14.
God accepts no price or reward, Isaiah
45:13.
Reward for pride, Zephaniah 2:9-10.
Content with one's income, Luke 3:14.
Doing good without expecting reward,
Luke 6:27-36.
See *Honorarium, Payment, Salary.*

RECONCILIATION
Jacob and Esau, Genesis 33:1-20.
David and Abner, 2 Samuel 3:6-21.
Unfaithful woman's return to husband,
Hosea 2:7.
Reconciled to God, Romans 5:10;
2 Corinthians 5:18-21.
Unity with Redeemer, Ephesians 2:14-18.

RECONNAISSANCE
The Lord lets His children discover for
themselves, Numbers 13:1-2.
Journey one should never make again,
Deuteronomy 28:68.
Spy report, Joshua 2:1-24.
Danite spies, Judges 18:2-10.
Satan's continual survey of earth, Job 1:7.
Babylon surveyed Hezekiah's treasures for
subsequent thievery, Isaiah 39:1-6.

RECREATION
Mighty hunter, Genesis 10:9.
Enjoying bow and arrow, Genesis 21:20.
Early morning revelry, Exodus 32:6.
Eating with rejoicing, Deuteronomy 27:7.
Telling riddles, Judges 14:12-18.
Sadistic entertainment, Judges 16:25.
Gross recreation of indecency, Judges
19:22-26.
Boxing and wrestling, 2 Samuel 2:14.
Camping out on rooftop, Nehemiah 8:13-
17.
Dancing children, Job 21:11.
Meaningless pleasures, Ecclesiastes 2:1-
11.
Renewal of strength, Isaiah 40:30-31.

Instrumental jam session, Amos 6:5.
Children play in streets, Zechariah 8:5.
Childish adults, Matthew 11:16-17.
Relaxed eating, Mark 14:3.
See *Athletics.*

RECRUITMENT
Taking care of business, Deuteronomy
20:5-9.
Choosing mighty and brave for service,
1 Samuel 14:52.
Leadership for those in trouble, 1 Samuel
22:2.
Inheritance of spirit, 2 Kings 2:9-10.
Recruited to turn against their own king,
2 Kings 9:14-24.
Finest young men chosen for service,
Daniel 1:3-4.
Those who united to follow Jesus, Luke
8:1-3.

RECUPERATION
Restored to health, Isaiah 38:16.

REDEEMER
Job's cry for someone to mediate between
him and God, Job 9:33-35.
Strength of a great Redeemer, Jeremiah
50:34.
Ezekiel bearing sin of people, Ezekiel 4:4-
6.
Statement of Jesus to John on Patmos,
Revelation 1:17-18.
Worthy to open scroll of judgment,
Revelation 5:1-10.

REDEMPTION
Job's search for salvation, Job 9:2.
Job saw his advocate at God's throne, Job
16:19-21.
Depth of God's mercy and forgiveness,
Psalm 51:1-2.
Total removal of sins from God's memory,
Psalm 103:11-12.
God's forgiveness and the multitude of our
sins, Psalm 130:3-4.
Unique parable of redemption,
Ecclesiastes 9:14-15.
Come let us reason, Isaiah 1:18.
Guilt atoned by fire, Isaiah 6:6-7.
Joy of salvation, Isaiah 12:2; 35:1-2.
Sins paid for, Isaiah 40:1-2.
Creator cares for His creation, Isaiah 42:5-
7.

Declaring the one and only Saviour, Isaiah 43:10-13.
Sold and then redeemed, Isaiah 52:3.
All ends of earth will see, Isaiah 52:10.
Prophetic description of Jesus, Isaiah 53:1-12.
Prophecy of coming of Christ and proclamation of Gospel, Isaiah 61:1-3.
The God who saves and heals, Jeremiah 17:14.
Strength of a great Redeemer, Jeremiah 50:34.
Ezekiel bearing sin of people, Ezekiel 4:4-6.
Mark of repentance, Ezekiel 9:3-6.
Beyond redemption, Hosea 7:13.
Seeking atonement for sin, Micah 6:7.
Healing sun of Righteousness, Malachi 4:2.
Parable of landowner and son, Matthew 21:33-44.
Rejected by His Father in heaven, Matthew 27:46.
Disciples could not understand, Mark 9:30-32.
Jesus foretold death and resurrection, Mark 10:32-34.
Son of vineyard owner killed by tenants, Mark 12:1-12.
Weight of sin, not pain of the cross, took life of Jesus, Mark 15:33-37, 44.
Jesus could not die before His time had come, Luke 4:28-30.
Misunderstanding role of Jesus in ministry, Luke 12:13-14.
Redeemer and judge, John 5:22-23.
Jesus willingly lay down His life, John 10:17-18.
All-encompassing goodness of God, Romans 4:16.
God's perfect timing in Christ, Romans 5:6.
Work of Christ in setting us free from power of sin, Romans 8:1-4.
He who was rich became poor, 2 Corinthians 8:9.
Christ became a curse on the cross, Galatians 3:13-14.
From Law to grace, Galatians 4:1-7.
Result of promise, Galatians 4:21-31.
God's love for unlovely, Ephesians 2:1-5.
Rescued from dominion of darkness, Colossians 1:13-14.
Sins of ignorance, 1 Timothy 1:12-14.
God's grace to worst of sinners, 1 Timothy 1:15-16.

God wants all to be saved, 1 Timothy 2:3-4.
Divine plan from beginning of time, 2 Timothy 1:8-10.
Salvation not possible through the Law, Hebrews 7:11.
First covenant not put into effect without blood, Hebrews 9:18-22.
Supreme sacrifice, Hebrews 9:24-28; 1 John 4:9-10.
Redemption planned before Creation of world, 1 Peter 1:18-20.
All must give account of themselves to God, 1 Peter 4:4-6.
Only the One who redeemed us qualified to be our Judge, Revelation 5:1-14.
Those from all nations who have been redeemed, Revelation 7:9-17.
Inevitable defeat of Satan, Revelation 12:1-9.
See *Salvation.*

REFUGE
Cities of refuge, Exodus 21:13; Numbers 35:6; Deuteronomy 4:41-42; 19:3; Joshua 20:2, 9; 1 Chronicles 6:67.
Covered by God's hand, Exodus 33:22.
Everlasting arms, Deuteronomy 33:27.
Strong tower in besieged city, Judges 9:51.
Fortress and deliverer, 2 Samuel 22:1-4; Psalm 18:2.
Protection for future king, 2 Kings 11:1-3.
Shadow of divine wings, Psalm 17:8-9.
Shelter from angry tongues, Psalm 31:20.
Hiding place, Psalm 32:7.
Refuge and strength, Psalm 46:1-3.
Shelter and shade, Isaiah 25:4; 32:2.
Egypt, a place of refuge, Jeremiah 41:16-18.
Scattered to all nations, Jeremiah 49:36.
Refuge for those who trust the Lord, Nahum 1:7.
Double blessing, Zechariah 9:12.
See *Protection, Shelter.*

REFUGEE
Cain, the wanderer, Genesis 4:13-14.
Abram's calling, Genesis 12:1
Founder of Luz, Judges 1:22-26.
Escape from famine, Ruth 1:1-3.
Joseph, Mary, and Jesus, Matthew 2:13-18.
Pilgrims on earth, Hebrews 11:13; 1 Peter 2:11.

REFUTE
Satan questioned truth spoken by God,
Genesis 3:2-5.
Approval of parents, Numbers 30:3-5.
Youth chides wisdom of age, Job 32:6-9.
Elihu challenged Job to refute, Job 33:31-33.
Refraining from response to one who
affronted name of the Lord, Isaiah
36:18-22. (See 37:1-7.)
False prophets foiled, Isaiah 44:25.
See *Demean.*

REGENERATION
New heart and spirit, Jeremiah 24:7;
Ezekiel 11:19-20; 36:26-29.
Born again, John 3:3; Titus 3:5; 1 Peter
1:23.
Depth of redemption, Romans 6:3-23.
Positive conduct of those who have died
with Christ, Colossians 2:20-23.
See *Conversion.*

REGRESSION
Silver to dross, wine to water, Isaiah 1:22.

REGRET
Regret of Creator, Genesis 6:6.
Foolish sins, Numbers 12:11.
Sacrifice of daughter, Judges 11:30-40.
Chasing wind, Ecclesiastes 1:17-18.
Ashamed and silent before the Lord,
Ezekiel 16:63.
Remorse of king, Daniel 6:13-18.
Remembering glory of better days, Haggai
2:3.
Guilt of Judas, Matthew 27:3.
Second Coming will bring mourning to
those unprepared, Revelation 1:7.
See *Disappointment, Discouragement,
Remorse.*

REGULATIONS
Ultimate in demands for obeying Law,
Joshua 1:18.
Pagan king persuaded to permit rebuilding
of temple, Ezra 4–8.
Example of carrying rules too far, Mark
2:23-27.

REHABILITATE
Avoid ways of heathen, Deuteronomy 18:9.
Defilement in sanctuary, 2 Chronicles
29:1-11.

Beauty for ashes, Isaiah 61:1-3.
Restoring backslider to fellowship, James
5:19-20.

REINCARNATION
John the Baptist not reincarnation of
Elijah, Matthew 11:13-14.

REINFORCEMENT
Joshua gave instructions God had initially
given to him, Joshua 23:6. (See 1:8.)
Importance of repetition, 2 Peter 1:12-15.
Word of the prophets validated, 2 Peter
1:19.
Giving emphasis to former command,
1 John 2:7-8.
See *Instruction, Teaching.*

REINSTATE
Making wrong right to another person,
Numbers 5:6-7.
Debt canceled every seven years,
Deuteronomy 15:1.
Brother spared, 1 Kings 1:49-53.
The Lord vindicated beleaguered Job, Job
42:7-10.
Making and breaking promise to slaves,
Jeremiah 34:8-22.
The Lord returns to those who return to
Him, Zechariah 1:3.
See *Restoration.*

REJECTION
Those who refuse to hear God's message,
Judges 6:10.
Turning to rejected brother in time of
need, Judges 11:1-10.
Prophecy of cry from cross, Psalm 22:1.
Rejecting divine truth, Isaiah 30:10.
God revealed Himself to those who did not
ask, Isaiah 65:1.
Those who do not respond to God's grace,
Isaiah 65:12.
Backs turned to God, Jeremiah 2:27.
The Lord turns His back on disobedience,
Jeremiah 18:17.
Message of Jeremiah brings threat of death
to prophet, Jeremiah 26:1-16.
Those who will not respond, Jeremiah
32:33.
Jehoiakim burned scroll dictated by
Jeremiah, Jeremiah 36:1-26.
Message of Jeremiah rejected, Jeremiah
43:1-7. (See 44:15-19.)

Broken jar no one wants, Jeremiah 48:38.
Babylon could not be healed, Jeremiah 51:9.
When God turns deaf ear to praise, Amos 5:23. (See 8:3, 10.)
Gospel divides world and households, Matthew 10:32-36.
Witnessing miracles with hard hearts, Matthew 11:20.
Parable of landowner and son, Matthew 21:33-44.
Rejecting wedding banquet invitation, Matthew 22:1-14.
Prayer of Jesus over rebellious Jerusalem, Matthew 23:37.
Jesus, the sin-bearer, rejected by His Father in heaven, Matthew 27:46; Mark 15:34.
Sowing seed on various kinds of soil, Mark 4:3-20.
Rejecting those who witness, Luke 10:16.
Christ rejected by His own people, John 1:11.
Accepting and rejecting the Messiah, John 7:25-31.
Doubt can be augmented by hearing truth, John 8:45-47.
Unbelief in face of proof, John 12:37-40.
Those who act in ignorance, Acts 3:17.
Rejection of Gospel caused by religious jealousy, Acts 13:45.
Paul and Barnabas turn to Gentiles, Acts 13:46-48; 18:6.
Entire city in uproar, Acts 19:23-41.
Those who stumble over provision for redemption, Romans 9:33.
Divine compassion to disobedient, Romans 10:21.
Differing reactions to truly Christian personality, 2 Corinthians 2:15-16.
Witnessing to those blinded by Satan, 2 Corinthians 4:1-6.
Those who will follow Antichrist, 2 Thessalonians 2:4-12.
Those who could not hold true to faith, 1 Timothy 1:18-20.
Failure to combine hearing with believing, Hebrews 4:1-3.
Rejection caused by disobedience, 1 Peter 2:8.
Those who do not obey Gospel, 1 Peter 4:17.

RELATIONSHIP

Three forefathers of mankind, Genesis 9:18-19.
Marriage of Abraham to his stepsister, Genesis 20:12, 16.
Forbidding marriage to foreigners, Genesis 24:3.
Bond between relatives, Genesis 29:1-14.
Change in relationship, Genesis 31:2.
Rejecting brother born of evil woman, Judges 11:1-10.
Broken circle among 12 tribes, Judges 21:1-6.
Ruth's love for mother-in-law, Ruth 1:8-18.
Hatred of wife for husband, 2 Samuel 6:16-23.
Marriage confirms alliance, 1 Kings 3:1.
Apple of God's eye, Psalm 17:8.
Being recognized as one who follows the Lord, Psalm 119:74.
Golden Rule, Matthew 7:12.
Jesus' evaluation of earthly relationships, Matthew 12:46-50; Mark 3:31-35.
Prayers answered when all is well with relationships, Mark 11:25.
Marriage on earth compared to relationship in heaven, Mark 12:18-27.
Relationship to God and to neighbors, Mark 12:28-34.
Presumed relationship to the Lord, Luke 13:22-30.
Putting Christ first above family, Luke 14:26.
Love the supreme identity of relationship, John 13:34.
True meaning of a friend, John 15:12-17.
New relationships in Christ, John 19:26-27.
Differing reactions to truly Christian personality, 2 Corinthians 2:15-16.
Identified in Christ, Ephesians 1:11-12.
God lives in us by His Spirit, Ephesians 2:22.
Slave and master have same Master, Ephesians 6:9.
Paul's concern for spiritual development of followers, Colossians 2:1-5.
Timothy, spiritual son of Paul, 1 Timothy 1:2, 18; 2 Timothy 1:2; 2:1.
Depth of relationship with Christ, 2 Timothy 2:11-13; Hebrews 2:11-13.
Known as God's friend, James 2:21-23.
Confessing sins one to another, James 5:16.
Becoming children of God, 1 John 3:1-3.

Loved and kept, Jude 1.
See *Body of Christ, Brotherhood, Family.*

RELATIVITY
God compresses millennia into moments,
2 Peter 3:8-9.

RELAXATION
Sure rest in the Lord's protection,
Deuteronomy 33:12.
David frequently played harp, 1 Samuel
18:10.
Steadfast heart, Psalm 57:7.
The Lord will bring quietness and
rejoicing, Zephaniah 3:17.
Importance of quietness and rest, Mark
6:31.
See *Recreation.*

RELEASE
King imprisoned and set free, 2 Kings
24:15; 25:27-29.
Making and breaking promise to slaves,
Jeremiah 34:8-22.
Rescued from dominion of darkness,
Colossians 1:13-14.

RELENTLESS
Times of trouble, Proverbs 24:10.
That which is never satisfied, Proverbs
30:15-16.
Doing what you do with all your might,
Ecclesiastes 9:10.
Greedy for gain, Jeremiah 8:10.
See *Determination.*

RELEVANCE
Discerning the prophets, Deuteronomy
18:21-22.
Samuel's unwasted words, 1 Samuel 3:19.

RELIABLE
Still standing at end of struggle, Ephesians
6:13.
Steadfast whatever circumstances,
Philippians 1:27-30.
Meaning of "today" in God's reckoning,
Hebrews 4:7.
No lie comes from truth, 1 John 2:20-21.
See *Dependability.*

RELICS
Historical items kept in earthly tabernacle,
Hebrews 9:3-4.

RELIEF
God ever present in times of trouble, Psalm
14:4-5.
Padding for Jeremiah's comfort in
deliverance, Jeremiah 38:11-13.

RELIGION
Job could not depend on his own piety, Job
4:6.
Natural perception, Job 12:7-16.
Difference between man's way and right
way, Proverbs 14:12; 16:25.
Rules taught by men, Isaiah 29:13.
Digging their own cisterns, Jeremiah 2:13.
Idols in heart, Ezekiel 14:1-11.
Those who simply say, "Lord, Lord,"
Matthew 7:21-23.
Jesus criticized for picking grain on
Sabbath, Matthew 12:1-8.
Faith of gross sinners compared to religion
of Pharisees, Matthew 21:31-32.
Clean outside, filthy inside, Matthew 23:25-
28.
Mere lip service to the Lord, Mark 7:6-7.
Morality and materialism, Mark 10:17-25.
Practice what you proclaim, Luke 3:7-8.
Attitude of Pharisees toward helping
others on Sabbath, Luke 13:10-17.
Pharisees and tax collector, Luke 18:9-14.
Reading Bible in vain, John 5:39-40.
Those who erroneously think they are
serving God, John 16:1-4.
Pagans certain of false belief, Acts 19:35-
36.
See *Formality, Legalism.*

RELUCTANCE
Reluctance of Lot to leave Sodom, Genesis
19:15-16.
Negative and positive viewpoints,
Numbers 13:17-33.
Ignoring word of the Lord, Jeremiah 7:13.
Reluctance of demon to leave one
possessed, Mark 1:21-26.
Man who feared Jesus might be reluctant
to heal him, Luke 5:12-14.
At tomb of Jesus, John 20:5, 8.

REMARRIAGE
Remarriage of divorced persons,
Deuteronomy 24:1-4.
Ruth and Boaz, Ruth 4:10.
Bible instruction concerning remarriage,
Romans 7:1-3.

Paul's view of marriage for widows,
1 Corinthians 7:8-9.
See *Divorce, Marriage.*

REMEDIES
Poultice of figs, 2 Kings 20:7.
Soothing oil, Isaiah 1:6; Luke 10:34.
No balm in Gilead, Jeremiah 8:22.
Wine for stomach, 1 Timothy 5:23.
Anointing oil, James 5:14.
See *Medicine, Therapy.*

REMINISCENCE
Asking about former days, Deuteronomy
4:32-35.
Past not brought to mind, Isaiah 65:17.
Bitterly remembering days of old,
Lamentations 1:7.
Glory of better days, Haggai 2:3.
Prodigal's memories of home, Luke 15:17.
See *Memory, Retrospect.*

REMNANT
Righteous remnant on earth, Genesis 6:5-
14.
Not one upright man remaining, Micah 7:2.
Remnant of believers in Israel, Romans
11:1-5.
Those clean in society of deceit, Revelation
3:4.
See *Israel.*

REMORSE
Divine grief of God, 1 Chronicles 21:14-15.
Tears of contrition and confession, Ezra
10:1.
Lamenting personal sin, Psalms 31:10;
38:2-6; 51:1-19.
Isaiah's self-analysis, Isaiah 6:5.
Cutting off hair to show remorse, Jeremiah
7:29.
Weeping and wailing as judgment comes,
Jeremiah 25:34.
Eyes dry from weeping, Lamentations 2:11.
Remorse of king, Daniel 6:13-18.
Remembering glory of better days, Haggai
2:3; Luke 15:17.
Guilt of Judas, Matthew 27:3-5.
Eternal remorse of lost souls, Luke 13:28.
Ashamed for past conduct, Romans 6:21.
Role of grief in repentance, 1 Corinthians
5:1-2.
Second Coming will bring mourning to
those unprepared, Revelation 1:7.

Agony of those who refuse to repent,
Revelation 16:10-11.
See *Conviction, Regret, Sorrow.*

REMUNERATION
Requesting payment for spiritual ministry,
2 Kings 5:20-27.
God accepts no price or reward, Isaiah
45:13.
Daniel's refusal of bribes or rewards,
Daniel 5:17.
Worker deserves wages, Luke 10:7;
1 Corinthians 9:9-14.
Wages of sin, Romans 6:23; 2 Peter 2:15.
See *Honorarium, Stipend, Wages.*

RENEGADE
Recruited to turn against their own king,
2 Kings 9:14-24.
Infamy to daughter of king, 2 Kings 9:30-
37.
Mistaken praise, Esther 6:1-12. (See 5:9-
14.)
Lamp of wicked, Job 18:5-6.
Worthless idols make worthless people,
Jeremiah 2:5.
Refusal to go God's way, Jeremiah 11:7-8.
Fed up with wild life, Luke 15:17.
See *Rebellion.*

RENEWAL
Tear down old and build new, Judges 6:25-
26.
Renewed by Scripture, Psalm 119:93.
Streams on dry ground, Isaiah 44:3.
Ask for ancient paths, the good way,
Jeremiah 6:16.
Examine one's ways and return to Lord,
Lamentations 3:40.
New heart and new spirit, Ezekiel 36:26.
Fan into flame the gift of God, 2 Timothy
1:6.

RENTAL
Difference between borrowing and
renting, Exodus 22:14-15.
Paul's rented house, Acts 28:30.

RENUNCIATION
Leaving all to follow Jesus, Matthew 10:38;
Luke 5:27-28; 18:29-30.
Supreme example of rejection, Matthew
27:46.
Peter's denial of Christ, Mark 14:66-72.

Dead to sin, Romans 6:2, 11; Colossians
3:3.
Old nature crucified, Galatians 5:24;
1 Peter 2:24.
All things as loss, Philippians 3:8.
See *Repentance.*

REPAIR
Lazy man's house, Ecclesiastes 10:18.
Proper repair of garment, Matthew 9:16.

REPENTANCE
Pharaoh's insincere repentance, Exodus
9:27.
Repentance brings forgiveness and
blessing, Leviticus 26:40-42;
Deuteronomy 30:1-10; Nehemiah 1:9.
A merciful God, Deuteronomy 4:29-31.
National repentance and commitment,
Joshua 24:16-27.
When people repent, God provides, Judges
3:9-15.
National repentance, 1 Samuel 7:3;
2 Chronicles 7:14.
King Saul's repentance, 1 Samuel 15:13-
35.
Tears of contrition and confession, Ezra
10:1.
Guilt of limited admission, Job 34:31-33.
After all his contests with God and
circumstances, Job submitted, Job 42:1-
9.
Sure forgiveness, Psalm 32:5-6.
David's prayer for the Lord's mercy, Psalm
41:4.
Source of new joy, Psalm 51:12-13.
Those who should be weeping engage in
merriment, Isaiah 22:12-13.
Do not miss opportunity, Isaiah 55:6-7.
Need for repentance, Isaiah 64:5.
God's great love to faithless Israel,
Jeremiah 3:11-17.
Sincere disgrace of those who realize
sinfulness, Jeremiah 3:24-25.
Break up unplowed ground, Jeremiah 4:3.
Asking for old paths, Jeremiah 6:16.
Sackcloth and ashes, Jeremiah 6:26.
Reward for repentance, Jeremiah 7:3.
Those who refuse to repent, Jeremiah 8:6.
Pride hinders repentance, Jeremiah 13:15.
Prayer of truly repentant, Jeremiah 14:20-
22.
Coming with weeping, Jeremiah 31:9.
Repentance from disgrace of youth,

Jeremiah 31:19.
Need for individual repentance, Jeremiah
36:1-3.
Tears of repentance, Jeremiah 50:4-5.
Sparing lives of those with mark of
repentance, Ezekiel 9:3-6.
Turning from wicked past, Ezekiel 16:59-
63.
Contrast between backsliding and
repentance, Ezekiel 18:24-28.
The Lord wants all to live, Ezekiel 18:32.
Conscious of need for repentance, Ezekiel
20:43.
The Lord prefers repentance to judgment,
Ezekiel 33:10-12.
Daniel's prayer of repentance, Daniel 9:4-
19.
Break up unplowed ground and sow
righteousness, Hosea 10:12.
Key to God's guidance, Hosea 12:6.
Sins cause downfall, Hosea 14:1.
Congregational response, Joel 1:14; 2:12-
17.
Testing and trials fail to bring disobedient
back to the Lord, Amos 4:6-11.
Ninevites heeded Jonah's warning, Jonah
3:3-6.
God's response to those who repent, Jonah
3:10.
Those who fall may rise, Micah 7:8-9.
Insincere fasting and repentance,
Zechariah 7:1-6; Malachi 2:13.
Preaching of John the Baptist, Matthew
3:1-3.
Unrepentant guilt of Judas, Matthew 27:3.
Sinful woman who washed feet of Jesus
with her tears, Luke 7:36-50.
Confessing evil deeds, Acts 19:18-19.
Ashamed of sin in one's past, Romans
6:21.
Role of grief in repentance, 1 Corinthians
5:1-2.
Godly sorrow brings repentance,
2 Corinthians 7:10.
Turning to God from idols,
1 Thessalonians 1:9.
Those who refuse to repent, Revelation
9:20-21; 16:10-11.
Evil queen refused to admit sin, Revelation
18:7-8.
See *Remorse, Renunciation.*

REPETITION
Repetition of miraculous provision at Red

Sea and River Jordan, Joshua 4:23.
Joshua gave people instructions God had initially given to him, Joshua 23:6. (See 1:8.)
History repeats itself, Ecclesiastes 3:15.
Farmer does not plow continuously, Isaiah 28:24.
Jeremiah proclaimed message "again and again," Jeremiah 25:3-4.
Identical trouble does not happen twice, Nahum 1:9.
Repetitious prayer, Matthew 6:7.
Paul repeats himself for emphasis, Philippians 3:1.
Importance of repetition, 2 Peter 1:12-15.
See *Emphasis.*

REPLY
See *Answer, Response.*

REPORT
Moses' report to father-in-law, Exodus 18:5-12.
Good news expected from good man, 2 Samuel 18:27.
One message after another of bad news, Jeremiah 51:31-32.
Paul's summary of ministry, Acts 21:19.
Speaking only of what Christ has done, Romans 15:18-19.
Timothy's report concerning Thessalonian believers, 1 Thessalonians 3:6-10.

REPOSE
Place of certainty, Deuteronomy 33:27.
Steadfast heart, Psalm 57:7.
See *Rest.*

REPRESENTATIVE
Representatives for people, Exodus 18:14-27.
Looking out for welfare of people, Esther 10:3.
Christ's ambassadors, 2 Corinthians 5:20.
See *Government.*

REPRESSION
Futile effort to suppress truth, Jeremiah 38:1-6.

REPRIEVE
Slow to anger, Numbers 14:18.
Disaster delayed, 1 Kings 21:29.
Need for quick punishment, Ecclesiastes 8:11.
Restrained wrath of God, Isaiah 48:9.
Partial reprieve, Jeremiah 37:21.
Judgment against tree, Luke 13:7-9.
Divine power restrained, Romans 9:22.
Divine patience in days of Noah, 1 Peter 3:20.
See *Mercy.*

REPRIMAND
The Lord speaking to Job's friends, Job 42:7-9.
Wounds of friend, Proverbs 27:6.
Worth of honest rebuke, Proverbs 28:23.
Jesus scolding an evil spirit, Mark 1:23-26.
Mother's reprimand, Luke 2:48.
See *Rebuke, Reproof, Scolding.*

REPRISAL
Reprisal invited, 1 Kings 19:2.
Stark picture of vengeance, Psalm 58:10. (See 68:23.)
When not to do as others have done, Proverbs 24:29.
Showing love to those who cause grief, 2 Corinthians 2:5-11.
Leave revenge with the Lord, 1 Thessalonians 5:15.
See *Revenge.*

REPROACH
King Saul silent toward those who insulted him, 1 Samuel 10:27.
Causing utter contempt, 2 Samuel 12:14; Nehemiah 5:9.
Daring to scoff at the name of the Lord, Isaiah 36:18-21. (See 37:6.)
Haunt of jackals, Jeremiah 9:11.
Facing grim destiny, Jeremiah 15:2-3.
Disrespect for the sanctuary, Ezekiel 25:1-4.
Dishonoring the Lord's name, Ezekiel 36:20; Romans 2:23-24.
Public insult, Hebrews 10:33.
Suffering reproach, Hebrews 11:24-26.
Blessing from persecution, 1 Peter 4:4.
See *Disobedience, Sacrilege.*

REPROBATE
Worldwide iniquity, Genesis 6:5-7.
Divine warning, Deuteronomy 28:15-68.
Contemptible sons, 1 Samuel 3:13.
The Lord provoked to anger, 1 Kings 21:22.

Deaf ears to divine warning, Isaiah 65:12.
Those who do not know how to blush,
    Jeremiah 6:15.
Beyond help of prayer, Jeremiah 7:16.
When who you know does not help,
    Jeremiah 15:1.
Anger beyond measure, Lamentations
    5:21-22.
For continued sinning, certain judgment,
    Amos 1:3, 6, 9, 11, 13; 2:1, 4, 6. (Note
    nature of sin in each of these
    judgments.)
Once the door is closed, Luke 13:25-28.
Total depravity, Romans 1:28.
Sin in broad daylight, 2 Peter 2:13-22.

REPRODUCTION
God's command to His creation, Genesis
    1:22, 27-28.
Good land and unproductive land,
    Hebrews 6:7-8.
See *Fruit, Propagation.*

REPROOF
Rebuking a neighbor, Leviticus 19:17.
Levites had gone too far, Numbers 16:7.
He who helped others himself becomes
    discouraged, Job 4:3-5.
Received as kindness, Psalm 141:5.
Parental reproof, Proverbs 15:5.
Corrective proof to receptive ear, Proverbs
    17:10.
Like fine gold, Proverbs 25:12.
Wounds of friend, Proverbs 27:6.
Worth of honest rebuke, Proverbs 28:23.
Song of fools, Ecclesiastes 7:5.
Discipline with justice, Jeremiah 30:11.
Scolding evil spirit, Mark 1:23-26.
Rebuke sinful brother, Luke 17:3.
Expose darkness, Ephesians 5:11.
Public rebuke, 1 Timothy 5:20.
Preaching and teaching, 2 Timothy 4:1-2;
    Titus 2:15.
Commendation before reproof, Revelation
    2:2-6, 13-16, 19-20.
See *Reprimand.*

REPUTATION
Righteous man without blame, Genesis
    6:9.
Abraham's reputation, Genesis 21:22.
A desert named Sin, Exodus 17:1.
Holiness by virtue of occupation, Leviticus
    21:8.

Holy community, Numbers 16:3.
No fault found in David, 1 Samuel 29:3.
High compliments for David, 1 Samuel
    29:6-9.
Reputation as troublemaker, 2 Samuel
    20:1.
Some good in Judah, 2 Chronicles 12:12.
David known as man of prayer, Psalm
    109:4.
Priceless value of good name, Proverbs
    22:1; Ecclesiastes 7:1.
Seeking one's own honor, Proverbs 25:27.
Parables to a fool, Proverbs 26:1-12.
Damaged reputation of parents, Proverbs
    27:11.
Looking for one honest person in
    Jerusalem, Jeremiah 5:1.
Least and greatest, Jeremiah 42:1-3.
Reputation of Daniel known to queen,
    Daniel 5:10-12.
Integrity in government affairs, Daniel 6:1-
    3.
Jealousy incited, Daniel 6:4-8.
Haggai called the Lord's messenger,
    Haggai 1:13.
People seek for those who know the Lord,
    Zechariah 8:23.
Joseph did not want to make public
    presumed sin of Mary, Matthew 1:19.
False prophets, Matthew 7:15-20.
Role of humility in greatness, Matthew
    23:12.
Neighbors of Joseph did not expect divinity
    in Jesus, Luke 4:22-24.
Lasting reputation for wrongdoing, Luke
    17:32.
Low reputation of Nazareth, John 1:46.
Mistrust of Paul by other disciples, Acts
    9:26.
Respect of Cornelius for Peter, Acts 10:25-
    26.
Good motivation of David, Acts 13:22.
Noble character of Bereans, Acts 17:11.
Paul speaking as former Pharisee, Acts
    23:6.
Faith of Christians at Rome known across
    world, Romans 1:8.
Always doing what is right, Romans 12:17.
Reputation for obedience, Romans 16:19.
Mark of integrity, 2 Corinthians 8:18-24.
Report of Paul's new faith encouraged
    others, Galatians 1:23-24.
Living life worthy of your calling,
    Ephesians 4:1.

Care of one's conduct toward unbelievers, Colossians 4:5.
Prostitute delivered by faith and obedience, Hebrews 11:31.
Joy of good reputation, 3 John 3-6.
Those of whom you can speak well, 3 John 12.
Strength and weakness of church at Ephesus, Revelation 2:1-6.
Place of residence for demons and evil spirits, Revelation 18:2.
See *Conduct, Esteem.*

REQUEST
Asking for special favor, Judges 1:13-15.
Desiring double portion of prophet's spirit, 2 Kings 2:9.
Blind man's simple request, Mark 10:46-52.

REQUIREMENT
Abstaining from wine and all fruit of grape, Numbers 6:2-4.
What the Lord requires of His people, Deuteronomy 10:12-13; Micah 6:8.
Do not take on ways of heathen, Deuteronomy 18:9.
The ultimate in demands for obeying the Law, Joshua 1:18.
What God requires, He provides, Isaiah 2:3.
Building a good society, Zechariah 7:9; 8:16.
See *Responsibility.*

RESCUE
Kidnapping and rescue of Lot, Genesis 14:12-16.
Queen Esther, advocate for her people, Esther 8:3-11.
Mercy to suffering Jeremiah, Jeremiah 38:6-13.
Too little, too late, Amos 3:12.
Jonah and great fish, Jonah 1:17.
See *Deliverance.*

RESEARCH
The Lord investigates situation at Sodom and Gomorrah, Genesis 18:20-21.
Searching royal archives, Ezra 5:17.
Good and bad sources for advice, Proverbs 12:5.
Kings must search out concealed matters, Proverbs 25:2-3.

RESENTMENT
Revenge left to divine timing, 1 Samuel 26:1-11.
Resentful citizens, 1 Samuel 30:3-6.
Detesting display of emotion, 2 Samuel 6:14-16.
Misunderstanding gesture of goodwill, 2 Samuel 10:1-4.
Inequity among citizens, Nehemiah 5:1-5.
Wealth and prestige could not numb resentment, Esther 5:10-14.
At odds with one's Maker, Isaiah 45:9.
Attitude of Pharisees toward helping others on Sabbath, Luke 13:10-17.
Pharisees resentment toward Jesus, Luke 15:1-7.
Prodigal son and resenting brother, Luke 15:11-32.
See *Hatred.*

RESIDENCE
Living in cave, Genesis 19:30.
Solomon took less time to build temple than palace, 1 Kings 6:37-38; 7:1.
Tent or cottage, Isaiah 38:12.
Jesus had no place of residence, Matthew 8:20.
Many demons in one man, Luke 8:30.
Place where Jesus stayed, John 1:37-39.
House convenient to synagogue, Acts 18:7.
Paul's rented house, Acts 28:30.
Living in tent en route to city of God, Hebrews 11:9-10.
See *Home, House, Palace, Parsonage*

RESIDUE
Ashes from altar ceremonially clean, Numbers 19:9.
Some juice left in grapes, Isaiah 65:8.
See *Remnant.*

RESILIENT
Race not to swift or strong, Ecclesiastes 9:11.

RESISTANCE
Sinful enticement, Proverbs 1:10; 4:14.
Made strong by God's power, Jeremiah 1:17-19.
Giving up to enemy, Lamentations 1:5.
Reluctance of demon to leave one possessed, Mark 1:21-26.
Jesus offered no resistance to His oppressors, Luke 22:47-53.

Mob incited against Paul and Silas, Acts 17:5-7.

Personal purity, Romans 6:13.

Stability to resist Satan, Ephesians 6:13.

Resisting ungodliness and passions of the world, Titus 2:11-12.

Do not harden your heart, Hebrews 3:7-8, 15.

Alert to spiritual error, 2 Peter 3:17.

See *Discipline.*

RESISTANT

Only Levites responded, Exodus 32:25-26.

Choice between life or death, Deuteronomy 30:19.

Hindered from choosing the true God, Joshua 24:15; 1 Kings 18:21.

Resisting the Son of God, Matthew 23:37.

Hindrance of wealth, Luke 18:18-25.

Resisting temptation through prayer, Luke 22:40.

See *Rebellion, Unbelief.*

RESOLUTE

Unending faithfulness, Joshua 24:14.

Moving ahead in spite of circumstances, Psalm 44:18.

Times of trouble, Proverbs 24:10.

See *Determination.*

RESOURCE

People more valuable than material, Genesis 14:21.

Dependability of divine strength, Isaiah 40:28-31.

Wood for making gods and cooking fires, Isaiah 44:14-20.

Dying earth, Isaiah 51:6.

Nothing too hard for God, Jeremiah 32:27.

Strength received from the Lord, Habakkuk 3:19.

Gold and silver of earth belong to God, Haggai 2:8.

See *Natural resources.*

RESPECT

Harm to parents forbidden, Exodus 21:15.

Stand when older person appears, Leviticus 19:32.

Mutual respect between enemies, Deuteronomy 2:4-5.

Show respect to church and court, Deuteronomy 17:12.

Do not respect prophet who proclaims error, Deuteronomy 18:21-22.

Samuel's unwasted words, 1 Samuel 3:19.

Reverence of god of stone for ark of God, 1 Samuel 5:1-5.

David's respect for King Saul's position and anointing, 1 Samuel 24:1-7; 26:7-11.

Success through blessing and guidance, 2 Samuel 22:44-45.

Respect for prophet born by fear, 2 Kings 1:1-15.

Little boy showed no respect for Job, Job 19:18.

Respect at city gate, Job 29:7-10.

Respect for those older, Job 32:4-6; 1 Timothy 5:1-2; 1 Peter 5:5.

Attitude toward older parents, Proverbs 23:22.

Promise of peaceful and honorable death, Jeremiah 34:4-5.

Honor to whom due, Malachi 1:6.

Levi truly worshiped the Lord, Malachi 2:4-5.

Empty sincerity of Pharisees, Mark 12:15-17.

Jesus accused of disrespect, John 18:19-24.

Respect of Cornelius for Peter, Acts 10:25-26.

The recognition of an apostle, 1 Corinthians 9:1-6.

Accused yet admired, 1 Peter 2:12.

Consideration for everyone, 1 Peter 2:17.

Those who take Scriptures to heart, Revelation 1:3.

See *Courtesy, Genuflect.*

RESPONSE

Agreement voiced by congregation, Deuteronomy 27:14-26.

Regret of poor student, Proverbs 5:12-13.

Refraining from response to one who affronted the name of the Lord, Isaiah 36:18-22. (See 37:1-7.)

Ignoring word of the Lord, Jeremiah 7:13.

Communicating to those who ought to listen eagerly, Ezekiel 3:4-9.

Nineveh more responsive than Jerusalem, Matthew 12:41-42.

Do not harden your heart, Hebrews 3:7-8, 15.

Opening door to Him who knocks, Revelation 3:20.

See *Answer.*

RESPONSIBILITY

Moses wanted substitute for his responsibility, Exodus 4:10-13. (See 6:30.)

Conditions for experiencing God's blessing, Exodus 15:26.

Responsibility delegated to father-in-law, Exodus 18:13-26.

The Lord delegates responsibility, Deuteronomy 1:9-18.

Remembering and following divine teaching, Deuteronomy 4:9.

Taking care of business, Deuteronomy 20:5-9.

Personal grief put aside to lead people, 2 Samuel 19:1-8.

Assigned as gatekeepers, 1 Chronicles 9:22-27.

Willingly assuming responsibility, Nehemiah 10:32, 35.

One threshes grain, one grinds flour, Isaiah 28:28.

Responsibility for warning wicked, Ezekiel 3:17-19.

Parents and children responsible for their own sin, Ezekiel 18:4-20.

Responsibility of watchman as danger approaches, Ezekiel 33:1-9.

Privilege brings responsibility, Amos 3:2.

Jonah's refusal to obey, Jonah 1:3.

Responsible for nation's sin, Micah 1:13.

Danger of wrong influence over children, Matthew 18:6.

Burden of responsibility lightened, Matthew 11:28-30.

Use of talents, Matthew 25:14-30.

Forgetting to bring necessities, Mark 8:14.

Care of unproductive fig tree, Luke 13:6-9.

Influencing others to sin, Luke 17:1.

Doing one's duty, Luke 17:10.

Responsible stewardship, Luke 21:1-4.

Personal responsibility to hearing truth, John 3:18-19.

Those who truly care for the sheep, John 10:11-13.

Delegating distribution of welfare to widows, Acts 6:1-4.

Paul's sense of responsibility to all cultures, Romans 1:14-17.

Result of Adam's disobedience, Romans 5:12.

Strong looking after weak, Romans 15:1.

Teamwork in reaching others, 1 Corinthians 3:6-9.

Entrusted with secret things of God, 1 Corinthians 4:1-2.

Responsibility of leadership regarding gifts of Spirit, 1 Corinthians 12:27-30.

Aim for perfection, 2 Corinthians 13:11.

Carrying one's own load, Galatians 6:5.

Do not neglect your gift, 1 Timothy 4:14.

Families should take care of those in need, 1 Timothy 5:3-8.

Responsibility of obtaining wealth, 1 Timothy 6:17-19.

Paul's responsibility to proclaim message, Titus 1:1-3.

Given responsibility for one's own affairs, Titus 1:5.

Providing for personal needs, Titus 3:14.

Human responsibility for evil, James 1:13-15.

Responsibility to do good, James 4:17.

All must give account of themselves, 1 Peter 4:4-6.

Danger of seeing light but walking in darkness, 2 Peter 2:21.

See *Leadership*.

REST

Time set aside, Exodus 23:12; 34:21.

Exhausted in battle, 2 Samuel 21:15.

Lie down without fear, Job 11:19.

Assurance in rest, Psalm 3:5.

Love, faithfulness, and peace, Psalm 85:10.

Uncomfortable accommodations, Isaiah 28:20.

Avoiding work on Sabbath, Jeremiah 17:21-27.

Pleasant sleep, Jeremiah 31:26.

Rest for weary and burdened, Matthew 11:28-30.

No chance for rest in busy ministry, Mark 6:30-34.

Repose of death, Revelation 14:13-14.

RESTAURANT

Abraham as table waiter, Genesis 18:7-8.

Public eating places, Exodus 32:6; Psalm 23:5.

RESTITUTION

Good returned for evil, Genesis 47:1-11.

Responsibility for injury, Exodus 21:33-36.

Restitution for stolen property, Exodus 22:1-15.

Setting things right with one's neighbor, Leviticus 6:1-6.

Making wrong right, Numbers 5:6-7;
   Nehemiah 5:1-13.
Practice of prolonged retribution,
   Deuteronomy 23:2-6.
Guilt offering for desecrating ark of God,
   1 Samuel 6:17.
Conflict between David and Saul,
   1 Samuel 26:1-25.
Putting end to jealous conflict, 2 Samuel
   2:26-29.
Showing kindness to kin of enemy,
   2 Samuel 9:1-13.
David accused of reaping what he had
   sown, 2 Samuel 16:5-8.
Restitution between nations, 1 Kings
   20:34.
Return of property and income, 2 Kings
   8:1-6.
Defilement in sanctuary, 2 Chronicles
   29:1-11.
Fate of Job's friends, Job 42:7-10.
Forced to restore what was not stolen,
   Psalm 69:4.
Repaying sevenfold, Proverbs 6:31.
Our Lord's reward for giving us salvation,
   Isaiah 53:10-12.
Beauty for ashes, Isaiah 61:1-3.
Mercy for nation that repents, Jeremiah
   18:1-12.
Setting things right with the Lord,
   Lamentations 3:40.
Reprieve from death, Ezekiel 33:15.
Making things right begins in the heart,
   Joel 2:13.
Stone rejected by builders, Matthew 21:42.
Example of Zaccheus, Luke 19:8.
Peter restored to full fellowship, John
   21:15-18.
Adam's guilt and grace of God in Christ,
   Romans 5:12-19. (See 8:1-4.)

RESTLESS
Restless wanderer, Genesis 4:8-12.
Instability caused by disobedience,
   Deuteronomy 28:64-67.
Social and political unrest, 2 Chronicles
   15:3-7.
Insomnia, Job 7:2-3.
Unrequited love, Song of Songs 3:1-2.
Wicked like restless waves of tossing sea,
   Isaiah 57:20-21.
Restless pursuit, Lamentations 5:5.
Unrewarded search for peace, Ezekiel
   7:25.

Divine therapy for restlessness, Philippians
   4:4-7; 1 Peter 5:7.
See *Anxiety, Insomnia, Unrest.*

RESTLESSNESS
Endless passing of days, Deuteronomy
   28:67.
Citizens in turmoil, 2 Chronicles 15:5.
Restless thoughts into night, Ecclesiastes
   2:23.
No peace for wicked, Isaiah 48:22; 57:20-
   21; 59:8; Ezekiel 7:25.
In constant pursuit, Lamentations 5:5.
No rest day or night, Revelation 14:11.
See *Anguish, Turmoil.*

RESTORATION
Backslider returning to the Lord, 1 Samuel
   15:24-25.
Parable used to convince King David of
   forgiving Absalom, 2 Samuel 14:1-21.
Partial restoration of captive king, 2 Kings
   24:15; 25:27-30.
Transgressors restored, Psalm 51:12.
Restoration and guidance, Isaiah 57:18.
Ruins rebuilt, Isaiah 58:12.
Divine offer of restoration, Jeremiah 3:22;
   Hosea 14:4.
Certainty of national restoration, Jeremiah
   33:23-26.
Magnitude of divine restoration, Micah
   7:19.
Stone rejected by builders, Matthew 21:42.
Son received back as from dead, Hebrews
   11:19.
Restoring backslider to fellowship, James
   5:19-20.
See *Redemption.*

RESTRAINT
Forbidden to taste food, 1 Samuel 14:24-
   28.
Imbibing without restraint, Esther 1:7-
   8.
Nations resisting Law of God, Psalm 2:3.
Keeping oneself under control, Proverbs
   29:11.
Refraining from response to one who
   affronted the Lord, Isaiah 36:18-22;
   37:1-7.
Anger beyond measure, Isaiah 64:9.
Demons refused permission to speak,
   Mark 1:33-34.
See *Discipline, Hindrance.*

Vision of resurrected Christ, Revelation
1:13-16.
Statement of Jesus to John on Patmos,
Revelation 1:17-20.
Resurrection of two witnesses, Revelation
11:3-12.
Martyrs restored to life, Revelation 20:4-6.

RETALIATION
Eye for an eye, Exodus 21:23-24;
Deuteronomy 19:19. (See Matt. 5:38-
44.)
Love those who mistreat, Leviticus 19:18.
Dramatic reversal of fortunes, Esther
5:9–7:10.
Jews liquidated their enemies, Esther 9:1-
17.
Stark picture of vengeance, Psalm 58:10.
(See 68:23.)
When not to do as others have done,
Proverbs 20:22; 24:29.
Leave works of enemy in God's hands,
Lamentations 3:55-66.
Basics of Golden Rule, Luke 6:27-36.
Do not return evil for evil, Romans 12:17;
1 Peter 3:9.
Showing love to those who cause grief,
2 Corinthians 2:5-11.
Leave revenge in God's hands,
2 Thessalonians 1:6-7.
See *Retribution, Revenge.*

RETARDED
Senseless, Psalm 92:6; Jeremiah 10:8;
51:17.
Weak-minded youth, Proverbs 7:7; 9:14-
18.
Animal mentality, Daniel 4:16; 2 Peter
2:12; Jude 10.
Cretinism, Titus 1:12.

RETICENT
Testing of divine patience, Numbers 14:18.
Taking care of business, Deuteronomy
20:5-9.
Paul's reluctance in expressing deep
spiritual concern, Romans 9:1-2.
Timidity of Paul, 2 Corinthians 10:1.
See *Shy, Timidity.*

RETIREMENT
Recognizing time to retire, Deuteronomy
31:2.
Moses retained virility until death,

Deuteronomy 34:7.
Going strong at 85, Joshua 14:10-11.
Joshua's farewell, Joshua 23:1-16.
Looking back across exemplary life,
1 Samuel 12:3.
When others relaxed, David prepared for
action, 1 Samuel 24:22.
Denied fruit of life's labor, Ecclesiastes 6:1-
2.
Darius became king at age 62, Daniel 5:30-
31.
Those of old age sitting in streets,
Zechariah 8:4.
Relentless in worship during advanced
age, Luke 2:36-38.
Families should take care of those in need,
1 Timothy 5:3-8.
See *Geriatrics.*

RETREAT
One warrior stumbling over another,
Jeremiah 46:12, 16.
Hiss of fleeing serpent, Jeremiah 46:22.
Brave warriors flee naked, Amos 2:16.
Quiet place for rest, Mark 6:31.
Jesus withdrew from crowd to pray, Luke
5:16.
Praying through the night, Luke 6:12.
Futile attempt to hold retreat, Luke 9:10-
11.
Paul found Athens suitable place to be left
alone, 1 Thessalonians 3:1.
See *Defeat.*

RETRIBUTION
Servant's attitude toward unfair employer,
Genesis 16:1-10.
Practice of prolonged retribution,
Deuteronomy 23:2-6.
Folly of David's relationship with
Bathsheba, 2 Samuel 12:1-13.
Executing unfaithful fathers but sparing
sons, 2 Kings 14:5-6.
Man who built gallows for his own neck,
Esther 5:11-14. (See also 9:25.)
Enemy falls into pit he himself designed,
Psalm 57:6.
Stark picture of vengeance, Psalm 58:10;
68:23.
When not to do as others have done,
Proverbs 24:29.
Showing kindness to enemy, Proverbs
25:21-22.
Destroyer is destroyed, Isaiah 33:1.

Sins paid back, Isaiah 65:6.
Israel to strike back against enemies,
    Jeremiah 49:2.
Folly of taking revenge, Ezekiel 25:15-17.
Punishment for those who mock the
    Lord's people, Zephaniah 2:9-10.
Leave revenge in God's hands,
    2 Thessalonians 1:6-7.
Harm received for harm done, 2 Peter
    2:13.
Golden rule stated negatively, Revelation
    18:6.
See *Retaliation, Revenge.*

RETROGRESS
Journey one should never make again,
    Deuteronomy 28:68.
Go forward but fall backward, Isaiah 28:13.
Haunt of jackals, Jeremiah 9:11.

RETROSPECT
Looking back on long years of divine
    goodness and faithfulness, Psalm 37:25.
Remembering glory of better days, Haggai
    2:3.
Looking back on history, Acts 7:1-53.
See *Memory.*

REUNION
Reunion between Jacob and Esau, Genesis
    33:1-20.
Reunion between Joseph and brothers,
    Genesis 45:1-15.
Joseph's eagerness to meet his father,
    Genesis 46:29.
Return of Absalom to King David,
    2 Samuel 14:1-33.
Prodigal Son, Luke 15:11-32.
Paul was fearful of reunion with
    Corinthians, 2 Corinthians 12:20-21.
Coming reunion of all believers,
    1 Thessalonians 4:13-18.

REVEAL
See *Discovery, Display.*

REVELATION
God's message to Abram in deep sleep,
    Genesis 15:12-16.
Abraham's heavenly visitors, Genesis 18:1-
    10.
Reunion between Joseph and brothers,
    Genesis 45:1-15.
God's revelation of Himself to Moses,

Exodus 3:1-6, 14; 6:1-3.
Do not worship God in nature,
    Deuteronomy 4:15-20.
God speaks to man in different ways, Job
    33:14.
Skies proclaim glory of God, Psalm 19:1-6.
    (Note how role of skies has similarity to
    function of Scriptures, vv. 7-11.)
God-given ability to understand Scripture,
    Psalm 119:125.
New and hidden things, Isaiah 48:6.
Ezekiel's vision, Ezekiel 1:1.
God reveals Himself through judgment,
    Ezekiel 5:13; 6:7, 10, 13-14; 7:4, 9, 27.
Daniel received information in vision,
    Daniel 2:19.
Prophets informed of divine plans, Amos
    3:7.
Creator reveals His thoughts to man, Amos
    4:13.
Those who could not accept identity of
    Jesus, John 10:24-30.
Mistaking voice of God for thunder, John
    12:28-29.
God's message revealed in Creation,
    Romans 1:18-20.
God revealed Himself to those who did not
    seek Him, Romans 10:20.
Paul caught up into third heaven,
    2 Corinthians 12:1-4.
First the prophets, then the Son, Hebrews
    1:1-2.

REVELRY
Spiritual festival turns to wantonness,
    Exodus 32:5-6.
Celebration of harvest, Judges 9:27.
Evil mob in high spirits, Judges 16:23-25.
Celebrating plunder, 1 Samuel 30:16.
Entertainment with no thought of spiritual
    need, Isaiah 5:12.
Revelry of Tyre and Sidon, Isaiah 23:6-12.
Revelry brought to halt, Isaiah 24:8-9.
Noise of carefree crowd, Ezekiel 23:42.
See *Carousing, Hedonism, Orgy.*

REVENGE
First murder, Genesis 4:1-16.
Servant attitude to unfair employer,
    Genesis 16:1-10.
Revenge forbidden, Leviticus 19:18.
Sharing honors in military victory, Judges
    12:1-3.
Samson's method for burning Philistine

fields, Judges 15:4-5.
Massive act of revenge, Judges 20:1-48.
David's gratitude for not taking revenge, 1 Samuel 25:32-34.
Murder of Abner, 2 Samuel 3:22-34.
David's attitude toward murder of King Saul's son, 2 Samuel 4:1-12.
Absalom's murder of Amnon for disgracing his sister, 2 Samuel 13:23-29.
Strength of family ties in seeking vengeance, 2 Samuel 16:5-8.
Reward of evil, 1 Kings 2:5-6.
Destruction of royal family, 2 Kings 11:1.
Revenge against those who did not assist Israelites, Nehemiah 13:1-3.
Evil brings about its own retribution, Psalm 9:15.
Enemy falls into pit he himself designed, Psalm 57:6.
Stark picture of vengeance, Psalm 58:10. (See 68:23.)
Revenge against those who gossip, Psalm 64:8.
Let the Lord vindicate, Psalm 135:14; Ezekiel 25:12-17; 2 Thessalonians 1:6-7.
Counsel against taking revenge, Proverbs 24:29.
Traitor suffers what he imposed, Isaiah 33:1.
Time for divine vengeance, Jeremiah 51:6, 56.
Babylon must fall, Jeremiah 51:49.
Leave works of enemy in God's hands, Lamentations 3:55-66.
Vengeful spirit punished, Amos 1:11-12.
Punishment for those who mock God's people, Zephaniah 2:9-10.
Turn opposite cheek, go extra mile, Matthew 5:38-41.
Basics of Golden Rule, Luke 6:27-36.
Calling down fire from heaven, Luke 9:54-55.
Forgiving spirit of martyr, Acts 7:60.
Do not return evil for evil, Romans 12:17.
Showing love to those who cause grief, 2 Corinthians 2:5-11.
Kindness in place of vengeance, 1 Thessalonians 5:15.
Do not retaliate against those who do wrong, 1 Peter 2:23.
Do not repay evil with evil or insult with insult, 1 Peter 3:9.
Harm received for harm done, 2 Peter 2:13.
Those who crucified Jesus shall see Him coming in clouds, Revelation 1:7.
Martyrs call out for revenge, Revelation 6:9-11.
Judgment of God on evil, Revelation 16:5-7.
Golden Rule stated negatively, Revelation 18:6.
See *Retaliation, Sadistic.*

REVERENCE

Reverence for God, Genesis 17:3; Exodus 3:5.
Reverence for place of worship, Leviticus 19:30; 26:2.
Worship only at place designated by God, Deuteronomy 12:13-14.
Do not respect prophet who speaks in error, Deuteronomy 18:21-22.
Those who honor God and those who do not, 1 Samuel 2:30.
A god of stone shows reverence for ark of God, 1 Samuel 5:1-5.
Death from looking into ark of God, 1 Samuel 6:19-20.
Touching ark of God, 2 Samuel 6:6-11.
David's fear of God, 1 Chronicles 13:12.
Nehemiah's prayer, Nehemiah 1:4-11.
Recognizing God's majesty, Job 37:23-24.
Levi truly worshiped the Lord, Malachi 2:4-5.
Observance of Sabbath, Matthew 12:1-13.
Call no one on earth "Father," Matthew 23:8-10.
Use of head covering in worship, 1 Corinthians 11:3-10.
Those who take Scriptures to heart, Revelation 1:3.
Living creatures and elders, Revelation 4:8-11.
Drama of worship in heaven, Revelation 7:11-12.
See *Worship.*

REVISION

Book that cannot be revised, Revelation 22:18.

REVIVAL

Tear down the old, build new, Judges 6:25-26.
Disobedience of faithful, 1 Samuel 12:20.

Backslider returning to the Lord, 1 Samuel 15:24-25.

Prayer for revival, Psalm 85:1-7.

Streams on dry ground, Isaiah 44:3.

Self-examination in midst of testing, Lamentations 3:40-42.

Heart of flesh or heart of stone, Ezekiel 11:19.

Coming spiritual revival in Israel, Ezekiel 39:28-29.

Acknowledge the Lord, Hosea 6:3.

Break up unplowed ground and sow righteousness, Hosea 10:12.

Divine response to those who repent, Joel 2:12-13.

Fan into flame the gift of God, 2 Timothy 1:6.

Time to awaken, Revelation 3:2.

See *Repentance.*

REWARD

Reward for honoring parents, Exodus 20:12; Ephesians 6:1-3.

National obedience rewarded, Leviticus 25:18-19; Deuteronomy 4:40; 6:3.

Good weather and security, Leviticus 26:3-45; Deuteronomy 11:13-29.

Honesty and longevity, Deuteronomy 25:15.

Reward of accomplishment, Judges 8:22-23.

Ruth rewarded for faithfulness to mother-in-law, Ruth 2:7-12. (See 1:8-18.)

Mother's reward for giving son to the Lord, 1 Samuel 2:18-21.

Reward for act of kindness, 1 Samuel 30:11-18.

Haman plotted death of Mordecai but was commanded by king to be part of rewarding Mordecai, Esther 5:14; 6:10.

Reward for good mother, Proverbs 31:31.

Bread cast on waters, Ecclesiastes 11:1.

All is in God's hands, Isaiah 49:4.

Fate of good and evil, Isaiah 65:13-14.

God, who sees all, rewards good, Jeremiah 32:19.

Ebed-Melech rewarded for kindness to Jeremiah, Jeremiah 38:7-13; 39:15-18.

Daniel's refusal of bribes or rewards, Daniel 5:17.

Heavenly reward following resurrection, Daniel 12:13.

Receiving what one deserves, Zechariah 1:6.

Reward for self-denial, Matthew 16:24-27.

Good works rewarded, Matthew 25:34-46; Romans 2:5-11.

Leaving all to follow Jesus, Mark 10:28-31.

Persecution rewarded, Luke 6:22-23.

Runner and prize, 1 Corinthians 9:24-27.

Followers are joy and crown of those who proclaim, 1 Thessalonians 2:17-19.

Paul's prayer that friend would be rewarded, 2 Timothy 1:16-18.

Farmer receives first share of crop, 2 Timothy 2:6.

Sure reward for obedience and disobedience, 2 Timothy 2:11-13.

Crown of righteousness for faithful ministry, 2 Timothy 4:6-8.

Those who forfeited reward, Hebrews 3:16-19.

God does not forget good works, Hebrews 6:10.

Confidence will be rewarded, Hebrews 10:35.

Crown of life for those who persevere under trial, James 1:12.

Danger of losing one's full reward, 2 John 8.

Seated one day on the throne, Revelation 3:21.

Reward for what one has done, Revelation 22:12.

See *Recompense.*

RHEUMATISM

Filled with searing pain, Psalm 38:7.

RIDDANCE

Infamy to daughter of king, 2 Kings 9:30-37.

Egypt's dread of Israel, Psalm 105:38.

Quandary for ignorant man, Proverbs 30:2-4.

Pharisees' supposed concern for safety of Jesus, Luke 13:31.

RIDDLE

Abraham laughed at God, Genesis 17:17. (See 18:10-15.)

Riddles learned from dreams, Genesis 37:5-11; 40:9-22; 41:15-31; Daniel 2:29-45; 4:4-33.

Riddle of dead lion, Judges 14:8-17.

Two eagles and vine, Ezekiel 17:1-21.

RIDICULE
Job ridiculed by friends, Job 12:4.
Scorn for acts of humility, Psalm 69:10-11.
Youth ridiculed for faith, Psalm 129:1-2.
Do not fear reproach of men, Isaiah 51:7.
Lord was despised and rejected, Isaiah 53:3.
Moab an object of ridicule, Jeremiah 48:39.
Once-exalted city, Lamentations 2:15.
Jerusalem became laughingstock, Lamentations 3:14.
God's people ridiculed, Micah 2:4.
Those who dared to laugh at Jesus, Matthew 9:23-24; Luke 4:33-35; 8:50-53.
Crucifixion of Jesus, Mark 15:21-32.
Day of Pentecost, Acts 2:13.
See *Demean, Humiliation.*

RIGHT
Led the right way, Job 23:10; Psalm 119:35.
The right path, Psalm 16:11.
Following the Good Shepherd, Psalm 23:1-2; Luke 1:79.
Trust and commitment rewarded, Proverbs 3:5-6.
Tutored in the right way, Isaiah 2:3.
Level path, Isaiah 26:7.
Source of right guidance, Jeremiah 42:3.
The narrow way, Matthew 7:13-14.

RIGHTEOUSNESS
Made righteous by God's presence, Exodus 33:16.
Some good in Judah, 2 Chronicles 12:12.
Man who truly walked with God, Job 1:1.
Bildad's correct assessment, Job 8:5-6.
Meaning of personal righteousness to God, Job 34:1-8; Psalm 18:20-21.
Definition of righteous man, Psalm 1:1-3.
Marks of righteous person, Psalm 15:1-5; Proverbs 13:5.
David could see himself blameless before the Lord, Psalm 26:1, 11.
Purity of heart, gift from God, Psalm 51:10.
Right prevails, Psalm 58:11.
Righteous person and good, full life, Psalm 112:1-10.
God blesses those who walk according to Scripture, Psalm 119:1-16.
Growth in perception, Proverbs 4:18.
Man's ways may seem right, Proverbs 21:2.
National righteousness, Jeremiah 31:12-34.
God's total forgiveness, Jeremiah 50:20.
Neither good nor evil transmitted from father to son, Ezekiel 18:3-20.
Absolute holiness of God, Daniel 9:14.
Beatitudes, Matthew 5:3-16.
Test of righteousness in time of wickedness, Matthew 24:12-13.
Righteousness comes from God by faith, Romans 1:17.
Hate evil, cling to good, Romans 12:9.
Seeking righteousness by human effort, Galatians 3:3.
Be not judged by observance of legalism, Colossians 2:16.
Lifestyle of those risen with Christ, Colossians 3:1-17.
The Law makes nothing perfect, Hebrews 7:18-19.
See *Consecration, Discipleship, Discipline.*

RIGHTS
Right of first son, Deuteronomy 21:15-17.
Protection for Roman citizen, Acts 22:25-29.

RIGHT WING
See *Conservative.*

RING
Signet ring denoting government position, Genesis 41:42; Esther 3:10.
Rings given for use in temple, Exodus 35:22.
Signet ring used for placing seal on document, Esther 8:8.
Item of finery, Isaiah 3:18-23.
Symbol of relationship, Luke 15:22.
See *Jewelry.*

RITUAL
Circumcision at advanced age, Genesis 17:10-27.
Envious brothers, Genesis 37:4.
Prayer for protection, Numbers 10:35.
Misuse of sacrifice, 1 Samuel 2:12-17.
Religious works involved in idolatry, Isaiah 46:1.
Barrier of Law broken in Christ, Ephesians 2:14-16; Colossians 2:13-15; Hebrews 7:18; 8:13; 10:1.
See *Formality, Liturgy.*

RIVAL
Jealous wife, 1 Samuel 1:2-7.

Frustrated King Saul, 1 Samuel 18:8.
Conflict between David and Saul,
1 Samuel 26:1-25.
A brother spared, 1 Kings 1:49-53.
At peace with one's enemies, Proverbs
16:7.
Bickering among laborers, Matthew 20:12.
Evaluating military logistics, Luke 14:31-
32.
Prodigal and his brother, Luke 15:25-32.
See *Competition, Jealousy.*

RIVER
Bible rivers, Genesis 2:11-14; Exodus 1:22;
Deuteronomy 2:36; Judges 5:21;
2 Kings 5:12; 17:6; Ezekiel 1:1; Daniel
8:16.
Substitute for bridge to cross Jordan,
2 Kings 2:13-14.
Egypt's claim of possessing the Nile,
Ezekiel 29:3-5.
River of life, Revelation 22:1-2.

ROAD
Keeping to main road through country,
Deuteronomy 2:27.
Military route, Joshua 10:9-11; Judges
20:31.
Only one right road to take, Proverbs
16:17.
Highway for Israel's remnant, Isaiah 11:16.
Way of holiness, Isaiah 35:8-10.
Prepared way for the Lord, Isaiah 40:3-4.
(See Matt. 3:1-3.)
Broad and narrow roads, Matthew 7:13-14.
Adventure on the Jericho road, Luke
10:30-37.
See *Highway, Journey, Transportation,
Travel.*

ROBBERY
Responsibility for killing thief, Exodus
22:2-3.
Forbidden by law, Leviticus 19:13; Isaiah
61:8.
Need for two or three witnesses,
Deuteronomy 19:15.
Lurking in ambush, Judges 9:25.
Protection against enemies of the road,
Ezra 8:21-23.
Breaking and entering, Job 24:16.
Larceny as career, Proverbs 1:11-16.
Babylon surveyed Hezekiah's treasures for
subsequent thievery, Isaiah 39:1-6.

Robbers' den, Jeremiah 7:11.
Death penalty, Ezekiel 18:10-13.
Robbery and extortion, Ezekiel 22:29.
Robber bands, Hosea 6:9; 7:1.
High-level thievery of tax collectors and
soldiers, Luke 3:12-14.
Danger on Jericho road, Luke 10:25-37.
See *Stealing, Thieves.*

ROBE
Robe of righteousness, 2 Chronicles 6:41;
Isaiah 61:10; Revelation 6:11; 7:9-13.
Purple robe, Esther 8:15; Daniel 5:7; Luke
16:19.
Threads of gold, Psalm 45:13.
Priests' garments considered holy, Ezekiel
42:14; 44:19.
Herod's royal robes, Acts 12:21.
See *Wardrobe.*

ROCK
Rock struck by Moses, Deuteronomy 8:15;
Psalm 78:18-22.
The Lord our Rock, Deuteronomy 32:4;
2 Samuel 22:32, 47; 23:3; Psalms 18:2;
31:2; Isaiah 17:10.
Source of oil, Deuteronomy 32:13; Job
29:6.
Sure footing, Psalm 40:2.
God's resourceful followers, Isaiah 32:2.
Christ the Living Stone, believers lesser
stones, 1 Peter 2:4-5.

ROCK AND ROLL
End to noisy songs, Ezekiel 26:13.

ROMAN CATHOLICS
Roman Catholic view of celibacy
advocated by Jesus, Matthew 19:12.
Relationship of Jesus to His mother, Mark
3:31-35.
Celibacy taught by Apostle Paul,
1 Corinthians 7:8, 27.

ROMANCE
Abraham's search for bride for Isaac,
Genesis 24:1-58; 25:19-20.
Strange relationship toward captive
women, Deuteronomy 21:10-14.
Love seemingly mistaken as infatuation,
1 Samuel 18:20-29.
David demanded that Michal be taken
from her husband, 2 Samuel 3:12-
16.

A man and a maid, Proverbs 30:18-19.
Stealing the heart, Songs of Songs 4:9.
See *Courtship.*

ROOM
See *Accommodations, Hospitality.*

ROOTS
See *Ancestors, Background, Family,
Heritage.*

ROPE
Pegs and ropes for tabernacle, Exodus
35:18; 39:40.
Rope of deliverance in Jericho, Joshua
2:15.
Samson bound with inadequate new ropes,
Judges 15:13-14.

ROTATION
Seventh-year rest for fields, Exodus 23:10-
11.

ROTTEN
See *Decay, Putrid, Stench.*

ROUNDELAY
History repeats itself, Ecclesiastes 3:15.

ROYALTY
Choosing king from among trees, Judges
9:7-15.
King and queen brought to judgment,
Jeremiah 13:18.
King in respectable exile, Jeremiah 52:31-
34.
Pilate's question to Jesus, Mark 15:2.
King of the Jews, John 19:1-16.

RUBBISH
Silver thrown into streets, Ezekiel 7:19.
Earth's content compared to God's best,
Philippians 3:7-10.

RUDENESS
Staring at those God uses, Acts 3:12.

See *Discourtesy.*

RULES
Regulation of music used in worship,
1 Chronicles 6:31-32.
Carrying rules too far, Mark 2:23-27.
Need for proper credentials, Acts 15:22-31.
Playing according to rules, 2 Timothy 2:5.
Regulations for worship, Hebrews 9:1.
See *Regulations.*

RUMOR
Fear of rumor to enemy, Numbers 14:13-
16.
Evil motivations discerned, Nehemiah
6:10-13.
Disbelieving threat of murder, Jeremiah
40:13-16; 41:1-2.
First one rumor, then another, Jeremiah
51:46.
See *Gossip.*

RUNNING
Renewal of strength, Isaiah 40:30-31.
Running long race, Jeremiah 12:5.
See *Athletics.*

RURAL
Contrast between Abram and Lot, Genesis
13:12.
Town and country, Deuteronomy 28:3.

RUSE
Circumstantial evidence against Joseph,
Genesis 39:6-20.
Deceitful plan to destroy Paul, Acts 23:12-
22.

RUSH
Paul's hurry to reach Jerusalem, Acts
20:16.

RUST
Oil as protection against rust, Isaiah 21:5.
Gold and silver corroded, James 5:3.
See *Corrosion.*

S

SACRAMENT
Sacrifice of a son, 2 Kings 16:3.
Religious works involved in idolatry, Isaiah 46:1.
The Lord's Supper, Matthew 26:17-30; Mark 14:12-26; 1 Corinthians 11:17-30.
Those circumcised who do not keep the Law, Romans 2:25-27.
Circumcision did not bring salvation, Romans 4:1-13.
Personal righteousness not obtained through observing sacraments, Hebrews 9:8-10.
Physical act in worship cannot bring spiritual result, Hebrews 10:1-4.

SACRED
Sacred location for altar, Deuteronomy 12:5-6.
Sacred courtroom, Deuteronomy 17:8.
Grave of Moses, Deuteronomy 34:6.
Purpose of Solomon's temple, 2 Chronicles 2:5-6.
Articles from temple in Jerusalem put into pagan temple, Daniel 1:1-2.
Truly sacred, Matthew 23:16-17.
Sacred mountain that could not be touched, Hebrews 12:18-21.

SACRIFICE
Aroma of good sacrifice, Genesis 8:20-21. (See Lev. 23:18; 2 Cor. 2:15; Eph. 5:1-2.)
Test of father's love to God and his son, Genesis 22:1-14.
Infanticide forbidden, Leviticus 18:21; Deuteronomy 12:31.
Fate of favorite daughter, an only child, Judges 11:29-39.
David refused to drink water which his men had risked their lives to get,

2 Samuel 23:15-17.
Cheap stewardship refused, 2 Samuel 24:21-24.
Pagan practice of infanticide, 2 Kings 3:26-27; 16:1-3; 17:17; 2 Chronicles 28:3; Isaiah 57:5; Jeremiah 19:5; Ezekiel 16:20; 23:37.
Finest youth killed in battle, Jeremiah 48:15.
Death of Ezekiel's wife a lesson for wicked Israel, Ezekiel 24:15-24.
Persistent sacrifices offered in temple, Ezekiel 43:18-27.
Abundant sacrifices, Micah 6:7.
Leaving all to follow Jesus, Mark 10:28-31; Luke 18:28-30.
Mixing blood of man with sacrificial blood, Luke 13:1.
Death of kernel of wheat, John 12:24-26.
Willingness of Jesus to be sacrificed, John 18:1-11.
Giving up that which has value, Acts 19:19.
Poured out like an offering, 2 Timothy 4:6.
Power and meaning of blood of Christ, Hebrews 9:8-15.
Willing to lay down one's life, 1 John 3:16.

SACRILEGE
Taunting Pharaoh, Exodus 5:2.
Tempting the Lord, Exodus 17:7.
Unauthorized fire, Leviticus 10:1.
Punishment of expulsion, Leviticus 19:8.
Gathering wood on Sabbath, Numbers 15:32-36.
Mixing immorality with worship, Numbers 25:1-2.
Making idol to please the Lord, Judges 17:3.
Illicit relationship between those in spiritual service, 1 Samuel 2:22.
Using sacred offering for personal gain,

1 Samuel 2:29.
Desecration of ark of God, 1 Samuel 5:1-2.
Death from looking into ark of God, 1 Samuel 6:19-20.
Touching ark of God, 2 Samuel 6:6-11.
Breaking and entering temple, 2 Chronicles 24:7.
Insulting the Lord, 2 Chronicles 32:17.
Mocking God's messengers, 2 Chronicles 36:16.
Sin of challenging God, Isaiah 5:18-19.
God spoken of as if He were one of many gods, Isaiah 37:10. (See vv. 6, 23.)
Pagan temple profaned by murder, Isaiah 37:38.
Wrong kind of offering, Isaiah 66:3.
Disrespect for sanctuary, Ezekiel 25:1-4.
Misuse of temple furnishings, Daniel 5:2.
Laughing at Jesus, Matthew 9:23-24; Luke 4:33-35; 8:50-53.
Attributing work of God to demons, Matthew 9:34.
Using temple for business purposes, Matthew 21:12-13; Mark 11:15-17.
Empty sincerity of Pharisees, Mark 12:15-17.
Scoffing at Jesus on cross, Mark 15:29-32.
Mixing human blood with sacrifices, Luke 13:1.
Destroying temple, 1 Corinthians 3:17.
Slandering angels, 2 Peter 2:10-11.
See *Irreligious, Irreverence.*

SADISTIC

Cutting off thumbs and big toes, Judges 1:7.
Violent murder, Judges 4:21; Judges 5:24-27.
Dismembered concubine, Judges 19:27-30.
Gouging out eye, 1 Samuel 11:1-2.
Destroying entire population, 1 Samuel 15:3.
King Saul's vulgar request for dowry, 1 Samuel 18:25.
Sadistic amusement, 2 Samuel 2:12-16.
Enjoying misfortune of others, Lamentations 2:15.
Plundering with glee, Ezekiel 36:5.
See *Torture.*

SADNESS

See *Mourning, Regret, Sorrow.*

SAFETY

No safe place to be found, Genesis 8:8-9. (See v. 12.)
Built-in safety devices, Deuteronomy 22:8.
Safety for Ruth in fields of Boaz, Ruth 2:4-22.
Making sure of king's safety, 2 Samuel 19:24.
Enemies lurk along roads and fields, Jeremiah 6:25.
Wise dove, Jeremiah 48:28.
Daniel in lions' den, Daniel 6:13-24.
Security in lions' habitat, Nahum 2:11.
Children playing in streets, Zechariah 8:5.
Safety of darkness, Acts 17:10.
Paul's experience in storm and shipwreck, Acts 27:13-44.
Shielded by God's power, 1 Peter 1:5.
See *Protection, Security, Shelter.*

SAGACITY

Wisdom of Gamaliel, Acts 5:34-39.
Eyes of heart, Ephesians 1:18-19.
See *Discernment, Intelligence, Wisdom.*

SALARY

Priests to eat from food offerings, Numbers 18:11-13.
Earnings from prostitution unacceptable as gift to God, Deuteronomy 23:18. (Compare Ezek. 16:32-34.)
Priests and singers required to work to support themselves, Nehemiah 13:10-11.
Income for 12 apostles, Matthew 10:9-10.
Parable of Workers in Vineyard, Matthew 20:1-16.
Content with earnings, Luke 3:14.
Sending out of Twelve to minister, Luke 9:1-6.
Spiritual wages, John 4:36.
Paul made tents during week, ministered on Sabbath, Acts 18:1-5; 20:33-35; 1 Thessalonians 2:9; 2 Thessalonians 3:6-10.
Right of apostle to receive material support, 1 Corinthians 9:6-14.
Concern for pastor, Philippians 4:10-19.
Payment for those in Christian work, 1 Timothy 5:17-18.
Dignity of labor, Titus 3:14.
Withholding payment from those who labor, James 5:4.
Danger of greed in ministry, 1 Peter 5:2-3.

Grain for a day's wages, Revelation 6:6.
See *Honorarium, Wages.*

SALESMEN
Sale of burial plot, Genesis 23:12-16.
Young brother for sale, Genesis 37:19-36.
Solomon the salesman and purchaser,
 1 Kings 10:14-15, 28; 2 Chronicles
 9:13-14.
Varied merchandise for sale, Nehemiah
 13:20.
Selling to sailors, Isaiah 23:2.
Selling by barter system, Ezekiel 27:12-25.
Dishonest sales technique, Hosea 12:7.
Lady cloth salesperson, Acts 16:13-15.

SALT
Lot's wife, Genesis 19:26.
Salt as condiment, Leviticus 2:13; Job 6:6.
Covenant of salt, Numbers 18:19.
Land made sterile, Judges 9:42-45.
Valley of Salt, 2 Samuel 8:13.
Water softener and conditioning, 2 Kings
 2:19-22.
Wasteland forever, Zephaniah 2:9.
Believers called salt of earth, Matthew 5:13;
 Mark 9:50.

SALUTATION
Greeting to angels, Genesis 19:1-2.
Invoking God's blessing, Genesis 43:29;
 Ruth 2:4.
Wishing good health and long life,
 1 Samuel 25:6.
Greeting with, "Peace," Luke 10:5; John
 20:21.
See *Greeting.*

SALVATION
Strong tower in besieged city, Judges 9:51.
Forgiving, gracious, and compassionate
 God, Nehemiah 9:17.
Loss of salvation, Psalm 69:28.
God does not deal with us according to
 what we deserve, Psalm 103:9-10.
Walking in the Way, Isaiah 35:8.
Come and buy without money, Isaiah 55:1.
Seek the Lord while He may be found,
 Isaiah 55:6-7.
Sin causes God not to hear sinner's cry,
 Isaiah 59:1-3.
Need for repentance, Isaiah 64:5.
God revealed Himself to those who did not
 ask for Him, Isaiah 65:1.

The God who saves and heals, Jeremiah
 17:14.
Those found written in the book, Daniel
 12:1.
No God but the Lord, Hosea 13:4.
All who call on the Lord will be saved, Joel
 2:32.
Burning stick snatched from fire,
 Zechariah 3:2.
Healing sun of righteousness, Malachi 4:2.
Jesus chose the only way, Matthew 26:50-
 54.
Those who need the Great Physician, Mark
 2:17.
Rich young man who kept the Law, Mark
 10:17-27.
Those who will receive and believe, John
 1:12.
Being born again, John 3:1-8.
Message of salvation, John 5:24.
Drawn to Christ by the Heavenly Father,
 John 6:44.
Entering the right gate, John 10:9.
Turning to the light before darkness
 comes, John 12:35-36.
Jesus came to save the world, not judge it,
 John 12:47.
Salvation in no other name but Christ, Acts
 4:12.
Salvation through faith apart from
 legalism, Acts 15:1-11; Romans 3:22-24.
Salvation a gift, not earned, Romans 4:4-8.
All-encompassing goodness of God,
 Romans 4:16.
Justification by faith alone, Romans 5:1-2.
God's love demonstrated toward sinners,
 Romans 5:8.
Death through Adam, life in Christ,
 Romans 5:12-19.
The gift of God, Romans 6:23.
Deliverance from sin through Christ alone,
 Romans 7:24-25.
No condemnation in Christ, Romans 8:1-2.
Trying to establish one's own
 righteousness, Romans 10:3.
Role of witness in salvation, Romans 10:9-
 10.
Salvation for individual who calls on the
 Lord, Romans 10:13.
Message of salvation came through
 Abraham, Galatians 3:6-9.
Mercy and grace of God, Ephesians 2:1-10.
Rescued from dominion of darkness,
 Colossians 1:13-14.

Christ Jesus came to save sinners,
1 Timothy 1:15.
Mediator between God and men,
1 Timothy 2:5.
Unmerited grace of God, Titus 3:4-8.
Message to be carefully heeded, Hebrews
2:1-3.
True rest for people of God, Hebrews 4:9-
11.
Total salvation for those who trust the
Lord, Hebrews 7:25.
Power and meaning of blood of Christ,
Hebrews 9:8-15.
First covenant put into effect with blood,
Hebrews 9:18-22.
Supreme sacrifice, Hebrews 9:24-28;
1 John 4:9-10.
A perfect Saviour offers perfect salvation,
Hebrews 10:11-14.
Not redeemed with silver and gold but with
the blood of Christ, 1 Peter 1:18-19.
Born again of imperishable seed, 1 Peter
1:23.
Not an easy way, 1 Peter 4:17-18.
Fact of sin and provision for cleansing,
1 John 1:8-10.
Gift of eternal life, 1 John 5:11-12.
Opening door to Him who knocks,
Revelation 3:20.
See *Redemption.*

SAMPLE
Moses saw but did not experience,
Numbers 27:12-14.
Fruit of the land, Deuteronomy 1:24-25.
Tasting that the Lord is good, 1 Peter 2:3.
See *Taste.*

SANCTIFICATION
Setting aside day for rest, Genesis 2:2-3.
Firstborn, Exodus 13:2.
Those truly holy, Numbers 16:3-7.
Made pure through testing, Job 23:10.
Covenant to avoid lust, Job 31:1.
Sanctified before birth, Jeremiah 1:5.
Sanctifying work of Holy Spirit and impact
of Scripture, John 17:17;
2 Thessalonians 2:13.
Scriptural basics of sanctification, Romans
6:13; 8:1-2; 12:1-2; 1 Corinthians 6:19-
20; Galatians 5:16-18; Ephesians 4:17-
24; 5:17; Philippians 3:7-11; Colossians
3:1-3.
See *Consecration.*

SANCTIMONIOUS
Claiming perfection, Job 33:9.
Seeming piety, Isaiah 58:2.
Holier-than-thou, Isaiah 65:5.
Ego displayed by teachers of the Law,
Matthew 6:5; Mark 12:38-40; Luke
18:11.
Pharisees' resentment of Jesus, Luke 15:1-
7.
Wretched and blind, Revelation 3:17.
See *Hypocrisy.*

SANCTUARY
Worship among trees, Genesis 13:18. (See
14:13; 18:1.)
Committing all of sanctuary to the Lord,
Numbers 7:1.
Frightened of place of worship, Numbers
17:12-13.
Place chosen by God, Deuteronomy 12:11.
King Solomon dedicated temple, 1 Kings
8:22-53.
Repairing the temple, 2 Kings 12:4-5.
Murder in pagan temple, 2 Kings 19:37.
Setting fire to temple, 2 Kings 25:8-9.
Temple cannot truly be house of God,
2 Chronicles 2:6.
Love for house of God, Psalm 26:8.
Meditation in temple, Psalm 48:9.
Beauty of sanctuary and longing for
worship, Psalm 84:1-2.
Filled with glory of the Lord, Ezekiel 10:4.
God's glory seen but not God Himself,
Ezekiel 43:1-5.
Gate closed during working days, Ezekiel
46:1.
The Lord is in His holy temple, Habakkuk
2:20.
People lived in fine houses while temple
stood in ruins, Haggai 1:1-4.
Bring tithes to storehouse, Malachi 3:10.
Money changers driven out of temple,
Matthew 21:12-13; Mark 11:15-17.
Truly sacred, Matthew 23:16-17.
Lack of permanence in temple, Mark 13:1-
2.
Ultimate "holy of holies," 1 Corinthians
3:16.
Heavenly sanctuary entered by Christ,
Hebrews 9:24.
Measure temple, count worshipers,
Revelation 11:1.
Temple court defiled, Revelation 11:2.
Name of temple in heaven, Revelation

15:5.
Filled with the glory of God, Revelation
15:8.
No need for temple of worship, Revelation
21:22.

SANITATION
Provision of pure food, Exodus 16:19-24.
Skin infection, Leviticus 13:6.
Care of venereal disease, Leviticus 15:2-7.
Procedure with those suffering disease,
Numbers 5:1-3.
Care in touching dead body, Numbers
19:14-21.
Disposal of excrement, Deuteronomy
23:12-13.
Purifying bad water, 2 Kings 2:19-22.
Purifying rooms of temple, Nehemiah 13:9.
Bodies lying unburied, Jeremiah 9:22.
Place of disease and death, Jeremiah 16:1-
9.
Improper care of newborn, Ezekiel 16:4-5.
Washing hands before eating, Matthew
15:1-9.
See *Health.*

SANITY
The rash understand, Isaiah 32:4.
Restored to sanity, Daniel 4:29-37; Mark
5:2-20.

SARCASM
Stimulant to action, Joshua 17:14-18.
Parable of trees, Judges 9:7-15.
Challenging pagan gods, Judges 10:14.
Neglected duty, 1 Samuel 26:15.
Elijah taunted prophets of Baal, 1 Kings
18:27.
Taunting pride, 1 Kings 20:10-11.
Botanical communication, 2 Kings 14:9.
Mocking builders of wall, Nehemiah 4:1-3.
Scarecrow in melon patch, Jeremiah 10:5.
Speaking truth in sarcasm, Matthew 27:28-
29; Luke 23:35-39; John 19:19.
Paul chided "super apostle,"
2 Corinthians 11:5.
See *Irony.*

SATAN
Brief history of fall from heaven, Isaiah
14:12-15.
Satan's fall likened to king of Tyre, Ezekiel
28:11-19.
Satan's role as accuser, Zechariah 3:1-2.

Satan confronted with Scripture, Matthew
4:1-11; Luke 4:1-13.
Pharisees accused Jesus of satanic power,
Matthew 9:32-34.
Satan as teacher, 1 Timothy 1:18-20.
Battleground in which Satan attacks,
1 John 2:15-17.
Work of the devil, 1 John 3:7-8.
Only authority over evil, Jude 9.
Star fallen from sky, Revelation 9:1-2.
Birth of Christ reviewed, Revelation 12:1-5.
Conquered and yet conqueror, Revelation
12:7-10.
Angel capable of overpowering and
binding Satan, Revelation 20:1-3.
See *Demons, Evil.*

SATIRE
Young Joseph called a dreamer by his
brothers, Genesis 37:19.
Satirical parable, Judges 9:8-15.
Divine satire against idolatrous Egyptians,
Judges 10:11-14.
Goliath's disdain of David, 1 Samuel
17:41-44.
Acrid speech from wife to husband,
2 Samuel 6:20. (Note v. 16.)
Elijah chided prophets of Baal, 1 Kings
18:27-28.
Taunts of Job's three "friends," Job 4:1-6;
8:2; 11:1-12; 15:1-3; 22:1-4.
Pessimistic assessment of life, Ecclesiastes
2:1-11.
Scoffing at futility of military might be
compared to divine intervention, Isaiah
8:9-10.
The Lord's use of literary device
concerning freedom, Jeremiah 34:17.
Medicine has no value for one who will not
be healed, Jeremiah 46:11.
Ironical message from the Lord
concerning idols, Ezekiel 20:39-42.
Folly of rebellious people, Hosea 8:7-9.
Satire used by Jesus, Matthew 23:1-33.
Jesus chided Nicodemus, John 3:10.

SATISFACTION
Pleased populace, 2 Samuel 3:36.
Desires satisfied and strength renewed,
Psalm 103:5.
Security in the Lord, Psalm 127:1-2.
What the righteous desire, Proverbs 10:24.
Voicing simple need, Proverbs 30:7-8.
Reward for obedience, Isaiah 48:17-18.

Joy of good reputation, 3 John 3-4.

SATURATION
Potential of worldwide turning to the Lord, Mark 16:15.
Widespread acceptance in Samaria, Acts 8:14.
All Jews and Greeks heard message, Acts 19:10.

SAVAGE
People like animals in times of distress, Deuteronomy 28:53-57.
Gross recreation, Judges 19:22-26.
Women's hair and lions' teeth, Revelation 9:8.

SAVINGS
Careful frugality, Proverbs 13:11.
Treasures on earth or in heaven, Matthew 6:19-21.

SCANDAL
Joseph falsely accused, Genesis 39:11-20.
Giving false testimony, Deuteronomy 19:16-21.
Hatred without reason, Psalm 69:4.
Lying lips and deceitful tongues, Psalm 120:2.
Choice morsels to those who wish to hear, Proverbs 26:22.
Do not fear reproach of men, Isaiah 51:7.
Impeccable witness of Daniel, Daniel 6:3-5.
Rejoice when people speak falsely of you, Matthew 5:11-12.

SCAPEGOAT
Function of Old Testament scapegoat, Leviticus 16:8-22.

SCAVENGER
The eagle, Job 39:27-30.
Food for jackals, Psalm 63:10.
Flesh of people becomes food for birds, Jeremiah 7:33.
Feast for animals after battle, Ezekiel 39:14-20.
See *Gleaners.*

SCHEDULE
Offerings given three times annually, Deuteronomy 16:16-17.
Solomon's schedule for sacrifices, 1 Kings 9:25.
Working from morning to night, Nehemiah 4:21.
Time for everything, Ecclesiastes 3:1-8.
The Lord plans far in advance, Isaiah 25:1.
God's perfect timing, Isaiah 49:8.
Noon schedule delayed until night, Jeremiah 6:4-5.
Temple activity concluded, Mark 11:11.
Itinerary of Jesus, Luke 4:42-44.
Paul asked to reschedule Ephesus, Acts 18:19-21.
Example of Paul's ministry and travel schedule, Acts 20:1-6. (See also vv. 13-16 and 21:1-8.)
God always on schedule, Romans 5:6.
Satan's awareness of shortage of time, Revelation 12:12.

SCHEME
Cain's scheme for killing Abel, Genesis 4:8.
Counselors hired to frustrate plans for building temple, Ezra 4:5.
Sanballat's scheme to hinder Nehemiah, Nehemiah 6:1-9.
Strategy of Judas to betray Jesus, Mark 14:10-11, 43-46.
See *Deceit.*

SCHISM
Entire congregation in rebellion, Numbers 14:1-4.
Deliberately writing falsehoods concerning the Law, Jeremiah 8:8.
Argument over washing, John 3:25.
Pagans certain of erroneous belief, Acts 19:35-36.
Accusing Paul of mishandling truth, Acts 21:19-24.
Division among believers, 1 Corinthians 1:12. (See 3:1-9.)
Quarreling about words, 2 Timothy 2:14.
Those who preach and teach for dishonest gain, Titus 1:10-16.
See *Disruption.*

SCHOLARSHIP
Daniel and friends passed royal exam, Daniel 1:18-20.
Folly of intellectual pride, 1 Corinthians 3:18-20.

SCHOOL
Study at home, Deuteronomy 4:9-10; 6:7-9;

11:19-21; Psalm 78:5-6.
Specialized Bible training, Deuteronomy 31:10-13.
Small classroom, 2 Kings 6:1.
Babylonian training, Daniel 1:3-21.
Tutor and teacher, Acts 22:3.
See *Education, Teaching.*

SCOFF

Avoid criticizing those whom the Lord has not denounced, Numbers 23:8.
Scoffing at pagans whose prayers went unanswered, 1 Kings 18:22-38.
Mocking God's messengers, 2 Chronicles 36:16.
Daring to evaluate divinity, Job 21:14-15.
Scorn for acts of humility, Psalm 69:10-11.
Questioning divine wisdom, Psalm 73:6-11.
Put out the scornful, Proverbs 22:10.
Daring to scoff at the name of the Lord, Isaiah 36:18-21. (See 37:6.)
Those who mock, Isaiah 57:3-4; Zephaniah 2:10.
God scoffs at idols, likens them to scarecrows, Jeremiah 10:5.
Disrespect for sanctuary, Ezekiel 25:1-4.
Scoffing at alleged unfairness, Ezekiel 33:20.
Mocking Jesus, Mark 15:16-20.
Demon who laughed at Jesus, Luke 4:33-35.
Demeaning Jesus, Luke 22:63-65.
Scoffing incited by envy, Acts 13:45.
Some rejected the message, others asked to hear more, Acts 17:32.
Scoffers in last days, 2 Peter 3:3-4.
See *Criticism, Demean, Rudeness, Scorn.*

SCOLDING

Levites had gone too far, Numbers 16:7.
Wounds of a friend, Proverbs 27:6.
Jesus scolded an evil spirit, Mark 1:23-26.
See *Criticism.*

SCOPE

Small and insignificant greatness, Proverbs 30:24-28.
Given eternal viewpoint, Jeremiah 33:3.

SCORCHED EARTH

Towns destroyed by Israelite army, Numbers 31:10.
Devastated Jericho, Joshua 6:20-21.

Laying land completely waste, 2 Kings 3:19.
Land like Garden of Eden becomes desert waste, Joel 2:3.
See *War.*

SCORN

Veteran soldier underrated abilities of boy, 1 Samuel 17:42-43.
Contempt for unfortunate, Job 12:5.
Jehoiakim burned scroll dictated by Jeremiah, Jeremiah 36:1-26.
Object of ridicule, Jeremiah 48:39.
Object of horror, Jeremiah 49:17.
Ridicule of once-exalted city, Lamentations 2:15.
Supreme example of rejection, Matthew 27:46.
Those who laughed at Jesus, Mark 5:39-40.
Message of the Cross foolishness to the lost, 1 Corinthians 1:18.
See *Scoff.*

SCRIPTURE

Scripture contains both blessings and curses, Joshua 8:34.
Complete reading of the Law, Joshua 8:35.
Joshua gave instructions God had initially given him, Joshua 23:6. (See 1:8.)
Joshua's blessing and warning as his death approached, Joshua 23:14-16.
Small emphasis given to Word of the Lord, 1 Samuel 3:1.
God reveals Himself through His word, 1 Samuel 3:21.
Words of God are trustworthy, 2 Samuel 7:28; Nehemiah 9:8; Psalm 12:6.
The Lord our lamp, 2 Samuel 22:29.
Not one word of God's promise can fail, 1 Kings 8:56.
Reading of Scripture long neglected, 2 Kings 22:10-20.
The Lord does what He promises, 2 Chronicles 6:4, 14-15.
No God, no priest, no Law in Israel, 2 Chronicles 15:3.
Book of the Law lost in temple, 2 Chronicles 34:14-15.
Day after day devoted to reading Scriptures, Nehemiah 8:17-18.
Bread from heaven, Nehemiah 9:15.
Delight in Law of the Lord, Psalm 1:2.
Obeying teachings of God's Word, Psalm 18:22.

Flawless Word of God, Psalms 18:30; 19:7-8; Proverbs 30:5.

Seeing light in God's light, Psalm 36:9.

Undergirding of God's Word gives credence to speech of righteous, Psalm 37:30-31.

Knowledge of God's Word leads to desire for His will, Psalm 40:8.

Giving praise to God's Word, Psalm 56:10.

God's covenant never changes, Psalms 105:8-9; 111:5.

Delight in the Lord's commands, Psalm 112:1.

God blesses those who walk according to guidance of Scripture, Psalm 119:1-16.

Prayer for perception in study of Scripture, Psalm 119:18.

Seeking, considering, hastening to obey Scripture, Psalm 119:57-64.

Value of affliction to turn us to Scripture, Psalm 119:71.

Eternal Word of the Lord, Psalm 119:89.

God-given ability to understand, Psalm 119:125.

Trusting confidently in God's promises, Psalms 130:5-6; 145:13.

King Hezekiah's dependence on God's promises, Isaiah 37:1-38.

Word of God stands forever, Isaiah 40:8.

God's Word will not return empty, Isaiah 55:10-11.

Delight in God's Word, Jeremiah 15:16.

Challenging fulfillment of Scripture, Jeremiah 17:15.

Jeremiah blamed the Lord for persecution suffered by proclaiming His Word, Jeremiah 20:7-8.

Substituting dreams for the Word of God, Jeremiah 23:25-32.

Command to write, Jeremiah 30:2.

Jeremiah imprisoned for faithfulness to God's Word, Jeremiah 37:1-21.

Promise of judgment fulfilled, Lamentations 2:17.

Scroll eaten by Ezekiel was as sweet as honey, Ezekiel 3:1-3.

Certainty of God's Word, Ezekiel 12:26-28; Habakkuk 2:3.

Famine for the words of the Lord, Amos 8:11-12.

Satan's misuse of Scripture and response of Jesus, Matthew 4:1-11; Luke 4:1-13.

All truth will be fulfilled, Matthew 5:17-18.

Parable of Sower, Matthew 13:1-23; Luke 8:4-15.

Believe the Good News, Mark 1:14-15.

Wealth and worry numb understanding of Scripture, Mark 4:19.

Divine revelation does not require external evidence, Mark 8:11-12.

Many writers attempted to record New Testament events, Luke 1:1-4.

Living Word pierces heart, Luke 2:34-35.

Taking Jesus at His word, John 4:50.

Message of salvation, John 5:24.

Those who read Bible in vain, John 5:39-40.

Living Scripture, John 6:63.

Sanctifying truth, John 17:17.

Conversion of Ethiopian eunuch, Acts 8:26-39.

Use of Scripture in bold witness, Acts 13:13-52.

Basis for persuasion and teaching, Acts 17:2-4.

More noble and eager to examine Scriptures, Acts 17:11.

Thorough knowledge of Scriptures, Acts 18:24-26.

Scriptures as authority concerning Jesus, Acts 18:28.

Those who do not have scriptural guidance, Romans 2:14-15.

God's Word does not fail, Romans 9:6-7.

Faith comes through the Word of Christ, Romans 10:17.

Holy Spirit's guidance in Bible study, 1 Corinthians 2:6-16.

Milk and solid food, 1 Corinthians 3:1-2; Hebrews 5:11-14. (See also 6:1-3.)

Bread of truth, 1 Corinthians 5:8.

Paul's recognition of writings as authentic Scripture, 1 Corinthians 14:37-38.

Received by revelation, Galatians 1:12.

Helmet and sword, Ephesians 6:17.

Power of Gospel in whatever manner proclaimed, Philippians 1:15-18.

Richness of the Word in one's life, Colossians 3:16.

Public reading of Scripture, 1 Timothy 4:13.

Word of God not chained, 2 Timothy 2:9.

Correctly handling Word of truth, 2 Timothy 2:15.

Foundation stands firm, 2 Timothy 2:19.

Influence of Scriptures since childhood, 2 Timothy 3:14-15.

Fourfold use of Scripture in teaching and

training, 2 Timothy 3:16.
Paying attention to Scripture, Hebrews 2:1-3.
Double-edged sword, Hebrews 4:12.
Birth through the Word of truth, James 1:18.
Cleansing work of Scripture, James 1:21.
Scriptural teaching put into action, James 1:22-25.
Royal law of Scripture, James 2:8.
Purified by obeying truth, 1 Peter 1:22.
Men like grass but the Word stands forever, 1 Peter 1:24-25.
Divine purpose in giving Scriptures, 2 Peter 1:15.
Inspired by Holy Spirit, 2 Peter 1:20-21.
Bringing Scripture to mind, 2 Peter 3:2.
God's Word fulfilled in those who obey, 1 John 2:5.
Love results from obedience to Scripture, 2 John 6.
Book of Revelation given by angel, Revelation 1:1.
Promised blessing for those who read and take to heart, Revelation 1:3.
Example of verbal inspiration in Scriptures, Revelation 1:11.
Word of God incarnate, Revelation 19:13.
All Scripture must be fulfilled, Revelation 22:10.
Finality of Scripture record, Revelation 22:18-19.
See *Revelation.*

SCRUTINY
Identification by manner of speech, Judges 12:5-6.
Veteran soldier underrated the abilities of a boy, 1 Samuel 17:42.
Seeing is believing, 1 Kings 10:6-9.
Evil eye on earth, Job 1:6-7.
The Lord examines mankind from heavenly throne, Psalm 11:4.
Jesus was carefully watched by critics, Luke 14:1.

SCULPTURE
Chisel at work, Deuteronomy 10:1.
Idol-maker burns wood for carving, Isaiah 44:15-17.
Decorative images in temple, Ezekiel 41:17-20.
See *Artist, Talent.*

SEAL
Signet ring, Genesis 41:42.
Marked by seal, Nehemiah 10:1-27.
Business transaction, Jeremiah 32:11-14.
Prophecy verified, Daniel 9:24.

SEAMSTRESS
Edenic garments, Genesis 3:7.
Time to mend, Ecclesiastes 3:7.
Sewing magic charms, Ezekiel 13:17-18.
Technique for repairing an old garment, Matthew 9:16; Mark 2:21.
Woman who helped poor, Acts 9:36-42.

SEANCE
Sorcery forbidden, Exodus 22:18.
Sorcery abandoned, Numbers 24:1.
Prophet of God called seer, 1 Samuel 9:8-9.
Dead cannot return, 2 Samuel 12:22-23.
Putting end to mediums and spiritists, 2 Kings 23:24.
Inquire of God rather than spiritists, Isaiah 8:19.
Spirits of the departed, Isaiah 14:9-10.
Making fools of diviners, Isaiah 44:25.
Fortune and destiny, Isaiah 65:11.
Diviners and mediums who tell lies, Jeremiah 27:9-15.
See *Fortune-telling, Sorcery, Spiritism.*

SEARCH
Truly holy, Numbers 16:3-7.
Mining deep into earth, Job 28:1-4.
Glory of kings, Proverbs 25:2.
Chasing wind, Ecclesiastes 1:17-18.
No one to give answers, Isaiah 41:28.
Ask for ancient paths, Jeremiah 6:16.
See *Exploration.*

SEASONS
Role of stars in marking seasons, Genesis 1:14.
Establishment of seasons after Flood, Genesis 8:22.
Spring: time kings go to war, 2 Samuel 11:1.
Lunar designation, Psalm 104:19.
Birds know when to migrate, Jeremiah 8:7.
Creator changes seasons, Daniel 2:10-21.
Confusion in planting and harvest, Amos 9:13.

SECLUSION
No place to hide, Leviticus 26:25.
Cities of refuge, Numbers 35:6-15.
Paul found Athens suitable place to be left
 alone, 1 Thessalonians 3:1.

SECOND COMING
Need to evangelize, Isaiah 21:11-12.
Time of judgment, Isaiah 26:21.
Yearning for Messiah, Isaiah 64:1.
The Lord coming in judgment, Isaiah
 66:15-16.
Daniel's vision of Christ's coming, Daniel
 7:9-14.
Silence before the Lord, Zephaniah 1:7.
Desire of all nations will come, Haggai 2:7.
Day of His coming, Malachi 3:2.
Watching for the Lord to come, Luke
 12:35-40.
Promise of Christ's return, John 14:3; Acts
 1:10-11.
Mistaken information as to return, John
 21:20-23.
Certain judgment coming on earth,
 Romans 9:28.
Resurrection at coming of Christ,
 1 Corinthians 15:51-55.
Waiting for Christ's return,
 1 Thessalonians 1:10.
Those prepared for return of Christ,
 1 Thessalonians 3:13.
Man of sin overthrown, 2 Thessalonians
 2:8.
Faithful until Christ returns, 1 Timothy
 6:11-16.
Conduct and attitudes in last days,
 2 Timothy 3:1-5.
Purified by blessed hope, Titus 2:11-14.
Christ's return as Lord and King, Hebrews
 9:24-28.
Reward for faithful, Hebrews 10:35-38.
Waiting for the Lord's return, James 5:7-8.
Birth into living hope, 1 Peter 1:3-5.
Christ's return an impetus for holy living,
 1 Peter 4:7-8.
Scoffers in last days, 2 Peter 3:3-4.
Like a thief, 2 Peter 3:10.
Unashamed at His coming, 1 John 2:28.
Scoffers and divisive influences, Jude 17-
 18.
Coming in clouds, Revelation 1:7.
Coming soon, Revelation 3:11.
Promised return of Christ, Revelation 22:7,
 12, 20.

See *Messiah, Rapture.*

SECRECY
Identification of evil act, Numbers 25:14.
Sweetness of stolen things, Proverbs 9:17.
Adulterous sites, Jeremiah 3:6.
Whispers to be proclaimed, Matthew
 10:27.
Jesus could not keep His presence secret,
 Mark 7:24.
Revealing thoughts of the heart, Luke 2:34-
 35.
Betrayal of Jesus by Judas, Luke 22:3-6.
Jesus withdrew from public activity, John
 11:54.
Hidden motives brought to light,
 1 Corinthians 4:5.
Deeds of darkness, Ephesians 5:8-14.
See *Confidential.*

SECRET
Deepest secret known to God,
 Deuteronomy 29:29; Job 12:22; 34:21-
 22; Ecclesiastes 12:14; Isaiah 29:15-16;
 Hebrews 4:13.
Animals of nature born in secret, Job 39:1.
The Lord knows our thoughts, Psalm
 94:11.
Thoughts and motives, Psalm 139:1-4.
Laughter with an aching heart, Proverbs
 14:13.
Secrets made known, Matthew 13:35.
Time of Christ's coming held secret,
 Matthew 24:36; Mark 13:32.
Nothing hidden will not be known, Luke
 8:17; 12:2-3.
God's secret made known, Ephesians 1:9-
 10.

SECRETARY
In charge of money, 2 Kings 12:10-12.
Person of versatility, 1 Chronicles 27:32.
Dispatching orders, Esther 3:12; 8:9.
Jeremiah dictated to Baruch, Jeremiah
 36:4, 15-16.
See *Dictation.*

SECRET BELIEVERS
Secret believer in king's palace, Esther
 4:12-16.
Secret believers, John 12:42-43; 19:38.

SECTARIAN
Rules taught by men, Isaiah 29:13.

Wrong interpretation of Scripture,
Jeremiah 8:8.
Proclaiming dreams instead of Word of
God, Jeremiah 23:25-32.
Pagans certain of erroneous belief, Acts
19:35-36.
See *Cult, Denomination, Syncretism.*

SECULAR
Need for building roads, Deuteronomy
19:1-3.
Seeing and hearing but not understanding,
Mark 4:11-12.
Turning God's house into marketplace,
John 2:16.
Bringing theological dispute into secular
courtroom, Acts 18:12-17.
City director of public works, Romans
16:23.
Praying for those in authority, 1 Timothy
2:1-4.
Viewpoint of world, 1 John 4:5.
See *Labor.*

SECURITY
Security at entrance to Garden of Eden,
Genesis 3:24.
A dove's security, Genesis 8:6-12.
Strong tower in a besieged city, Judges
9:51.
Desire for peace and security, 2 Kings
20:19.
City built around fortress, 1 Chronicles
11:7-9.
David's sin in depending on the number of
fighting men, 1 Chronicles 21:17.
Lie down without fear, Job 11:19.
Eagle finds its security in height, Job 39:27-
28.
The Lord is my rock, Psalm 18:1-2.
Trusting solely in the Lord, Psalm 20:7.
God our refuge and strength, Psalm 46:1-3.
Blotted out of Book of Life, Psalm 69:28.
Living under shadow of the Almighty,
Psalm 91:1-2.
Those who trust in the Lord cannot be
shaken, Psalm 125:1.
Name of the Lord a strong tower, Proverbs
18:10.
Labor and good food, Ecclesiastes 5:18-20.
In clefts of the rock, Song of Songs 2:14.
Tested stone in Zion, Isaiah 28:16.
Looking to earthly leadership, Isaiah 30:1-
3.

False trust in deeds and riches, Jeremiah
48:7; Mark 4:19.
Wise dove, Jeremiah 48:28.
Safety in midst of peril, Ezekiel 34:25.
Security in lions' habitat, Nahum 2:11.
False security of dishonest gain, Habakkuk
2:9.
Man-made idols, Habakkuk 2:18-19.
Jesus avoided those who would take His
life, John 7:1.
Function of good shepherd, John 10:1-15.
Jesus avoided public places, John 11:54.
Still standing at end of struggle, Ephesians
6:13.
Absolute confidence in the One whom we
believe, 2 Timothy 1:12.
Jesus our guarantee, Hebrews 7:22.
Kingdom that cannot be shaken, Hebrews
12:28-29.
Our eternal inheritance, 1 Peter 1:3-4.
Keeping power, Jude 1.
Gates of New Jerusalem never shut,
Revelation 21:25.
See *Protection, Shelter.*

SEDATIVE
Wine at Crucifixion, Mark 15:23-24, 36.

SEDENTARY
Loss of physical sensitivities with age,
2 Samuel 19:35.
See *Geriatrics, Old age, Senility.*

SEDUCTION
Wickedness of Amnon toward Tamar,
2 Samuel 13:1-20.
Led astray nationally, 2 Kings 21:9; Ezekiel
13:10-11.
Seductive ways of prostitute, Proverbs 7:6-
27; Jeremiah 3:1-2.
Naughty women of Zion, Isaiah 3:16-17.
Worst of women, Jeremiah 2:33.
Merchandising feminine beauty, Ezekiel
16:15.
Adulterous look, Hosea 2:2.
False Christs and fake prophets, Mark
13:22.
Young distorters of truth, Acts 20:30.
False spirits, 1 Timothy 4:1.
Taking advantage of weak-willed women,
2 Timothy 3:6.
Deceiving and being deceived, 2 Timothy
3:13.
Warning sounded, 1 John 2:26.

See *Deceit.*

SEED
Cycle of seasons, Genesis 8:22.
Good crops and weeds, Hebrews 6:7-8.

SEEKERS
Tent for inquirers, Exodus 33:7.
Intently seeking the Lord, 2 Chronicles 31:21.
Thirsting for God, Psalms 42:1-4; 63:1-8; 143:6.
Those who wanted to see Jesus, John 12:20-22.

SEGREGATION
Same rules for all, Numbers 15:15.
Revenge against those who did not assist Israelites, Nehemiah 13:1-3.
Mutual hatred of Samaritans and Jews, Luke 9:51-56; John 4:9.
Prophet from Galilee, John 7:41-52.
See *Prejudice, Racism.*

SELECTION
Improving species of animals, Genesis 30:41-42.
Choice of Jesus or Barabbas, Matthew 27:15-26.

SELF-ACCEPTANCE
Loss of personal worth, Deuteronomy 28:68.
Nehemiah requested God's favor in response to his faithfulness, Nehemiah 5:19.
Admitting wrong, Zechariah 1:6.
Paul accepted himself for what he was, 1 Corinthians 15:10.

SELF-CONFIDENCE
Lack of self-confidence, Job 9:20.
Righteous in one's own eyes, Job 32:1.
Boast only about the Lord, Jeremiah 9:23-24.
Paul could be timid and bold, 2 Corinthians 10:1.

SELF-CONTROL
Tongue control, Psalm 39:1-2.
Controlling one's temper, Proverbs 16:32.
Keeping oneself under control, Proverbs 29:11.
Refusal to drink wine, Jeremiah 35:6.

The exercise of tact in times of duress, James 1:19-20.
No one perfect, James 3:2.
Mature, gracious Christianity, 2 Peter 1:5-7.
See *Discipline.*

SELF-DEFENSE
Vindication by earthquake, Numbers 16:28-34.
Cities of refuge, Numbers 35:6-15.
David's lack of confidence, 1 Samuel 27:1.
Killing in self-defense, 2 Samuel 2:22-23.
Those fearful of personal safety, Acts 5:13-14.
See *Protection.*

SELF-DENIAL
Self-denial demonstrated, Genesis 22:1-12.
Avoid overeating, Proverbs 23:1-2, 20.
Taking up the cross, Matthew 10:38.
Take up your cross and follow, Matthew 16:24; Luke 14:27.
Leaving all, Mark 10:28; Luke 14:33.
Leaving family, Luke 18:29-30.
Bodily slavery, 1 Corinthians 9:27.
Flesh crucified, Galatians 5:24.
Put off old self, Ephesians 4:22-24.
Everything loss by comparison, Philippians 3:8.
Earthly nature put to death, Colossians 3:5.
Practicing "won't" power, Titus 2:12.
Abstain from sinful desires, 1 Peter 2:11; 4:2.
See *Discipline.*

SELF-ESTEEM
Lost self-esteem, Lamentations 4:2.
Proper love of self, Mark 12:31.
Danger of falsely evaluating oneself, 2 Corinthians 10:12.
See *Pride, Vanity.*

SELF-EXAMINATION
Immeasurable greatness of God, 2 Chronicles 6:12-19.
Examine and test our ways, Lamentations 3:40.
Repentance of the heart, Joel 2:13.
Specks and planks, Matthew 7:5.
Need for personal evaluation, Romans 2:17-28.
Examine oneself before the Lord's table, 1 Corinthians 11:29.

Examination of faith, 2 Corinthians 13:5.
Refusing to see oneself with reality, James
1:23-25.
See *Introspection.*

SELF-IMAGE
Pride and arrogance, 1 Samuel 2:3.
Rebuttal against oppressors, Job 12:1-3.
Low evaluation of man, Job 25:6.
Youth chides wisdom of age, Job 32:6-9.
Wrong and right boasting, Jeremiah 9:23-24.
More than wealth makes a king, Jeremiah
22:14-15.
Religious performance in public, Matthew
6:1-4.
Drawing attention to alleged piety,
Matthew 6:16-18.
Determining who is greatest, Mark 9:33-37.
Love of neighbor and of oneself, Mark
12:31.
Loyalty exaggerated, Mark 14:31.
Prodigal's opinion of himself, Luke 15:21.
Justified in eyes of men, Luke 16:15.
Folly of Herod, Acts 12:21-23.
Paul's estimation of himself, 1 Corinthians
15:9.
Danger of falsely evaluating oneself,
2 Corinthians 10:12.
Paul's image of himself compared to
others, 2 Corinthians 11:5-6. (See
12:11.)
Aware of one's weakness, 2 Corinthians
11:30.
Refusal to see oneself with reality, James
1:23-25.
See *Ego.*

SELF-INTEREST
Morose selfishness, Exodus 16:2-3.
Selfish marital relationship, Deuteronomy
22:13-19.
Chapter depicting personal motivations as
key to status and well-being,
Deuteronomy 28:1-68. (Note: Rewards
for obedience, vv. 1-14, and warning
against disobedience, vv. 15-68.)
Fortunes restored, Deuteronomy 30:1-3.
Art of careful negotiation, Ruth 4:1-8.
Leadership for those in trouble, 1 Samuel
22:2.
David's lack of confidence, 1 Samuel 27:1.
Showing favor for personal interest,

1 Samuel 27:12.
Share and share alike, 1 Samuel 30:24.
Dishonest report for personal gain,
2 Samuel 1:2-16. (See 1 Sam. 31:4.)
Looking in two perspectives, 2 Samuel
12:1-13.
Requesting payment for his master's
spiritual ministry, 2 Kings 5:20-27.
Providing for oneself at expense of others,
2 Kings 6:24-31.
Evaluating personal options, 2 Kings 7:3-4.
Trampled by hungry mob, 2 Kings 7:17-20.
(See entire chapter.)
Concern of one man, action of another,
2 Kings 8:7-15.
Overcome by personal pride, 2 Chronicles
26:16.
God's provision and man's pride,
2 Chronicles 32:24-26.
Pleasing the king, Esther 2:1-4.
Man who built gallows for his own neck,
Esther 5:11-14. (See also 9:25.)
Mistaken praise, Esther 6:1-12.
Satanic view of man's motivations, Job 2:1-10.
The Lord on our side, Psalm 124:1-5.
Looking back on academic folly, Proverbs
5:13-14.
Treasures of no value, Proverbs 10:2.
Dread and desire, Proverbs 10:24.
Self-interest principle functioning,
Proverbs 11:24-25.
Submitting personal plans to the Lord's
purpose, Proverbs 19:21.
Birds know seasons of migration, Jeremiah
8:7.
Refusal to go God's way, Jeremiah 11:7-8.
Provision of choice for national well-being,
Jeremiah 27:12-15.
Making and breaking promise to slaves,
Jeremiah 34:8-22.
Shepherds who care more for themselves
than for their flocks, Ezekiel 34:2.
Personal desire above need of others,
Amos 6:6.
Fate of carefree city, Zephaniah 2:15.
Concerned for self more than for the Lord,
Zechariah 7:4-6.
Reward for tithing, Malachi 3:10.
Personal gain from serving God, Malachi
3:14-15.
Self-interest in its highest function,
Matthew 6:33.
Complaining about another's generosity,

Matthew 20:1-16.
Self-interest wrongly pursued, Mark 8:36.
Selfish request for honor, Mark 10:35-45.
Slumbering disciples, Mark 14:32-42.
Jesus deserted by followers, Mark 14:50-52. (Note v. 54.)
Thievery of tax collectors and soldiers, Luke 3:12-14.
Stewardship and self-interest, Luke 6:38.
Desiring healing of valuable servant, Luke 7:1-3.
Denial of self for best interest of self, Luke 9:23-25.
Greatest among apostles, Luke 9:46-48; 22:24-27.
Right spirit in victory over evil, Luke 10:17-20.
Martha's distraction, Luke 10:38-42.
Evil of vanity, Luke 11:43.
All kinds of greed, Luke 12:15-21.
Desiring place of honor at table, Luke 14:7-11.
Reaching out to those in need, Luke 14:12-14.
Deciding whether to go to war or negotiate peace, Luke 14:31-32.
Prodigal son and resenting brother, Luke 15:11-32.
Attitude of employer toward labor, Luke 17:7-10.
Pharisees desired visible kingdom, Luke 17:20-21.
Difficulty of rich man to find kingdom of God, Luke 18:18-25.
Disciples desired earthly status, Acts 1:6.
Fearful of personal safety, Acts 5:13-14.
Desiring spiritual power for personal gain, Acts 8:18-24.
Disturbed over loss of revenue from manufacturing idols, Acts 19:23-26.
Judging others and ignoring personal guilt, Romans 2:1-16.
Christian attitude toward others, Romans 12:10.
Remuneration expected for effort, 1 Corinthians 9:7.
Reaping what one sows, 2 Corinthians 9:6-8.
Wisdom of self-examination, 2 Corinthians 13:5.
Serving the Lord with wrong motives, Philippians 1:15-19.
Syndrome of last days, 2 Timothy 3:1-5.
Unsatisfied inner desires, James 4:1-2.

Methods of disruptive hypocrite in the church, 3 John 9-10.
See *Hedonism, Narcissism, Selfishness.*

SELFISHNESS
Attitude of management toward labor, Exodus 5:2-5.
Conflict between David and Saul, 1 Samuel 26:1-25.
Cursed for hoarding, Proverbs 11:26.
Denying food and drink, Isaiah 32:6.
Shepherds care more for themselves than for flocks, Ezekiel 34:2, 18.
Putting cheap value on human beings, Amos 2:6.
People lived in fine homes while temple lay in ruins, Haggai 1:1-4.
Give to those who ask, Matthew 5:42.
Ignoring need of others, Matthew 25:43.
Seeking best for themselves, Mark 10:37.
Greed over one's possessions, Luke 12:14-15.
Choosing place of honor for yourself, Luke 14:7-11.
Preaching of Gospel hindered business of idol-makers, Acts 19:20-41.
Self-seeking, Philippians 2:21.
Those who would not share with Paul in ministry financing, Philippians 4:15-19.
Good deeds will be made known, 1 Timothy 5:25.
Love of self, 2 Timothy 3:2.
Unsatisfied inner desires, James 4:1-2.
See *Greed, Self-interest.*

SELF-PITY
Those who complained about leadership of Moses, Numbers 16:12-14.
King feeling sorry for himself, 1 Samuel 22:6-8.
Rebuffed by subordinate, Esther 5:9-10.
Weight of misery, Job 6:2-3.
Yearning for death, Job 7:13-16.
Job's plight, Job 19:13-21.
Living righteously for no seeming purpose, Psalm 73:12-13.
Daughters taught how to wail, Jeremiah 9:20.
Seeing inequity of testing, Jeremiah 15:15-18.
Jeremiah blamed the Lord for persecution, Jeremiah 20:7-8.
Jeremiah lamented day of his birth, Jeremiah 20:14-15.

Blaming the Lord for problems, Habakkuk 1:1-4.
Martha's distraction, Luke 10:38-42.
Refusal of Jesus to accept pity, Luke 23:27-28.
Avoid complaining in whatever circumstances, Philippians 2:14-16.
See *Complain.*

SELF-RIGHTEOUS
Self-righteousness affronted, Deuteronomy 3:3-11.
Attitude of Job, Job 9:20.
Job accused of self-righteousness, Job 33:8-13; 34:1-9; 36:4.
Those pure in their own eyes, Proverbs 30:12.
Filthy rags, Isaiah 64:6.
Scorning those who have done wrong, Ezekiel 16:56-57.
Vanity over wealth and self-righteousness, Hosea 12:8.
Claiming piety superior to ancestors', Matthew 23:30.
Seeking self-justification, Luke 10:29; 16:15.
Holier than thou, Luke 18:9.
Woman caught in adultery, John 8:3-11.
Boasting before men not valid before God, Romans 4:2.
Those who commend themselves, 2 Corinthians 10:12.
Paul's personal example, Philippians 3:3-11.
See *Hypocrisy.*

SELF-WILL
See *Stubborn.*

SENILITY
Work for old man to do, Joshua 13:1; 14:10-11.
Loss of sensitivities, 2 Samuel 19:35.
David's senility, 1 Kings 1:1-4.
See *Geriatrics, Old age, Sedentary.*

SENSATIONALISM
Shem's attitude toward father's privacy, Genesis 9:20-27.
Jesus asked miracles be kept private, Matthew 9:29-31.
Spectacular prophecies, 2 Thessalonians 2:1-2.
See *Spectacular.*

SENSES
Temple fragrance not for personal enjoyment, Exodus 30:34-38.
Eyes that see, ears that hear, Deuteronomy 29:2-4.
Perfume for lady, Ruth 3:3.
Partial blindness threatened as disgrace, 1 Samuel 11:2-11.
Loss of physical sensitivities with age, 2 Samuel 19:35.
Motivated by hook and bit, 2 Kings 19:28.
Satanic view of man's motivations, Job 2:1-10.
Eyes and ears that do not function, Jeremiah 5:21; Ezekiel 12:2.
Birds know seasons of migration, Jeremiah 8:7.
Demon-possessed, blind, and mute, Matthew 12:22-30.
Hunger caused Peter to fall into trance, Acts 10:10.
See *Perception.*

SENSITIVITY
Yearning for the Lord, Isaiah 26:9.
Jesus knew when He had been touched, Luke 8:43-48.
Physical illustration of spiritual truth, John 6:53-64.
Lack of spiritual perception, John 8:47.
Some thought they heard thunder; others, voice of an angel, John 12:29.
Trouble prepares us to help others, 2 Corinthians 1:3-4.
New awareness in hearts of Corinthians, 2 Corinthians 7:10-13.
Eyes of heart, Ephesians 1:18-19.
Knowledge of Scriptures gives discernment, Hebrews 5:11-14.
See *Perception.*

SENSUAL
Lust that seemingly turned to love, Genesis 34:1-4.
Mixing pagan religion with immorality, Numbers 25:1-2.
Evil earnings forbidden in house of the Lord, Deuteronomy 23:18.
Immoral use of place of worship, 1 Samuel 2:22-25.
Imbibing without restraint, Esther 1:7-8.
Replacing queen, Esther 2:1-4.
Covenant to avoid lust, Job 31:1.
Captivated by sensual beauty, Proverbs

6:25.
Haughty women, Isaiah 3:16.
From one sin to another, Jeremiah 9:3.
Continual lust for more, Ephesians 4:19.
See *Immorality, Lust.*

SENTENCE
Capital punishment, Exodus 21:12-14.
Facing grim destiny, Jeremiah 15:2-3.
Daniel sentenced to death, Daniel 6:16.
See *Prison.*

SEPARATION
God commanded separation in Garden of
Eden, Genesis 2:16-17.
Old Testament command to separate from
unbelievers, Exodus 34:11-16.
Early joys of marriage, Deuteronomy 24:5.
Samson desired Philistine wife, Judges
14:1-2.
Partial commitment of King Solomon,
1 Kings 3:3.
Pledge to avoid intermarriage, Nehemiah
10:30.
Separated from evil by choice, Psalm 1:1.
Godly set apart, Psalm 4:3.
Do not envy sinners, Proverbs 23:17.
Touch no unclean thing, Isaiah 52:11.
Sitting apart from revelers, Jeremiah
15:16-17.
Daniel resolved not to defile himself,
Daniel 1:8-20.
Daniel's friends refused to worship idols,
Daniel 3:8-12.
Two in agreement, Amos 3:3.
Jesus criticized for fellowship with sinners,
Matthew 9:10-12; Mark 2:15-17; Luke
5:27-31.
Test of righteousness in time of
wickedness, Matthew 24:12-13.
That which enters into man and that which
comes out, Mark 7:15-23.
You cannot serve two masters, Luke 16:13.
Those who refuse to separate themselves
from praise of men, John 12:42-43.
Not of the world, John 17:15-16.
Peter and Gentiles, Acts 11:1-3.
Christian lifestyle, Romans 13:12-14.
True measure of spirituality, Romans
14:17-18.
Do not cause another to stumble, Romans
14:20-23.
Marriage of Christians to non-Christians,
1 Corinthians 7:10-16.

Food sacrificed to idols, 1 Corinthians 8:1.
Exercise of liberty in eating and drinking,
1 Corinthians 8:7-13; 10:23-33.
Believers not to join with unbelievers,
2 Corinthians 6:14-18.
Those who live by standards of world,
2 Corinthians 10:2.
Crucified with Christ, Galatians 2:20.
Do not be judged by observance of
legalism, Colossians 2:16.
Turn away from wickedness, 2 Timothy
2:19.
To the pure, always pure, Titus 1:15.
Resisting ungodliness and passions, Titus
2:11-12.
Moses refused to be known as son of
Pharaoh's daughter, Hebrews 11:24-25.
Faithfully running race, Hebrews 12:1-2.
Submit to God, resist devil, James 4:7.
Strangers in the world, 1 Peter 1:1-2.
Call to holiness, 1 Peter 1:13-16.
Love of world, 1 John 2:15-17.
Come out from iniquity, Revelation 18:4-5.
See *Legalism, Worldliness.*

SEPULCHER
Choicest of tombs, Genesis 23:6.
Festive burial, 2 Chronicles 16:14.
Graves hewn out of rock, Isaiah 22:16.
Easter burial prophesied, Isaiah 53:9.
See *Burial, Tomb.*

SERIOUS
Value of sorrow over laughter, Ecclesiastes
3:4.
Serious question, Matthew 22:42; 26:66;
Mark 14:64.
Pondering mother, Luke 2:19.
Serious assessment, Philippians 4:8.

SERENDIPITY
Altered events for Abraham and Isaac,
Genesis 22:6-18.
Joy in home of Laban and Rachel, Genesis
29:9-14.
Drama at the Red Sea, Exodus 14:21-28.
Surprise for Boaz, blessing for Ruth, Ruth
3:1-15.
Fourth figure in fiery furnace, Daniel 3:19-
28.
Pagan king's experience of joy, Daniel
6:16-27.
Terrified shepherds, Luke 2:8-18.
Discovering water of life, John 4:4-15.

Ethiopian eunuch, Acts 8:26-39.
Road to Damascus, Acts 9:1-8.
Deliverance by earthquake, Acts 16:23-34.
See *Blessing, Surprise.*

SERMON
Good things from God's house, Psalm
  65:4.
"Amen" of agreement to God's message,
  Jeremiah 28:5-6.
Mistaking voice of God for thunder, John
  12:28-29.
Paul's resumé of Old Testament and
  proclamation of Gospel, Acts 13:16-41.
Long sermon, Acts 20:7.
See *Preaching.*

SERVANT
Servant's attitude toward unfair employer,
  Genesis 16:1-10.
Declining freedom, Exodus 21:5.
Servants who disobey masters, 1 Samuel
  25:10.
Loyalty of servant to king, 2 Samuel 15:19-
  21.
Servant earns role of brother, Proverbs
  17:2.
Honored servant, Proverbs 27:18.
Maintaining servant attitude, Matthew
  10:24.
Spiritual greatness through humility and
  servitude, Matthew 20:20-28; Mark
  10:35-45.
Faithful and unfaithful service, Matthew
  24:45-51.
Black man helped Jesus carry cross, Mark
  15:21. (Note: Cyrene was a city in North
  Africa.)
John the Baptist, forerunner of Jesus, Luke
  3:1-20.
First servant, then minister, Romans 1:1.
Paul considered himself least of apostles,
  1 Corinthians 15:9; Ephesians 3:8-9.
Submission to each other, 1 Corinthians
  16:15-16.
Serve one another in love, Galatians 5:13.
God's workmanship, Ephesians 2:10.
Slaves and masters, Ephesians 6:5-9;
  Colossians 3:22; 1 Timothy 6:1; Titus
  2:9; 1 Peter 2:18.
Tools through whom God ministers, Titus
  1:1-3.
In His own words, Christ defined
  Incarnation, Hebrews 10:5-7.

Humble circumstances are high position,
  James 1:9.
See *Discipleship.*

SERVICE
Anointing of object, Exodus 40:9-10.
Material security versus God's will,
  Numbers 32:14-27.
Eagerly volunteering, 1 Kings 19:20.
Requesting payment for spiritual ministry,
  2 Kings 5:20-27.
Those assigned as gatekeepers,
  1 Chronicles 9:22-27.
Motivated by fear, Psalm 2:11.
Serve the Lord with gladness, Psalm 100:1-
  2.
Blameless ministers, Psalm 101:6.
Writing with ordinary pen, Isaiah 8:1.
Conditional freedom, Jeremiah 34:8-11.
Women who command husbands, Amos
  4:1.
Total loyalty, Matthew 6:24.
Authority of teachers and masters,
  Matthew 10:24.
Last act of Jesus prior to Crucifixion,
  Matthew 20:29-34.
Donkey chosen to serve Jesus, Matthew
  21:1-7; Mark 11:1-7.
Parable of Two Sons, Matthew 21:28-31.
Attitude of servant in spiritual service,
  Matthew 23:8-12.
Faithful and unfaithful service, Matthew
  24:45-51.
Wanting to be first in God's kingdom the
  easy way, Mark 10:35-45.
Joy of serving Christ, Luke 10:17.
Putting first things first, Luke 10:38-42.
Serving God seven days a week, John 5:16-
  17.
Jesus washed feet of disciples, John 13:1-
  17.
Love of the Lord involves outreach to
  others, John 21:15-18.
John the helper, Acts 13:5.
Service with humility, Acts 20:19.
Relationship between talent and call to
  service, Romans 11:29.
Strong looking after weak, Romans 15:1.
Paul's servant attitude in preaching
  Gospel, 1 Corinthians 9:19-23.
In serving God, all may win, 1 Corinthians
  9:24-27.
Different kinds of gifts and service,
  1 Corinthians 12:4-11.

Total function of body of Christ,
1 Corinthians 12:14-20.
Labor of love, Galatians 5:13.
God's workmanship, Ephesians 2:10.
Varied talents in body of Christ, Ephesians
4:11-13.
"Work" and "labor," 1 Thessalonians
1:3.
Need for full-time Christian service,
2 Timothy 2:1-4.
See *Ministry, Vocation.*

SEWING
First tailor and seamstress, Genesis 3:7.
Skilled tailors, Exodus 28:3.
Time to mend garments, Ecclesiastes 3:7.
Sewing on magic charms, Ezekiel 13:18.
How not to patch old garment, Matthew
9:16.
See *Wardrobe.*

SEXUAL
Relationship between Adam and Eve,
Genesis 4:1-2, 25.
Animals offered in sacrifice, Leviticus
22:24-25.
Injury to sexual organs, Deuteronomy
23:1.
Chastity in conduct, Deuteronomy 25:11-
12.
Morality a vital part of spirituality,
Jeremiah 3:1-5.
Marriage on earth compared to
relationship in heaven, Mark 12:18-27.
Paul's instructions on restraint in
marriage, 1 Corinthians 7:5.
Modesty in regard to body organs,
1 Corinthians 12:22-25.
See *Chastity, Immorality, Passion.*

SHADING
Separation of light from darkness, Genesis
1:4.

SHADOW
Strange movement of shadow, 2 Kings
20:8-11.
Valley of death's shadow, Psalm 23:4;
Matthew 4:16.
Shadow of divine wings, Psalm 57:1.
Shadow of God's hand, Isaiah 51:16.

SHALLOWNESS
People quick to complain, Numbers 11:4-
11.
Pride and arrogance, 1 Samuel 2:3.
Beautiful but dumb, Proverbs 11:22.
Likeness of a fool, Proverbs 26:1-11.
Forever unsatisfied, Proverbs 30:15-16.
Avoid meaningless offerings, Isaiah 1:13.
Haughty women, Isaiah 3:16.
Skilled at art of seduction, Jeremiah 2:33.
An end to noisy songs, Ezekiel 26:13.
Merely lip service, Ezekiel 33:31-32.
Roots near surface, Mark 4:16-17.
Weak foundation, Luke 6:49.
Pharisees resented Jesus for reaching out,
Luke 15:1-7.
Marginal commitment, John 6:66.
Paul chided Corinthians, 2 Corinthians
11:16-21.
Quickly turned from one doctrinal opinion
to another, Galatians 1:6-9.
Infants tossed by wind, Ephesians 4:14.
See *Immaturity.*

SHAM
King Herod and the magi, Matthew 2:7-8,
12.
Pharisees and religion of sham, Matthew
23:5-7; Mark 12:15-17.
False humility, Colossians 2:18.
Making hypocritical claim of holy life,
1 John 1:8-10.
Methods of disruptive conduct in church,
3 John 9-10.
Feigning life when spiritually dead,
Revelation 3:1.
See *Deception, Falsehood, Immaturity.*

SHAME
First display of conscience, Genesis 3:10.
Regret of Creator, Genesis 6:6.
Ham's attitude toward father's privacy,
Genesis 9:20-27.
Shame of prostitute, Genesis 38:15.
Father's shame for immoral sons,
1 Samuel 2:22-23.
Samuel's disappointing sons, 1 Samuel
8:1-3.
Death of King Saul, 1 Samuel 31:8-10.
Over their heads in guilt and shame, Ezra
9:6.
Those who are and are not put to shame,
Psalm 25:3.
Deep sense of disgrace, Psalm 44:15.
Arrogant ashamed, Psalm 119:78.
Disgrace of carelessness in harvest,

Proverbs 10:5.
Mother's disgrace, Proverbs 29:15.
Put to shame by zeal of others, Isaiah 26:11.
Idol-makers put to shame, Isaiah 45:16.
Brazen shamelessness, Jeremiah 3:3.
Those who do not know how to blush, Jeremiah 6:15.
Nudity as form of shame, Ezekiel 16:35-38.
Fallen princes, Ezekiel 32:30.
Committing sin in broad daylight, 2 Peter 2:13-23.
See *Embarrassment, Humiliation.*

SHARING
Iron sharpens iron, Proverbs 27:17.
Two in agreement, Amos 3:3.
Faith of friends resulted in man's healing, Mark 2:1-12.
Sharing with others, Luke 3:11.
Bringing message to others, John 1:41.
Christian kind of sharing, Acts 2:44.
Early Christians had all things in common, Acts 4:32.
Sharing scriptural insights, Acts 18:24-26; Romans 15:14.
Sharing both suffering and comfort, 2 Corinthians 1:7.
Sharing equally in stewardship, 2 Corinthians 8:11-15.
Some pay, others receive, 2 Corinthians 11:7-8.
Abraham, blessed and a blessing, Galatians 3:9.
Carrying each other's burdens, Galatians 6:2.
Student sharing with teacher, Galatians 6:6.
See *Fellowship.*

SHAVING
Shave and clean clothes, Genesis 41:14.
Shaving head, Numbers 6:9; Job 1:20.
Body hair removed, Numbers 8:7.
Losing half of beard, 2 Samuel 10:4.
Sharp sword used for shaving, Ezekiel 5:1.
No razor cuts allowed, Ezekiel 44:20.
Mark of distinction, Acts 21:24.
See *Barber.*

SHEEP
Initial object of sacrifice, Genesis 4:4-8.
Divine provision for sacrifice, Genesis 22:3-14.

Wool for cloth, Genesis 31:19; 38:12-17.
Wool for clergy, Deuteronomy 18:3-5.
Milk and mutton, Deuteronomy 32:13-14.
Tribute from king to king, 2 Kings 3:4.
Lost sheep, Matthew 18:11-13; Luke 15:4-7.
Lamb of God, John 1:29.
See *Shepherd.*

SHELTER
Springs and palm trees, Exodus 15:27.
Conditions for protection of Rahab and family, Joshua 2:17-21.
Careless about danger, Proverbs 22:3.
No place to escape, Jeremiah 25:35.
Protection from evil one, John 17:15.
Hiding in caves, crying out to mountains, Revelation 6:15-17.
See *Protection.*

SHEPHERD
Shepherds of Bible, Genesis 4:2; 13:5; 29:9; 37:2; 46:32; Exodus 2:17; 3:1; 1 Samuel 16:11; 17:20; 1 Chronicles 4:39; Amos 3:12.
Assistance for overworked shepherd, Exodus 18:14-27.
Fearless shepherd, 1 Samuel 17:34-36.
Shepherd of shepherds, Psalm 23:1-6; John 10:1-16.
Lambs in shepherd's arms, Isaiah 40:11.
Good shepherds, Jeremiah 3:15; 23:4.
Every sheep counted, Jeremiah 33:13.
False shepherds, Jeremiah 50:6; Ezekiel 34:3.
Search for lost sheep, Ezekiel 34:12-16.
Broken staff called Favor, Zechariah 11:10.
Sheep with no shepherd, Matthew 9:36.
One lost sheep, Matthew 18:10-14.
Sheep and goats, Matthew 25:32.
Christmas shepherds, Luke 2:8-18.
Spiritual shepherd, John 21:17; Acts 20:28; 1 Peter 5:2.
See *Pastor, Sheep.*

SHIFTS
Sabbath duty on shifts, 2 Kings 11:4-8.
People who served double duty, Nehemiah 4:22.

SHIPPING
Grain of Nile brought to Tyre, Isaiah 23:3.
Paths in sea, Isaiah 43:16.
See *Navigation.*

SHOCK
Startling information, Genesis 45:25-28.
Death caused by shock, 1 Samuel 4:12-18.
Nations in anguish, Joel 2:6.
See *Trauma.*

SHOES
Bare feet in God's presence, Exodus 3:5;
  2 Samuel 15:30. (See Acts 7:30-35.)
Sandal used to express resentment,
  Deuteronomy 25:8-9.
Removal of sandal as nonverbal
  communication, Ruth 4:8.
Expression of disdain, Psalm 60:8.
Dainty feet, Song of Songs 7:1.
Boots worn in battle, Isaiah 9:5.
Poor and needy exchanged for shoes,
  Amos 2:6.
Unworthy to touch shoes, Matthew 3:11;
  Mark 1:7; Luke 3:16; John 1:27; Acts
  13:25.
See *Feet, Walk.*

SHORT
Shortest short story, Ecclesiastes 9:14-
  15.
Short chapter with message of judgment
  and mercy, Jeremiah 45:1-5.
One-chapter books, Obadiah 1-21;
  Philemon 1-25; 2 John 1-13; 3 John 1-
  14; Jude 1-25.
Man of short stature, Luke 19:1-6.
Verse with two words, John 11:35.
See *Brevity.*

SHORTAGE
Shortage of wives, Judges 21:14.

SHORT STORY
Short story with moral for disobedient
  man, 2 Samuel 12:1-4. (Note vv. 5-
  11.)
Shortest short story ever written,
  Ecclesiastes 9:14-15.

SHOUTING
Joyful altar, Leviticus 9:24.
Walls of Jericho, Joshua 6:20.
Saluting the ark, 2 Samuel 6:14-15;
  1 Chronicles 15:28.
Shouts of affirmation, 2 Chronicles 13:14-
  15; 15:12-14.
Loudly praising the Lord, Ezra 3:11-13;
  Psalms 5:11; 47:1.

SHREWDNESS
Identification by manner of speech, Judges
  12:5-6.
Art of careful negotiation, Ruth 4:1-8.
Wisdom of Solomon, 1 Kings 4:29-34.
Eyes fixed directly ahead, Proverbs 4:25.
Wise as snakes, innocent as doves,
  Matthew 10:16.
Shrewd manager, Luke 19:11-27.
Wisdom of Gamaliel, Acts 5:34-39.
See *Perception.*

SHY
Samuel reluctant to inform Eli of vision,
  1 Samuel 3:15-16.
Saul's humility concerning anointing,
  1 Samuel 10:13-22.
Tongues stick to roof of mouth, Job 29:10.
Fear of speaking to those who are older,
  Jeremiah 1:6-7.
Coming to Jesus at night, John 3:1-2.
Paul could be timid and bold,
  2 Corinthians 10:1.
Paul prayed not to be ashamed, Philippians
  1:20.
Courage to witness in spite of opposition,
  1 Thessalonians 2:2.
Counsel from brave man to timid man,
  2 Timothy 1:7.
See *Reticent, Timidity.*

SICKNESS
Infirm eyesight, 1 Samuel 4:14-15.
Anguish of one ill and in great pain, Psalm
  38:1-22.
The Lord sustains on sickbed, Psalm 41:3.
God the great healer, Psalm 103:3.
Value of affliction, Psalm 119:71.
Prayer for coming of another day, Psalm
  143:8.
Love's times of testing, Proverbs 3:11-12.
Sustaining spirit, Proverbs 18:14.
Furnace of affliction, Isaiah 48:10.
Do not despise rod of testing, Ezekiel
  21:13.
Epilepsy caused by demon, Matthew
  17:14-20.
Purpose of suffering, Romans 5:3.
Made perfect through suffering, Hebrews
  2:10.
See *Health, Medicine, Therapy.*

SIGHT
Eli may have suffered from cataracts,

1 Samuel 4:14-15.
Opening eyes to see God's provision,
2 Kings 6:16-17.
Bodies full of eyes, Ezekiel 10:12.
Using eyes for good or evil, Matthew 6:22-23.
Partial, then full vision for blind man, Mark 8:22-25.
Special gift of sight, Galatians 4:15.
Eyes of heart, Ephesians 1:18-19.
See *Eyes.*

SIGHTSEEING
Seeing unpleasant sights, Deuteronomy 28:34.

SIGN
Asking God for sign of guidance, Genesis 24:12-14.
Wet and dry fleece, Judges 6:36-40.
Decimated altar, 1 Kings 13:3.
Sign of the shadow, 2 Kings 20:9-11.
Refusing to put God to test, Isaiah 7:11-14.
See *Guidance, Token.*

SIGNING
Hands held high, Exodus 17:8-13.
Speaking with signing, Luke 1:62.
See *Deafness.*

SIGNS OF THE TIMES
Characteristics of last days, 2 Timothy 3:1-7.

SILENCE
Wisdom of speaking neither good nor evil, Genesis 31:24.
Silent toward those who insulted, 1 Samuel 10:27.
Stand still to see what God will do, 1 Samuel 12:16.
Left with nothing to say, Nehemiah 5:8.
Respect for those older, Job 32:4.
Wisdom of silence, Proverbs 10:19; 17:28.
Good counsel when tempted to quarrel, Proverbs 17:14.
Guarding tongue, Proverbs 21:23.
Those who speak in haste, Proverbs 29:20.
Dramatic use of silence, Isaiah 36:13-21.
Silence of the Saviour, Isaiah 53:7.
Futile effort to suppress truth, Jeremiah 38:1-6.
Wise man remains quiet in times of evil, Amos 5:13.

Ashamed to mention name of the Lord, Amos 6:10.
Silent prophets, Zechariah 13:1-5.
Silence of Jesus before accusers, Matthew 26:57-67; Mark 14:53-62; John 19:8-9.
Demons refused permission to speak, Mark 1:33-34.
Pondering in heart, Luke 2:19.
Cynical tongues silenced, Luke 20:20-26.
Be slow to speak, James 1:19.
Musicians put to silence, Revelation 18:22.
See *Tact.*

SIMILARITY
Common destiny, Ecclesiastes 9:1-2.
Similar names of father and son, Jeremiah 22:24.
Like teacher, like student, Luke 6:40.
Compare John 1:1-9 with 1 John 1:1-7.
See *Like-minded.*

SIMILE
Like tree, like chaff, Psalm 1:3-4.
As with shield, Psalm 5:12.
Apple of eye, Psalm 17:8.
Compacted city, Psalm 122:3.
Like weaned child, Psalm 131:2.
Like Sodom and Gomorrah, Isaiah 1:9.
"Freedom" in quotation marks, Jeremiah 34:17.
Those who move boundaries, Hosea 5:10.
Like unmarked graves, Luke 11:44.
As in mirror, 2 Corinthians 3:18.
See *Figure of speech.*

SIMPLICITY
Great things, small things, 2 Kings 5:13.
Special protection for simple folk, Psalm 116:6.
Understanding to simple, Psalm 119:130.
Understanding for those of simple ways, Proverbs 9:6.
Writing with ordinary pen, Isaiah 8:1.
Comprehension of children, Matthew 11:25; Luke 18:17.
Attitude of Jesus to children, Matthew 18:1-6; Mark 10:13-16.
Simple truth difficult to understand, Mark 4:13.
Disciples to travel with humble equipment, Mark 6:8-11.
Blind man's request, Mark 10:46-52.
Simple men confounded scholars, Acts 4:13.

Spiritual truth communicated in human terms, Romans 6:19.

Some confounded by simple message, 1 Corinthians 1:18-21.

God calls those of humble backgrounds and abilities, 1 Corinthians 1:26.

Faith the ultimate intelligence, 1 Corinthians 3:18-23.

See *Naive.*

SIN

Image of God and image of man, Genesis 5:1-3.

Sin against man and sin against God, 1 Samuel 2:25.

Disobedience of faithful, 1 Samuel 12:20.

One sin as great as another, 1 Samuel 15:23.

Son less evil than parents, 2 Kings 3:1-3.

Sin cherished becomes like venom of serpents, Job 20:12-14.

Nothing hidden from God, Job 34:21-22.

Sinful nature inherited at birth, Psalms 51:5; 58:3-5.

Prayer unanswered when sin is cherished, Psalm 66:18-19.

Key to victory over sin, Psalm 119:11, 128.

Ravages of wickedness, Isaiah 9:18.

Need for repentance, Isaiah 64:5.

Leopard cannot change spots, Jeremiah 13:23.

Wages of sin, Lamentations 1:14.

Degrees of sin in God's sight, Ezekiel 16:48-52.

Death to soul that sins, Ezekiel 18:4.

Certain wages of sin, Ezekiel 33:13.

Three sins, even four, Amos 1:3, 6, 9, 11, 13; 2:1, 4, 6.

Old Testament ends with curse, Malachi 4:6.

Weight of sin, not pain of the cross, took the life of Jesus, Mark 15:33-37, 44.

Those guilty of much and those guilty of less, Luke 7:36-50.

Nothing hidden that will not be made known, Luke 12:2-3.

Men love darkness rather than light, John 3:19-21.

Sin done in ignorance, Acts 3:17; 1 Timothy 1:12-14.

No one righteous, Romans 3:10-18.

Seeking pleasure from those things which cause spiritual death, Romans 6:21.

Purpose of Law in revealing sin, Romans 7:7-12, 14.

Way of death, Ephesians 2:1.

Life prior to regeneration, Titus 3:3.

Unintentional sin, Hebrews 9:7.

Our sins forgotten in mercy of salvation, Hebrews 10:17.

Role of evil desire in causing sin, James 1:13-15.

Breaking just one point of Law, James 2:10.

Sin of neglect, James 4:17.

Love of world, 1 John 2:15-17.

Definition of sin, 1 John 5:17.

Whole world controlled by evil one, 1 John 5:19.

When evil serves God's purpose, Revelation 17:17.

See *Depravity, Evil, Iniquity, Wrong.*

SINCERITY

New clergy comes in all earnestness, Deuteronomy 18:6-7.

Avoiding flattery, Job 32:21.

Sackcloth and ashes, Jeremiah 6:26.

Hyper-piety, Matthew 6:16-18.

Faith of Canaanite woman tested, Matthew 15:21-28.

Fullest measure of the Law, Matthew 23:23.

Mary questioned cordial greeting of angel, Luke 1:28-31.

Practice what you proclaim, Luke 3:7-8.

Insincerity of spiritual expression, Romans 9:1-2.

Bread of sincerity and truth, 1 Corinthians 5:8.

Boldness and sincerity, 2 Corinthians 1:12; 2:17.

Working hard for the Lord, Colossians 3:23-24.

Love that comes from the heart, 1 Peter 1:22; 4:8.

Actions speak louder than words, 1 John 3:18.

Those who take Scriptures to heart, Revelation 1:3.

See *Motivation.*

SINGING

Songs to the Lord, Psalms 81:1; 95:1.

Mountain songs, Isaiah 30:29.

Potential of singing stones, Luke 19:37-40.

Inner music, 1 Corinthians 14:15.

Singing as mutual ministry, Ephesians 5:19.

See *Hymn, Music.*

SINGLE
Accepting either married or unmarried
state, 1 Corinthians 7:32-35.

SINNER
Endless anguish of conscience,
Deuteronomy 28:67; Job 15:20;
Ecclesiastes 2:23; Romans 2:9.
Shallow joy, Proverbs 14:13.
Isaiah's conviction of sin, Isaiah 6:5. (Note:
Scripture nowhere shows Isaiah as an
evil person.)
Friend of sinners, Luke 7:39; 19:7; John
8:11; Romans 5:8.
See *Disobedience, Sin, Wrong.*

SISTER
Wife who was also sister, Genesis 20:12.

SITUATION ETHICS
Folly of listening to Satan's reasoning,
Genesis 3:1-5.
Deceit of Abraham concerning his wife,
Genesis 12:10-13; 20:1-18.
Lot offered daughters in immorality,
Genesis 19:4-8.
Isaac claimed his wife was his sister to
protect himself, Genesis 26:7-11.
Making oneself purposely unclean,
Leviticus 21:1-4.
Rahab lied to protect spies, Joshua 2:1-6.
Lauding woman murderer, Judges 5:24-27.
Use of untruth for protection, 1 Samuel
19:14. (See also 20:4-8.)
Pretense of prophet, 1 Kings 20:35-43.
Pagan prophets, ministers, and priests
destroyed, 2 Kings 10:15-29.
Stealing to satisfy hunger, Proverbs 6:30.
Doing wrong for piece of bread, Proverbs
28:21.
Jeremiah commanded to lie by King
Zedekiah, Jeremiah 38:24-27.
See *Compromise.*

SIZE
Taking credit for divine blessing, Judges
7:2-3.
Big family, Judges 12:9.
Day of small things, Zechariah 4:10.

SKELETON
See *Bones.*

SKEPTICISM
Abraham's incredulity, Genesis 17:17.
Only a joke, Genesis 19:14.
Questioning divine capability, 2 Kings 7:2.
Lack of faith hinders blessing, Matthew
13:58.
Mother of Jesus too frightened to
comprehend, Mark 16:1-8.
Cost for doubting an angel, Luke 1:18-20.
Unable to believe in face of certain
evidence, Luke 24:36-43.
Skepticism of Nathanael, John 1:45-49.
People questioned conversion of Saul, Acts
9:19-26.
Lack of faith does not change God's
faithfulness, Romans 3:3.
Put truth to test, 1 Thessalonians 5:21.
Godless chatter and opposing ideas,
1 Timothy 6:20-21.
Faith the sure antidote for doubt, Hebrews
11:1-3.
See *Doubt, Pragmatic.*

SKILL
Lost skill for farming, Genesis 4:9-12.
Maker of tools, Genesis 4:22.
Building Tower of Babel, Genesis 11:1-6.
Skill put to use, Exodus 28:3.
Special gifts from God through the Holy
Spirit, Exodus 31:1-5.
Ability to both design and produce, Exodus
38:23.
Elimination of blacksmiths, 1 Samuel
13:19.
Various skills, 1 Chronicles 5:18;
2 Chronicles 2:7-14; 34:12; Daniel 1:4,
17; 9:22.
Variety of skilled workmen, 1 Chronicles
22:15.
Victory not necessarily to swift and strong,
Ecclesiastes 9:11.
Success requires more than ability, Isaiah
25:11.
Artist is mortal, Isaiah 44:11.
Disaster to swift and strong, Jeremiah 46:6.
Skilled crew on ships of Tyre, Ezekiel 27:8-
9.
Trying to purchase spiritual skill, Acts 8:18-
23.
Those expert in iniquity, 2 Peter 2:14.
See *Ability, Athletics, Talent.*

SKY
Rider in the sky, Deuteronomy 33:26.

Rain clouds become God's canopy,
2 Samuel 22:12; Psalm 18:11.
He who spreads out the skies, Job 37:18.
Resounding skies during heavy rainfall,
Psalm 77:17.
Raining righteousness, Isaiah 45:8.
Dimensions of judgment reach to the
skies, Jeremiah 51:9.
Weather forecasting, Matthew 16:2-3; Luke
12:54-56.
Stars of the sky, Hebrews 11:12.
See *Astronomy.*

SLANDER

False report, Exodus 23:1.
Criticism of king, 2 Samuel 6:17-
23.
Mistrust of good motive, 2 Samuel 10:3.
Scourge of tongue, Job 5:21.
Concerned with error of others, Job 19:4.
Slander of many, Psalm 31:13.
Secret slander, Psalm 101:5.
Let the Lord vindicate, Psalm 135:14.
Hatred and slander, Proverbs 10:18.
Destructive mouths, Proverbs 11:9.
Power of words, Isaiah 29:20-21.
Those who attack with tongues, Jeremiah
18:18; Micah 2:4.
Undercutting prophet's message, Amos
7:10.
Jesus criticized on the cross, Matthew
27:39-44.
Pharisees looked for point against Jesus,
Mark 3:1-6.
False accusation of demon-possession,
Luke 7:33.
Poisoning the mind, Acts 14:2.
Slandering type, Romans 1:29.
Slander no one, Titus 3:2; James 4:11-
12.
See *Gossip, Scoff, Scorn.*

SLAUGHTER

David's reasoning for mass slaughter,
1 Samuel 27:8-11.
Trampled to death by mob, 2 Kings 7:17-
20.
Slaughter on battlefield, Isaiah 37:36;
Amos 5:3.
Facing grim destiny, Jeremiah 15:2-3.
Too little, too late, Amos 3:12.
Third of mankind destroyed, Revelation
9:18.
See *Carnage.*

SLAVERY

Circumcision of Abraham's slaves,
Genesis 17:27.
Plight of conquered, Deuteronomy 20:10-
11.
Solomon's use of forced labor, 1 Kings
9:15.
Slaves set free, then again enslaved,
Jeremiah 34:8-22.
Special purpose for selling slaves, Joel 3:6.
Enslaved by sin, John 8:34; Acts 8:23;
Romans 6:16; 7:23; 2 Timothy 2:26.
Paul's introduction of Onesimus to
Colossians, Colossians 4:9. (See Phile.
10-11.)
Man a slave to whatever masters him,
2 Peter 2:19.
Bodies and souls of men, Revelation 18:13.
See *Bondage, Servant.*

SLEEP

Deep sleep, Genesis 2:21; 15:12; Job 4:13;
Daniel 8:18; Jonah 1:5.
Angels retired in Lot's home, Genesis
19:1-4.
Potentially perilous sleep, 1 Samuel 26:12.
Little time for sleep, Nehemiah 4:21-23.
Companion of night creatures, Job 30:29.
Time for heart searching, Psalm 4:4.
Plotting evil while falling asleep, Psalm
36:4.
Songs in the night, Psalm 77:6.
Frogs in bedrooms of Egypt, Psalm 105:30.
Giving thanks at midnight, Psalm 119:62,
148.
Gift of sleep, Psalm 127:2.
Lazy slumber, Proverbs 6:9-11.
Early morning religiosity can be mistaken,
Proverbs 27:14.
Poor man sleeps better than rich man,
Ecclesiastes 5:12.
Uncomfortable accommodations, Isaiah
28:20.
In time of their Lord's greatest need,
disciples slept, Matthew 26:36-45.
Man who fell asleep during sermon, Acts
20:7-12.
See *Rest.*

SLINGSHOT

Southpaw expertise, Judges 20:16.
David and Goliath, 1 Samuel 17:40-50.
Slingshots as arms of battle, 2 Kings 3:25;
2 Chronicles 26:14.

Stones must lie loose in slingshot, Proverbs 26:8.

SLOGAN
Trustworthy saying, 1 Timothy 4:9-10.
See *Graffiti.*

SLOW
Danger to those who lag behind, Deuteronomy 25:17-19.

SMALL
Branch of a tree, Jeremiah 1:11-12.
One chapter books, Obadiah 1-21; Philemon 1-25; 2 John 1-13; 3 John 1-14; Jude 1-25.
Day of small things, Zechariah 4:10.
As a mustard seed, Mark 4:31; Luke 13:19.
Power of a small faith, Luke 17:5-6.
Man short of stature, Luke 19:1-10.
Widow's mite, Luke 21:1-4.
Remnant of Israel, Romans 11:1-5.
See *Insignificant.*

SNAKE CHARMER
Cobra refuses to listen, Psalm 58:4-5.
Snake bites before charmed, Ecclesiastes 10:11.
Snakes that cannot be charmed, Jeremiah 8:17.

SNAKES
Curse on serpent, Genesis 3:14.
Staff turned into snake, Exodus 4:1-5; 7:8-12.
Perilous snakebite, Numbers 21:6; Deuteronomy 8:15.
Bronze serpent, Numbers 21:9; 2 Kings 18:4; John 3:14.
Wine like venom, Proverbs 23:32.
Snake on rock, Proverbs 30:19.
Beware of breaking into wall, Ecclesiastes 10:8.
Child will play safely near cobra, Isaiah 11:8.
Adders and darting snakes, Isaiah 30:6.
Serpents eating dust, Isaiah 65:25.
Bitten by surprise, Amos 5:19.
Fish or snake, Matthew 7:10.
Wise as serpents, Matthew 10:16.
No fear of serpents, Mark 16:17-18; Luke 10:19.
Paul bitten by snake, Acts 28:1-6.

SNARE
Evil nations become snares and traps, Joshua 23:12-13.
Danger along path, Job 18:10; Psalm 142:3; Proverbs 28:10; Jeremiah 18:22.
Wicked ensnared by their own hands, Psalm 9:16.
Hidden net, Psalm 35:7.
Deliverance from fowler's snare, Psalm 91:3.
Arrogant dig pitfalls, Psalm 119:85.
Snare of wicked avoided, Psalms 119:110; 141:9.
Traps to catch men, Jeremiah 5:26.
Nets and snares, Hosea 5:1.
Brother setting nets for brother, Micah 7:2.
See *Trap.*

SNOW
Hunting in snowfall, 2 Samuel 23:20.
Streams flow with melting snow, Job 6:16.
Divine command, Job 37:6.
Inexhaustible design in snowflake, Job 38:22.
Summer snow, Proverbs 26:1.
Whiter than snow, Isaiah 1:18.
Mountain peaks, Jeremiah 18:14.

SOAP
Unable to wash away stain of guilt, Jeremiah 2:22; Matthew 27:24.
Laundry soap, Malachi 3:2.

SOBRIETY
Alcohol not for those in leadership, Proverbs 31:4-5.
Refusal to drink wine, Jeremiah 35:1-6.
Silence before the Lord, Zephaniah 1:7.
Alert and self-controlled, 1 Thessalonians 5:6; 1 Timothy 3:2.
Temperate use of wine, Titus 1:7.
Temperate disposition, Titus 2:2, 12.
See *Alcohol, Drunkenness.*

SOCIALISM
All things in common, Acts 4:32-35.

SOCIETY
Those who spoke one common language, Genesis 11:1.
Dislike of neighbors who become wealthy, Genesis 26:12-17.
Separated from evil by choice, Psalm 1:1.
Seldom visit your neighbor, Proverbs

25:17.
Salt of earth, Matthew 5:13.
As in the days of Noah, Luke 17:26-30.
Kinship of all people, Acts 17:26.
Many simple people brought to Christ,
1 Corinthians 1:26-31.
See *Community, Neighborhood.*

SOIL
Good soil and poor soil, Ezekiel 19:10-14.
Various types of quality, Luke 8:1-15.
See *Agriculture.*

SOLDIER
Census involved men 20 years or older,
Numbers 26:2.
Large army, Joshua 4:13; 2 Chronicles
14:8; 17:14-18; 26:13.
Reckless adventurers, Judges 9:4. (See
11:3.)
No weapon in Israel, 1 Samuel 13:19-22.
Choosing the mighty and brave for service,
1 Samuel 14:52.
David fought the Lord's battles, 1 Samuel
25:28.
Military family, 1 Chronicles 8:40.
Defecting soldiers, 1 Chronicles 12:1-2, 8,
20.
Abundant young recruits, 2 Chronicles
25:5.
Angel in the military, Isaiah 37:36.
No one to go into battle, Ezekiel 7:14.
Cornelius and his devout family, Acts 10:1-
2. (See also vv. 7, 22.)
See *Mercenaries.*

SOLICITATION
Invitation to immorality, Numbers 25:1-2.
Asking for much, 2 Kings 4:3.

SOLITUDE
Invasion of solitude, Genesis 32:24.
Desire for the desert, Psalm 55:7; Jeremiah
9:2.
Jesus alone in the hills, Matthew 14:23;
15:29.
Jesus and three disciples, Matthew 17:1.
Rest from time of labor, Mark 6:31; Luke
9:10.
Solitude of Jesus disturbed, Mark 7:24.
Jesus often spent time alone, Luke 5:16.
Jesus alone for prayer, Luke 22:41.
Paul found Athens a suitable place to be
left alone, 1 Thessalonians 3:1.

See *Meditation, Quiet time.*

SOLO
Miriam's song of praise, Exodus 15:21.
Inner, unvoiced solo in worship,
1 Corinthians 14:15.
Sing by yourself, James 5:13.
See *Hymn, Music, Singing.*

SON
Abraham's willingness to sacrifice Isaac,
Genesis 22:1-18.
Threat to children if God's commands
disobeyed, Joshua 6:26.
Father's shame for immoral sons,
1 Samuel 2:22-23.
Son's influence over father, 1 Samuel
19:1-6.
Father and son together in death,
2 Samuel 1:23.
Rivalry between father and son, 2 Samuel
15:1-37.
Attitude of David toward rebellious son,
Absalom, 2 Samuel 18:5.
No son to carry Absalom's name,
2 Samuel 18:18.
Father who would have died in place of
son, 2 Samuel 18:32-33.
Father's greatness and son's greater fame,
1 Kings 1:47-48.
Aged father's counsel to son, 1 Kings 2:1-
9.
King Solomon succeeded by his son,
Rehoboam, 1 Kings 11:41-42.
Son less evil than parents, 2 Kings 3:1-3.
Sacrifice of son, 2 Kings 16:3.
Fate of father becomes fate of sons, Esther
9:12-14.
Neither good nor evil transmitted from
father to son, Ezekiel 18:3-20.
Joy and delight to parents, Luke 1:14-15.
Obedience of the Child Jesus to His
parents, Luke 2:41-52.
A son yet in body of ancestor, Hebrews 7:9-
10.
Son received back as from dead, Hebrews
11:19.
See *Children, Family.*

SORCERY
Confronting magicians of Egypt, Exodus
7:6-12. (See 4:1-5.)
Sorcery abandoned, Numbers 24:1.
Substitute for prayer, 1 Samuel 28:5-20.

False prophets foiled, Isaiah 44:25.
Fortune and destiny, Isaiah 65:11.
Those who prophesy lies, Jeremiah 27:9-
15.
Use of magic charms, Ezekiel 13:20.
So-called men of wisdom, Daniel 2:1-4.
Failure of sorcerers and astrologers, Daniel
5:7-8.
Simon in Samaria, Acts 8:9-11.
See *Fortune-telling, Magic.*

SORDID
Mixing human blood with sacrifice, Luke
13:1.

SORROW
Time to conclude mourning, Genesis 50:4.
Shaving head of mourner, Deuteronomy
14:1-2.
All Israel assembled to mourn Samuel,
1 Samuel 25:1.
Weeping until exhausted, 1 Samuel 30:4.
David's song of lament, 2 Samuel 1:17-27.
David's grief over death of Absalom,
2 Samuel 18:19-33.
Sorrow will pass as waters gone by, Job
11:16.
Weeping through night, Psalm 6:6.
Tears become as food, Psalm 42:3.
Recording one's tears, Psalm 56:8.
Sorrow of death brings joy to the Lord,
Psalm 116:15.
Laughter with aching heart, Proverbs
14:13.
Song for heavy heart, Proverbs 25:20.
Tears wiped away, Isaiah 25:8.
Judgment brings righteousness, Isaiah
26:9.
Gladness and joy overcome sorrow and
sighing, Isaiah 35:10.
Sorrow banished, Isaiah 65:19.
Sorrow of disobedience, Jeremiah 3:21.
No balm in Gilead, Jeremiah 8:22.
Mourning forbidden in time of judgment,
Jeremiah 16:5-7.
Joy and gladness gone, Jeremiah 48:33.
Weeping with no one to comfort,
Lamentations 1:16.
Eyes dry from weeping, Lamentations 2:11.
Joy turns to sorrow, Lamentations 5:15.
Tears of false repentance, Malachi 2:13.
Comfort for those who mourn, Matthew
5:4.
Grief of disciples, Matthew 17:22-23.

Laughter can follow tears, Luke 6:21.
Death of Lazarus, John 11:1-44.
Grief turns to joy, John 16:20.
Grief at burial of Stephen, Acts 8:2.
Counselor shares what has been
experienced, 2 Corinthians 1:3-4.
Sorrow at time of death, 1 Thessalonians
4:13-18.
Paul remembered tears of others,
2 Timothy 1:3-4.
Second Coming will bring mourning to
those unprepared, Revelation 1:7.
Tears forever wiped away, Revelation 7:17;
21:4.
Agony of those who refuse to repent,
Revelation 16:10-11.
See *Grief.*

SOUL
Spirit returns to God, Ecclesiastes 12:6-7.
Body destroyed but not soul, Matthew
10:28.
Worth of one lost soul, Matthew 18:12-14;
Luke 15:1-32.
Eternal value of soul compared to temporal
values of life, Mark 8:35-37.
Assured immortality, John 8:51; 11:25-26;
1 Corinthians 15:53-54.
Assembled in heaven, Revelation 20:4.

SOUL-WINNING
Outreach to lost, Psalm 51:13.
Compassion for soul-winning, Psalm
126:6.
The wise who win souls, Proverbs 11:30.
Harvest past, summer ended, no salvation,
Jeremiah 8:20.
Day coming when soul-winning not
necessary, Jeremiah 31:34; Hebrews
8:10-11.
Penalty for failing to witness, Ezekiel 3:18-
19.
Mark of identification on forehead of those
who repent, Ezekiel 9:3-11.
Shepherds who refuse to look for lost
sheep, Ezekiel 34:1-31.
Those who witness shine like stars, Daniel
12:3.
Rescue too late at lion's mouth, Amos 3:12.
Inviting others to come and seek the Lord,
Zechariah 8:20-22.
Becoming fishers of men, Matthew 4:19;
Luke 5:10.
Plentiful harvest but few workers, Matthew

Things shut and things opened, Revelation 3:7.
Lord of lords and King of kings, Revelation 17:14; 19:16.
Totality of Son of God, Revelation 22:13.
See *Determinism, Predestination.*

SPACE
Expanse of sky, Genesis 1:17.
Wonders of space turn thinking inward, Psalm 8:3-8.
Creation proclaims God's righteousness, Psalm 50:6.
All space cannot contain God's love, Psalm 108:4-5.
Material universe vanishes but salvation endures, Isaiah 51:6.
See *Astronomy.*

SPACE/TIME
Vastness of Creation, Genesis 2:1.
Job's concept of space/time, Job 26:7-14.
In the hollow of God's hand, Isaiah 40:12.
Role of heaven and earth, Isaiah 66:22-23.
Creator continuing at work, John 5:17.
Ultimate purpose of creation and human life, Romans 8:18-23.
One who fills the whole universe, Ephesians 4:10.
Universe formed at God's command, Hebrews 11:3.
Earth and sky flee from the eternal, Revelation 20:11.

SPARROW
Sparrow finds nest, Psalm 84:3.
Lonely as a sparrow, Psalm 102:7.
Monetary value, Matthew 10:29; Luke 12:6.

SPECIES
Genetic distinction of species, Genesis 1:25; 1 Corinthians 15:39.

SPECTACLE
First rainbow, Genesis 9:12-17.
Migration of Joseph's family with all their possessions, Genesis 46:5-7.
Vindication by earthquake, Numbers 16:28-34.
Angel who ascended in flame of fire, Judges 13:20.
Chariot of fire and whirlwind, 2 Kings 2:11-12.
Stripped and barefoot, Isaiah 20:2-4.

God's glory seen but not God Himself, Ezekiel 43:1-5.
Something beyond belief, Habakkuk 1:5.
Mountain of Transfiguration, prelude to Resurrection, Mark 9:1-13.
Crucifixion of Jesus, Mark 15:21-32.
Shepherds frightened by shining glory of the Lord, Luke 2:8-10.
Day of Pentecost, Acts 2:1-21.
Staring at those God uses, Acts 3:12.
Conversion of Saul, Acts 9:1-6.
Tongues a sign for unbelievers, 1 Corinthians 14:22-25.
Contemplating resurrection and exaltation of Christ, Ephesians 1:18-23.
Coming to Mount Zion, Hebrews 12:22-24.
Christ coming in clouds, Revelation 1:7.
John's vision of Christ among seven golden lampstands, Revelation 1:12-16.
All creation singing praises to the Lamb, Revelation 5:13-14.
Destruction on earth and in sky, Revelation 6:12-14; 8:4-5.
Cloud for robe, rainbow for hat, Revelation 10:1.
Earth illuminated by angelic splendor, Revelation 18:1.

SPECTACULAR
Proclaiming dreams instead of the Word of God, Jeremiah 23:25-32.
Nothing like this has happened before, Joel 1:2-3.
Army of locusts, Joel 2:1-9.
Flying scroll, Zechariah 5:1-2.
Mountain of Transfiguration, Matthew 17:1-8.
Events at time of Crucifixion, Matthew 27:15-54.
Pharisees wanted sign from heaven, Mark 8:11-12.
Frightened at the sight of an angel, Luke 1:11-12.
Spectacular communication from heaven, Luke 2:8-14.
Excited about the wrong phenomena, Luke 10:17-20.
People curious to see miracles performed, John 6:1-2, 26-27.
Paul caught up into third heaven, 2 Corinthians 12:1-4.
Censer hurled to earth, Revelation 8:5.

SPEECH
Authority of Creator's command, Genesis
1:3, 6, 9, 14, 20, 24, 26.
Samuel's unwasted words, 1 Samuel 3:19.
Left with nothing to say, Nehemiah 5:8.
Elihu's forthright introduction, Job 33:1-5.
Words of enemy not to be trusted, Psalm
5:9.
Speaking lies and flattery, Psalm 12:2.
Resolving not to sin with one's mouth,
Psalm 17:3.
Words pleasing to God, Psalm 19:14.
Blessing of honest speech, Psalm 34:12-13.
Undergirding of God's Word gives
credence to speech of righteous, Psalm
37:30-31.
Keeping tongue from speaking wrong,
Psalm 39:1.
Slander against one's own relative, Psalm
50:20.
Speech of the righteous and of the wicked,
Proverbs 10:11.
Fruit of one's lips, Proverbs 12:14.
Speaking with knowledge the rarest of
jewels, Proverbs 20:15.
Honest answer like kiss, Proverbs 24:26.
Words aptly spoken, Proverbs 25:11.
Speaking with gentle tongue, Proverbs
25:15.
Healing blind, deaf, and dumb, Isaiah 35:5-
6.
Speaking cordially but with deceitful heart,
Jeremiah 9:8.
Importance of worthy speech, Jeremiah
15:19.
Daniel spoke with wisdom and tact, Daniel
2:14.
Quiet in times of evil, Amos 5:13.
Kind and comforting words, Zechariah
1:13.
Lips that preserve knowledge, Malachi 2:7.
Attempting to trap Jesus in His words,
Matthew 22:15; Mark 12:13-17.
Two-word command, Mark 2:14.
Father of John the Baptist stricken with
muteness, Luke 1:11-22.
Use of gracious words, Luke 4:22.
Mute demon, Luke 11:14.
Given words in difficult time, Luke 12:11-
12.
No one ever spoke like Jesus, John 7:46.
Speaking without figures of speech, John
16:29-30.
Writing more effectively than speaking,
2 Corinthians 10:10-11.
Whatever you say or do, Colossians 3:17.
Conversation full of grace, Colossians 4:6.
Deceit of unruly tongue, James 1:26.
Guard well the tongue, James 3:3-6.
See *Communication, Eloquence.*

SPEECHLESS
Speechless in prayer, 1 Samuel 1:9-15.
Tongues stick to roof of mouth, Job 29:10.
Wise put to shame, Jeremiah 8:9.
Ashamed and silent before the Lord,
Ezekiel 16:63.
Embarrassed disciples, Mark 14:40.
Muteness caused by skepticism, Luke 1:19-
20. (See also vv. 62-64.)
Cynical tongues made silent, Luke 20:20-
26.
Silence in heaven, Revelation 8:1.
See *Mute.*

SPEED
Abraham knew how to prepare fast food,
Genesis 18:6-7.
Reckless driving, 2 Kings 9:20.
Verse thought to be prophecy of modern
traffic, Nahum 2:4.
See *Haste.*

SPELLBOUND
Seeing is believing, 1 Kings 10:6-7.
Ezekiel overwhelmed, Ezekiel 3:15.
Ashamed and silent before the Lord,
Ezekiel 16:63.
Reaction of Jesus' parents to Simeon's
attestation, Luke 2:28-33.

SPENDING
Purses with holes in them, Haggai 1:6.

SPIDER
Fragile as spider's web, Job 8:14.
Cobwebs for clothing, Isaiah 59:5-6.

SPINSTER
Remaining unmarried, 1 Corinthians 7:27-
28.

SPIRITISM
Seeking God's will by divination, Genesis
30:27.
Pretending to believe in divination,
Genesis 44:5.
Dead cannot return, 2 Samuel 12:22-23.

Consulting dead concerning living, Isaiah 8:19.

Seeking omen at fork in road, Ezekiel 21:18-23.

So-called men of wisdom in Nebuchadnezzar's court, Daniel 2:1-4.

Failure of the sorcerers and astrologers, Daniel 5:7-8.

Diviners lose skill, Micah 3:7.

Witchcraft destroyed, Micah 5:12.

Wickedness of Nineveh, Nahum 3:3-4.

False visions of diviners, Zechariah 10:2.

Simon in Samaria, Acts 8:9-11.

Those cast into lake of fire, Revelation 21:8.

See *Seance, Sorcery.*

SPIRITUAL HUNGER
Seeking eagerly, 2 Chronicles 15:15.

Longing heart, Psalms 38:9; 73:25.

Chasing wind, Ecclesiastes 1:17-18.

Yearning soul, Isaiah 26:9.

Famine for the words of the Lord, Amos 8:11-12.

Earth filled with the Lord's glory, Habakkuk 2:14.

Blessed are those who hunger, Matthew 5:6; Luke 6:21.

Newborn hunger, 1 Peter 2:2.

SPIRITUALITY
Righteous in one's own eyes, Job 32:1.

Yearning for the Lord, Isaiah 26:9.

Fullest measure of the Law, Matthew 23:23.

Experiencing God's kingdom within, Luke 17:20-21.

Keeping soul in good health, 3 John 2.

Difference between temporal wealth and spiritual wealth, Revelation 3:15-18.

See *Commitment, Discipleship, Holiness, Piety.*

SPIRITUAL PRIDE
Being truly holy, Numbers 16:3-7.

Wise put to shame, Jeremiah 8:9.

Spiritual pride of disobedient people, Amos 4:5.

Paul's concern not to be spiritually proud, Romans 9:1-2.

See *Hypocrisy, Vanity.*

SPLENDOR
Splendor of God, Psalm 8:1-9.

The Lord's splendor in temple, Isaiah 6:1-4.

No more need for sun and moon, Isaiah 60:19-20.

Palace built by unrighteousness, Jeremiah 22:13-15.

Mountain of Transfiguration, Mark 9:2-13.

Description of New Jerusalem, Revelation 21:15-27.

See *Spectacular.*

SPOILS
Plunder permitted at Ai, Joshua 8:1-2. (See 22:8.)

Crops and animals taken by enemy, Judges 6:3-6.

Plunder taken in battle, 1 Samuel 30:16.

Robbing dead after battle, 2 Samuel 23:10.

Grain and wine to enemy, Isaiah 62:8-9.

Do not take from those experiencing disaster, Obadiah 13.

Temptation of soldier to extort, Luke 3:14.

SPORTSMAN
Nimrod, the hunter, Genesis 10:8-9.

Ishmael, the archer, Genesis 21:20.

Esau, the hunter, Genesis 25:27.

Setting traps for men, Jeremiah 5:26.

Men cannot outrun horses, Jeremiah 12:5.

Ready with bow and arrow, Lamentations 2:4.

Swift race horses, Habakkuk 1:8.

Growing up in desert, Luke 1:80.

Invitation to go fishing, Luke 5:1-11.

Peter, the fisherman, John 21:3-11.

Running race with perseverance, Hebrews 12:1.

See *Fisherman, Hunting.*

SPRING
Seedtime and harvest, Genesis 8:22.

Time for kings to go to war, 2 Samuel 11:1.

New growth appears, Proverbs 27:25.

Winter past and flowers appearing, Song of Songs 2:11-12.

Time for birds to migrate, Jeremiah 8:7.

See *Seasons.*

SPY
Joseph a spy against his brothers, Genesis 37:2.

Joseph's brothers accused, Genesis 42:8-9.

Sent to explore Canaan, Numbers 13:1-16.

Ammonites mistrusted David's men who came to show condolence, 2 Samuel

10:1-4.
Searching for Elijah, 2 Kings 2:15-18.
Looking from one's window to activity on
street, Proverbs 7:6-13.
Spying for Pharisees, Luke 20:20.

STABILITY
The God greater than numbers,
Deuteronomy 20:1-4.
Lack of discernment, Deuteronomy 32:28.
The Lord on our side, Psalm 124:1-5.
Voicing simple need, Proverbs 30:7-8.
Looking to flesh for strength, Jeremiah
17:5.
Need for stability in congregation,
Galatians 1:6-9.
Standing at end of struggle, Ephesians
6:13.
That which was from beginning, 1 John
1:1.
See *Dependability*.

STAFF
Choosing mighty and brave for service,
1 Samuel 14:52.
King Solomon's fortunate officials, 1 Kings
10:8.
See *Organization*.

STAMINA
Virility retained until death, Deuteronomy
34:7.
Work for old man, Joshua 13:1.
Not giving up to weariness, Judges 8:4.
Satanic view of man's motivations, Job 2:1-
10.
Times of trouble, Proverbs 24:10.
Race not to swift or strong, Ecclesiastes
9:11.
Renewal of strength, Isaiah 40:30-31.
Men cannot outrun horses, Jeremiah 12:5.
Here we stand, Romans 5:2; 1 Corinthians
7:37.
Stand fast in faith, 1 Corinthians 16:13;
1 Thessalonians 3:8.
See *Strength, Virility*.

STAND
Standing till mission accomplished,
1 Samuel 16:11.
Stand against evil, Ephesians 6:11.

STANDARD
Evil earnings forbidden in house of the

Lord, Deuteronomy 23:18.
Honest weights and measures,
Deuteronomy 25:13-16.
Working by high standards, Proverbs
22:29.
New Testament measure for greatness,
Matthew 20:25-28.
Do not cause another to stumble, Romans
14:20-23.

STARVATION
See *Famine, Hunger*.

STATISTICS
Innumerable dust and stars, Genesis 13:15;
15:5.
Specific enumeration of trained men,
Genesis 14:14.
Greater than numbers, Deuteronomy 20:1-
4.
Thirty sons and 30 daughters, Judges 12:9.
(See v. 14.)
Saul's thousands and David's tens of
thousands, 1 Samuel 18:7. (See 21:11;
29:5.)
Death by measurement, 2 Samuel 8:2.
Depending on number of fighting men,
1 Chronicles 21:17.
Exact number of musicians, 1 Chronicles
25:7.
Census of aliens, 2 Chronicles 2:17-18.
Inventory of temple, Ezra 1:9-11.
People taken into Exile, Jeremiah 52:28-
30.
Measuring width and length of Jerusalem,
Zechariah 2:1-2.
Measurement of flying scroll, Zechariah
5:2.
Genealogy of Jesus, Matthew 1:1-17.
Each sparrow known, hairs of head
numbered, Matthew 10:28-30; Luke
12:7.
Census of Roman world, Luke 2:1-
3.
Number of fish caught, John 21:11.
Growing New Testament church, Acts
16:5.
Number of people saved in ark, 1 Peter
3:20.
Those sealed against judgment, Revelation
7:3-8.
Measure temple, count worshipers,
Revelation 11:1. (See 21:15-21.)
See *Population*.

STATUS
Dislike of neighbors who become wealthy, Genesis 26:12-17.
Least and greatest in society, 2 Kings 23:2.
Blessed in heavenly realms, Ephesians 1:3.
Paul could boast of former status, Philippians 3:2-11.

STATUTE OF LIMITATIONS
Debts canceled every seven years, Deuteronomy 15:1-6.

STEADFAST
Standing at the end of struggle, Ephesians 6:13.
Example of those who lived by faith, Hebrews 12:1-3.
Learning perseverance through trials and testing, James 1:2-4.
Reward for Job's patience, James 5:11.
See *Courage, Perseverance, Stand.*

STEALING
Need for two or three witnesses, Deuteronomy 19:15.
Definition of stealing, Deuteronomy 23:24-25.
Riches gained unjustly, Jeremiah 17:11.
See *Thieves.*

STEALTH
Mode for murder, Judges 4:21; 5:24-27.
King Herod and magi, Matthew 2:7-8, 12.
See *Ruse.*

STENCH
Foul odor of disobedience, Exodus 16:19-20. (See also vv. 22-24.)
Sick drunk, Isaiah 28:7.
Worms in dead bodies, Isaiah 66:24.
Blood of dead man, Revelation 16:3.
See *Putrid.*

STERILE
Women's barrenness, Genesis 11:30; 15:2; 1 Samuel 1:2; 2 Samuel 6:23; 2 Kings 4:11-17; Luke 1:7.
Unable to have children, Hosea 9:11.
See *Barren, Childless.*

STEWARDSHIP
Abram's tithe to Melchizedek, Genesis 14:18-20; Hebrews 7:1-2.
Coming before the Lord empty-handed,
Exodus 23:15.
Giving with willing heart, Exodus 25:2.
Giving to the Lord in overabundance, Exodus 36:2-7.
Offering required from those of limited means, Leviticus 5:7-11.
Offering of thanksgiving, Leviticus 7:12.
Giving less than best to God, Leviticus 22:17-22; Numbers 18:29.
Value of silver in giving, Numbers 7:13-85. (See also 10:2.)
Gifts expected from those who gave most in battle, Numbers 31:27-31.
Items consecrated in advance of offering, Deuteronomy 12:26.
Offerings given three times annually, Deuteronomy 16:16-17.
Earnings from prostitution unacceptable, Deuteronomy 23:18.
Giving to the Lord the child given to praying woman, 1 Samuel 1:25-28.
Bizarre offering, 1 Samuel 6:4-5.
Offering required to obtain divine leadership, 1 Samuel 9:1-9.
David refused cheap stewardship, 2 Samuel 24:21-24.
Three sources of funds for temple, 2 Kings 12:4-5.
Personal treasures given to temple, 1 Chronicles 29:3-4.
Giving to God what He has given to us, 1 Chronicles 29:14.
Money, food, and drink for temple workers, Ezra 3:7.
Giving generously, Psalm 37:21, 26.
Value of sacrifice and offering, Psalm 50:23.
The kind of sacrifice God blesses, Psalm 51:15-17.
Giving out of gratitude for deliverance, Psalm 54:6-7.
Blessing on generous, Psalm 112:5.
Honor the Lord with one's wealth, Proverbs 3:9-10.
Doing good to others, Proverbs 3:27-28.
Blessing for generous man, Proverbs 22:9.
Those who boast of giving but do not give, Proverbs 25:14.
Bread cast on waters, Ecclesiastes 11:1.
Meaningless offerings brought by Israel, Isaiah 1:11-17.
Prophecy concerning Tyre, Isaiah 23:15-18.
Relating fasting to care of others, Isaiah

58:3-7.
Wrong kind of offering, Isaiah 66:3.
Bringing offerings unsuitable to the Lord, Jeremiah 6:20.
Paying tithes every three years, Amos 4:4.
People lived in fine homes while temple lay in ruins, Haggai 1:1-4.
Defiled offerings from defiled people, Haggai 2:13-14.
Priests who defiled altar, Malachi 1:6-14.
Refined gold and silver, Malachi 3:2-4.
Stealing from God, Malachi 3:8-10.
Giving with clean heart, Matthew 5:23-24.
Private stewardship, Matthew 6:2-4.
Treasures on earth and treasures in heaven, Matthew 6:19-21.
Losing life to find it again, Matthew 10:39.
Paying taxes to government, Matthew 22:15-22; Mark 12:13-17.
Fullest measure of giving, Matthew 23:23.
Anointing of Jesus, Matthew 26:6-13.
Rich man who provided tomb for Jesus, Matthew 27:57-61.
Those given much and those given little, Mark 4:24-25.
Widow's small offering, Mark 12:41-44; Luke 21:1-4.
Expensive perfume used to prepare Jesus for burial, Mark 14:3-9.
Sharing with others, Luke 3:11.
Abundance rewarded those who give, Luke 6:38.
Man who built synagogue, Luke 7:1-5.
Women who helped Jesus in support of His ministry, Luke 8:1-3.
Those who tithe but neglect justice, Luke 11:42.
Selling one's possessions for the poor, Luke 12:33-34.
Ananias and Sapphira, Acts 5:1-11.
Woman who helped the poor, Acts 9:36-42.
Devout centurion, Acts 10:2.
Reaching out to help others, Acts 11:27-30.
Paul worked to provide for his own needs, Acts 20:33-35.
Sharing spiritual blessings and material blessings, Romans 15:26-27.
Need to prove faithful, 1 Corinthians 4:2.
Right of apostle to receive material support, 1 Corinthians 9:7-14.
Seeking good of others above one's self, 1 Corinthians 10:24.
Greater gift than money, 1 Corinthians

13:3.
Giving on first day of week, 1 Corinthians 16:2.
Not making profit of the Gospel, 2 Corinthians 2:17.
Persecution brought overflowing joy and generosity, 2 Corinthians 8:1-5.
Sowing and reaping, 2 Corinthians 9:6-7.
Giving from continuity of desire, 2 Corinthians 9:10.
Some pay, others only receive, 2 Corinthians 11:7-8.
Financial responsibility of children, 2 Corinthians 12:14-15.
Concern of early Christians for poor, Galatians 2:9-10.
Student sharing with teacher, Galatians 6:6.
Concern for pastor, Philippians 4:10-19.
Paul avoided greed, 1 Thessalonians 2:5.
Wealth of money and wealth of good deeds, 1 Timothy 6:17-19.
Gifts and sacrifices, Hebrews 8:3.
Abel's good offerings, Hebrews 11:4.
Share with others, Hebrews 13:16.
Using one's gift for good of others, 1 Peter 4:10.
See *Benevolence, Donation, Philanthropy, Tithe.*

STINGY
Result of stinginess, Proverbs 11:24; 21:13; 28:27.
Food of stingy man, Proverbs 23:6-8.
Folly of hoarding, Ecclesiastes 5:13.
Those who would not share in financing Paul's ministry, Philippians 4:15.
See *Frugality, Miser.*

STIPEND
Salary arrangement for priest, Deuteronomy 18:1-2.
Evil earnings forbidden in house of the Lord, Deuteronomy 23:18.
Requesting payment for spiritual ministry, 2 Kings 5:20-27.
High cost of a dance, Mark 6:21-29.
See *Honorarium, Payment, Salary, Wages.*

STOMACH
Knife to the throat, Proverbs 23:2.
To swallow camel, Matthew 23:24.
Making stomach god, Philippians 3:19.
See *Diet, Digestion, Food, Gluttony,*

fighting men, 1 Chronicles 21:17.
Prayer for physical strength, Nehemiah 6:9.
Strength of elephant, Job 40:15-24.
Strength comes from God, Psalm 18:32.
Working with dull ax, Ecclesiastes 10:10.
Trust in the Lord, not horses and chariots,
    Isaiah 31:1-3.
Strength and repose from the Lord, Isaiah
    35:3-4.
Mount up on wings like eagles, Isaiah
    40:29-31.
Sufficiency of our God, Isaiah 41:10.
Least becomes great, Isaiah 60:22.
Made strong by God's power, Jeremiah
    1:17-19.
Boasting only in the Lord, Jeremiah 9:23-
    24.
Lord like mighty warrior, Jeremiah 20:11.
Nothing too hard for God, Jeremiah 32:27.
Strength of great Redeemer, Jeremiah
    50:34.
Weaker sex, Jeremiah 51:30.
Mighty are those who obey the Lord, Joel
    2:11.
Filled with power, Micah 3:8.
Feet like feet of deer, Habakkuk 3:19.
Not by might nor by power, Zechariah 4:6.
Faith in God the greatest strength,
    Zechariah 12:5.
Strong looking after weak, Romans 15:1.
Standing firm in faith, 1 Corinthians 16:13-
    14.
We are promised same power which
    brought Jesus back from grave,
    Ephesians 1:18-21.
Holy Spirit's power working within us,
    Ephesians 3:20-21.
Undying love, Ephesians 6:24.
One angel overpowering and binding
    Satan, Revelation 20:1-3.
See *Power, Vigorous, Vitality.*

STRESS
Delegating work to others, Exodus 18:17-
    27.
The God who is greater than numbers,
    Deuteronomy 20:1-4.
Jealous wife, 1 Samuel 1:2-11.
King's business urgent, 1 Samuel 21:8.
Leadership for those in trouble, 1 Samuel
    22:2.
Where to look for help in desperate times,
    2 Kings 6:24-31.
Ultimate in distressing circumstances, Job

1:6-22.
Refining finest gold, Job 23:10; Isaiah
    48:10.
New attitude and confidence, Psalm 40:1-
    3.
Refuge and strength for every trouble,
    Psalm 46:1-3.
The One who helps and sustains, Psalm
    54:4.
For times of anguish, the God who hears,
    Psalm 55:1-17.
No need for fear, Psalm 56:3-4.
Steadfast, singing heart, Psalm 57:7-8.
Rest in God alone, Psalm 62:1-2.
Waters up to neck, Psalm 69:1.
Dwelling place for yearning soul, Psalm
    84:1-12.
Sheep of His pasture, Psalm 100:1-5.
Steadfast heart, Psalm 108:1-5.
Refuge in times of anguish, Psalm 118:1-9.
Answer to those who taunt, Psalm 119:41-
    48.
The Lord on our side, Psalm 124:1-5.
The Lord grants sleep, Psalm 127:2.
Out of depths, Psalm 130:1-6.
Made bold and stouthearted, Psalm 138:3.
Turning to the Lord when no one else
    cares, Psalm 142:1-7.
Pleasant ways and paths of peace, Proverbs
    3:13-18.
Cheerful heart, Proverbs 17:22. (See
    18:14.)
Prayer for contentment, Proverbs 30:7-8.
Prayer for strength in time of distress,
    Isaiah 33:2.
Renewal of strength, Isaiah 40:30-31.
One who strengthens and helps, Isaiah
    41:10.
Peace comes to those who obey and follow
    the Lord's direction, Isaiah 48:17-18.
The Lord will guide, satisfy, and
    strengthen, Isaiah 58:11.
Beauty for ashes, Isaiah 61:1-3.
The Lord shared their distress, Isaiah 63:9.
Where to find rest for the soul, Jeremiah
    6:16.
The Lord who understands and gives
    counsel, Jeremiah 15:15-16.
Sure resource in time of trouble,
    Lamentations 3:19-33.
Sleepless king, relaxed prisoner, Daniel
    6:16-23.
Witness in time of stress, Jonah 1:4-9.
Acknowledging the Lord in times of great

distress, Jonah 2:1-9.
Strength from the Lord, Habakkuk 3:19.
Reacting as a Christian to those who
persecute, Matthew 5:11-12.
Trusting the Lord for needs, Matthew 6:25-
34; Luke 12:22-34.
The One who lifts burdens and gives rest,
Matthew 11:28-30.
Mastery of Jesus over fear, Luke 8:22-
25.
Small faith in a great God, Luke 11:20.
Never give up, Luke 18:1-8.
Advanced determination not to worry,
Luke 21:14.
Light of Scripture dispels darkness, John
1:5.
Jesus is our light, John 8:12.
Confidence in future brings stability to
present, John 14:1-6.
Futility of life apart from faith, John 15:5-
11.
Trusting the One who gives true peace,
John 16:33.
Going without food in times of anxiety,
Acts 27:33-36.
Role of suffering in strengthening faith,
Romans 5:1-11.
More than conquerors, Romans 8:12-39.
(Note victory over fear, v. 15.)
Strength and confidence in sufficient Lord,
1 Corinthians 1:8-9.
Facing problems, yet victorious,
2 Corinthians 4:7-18.
Facing life with dimensions of faith,
Ephesians 3:14-21.
Paul experienced anxiety, Philippians
2:25-30.
Sure way to inner peace, Philippians 4:4-
7.
Captive of wrong thinking, Colossians 2:8.
Capsule antidote for stress,
1 Thessalonians 5:16-18.
The Lord knows what He is doing,
2 Thessalonians 1:3-5.
Anchor for soul, Hebrews 6:19-20.
Restoration for those who suffer, 1 Peter
5:10.
Grace and peace in abundance, 2 Peter
1:2.
Testing as an act of divine love, Revelation
3:19.
Absence of stress in New Jerusalem,
Revelation 21:1-5.
See *Anxiety, Duress, Tension.*

STRIFE
Abraham's effort to avoid strife, Genesis
13:8.
The God who is greater than numbers,
Deuteronomy 20:1-4.
Jealous wife, 1 Samuel 1:2-7.
Conflict between David and Saul,
1 Samuel 26:1-25.
Reputation as troublemaker, 2 Samuel
20:1.
The Lord on our side, Psalm 124:1-5.
Cause and solution, Proverbs 12:10; 15:18;
17:14.
Wise in his own eyes, Proverbs 26:16.
Avoid quarrels of others, Proverbs 26:17.
Blessed are peacemakers, Matthew 5:9.
Division in communities and families,
Matthew 12:25.
Christian leaders part company, Acts
15:36-41.
Devouring each other, Galatians 5:15.
Mark of good disciple, 2 Timothy 2:24.
See *Abrasion, Conflict, Jealousy.*

STRUGGLE
Becoming master over sin, Genesis 4:7.
David fought the Lord's battles, 1 Samuel
25:28.
Turning battle back at gate, Isaiah 28:6.
Test of righteousness in time of
wickedness, Matthew 24:12-13.
Fight good fight of faith, 1 Timothy 6:11-
12.
See *Duress.*

STUBBORN
Those who change only under pressure of
circumstances, Psalm 32:9
Cobra refuses to listen, Psalm 58:3-5.
Fool airs own opinion, Proverbs 18:2.
Those who refuse counsel, Proverbs 29:1.
Break up unplowed ground, Jeremiah 4:3.
Hearts hard as flint, Zechariah 7:11-12.
See *Resistance.*

STUDENTS
King Solomon's fortunate officials, 1 Kings
10:8.
Learning what cannot be seen, Job 34:32.
True wisdom obtained from Scriptures,
Psalm 119:97-100.
Giving heed to instruction, Proverbs 16:20.
Discernment provides knowledge,
Proverbs 18:15.

Those who will not respond, Jeremiah 32:33.
The God who helps students, Daniel 1:17. (See vv. 3-20.)
Students and servants beneath teachers and masters, Matthew 10:24.
Hearing but not understanding, Mark 4:11-12.
Thoroughness of Jesus with disciples, Mark 4:34.
Willingness to learn, Luke 11:1.
Listening with eagerness, Acts 17:11-12.
Thorough knowledge of Scriptures, Acts 18:24-26.
Holy Spirit's guidance in Bible study, 1 Corinthians 2:6-16.
Folly of intellectual pride, 1 Corinthians 3:18-20.
Supreme examination, 2 Corinthians 13:5.
Student sharing with teacher, Galatians 6:6.
Properly receiving the Word of God, 1 Thessalonians 2:13.
Correctly handling Scripture, 2 Timothy 2:15.
Those slow to learn, Hebrews 5:11-14.
Faith as sure antidote for doubt, Hebrews 11:1-3.
Those who take Scriptures to heart, Revelation 1:3.
Questions and answers between teacher and student, Revelation 7:13-17.
See *Academic, Learning.*

STUDY
Do not neglect God's Word, Psalm 119:16.
Prayer for perception in study of Scripture, Psalm 119:18.
Wisdom a gift from God for study of Scriptures, Psalm 119:33-38.
Glory of kings, Proverbs 25:2.
Those who do not know Scriptures, Matthew 22:29.
Wealth and worry limit understanding, Mark 4:19.
Putting good teaching into action, John 13:17.
Eager to examine Scriptures, Acts 17:11.
Sharing together insights into Scriptures, Acts 18:24-26.
Holy Spirit's guidance in Bible study, 1 Corinthians 2:6-16.
Diligent in quest for spiritual maturity, 1 Timothy 4:13.

Searching prophets, 1 Peter 1:10-12.

STYLE
Clothed with righteousness and faithfulness, Isaiah 11:5.
Fine clothing belongs in kings' palaces, not on prophet in desert, Matthew 11:7-9.
Those wearing clean robes, Revelation 22:14.
See *Wardrobe.*

SUBCONSCIOUS
In-depth corruption of thought, Genesis 6:5; Jeremiah 4:14; Matthew 15:19; Romans 1:28.
Fortified mind, Deuteronomy 6:5-6.
Heart and spirit, Psalm 51:10.
Motivational resources, Psalm 119:11.
Fountain in the heart, Proverbs 4:23.
Poisoned subconscious, Proverbs 18:18; 26:22.
Deceitfulness of heart, Jeremiah 17:9.
Vitality for subconscious, Romans 12:2; Ephesians 4:22.
Thought motivation, Romans 14:14.
Cultivating the subconscious, Philippians 4:8.
Function of evil subconscious, 2 Timothy 3:2.
Mental purity and corruption, Titus 1:15.
Inner mind perceived, Hebrews 4:12.
Written in the heart, Hebrews 10:16.
See *Motivation, Thought.*

SUBJECTION
Partial blindness inflicted as disgrace, 1 Samuel 11:2-11.
Becoming subjected by need for protection, 1 Samuel 27:12.
Inequity among citizens, Nehemiah 5:1-5.
If I perish, I perish, Esther 4:16.
Subjecting oneself to the Lord's commands, Isaiah 48:17-18.
Conditional freedom, Jeremiah 34:8-11.
No chance for escape, Jeremiah 48:44.
Knowing who is the Lord, Ezekiel 6:10, 14; 7:4, 9, 27; 12:16, 20; 13:9, 23; 14:11.
Ashamed and silent before the Lord, Ezekiel 16:63.
Demons refused permission to speak, Mark 1:33-34.
Right spirit in victory over evil, Luke 10:17-20.
See *Bondage.*

7:1-16.
Strength from God, 2 Samuel 22:33.
Solomon's prayer for wisdom rather than material gain, 1 Kings 3:5-15; 4:29-34.
Believer assured true success, Psalm 1:3.
Sure success a delight to the One who guides us, Psalm 37:23-24.
Letting God fulfill His purpose, Psalm 57:2.
Giving God glory for success, Psalm 118:1-16.
Hiding God's Word in the heart, Psalm 119:11.
Good influence written on tablet of heart, Proverbs 3:1-4.
Key to success, Proverbs 16:3; 21:30.
Seeking first the kingdom of God, Proverbs 21:21.
Humility and faith, Proverbs 22:4.
Righteous man rises again and again, Proverbs 24:15-16.
Emptiness of success and affluence, Ecclesiastes 2:4-11.
Victory not necessarily to swift and strong, Ecclesiastes 9:11.
Noble man makes noble plans, Isaiah 32:8.
Definition of man who refuses bribes, Isaiah 33:15-16.
Those whom the Lord commissions achieve success, Isaiah 48:15.
Success assured those who trust the Lord, whatever circumstances, Jeremiah 17:7-8.
King's prosperity linked to conduct, Daniel 4:27.
Not by might nor by power, Zechariah 4:6
New Testament measure for greatness, Matthew 20:25-28.
Failure turned to success for fishermen, Luke 5:1-11.
Excited about wrong phenomena, Luke 10:17-20.
Vine and fruit, John 15:1-8.
Chosen for guidance and blessing, John 15:16.
Speaking only of what Christ has done in us, Romans 15:18-19.
Success comes only from God, 1 Corinthians 3:6-8; 2 Corinthians 4:7.
Building on good foundation, 1 Corinthians 3:10-15.
Need to prove faithful, 1 Corinthians 4:2.
In race, only one wins. In serving God, all may win, 1 Corinthians 9:24-27.
Spreading fragrance of Christ,

2 Corinthians 2:14.
Let the Lord commend, 2 Corinthians 10:17-18.
Paul's commendation of Timothy, Philippians 2:19-23.
Work of God reported widely, 1 Thessalonians 1:8-10.
Joy and crown of those who present message, 1 Thessalonians 2:17-19.
Timothy's encouraging report from Thessalonians, 1 Thessalonians 3:6-7.
Abundant praise to God for success in ministry, 1 Thessalonians 3:8-10.
Good purpose fulfilled, 2 Thessalonians 1:11.
Purpose and means of spiritual success, 2 Thessalonians 1:11-12.
Prepared by God to succeed as believer, Hebrews 13:20-21.
Success in business succumbs to certainty of death, James 1:10-11.
Mentality of success, 1 Peter 1:15.
Attributes of mature Christian life, 2 Peter 1:5-9.
Certainty of success in Christian life, Jude 24-25.
See *Accomplishment, Achievement, Victory.*

SUCCESSOR
Moses turned control over to Joshua, Deuteronomy 31:1-8.
Moses laid hands on Joshua, Deuteronomy 34:9.
David's words on taking over as king after death of Saul, 2 Samuel 2:7.
Mother's role in advancement of son, 1 Kings 1:11-31.
Divided into factions, 1 Kings 16:21-22.
Secret anointing of king, 2 Kings 9:1-13.
Chosen to build temple, 1 Chronicles 28:2-10.
Son fulfills father's dream, 2 Chronicles 6:3-11.
Candidates to replace Queen Vashti, Esther 2:1-4.

SUFFERING
Purpose of testing, Deuteronomy 8:1-5.
Experiencing suffering and reversal without blaming God, Job 1:22.
Tested to come forth as gold, Job 23:10.
God speaks through suffering, Job 33:14.
Suffering becomes God's avenue for counsel, Job 36:15.

Desperate times, Psalm 60:3.
Refined like silver, Psalm 66:10.
Discipline meant to be blessing, Psalm 94:12.
The Lord does as He pleases, Psalm 135:6.
Going through crucible, Proverbs 17:3.
Description of physical beating, Isaiah 1:6.
Furnace of affliction, Isaiah 48:10.
The Lord takes our infirmities and sorrows, Isaiah 53:4.
God's thoughts higher than man's, Isaiah 55:9.
Suffering on just and unjust, Jeremiah 49:12.
Suffering can be means of learning, Matthew 11:28-30.
Peter saw suffering of Christ as material event, not in its deep redemptive meaning, Matthew 16:21-23.
Suffering of Jesus in spite of His innocence, Luke 23:15-16.
Marks of suffering, Luke 24:40.
Purpose of sickness, John 11:4.
Persecution implements spread of Gospel, Acts 8:3-4.
Purpose of suffering, Romans 5:3.
Present suffering not to be compared with coming glory, Romans 8:18.
Patience in affliction, Romans 12:12.
Christ, who is faithful, will keep you strong, 1 Corinthians 1:8-9.
Purpose of trouble, 2 Corinthians 4:17-18.
Bearing marks of Jesus, Galatians 6:17.
Suffering a privilege, Philippians 1:29-30.
Anticipating persecution in advance, 1 Thessalonians 3:4.
Made perfect through suffering, Hebrews 2:10.
Benefit of bodily suffering, 1 Peter 4:1-2.
Suffering in name of Christ, 1 Peter 4:12-16.
Temporary suffering as reward for faithfulness, Revelation 1:9.
The Lord disciplines those He loves, Revelation 3:19.
Those who wish to die but cannot, Revelation 9:4-6.
Agony of those who refuse to repent, Revelation 16:10-11.
All tears wiped away, Revelation 21:4.
See *Persecution.*

SUFFICIENT
All-sufficiency of our Lord, Isaiah 44:24-28.

God's righteousness lasts forever, Isaiah 51:8.
Nothing too hard for God, Jeremiah 32:27.
Needs supplied, Philippians 4:13, 19.
All we need to live life of godliness, 2 Peter 1:3.

SUFFRAGE
God's plan for women and their rights, Genesis 3:16.
Businesswoman at Thyatira, Acts 16:13-15.
Paul's view of woman's role in marriage, 1 Corinthians 7:4.
See *Equal rights, Women's rights.*

SUICIDE
Contemplating suicide, Genesis 27:46.
Death of King Saul on battlefield, 1 Samuel 31:1-6. (See also 2 Sam. 1:1-12.)
Death of Ahithophel, 2 Samuel 17:23.
Death by fire, 1 Kings 16:18.
Covenant with death, Isaiah 28:15, 18.
Death of Judas, Matthew 27:3-5.
Man who almost killed himself, Acts 16:25-28.

SUITOR
See *Courtship, Romance.*

SUMMER
Summer assured, Genesis 8:22.
Intense heat, Psalm 32:4.
The Creator's design, Psalm 74:17.
Learn from the ants, Proverbs 6:6-8; 30:25.
Summer snow, Proverbs 26:1.
Ripened fruit, Jeremiah 40:10-12.
Chaff on threshing floor, Daniel 2:35.
Summer house, Amos 3:15.
Approaching summer, Matthew 24:32; Mark 13:28; Luke 21:30.

SUMMONS
See *Decree, Mandate.*

SUN
Causing sun to stand still, Joshua 10:12-13.
Reversal of sun's shadow, 2 Kings 20:9-11; Isaiah 38:7-8.
Canopy for sun, Psalm 19:4.
Immune to sunstroke and sunburn, Psalm 121:6.
Perpetual routine, Ecclesiastes 1:5.
Turned to darkness, Joel 2:31.
Brighter than sunshine, Acts 26:13.

See *Astronomy, Sunset.*

SUNDAY
Not doing business on Sabbath, Nehemiah
10:31.
Proper observance of Sabbath, Isaiah
58:13-14; Matthew 12:1-13.
Serving God seven days a week, John 5:16-
17.
Paul regularly attended Sabbath worship,
Acts 14:1; 17:2.
Those who consider one day more sacred
than another, Romans 14:5.
See *Legalism.*

SUNSET
Creator's design of sunset, Genesis 1:5.
Accuracy of sunset, Psalm 104:19.
Jesus healed at sunset, Luke 4:40.
See *Sun.*

SUPERFICIAL
Pride and arrogance, 1 Samuel 2:3.
Laughter with aching heart, Proverbs
14:13.
Deceitful, malicious man, Proverbs 26:24-
26.
Avoid meaningless offerings, Isaiah 1:13.
End to noisy songs, Ezekiel 26:13.
Mere lip service instead of true
commitment, Ezekiel 33:31-32.
Lacking roots, Mark 4:16-17.
Doing good without expecting
reciprocation, Luke 6:27-36.
Like children in marketplace, Luke 7:31-
32.
No spiritual depth, John 6:66.
Desiring earthly kingdom rather than
spiritual dynamics, Acts 1:6-8.
Superficial service for the Lord,
1 Corinthians 3:10-15.
Blown about by varying winds of teaching,
Ephesians 4:14.
See *Hypocrisy, Phony, Pretense,
Shallowness, Sham.*

SUPERIORITY
God as first priority, Genesis 1:1.
Protected from superior enemy, Exodus
14:15-31.
Measure of holiness, Numbers 16:3-7.
The God greater than numbers,
Deuteronomy 20:1-4.
Nothing equal to Solomon's wisdom,

1 Kings 4:29-34.
Race not to swift or strong, Ecclesiastes
9:11.
Wrong and right boasting, Jeremiah 9:23-
24.
God the Creator and gods who perish,
Jeremiah 10:11-12.
Knowing who is the Lord, Ezekiel 6:10, 14;
7:4, 9, 27; 12:16, 20; 13:9, 23; 14:11.
All one in Christ, Galatians 3:28.
God's Son superior to angels, Hebrews
1:3-4.

SUPERLATIVE
Greatness of David and anticipated greater
fame of Solomon, 1 Kings 1:47-48.
Great, mighty, and awesome God,
Nehemiah 9:32.
Immeasurable anticipations, Jeremiah
33:3.
Beyond human conception and
perception, 1 Corinthians 2:9.
Lavished with blessing, Ephesians 1:7-8.
Holy Spirit's power working within us,
Ephesians 3:20-21.
Christ above all, Colossians 1:15-20.
Joy of problems and testing, James 1:2-4.
See *Hyperbole.*

SUPERSTITION
Depending on ark of covenant for good
luck, 1 Samuel 4:3.
Dangerous gods of hills, 1 Kings 20:23.
Use of incense, Jeremiah 44:18.
Use of magic charms, Ezekiel 13:18.
Disciples thought to be gods, Acts 14:11-
15.
Sign of the serpent, Acts 28:3-5.

SUPERVISION
Rebelling against supervision, Numbers
14:1-4.
Approval of parents, Numbers 30:3-5.
Faithful service without pastoral
supervision, Philippians 2:12-13.
See *Discipline.*

SUPPLICATION
Persistent prayer, 1 Samuel 1:20; 7:8;
Philippians 4:6.
Looking persistently to the Lord, Psalm
123:2.
Friend in need, Luke 11:5-8.
See *Intercession.*

SUPPLY
Unhappy with God's provision, Numbers 11:4-6.
Shortage of wives, Judges 21:14.
Dying earth, Isaiah 51:6.
No wine at wedding, John 2:1-5.
See *Provision.*

SUPPORT
Commission with encouragement, Deuteronomy 3:28.
Weak as spider's web, Job 8:14.
God ever-present in times of trouble, Psalm 14:4-5.
Overt generosity of Macedonian churches, 2 Corinthians 8:1-5.
Some pay and others only receive, 2 Corinthians 11:7-8.
See *Assistance.*

SUPPRESSION
Futile effort to suppress truth, Jeremiah 38:1-6.
Those who tried to prevent resurrection of Jesus, Matthew 27:62-66. (See also 28:11-15.)
Demons refused permission to speak, Mark 1:33-34.
See *Censure.*

SUPREMACY
Prenatal superiority, Genesis 25:23.
Subservient sheaves, Genesis 37:5-7.
Hand on neck, Genesis 49:8.
Power in numbers, Numbers 22:2-4.
The God who overcomes great enemies, Deuteronomy 20:1.
Apparent supremacy of enemy invalidated, Joshua 11:1-6.
Praising subject above king, 1 Samuel 21:11.
Immeasurable greatness of God, 2 Chronicles 6:12-19.
The God who speaks and acts, Isaiah 44:24-28.
No other God like the Lord, Isaiah 46:9.
Wrong and right boasting, Jeremiah 9:23-24.
God the Creator and gods who perish, Jeremiah 10:11-12.
Sovereignty of Jesus over all earth, Revelation 1:5.
See *Conquest.*

SURETY
Reuben's guarantee to his father, Genesis 42:37.
Words of caution, Proverbs 6:1-5; 11:15; 22:26.

SURGERY
Circumcision at advanced age, Genesis 17:10-27.

SURPRISE
Harvesters see ark of God, 1 Samuel 6:13.
Awesome, unexpected acts of God, Isaiah 64:3.
Grapes in desert, Hosea 9:10.
Return of Christ at unexpected hour, Matthew 24:44.
Frightened at sight of angel, Luke 1:11-12.
Message heard by those who did not ask, Romans 10:20.
Like a thief, 2 Peter 3:10.
See *Amazement, Awe, Speechless.*

SURRENDER
Fortunes restored, Deuteronomy 30:1-3.
Partial blindness inflicted as disgrace, 1 Samuel 11:2-11.
Surrender to power of God, 1 Samuel 14:1-14.
Ammonites surrendered to David, 2 Samuel 10:1-19.
After all his contests with God and circumstances, Job submitted, Job 42:1-9.
Potter and clay, Isaiah 45:9; 64:8.
Reward for obedience, Isaiah 48:17-18.
Hands on head, Jeremiah 2:37.
In desperation, Zedekiah listened to Jeremiah, Jeremiah 38:14-28.
See *Defeat.*

SURROGATE
One woman bearing a child for another, Genesis 16:1-5; 30:1-6.
True mother served as surrogate, Exodus 2:1-9.
Surrogate mother among birds, Jeremiah 17:11.

SURVEILLANCE
Satan's continual survey of earth, Job 1:7.
Mankind observed from heavenly throne, Psalm 11:4.
Looking from window to activity on street,

Proverbs 7:6-13.
Faithful service without pastoral
supervision, Philippians 2:12-13.

SURVEY
Situation investigated at Sodom and
Gomorrah, Genesis 18:20-21.
Questions for spies sent to Canaan,
Numbers 13:18-20.
Seeing unpleasant sights, Deuteronomy
28:34.
Babylon's preparation to plunder
Hezekiah's treasures, Isaiah 39:1-6.
Paul's survey concerning Thessalonians,
1 Thessalonians 3:1-11.

SURVEYOR
Measurement for judgment, Lamentations
2:8.

SURVIVAL
People divided for protection, Genesis
32:6-8.
Protection against enemies of road, Ezra
8:21-23.
The Lord on our side, Psalm 124:1-5.
Ask for ancient paths, Jeremiah 6:16.
Birds know seasons of migration, Jeremiah
8:7.
Empty cisterns, parched fields, Jeremiah
14:1-6.
Ten percent survival, Amos 5:3.
Whether to contest enemy or seek terms of
peace, Luke 14:31-32.
Desiring food of pigs, Luke 15:16.

SUSPICION
Negative and positive viewpoints,
Numbers 13:17-33.
Proof of virginity, Deuteronomy 22:13-19.
Identification by manner of speech, Judges
12:5-6.
Wrongly suspecting woman of
drunkenness, 1 Samuel 1:9-16.
Mistrusting men who came to show
condolence, 2 Samuel 10:1-4.
See *Mistrust.*

SUSTENANCE
Need for food and water, Job 22:7-8.
Wickedness and violence, Proverbs 4:17.

SWEETNESS
Tempting to taste, 1 Samuel 14:24-28

Honey from rock, Psalm 81:16.
Eating too much honey, Proverbs 25:16.
See *Taste.*

SWIFTNESS
Disciple who outran Peter, John 20:4.

SWIMMING
Spreading hands to swim, Isaiah 25:11.
Jonah's plunge into sea, Jonah 2:1-10.
Swim to freedom and safety, Acts 27:42-44.

SYMBOLISM
God's rainbow, Genesis 9:12-17.
Hand under thigh, Genesis 24:2, 9.
Avoid architecture which detracts from
worship, Deuteronomy 16:21-22.
Symbol of judgment and forgiveness,
1 Chronicles 21:27-30.
Prophecy of boiling pot, Jeremiah 1:13-15.
Smashing jar from potter, Jeremiah 19:1-
13.
Good figs and bad figs, Jeremiah 24:1-10.
Act of rebellious idolatry, Ezekiel 8:17.
Symbol of Holy Spirit's power, Zechariah
4:1-6.
Jesus washed feet of disciples, John 13:2-
17.
See *Nonverbal communication, Visual.*

SYMPATHY
Mistrusting men who came to show
condolence, 2 Samuel 10:1-4.
Those at ease have contempt for others,
Job 12:5.
Divine sympathy, Psalms 78:39; 103:13;
Isaiah 63:9.
Sympathy put into action, Isaiah 58:7.
Help in time of need, Luke 10:33-35; Acts
20:35.
Shared sorrow, John 11:19-33.
Tears of Jesus, John 11:35.
Bearing burdens of others, Galatians 6:2;
Hebrews 13:3.
Remembering another's tears, 2 Timothy
1:4.
Divine empathy, Hebrews 4:15.
See *Caring, Compassion, Empathy,
Involvement.*

SYNCRETISM
Confused mother and son, Judges 17:1-6.
No relationship between ark of God and
god Dagon, 1 Samuel 5:1-5.

Using idol to provide divine deliverance,
1 Samuel 19:11-17.
Solomon's involvement with other gods,
1 Kings 11:4-6.
Procedure of Jeroboam to dilute faith of
Israel, 1 Kings 12:25-33.
Appointing those unqualified to office of
priest, 1 Kings 13:33.
Mixing paganism with worship of true God,
1 Kings 14:1-18.
Worthless idols, 1 Kings 16:25-26.
No God in Israel, 2 Kings 1:1-4.
Pagan prophets, ministers, and priests
destroyed, 2 Kings 10:18-29.
Partial obedience to the Lord, 2 Kings
15:1-4.
Worshiping the Lord and other gods,
2 Kings 17:33.
Defilement in sanctuary, 2 Chronicles
29:1-11.
True God spoken of as if He were one of
many gods, Isaiah 37:10. (See vv. 6, 23.)
Clearly stated divine rule, Isaiah 42:8.
No place for foreign gods, Isaiah 43:12-13.
Blending teaching of Law with idolatry,
Jeremiah 2:8.
None handle truth honestly, Jeremiah 5:1-
2.
Defiling house of the Lord, Jeremiah 7:9-
11.
Harm to those who dilute worship,
Jeremiah 7:16-19.
Do not involve idols in worship, Ezekiel
20:7-8.
Those who swear by the Lord and Molech,
Zephaniah 1:4-6.
Worshiping created things rather than the
Creator, Romans 1:21-25.
Cannot blend holiness with evil,
1 Corinthians 10:21.
Diluting Gospel message, Galatians 1:6-9.
Deceptive philosophy and human
tradition, Colossians 2:8, 23.
Confusion at church in Ephesus,
1 Timothy 1:3-7.
Blending secular interests with spiritual,
1 Timothy 6:3-10.
Turning from truth to myths, 2 Timothy
4:4.
Avoid those who dilute Gospel message,
2 Thessalonians 3:6.
Danger of worldly adaption to life of
believer, 1 John 2:15-17.
See *Heresy.*

T

TABLE
Furniture makers' specifications, Exodus 25:23; 37:10.
Bread set before the Lord, Exodus 40:22.
Responsible for care of table, Numbers 3:31.
Scraps under table, Judges 1:7.
Always welcome to table, 2 Samuel 9:7.
Table set for visiting queen, 1 Kings 10:4-5.
Table set for large number of guests, 1 Kings 18:19; Nehemiah 5:17.

TACT
Diplomacy of Joseph, Genesis 41:33-46.
Tactful comparison of accomplishments, Judges 8:2.
David's skill with compliments, 2 Samuel 2:4-5.
Waiting for proper time to speak, Job 32:4-6.
Anger turned away by gentle words, Proverbs 15:1.
Proper time and procedure, Ecclesiastes 8:5-6.
Jeremiah gave initially positive response to false prophecy, Jeremiah 28:1-17. (Note vv. 5-9.)
Daniel spoke with wisdom and tact, Daniel 2:14.
Wise as snakes, innocent as doves, Matthew 10:16.
Response of Jesus to critics, Matthew 21:23-27.
Use of gracious words, Luke 4:22.
Tact of Jesus with Samaritan woman, John 4:4-26.
Paul's timely validation of his ministry, Acts 23:6.
Relating to unbelievers, 2 Corinthians 2:15-16.
Avoidance of stumbling blocks, 2 Corinthians 6:3-13.
Speaking truth in love, Ephesians 4:15.
Tactful in conversation with others, Colossians 4:6.
Paul's tact concerning debt, Philemon 18-19.
Dealing gently with those who need guidance, Hebrews 5:2.
Tact in times of duress, James 1:19-20.
Wisdom that comes from heaven, James 3:17-18.

TACTICS
Military maneuver and ambush, Joshua 8:3-23.
Perfume for lady, Ruth 3:3.
Setting traps for men, Jeremiah 5:26.
See *Military*.

TAILOR
Clothing for high priest, Exodus 28:3.
Apparel worn by members of opposite sex, Deuteronomy 22:5
Mixing wool and linen, Deuteronomy 22:11.
Proper repair of garment, Matthew 9:16; Mark 2:21; Luke 5:36.
See *Sewing, Wardrobe*.

TALENT
Lost skill for farming, Genesis 4:9-12.
Playing musical instruments, family tradition, Genesis 4:21.
All talent and ability come from God, Exodus 4:10-12. (See 6:30.)
Skillful minds and hands, Exodus 28:3; 31:3; 38:23; 1 Kings 7:14; 1 Chronicles 22:15-16; 2 Chronicles 2:13-14; 26:15.
Divine purpose in giving skill, Exodus 35:10, 35.
God-given ability to produce wealth,

Deuteronomy 8:18.
Elimination of blacksmiths, 1 Samuel 13:19.
Solomon's many proverbs and songs, 1 Kings 4:32.
Farmer cannot manage wild ox, Job 39:9-13.
God's blessing on work of hands, Psalm 90:17.
Race not to swift or strong, Ecclesiastes 9:11.
Those wise in their own eyes, Isaiah 5:21.
Victory requires more than ability, Isaiah 25:11.
Farmer's God-given skills, Isaiah 28:24-29.
Artist is mortal, Isaiah 44:11.
Skilled in doing evil, Jeremiah 4:22.
Men have talent but God is sovereign, Jeremiah 10:8-10.
Disaster to swift and strong, Jeremiah 46:6.
Finest of young men chosen for service, Daniel 1:3-4.
Parable of Talents, Matthew 25:14-30.
Those given much and those given little, Mark 4:24-25; Luke 12:48.
Neighbors of Joseph did not expect divinity in Jesus, Luke 4:22-24.
Jesus challenged to display His prowess, John 7:2-9.
Relationship between talent and God's call, Romans 11:29.
Function of various body members, Romans 12:4-8; 1 Corinthians 12:14-20.
Not making profit of Gospel, 2 Corinthians 2:17.
God intends diversity to produce unity, Ephesians 4:11-13.
Do not neglect your gift, 1 Timothy 4:14.
Fan gift of God into flame, 2 Timothy 1:6.
The Holy Spirit designates distribution of gifts, Hebrews 2:4.
Prepared by God to succeed as believer, Hebrews 13:20-21.
Using one's gift for good of others, 1 Peter 4:10.
See *Ability, Skill.*

TALKATIVE
Slow of speech, Exodus 4:10.
Words like blustering wind, Job 8:2.
Deceitful, malicious man, Proverbs 26:24-26.
Quick mouth, Ecclesiastes 5:2.

Words unwisely spoken, Ecclesiastes 5:6.
Pharaoh only loud noise, Jeremiah 46:17.
Paul accused of babbling, Acts 17:18.
See *Loquacious.*

TALL
Towering enemies, Numbers 13:33; Deuteronomy 2:21.
King-sized bed, Deuteronomy 3:11.
Bearing of prince, Judges 8:18.
Stature of King Saul, 1 Samuel 10:23-24.
Nine feet tall, 1 Samuel 17:4.
See *Giant.*

TAME
Noah and dove, Genesis 8:9.
Future harmony of nature, Isaiah 11:6-9.
Training wild animals, James 3:7.

TANGIBLE
Clear communication, Numbers 12:4-8.
The Lord's demands within reach, Deuteronomy 30:11.
Faith more important than things tangible, 2 Corinthians 5:7.
Intangible made tangible, Hebrews 11:3.
See *Clarity, Comprehension.*

TANTALIZE
Wiles of evil woman, Judges 16:4-20.
Perfume for lady, Ruth 3:3.
Tempting taste of honey, 1 Samuel 14:24-28.
Haughty women of Zion, Isaiah 3:16-17.
Guilt of influencing others to sin, Luke 17:1.
See *Seduction.*

TARGET
The Lord's demands within reach, Deuteronomy 30:11.
Fortunate missing of target, 1 Samuel 19:9-10.
Using faulty bow, Hosea 7:16.

TASK
See *Assignment, Duty, Responsibility.*

TASTE
Sampling food offered for sacrifice, 1 Samuel 2:13-14.
Unpalatable food, 2 Kings 4:40.
Gall of bitterness, Lamentations 3:15.
See *Food.*

TAXES

Percentage to government, Genesis 47:13-26; 1 Samuel 8:15; 2 Kings 23:35; Esther 10:1.

Clergy tax-free, Ezra 7:24.

Borrowing money to pay taxes, Nehemiah 5:4.

Coin in mouth of fish to pay tax, Matthew 17:24-27.

Calling of tax collector, Mark 2:13-17; Luke 5:27-31.

Correct procedure in paying taxes, Mark 12:17; Luke 20:25.

Advice to tax collectors, Luke 3:12-13.

Citizen's obligation, Romans 13:6-7.

TEACHER

Divine instructor, Exodus 4:15; Deuteronomy 4:36; Psalms 25:12; 32:8; Isaiah 28:26; 48:17

Commissioned to teach, Leviticus 10:11.

Need for teacher, 2 Chronicles 15:3.

Itinerant teachers, 2 Chronicles 17:7-9.

Teacher who knows subject, Psalm 94:10.

Worthy things to say, Proverbs 8:6.

Teacher disciplines, Jeremiah 32:33.

Teaching truth, Malachi 2:6.

Promised Counselor, John 14:16-17, 26; 16:5-14.

Need for a teacher to explain truth, Acts 8:30-31.

Teachers of first Christians, Acts 11:26.

Abundance of teachers, Acts 15:35.

Thorough knowledge of Scriptures, Acts 18:12-17.

Compliment to those who faithfully followed teachings, 1 Corinthians 11:2.

Divine calling, Ephesians 4:11.

Teachers should be select group, James 3:1.

See *Education, Learning, School.*

TEACHING

Learning at home, Exodus 10:2; Deuteronomy 6:6-9; Isaiah 38:19; Ephesians 6:4.

Children taught to worship, Exodus 12:26-27.

Remembering and following divine teaching, Deuteronomy 4:9.

Duty of parents to children, Deuteronomy 11:1-7.

Joshua gave instructions God had initially given him, Joshua 23:6. (See 1:8.)

God revealed Himself through His word, 1 Samuel 3:21.

God's counsel darkened by words without knowledge, Job 32:2.

Those who hate divine instruction, Psalm 50:17.

Relating God's greatness from generation to generation, Psalm 78:1-7. (Note use of parables, v. 2.)

Way of purity for young man, Psalm 119:9.

Learning objectives of Book of Proverbs, Proverbs 1:1-6.

Advice of King Solomon to son, Proverbs 1:8-19.

Using pleasant words to instruct, Proverbs 16:21.

Understanding brings terror, Isaiah 28:19.

Technique illustrated by farmer, Isaiah 28:23-28.

Instructed tongue, Isaiah 50:4.

God's Word will not return empty, Isaiah 55:10-11.

Boldness of speech, a gift from God, Jeremiah 1:6-10.

Proclaiming dreams instead of God's Word, Jeremiah 23:25-32.

Trampled grass and muddied water, Ezekiel 34:18-19.

Lips that preserve knowledge, Malachi 2:7.

Hearing but not understanding, Mark 4:11-12.

Thoroughness of Jesus with disciples, Mark 4:34.

Causing child to go astray, Mark 9:42.

Living Word pierces heart, Luke 2:34-35.

Commission to preach and teach, Luke 4:14-21.

Jesus proclaimed depths of spiritual truth, John 6:60-69.

Theme of post-Resurrection apostles, Acts 4:2.

Comprehension of Ethiopian eunuch, Acts 8:26-39.

Barnabas and Saul, Acts 11:22-26.

Teacher experiences what he teaches, Acts 14:19-22.

Use of reasoning, Acts 17:1-3.

Listening with eagerness, Acts 17:11-12.

Teaching God's Word a year and a half, Acts 18:11.

Teaching with accuracy, Acts 18:25.

Paul's counsel and sad parting with friends at Ephesus, Acts 20:25-38.

Teaching boldly, Acts 28:31.

Spiritual truth communicated in human terms, Romans 6:19.

Instruct one another, Romans 15:14.

Teacher's request for prayer, Romans 15:31-32.

Speaking and knowledge enriched in Christ, 1 Corinthians 1:5-6.

Paul's compliment to those who faithfully followed teachings, 1 Corinthians 11:2.

Presenting understandable message, 2 Corinthians 1:13-14.

Making profit from Word of God, 2 Corinthians 2:17.

Information without eloquence, 2 Corinthians 11:6.

Example from life, Galatians 3:15.

Student shares with teacher, Galatians 6:6.

Proper instruction in home, Ephesians 6:4.

Praying for those who preach and teach, Ephesians 6:19-20.

Repetition for emphasis, Philippians 3:1; 2 Peter 1:12-15.

God's Word in its fullness, Colossians 1:25-26.

Paul's concern for spiritual development of followers, Colossians 2:1-5.

Encouragement and instruction for children, Colossians 3:20-21.

Preaching and teaching with more than words, 1 Thessalonians 1:4-5.

Letting message ring out, 1 Thessalonians 1:8.

Joy and crown of those who present message, 1 Thessalonians 2:17-19.

Praise to God for success in ministry, 1 Thessalonians 3:8-10.

Teaching by means of speech and writing, 2 Thessalonians 2:15.

Teaching those who wanted to adhere to Law, 1 Timothy 1:3-11.

Satan as teacher, 1 Timothy 1:18-20.

Purpose of becoming teacher, 1 Timothy 2:1-7.

Quality of a bishop, 1 Timothy 3:2.

Communication in person and by writing, 1 Timothy 3:14-15.

Giving caution concerning false teaching, 1 Timothy 4:1-6.

Devoting yourself to preaching and teaching, 1 Timothy 4:13-14.

Those who take pride in false doctrine, 1 Timothy 6:3-5.

God's plan for perpetuation of Gospel, 2 Timothy 2:1-4.

Basic rules for teacher in handling dispute, 2 Timothy 2:23-26.

Scriptures learned from infancy, 2 Timothy 3:15.

Ministry mandate to Timothy, 2 Timothy 4:1-5.

Responsibility to proclaim God-given message, Titus 1:1-3.

Talkers and deceivers, Titus 1:10-14.

Proper teaching for all ages, Titus 2:1-10. (Note importance of teacher's example, v. 7, and making subject attractive, v. 10.)

Teaching with authority, Titus 2:15.

Example of Christian leader, Titus 3:1-2.

Those slow to learn, Hebrews 5:11-14.

Depth perception in teaching and learning, Hebrews 6:1-3.

Teachers should be select group, James 3:1.

Speaking and serving to glory of God, 1 Peter 4:11.

Giving emphasis to former command, 1 John 2:7-8.

When oral teaching is superior to writing, 2 John 12. (See 3 John 13-14.)

Questions and answers, Revelation 7:13-17.

Nothing added or taken away, Revelation 22:18-19.

See *Children, Learning objectives.*

TEAMWORK

Taking care of business, Deuteronomy 20:5-9.

Leadership for those in trouble, 1 Samuel 22:2.

Working diligently together, Nehemiah 4:6.

Iron sharpens iron, Proverbs 27:17.

Skilled crew on ships of Tyre, Ezekiel 27:8-9.

Disciples sent out two-by-two, Mark 6:7.

Healing of paralytic man, Luke 5:17-26.

Set apart by laying on of hands, Acts 13:1-3.

Teamwork in reaching others, 1 Corinthians 3:6-9.

Body as unit, 1 Corinthians 12:12-30.

See *Cooperation.*

TEARS

Wiles of Samson's wife, Judges 14:11-19.

Tears of friendship, 1 Samuel 20:41.

Fears of confessing wrong to another,

1 Samuel 24:16-17.
Weeping until exhausted, 1 Samuel 30:4; Psalm 6:6.
Altered countenance, Job 16:16.
Weeping as part of prayer, Psalm 39:12.
Loss of appetite, Psalms 42:3; 80:5; 102:9.
Burdened soul-winning, Psalm 126:6.
Sorrow over death, Jeremiah 9:1.
Our Redeemer's sorrow, Luke 19:41.
See *Emotion, Grief, Sorrow.*

TECHNIQUE
Purifying bad water, 2 Kings 2:19-22.
Formula for success, Joshua 1:8.
Daughters taught how to wail, Jeremiah 9:20.

TEETH
Making lions harmless, Psalm 58:6.
Gnashing teeth, Psalm 112:10; Matthew 8:12; 13:42, 50; 22:13; Mark 9:18; Luke 13:28.
Sour taste, Proverbs 10:26.
Teeth like swords, Proverbs 30:14.
Lost ability for chewing, Ecclesiastes 12:3. (Some believe "grinders" refer to teeth of old man.)
Scoffing enemies, Lamentations 2:16.

TELEVISION
Verses suggested as guidance in assessing use of television, Proverbs 14:7; 19:27; Matthew 6:22-23; Romans 12:2; Ephesians 5:15-16; Philippians 4:8; 1 Thessalonians 5:21-22.

TEMPER
Those things done in rage, Deuteronomy 19:4-7.
The Lord is slow to anger, Psalm 86:15; Nahum 1:3.
Be slow to anger, James 1:19-20.
See *Anger.*

TEMPERAMENT
Ox and donkey cannot plow together, Deuteronomy 22:10.
Hotheaded fool, Proverbs 14:16-17; Ecclesiastes 7:9.
Controlling temper a major conquest, Proverbs 16:32.
Beware the hot-tempered man, Proverbs 22:24-25.
Lacking self-control, Proverbs 25:28.

A fool and a wise man, Proverbs 29:11.
Anger condemned by Jesus, Matthew 5:22.
An even temperament, James 1:19-20.

TEMPERANCE
Led astray by alcohol, Proverbs 20:1.
Too much wine and food cause laziness, Proverbs 23:20-21.
Lingering over wine, Proverbs 23:30-33.
Best of meats and finest wine, Isaiah 25:6.
Laid low by wine, Isaiah 28:1, 7.
Refusal to drink wine, Jeremiah 35:1-14.
Drinking of wine, 1 Timothy 5:23.

TEMPEST
See *Storm, Wind.*

TEMPLE
Realization and vision, 2 Samuel 7:1-7. (See 1 Chron. 22:1-19.)
Finishing the job, 1 Kings 6:1-38. (See 2 Chron. 3:1–5:1.)
Destruction, 2 Kings 24:10-13; 25:9-17.
Restoration, Ezra 1–3.

TEMPORAL
Abundant temporal blessings, Genesis 24:35; Isaiah 30:23; Amos 9:13.
Putting physical needs above spiritual needs, Exodus 16:1-30.
Promise of good health, Exodus 23:25.
Too much emphasis on temporal, Numbers 11:4-11.
Promised temporal blessings, 1 Kings 3:13.
Immeasurable greatness of God, 2 Chronicles 6:12-19.
Bread and honey, Psalm 81:16.
Evaluation of life, Ecclesiastes 5:15.
In hollow of God's hand, Isaiah 40:12.
Spiritual blessing key to temporal, Matthew 6:33.
Marriage on earth compared to relationship in heaven, Mark 12:18-27.
Earth and sky flee from eternal, Revelation 20:11.
See *Materialism, Physical.*

TEMPORARY
Death always imminent, 1 Samuel 20:3; Isaiah 2:22.
Rich and poor leave possessions to others, Psalm 49:10, 16-20.
Built-in obsolescence, Psalm 49:12.

Passing breeze, Psalm 78:39.
We are but dust, Psalm 103:14.
Life like the morning mist, James 4:14.
Human body as a tent, 2 Peter 1:13.
See *Transient.*

TEMPTATION
Satanic persuasion, Genesis 3:1-6;
 2 Corinthians 2:11.
Becoming master over sin, Genesis 4:7.
Enemy strikes in times of physical
 weakness, Genesis 14:10-13; 2 Samuel
 21:15-17.
Joseph's resistance to temptation, Genesis
 39:6-10.
Personal responsibility in resisting
 temptation, Deuteronomy 11:16.
Desire for plunder, Joshua 7:21.
Hedonistic inclinations, 1 Kings 11:1, 4.
Resolute Job, Job 2:9-10.
Overtly resisting temptation, Proverbs
 1:10-17.
Facility for resisting temptation, Proverbs
 2:10-12, 16.
Danger of playing with fire, Proverbs 6:27-
 29.
Man who pleases God escapes immorality,
 Ecclesiastes 7:26.
Made strong by God's power, Jeremiah
 1:17-19.
Divine illustration to rebellious Israel,
 Jeremiah 35:1-16.
Prior resolution to resist temptation,
 Daniel 1:8.
Temptation of Jesus, Matthew 4:1-11; Luke
 4:1-13.
Physical restraint, Romans 6:13.
Deliverance by the faithful God,
 1 Corinthians 10:13.
Standing at end of struggle, Ephesians
 6:13.
Shield of faith, Ephesians 6:16.
Supporting and surveying one another,
 1 Thessalonians 3:5.
Resisting ungodliness and passions, Titus
 2:11-12.
Christ suffered temptation so He might
 help those tempted, Hebrews 2:18; 4:15.
God, who cannot lie, provides anchor for
 soul, Hebrews 6:18-20.
God's promise of deliverance in Christ,
 Hebrews 7:23-28.
Avenue of joy, James 1:2.
God tempts no one, James 1:13-14.

Evil desires, 2 Peter 1:4.
Sure rescue in the Lord, 2 Peter 2:7-9.
Battleground in which Satan attacks,
 1 John 2:15-17.
Work of the devil, 1 John 3:7-8.
Keep yourself from idols, 1 John 5:21.
Immorality in body of Christ, Revelation
 2:20.

TEMPTRESS
Eve's influence over Adam, Genesis 3:6.
Wife and daughter, Deuteronomy 13:6.
Samson and Delilah, Judges 16:1-31.
David and Bathsheba, 2 Samuel 11:2-5.
Wanton weakness of world's wisest man,
 1 Kings 11:1, 4.
Wife's urging to evil, 1 Kings 21:25; Job
 2:9-10.
Folly of the temptress, Proverbs 5:3-5;
 Ezekiel 13:18-19; Mark 6:22.
Flirtation, Isaiah 3:16-17.
See *Seduction.*

TENACITY
Unending faithfulness, Joshua 24:14.
Not giving in to weariness, Judges 8:4.
Satanic view of man's motivations, Job 2:1-
 10.
The Lord on our side, Psalm 124:1-5.
Greatness of small and insignificant,
 Proverbs 30:24-28.
Race not to swift or strong, Ecclesiastes
 9:11.
Long durability of Jerusalem, Jeremiah
 31:38-40.
Following example of those who lived by
 faith, Hebrews 12:1-3.
Reward for Job's patience, James 5:11.
See *Perseverance, Persistence, Strength.*

TENDERHEARTED
Testing divine patience, Numbers 14:18.
Gentleness of strong man, Ruth 3:5-
 15.
Demonstrated concern, 2 Chronicles
 28:15; Luke 10:25-37; Acts 28:2.
Mortal and divine, Psalm 103:13.
Concern for others, Isaiah 63:9.
Joseph did not want to make Mary subject
 of public disgrace, Matthew 1:19.
Tenderness of Jesus, John 11:35-36;
 Hebrews 4:15.
Paul's example, Acts 20:35.
See *Caring, Compassion.*

TENSION
Description of anxiety, Deuteronomy 28:66-67.
Sure rest in the Lord's protection, Deuteronomy 33:12.
Desire for peace and security, 2 Kings 20:19.
Endless churning inside, Job 30:27.
Trusting the Lord despite circumstances, Psalm 3:1-8.
Rest without tension, Psalm 4:8.
Wrestling one's thoughts, Psalm 13:2, 5.
Relaxation in the Lord, Psalms 37:7; 62:5-8; Proverbs 19:23.
Be still and know, Psalm 46:10.
Fear of future, Psalm 55:4-5.
Casting cares on the Lord, Psalm 55:22.
Steadfast heart, Psalm 57:7.
God bears our burdens daily, Psalm 68:19.
Danger of coveting good fortune of wicked, Psalm 73:2-5.
Cry of distress, Psalm 77:2.
God rules surging sea, Psalm 89:9.
Consolation from anxiety, Psalm 94:19.
God delivers from distress, Psalm 107:6.
Storm becomes as whisper, Psalm 107:29.
Calling out to God in time of depression, Psalms 116:1-4; 120:1.
Release from anguish, Psalm 118:5.
Finding renewal through Scripture, Psalm 119:93.
Those who trust the Lord cannot be shaken, Psalm 125:1.
Prayer for instruction and confidence, Psalm 143:10.
Going through crucible, Proverbs 17:3.
Poor man sleeps better than rich man, Ecclesiastes 5:12.
Learn to banish anxiety, Ecclesiastes 11:10.
Kept in perfect peace, Isaiah 26:3.
Seek quietness and trust, Isaiah 30:15.
Quietness and confidence, Isaiah 32:17.
Anxiety as means of growth, Isaiah 38:15-16.
Mount up on wings like eagles, Isaiah 40:29-31.
Inner torment, Lamentations 1:20.
Quiet rejoicing in the Lord, Zephaniah 3:17.
Rest for weary and burdened, Matthew 11:28-30.
Stress between evil and good in human nature, Romans 7:14-20.
Divine deliverance, 1 Corinthians 10:13.

Turning to God of all comfort, 2 Corinthians 1:3-4.
God's peace available at all times, 2 Thessalonians 3:16.
Rest for people of God, Hebrews 4:9-11.
Promised help in time of trouble, Hebrews 4:14-16.
Grace and peace in abundance, 1 Peter 1:2.
Be self-controlled, 1 Peter 1:13.
Cast all cares on the Lord, 1 Peter 5:7.
See *Anxiety, Stress.*

TENT
Tent community, Genesis 4:20.
Place of residence, Genesis 9:21; 12:8; 13:5; Exodus 18:7.
Objects of beauty, Numbers 24:5-6.
Shelter for shepherds, Isaiah 38:12; Jeremiah 6:3.
Famous tentmaker, Acts 18:1-3.

TENURE
King Saul's long reign over Israel, 1 Samuel 13:1.
Long reign of King David, 2 Samuel 5:4.
Birds know seasons of migration, Jeremiah 8:7.
No permanent place, Jeremiah 16:1-13.

TERMINAL
Visiting one terminally ill, 2 Kings 13:14.
Desiring to die in one's home, Job 29:18.
Hezekiah's terminal illness, Isaiah 38:1.
Seeming inequity of death of righteous, Isaiah 57:1-2.
See *Death.*

TERMINATION
Debt canceled every seven years, Deuteronomy 15:1.
Lamp of wicked, Job 18:5-6.
God pronounces "the end," Ezekiel 7:2.
Conclusion of wrath of God, Revelation 15:1.
See *Conclusion, Ending.*

TERRAIN
Rainless sky and parched earth, Leviticus 26:19-20.
Proper marking of boundaries, Numbers 34:1-12.
Blessing in city and country, Deuteronomy 28:3.

Boasting of land possessed, Jeremiah 49:4.
Exceptionally large city, Jonah 3:3.
Level place in hilly area, Luke 6:17.
See *Geography*.

TERRITORY
Entry refused into Promised Land,
   Numbers 14:35.
Footstep ownership, Joshua 1:2-4.
Lands of other nations, Psalm 111:6.
Greatness of the small and insignificant,
   Proverbs 30:24-28.
Those who live by sea, Zephaniah 2:5-6.
See *Property*.

TERRORISM
Bodily mutilation, Judges 1:7; 1 Samuel
   11:2-11.
Intimidation of a city, 2 Chronicles 32:18.
Protection against enemies of road, Ezra
   8:21-23.
No fear of terror at night, Psalm 91:5; Song
   of Songs 3:8.
Security against attack, Psalm 124:1-5.
Impending terror, Isaiah 24:17.
Danger on streets, Jeremiah 6:25.
Surrounded by terror, Jeremiah 49:29.
Fearful events on earth, Luke 21:11-
   13.
Mob of bad characters incited against Paul
   and Silas, Acts 17:5-7.
Paul accused of being terrorist, Acts 21:38.
See *Plunder*.

TESTIMONY
Backslidden believers a laughingstock,
   Exodus 32:25.
Invitation to hear, Psalm 66:16.
Children damage reputation of parents,
   Proverbs 27:11.
Solomon's summation of testimony,
   Ecclesiastes 12:13-14.
We are the Lord's witnesses, Isaiah 43:10.
Constant watchman, Isaiah 62:6.
Tell what the Lord has done, Mark 5:18-19;
   Acts 5:20-21; 22:15.
Commission to witness, Acts 1:8.
Speaking only of what Christ has done in
   us, Romans 15:18-19.
Paul, worst of sinners, a testimony to
   others, 1 Timothy 1:15-16.
Unashamed witness, 2 Timothy 1:8.
Constantly prepared, 1 Peter 3:15.
See *Witness*.

TESTING
Test of father's love to God and son,
   Genesis 22:1-14.
When God permits testing to prove worth,
   Deuteronomy 13:1-4.
Tested to come forth as gold, Job 23:10.
Dual function of clouds, Job 37:13-14.
Facing disaster with confidence, Psalm
   57:1.
Desperate times, Psalm 60:3.
Refined like silver, Psalm 66:10.
Blessing of divine discipline, Psalm 94:12-
   13.
Light dawns in darkness, Psalm 112:4.
Chastening but deliverance, Psalm 118:18.
Role of Scripture in time of trouble, Psalm
   119:14.
Value of affliction to turn us to Scripture,
   Psalm 119:71.
Going through crucible, Proverbs 17:3.
Do not falter in times of trouble, Proverbs
   24:10.
Dross from silver, Proverbs 25:4.
Gentle flowing waters or mighty flood
   waters, Isaiah 8:6-7.
God's glory first in time of trouble, Isaiah
   37:14-20.
Humility caused by anguish of soul, Isaiah
   38:15.
No need to fear danger, Isaiah 43:1-2.
Confidence in dark, Isaiah 50:10.
God's thoughts higher than man's, Isaiah
   55:9.
Tester of metals, Jeremiah 6:27.
Impervious to refiner's fire, Jeremiah 6:28-
   30.
Thanking God in adverse circumstances,
   Jeremiah 33:10-11.
Burden of Jeremiah for his people,
   Lamentations 3:40-51.
Rod of testing, Ezekiel 21:13.
Confidence of Daniel's friends in
   deliverance from fiery furnace, Daniel
   3:16-17, 22-27.
Daniel in lions' den, Daniel 6:13-24.
Torn but healed, Hosea 6:1.
Refuge for those who trust, Nahum 1:7.
Building on rock or sand, Matthew 7:24-27.
Jesus makes burden light, Matthew 11:28-
   30.
Faith of Canaanite woman tested, Matthew
   15:21-28.
Teacher experiences what he teaches, Acts
   14:19-22. (Note role of hardship, v. 22.)

Purpose of suffering, Romans 5:3.
God works out everything according to His will, Romans 8:28; Ephesians 1:11-12.
The God who is faithful and will deliver, 1 Corinthians 10:13.
Certain victory in Christ, 1 Corinthians 15:57-58.
Purpose of testing, 2 Corinthians 1:2-11.
Standing at end of struggle, Ephesians 6:13.
Shield of faith, Ephesians 6:16.
Adverse circumstances can be special blessing, Philippians 1:12.
Destined for persecution and trials, 1 Thessalonians 3:1-5.
Made perfect through suffering, Hebrews 2:10.
Jesus tempted as we are, Hebrews 4:15.
God's promise of deliverance in Christ, Hebrews 7:23-28.
Confident now of fulfillment in future, Hebrews 11:13.
Recognizing persecution as avenue of blessing, Hebrews 11:35.
Testing resisted short of shedding blood, Hebrews 12:4.
The Lord disciplines those whom He loves, Hebrews 12:5-11; Revelation 3:19.
Maturing value of testing, trials, problems, James 1:2-4, 12.
Positive result of testing, James 5:11.
Purpose of trials and grief, 1 Peter 1:6-7.
Temporary suffering as reward for faithfulness, Revelation 1:9.
Do not fear suffering, Revelation 2:10.
Faithful in face of persecution, Revelation 2:13.
Satan given temporary power to persecute believers, Revelation 13:5-7.
See *Affliction, Deliverance, Persecution, Suffering.*

TEXTILES
Blue, purple, and scarlet yarn and fine linen, Exodus 35:35.
Apparel worn by opposite sex, Deuteronomy 22:5.
Mixing wool and linen, Deuteronomy 22:11.
Combing flax for linen, Isaiah 19:9.
Extensive merchandising, Ezekiel 27:12-23.
See *Clothing.*

THANKSGIVING
Token of harvest, Leviticus 19:24; Deuteronomy 26:10; Proverbs 3:9-10.
Prayer after meal, Deuteronomy 8:10; Joel 2:26.
Gratitude of Ruth, Ruth 2:10.
Prayer of gratitude, 2 Samuel 7:18-29.
David's song of praise, 2 Samuel 22:1-51.
Gratitude for divine faithfulness and goodness, 1 Kings 8:14-21.
Songs of gratitude, Psalms 9:11; 33:2.
Perpetual gratitude, Psalm 35:28.
Value of sacrifice and offering, Psalm 50:23.
Song of praise, Psalm 98:1.
Thanking God for enduring love, Psalm 106:1.
Thanksgiving leads to witnessing, Psalm 107:1-3.
Refusing to glorify God for harvest, Jeremiah 5:24.
Daniel's gratitude to God for wisdom, Daniel 2:19-23.
Gratitude for food, Joel 2:26.
Jesus gave thanks, John 6:11.
Key to answered prayer, Philippians 4:6.
Overflow with thankfulness, Colossians 2:6-7.
Thankful for everything, 1 Thessalonians 5:18.
See *Gratitude, Praise.*

THEATER
Paul urged not to enter, Acts 19:29-31.

THEOCRACY
The divine plan, Exodus 24:1-7.
Lord over all, Deuteronomy 4:39; 5:25-29; 33:2-5; 1 Chronicles 29:12; Psalms 47:2; 135:6.
Unfailing promises, Joshua 23:4.
Danger of taking credit for God's blessing, Judges 7:2-3.
Gideon's definition of theocracy, Judges 8:22-23.
Change from divine leadership to mortal, 1 Samuel 8:1-9.
Bridge between theocratic and temporal rule, 1 Samuel 15:1.
Monarch turning against the Lord's servants, 1 Samuel 22:17.
Leadership by hook and bit, 2 Kings 19:28.
Surest mode for guidance and success, Nehemiah 1:1-11.

Divine superiority over earthly monarchy, Proverbs 21:1.

Creator and Ruler of universe, Isaiah 40:12-17. (Note v. 11.)

Earth filled with the Lord's glory, Habakkuk 2:14.

Coming kingdom, Revelation 19:6.

See *Sovereignty.*

THEOLOGY

Full gamut of theology, Genesis 1:1; Revelation 22:20-21.

God of Israel spoken of as "god" by pagan king, Isaiah 37:10.

Deceitful theology, Jeremiah 8:8.

Reading Bible in vain, John 5:39-40.

Wisdom of Jesus, John 7:14-15.

Concise purpose of divine revelation, John 20:30-31; 2 Timothy 3:16; 2 Peter 1:21.

Lacking theological training, Acts 4:13.

Bringing theological dispute into secular courtroom, Acts 18:12-17.

Simplicity of Paul's message, 1 Corinthians 2:1-5.

Message of wisdom to mature Christians, 1 Corinthians 2:6.

See *Error, Heresy, Syncretism.*

THERAPY

Deliverance from snakebite, Numbers 21:4-9.

Body-to-body resuscitation, 2 Kings 4:32-37.

Ceremonial procedures, 2 Kings 5:8-14; John 5:7.

Healing attitude, Proverbs 17:22.

Soothing oil, Isaiah 1:6; Luke 10:34.

Poultice of figs, Isaiah 38:21.

Where to find rest for your soul, Jeremiah 6:16.

No balm in Gilead, Jeremiah 8:22.

Incurable ailment, Jeremiah 30:12-13; 46:11.

Leaves used for healing, Ezekiel 47:12; Revelation 22:2.

Attitude of Pharisees toward healing on Sabbath, Luke 13:10-17.

Use of wine, 1 Timothy 5:23.

Efficacy of prayer, James 5:14.

See *Medicine.*

THESIS

Unfailing promises, Joshua 23:4.

Paul's concise thesis concerning Gospel,

1 Timothy 4:9-10.

THIEVES

Eat but do not take away, Deuteronomy 23:24.

Honest weights and measurements, Deuteronomy 25:13-16.

Disgrace of being caught, Jeremiah 2:26.

Riches gained unjustly, Jeremiah 17:11.

Honor among thieves, Jeremiah 49:9.

Temptation of tax collectors and soldiers, Luke 3:12-14.

Mark of conversion, Ephesians 4:28.

See *Stealing.*

THINKING

Psychological effects of resentment and envy, Job 5:2.

Personal evaluation, Psalm 119:59.

Danger of evil thoughts, Jeremiah 4:14.

God's Law in mind and heart, Jeremiah 31:33.

Revealing thoughts of heart, Luke 2:34-35.

Poisoning mind, Acts 14:2.

Natural mind and Spirit-controlled mind, Romans 8:6-8.

Renewing mind, Romans 12:2-3.

Attitude of mind dictates life conduct, Philippians 4:8-9.

Fix thoughts on Jesus, Hebrews 3:1.

Prepare minds for action, 1 Peter 1:13.

God searches mind and heart, Revelation 2:23.

See *Frame of reference.*

THIN-SKINNED

Homicidal jealousy, Genesis 4:3-16.

Joseph's thin-skinned brothers, Genesis 37:3-4.

Thin-skinned Haman, Esther 5:9-13.

Avoid envy of wrongdoers, Psalm 37:1.

Disease of envy, Proverbs 14:30.

Busy homemaker offended, Luke 10:38-42.

Thin-skinned Pharisee, Luke 13:13-17.

Prodigal son's jealous brother, Luke 15:25-32.

Unable to hear rebuke, Acts 7:51-58.

Leadership clash between Barnabas and Saul, Acts 15:36-40.

See *Envy, Jealousy.*

THIRST

Water for thirsty child, Genesis 21:14-19.

Importance of well in dry country, Genesis 21:25-31. (See also 26:12-17.)
Singing at watering places, Judges 5:11.
Strong man's need for liquid, Judges 15:17-19.
Water from special well, 2 Samuel 23:15.
God offers joyful river, Psalm 36:8.
Spiritual thirst, Psalm 42:1-4.
Awakening to reality, Isaiah 29:8.
Burning sand becomes pool, Isaiah 35:7.
Israel turned away from Living Water, Jeremiah 2:13, 18.
Poisoned water to drink, Jeremiah 8:14; 23:15.
Empty jars return from cisterns, Jeremiah 14:3.
Springs that fail, Jeremiah 15:18.
Children without food and drink, Lamentations 4:4.
Water for sale, Lamentations 5:4.
Scant rainfall, Amos 4:7-8.
Cup of cold water, Matthew 10:42.
Holy Spirit spoken of as satisfying drink, 1 Corinthians 12:13.
Springs of living water, Revelation 7:16-17.

THORNS
Relevant to sin's curse, Genesis 3:18; Hebrews 6:8.
Communication between thistle and tree, 2 Kings 14:9.
Judgment on harvest, Job 31:40.
Fuel for cooking, Psalm 58:9; Ecclesiastes 7:6.
Flash fire, Psalm 118:12.
Blemished altars, Hosea 10:8.
Used for hedge, Micah 7:4.
Fruit not found on thistle, Matthew 7:16.
Choking thorns, Matthew 13:7.
Crown of thorns on Jesus' head, Matthew 27:28-29.

THOROUGH
Taking care of business, Deuteronomy 20:5-9.
Complete reading of the Law, Joshua 8:35.
Nehemiah's skill in rebuilding wall, Nehemiah 6:1.
Thoroughly keeping divine commands, Proverbs 7:2.
Making most of every opportunity, Ephesians 5:15-16.
See *Dependability.*

THOUGHT
Keeping one's thoughts pleasing to God, Psalm 19:14.
Submitting to God's tests of motive and thought, Psalm 26:2.
Those of warped minds, Proverbs 12:8.
The Lord searches the heart, examines the mind, Jeremiah 17:10.
Self-evaluation, Haggai 1:5-6.
Relationship of thought and action, Romans 2:1-11.
Humility of thinking, Romans 12:3.
Thing worth thinking about, Philippians 4:8-9.
See *Frame of reference, Mind, Motivation.*

THOUGHTFULNESS
Providing for need of another, Ruth 2:15-16.
Thoughtfulness of Ebed-Melech in rescuing Jeremiah, Jeremiah 38:7-13.

THREAT
Lot threatened by deviates, Genesis 19:9.
Wicked bend their bows, Psalm 11:2.
Song of ruthless made silent, Isaiah 25:5.
Thousand flee from one enemy, Isaiah 30:17.
Hezekiah intimidated, Isaiah 36:4-10.
Disbelieving threat of murder, Jeremiah 40:13-16; 41:1-2.
Only loud noise, Jeremiah 46:17.
Threat of death to Daniel's friends, Daniel 3:8-15.
See *Menace, Warning.*

THRIFT
See *Frugality, Stingy.*

TIDINGS
Destiny set for rebellious people, Numbers 14:35.
False prophets, Jeremiah 23:16-18.
Prophet's certainty of voice of the Lord, Jeremiah 32:1-12.
One message after another of bad news, Jeremiah 51:31-32.
Bearer of bad news, Ezekiel 33:21.

TIME
Love causes time to pass quickly, Genesis 29:14-20.
The Lord took an entire night to open Red Sea to Israel, Exodus 14:21-22.

Days like shadow, 1 Chronicles 29:15.
Wishing for given day not to exist, Job 3:6.
Quick passing of our days, Job 7:6; 9:25-26;
16:22; Psalm 89:47.
End of life comes quickly, Psalm 39:4-6.
Ancient skies, Psalm 68:32-33.
Thousand years as one day, Psalm 90:4.
Varied times of day at moment when Christ
returns, Luke 17:30-35.
Man who waited 38 years, John 5:1-9.
Those who did not understand measure
Jesus gave to time, John 16:17-18.
Rapid deterioration of human body,
2 Corinthians 4:16-18.
Fulfillment of times, Ephesians 1:9-10.
Beginning of time, 2 Timothy 1:9.
Meaning of "today" in God's reckoning,
Hebrews 4:7.
Eternal existence of God, Revelation 1:8.
No more delay, Revelation 10:6.
Satan's awareness of shortage of time,
Revelation 12:12.
The beginning and the end, Revelation
22:13.

TIMIDITY
Guilty people frightened of place of
worship, Numbers 17:12-13.
Samuel reluctant to inform Eli of his vision,
1 Samuel 3:15-16.
Tongues stick to roof of mouth, Job 29:10.
The Lord on our side, Psalms 124:1-5;
139:1-18.
Those afraid to profess faith, John 12:42-
43; Acts 5:13-14.
Paul could be timid and bold,
2 Corinthians 10:1.
Counsel from brave to timid man,
2 Timothy 1:7.
Those not embarrassed because of Paul's
chains, 2 Timothy 1:16-18.
See *Apprehension, Fear*.

TIMING
Leave revenge to God's timing, 1 Samuel
26:1-11.
Time for everything, Ecclesiastes 3:1-8.
Proper time and procedure, Ecclesiastes
8:5-6.
Time to prepare and time to plant, Isaiah
28:24-25.
God's perfect timing, Isaiah 49:8.
Seeking at right time, Isaiah 55:6.
God moves in His time, Isaiah 60:22.

Jesus could not die before His time had
come, Luke 4:28-30.
Jesus offered no resistance to oppressors,
Luke 22:47-53.
God's perfect timing in Christ, Romans 5:6.
See *Destiny, Fortuity*.

TIRELESS
Creator continuing at work, John 5:17.

TITHE
Abram's tithe to Melchizedek, Genesis
14:18-20; Hebrews 7:1-2.
Jacob's pledge to give God a tenth, Genesis
28:22.
Value of silver in giving, Numbers 7:13-85.
(See also 10:2.)
The tenth used for personal consumption,
Deuteronomy 14:22-23.
Evil earnings forbidden in house of the
Lord, Deuteronomy 23:18.
Keeping one's word when making pledge,
Deuteronomy 23:23.
Use of tithe in welfare, Deuteronomy
26:12.
Avoid meaningless offerings, Isaiah 1:13.
Challenge to tithe, Malachi 3:6-10.
Giving a meaningless tenth, Matthew
23:23.
Tithing without good spiritual conduct,
Luke 11:42.
See *Stewardship*.

TITLE
Property involved in inheritance, Numbers
36:1-9.
See *Property*.

TODAY
Living for today in God's favor,
Ecclesiastes 9:7.
The "now" of salvation, 2 Corinthians 6:2.
Meaning of "today" in God's reckoning,
Hebrews 4:7.

TOGETHERNESS
Wrong kind of togetherness, Exodus 23:2;
Numbers 11:4-10.
Do not take on ways of heathen,
Deuteronomy 18:9.
People working diligently together,
Nehemiah 4:6.
Language confused by intermarriage,
Nehemiah 13:23-27.

Glorify the Lord together, Psalm 34:3.
Iron sharpens iron, Proverbs 27:17.
Like teacher, like student, Luke 6:40.
See *Cooperation, Rapport.*

TOILET
Disposal of excrement, Deuteronomy
23:12-13.

TOKEN
Promise in sky, Genesis 9:12-13.
Circumcision, Genesis 17:11.
Token of love between brothers, Genesis
33:1-11.
Sign of blood, Exodus 12:13.
Evidence of divine provision for future
generations to see, Exodus 16:32-34.
Token of harvest, Leviticus 23:9-13.
Removal of sandal, Ruth 4:7-8.
Nominal piety of King Zedekiah, Jeremiah
37:1-3.
Break bow, Jeremiah 49:35.
Likened to the Lord's signet ring, Haggai
2:23.
One who dipped his hand, Matthew 26:23-
25.
See *Visual.*

TOLERANCE
Tolerant of strangers, Exodus 23:9.
Unwilling to tolerate food, Numbers 11:4-
6.
Slow to anger, great in power, Nahum 1:3.
Attitude toward lost, Matthew 9:10.
Tolerance of Jesus for sleeping disciples,
Matthew 26:37-46.
Those of differing views, Mark 9:38-39;
Luke 9:49-50; Philippians 1:17-18.

TOMB
Choicest tombs, Genesis 23:6.
Unknown tomb of Moses, Deuteronomy
34:6.
Self-made tomb, 2 Chronicles 16:14.
Hewing out his own tomb, 2 Chronicles
16:14.
Graves hewn out of rock, Isaiah 22:16.
The empty tomb, Matthew 28:1-10; Mark
16:1-7; Luke 24:1-8; John 20:1-9.
See *Burial, Grave.*

TOMBSTONE
Rachel's pillar, Genesis 35:20.
Absalom's memorial to himself, 2 Samuel
18:18.
Prophet's resting place, 2 Kings 23:16-18.

TOMORROW
Destiny set for rebellious people, Numbers
14:35.
Better days coming, Proverbs 4:18; Isaiah
25:8; Revelation 7:14-17.
Overconfidence about future, Proverbs
27:1; James 4:14.
Future can be left safely in God's hands,
Isaiah 46:8-11.
Certainty of day and night, Jeremiah 33:19-
22.
Future day established, Acts 17:31;
Romans 2:16.
See *Future.*

TONGUE
Spreading false reports, Exodus 23:1.
Rabble of complaint, Numbers 11:4-6.
Avoid criticizing those whom the Lord has
not denounced, Numbers 23:8.
Talk about spiritual matters, Deuteronomy
6:4-7.
Stewardship of speech, Deuteronomy
23:23.
Pride and arrogance, 1 Samuel 2:3.
Cruelty of words, Job 19:2.
Agent of inner expression, Psalm 34:13;
Proverbs 13:3; 21:23.
Purity of speech, Proverbs 4:24.
Rare jewel, Proverbs 20:15.
Word aptly spoken, Proverbs 25:11.
Deceitful, malicious man, Proverbs 26:24-
26.
Vileness from every mouth, Isaiah 9:17.
Refraining from response to one who
affronted the name of the Lord, Isaiah
36:18-22. (See 37:1-7.)
Like deadly arrow, Jeremiah 9:8.
Wrong and right boasting, Jeremiah 9:23-
24.
Critical tongues made silent, Luke 20:20-
26.
Whatever you say or do, Colossians 3:17.
Do not talk back, Titus 2:9.
Guard tongue well, James 3:3-6.
Insuring good relationships, 1 Peter 3:10.
See *Conversation, Gossip, Slander, Speech.*

TONGUES
Those who spoke one common language,
Genesis 11:1.

Speaking in language understood, Isaiah
36:11.
Paul and gift of tongues, Acts 19:1-7.
Words beyond normal vocabulary,
Romans 8:16, 26-27.
Paul did not mention gift of tongues in
Romans, Romans 12:4-8; 15:17-19.
Role of tongues in body of Christ,
1 Corinthians 12:27-31.
See *Glossalalia.*

TOOL
Maker of tools, Genesis 4:22.
Tools do not defy craftsmen, Isaiah 10:15.
Tools through whom God ministers, Titus
1:1-3.

TORMENT
Desperate times, Psalm 60:3.
Torment in hell, Luke 16:22-23.
Those who wish to die but cannot,
Revelation 9:4-6.
Aftermath of mark of beast, Revelation
14:9-11.
Agony of those who refuse to repent,
Revelation 16:10-11.
Lake of fire, Revelation 20:10.
See *Punishment, Suffering, Torture.*

TORTURE
Cutting off thumbs and big toes, Judges
1:7.
Partial blindness threatened as disgrace,
1 Samuel 11:2-11.
Satanic view of man's motivations, Job 2:1-
10.
Sadistic killing of children, Psalm 137:9.
Intoxicated by torture, Isaiah 51:21-23.
Wicked find no rest, Isaiah 57:20-21.
Haunt of jackals, Jeremiah 9:11.
Facing grim destiny, Jeremiah 15:2-3.
No chance for escape, Jeremiah 48:44.
Leaders and common people subjected to
torture, Lamentations 5:11-13.
Fear of sword, Ezekiel 11:8.
Those who wish to die but cannot,
Revelation 9:4-6.
See *Sadistic.*

TOTALITARIAN
Rehoboam more oppressive than
Solomon, 1 Kings 12:1-11.
Those who live under non-Christian
governments, Isaiah 26:13; Romans

13:1; 1 Peter 2:13-14.
Tyranny abolished, Isaiah 54:14.
Temporary authority of the beast,
Revelation 13:5.
See *Communism, Despot, Dictator.*

TOURIST
Seeing unpleasant sights, Deuteronomy
28:34.
Protection against enemies of road, Ezra
8:21-23.
Provision for safe conduct, Nehemiah 2:7.
Road signs and guideposts, Jeremiah
31:21.
Things packed for Exile, Ezekiel 12:7.
Jonah as tourist, Jonah 1:3.
Traveling with light baggage, Mark 6:8.
See *Travel.*

TOWER
Towers of the Bible, Genesis 11:4-9;
Judges 8:17; 9:46, 49; Song of Songs 4:4;
7:4; Luke 13:4.

TOWN
Small town spared disaster of large city,
Genesis 19:15-22.

TRADE
Career in trading, Genesis 34:10.
Conditions given by Joseph, Genesis 42:34.
Elimination of blacksmiths, 1 Samuel
13:19.
Import and export in Solomon's time,
1 Kings 10:14-15, 28-29.
Deceitful buyer, Proverbs 20:14.
Balance of trade, Isaiah 61:6.
Barter for merchandise, Ezekiel 27:12.
See *Barter, Commerce.*

TRADITION
Do not take on ways of heathen,
Deuteronomy 18:9.
Putting foot to neck, Joshua 10:24.
Traditional wearing of jewelry, Judges
8:24.
Sacrifice of daughter, Judges 11:30-40.
Removal of sandal, Ruth 4:7-8.
Ancient boundary stone, Proverbs 22:28;
23:10-11.
Communicating God's message to
children, Joel 1:1-3.
Washing hands before eating, Matthew
15:1-9.

Myths and tales, 1 Timothy 4:7.
See *Culture.*

TRAFFIC
No traffic during Sabbath, Nehemiah
13:15-22.
Wild animals laugh at man's commotion,
Job 39:5-7.
Verse some think to be prophecy of
modern traffic, Nahum 2:4.
Children playing in streets, Zechariah 8:5.

TRAGEDY
More powerful and victorious in death than
in life, Judges 16:30.
Death caused by bad news, 1 Samuel 4:12-
18.
End of dissolute life, 2 Kings 9:30-37.
Job wanted written record of agony, Job
19:23-24.
Tragedy with respect predicted for
Jeremiah, Jeremiah 34:1-7.
End of young marriage, Joel 1:8.
Too little and too late, Amos 3:12.
Desire of Jesus for judgment to come,
Luke 12:49.
See *Catastrophe, Disaster, Trauma.*

TRAINING
Trained men in Abram's household,
Genesis 14:14.
Training Joshua for future leadership,
Numbers 27:18-23.
Eagle training young to fly, Deuteronomy
32:11.
Men trained for service, 1 Chronicles 5:18.
Wild ox must be tamed, Job 39:9-12.
Instructions given by Jesus to 12 Apostles,
Matthew 10:5-32. (See also 11:1.)
Family of elder must be exemplary, Titus
1:6.
See *Apprentice, Instruction.*

TRAITORS
Aaron and Miriam opposing Moses,
Numbers 12:1-11.
Disloyalty to Moses and Aaron, Numbers
16:1-33.
Traitor to evil city, Joshua 2:1-24.
Uprising against King Saul, 1 Samuel
10:27.
Plot to overthrow government, 2 Samuel
15:10.
Amnesty to traitors, 2 Samuel 19:16-23.

Recruited to turn against their own king,
2 Kings 9:14-24.
Frustrated traitor, 2 Kings 11:13-14.
King destroyed by associates, 2 Kings
12:19-20.
Death penalty for treason, Esther 2:23.
Pretense of righteousness, Luke 20:20.
Ultimate end for Judas, Acts 1:18-20.
Those who turn their backs, 2 Peter 2:20-
22.
Deception among believers, Jude 3-4.
See *Disloyalty.*

TRAITS
See *Character, Habits.*

TRANCE
Vision of the Lord, Numbers 24:2-4.
Peter's vision, Acts 10:9-16; 11:1-10.
Direction by vision, Acts 22:12-21.
Paul unsure of mode of his experience,
2 Corinthians 12:1-4.

TRANQUILITY
Place of certainty, Deuteronomy 33:27.
Love, faithfulness, and peace, Psalm 85:10.
Keeping oneself under control, Proverbs
29:11.
Voicing simple need, Proverbs 30:7-8.
Reward of labor, Ecclesiastes 5:12.
Great peace to those who obey, Isaiah
48:17-18. (See Ps. 119:165.)
New every day, Lamentations 3:22-24.
Living in peace and contentment, Micah
4:4.
Quiet rejoicing in the Lord, Zephaniah
3:17.
See *Peace, Relaxation, Repose.*

TRANSFORMATION
Tear down the old and build new, Judges
6:25-26.
Different person by power of Holy Spirit,
1 Samuel 10:6-9.
Poor and needy lifted, Psalm 113:7-8.
Scarlet sin to transformation like snow,
Isaiah 1:18.
Potter and clay, Jeremiah 18:1-4.
Heart of stone to heart of flesh, Ezekiel
11:19.
Clean hearts and changed lives, Ezekiel
36:25-27.
Satan rebuked, Zechariah 3:1-7.
Being born again, John 3:1-8.

Conversion of sorcerer, Acts 8:9-
13.
Conversion of Saul, Acts 9:1-18.
Repentance in action, Acts 19:18-
19.
Dead to sin, alive to God, Romans 6:11.
Do not conform to world, Romans 12:2;
1 Peter 1:14.
New creation in Christ, 2 Corinthians 5:17;
Ephesians 4:22-24.
From darkness to light, Ephesians 5:8-10.
Positive conduct of those who have died
with Christ, Colossians 2:20-23.
Blasphemer becomes minister of Gospel,
1 Timothy 1:12-16.
Doing what is right, 1 John 2:29.
See *Regeneration, Salvation.*

TRANSIENT
Destiny set for rebellious people, Numbers
14:35.
Rich and poor die, leave possessions to
others, Psalm 49:10, 16-20.
Even royalty is not secure, Proverbs 27:24.
Our bodies but tents, 2 Peter 1:13.
See *Pilgrim, Tourist.*

TRANSITION
God's command to Abraham, Genesis
12:1-9.
After death of Moses, the Lord moved
decisively in naming Joshua leader,
Joshua 1:1-2.
Duty of citizens to leadership change,
Joshua 1:16-17.
Wide contrast between temporal and
spiritual, Isaiah 40:7-8.
Foolishness of depending on mortal flesh,
Jeremiah 17:5.
See *Change, Progress.*

TRANSLATION
Speaking in language understood, Isaiah
36:11.

TRANSMUTATION
Indifference to others causes limitation to
oneself, Proverbs 19:17.
Earthly obedience evokes heaven's
blessing, Malachi 3:8-12.
Transmuting earthly wealth to eternal
wealth, Matthew 6:19-20.
Divine principle for stewardship,
2 Corinthians 9:6.

TRANSPORTATION
Carts provided for Joseph's brothers,
Genesis 45:16-20.
Transportation for 40 sons and 30
grandsons, Judges 12:14.
Chariot of fire and whirlwind, 2 Kings
2:11-12.
Mountains turned into roads, Isaiah 49:11.
Wealth to those who lived by many waters,
Jeremiah 51:13.
Donkey chosen to serve Jesus, Matthew
21:1-7; Mark 11:1-7.

TRAP
The tar pits of Siddim, Genesis 14:10.
Net and pit, Psalms 35:7; 119:85, 110;
140:5; 141:9.
Men like trapped birds, Jeremiah 5:26.
Attempts to trap Jesus, Matthew 16:1;
22:15; Mark 12:13; Luke 11:53-54; John
8:6.
See *Snare.*

TRAUMA
Startling information given father about
son, Genesis 45:25-28.
The God greater than numbers,
Deuteronomy 20:1-4.
Satanic view of man's motivations, Job 2:1-
10.
Hurting another brings greater hurt to
oneself, Jeremiah 7:18-19.
Haunt of jackals, Jeremiah 9:11.
Numerous widows, Jeremiah 15:8.
Men as in pains of childbirth, Jeremiah
30:6.
Peril outside, plague inside, Ezekiel 7:15-
17.
Nations in anguish, Joel 2:6.
From one fear to another, Amos 5:18-19.
Singing turns to wailing, Amos 8:3.
Avoid those experiencing disaster,
Obadiah 13.
Terrified by glory of the Lord, Luke 2:9.
Fear of drowning, Luke 8:22-25.
Hard pressed from every side,
2 Corinthians 4:8.
See *Distress, Shock.*

TRAVEL
Washing feet common for those who
walked, Genesis 18:4; 19:2.
Not traveling after sunset, Genesis 28:11.
Taking care to check family welfare,

Exodus 4:18.
Traveling by divine instructions, Numbers 9:23.
Prayer for protection, Numbers 10:35.
Passage denied, Numbers 20:14-21.
Roads to cities of refuge, Deuteronomy 19:1-3.
Journey by an entire nation, Joshua 4:1.
Transportation for 40 sons and 30 grandsons, Judges 12:14.
Journey with the Lord's approval, Judges 18:6.
Leaving early in morning, 1 Samuel 17:20.
Fatal detour, Job 6:18.
Avoiding lighted pathway, Job 24:13.
Sleeping on the high seas, Proverbs 23:34.
Mountains turned into roads, Isaiah 49:11.
Crooked roads, Isaiah 59:8.
Frailty of foot, Jeremiah 12:5.
Road signs and guideposts, Jeremiah 31:21.
Divine obstruction, Hosea 2:6.
Journey of Joseph and Mary to Bethlehem, Luke 2:1-5.
Transportation at high speed, John 6:21.
Wife traveling with husband, 1 Corinthians 9:5.
Letters of introduction, 1 Corinthians 16:3.
Care in planning journey, 2 Corinthians 1:15-17.
See *Itinerary, Journey, Transportation.*

TREACHERY
False affection, Judges 16:18-19.
Refusal to use treachery against enemy, 1 Samuel 26:1-25.
Conversation of death, 2 Samuel 3:27.
Pretense of securing food, 2 Samuel 4:5-7.
Misunderstanding gesture of goodwill, 2 Samuel 10:1-4.
Strategy for legal murder, 2 Samuel 11:15.
Avoiding evil scheme, Nehemiah 6:2-4.
Trumped-up charges, Esther 3:8.
Security against attack, Psalm 124:1-5.
Deceitful, malicious man, Proverbs 26:24-26.
Friends and brothers not to be trusted, Jeremiah 9:4-8.
Toleration of treachery, Habakkuk 1:13.
King Herod and magi, Matthew 2:7-8, 12.
Guilt of influencing others to sin, Luke 17:1.
Cynical tongues made silent, Luke 20:20-26.

See *Deception.*

TREASON
See *Disloyalty, Traitors.*

TREASURE
Searching for treasure, Job 28:1-4, 9-11.
Silver thrown into streets, Ezekiel 7:19.
Gold and silver of earth belong to God, Haggai 2:8.
The Lord's treasured possessions, Malachi 3:17.
Precious faith, 2 Peter 1:1.
See *Value.*

TREES
Varieties of trees, Genesis 35:4; Exodus 15:27; 36:20; Numbers 17:8; Judges 9:10; 1 Samuel 14:2; 2 Samuel 5:23; 1 Kings 19:4; Nehemiah 8:15; Song of Songs 2:3; Isaiah 6:13; 14:8; 41:19; 44:14.
Three years of purification, Leviticus 19:23.
Trees and tithe, Leviticus 27:30.
Neutrality of timber, Deuteronomy 20:19-20.
Beautiful tree destroyed in judgment, Jeremiah 11:16.
Agency of punishment, Jeremiah 6:6.
Good and bad, Matthew 12:33.
See *Forestry.*

TRIBULATION
Daughters taught how to wail, Jeremiah 9:20.
Facing grim destiny, Jeremiah 15:2-3.
No chance for escape, Jeremiah 48:44.
Words of Jesus concerning end times, Mark 13:1-37.
See *Second Coming.*

TRIBUTE
David's tribute to Abner following Abner's death, 2 Samuel 3:33-39.
Jesus' evaluation of John the Baptist, Matthew 11:11-14.
Commending great faith, Matthew 15:28; Luke 7:9.
Empty sincerity of Pharisees, Mark 12:15-17.
Complimentary service, Mark 14:3-9.
Greatness and subservience, Luke 7:28.
Widow's mite, Luke 21:1-4.
See *Citation, Praise.*

TRINITY
Plural Godhead "Us" at work, Genesis 1:26; 3:22.
Threefold benediction, Numbers 6:24-26.
Father and Son in Old Testament, Proverbs 30:2-4.
Holy, holy, holy is the Lord, Isaiah 6:3.
God and Holy Spirit, Isaiah 48:16.
Prophecy of Jesus and Holy Spirit, Isaiah 61:1-3.
Trinity in one verse, Matthew 12:28; 28:19; Luke 3:22; John 1:32.
Oneness of Jesus and God, John 12:44-45.
Teaching of Christ concerning Trinity, John 14:25-31; 15:26-27.
Benediction involving grace, love, and fellowship of the Trinity, 2 Corinthians 13:14.
Fullness of Deity, Colossians 2:9-10.
Spiritual function of Father and Son, 2 Thessalonians 3:5.
Three who bear record, 1 John 5:6-7.

TRITE
See *Insignificant.*

TRIUMPH
See *Conquest, Victory.*

TROPHY
Trophy of God's goodness, Exodus 16:32-34.
People as the Lord's treasure, Deuteronomy 26:18.
David kept weapons of Goliath, 1 Samuel 17:54.
Likened to the Lord's signet ring, Haggai 2:23.

TROUBADOUR
Walking through city with harp and sad song, Isaiah 23:16.
End to noisy songs, Ezekiel 26:13.
See *Music.*

TROUBLE
Certainty for all, Job 5:7; 14:1; Ecclesiastes 2:22-23.
Questioning ways of God, Job 10:3.
Calamity hungered for Job, Job 18:12.
God ever-present in times of trouble, Psalm 14:4-5.
Prayer in time of trouble, Psalm 18:6.
Those who change only under pressure of circumstances, Psalm 32:9.
Facing disaster with confidence, Psalm 57:1.
Help in time of trouble, Psalm 60:11-12.
Waters up to neck, Psalm 69:1.
Calling on the Lord in time of distress, Psalm 120:1.
Leaders captured without fight, Isaiah 22:3.
Putting God's glory first in time of trouble, Isaiah 37:14-20.
Punishment brought on disobedient by themselves, Jeremiah 4:18; Ezekiel 22:1-5.
Faithfulness causing imprisonment, Jeremiah 37:1-21.
Assurance to Israel in Egypt, Jeremiah 46:27.
Rod of testing, Ezekiel 21:13.
Saved from trouble and in trouble, Daniel 3:16-18.
Famine turning people to the Lord, Amos 4:6.
Dawn to darkness, Amos 4:13.
From frying pan to fire, Amos 5:19.
Refuge for those who trust the Lord, Nahum 1:7.
Those who are persecuted, Matthew 5:10.
Persecution implements spread of Gospel, Acts 8:3-4.
Paul's experience in storm and shipwreck, Acts 27:13-44.
Those who purposely cause trouble, Romans 16:17.
Turning to God of all comfort, 2 Corinthians 1:3-4.
Reason for circumstances, Philemon 15-16.
Purpose of trials and grief, 1 Peter 1:6-7.
See *Testing.*

TROUBLEMAKER
Community of troublemakers, Exodus 16:2.
Negligence in care of dangerous animal, Exodus 21:35-36.
Augmenting gossip and trouble, Exodus 23:1.
Sin of only one person, Numbers 16:22.
Successfully facing formidable opponent, Numbers 21:21-26.
Troubler of Israel, 1 Kings 18:16-18.
Man who built gallows for his own neck, Esther 5:11-14. (See also 9:25.)
Marks of evil character, Proverbs 6:16-19.

One who affronted the Lord's name, Isaiah 36:18-22. (See 37:1-7.)
Boomerang principle of harming others, Jeremiah 7:18-19.
Fine-sounding arguments, Colossians 2:4.
What to do with divisive person, Titus 3:10.
Suffering as meddler, 1 Peter 4:15.
See *Abrasion, Meddle.*

TRUST
Remembering Egypt instead of trusting God, Exodus 16:2-3.
Exemplary leadership, 2 Kings 18:5.
Confidence against all circumstances, Job 13:15.
Trusting God like small child, Psalm 131:2.
Betraying confidence, Proverbs 11:13.
Kept in perfect peace, Isaiah 26:3.
Confidence in the Lord rather than men, Isaiah 36:4-10.
Confidence in the potter, Isaiah 45:9.
Confidence in difficult times, Jeremiah 1:17.
Those who trust in man, Jeremiah 17:5.
Safer to trust God than run away, Jeremiah 42:1-22.
Trust in midst of trouble, Habakkuk 3:17-18.
Needless fear in time of storm, Mark 4:35-41.
Assurance to those who come to the Lord for help, John 6:37.
Do not test the Lord, 1 Corinthians 10:9-10.
Invisible reality, Hebrews 11:1.
Cast all cares upon the Lord, 1 Peter 5:7.
See *Confidence, Faith.*

TRUSTWORTHY
The Lord does what He promises, 2 Chronicles 6:4, 14-15.
Looking for one honest person in Jerusalem, Jeremiah 5:1.
Always doing what is right, Romans 12:17.
Faithful service without pastoral supervision, Philippians 2:12-13.
Employees who can be trusted, Titus 2:9-10.
See *Dependability.*

TRUTH
Scripture contains both blessings and curses, Joshua 8:34.
Let God be judge, Job 32:13.

God's covenant never changes, Psalms 105:8-9; 111:5.
Good men and sinners taking oaths, Ecclesiastes 9:2.
Sincere search for God, Jeremiah 29:10-14.
Faithfulness rewarded with imprisonment, Jeremiah 37:1-21.
Futile effort to suppress truth, Jeremiah 38:1-6.
Listening out of desperation, Jeremiah 38:14-28.
Those who refused to believe Jeremiah's prophecy of protection, Jeremiah 43:1-3; 44:15-19.
Those who would silence God's Word, Jeremiah 47:6-7.
God's message proclaimed with boldness, Ezekiel 33:21-33.
Witnessing miracles with hard hearts, Matthew 11:20.
Why Jesus used parables, Matthew 13:10-13.
Believe the Good News, Mark 1:14-15.
Mother of Jesus too frightened to comprehend, Mark 16:1-8.
Message of Christ gives life and destruction, Luke 20:17-18.
Doubt can be augmented by hearing truth, John 8:45-47.
Spiritual blindness and spiritual sight, John 9:39-41.
Walking in light, John 12:35-36.
Pilate's immortal question, John 18:38.
Varying response to resurrection message, Acts 17:32.
Truth declared with power, Romans 1:4.
Those who stumble over means of their redemption, Romans 9:33.
Implications of doubting resurrection, 1 Corinthians 15:12-19.
Truth proclaimed with false motives, Philippians 1:18.
Teachings which cause controversy, 1 Timothy 1:3-4.
God cannot lie, Titus 1:2; Hebrews 6:18.
Certain of truth, 1 John 2:21.
Truth and love united, 2 John 1:3, 5-6.
Love in truth, 3 John 1.
Nothing to be added or taken away, Revelation 22:18-19.
See *Orthodoxy.*

TURMOIL
Unable to tolerate food, Numbers 11:4-6.
Uproar in town, 1 Samuel 4:12-17.
Army shaken by power of God, 1 Samuel 14:15.
Warriors stumbling over each other, Jeremiah 46:12.
See *Unrest.*

TWINS
Jacob and Esau, Genesis 25:21-26.
Obstetrical trickery, Genesis 38:27-30.
Strife before birth, Hosea 12:3.

TYRANT
Life under tyranny, Exodus 1:14; 5:8; Ecclesiastes 4:1-5.
Rehoboam more oppressive than father, King Solomon, 1 Kings 12:1-11.
Oppressive ruler, Proverbs 28:3.
See *Despot, Dictator, Totalitarian.*

U

10.
Only 1 in 10 expressed appreciation, Luke 17:11-19.

UNAWARE
Generation in spiritual ignorance, Judges 2:10.
Unaware of God's plan for man, 1 Samuel 27:12.
Wealth numbs conscience, Hosea 12:8.

UNBELIEF
Making joke of divine truth, Genesis 17:17; 19:14.
Taunting the presence of the Lord, Exodus 17:7.
Israel's failure to trust promises, Deuteronomy 1:28-33.
Sure victory or sure defeat involving same enemy, Joshua 23:6-13.
Pessimism of unbelief, 2 Kings 18:29-35.
No God, no priest, no Law, 2 Chronicles 15:3.
Rebellion of prosperous wicked, Job 21:7-16.
Contrasting walks of belief and unbelief, Psalm 1:1-6.
Sin abounded in spite of God's mercy and judgment, Psalm 78:32.
God made known through judgment, Ezekiel 11:7-12.
Idols in heart, Ezekiel 14:1-11.
Laughing at truth spoken by Jesus, Matthew 9:23-24.
Attributing work of God to demons, Matthew 9:34.
Hindrance to miracles, Matthew 13:58.
Unbelief in face of proof, John 12:37-40.
Acting in ignorance, Acts 3:17.
Unable to believe when prayer is answered, Acts 12:13-15.
Paul's confrontation with intellectual idolatry, Acts 17:16-34.
Pagans certain of erroneous belief, Acts 19:35-36.
Message like smell of death to some, 2 Corinthians 2:16.
Witnessing to those blinded by Satan, 2 Corinthians 4:1-6.
Danger of intellectual pride, 2 Timothy 3:7.
Deceiving others while themselves deceived, 2 Timothy 3:13.
Failure to combine hearing with believing, Hebrews 4:1-3.

Scoffers in last days, 2 Peter 3:3-4.
Denying that Jesus is the Christ, 1 John 2:22-23.
Those cast into lake of fire, Revelation 21:8.

UNCERTAINTY
Boasting about tomorrow, Proverbs 27:1.
Going with confidence into difficult places, Acts 20:22-24.
Obedience toward unknown objectives, Hebrews 11:8.
See *Hesitation.*

UNCHANGEABLE
Unfailing promises, Joshua 23:4.
Unending faithfulness, Joshua 24:14.
Certainty of day and night, Jeremiah 33:19-22.
The One who never changes, Hebrews 1:10-12.
See *Dependability.*

UNCLE
Quarreling herdsmen and wise uncle, Genesis 13:7-9.
Loving uncle, Genesis 29:13-14.
Neither uncle nor father, Leviticus 20:21.
Uncle becomes father, Deuteronomy 25:5-6
Uncle Paul and courageous nephew, Acts 23:12-22.

UNCLEAN
Edible and inedible insects, Leviticus 11:20-23.
Washing prostitutes and chariots, 1 Kings 22:38.
Purifying bad water, 2 Kings 2:19-22.
Men of bad circumstances share good fortune, 2 Kings 7:3-9.
King afflicted with leprosy, 2 Kings 15:5.
Soap that does not wash away guilt, Jeremiah 2:22.
Place of disease and death, Jeremiah 16:1-9.
Uncleanness in God's sight, Ezekiel 36:17.
Clothing of those engaged in immorality, Jude 23.

UNCOMPLICATED
Great things and small things, 2 Kings 5:13.
Simple can understand, Psalm 119:130.
Content with simple things, Psalm 131:1-2.

Understood by children, Matthew 11:25; Luke 18:17.
See *Simplicity*.

UNCONCERNED
Ignoring the Word of the Lord, Jeremiah 25:3.
Those who pass by, Lamentations 1:12.
One's own spiritual welfare, Luke 13:34.
Pharisees' resentment to reaching out, Luke 15:1-7.
Caring neither for God nor man, Luke 18:1-5.
See *Complacency*.

UNCOOPERATIVE
See *Resistant, Stubborn*.

UNCOUTH
See *Vulgar*.

UNCTION
Being truly holy, Numbers 16:3-7.
Speaking words given by the Lord, Numbers 23:12.
Given words to speak, Numbers 24:1-2; 2 Samuel 23:2; Matthew 10:19-20.
Discerning the prophets, Deuteronomy 18:21-22.
Touched by Spirit of the Lord, 1 Samuel 10:6.
The Lord's hand on Ezra, Ezra 7:6.
Instructed tongue, Isaiah 50:4.
Living creatures led by the Spirit, Ezekiel 1:12.
Empowered by the Spirit of the Lord, Micah 3:8.
Strength from the Lord, Habakkuk 3:19.
Holy Spirit's influence over unborn child, Luke 1:41.
Power of Holy Spirit, Luke 4:14-15.
Danger of pride in conquest of demons, Luke 10:16-20.
Asking the Lord for unction, Luke 11:9-13.
Witnessing boldly in Holy Spirit's guidance, Acts 4:5-13.
Living evidence of Holy Spirit in Christian, Acts 6:8-13.
Rebuking Satan, Acts 13:6-12.
No difference between Jew or Gentile, Acts 15:8-9.
Weapons of world versus divine weapons, 2 Corinthians 10:3-5.
Scripture given by Holy Spirit, 2 Peter 1:21.

See *Holiness, Holy Spirit*.

UNDEPENDABLE
Those who broke faith with God, Deuteronomy 32:51.
Weak as spider's web, Job 8:14.
Too much food and drink, Proverbs 23:20.
Friends and brothers untrustworthy, Jeremiah 9:4-8.
Slaves set free, again enslaved, Jeremiah 34:8-11.

UNDERESTIMATE
Positive and negative viewpoints, Numbers 13:17-33.
Underestimating enemy, Deuteronomy 1:41-44.
Small and insignificant greatness, Proverbs 30:24-28.
Contrasting temporal and eternal values, Matthew 6:19-21; Mark 8:36-37.
Underestimating the Son of God, Matthew 13:57; John 1:46.
Understanding individual worth, 1 Corinthians 6:20; 1 Peter 1:18-19.
See *Assessment*.

UNDERHANDED
See *Connivance, Deceit, Deception*.

UNDERMINE
See *Betrayal*.

UNDERPRIVILEGED
Providing for underprivileged, Leviticus 23:22.
Inequity among citizens, Nehemiah 5:1-5.
Sons of sorceress, Isaiah 57:3.
Status of servant, Luke 17:7-10.

UNDERSCORE
See *Emphasis*.

UNDERSTANDING
Eyes that see and ears that hear, Deuteronomy 29:2-4.
Purposeful comprehension, 1 Chronicles 22:12.
Seeing light in God's light, Psalm 36:9.
God-given ability to understand Scripture, Psalm 119:125.
Reward of persistent search for wisdom and insight, Proverbs 2:1-6.
Refusal and inability to read, Isaiah 29:11-

12.
Effect of attitudes on understanding,
Matthew 13:14-15.
Truth understood by children, Luke 10:21.
Sharing together insights into Scriptures,
Acts 18:24-26.
Seeing light but not understanding voice,
Acts 22:9.
Milk and solid food, 1 Corinthians 3:1-2.
Paul showed tolerance toward bad reports
concerning Corinthians, 1 Corinthians
11:18-19.
Filled with knowledge of God's will,
Colossians 1:9-12.
See *Discernment.*

UNDISCIPLINED
Lack of discernment, Deuteronomy 32:28.
Destructive duplicity, Proverbs 11:3.
Warped minds, Proverbs 12:8.
Too much food and drink, Proverbs 23:20.
Disciplined attitude, Isaiah 30:15.
Spiritual vagabonds, Jeremiah 2:31.
Undisciplined nation, Ezekiel 9:9.
See *Irresponsible.*

UNEXPECTED
Burning bush, Exodus 3:1-3.
Awesome, unexpected acts of God, Isaiah
64:3.
Banquet disrupted, Daniel 5:5-28.
Grapes in desert, Hosea 9:10.
Confronted by dazzling light, Acts 9:3-4.
Message heard by those who did not ask,
Romans 10:20.
See *Surprise.*

UNFAIRNESS
Rights of oldest son, Deuteronomy 21:15-
17.
Making and breaking promise to slaves,
Jeremiah 34:8-22.
Cheating on weight and cost, Amos 8:5-6.

UNFAITHFUL
Destiny set for rebellious people, Numbers
14:35.
Turning quickly to heathen gods, Judges
8:33-34.
Woman unfaithful to husband, Judges
19:1-3.
Neglecting the Lord's Word, 1 Samuel 3:1.
Divine disappointment, Isaiah 5:7.
Eyes and ears that do not function, Ezekiel

12:2.
Peter's denial, Matthew 26:31-35,
69-75.
Test of faithfulness, Luke 16:12.
See *Disloyalty.*

UNFIT
Sold for nothing, Isaiah 52:3.
High cost of spiritual fitness, Matthew
10:37-38.
Unfit banquet guests, Matthew 22:8.
Self-condemnation, Acts 13:46.

UNFORGIVABLE SIN
Context of unforgivable sin, Mark 3:20-30.
Blasphemy against Holy Spirit, Luke 12:10.

UNFORGIVING
Practice of prolonged retribution,
Deuteronomy 23:2-6.
Stark picture of vengeance, Psalm 58:10.
(See 68:23.)
See *Retaliation.*

UNFULFILLED
Destiny set for rebellious people, Numbers
14:35.
Partial fulfillment, Deuteronomy 32:48-52.
Three things never satisfied, Proverbs
30:15-16.
Emptiness of success and affluence,
Ecclesiastes 2:4-11.
Life's emptiness, Isaiah 55:2.
No rest for wicked, Isaiah 57:20-21.
Empty cisterns, parched fields, Jeremiah
14:1-6.
Visions come to nothing, Ezekiel 12:21-
25.
Wealth plundered, houses demolished,
wine unused, Zephaniah 1:13.
Those never satisfied, Haggai 1:5-6.
Continual lust for more, Ephesians 4:19.
See *Emptiness.*

UNHAPPINESS
Leadership for those in trouble, 1 Samuel
22:2.
Inequity among citizens, Nehemiah 5:1-5.
Never satisfied, Proverbs 30:15-16.
Bitterness of forsaking the Lord, Jeremiah
2:19.
Judgment bringing absence of joy,
Jeremiah 25:10.
See *Grief, Sorrow.*

UNINTELLIGENT
Willful ignorance, 2 Chronicles 30:10;
36:16; Job 21:13-15; Zechariah 7:11-12;
Matthew 13:15; Romans 1:28; 2 Peter
3:5.
Wild donkey's colt, Job 11:12.
Boastful of ignorance, Proverbs 1:7.
Likenesses of fool, Proverbs 26:1-11.
See *Ignorance.*

UNISEX
Men and women not to wear each other's
clothing, Deuteronomy 22:5.

UNITED STATES
Area of Scripture some believe descriptive
of United States, Isaiah 18:1-2, 7.

UNITY
Wrong kind of unanimity, Numbers 11:4-
10.
Heart and soul in unity, 1 Samuel 14:7.
Two becoming one in spirit, 1 Samuel
18:1-4.
Mutual love between friends, 1 Samuel
20:17.
Multitude as one, Nehemiah 8:1.
Power of love, Proverbs 10:12.
At peace with one's enemies, Proverbs
16:7.
Tiny grains of sand hold back ocean,
Jeremiah 5:22.
Two sticks become as one, Ezekiel 37:17-
23.
Two in agreement, Amos 3:3.
Serving shoulder to shoulder, Zephaniah
3:9.
People at peace with each other, Mark
9:50.
Prayer of Jesus for His own, John 17:20-
23.
Devotion to one another, Romans 12:10.
Divine call to unity, 1 Corinthians 1:10-17;
2 Corinthians 13:11; Ephesians 4:3;
1 Peter 3:8.
Abraham and his seed, Galatians 3:15-
16.
Unity in Christ, Ephesians 2:14.
Diversity producing unity, Ephesians 4:11-
13.
Becoming as one person, Philippians 1:27.
Instructions on unity, Philippians 4:1-9.
Faith held in common, Titus 1:4.
See *Cooperation, Rapport, Unanimity.*

UNIVERSALISM
One Lord over all earth, Zechariah 14:9.
Works insufficient for salvation, Matthew
7:22-23; Romans 3:20; Ephesians 2:8-9;
Titus 3:5.
Only those who pass through narrow door,
Luke 13:22-30.
God wants all to be saved, 1 Timothy 2:3-4.
All must give account of themselves,
1 Peter 4:4-6.

UNIVERSE
Greatness of heavens attests to smallness
of man, Psalm 8:3-4.
Formed at God's command, Hebrews 11:3.
See *Astronomy, Space/time.*

UNKIND
Purposeful oppression, Exodus 1:8-14; 5:6-
18.
Taking advantage of employees,
Deuteronomy 24:14.
Illustration of unkindness, 2 Samuel 12:1-
6.
Attribute of arrogance, Psalm 10:2.
No thought of unkindness, Psalm 109:16.
Unkindness affronts God, Proverbs 14:31.
Unkind to relatives, Isaiah 58:7.
Purposeful practice of unkindness, Ezekiel
22:27-29.
Example to others, Acts 20:35.
Unpaid wages, James 5:4.
See *Cruelty, Heartless.*

UNKNOWN
Forgotten deliverer, Ecclesiastes 9:13-14.
Athenian god, Acts 17:23.
See *Anonymity, Secrecy, Stranger.*

UNPALATABLE
Polluting wheat, Amos 8:6.
Salt that loses its saltiness, Luke 14:34-
35.
Neither cold nor hot, Revelation 3:15-16.
See *Appetite.*

UNPARDONABLE
Anger beyond measure, Lamentations
5:21-22.
Beyond redemption, Hosea 7:13.
Attributing work of God to demons,
Matthew 9:34.
Unpardonable sin, Matthew 12:31-32.
See *Reprobate.*

UNPRECEDENTED
Wisdom of Solomon, 1 Kings 4:29-34.
The God without precedent, Isaiah 64:4.
Believer's anticipation, Jeremiah 33:3.
Something that had not happened before,
   Joel 1:2-3.
Army of locusts, Joel 2:1-9.
See *Original.*

UNPREPARED
Guilty people frightened by place of
   worship, Numbers 17:12-13.
Unexpected evil times, Ecclesiastes 9:12.
Sudden appearance, Malachi 3:1.
Conduct before the Flood, Matthew 24:38-
   39.
Prepared for Second Coming, Matthew
   24:44.
Unworthy servant, Matthew 24:45-51.
Parable of Ten Virgins, Matthew 25:1-13.
Startled jailer, Acts 16:25-32.

UNPRODUCTIVE
Land that produces sparingly, Isaiah 5:10.
Visions come to nothing, Ezekiel 12:22-25.

UNQUALIFIED
Unworthy to build house of God,
   1 Chronicles 28:2-3.

UNRELIABLE
Lack of discernment, Deuteronomy 32:28.
Learn from ant, Proverbs 6:6.
Unfit for job, Proverbs 18:9; 24:30-31.
Inept workman, Ecclesiastes 10:18.
Using dishonest scales, Hosea 12:7.
See *Deceit.*

UNREPENTANT
Judgment on those who persistently reject,
   Leviticus 26:18-20.
Defiant sin, Numbers 15:30-31.
Divine patience with unrepentant, 2 Kings
   8:16-19.
Lamp of wicked, Job 18:5-6.
Playing with fire, Proverbs 6:27-29.
Proclaiming innocence when guilt is
   obvious, Jeremiah 2:34-35.
Hard as stones, Jeremiah 5:3.
Deceit with no shame, Jeremiah 8:8-12.
Burning prophecy of Jeremiah, Jeremiah
   36:20-24.
Nonfunctioning eyes and ears, Ezekiel
   12:2.

See *Depravity, Wickedness.*

UNRESPONSIVE
Failure to respond, Leviticus 5:1.
Refraining from response, Isaiah 36:18-22.
   (See 37:1-7.)
People unresponsive to discipline,
   Jeremiah 2:30.
Ignoring Word of the Lord, Jeremiah 25:3-
   4, 7.
Refusing to see and hear, Ezekiel 12:1-2.
See *Calloused.*

UNREST
Complaining community, Exodus 16:2.
Daily instability, Deuteronomy 28:67.
Caused by troublemaker, 2 Samuel 20:1-2.
Inequity among citizens, Nehemiah 5:1-5.
Chasing wind, Ecclesiastes 2:11.
Unrest day and night, Ecclesiastes 2:23.
Wicked find no rest, Isaiah 57:20-21.
Torment for false worship, Revelation
   14:11.
See *Restless.*

UNRIGHTEOUSNESS
Godlessness and wickedness, Romans
   1:18-25.
Instruments of wickedness, Romans 6:13.
Refused to believe truth, 2 Thessalonians
   2:9-10.
See *Evil.*

UNSATISFIED
Prayer for protection, Numbers 10:35.
Unable to tolerate food, Numbers 11:4-6.
All things wearisome, Ecclesiastes 1:2.
Futility of thought, Ephesians 4:17.
Continual lust for more, Ephesians 4:19.
See *Discontent.*

UNSCRUPULOUS
Blatant display of immorality, Numbers
   25:6-9.
Discerning the prophets, Deuteronomy
   18:21-22.
Selfish marital relationship, Deuteronomy
   22:13-19.
Palace built by unrighteousness, Jeremiah
   22:13-15.
Making and breaking promise to slaves,
   Jeremiah 34:8-22.
Daring to burn prophecy of Jeremiah,
   Jeremiah 36:21-23.

Prophets who see nothing, Ezekiel 13:1-3.
Despising those who speak truth, Amos 5:10.
Cheating in business, Amos 8:5-6.
Mixing human blood with sacrifices, Luke 13:1.
Gaining benefit by taking advantage of others, James 5:4-5.

UNSEEN
Cannot see God and live, Exodus 33:20.
Invisible God, John 1:18; 5:37; Colossians 1:15; 1 Timothy 1:17; 6:16.
God's best beyond visibility, 1 Corinthians 2:9-10.
Visible from invisible, Hebrews 11:3.
Reality of unseen, 1 Peter 1:8-9.
See *Invisible.*

UNSELFISHNESS
Abraham's example, Genesis 13:6-9.
Unselfishness between brothers, Genesis 33:1-11.
Though he loved Ruth, Boaz sought younger husband for her, Ruth 4:1-6.
Expression of comradeship, 1 Samuel 18:4.
Share and share alike, 1 Samuel 30:24.
Room for prophet, 2 Kings 4:8-10.
Men of bad circumstances share good fortune with others, 2 Kings 7:3-9.
Unselfish prayer of wise king, 2 Chronicles 1:7-12.
Woman's willingness to do her duty, Esther 4:12-16.
Concern for others, 1 Corinthians 10:33.
Supreme model of unselfishness, 2 Corinthians 8:7-9.
Student sharing with teacher, Galatians 6:6.
Enduring to help others, 2 Timothy 2:10.
See *Generosity.*

UNSTABLE
Unable to tolerate food, Numbers 11:4-6.
Lack of discernment, Deuteronomy 32:28.
Giving vent to anger, Proverbs 29:11.
Spiritual vagabonds, Jeremiah 2:31.
Easily deceived, Hosea 7:11.
Doctrinal instability, Galatians 1:6-7; Ephesians 4:14.

UNWILLING
First example of unwillingness, Genesis
2:16-17; 3:6.
Daughter-in-law's unwillingness, Ruth 1:14-18.
Unwilling to hear God's message, 2 Chronicles 30:10; 36:16; Proverbs 5:12; Isaiah 30:12; Jeremiah 6:10; 26:23; Zechariah 7:12.
Refusal to obey the Lord, Psalm 81:11; Isaiah 65:12.
Jonah's example, Jonah 1:1-3.
Banquet invitation refused, Matthew 22:3.
Unwilling to accept divine blessing, Matthew 23:37; Luke 13:34.
Divine reluctance to invoke judgment, 2 Peter 3:9.

UNWORTHY
Destiny set for rebellious people, Numbers 14:35.
Evil earnings forbidden in house of Lord, Deuteronomy 23:18.
Unworthy to build house of God, 1 Chronicles 28:2-3.
Parables to fool, Proverbs 26:1-12.
Calling on God because of His great mercy, Daniel 9:18.
Absolute loyalty, Matthew 10:37-39.
Invitation to undeserving, Matthew 22:8.
Sense of self-unworthiness, Acts 13:46.

UPWARD
Elijah to heaven in whirlwind, 2 Kings 2:11.
Christ's ascension, Acts 1:9.
High journey, Deuteronomy 33:26-27; 2 Samuel 22:10-14.
Creator of skies, Job 37:17-18.
Upward look, Psalm 121:1.

URBAN
Building first city, Genesis 4:17.
Urban development, Genesis 10:11-12.
Lifestyle contrast between Abram and Lot, Genesis 13:12.
Cities totally given to debauchery, Genesis 18:16-33.
Dynamic communities, Numbers 13:27-28; Deuteronomy 6:10-12.
Town and country, Deuteronomy 28:3.
Struggle for ownership, 2 Kings 13:25.
Violent streets, Psalm 55:9-11.
New Jerusalem, Revelation 21:2, 15-27.
See *City.*

URGENCY
Ready for quick action, Exodus 12:11.
King's business urgent, 1 Samuel 21:8.
Depart in haste, 2 Samuel 15:14.
Making most of time, Psalm 90:12;
 Ecclesiastes 9:10; Ephesians 5:15-16.
Urgent proclamation, Isaiah 62:1.
Hurry with good news, Matthew 28:5-10.

Extend invitations quickly, Luke 14:21.
Shortness of time, 1 Corinthians 7:29-
 31.
Careful not to waste opportunities,
 Colossians 4:5.

UTILITIES
Water brought into city, 2 Kings 20:20.

V

VACATION
See *Holiday*.

VACILLATE
Wavering between two opinions, 1 Kings 18:21.
Vacillating between pessimism and optimism, Psalm 73:1-28.
Easily deceived, Hosea 7:11.
Changeable Galatians, Galatians 1:6-9.
See *Indecision*.

VAGABOND
Self-imposed wandering, Numbers 14:35.
Satan the vagabond, Job 1:7.
Straying like lost sheep, Psalm 119:176; 1 Peter 2:25; 2 Peter 2:15.
Leaving home, Proverbs 27:8.
Spiritual vagabonds, Jeremiah 2:31.
See *Wandering*.

VAGUE
Inept watchman, Isaiah 56:10.
Uncertain prophets, Micah 3:11.
Write message plainly, Habakkuk 2:2.
Trumpeting uncertain sound, 1 Corinthians 14:8-9.
Some of Paul's writing difficult to understand, 2 Peter 3:15-16.
Wandering stars, Jude 13.
See *Ambiguous*.

VALIDITY
Documentation of ministry of Jesus, Matthew 11:4-5.
Those who tried to prevent resurrection of Jesus, Matthew 27:62-66. (See also 28:11-15.)
Believe Good News, Mark 1:14-15.
Divine revelation does not require external evidence, Mark 8:11-12.
Living by truth, John 3:21.
Jesus had no need for human credentials, John 5:31-40.
Barnabas true friend to Saul, Acts 9:26-27.
Scripture authority concerning Jesus, Acts 18:28.
Ministry of radiance, 2 Corinthians 3:7-8.
Mark of apostle, 2 Corinthians 12:12.
Love validates faith, Galatians 5:5.
Marked by the Holy Spirit, Ephesians 1:13. (Note the "seal" is official identification as on document.)
Validity of faith made known, 1 Thessalonians 1:8-10.
Approved by God rather than men, 1 Thessalonians 2:4-6.
All Scripture God-breathed, 2 Timothy 3:16-17.
Faith credibility to what is heard, Hebrews 4:2.
Sureness and certainty of faith, Hebrews 11:1.
See *Genuine*.

VALOR
Not giving in to weariness, Judges 8:4.
David refused to drink water which endangered lives of his men, 2 Samuel 23:15-17.
Woman's willingness to do her duty, Esther 4:12-16.
Bold and stouthearted, Psalm 138:3.
Standing firm whatever circumstances, Philippians 1:27-30.
See *Courage*.

VALUE
People more valuable than material things, Genesis 14:21.
Importance of well in dry country, Genesis 21:25-31. (See also 26:12-17.)

Monetary value of human being, Leviticus 27:1-8.
Loss of personal worth, Deuteronomy 28:68.
Spoils for conqueror, Judges 5:30.
Silver not precious metal, 1 Kings 10:21, 27.
Low estimation of man's worth, Job 25:5-6.
God's love better than our lives, Psalm 63:3.
Greatest values in life, Psalm 119:36-37.
Value lost through lust, Proverbs 6:25-26.
Wisdom and understanding greater than money, Proverbs 16:16.
Better simple food with peace and quiet, Proverbs 17:1.
Pain of being poor, Proverbs 19:7.
Stealing from poor and giving to rich, Proverbs 22:16.
Devoting energy to becoming rich, Proverbs 23:4-5.
Man born naked, departs naked, Ecclesiastes 5:15.
Calling evil good and good evil, Isaiah 5:20.
Greatest treasure, Isaiah 33:6.
Sold for nothing, then redeemed, Isaiah 52:3.
That which money cannot buy, Isaiah 55:1-2.
Some juice left in grapes, Isaiah 65:8.
Losing in bad exchange, Jeremiah 2:11.
Gold and gems with lost value, Lamentations 4:1; Ezekiel 7:19-20.
Prostitute giving rather than receiving, Ezekiel 16:32-34.
Cheap value on human beings, Amos 2:6.
Silver and gold like dust and dirt, Zechariah 9:3.
Value of sparrow, and value of soul, Matthew 10:28-30.
Losing life to find it again, Matthew 10:39.
Purchase of sure investment, Matthew 13:44.
Worth of one lost sheep, Matthew 18:12-14.
Eternal value of soul, Mark 8:35-37.
First last and last first, Mark 10:31.
Widow's two small coins, Mark 12:41-44; Luke 21:1-4.
Putting first things first, Luke 10:38-42.
Worth of one of God's children, Luke 12:6-7.
Value of what is lost, Luke 15:1-32.
Spiritual economics, Acts 3:6.

Scrolls of value destroyed by converted sorcerers, Acts 19:19.
Wood, hay, and straw instead of gold, silver, and costly stones, 1 Corinthians 3:12-13.
Paul's supreme desire, Philippians 3:7-11.
Proper understanding of Law, 1 Timothy 1:8-11.
Instruments of gold, silver, wood, and clay, 2 Timothy 2:20-21.
Good land and unproductive land, Hebrews 6:7-8.
Moses regarded disgrace greater than treasures of Egypt, Hebrews 11:26.
Esau sold birthright, Hebrews 12:16-17.
Eternal inheritance, 1 Peter 1:3-4.
Not redeemed with silver and gold, 1 Peter 1:18-19.
The "stone" precious to some, rejected by others, 1 Peter 2:7-8.
Precious faith, 2 Peter 3:11-14.
See *Cost, Worth.*

VANITY
Success caused pride and downfall, 2 Chronicles 26:16.
King Hezekiah victim of pride, 2 Chronicles 32:24-26.
Six-month celebration and display of king's wealth, Esther 1:1-5.
Affronted ego, Esther 3:5; 5:9.
Accused of hypocrisy, Job 11:4-6.
Vanity numbs realization of sin, Psalm 36:2.
Obtaining divine attention, Psalm 138:6.
Pretending to be what one is not, Proverbs 12:9; 13:7.
Proud and arrogant, Proverbs 21:24.
Strutting rooster, Proverbs 30:31.
Haughty women become bald, Isaiah 3:16-17.
Those wise in their own eyes, Isaiah 5:21.
Pride of conqueror brought down, Jeremiah 50:11-12.
Deification of self, Ezekiel 16:23-25.
Skill in business brings vanity of heart, Ezekiel 28:4-5.
Egypt's claim of possessing the Nile, Ezekiel 29:3-5.
Vanity over wealth and self-righteousness, Hosea 12:8.
Destruction of wise men, Obadiah 8.
Seeking notice and acclaim, Luke 11:43.
Choosing place of honor for yourself, Luke

14:7-11.
High cost of flagrant vanity, Acts 12:19-23.
Pride over immorality, 1 Corinthians 5:1-2.
Danger of intellectual pride, 1 Corinthians 8:1-3.
Comparing oneself with oneself, 2 Corinthians 10:12.
Those who only seem to be important, Galatians 2:6.
Vain self-appraisal, Galatians 6:3.
Role of conceit in false doctrine, 1 Timothy 6:3-5.
Wealth of money and wealth of good deeds, 1 Timothy 6:17-19.
Empty, boastful words, 2 Peter 2:18.
Making false claim of holy life, 1 John 1:8-10.
Vanity causing disruption in congregation, 3 John 9-10.
Pride and blasphemy, Revelation 13:5.
Refusal to admit sin, Revelation 18:7-8.
See *Pride.*

VANQUISHED
Refusal to use treachery against enemy, 1 Samuel 26:1-25.
Enjoying plunder taken in battle, 1 Samuel 30:16.
Death by measurement, 2 Samuel 8:2.
Haunt of jackals, Jeremiah 9:11.
Break bow, Jeremiah 49:35.
Enemy put to silence, Jeremiah 51:55.
Deserted city, Lamentations 1:1.
Ashamed and silent before the Lord, Ezekiel 16:63.
See *Defeat.*

VANTAGE
Immeasurable greatness of God, 2 Chronicles 6:12-19.
Looking from one's window to activity on street, Proverbs 7:6-13.
Ezekiel lifted up between earth and heaven, Ezekiel 8:3.

VARIANCE
See *Argument, Conflict, Disagreement, Dispute.*

VARIETY
Variety in species, Genesis 1:24-25.
Same food for 40 years, Exodus 16:35.
Inexhaustible design in snowflake, Job 38:22.

New every day, Lamentations 3:22-24.
Wide variety of merchandise, Ezekiel 27:12-23.
Variety of gifts among Christians, 1 Corinthians 12:4-11.

VASTNESS
Army of locusts, Joel 2:1-9.
Contemplating resurrection and exaltation of Christ, Ephesians 1:18-23.
Holy Spirit's power working within, Ephesians 3:20-21.
See *Immensity.*

VEGETABLE
Remembered vegetables of Egypt, Numbers 11:4-6.
Vegetables for king, 1 Kings 21:2.
Garden slug, Psalm 58:8.
See *Horticulture.*

VEGETARIAN
Man and animals originally vegetarian, Genesis 1:29-30.
Using meat as food, Genesis 9:3.
Caution regarding eating of meat, Genesis 9:4.
Discontent over meatless diet, Numbers 11:4-6.
A meal of vegetables, Proverbs 15:17.
Daniel and friends refused royal food in Babylon, Daniel 1:8-16.
Those who only eat vegetables, Romans 14:2.

VENDETTA
See *Enemy, Revenge.*

VENGEANCE
No refuge in cities of refuge, Deuteronomy 19:11-13. (See Josh. 20:1-3.)
Dramatic reversal of fortunes, Esther 5:9–7:10.
When not to do as others have done, Proverbs 24:29.
Folly of taking revenge, Ezekiel 25:15-17.
Leave revenge in God's hands, 2 Thessalonians 1:6-7.
Those who crucified Jesus shall see Him coming again, Revelation 1:7.
See *Retribution, Revenge.*

VENOM
Venom of judgment, Numbers 21:6-9.

Venom of snakes, Deuteronomy 32:24; Job 20:16; Psalm 58:4-5.

People with venom on their lips, Psalm 140:3; James 3:7-8.

Pestilence of locusts in judgment, Revelation 9:7-11.

See *Poison, Snakes.*

VENTRILOQUIST
Voice coming from earth, Isaiah 29:4.

VERBOSE
Words like blustering wind, Job 8:2.

Wrong and right boasting, Jeremiah 9:23-24.

Cynical tongues made silent, Luke 20:20-26.

See *Long-winded, Loquacious, Talkative.*

VERDICT
Jury by plebiscite, Joshua 24:14-21; Matthew 27:15-23.

Wisdom of Solomon, 1 Kings 3:16-28.

See *Judge, Jury.*

VERSATILITY
Wood for making gods and cooking fires, Isaiah 44:14-20.

All-sufficiency of our Lord, Isaiah 44:24-28.

From one sin to another, Jeremiah 9:3.

New every day, Lamentations 3:22-24.

Training for Daniel and friends, Daniel 1:3-4.

VEXATION
Testing patience of Moses, Exodus 17:1-2.

Making wrong a right, Numbers 5:6-7.

Rebuffed by subordinate, Esther 5:9-10.

Giving heed to instruction, Proverbs 16:20.

See *Troublemaker.*

VICARIOUS
Sin's penalty taken for us, Isaiah 53:1-7; John 15:13; Galatians 3:13; Hebrews 2:9; 1 Peter 3:18.

Experiencing in thought what others do in performance, Romans 2:1-11.

Paul willing to be cursed for Israel's salvation, Romans 9:3-4.

Paul's concern for spiritual development of followers, Colossians 2:1-5.

See *Empathy.*

VICE
Evil earnings forbidden in house of the Lord, Deuteronomy 23:18.

Covenant to avoid lust, Job 31:1.

Playing with fire, Proverbs 6:27-28.

Haughty women, Isaiah 3:16.

Those who do not know how to blush, Jeremiah 6:15.

Lust and promiscuity of two sisters, Ezekiel 23:1-49.

For continued sinning, certain judgment, Amos 1:3, 6, 9, 11, 13; 2:1, 4, 6. (Note nature of sin in each of these judgments.)

Sin in broad daylight, 2 Peter 2:13-22.

See *Depravity.*

VICIOUS
Appeasement of jealousy, Genesis 37:23-24.

Weapons of violence, Genesis 49:5.

Destruction of children, Exodus 1:22.

Mutilation of hands and feet, Judges 1:6.

Violent murder, Judges 4:21; 5:24-27.

People burned to death, Judges 9:49.

Violent treaty, 1 Samuel 11:1-2.

Death of Absalom, 2 Samuel 18:9-15.

Sadistic killing, 2 Kings 25:7.

Prophet lowered into mud, Jeremiah 38:6.

See *Ferocity.*

VICTORY
Becoming master over sin, Genesis 4:7.

Powerful and victorious in death more than life, Judges 16:30.

God the resource in time of weakness, 2 Chronicles 14:11.

Certainty of God's promises, 2 Chronicles 20:17.

Victory or defeat in God's hands, 2 Chronicles 25:8.

Trusting God for deliverance, 2 Chronicles 32:1-21.

Power of God's name in time of trouble, Psalms 54:1; 118:8-12.

God, not man, can help in time of trouble, Psalm 60:11-12.

Key to victory over sin, Psalm 119:133.

Given strength to declare God's message, Jeremiah 1:6-10, 17-19.

Jesus responded to Satan with Scripture, Matthew 4:1-11.

Freedom from mastery of sin, Romans 6:14.

Nothing can separate us from love of God, Romans 8:37-39.

In serving God, all may win, 1 Corinthians 9:24-27.

Armor of God, Ephesians 6:10-18.

Timothy's encouraging report from Thessalonians, 1 Thessalonians 3:6-8.

Means by which the Lord Jesus will overthrow man of sin, 2 Thessalonians 2:8.

Attributes of mature Christian life, 2 Peter 1:5-9.

Deliverance from continual sin, 1 John 3:4-6.

Satan's work destroyed, 1 John 3:8.

Overcoming world through faith, 1 John 5:4.

Certainty of success in Christian life, Jude 24-25.

Inevitable defeat of Satan, Revelation 12:1-9.

Rejoicing in heaven over destruction of Babylon, Revelation 19:6-8.

See *Conquest.*

VIEWPOINT

Varied reactions of spies sent to Canaan, Numbers 13:26-33.

God's point of view and man's, Job 10:3-7; Isaiah 55:8-9.

Bible-centered mentality, Psalm 1:2.

Given eternal viewpoint, Jeremiah 33:3.

Paul and Peter face-to-face, Galatians 2:11.

See *Prejudice.*

VIGILANCE

Negative and positive viewpoints, Numbers 13:17-33.

Remembering and following divine teaching, Deuteronomy 4:9.

King's business urgent, 1 Samuel 21:8.

Total vigilance against attack, Nahum 2:1.

Paul's concern lest his vigilance appear mere hypocrisy, Romans 9:1-2.

Making most of every opportunity, Ephesians 5:15-16.

Ready to serve and witness, Ephesians 6:15.

Beware fine-sounding arguments, Colossians 2:4.

See *Alert.*

VIGOROUS

Not giving in to weariness, Judges 8:4.

Vigor of strong man, Judges 15:16.

Strength in numbers, Proverbs 30:25.

Doing what you do with all your might, Ecclesiastes 9:10.

Race not to swift or strong, Ecclesiastes 9:11.

Strength for weary, Isaiah 40:29-31.

Longevity like days of tree, Isaiah 65:22.

See *Virility.*

VINDICATION

Vindication by earthquake, Numbers 16:28-34.

Cities of refuge, Numbers 35:6-15.

Act of mercy rewarded, 1 Samuel 24:1-22.

Scoffing at pagans whose prayers went unanswered, 1 Kings 18:22-38.

The Lord vindicated beleaguered Job, Job 42:7-10.

Paul's vindication of himself, Acts 24:10-27.

See *Innocence.*

VINDICTIVE

David's attitude toward murder of King Saul's son, 2 Samuel 4:1-12.

Variance of attitudes, 2 Kings 6:20-23.

Revenge of bad conscience, 2 Chronicles 16:7-10; 18:23-27.

Contemplated genocide, Esther 3:2-9.

Stark picture of vengeance, Psalm 58:10. (See also 68:23.)

Evil to those who do evil, Psalm 137:8-9.

When not to do as others have done, Proverbs 24:29.

Confrontation between David's and Abner's men, 2 Samuel 2:12-17.

God permits evil government to punish His own people, Habakkuk 1:1-6.

Conflict between husband and wife, Mark 6:17-29.

Potential mob violence during Passover, Mark 14:1-2.

Call for divine vengeance, Luke 9:51-56.

Violence in believer's momentary anger, John 18:10-11.

Evil characters incited against Paul and Silas, Acts 17:5-7.

Argument which almost turned into physical violence, Acts 23:9-12.

See *Revenge.*

VIRGIN

Lot's offer of virgin daughters, Genesis

19:4-8.
Virgin defiled, Genesis 34:1-4.
Spared in time of war, Numbers 31:17-18.
Taken in plunder, Deuteronomy 21:10-14.
Medical proof of virginity, Deuteronomy 22:13-19.
Sacrifice of daughter, Judges 11:30-40.
Prophecy of Incarnation, Isaiah 7:14; Matthew 1:22-23.
Matrimonial happiness, Isaiah 62:5.
Virgin Birth, Matthew 1:18-21; Luke 2:1-7.
Ten virgins, Matthew 25:1-13.
A word about spinsters, 1 Corinthians 7:25-26.
Presented to husband, 2 Corinthians 11:2-3.
See *Chastity.*

VIRGIN MARY
Relationship of Jesus to His mother, Mark 3:31-35.
See *Roman Catholics.*

VIRILITY
Virility of old man, Genesis 17:17. (See 18:11-14.)
Virility of Joseph, Genesis 39:6.
Animals offered in sacrifice, Leviticus 22:24-25.
Moses retained virility until death, Deuteronomy 34:7.
Strong soldiers, 2 Samuel 10:12.
Old age and youth, 1 Kings 2:1-4.
Gadites who defected to fight for David, 1 Chronicles 12:8, 14.
Freedom from human illness, Psalm 73:5.
Fruitful in old age, Psalm 92:14-15.
Race not to swift or strong, Ecclesiastes 9:11.
Strength for weary, Isaiah 40:29-31.
True spiritual virility, Jeremiah 17:7-8.
Looking in vain for man among men, Ezekiel 22:30.
Egyptian men and a prostitute, Ezekiel 23:19-21.
Those whose own strength is their god, Habakkuk 1:11.
See *Athletics, Soldier.*

VIRTUE
Nakedness of Noah, Genesis 9:20-27.
Lot's offer of virgin daughters, Genesis 19:4-8.
Modesty of Rebekah, Genesis 24:61-65.

Dependable employees, 2 Chronicles 34:12; Nehemiah 13:13.
Looking for one honest person in Jerusalem, Jeremiah 5:1.
Act of shame, Jeremiah 13:26.
Daniel's impeccable virtues, Daniel 6:4.
Always doing what is right, Romans 12:17.
Virtue as means of witness, 1 Peter 3:1-2.
See *Chastity, Purity.*

VISA
Travel across national boundaries, Nehemiah 2:1-10.

VISAGE
Radiant face of spiritual experience, Exodus 34:29-32; 2 Corinthians 3:7-8.
Glowing countenance, Ecclesiastes 8:1.
Countenance betrays conscience, Isaiah 3:9.
Face shining like sun, Matthew 17:1-3.
Angel at empty tomb, Matthew 28:1-4.
Countenance of Stephen, Acts 6:15.
See *Countenance, Face.*

VISIBILITY
Vindication by earthquake, Numbers 16:28-34.
Not putting the Lord to the test, Isaiah 7:10-12.
Certainty of day and night, Jeremiah 33:19-22.
Ezekiel's vision, Ezekiel 1:4-28.
Blind man's ears caused eyes to open, Luke 18:35-43.
Seeing not necessarily believing, John 7:3-5.
Faith more important than things tangible, 2 Corinthians 5:7.
Light makes everything visible, Ephesians 5:14.
Reality of unseen, 1 Peter 1:8-9.

VISION
Appearance of the Lord to Abraham, Genesis 18:1.
Opening eyes to see God's provision, 2 Kings 6:16-17.
Divine message through dreams and visions, Job 33:14-17.
Not knowing what others will do with projects, Ecclesiastes 3:22.
Cause of dreams, Ecclesiastes 5:3.
Eloquent description of noble person,

Isaiah 32:8.
Man who dwells on heights, Isaiah 33:16.
God makes a new thing, Isaiah 43:19.
Time to enlarge, Isaiah 54:2-3.
Ezekiel's vision, Ezekiel 1:1.
Vision comes to nothing, Ezekiel 12:22-25.
Prophecy of imagination, Ezekiel 13:1-23.
Young prophesy, old dream dreams, Joel 2:28.
Time to build and extend, Micah 7:11.
Something beyond belief, Habakkuk 1:5.
Partial, then full vision, Mark 8:22-25.
Jesus saw abundant fishing where there had been none, Luke 5:1-11.
Looking only on surface, 2 Corinthians 10:7.
Paul caught up into third heaven, 2 Corinthians 12:1-4.
Eyes of heart, Ephesians 1:18-19.

VISITOR
Public relations approach, 1 Kings 1:42.
Visiting one terminally ill, 2 Kings 13:14.
Intended encouragement, Job 2:11-13.
Gift for departing visitor, Jeremiah 40:5.
Wise men and Jesus, Matthew 2:1-12.
Ministry to sick, Matthew 25:36; James 5:14.
Visit of a few days, John 2:12.
Coming in full measure of blessing, Romans 15:29.
Coming to stay awhile, 1 Corinthians 16:5-6.
Those who refresh spirit, 1 Corinthians 16:18.
Planning double visit, 2 Corinthians 1:16.
Paul's visit with Peter, Galatians 1:18.
Paul's eagerness to visit Thessalonians, 1 Thessalonians 3:11.
Use of guest room, Philemon 22.
See *Guests, Hospitality.*

VISUAL
Avoid architecture which detracts from worship, Deuteronomy 16:21-22.
God's arm coming down in punishment, Isaiah 30:30.
Prophecy of boiling pot, Jeremiah 1:13-15.
Old Testament object lessons, Jeremiah 13:1-11; 19:1-12.
Good figs and bad figs, Jeremiah 24:1-10.
Siege of Jerusalem illustrated, Ezekiel 4:1-3.
Basket of ripe fruit, Amos 8:1-2.

Measuring basket, Zechariah 5:5-11.
Seeing marks of cross as identity, John 20:20-29.
Using object to illustrate point, Acts 21:10-11.
Christ as visualization of Deity, Colossians 1:15; 2:9.

VITALITY
Vitality of loaf of bread, Judges 7:13-15.
Race not to swift or strong, Ecclesiastes 9:11.
Strength for weary, Isaiah 40:29-31.
River brings vitality to arid land, Ezekiel 47:6-12.
Daniel's vitality, Daniel 10:15-19.
Filled with power, Micah 3:8.
Strength received from the Lord, Habakkuk 3:19.
Resurrection power, Philippians 3:10.
Promise of life in Christ Jesus, 2 Timothy 1:1.
See *Health, Virility.*

VOCABULARY
Those who spoke common language, Genesis 11:1.
Peril from wrong use of words, Leviticus 24:13-16.
Resolving not to sin with one's mouth, Psalm 17:3.
Simple words with profound meaning, Psalm 23:1-6.
Apt choice of vocabulary, Proverbs 25:11.
Charming but malicious speech, Proverbs 26:24-26.
Speaking with instructed tongue, Isaiah 50:4.
Learning new language and literature, Daniel 1:3-4.
Use of gracious words, Luke 4:22.
Words beyond normal vocabulary, Romans 8:16, 26-27.
Paul did not use "wise and persuasive words," 1 Corinthians 2:4.
See *Eloquence.*

VOCATION
Different vocations of Cain and Abel, Genesis 4:2-3.
Unique role of priest, Deuteronomy 18:1-2.
Protecting debtor's earning power, Deuteronomy 24:6.
Evaluation of life, Ecclesiastes 5:15.

See *Employment, Labor, Skill.*

VOLCANO
Stream of burning sulphur, Isaiah 30:33.
Caused by falling star, Revelation 9:1-2.

VOLITION
Those moved of heart to do God's work,
    Exodus 35:20-29.
Sin of only one person, Numbers 16:22.
Not giving in to weariness, Judges 8:4.
King's business urgent, 1 Samuel 21:8.
Leadership under divine guidance,
    2 Chronicles 31:20-21.
Earth formed for a purpose, Isaiah 45:18.
Great peace to those who obey, Isaiah
    48:17-18. (See Ps. 119:165.)
Evil procedure and choices, Isaiah 65:11-
    12.
Birds know seasons of migration, Jeremiah
    8:7.
Valley of decision, Joel 3:14.
Influencing others to sin, Luke 17:1.
Filled with knowledge of God's will,
    Colossians 1:9-12.
See *Initiative, Motivation.*

VOTE
Appointment of leader, Numbers 27:16.
Choosing right leader, Deuteronomy
    17:14-15.
Trees seek king, Judges 9:7-15.
Choice of Jesus or Barabbas, Matthew
    27:15-26.
Casting lots to determine God's will, Acts
    1:23-26.
Agreeing with each other in united mind
    and thought, 1 Corinthians 1:10.
See *Politics.*

VOW
Conditioned vow, Genesis 28:20-21.
Keeping every word, Numbers 21:2;
    Deuteronomy 23:21; Psalm 65:1;
    Ecclesiastes 5:4-5.
Pledge not to be made lightly, Numbers
    30:2.
Excruciating condition of vow, Judges
    11:30-35.
Mother's promise for a son, 1 Samuel 1:11.
Vow to Queen of Heaven, Jeremiah 44:24-
    30.
Peter's pledge not to betray Christ, Mark
    14:27-31, 66-72.

Haircut in response to vow, Acts 18:18.
See *Pledge, Promise.*

VOYAGE
Voyage for gold, 1 Kings 22:48.
Experienced sailors, 2 Chronicles 8:18.
Widely divergent cargo, 2 Chronicles 9:21.
Paths in sea, Isaiah 43:16.
Dependable sea transportation, Isaiah
    60:9.
Perilous voyage, Acts 27:1-44.
See *Navigation.*

VULGAR
People who become like animals in times
    of distress, Deuteronomy 28:53-57.
King Saul's vulgar request for dowry,
    1 Samuel 18:25.
Sick drunk, Isaiah 28:7.
Eating filth and drinking urine, Isaiah
    36:12.
See *Debase.*

VULNERABILITY
Foolish sins, Numbers 12:11.
Negative and positive viewpoints,
    Numbers 13:17-33.
No success outside will of God, Numbers
    14:41-45.
Do not take on ways of heathen,
    Deuteronomy 18:9.
Perfume for lady, Ruth 3:3.
Surrender to power of God, 1 Samuel 14:1-
    14.
David's refusal to take advantage of Saul's
    vulnerability, 1 Samuel 26:1-25. (See
    also chap. 24.)
Lack of confidence, 1 Samuel 27:1.
Misunderstanding gesture of goodwill,
    2 Samuel 10:1-4.
Weariness lures enemy to strike, 2 Samuel
    21:15-17.
Protection against enemies along road,
    Ezra 8:21-23.
Times of trouble, Proverbs 24:10.
Those who trust in material security, Isaiah
    31:1-3.
Haunt of jackals, Jeremiah 9:11.
Looking to flesh for strength, Jeremiah
    17:5.
No chance for escape, Jeremiah 48:44.
Guilt of influencing others to sin, Luke
    17:1.
See *Weakness.*

W

WAGES
Wages due daily, Leviticus 19:13;
   Deuteronomy 24:15.
Evil earnings forbidden in house of Lord,
   Deuteronomy 23:18.
Proper care of servants, Job 31:13-14;
   Colossians 4:1.
Expecting free service from neighbor,
   Jeremiah 22:13.
No wages, no business opportunities,
   Zechariah 8:10.
Unfair laborers, Malachi 3:5; James 5:4.
Wages an obligation, not a gift, Romans
   4:4.
See *Honorarium, Salary, Stipend.*

WALK
Path of righteous and way of wicked,
   Proverbs 4:18-19, 25, 27.
Ask for ancient paths, Jeremiah 6:16.
Feet strengthened for conquest, Micah
   4:13.
One who brings good news, Isaiah 52:7;
   Nahum 1:15; Romans 10:15.
Living new life, Romans 6:4; Galatians
   5:16; Ephesians 4:1-32.
See *Hiking.*

WANDERING
Fate of murderer, Genesis 4:11-12.
Uprooted nation, Numbers 32:10-15;
   Hosea 9:17.
Groping in the streets, Lamentations 4:14.
Straying sheep, 1 Peter 2:25.
Eternal disorientation, Jude 11-13.
See *Vagabond.*

WANTONNESS
Evil earnings forbidden in house of the
   Lord, Deuteronomy 23:18.
People like animals in times of distress,

Deuteronomy 28:53-57.
Imbibing without restraint, Esther 1:7-8.
Playing with fire, Proverbs 6:27-28.
Delinquent son, Proverbs 29:3.
Adultery in profusion, Jeremiah 3:6.
Deceit with no shame, Jeremiah 8:8-12.
Prodigal squandering, Luke 15:13.
Continual lust for more, Ephesians 4:19.
Flagrant worldliness, James 5:5; 2 Peter
   2:18.
See *Debauchery, Depravity, Immorality,
Lust.*

WAR
Victory assured in advance, Numbers
   21:34.
Power in numbers, Numbers 22:2-4.
God greater than numbers, Deuteronomy
   20:1.
Civilian and military, Deuteronomy 20:5-9.
Price of possession, Joshua 1:12-15.
Use of ambush, Joshua 8:14-29.
Apparent supremacy of enemy, Joshua
   11:1-6.
Those excluded from battle, Judges 12:1-3.
Surrender to power of God, 1 Samuel 14:1-
   14.
Futility of war, 2 Samuel 1:27.
Trained for battle, 2 Samuel 22:35.
Courage in time of war, Psalm 27:3.
Those who hate peace, Psalm 120:6-7.
Time for war, Ecclesiastes 3:8.
Millennial peace among nations, Isaiah 2:4.
Devastating statement of God's judgment,
   Isaiah 34:1-7.
Daring to scoff at name of the Lord, Isaiah
   36:18-21. (See 37:6.)
Bodies unburied, Jeremiah 9:22.
Break bow, Jeremiah 49:35.
Coming great war against Israel, Ezekiel
   38–39.

World peace an impossibility without Christ, Matthew 24:6-8; Mark 13:6-8.

Four horsemen, Revelation 6:1-8.

See *Army, Military, Scorched earth, Soldier.*

WARDROBE

First clothing, Genesis 3:7, 21.

Widow's clothing, Genesis 38:13-14; 2 Samuel 14:2.

Gifts of clothing, Genesis 45:22.

Durability from good workmanship, Exodus 28:31-32.

Robes for pagan worship, 2 Kings 10:22.

Excessive variety, Job 27:16.

Clothing fit for king's daughter, Psalm 45:13.

Clothed with righteousness and faithfulness, Isaiah 11:5.

Dressed like bridegroom, Isaiah 61:10.

New garments for Joshua, Zechariah 3:1-7.

Dress code for weddings, Matthew 22:11.

Ego displayed by teachers of Law, Mark 12:38-40; Luke 20:46-47; 21:1-4.

John the Baptist avoided fine clothes, Luke 7:24-28.

Wardrobe of wealth, Luke 16:19.

Modest dress, 1 Timothy 2:9-10; 1 Peter 3:3.

Clothes do not necessarily make the man, James 2:1-5.

Clothing of those engaged in immorality, Jude 23.

Cloud for robe, rainbow for hat, Revelation 10:1.

Garments worn by the angels, Revelation 15:6.

Garments of bride in heaven, Revelation 19:7-8.

Those wearing clean robes, Revelation 22:14.

See *Clothing.*

WARNING

Warning of angels taken as joke, Genesis 19:14.

Joshua's blessing and warning, Joshua 23:14-16.

Letter of warning, 2 Chronicles 21:12-15.

Shout like trumpet, Isaiah 58:1.

Prophecy of boiling pot, Jeremiah 1:13-15.

Cry of terror, Jeremiah 49:29.

Responsibility to warn lost souls, Ezekiel 3:18-19.

Responsibility of watchman, Ezekiel 33:1-

9.

Prosperity linked to conduct, Daniel 4:27.

Ninevites heeded Jonah's warning, Jonah 3:3-6.

Warned in a dream, Matthew 2:13.

Information ahead of time, Matthew 24:22-25.

Example of Lot's wife, Luke 17:32.

Christian friends warned Paul not to go to Jerusalem, Acts 21:3-4.

Giving caution concerning false teaching, 1 Timothy 4:1-6.

How to deal with divisive person, Titus 3:10.

False teaching and wrong conduct, Jude 3-4.

Sounding forth cry of doom, Revelation 8:13.

No more delay, Revelation 10:6.

See *Admonition.*

WASHING

Washing for sanitary purpose, Leviticus 13:53-54.

Symbol of innocence, Deuteronomy 21:6; Psalm 26:6; Matthew 27:24.

Bathing in salt water, 2 Chronicles 4:6.

Stain that soda and soap will not cleanse, Jeremiah 2:22.

See *Bath.*

WASTE

Careful storage of food, Genesis 41:35-36; Proverbs 21:20.

Nothing wasted, Exodus 16:4-18.

Purifying bad water, 2 Kings 2:19-22.

Learn lesson from ant, Proverbs 6:6-8.

Purses with holes in them, Haggai 1:6.

Squandered wealth, Luke 15:13.

Attitude of Jesus to waste, John 6:12.

WATER

Importance of wells in dry country, Genesis 21:25-31. (See also 26:12-17.)

Dispute over water rights, Genesis 26:19-22.

Bitter water made sweet, Exodus 15:25.

No water for crops, Leviticus 26:18-20.

Song to desert well, Numbers 21:17-18.

Irrigation versus abundant rainfall, Deuteronomy 11:10-11.

Revitalizing water, Judges 15:19.

Municipal waterworks, 2 Kings 20:20.

Gift of the Creator, Psalm 148:4-5.

Reservoirs for irrigation, Ecclesiastes 2:6.
Water supply for Jerusalem, Isaiah 36:2.
Uninterrupted supply, Isaiah 58:11.
Israel turned away from living water,
    Jeremiah 2:13, 18.
Poisoned water, Jeremiah 8:14.
Springs that fail, Jeremiah 15:18.
Daily allotment, Ezekiel 4:11.
Praying for rain in springtime, Zechariah
    10:1.
Living water, John 4:4-14.
No longer any sea, Revelation 21:1.
See *Wells.*

WEAK-MINDED
Senseless thinking, Psalm 92:6; Jeremiah
    10:8.
Likenesses of fool, Proverbs 26:1-11.
Given animal's mind, Daniel 4:16; 2 Peter
    2:12.
Easily deceived, Hosea 7:11.
Futility of thinking, Ephesians 4:17.
See *Retarded.*

WEAKNESS
Fear of rumor, Numbers 14:13-16.
People quick to disobey, Judges 2:10-13,
    19; 3:7, 12; 4:1.
Struggle between strong and weak,
    2 Samuel 3:1.
Divine resource in time of weakness,
    2 Chronicles 14:11.
Unable to face enemy, 2 Chronicles 20:12.
Omnipotent God touches weak, Job 36:5.
Weakness from fasting, Psalm 109:24.
Futility of human effort, Psalm 127:1.
Faith greater than physical strength, Psalm
    147:10-11.
Too much food and drink, Proverbs 23:20.
Mount up on wings like eagles, Isaiah
    40:29-31.
Least becomes great, Isaiah 60:22.
Tiny grains of sand hold back ocean,
    Jeremiah 5:22.
Frailty of foot, Jeremiah 12:5.
Weaker sex, Jeremiah 51:30.
Easily deceived, Hosea 7:11.
God's blessing on meek and humble,
    Zephaniah 3:12.
Day of small things, Zechariah 4:10.
Dependence on divine strength, John 15:5.
Immaturity of new convert, Acts 8:13-24.
Strength in weakness, 1 Corinthians 1:27;
    Hebrews 11:33-34.

Human incompetence, 2 Corinthians 3:5.
Jars of clay, 2 Corinthians 4:7.
Antidote for vanity, 2 Corinthians 11:30;
    12:7-10.
Dynamic of the Cross, 2 Corinthians 13:4.
High priests men of human weakness,
    Hebrews 7:28.
See *Vulnerability.*

WEALTH
Earth's wealth, Genesis 2:11-12.
Promise and warning, Deuteronomy 6:10-
    12.
Wealth an impetus to backsliding,
    Deuteronomy 8:13-14; 31:20; 32:15;
    Psalm 62:10.
Divine ability to produce wealth,
    Deuteronomy 8:18; Ecclesiastes 5:19.
The Lord gives and takes away, 1 Samuel
    2:6-7.
Solomon's great wealth, 2 Chronicles 9:22.
Folly of trusting in wealth, Job 31:24-28;
    Psalm 49:5-12.
Producing wealth for others to enjoy,
    Psalm 39:6.
Riches without understanding, Psalm
    49:16-20.
Growing rich by harming others, Psalm
    52:7.
Greatest of all wealth, Psalm 119:14.
Barns filled and flocks abundant, Psalm
    144:13.
Honor the Lord with one's wealth,
    Proverbs 3:9-10.
Wealth stolen by strangers, Proverbs 5:8-
    10.
Wisdom the truest wealth, Proverbs 8:17-
    19; 16:16.
Wealth that is actually poverty, Proverbs
    13:7.
Greatest value, Proverbs 16:8.
Purchase of prestige, Proverbs 18:16.
Priceless value of good name, Proverbs
    22:1.
Power of money, Proverbs 22:7.
Stealing from poor and giving to rich,
    Proverbs 22:16.
Wearing yourself out to become rich,
    Proverbs 23:4-5.
Do not envy wicked, Proverbs 24:19-20.
Prayer of true wisdom, Proverbs 30:8-9.
Meaningless accumulation of wealth,
    Ecclesiastes 2:4-11.
Money alone never satisfies, Ecclesiastes

5:10.
Money as shelter, Ecclesiastes 7:12.
Presumed function of money, Ecclesiastes 10:19.
Wealth undeserved and unearned, Jeremiah 17:11.
Tyre, city of luxury, brought down, Ezekiel 27:1-36. (See also 28:1-19.)
Exploiting poor for personal gain, Amos 5:11.
Gold and silver belong to God, Haggai 2:8.
Eternal transmutation, Matthew 6:19-21.
Wealth a spiritual liability, Matthew 19:23; 1 Timothy 6:9.
Rich man who provided tomb for Jesus, Matthew 27:57-61.
Poor can inherit kingdom, Luke 6:20.
Much required of those given much, Luke 12:48.
Surprised beggar, Acts 3:1-8.
Sharing spiritual and material blessings, Romans 15:26-27.
God's grace lavished on us, Ephesians 1:7-8.
We bring nothing into the world, take nothing out, 1 Timothy 6:6-8.
What seems high position is, instead, low, James 1:10.
Eternal inheritance, 1 Peter 1:3-4.
Not redeemed with silver and gold, 1 Peter 1:18-19.
True wealth, Revelation 2:9.
Temporal wealth and spiritual wealth, Revelation 3:15-18.
See *Affluence, Materialism.*

WEAPONS
No weapons in Israel, 1 Samuel 13:19-22.
Spiritual weapons, 1 Samuel 17:45;
   2 Corinthians 10:4; Ephesians 6:17;
   Hebrews 4:12.
Primitive weapons, 2 Chronicles 26:14.
The Lord on our side, Psalm 124:1-5.
Satisfied sword, Jeremiah 46:10.
Break bow, Jeremiah 49:35.
Arsenal of the Lord, Jeremiah 50:25.
Trusting the Lord and trusting in weapons, Luke 22:35-38.
See *Army, Military, War.*

WEARINESS
Weary of life, Genesis 27:46; Ecclesiastes 4:2.
Bread for exhausted men, Judges 8:15.

Vulnerable to attack from enemy, 2 Samuel 17:1-2.
Exhausted in the battle, 2 Samuel 21:15.
Refusing opportunity for rest, Isaiah 28:11-12.
Strength for the weary, Isaiah 40:29-31.
Weariness induced by sin, Jeremiah 9:3-5.
Daniel's weariness, Daniel 8:27; 10:17.
Respite for weariness, Matthew 11:28-30; Romans 8:31-39.
No chance for rest in busy ministry, Mark 6:30-34.
Man who fell asleep during worship, Acts 20:7-12.
Not weary of doing good, Galatians 6:9.

WEATHER
Earth before rainfall, Genesis 2:4-6.
Cool time of day, Genesis 3:8.
First rainfall, Genesis 7:11-12. (See 2:4-6.)
Establishment of seasons after Flood, Genesis 8:22.
Rainless sky and parched earth, Leviticus 26:19-20.
Reward for obedience, Deuteronomy 11:13-29.
Abundant blessings of nature, Deuteronomy 33:13-16.
Praying for rain, 1 Samuel 12:18.
Good weather blessing from God, 1 Kings 8:35-36.
Rainy season affected worship and confession, Ezra 10:13.
Path for wind and storm, Job 28:25-27.
Accurate description of rainfall, Job 36:27-30; 37:6, 15-16.
Storehouses for snow and hail, Job 38:22.
Sky seen revealing reality of God, Psalm 18:9-14.
Rain for crops and pastures, Psalm 65:9-13; Joel 2:23-24.
Rain likened to blessing, Psalm 72:6.
Skies at God's command, Psalm 77:16-19.
God's chariot clouds, Psalm 104:3.
Lord of all kinds of weather, Psalm 135:6-7.
Snow and rain out of season, Proverbs 26:1.
Driving rain of little value, Proverbs 28:3.
Wind and rain, Ecclesiastes 1:6-7.
Too much concern for weather, Ecclesiastes 11:4.
Winter past and flowers appearing, Song of Songs 2:11-12.
Wind, rain, and hail, Isaiah 28:2.

Clouds rise, Jeremiah 10:13.
The God who made and sustains universe, Jeremiah 51:15-16.
Scant rainfall during growing season, Amos 4:7.
Violent storm and Jonah's voyage, Jonah 1:4, 10-15.
Whirlwind invokes judgment, Nahum 1:3.
Dew from heavens, Zechariah 8:12.
Prayer for rain in springtime, Zechariah 10:1.
Pharisees could forecast weather, Matthew 16:1-4.
Wind obedient to Creator's command, Mark 4:35-41.
Jesus forecasting weather, Luke 12:54-56.
Mistaking voice of God for thunder, John 12:28-29.
Inclement winds delayed progress by ship, Acts 27:6-9.
Mistaking gentle wind, Acts 27:13-14.
Wind forbidden to blow, Revelation 7:1.
Hailstones from sky, Revelation 16:21.
See *Meteorologist, Rain, Seasons, Snow, Storm.*

WEDDING
Long-delayed wedding, Genesis 29:22.
Payment of dowry, Genesis 34:12; Exodus 22:16-17.
Wedding riddle, Judges 14:12-13.
Esther's great banquet, Esther 2:18.
Arrival of bridegroom, Song of Songs 3:9-11.
Dressed like bridegroom, Isaiah 61:10.
Parable of Virgins, Matthew 25:1-13.
Site of Christ's first miracle, John 2:1-11.
Garments of bride, Revelation 19:7-8; 21:2.
See *Marriage, Romance.*

WEEDS
Eating that which grows of its own, 2 Kings 19:29; Isaiah 37:30.
Nettles and brambles, Isaiah 34:13.
Thorns spoil harvest, Matthew 13:3-8, 18-23.
Weeds planted by enemy, Matthew 13:24-29, 36-42.
Good crops and weeds, Hebrews 6:7-8.
See *Thorns.*

WEIGHT
Money by weight, Genesis 23:16; Ezra 8:24-27; Jeremiah 32:9.

Use of accurate scales, Leviticus 19:36; Deuteronomy 25:13; Ezekiel 45:10.
Divine delight in accuracy, Proverbs 11:1; 16:11.
Divine dislike of inaccuracy, Proverbs 20:10; Micah 6:11.
See *Measurement.*

WELCOME
Room for the prophet, 2 Kings 4:8-10.
Familiarity breeds contempt, Proverbs 25:17.
Abundance for all, Isaiah 55:1-2.
How not to take advantage of host, Luke 14:8-11.
Tax collectors and "sinners" welcomed to Jesus' table, Luke 15:1-7.
Receiving less than desired guest, Galatians 4:14.
Show welcome to strangers, Hebrews 13:2.
Divine invitation, Revelation 22:17.
See *Hospitality.*

WELFARE
Responsibility toward each other, Genesis 9:5.
Use of tithe for welfare, Deuteronomy 26:12.
Concern for those in need, Job 29:16.
Sharing with others, Job 31:16-22.
Blessing for generous man, Proverbs 22:9.
Outreach to enemy, Proverbs 25:21.
Concern for poor, Proverbs 28:27; 31:20.
Speak up for those who cannot help themselves, Proverbs 31:8-9.
Welfare as spiritual service, Isaiah 58:6-10.
Babylonian mercy to poor, Jeremiah 39:10; 40:7-9.
Protecting orphans and widows, Jeremiah 49:11; Zechariah 7:8-10.
Cheap value on human beings, Amos 2:6.
Responding to request for aid, Matthew 5:42.
Privately giving to poor, Matthew 6:2-4.
Giving cup of cold water, Matthew 10:42.
Reward for looking after needs of others, Matthew 25:34-40.
Expensive perfume used to prepare Jesus for burial, Mark 14:3-9.
Men who brought paralytic man to Jesus, Luke 5:17-26.
Good Samaritan, Luke 10:30-37.
True concern for less privileged, Luke 14:12-14.

Surprised beggar, Acts 3:1-8.
Early Christians took care of those in need, Acts 4:32-35.
Woman who helped the poor, Acts 9:36-42.
Devout centurion, Acts 10:2.
Kindness to poor recognized by the Lord, Acts 10:4.
Reaching out to help others, Acts 11:27-30.
Share with those in need, Romans 12:13.
Church looking after needs of poor, Romans 15:26-27.
Seeking good of others above oneself, 1 Corinthians 10:24.
Greater gift than money, 1 Corinthians 13:3.
Concern of early Christians for poor, Galatians 2:9-10.
Proper care for widows, 1 Timothy 5:3-8.
Widows who qualify for welfare, 1 Timothy 5:9-11.
God's blessing on those who help others, Hebrews 6:10.
Share with others, Hebrews 13:16.
Looking after those in need, James 1:27.
Proper attitude toward poor, James 2:1-8.
Faith without works, James 2:14-18.
Sharing material possessions with others, 1 John 3:17.
See *Benevolence, Philanthropy.*

WELLS
Needed in arid areas, Genesis 21:25-31.
Destroyed and restored, Genesis 26:12-18.
Abundant cisterns, 2 Chronicles 26:10.
Irrigation reservoirs, Ecclesiastes 2:6.
Jacob's well, John 4:4-10.
See *Water.*

WHIPPING
Whips and scorpions, 1 Kings 12:11.
A child's discipline, Proverbs 22:6, 15.
Rod for fools, Proverbs 26:3.
Horse whips, Nahum 3:2.
Jesus flogged before Crucifixion, Matthew 27:26; Mark 15:15; John 19:1.
Flogging of Apostle Paul, Acts 22:22-29.
See *Punishment.*

WHISKERS
Hygienic shave, Leviticus 14:9.
Stylized beard, Leviticus 19:27; 21:5.
Feigned madness, 1 Samuel 21:13.
Half-shaved beards, 2 Samuel 10:4.

Untended mustache, 2 Samuel 19:24.
Grasping man by beard, 2 Samuel 20:9.
Oil down Aaron's beard, Psalm 133:1-2.

WICKEDNESS
Wickedness diverted, Genesis 11:8; Job 5:12.
Defiant sin, Exodus 23:2; Numbers 15:30-31.
Sin of only one person, Numbers 16:22.
Divine patience with unrepentant, 2 Kings 8:16-19.
Infamy to king's daughter, 2 Kings 9:30-37.
Devious speech, Psalm 5:9.
Plotting against righteous, Psalm 37:12.
Preference for evil, Psalm 52:3.
Iniquitous insomnia, Proverbs 4:16.
Loaded with guilt, Isaiah 1:4.
Power of wickedness taken away, Isaiah 37:27.
False prophets and diviners, Isaiah 44:25.
Like restless sea, Isaiah 57:20.
Palace built by unrighteousness, Jeremiah 22:13-15.
Repentance of heart, Joel 2:13.
For continued sinning, certain judgment, Amos 1:3, 6, 9, 11, 13; 2:1, 4, 6. (Note nature of sin in each judgment.)
Hands skilled in doing evil, Micah 7:3.
Sin in broad daylight, 2 Peter 2:13-23.
See *Carnality, Debauchery, Evil.*

WIDOW
Not to be disadvantaged, Exodus 22:22.
Participants in tithe, Deuteronomy 26:12.
Three widows in one family, Ruth 1:1-5.
Besieged by creditor, 2 Kings 4:1.
Father to fatherless, Psalm 68:5.
Numerous widows, Jeremiah 15:8.
Sorrow of young virgin, Joel 1:8.
Widow's mite, Mark 12:42-44; Luke 21:1-4.
Long years of widowhood, Luke 2:36-37.
Caring for widows, 1 Timothy 5:3-16.
Congregational concern, James 1:27.

WIDOWER
Abraham and death of Sarah, Genesis 23:1-20.

WIFE
Creator's design, Genesis 2:18-24.
Husband's involvement in contracts made

by wife, Numbers 30:10-15.
Wiles of new bride, Judges 14:11-19.
Favorite among many wives, 2 Chronicles
11:21.
Bad influence of evil woman, 2 Chronicles
21:6.
Refusal to be put on display, Esther 1:9-21.
Fruitful vine, Psalm 128:3.
Husband's crown, Proverbs 12:4.
Favor of the Lord, Proverbs 18:22.
Woman of noble character, Proverbs
31:10-31.
Death of Ezekiel's wife, Ezekiel 24:15-27.
Joseph's enigma concerning Mary,
Matthew 1:18-19.
See *Marriage.*

WILDERNESS
See *Desert.*

WILD OATS
Reaping what is sown, Galatians 6:7-8.

WILES
Clever wiles of Samson's wife, Judges
14:11-19.
Perfume for lady, Ruth 3:3.
Influencing others to sin, Luke 17:1.
Schemes of Satan, 2 Corinthians 2:11;
11:3; Ephesians 6:11.
See *Flirtation, Seduction.*

WILL
Freedom of choice, Genesis 13:10-13.
No success outside God's will, Numbers
14:41-45.
Some may think it undesirable to serve the
Lord, Joshua 24:15.
Not our desires but desires placed in our
hearts, Psalms 20:4-5; 37:3-5.
Let God plan, Psalm 40:5.
Divine purposes fulfilled, Psalm 138:8.
Man's plans and God's will, Isaiah 30:1.
Valley of decision, Joel 3:14.
Human and divine motivation, Matthew
8:1-3.
Wisdom from doing God's will, John 7:17.
Relationship between talent and knowing
God's will, Romans 11:29.
Folly of missing God's will, Ephesians 5:17.
God's promise concerning knowing His
will, Colossians 1:9-14.
Good purpose fulfilled, 2 Thessalonians
1:11.

Position in life subordinate to witness and
will of God, Titus 2:9-10.
Hindered from will of God, 1 John 2:15-17.
See *Guidance, Obedient.*

WILLING
Abraham's willingness to sacrifice Isaac,
Genesis 22:1-18.
Spontaneous commitment, Judges 5:2.
Volunteers for Jerusalem, Nehemiah 11:2.
Motivating desire, Psalm 40:8.
Prerequisite to blessing, Isaiah 1:19.
Willing followers, Mark 1:16-18.
Willing candidate for faith, Mark 9:17-25.
See *Obedient.*

WIND
Wind over water, Genesis 8:1; Exodus
15:10.
From all four directions, Exodus 10:19; Job
27:21; 37:17; Song of Songs 4:16.
Provision of food, Numbers 11:31.
Conveying life, Ezekiel 37:9.
Windstorm, Mark 4:37; Acts 27:14.
Wind forbidden to blow, Revelation 7:1.
See *Storm.*

WINDBAG
Making promises to curry loyalty,
1 Samuel 22:6-8.
Words like blustering wind, Job 8:2.
Bragging about wealth, Psalm 49:6.
Boasting of imagined gifts, Proverbs 25:14.
Speaking with empty words, Isaiah 36:4-7.
Sin to brag, James 4:16.
See *Loquacious.*

WINE
Used in spiritual offering, Exodus 29:40.
Forbidden to priests, Leviticus 10:9.
Purchase of wine, Deuteronomy 14:26.
Social consumption, Esther 5:6.
Love of wine and fattening food, Proverbs
21:17; 23:1-2.
Wine and leadership, Proverbs 31:4.
Fermentation of wine, Mark 2:22.
Setting good example, Romans 14:21.
Digestive function, 1 Timothy 5:23.
See *Abstinence, Alcohol, Drunkenness,
Liquor, Temperance.*

WINK
Malicious wink, Psalm 35:19; Proverbs
10:10.

Gesture of scoundrel, Proverbs 6:12-14.
Haughty women of Zion, Isaiah 3:16-17.
See *Flirtation, Seduction.*

WINTER
Divine breath produces ice and cold, Job 37:10.
Good mother provides clothes, Proverbs 31:21.
Joy of winter's end, Song of Songs 2:11.
Cold journey, Matthew 24:20; 2 Timothy 4:21.
Paul's choice for spending winter months, Titus 3:12.
See *Cold, Seasons, Snow.*

WISDOM
Prayer for wisdom rather than material gain, 1 Kings 3:5-15; 4:29-34.
Reputation for wisdom, 2 Chronicles 9:23.
Need to obtain advice more than give it, 2 Chronicles 10:1-8.
Wisdom of youth and age, Job 32:4-9.
Words without knowledge, Job 38:2.
Divine supply of light, Psalm 36:9.
Fear of the Lord, Psalm 111:10.
Gift from God for study of Scriptures, Psalm 119:33-38, 97-100.
Asking God for discernment, Psalm 119:125.
Divine omniscience, Isaiah 40:13-14.
Learning of wise overthrown, Isaiah 44:25.
God's thoughts higher than man's, Isaiah 55:9.
Wisdom of trusting in the Lord, Hosea 14:9.
Wise as snakes, innocent as doves, Matthew 10:16.
Greater wisdom than Solomon's, Matthew 12:42.
Truth understood by children, Luke 10:21.
Given words to say in difficult time, Luke 12:11-12; 21:15.
Knowledge beyond classroom, John 7:15.
Tact in relating to unbelievers, 2 Corinthians 2:15-16.
Eyes of heart, Ephesians 1:18-19.
Knowledge and insight, Philippians 1:9.
Reward of careful reflection, 2 Timothy 2:7.
We are given understanding, 1 John 5:20.
See *Intellectual.*

WISH
Three choices for punishment, 1 Chronicles 21:8-13.
The God who grants desires, Psalms 20:4; 21:2; 37:4.
See *Desire.*

WITCHCRAFT
Witchcraft destroyed, Exodus 22:18; 2 Kings 23:24; Micah 5:12.
Abstinence from, Leviticus 19:31; 20:6; Isaiah 8:19.
Sin of divination, 1 Samuel 15:23.
King who consulted a witch, 1 Samuel 28:5-20.
See *Sorcery.*

WITNESS
Moses became like God to Pharaoh, Exodus 7:1-2.
Backslidden believers a laughingstock, Exodus 32:25.
Presence of God the ultimate identity, Exodus 33:15-16.
Samuel's unwasted words, 1 Samuel 3:19.
Wisdom and spiritual identity, 1 Kings 10:1.
Nehemiah's enemies recognized God-given success, Nehemiah 6:15-16.
Refused to bow down and honor man, Esther 3:1-5.
Role of prayer in effective witness, Job 33:26-28.
David's song of transformation, Psalm 40:1-4.
Purity of life necessary for effective witness, Psalm 51:10-13.
Witnessing all day long, Psalm 71:24.
Let the redeemed of the Lord speak, Psalm 107:1-3.
Courage to witness to those in authority, Psalm 119:46.
Sow in tears, reap with joy, Psalm 126:5-6.
Speaking in praise of the Lord, Psalm 145:21.
Isaiah's call to convey message, Isaiah 6:8-10.
Convey God's message to others, Isaiah 38:18-19.
Declaring one and only Saviour, Isaiah 43:10-13.
Words the Lord puts into your mouth, Isaiah 51:16.
Beautiful feet of those who bring Good

News, Isaiah 52:7.
God's Word will not return to Him empty,
Isaiah 55:10-11.
Those who witness dishonestly, Jeremiah
5:1-2.
Day coming when soul-winning not
necessary, Jeremiah 31:34.
Responsibility for failing to witness, Ezekiel
3:18-19; 33:7-9.
Wearing mark of repentance, Ezekiel 9:3-
6.
Looking in vain for someone to stand in
gap, Ezekiel 22:30.
Clear witness in court of king, Daniel 3:8-
18.
King's acknowledgment of Daniel's faith,
Daniel 4:8.
Impeccable witness of Daniel, Daniel 6:3-
4.
Faith ahead of loyalty to king, Daniel 6:5-
11.
Those who witness shine like stars, Daniel
12:3.
Ashamed to mention the Lord's name,
Amos 6:10.
Witness in time of stress, Jonah 1:4-9.
Prophet an exception to those whom he
warned, Micah 3:8.
Haggai called the Lord's messenger,
Haggai 1:13.
Like the Lord's signet ring, Haggai 2:23.
People seek those who know the Lord,
Zechariah 8:23.
Like jewels in crown, Zechariah 9:16.
Becoming fishers of men, Matthew 4:19.
Let your light shine, Matthew 5:14-16;
Mark 4:21-22.
Giving to those unprepared to receive,
Matthew 7:6.
Association with sinners, Matthew 9:10-12.
Brought before men of high standing,
Matthew 10:16-20.
Heavenly Father acknowledges those who
acknowledge Him, Matthew 10:32-33.
Peter's denial of his Lord, Matthew 26:31-
35, 69-75; Mark 14:27-31, 66-72.
Centurion compelled to witness, Matthew
27:54.
Sowing seed on various kinds of soil, Mark
4:3-20; Luke 8:4-15.
Man who wanted only to be with the Lord
rather than reach out to others, Mark
5:18-20.
Those ashamed of the Lord and His

message, Mark 8:38.
Shepherds saw, then "spread the word,"
Luke 2:16-18.
Witness of demons, Luke 4:33-41.
Fishers of men, Luke 5:1-11.
Reaching out to the lost, Luke 5:27-32.
Declaring lordship of Christ, Luke 9:18-20.
Rejecting those who witness, Luke 10:16.
Spiritual light from within, Luke 11:33-36.
Those who acknowledge Christ before
men and those who deny, Luke 12:8-9.
Given words to speak, Luke 21:15.
Those who display true light, John 1:8-9.
Friend of bridegroom, John 3:26-30.
Tact in witness, John 4:4-26.
Harvesttime now, John 4:35-38.
Effectiveness of woman's testimony, John
4:39-42.
Those who dare not witness, John 7:12-13.
Miracle caused many to believe, John 12:9-
11.
Those who testify, John 15:26-27.
Secret loyalty, John 19:38.
Spiritual conquest, not earthly possession,
should motivate follower of Christ, Acts
1:6-8.
Simple men like Peter and John
confounded scholars, Acts 4:13.
Courage in face of opposition, Acts 4:18-
20.
Requisite for bold proclamation of the
Word, Acts 4:31.
Persistence in witnessing, Acts 5:42.
Philip guided by angel, Acts 8:26.
Ananias guided to Saul, Acts 9:10-17.
People questioned conversion of Saul, Acts
9:19-22. (See also v. 26.)
Those scattered by persecution witnessed
wherever they went, Acts 11:19-21.
Use of Scripture in bold witness, Acts
13:13-52.
Basis for persuasion and teaching, Acts
17:2-4.
The power of personal testimony, Acts
21:37–22:21; 26:1-18, 28-29.
Paul's bondage became means for
ministry, Acts 28:17-28.
Not ashamed of Gospel, Romans 1:16.
Role of witness in salvation, Romans 10:9-
10.
Bringing message to those who have not
heard, Romans 10:14-15.
One plants, one waters, God gives growth,
1 Corinthians 3:5-9.

Witnessing effective only through the Holy Spirit, 1 Corinthians 12:3.

Importance of being understood, 1 Corinthians 14:13-19.

Sign for unbelievers, 1 Corinthians 14:22-25.

Gospel message in brief, 1 Corinthians 15:1-5.

Spreading fragrance of Christ, 2 Corinthians 2:14.

Convert was Paul's recommendation, 2 Corinthians 3:1-3.

Radiance of face, 2 Corinthians 3:18.

Deserving right to be heard, 2 Corinthians 4:1-2.

Witnessing to those blinded by Satan, 2 Corinthians 4:3-6.

Compelled by love of Christ, 2 Corinthians 5:14.

Christ's ambassadors in world, 2 Corinthians 5:18-21.

Clarity of Gospel message, Galatians 1:8.

Speaking truth in love, Ephesians 4:15.

Ready to serve and to witness, Ephesians 6:15.

Paul's imprisonment widened sphere of influence, Philippians 1:12-14.

Standing firm whatever circumstances, Philippians 1:27-30.

Paul struggled over converts, Colossians 2:1.

Make most of every opportunity, Colossians 4:5.

Importance of lifestyle in witness, 1 Thessalonians 4:11-12.

Those who have believed, 2 Thessalonians 2:13-15.

Paul the blasphemer became minister of Gospel, 1 Timothy 1:15-16.

Persevere in life and doctrine, 1 Timothy 4:16.

Good deeds made known, 1 Timothy 5:25.

Not ashamed to testify, 2 Timothy 1:8-9.

Word of God not chained, 2 Timothy 2:9.

Need for actively sharing faith, Philemon 6

Witness of living in good relationships, Hebrews 12:14-15.

Witness of good life, 1 Peter 2:12.

Prepared to give answer, 1 Peter 3:15.

Speaking and serving to glory of God, 1 Peter 4:11.

Sharing what has been experienced and learned, 2 Peter 1:16-21.

Experiencing reality of Christ, 1 John 1:1-4.

Evil conduct as negative witness, Jude 7.

Helping those who doubt, Jude 22-23.

Faithful to point of death, Revelation 2:13.

Put to death for witness, Revelation 6:9.

Witnessing in face of judgment, Revelation 11:3-12.

Proclaiming angel, Revelation 14:6-7.

Tabernacle of testimony in heaven, Revelation 15:5.

Beheaded for faithfulness and testimony, Revelation 20:4.

Reporting what is seen and heard, Revelation 22:8.

Combined ministry of Holy Spirit and church in evangelism, Revelation 22:17.

See *Soul-winning.*

WOLF

Wolf attacking people, Jeremiah 5:6.

In sheep's clothing, Matthew 7:15.

Sheep among wolves, Matthew 10:16; John 10:11-13; Acts 20:29.

See *Animals.*

WOMEN

Abraham's deceitfulness concerning Sarah, Genesis 20:1-18. (See 12:10-20.)

Miriam's song of praise, Exodus 15:21.

Sold as slave but granted rights, Exodus 21:7-11.

Daughters who had no brother, Numbers 27:1-11.

Husband's involvement in contracts made by wife, Numbers 30:10-15.

Death to both women and children of enemy, Numbers 31:7-18.

Asking for special favor, Judges 1:13-15.

Spoils for conqueror, Judges 5:30.

Kidnapping wife, Judges 21:20-21.

Role of Rachel and Leah in strengthening house of Israel, Ruth 4:11.

Daughter-in-law worth seven sons, Ruth 4:13-15.

Prompt gathering of food, 1 Samuel 25:18.

David's respect for concubines, 2 Samuel 20:3.

Historical mention of mothers, not fathers, in record of young kings, 2 Kings 23:31, 36; 24:8, 18.

Prophetess counseled king, 2 Chronicles 34:22-28.

Daughters assisting in rebuilding wall at Jerusalem, Nehemiah 3:12.

Beautiful queen refused to be put on display, Esther 1:9-21.
Beauty treatments, Esther 2:3, 9, 12.
Queen Esther's influence over king, Esther 9:12.
Blessing of good wife, Proverbs 12:4.
One upright man, no upright women, Ecclesiastes 7:28.
Women as weaker sex, Isaiah 19:16; Jeremiah 50:37; 51:30; Nahum 3:13.
Beautiful and delicate, Jeremiah 6:2.
Babylonians worshiped Queen of Heaven, Jeremiah 7:18; 44:18-19.
King and queen brought to judgment, Jeremiah 13:18.
Woman made superior to man, Jeremiah 31:22.
Wisdom of queen, Daniel 5:10-11.
Women who command husbands, Amos 4:1. (Note also implication of alcohol.)
Reactions of Mary compared to shepherds, Luke 2:19-20.
Ministry of aged widow, Luke 2:36-38.
Women who traveled with Jesus, Luke 8:1-3.
Effectiveness of woman's testimony, John 4:39-42.
Paul's ministry to women, Acts 16:13.
Lydia, businesswoman, Acts 16:14-15.
Prominent women at Thessalonica, Acts 17:4. (See also v. 12.)
Four unmarried daughters with gift of prophecy, Acts 21:9.
Woman like mother to Paul, Romans 16:13.
Paul's advice to unmarried women, 1 Corinthians 7:25-26.
Wife traveling with husband, 1 Corinthians 9:5.
Paul describes role of women, 1 Corinthians 11:2-16.
Women in worship, 1 Corinthians 14:33-36; 1 Timothy 2:9-15.
Responsibility of young wives, Titus 2:3-5.
Epistle dedicated to chosen lady, 2 John 1-5.
See *Mother, Wife.*

WOMEN'S RIGHTS
Protection for sister, Genesis 34:31.
Daughter sold as servant, Exodus 21:7-11.
Rights of pregnant woman, Exodus 21:22.
Husband's superiority over wife, Numbers 30:10-16.

Apparel worn by members of opposite sex, Deuteronomy 22:5.
Selfish marital relationship, Deuteronomy 22:13-19.
Women divided among spoils, Judges 5:30.
Sacrifice of daughter, Judges 11:30-40.
Substituting heterosexual activity for homosexual, Judges 19:22-25.
Stolen wives, Judges 21:15-23.
Recognizing woman of character, Ruth 3:1-13.
Value of woman, Ruth 4:9-12.
Beloved but barren, 1 Samuel 1:2-7.
Solomon's counsel with two mothers, 1 Kings 3:16-28.
Daughters working with fathers rebuilding wall, Nehemiah 3:12.
Queen's prerogative and influence, Esther 1:15-22. (Note role of husbands in v. 22.)
Haughty women, Isaiah 3:16.
Women in need of name, Isaiah 4:1.
Women who command their husbands, Amos 4:1.
Mother told name of son, Luke 1:59-66.
Responsibility of servant returned from fields, Luke 17:7-10.
Relationship of woman to man, 1 Corinthians 11:6-12.
Women who had questions in New Testament church, 1 Corinthians 14:34-35.
Women not to teach, 1 Timothy 2:12.
Relationship between husband and wife, 1 Peter 3:1-7.
See *Feminist.*

WONDER
Unsearchable horizons, Jeremiah 33:3.
Ezekiel overwhelmed, Ezekiel 3:15.
Staring at those God uses, Acts 3:12.
See *Awe.*

WOOD
See *Forestry, Trees.*

WOODWORKING
See *Carpenter, Lumber.*

WORD
God does what He says, Numbers 23:19.
Discerning the prophets, Deuteronomy 18:21-22.
Keeping one's word when making pledge,

Deuteronomy 23:23.
Unfailing promises, Joshua 23:4.
Neglecting Word of the Lord, 1 Samuel
3:1.
Play on words, Jeremiah 34:17.
See *Scripture.*

WORK (Physical)
Unfairness to workers, Exodus 5:6-18.
Priest different from laity, Deuteronomy
18:1-2.
Taking care of business, Deuteronomy
20:5-9.
Divine blessing on work, Psalm 90:17.
Profitability of work, Proverbs 14:23.
Strength in numbers, Proverbs 30:25.
Working with diligence, Ecclesiastes 9:10.
Potential power of a prophet's words,
Jeremiah 1:10.
Digging cistern, Jeremiah 2:13.
Avoiding work on Sabbath, Jeremiah
17:21-27.
See *Labor.*

WORK (Spiritual)
Religious works involved in idolatry, Isaiah
46:1.
Trusting in your own deeds, Jeremiah 48:7.
Rich young man who kept Law, Mark
10:17-27.
Mixing blood of man with sacrificial blood,
Luke 13:1.
Kindness to poor recognized by the Lord,
Acts 10:4.
Handling problem of legalism at
Jerusalem, Acts 15:1-11.
Reward for good works, Romans 2:5-11.
Obedience brings righteousness, Romans
2:13.
Difference between faith and works,
Galatians 3:2-5.
Working out your own salvation,
Philippians 2:12-13.
Widow known for good works, 1 Timothy
5:9-10.
Wealth of money and wealth of good
deeds, 1 Timothy 6:11-19.
The Law makes nothing perfect, Hebrews
7:18-19.
Role of Law in pointing to coming
perfection in Christ, Hebrews 10:1.
Faith without works, James 2:14-18.
Reward for what one has done, Revelation
22:12.

See *Legalism.*

WORLD
Creation and status of earth, Nehemiah 9:6;
Job 26:7; Psalm 102:25; Hebrews 11:3.
Divine proprietor, Psalm 24:1.
Census of entire Roman world, Luke 2:1-3.
Earth's termination, 2 Peter 3:10.
See *Earth.*

WORLDLINESS
Reluctance of Lot to leave Sodom, Genesis
19:15-16.
Making an idol to please the Lord, Judges
17:3.
Desire to be like unbelievers, 1 Samuel
8:1-22.
Partial commitment of King Solomon,
1 Kings 3:3.
No help from wrong friends, Jeremiah
2:37.
Sons and daughters sacrificed to idols,
Ezekiel 16:20.
Daniel resolved not to defile himself,
Daniel 1:8-20.
Potential of blessing lost to idols, Hosea
9:10.
Salt that loses flavor and lights that are
hidden, Matthew 5:13-16.
Cannot serve two masters, Matthew 6:24;
Luke 16:13.
Witnessing miracles with hard hearts,
Matthew 11:20.
Conditions prior to return of Christ,
Matthew 24:37-38.
Jesus ate with "sinners," Mark 2:15-17.
Definitions of worldliness, John 17:25;
Romans 1:21.
Not conforming to world, Romans 12:1-2;
1 Peter 1:14.
Food sacrificed to idols, 1 Corinthians 8:1.
Eating and drinking, 1 Corinthians 15:32.
Believers not to join unbelievers,
2 Corinthians 6:14-18.
Crucified with Christ, Galatians 2:20.
Purity through Holy Spirit, Galatians 5:16.
Way of death, Ephesians 2:1.
Do not grieve Holy Spirit, Ephesians 4:30.
Love for world greater than love of
ministry, 2 Timothy 4:9-10.
Resisting ungodliness and passions of
world, Titus 2:11-12.
Moses' choice to identify with God's
people, Hebrews 11:24-25.

Friendship with world, James 4:4.
Strangers in world, 1 Peter 1:1-2.
Strangers on earth, 1 Peter 1:17.
Suffering removes evil human desires,
1 Peter 4:1-2.
Evil desires, 2 Peter 1:4.
Those who carouse, 2 Peter 2:13-16.
Kept from will of God, 1 John 2:15-17.
World control by evil one, 1 John 5:19.
Keep yourself from idols, 1 John 5:21.
Influence of Jezebel in church at Thyatira,
Revelation 2:20.
Merchants of earth lamenting destruction
of Babylon, Revelation 18:11-19.

WORRY
Two things to worry about, 1 Samuel 9:5.
Unnecessary fear, 1 Kings 1:50-53.
Desire for peace and security, 2 Kings
20:19.
Wrestling one's thoughts, Psalm 13:2.
Songs in night, Psalm 42:8.
No fear of bad news, Psalm 112:7.
Do not dwell on the past, Isaiah 43:18.
Nonproductive worry, Matthew 6:27-28.
Permitting worry to blind one's eyes to
truth, Matthew 13:22; Mark 4:19.
Circumstances need not hinder
confidence, Luke 8:22-25.
No wine at wedding in Cana, John 2:1-5.
The Lord always at hand, Acts 2:25-28.
Exercising hope when no basis for hope,
Romans 4:18-22.
Paul experienced anxiety, Philippians 2:28.
Antidote to worry, Philippians 4:6-7.
God's best in abundance, Jude 2.
See Anxiety.

WORSHIP
Abram's place of worship, Genesis 13:3-4.
Worship among trees, Genesis 13:18. (See
14:13; 18:1.)
Unaware of the Lord's presence, Genesis
28:16.
Temple fragrance not for personal
enjoyment, Exodus 30:34-38.
Insincerity in worship, Exodus 32:6.
Sober worship, Leviticus 10:8-10.
Consciously doing what is right, Leviticus
22:29.
Death by fire during worship, Numbers
16:35.
Mixing immorality with worship, Numbers
25:1-2.

The God who never appears as an image,
Deuteronomy 4:15-16.
Do not worship God in nature,
Deuteronomy 4:17-20.
Agreement voiced by congregation,
Deuteronomy 27:14-26.
Priests who engaged in idol worship,
Judges 18:30-31.
Worshiping the Lord and other gods,
2 Kings 17:33.
Regulation of music used in worship,
1 Chronicles 6:31-32.
David's self-evaluation, 1 Chronicles
17:16-19.
Morning and evening worship,
1 Chronicles 23:30.
Temple for people more than for God,
2 Chronicles 2:6.
Lengthy reading of Scripture, Nehemiah
8:1-6.
Job's critics spoke of a God far removed
from man's affairs, Job 22:12-14.
Recognizing majesty of God, Job 37:23-24.
Love for house of God, Psalm 26:8.
Giving glory to the Lord, Psalm 29:1-2.
Thirst for the living God, Psalm 42:1-2.
Using harp as instrument of praise, Psalm
43:4.
Meditation in temple, Psalm 48:9.
The kind of sacrifice God blesses, Psalm
51:15-17.
Exalting God above heavens, Psalm 57:5.
Good things from God's house, Psalm
65:4.
Procession of singers into sanctuary, Psalm
68:24-25.
Beauty of sanctuary and longing for
worship, Psalm 84:1-2.
Cry of praise, Psalm 89:8.
Worship the Lord in splendor of holiness,
Psalm 96:9.
Praising God seven times daily, Psalm
119:164.
Joy of going to God's house, Psalm 122:1.
God who answers prayer, Psalm 138:1-3.
Recognizing God's greatness beyond
comprehension, Psalm 145:3.
Nature and people praise the Lord, Psalm
148:1-14.
Cautious words in God's presence,
Ecclesiastes 5:2.
Meaningless offerings brought by Israel,
Isaiah 1:11-17.
Lifeless worship, Isaiah 29:13.

God's glory only for Him, Isaiah 42:8.
Listeners who hear nothing, Isaiah 42:20.
None other but the Lord, Isaiah 45:5-6.
Proper observance of Sabbath, Isaiah 58:13-14.
Effect of wrong worship, Jeremiah 2:5.
Unsuitable offerings, Jeremiah 6:20.
Beware deceptive words, Jeremiah 7:4-8.
Fraudulent idols, Jeremiah 10:4.
Reverence for the Lord, Jeremiah 10:6-7.
Physical act of humility in worship, Jeremiah 41:4-5.
Worship of sun, Ezekiel 8:16.
Coming to prophet without true faith in heart, Ezekiel 14:4.
Worship of image built by Nebuchadnezzar, Daniel 3:1-6.
Awe of talking to God, Daniel 10:15-21.
Deeper meaning of worship, Hosea 6:6.
Those who feed on the wind, Hosea 12:1.
When God turns deaf ear to praise, Amos 5:22. (See 8:3, 10.)
Fisherman worshiping his net, Habakkuk 1:16.
Futility of worshiping idols, Habakkuk 2:18-19.
The Lord is in His holy temple, Habakkuk 2:20.
Be still before the Lord, Zechariah 2:13.
Priests unaware of blemished sacrifices, Malachi 1:6-14.
Levi truly worshiped the Lord, Malachi 2:4-5.
Herod feigned desire to worship Jesus, Matthew 2:8.
Jesus attended place of worship, Matthew 12:9; Mark 1:21.
Phony worship, Matthew 15:8-9.
Children give the Lord praise, Matthew 21:16.
Missing real purpose of worship, Matthew 23:23-24.
Lip service, Mark 7:6-7.
Jesus in home of Mary and Martha, Luke 10:38-42.
Vain man and humble man, Luke 18:9-14.
Paul regularly attended Sabbath worship, Acts 14:1; 17:2.
Paul's long sermon, Acts 20:7.
Ultimate "holy of holies," 1 Corinthians 3:16.
Use of head covering in worship, 1 Corinthians 11:3-7.
Wrong attitudes in worship, 1 Corinthians 11:17-32.
Led astray to dumb idols, 1 Corinthians 12:2.
Good order in worship, 1 Corinthians 14:1-40.
Conduct and activity in worship, Ephesians 5:19-21.
Rules concerning women in worship, 1 Timothy 2:9-15.
High Priest in heaven, Hebrews 8:1-2.
Regulations for worship, Hebrews 9:1.
Physical act in worship cannot bring spiritual result, Hebrews 10:1-4.
Impetus for worship, Hebrews 12:28-29.
Come near to God and He will come near to you, James 4:8.
Reverent fear of God, 1 Peter 1:17.
Living creatures and elders around throne, Revelation 4:8-11.
Worship in music and song, Revelation 5:11-14.
Drama of worship in heaven, Revelation 7:11-12.
Incense and prayers of saints, Revelation 8:3-4.
Concluding proclamation of faith, Revelation 15:3-4.
Rejoicing in heaven over destruction of Babylon, Revelation 19:6-8.
No churches in heaven, Revelation 21:22.
Not to pray to or worship angels, Revelation 22:8-9.
See *Congregation.*

WORTH
Monetary value of human being, Leviticus 27:1-8.
Truly holy, Numbers 16:3-7.
Debt canceled every seven years, Deuteronomy 15:1.
People as the Lord's treasure, Deuteronomy 26:18.
Total loss of personal worth, Deuteronomy 28:68.
Daughter-in-law better than seven sons, Ruth 4:15.
Silver of little value, 1 Kings 10:21.
Gold received annually by King Solomon, 2 Chronicles 9:13-14.
Precious metal replaces the ordinary, Isaiah 60:17.
Change in value of man, Lamentations 4:2.
Likened to the Lord's signet ring, Haggai 2:23.

Day of small things, Zechariah 4:10.
Salt loses its saltiness, Luke 14:34-35.
Dependability in God's sight, Luke 16:10-12.
Value of servant, Luke 17:7-10.
Faith as precious as ours, 2 Peter 1:1.
Stone precious to some, rejected by others, 1 Peter 2:7-8.
See *Value.*

WORTHLESS
Sold for nothing, Isaiah 52:3.
Silver thrown into streets, Ezekiel 7:19.
Value of personal attainment, Philippians 3:7-11.

WOUNDS
Value of injury to personal well-being, Proverbs 20:30.
Body covered with wounds and sores, Isaiah 1:6.
Good Samaritan, Luke 10:30-35.
See *Injury.*

WRESTLING
Jacob's divine encounter, Genesis 32:22-32.
Satan as opponent, Ephesians 6:12.
See *Athletics.*

WRITING
Handwriting of God, Exodus 31:18; 32:16; Deuteronomy 10:4.

Inscribing Law of God clearly on stones, Deuteronomy 27:8.
Moses as author, Deuteronomy 31:24.
Written plan, 1 Chronicles 28:19.
Early correspondence, 2 Chronicles 2:11.
Short, short story, Ecclesiastes 9:14-15.
Deceitful theology, Jeremiah 8:8.
Instructions to write a book, Jeremiah 30:2.
Danger of writing truth, Jeremiah 36:4-32.
Revelation made plain so all can read, Habakkuk 2:2.
Gigantic scroll, Zechariah 5:1-2.
Many writers attempted to record New Testament events, Luke 1:1-4.
Paul wrote convincing letters but lacked ability in public speaking, 2 Corinthians 10:10.
Command given to John, Revelation 1:10-11.
See *Author, Literature.*

WRONG
Unintentional sin, Leviticus 4:1-35.
Testing of divine patience, Numbers 14:18.
Defiant sin, Numbers 15:30-31.
Sin of only one person, Numbers 16:22.
Wrongly suspecting woman of drunkenness, 1 Samuel 1:9-16.
Limited admission of wrong, Job 34:31-33.
Pardon for bloodguilt of nation, Joel 3:21.
Accused yet admired, 1 Peter 2:12.
See *Error.*

X

XENOPHOBIA
Sarah and Hagar, Genesis 21:8-10, 21.
Abraham's concern for wife for Isaac,
    Genesis 24:1-4.
Courtesy to foreigners, Exodus 23:9.
Providing for strangers, Leviticus 23:22.
Report of spies who explored Canaan,
    Numbers 13:17-33.
Loaning money to foreigner, Deuteronomy
    23:19-20.
Showing kindness to foreigner, Ruth 2:10.
Misunderstanding goodwill gesture,
    2 Samuel 10:1-4.
No marriage to foreigners, Nehemiah
10:30.
Language confused by intermarriage,
    Nehemiah 13:23-27.
Hatred of Jews, Esther 3:8-15.
Do good to foreigners, Jeremiah 22:3.
Falling into hand of foreigners, Ezekiel
    11:9.
Delivered from malicious neighbors,
    Ezekiel 28:24.
Ingratitude to foreigner, Luke 17:11-19.
See *Foreigner*.

X-RAY
Divine penetration, Hebrews 4:12.

Y

YEAR
Designed by Creator, Genesis 1:14.
Measurement of life span, Genesis 11:10-29.
First month of year, Exodus 12:2.
Lunar determination of time, Numbers 10:10.
Divine reckoning of time, Psalm 90:4.

YIELDING
Yielding to temptation, Genesis 3:6; Joshua 7:21; 1 Kings 11:4.
Foolish sins, Numbers 12:11.
Potter and clay, Isaiah 45:9; 64:8.
See *Weakness.*

YOM KIPPUR
Day of Atonement, Leviticus 16:1-34.

YOUTH
Resentment toward youth in leadership, Genesis 37:5-11.
Census involved men 20 years or older, Numbers 26:2; 1 Chronicles 27:23.
Early joys of marriage, Deuteronomy 24:5.
Sacrifice only child, Judges 11:28-40.
Age variable between Boaz and Ruth, Ruth 3:10-13.
Growth in spirit and character, 1 Samuel 2:26.
Age of Saul when he became king, 1 Samuel 13:1.
Boldness of Jonathan against Philistines, 1 Samuel 14:1-14.
Choice of David over older brothers, 1 Samuel 16:4-12.
Veteran soldier underrated abilities of a boy, 1 Samuel 17:42.
King Saul went home but David prepared for action, 1 Samuel 24:22.
Father who would have died in place of son, 2 Samuel 18:32-33.
Advice of younger men rather than elders, 1 Kings 12:1-15.
Elisha ridiculed for baldness, 2 Kings 2:23-24.
Sixteen-year-old king, 2 Kings 14:21-22; 2 Chronicles 26:1.
Ages of young kings, 2 Kings 21:1, 19; 22:1; 23:31, 36; 24:8, 18; 2 Chronicles 33:1, 21; 34:1; 36:2, 5, 9, 11.
Father and inexperienced son, 1 Chronicles 22:5; 29:1.
Victim of bad influence, 2 Chronicles 13:7.
The Lord honored in early reign of young king, 2 Chronicles 17:1-4.
Longing for younger years, Job 29:4-6.
Wisdom of old and young, Job 32:4-9.
Afflicted from youth, Psalm 88:15.
Strength broken and days shortened, Psalm 102:23.
Purity for young man, Psalm 119:9.
More understanding than those older, Psalm 119:100.
Youth and old age, Proverbs 20:29.
Counsel to young, Ecclesiastes 12:1-7.
All have become ungodly, Isaiah 9:17.
Death in early years of life, Isaiah 38:10.
Finest youth killed in battle, Jeremiah 48:15.
Facing problems while young, Lamentations 3:27.
Chosen for royal service, Daniel 1:3-6.
Daniel resolved not to defile himself, Daniel 1:8-20.
Young prophesy, old dream dreams, Joel 2:28.
Attractive and beautiful young men, young women, Zechariah 9:17.
Role of recent convert, 1 Timothy 3:6.
Young not to be looked down on, 1 Timothy 4:12.

Evil desires of youth, 2 Timothy 2:22.
Respect for those who are older, 1 Peter 5:5.

Message for all ages, 1 John 2:12-14.

Z

ZEAL
Keep the fire burning, Leviticus 6:13.
Talk about spiritual matters, Deuteronomy 6:4-7.
New priest comes in all earnestness, Deuteronomy 18:6-7.
The Lord's demands within reach, Deuteronomy 30:11.
Do not envy sinners, Proverbs 23:17.
Zeal of the Lord, Isaiah 9:7.
Press on to acknowledge the Lord, Hosea 6:3.
Zealous fanatics, Matthew 23:15.
Eagerness to be baptized, Acts 8:36-37.
Zealous ministry of Apollos, Acts 18:24-28.
Zeal without knowledge, Romans 10:1-2.
Spiritual fervor sustained, Romans 12:11.
Galatians would have given Paul their eyes, Galatians 4:15.
Ready to serve and witness, Ephesians 2:10; 6:10-20.
Losing first love, Revelation 2:4.
See *Vision, Unction.*

ZODIAC
God's literal and trustworthy message in astronomy, Psalm 19:1, 6. (Note words "speech," "language," and "voice" in the text. Then compare vv. 7-13.)

ZOOLOGY
Clear distinction of species, Genesis 1:25; 1 Corinthians 15:39.
Naming of birds and animals, Genesis 2:20.
Solomon's expertise, 1 Kings 4:33-34.
Apes and baboons brought to King Solomon, 1 Kings 10:22.
See *Animals.*